Quirin Pinyin Upda

(QPUE)

New editions that update and revise classics of Western sinology in line with current scholarship and practices (e.g. the older Wade-Giles transliteration of Chinese words updated to the current Pinyin standard). All QPUE titles are published in both paperback and E-book formats.

Series titles include the following ***Revised Editions***:

The Poetry of the Early Tang, by Stephen Owen

The Great Age of Chinese Poetry: The High Tang, by Stephen Owen

Taoism and Chinese Religion, by Henri Maspero

China in Antiquity, by Henri Maspero

Zen Dust: The History of the Koan and Koan Study in Rinzai (Linji) Zen, by Isshu Miura and Ruth Fuller Sasaki

Lunheng: The Complete Essays of Wang Chong, Translated & annotated by Alfred Forke

For further details visit:

www.quirinpress.com

Twitter: @quirinpress

Zen Dust

The History of the Koan and Koan Study in Rinzai (Linji) Zen

Zen Dust

The History of the Koan and Koan Study in Rinzai (Linji) Zen

Revised Edition

Isshū Miura

Ruth Fuller Sasaki

with Background Notes, Descriptive Bibliography, Genealogical Charts, Maps, Indexes, and Reproductions of Drawings by Hakuin

QUIRIN PRESS
Melbourne & Basel
2015

Published by Quirin Press
P.O. Box 4226, Melbourne University, Vic. 3052, Australia
E-mail: enquiries@quirinpress.com
http://www.quirinpress.com

The National Library of Australia Cataloging-in-Publication entry:
Miura, Isshu, 1903-1978, author.
Zen dust : the history of the Koan and Koan study in Rinzai (Linji) Zen / Isshū Miura, Ruth Fuller Sasaki.
Revised edition.
ISBN: 9781922169129 (paperback)
Quirin Pinyin Updated Editions (QPUE)
Includes bibliographical references and index.
Koan. | Zen Buddhism. | Rinzai (Sect)
Sasaki, Ruth Fuller, 1883-1967, author.
294.3927

ISBN: 978-1-922169-12-9 (pbk.)
ISBN: 978-1-922169-13-6 (E-book)

♾ Printed on acid-free paper

Parts I, II, and III originally published under the title *The Zen Koan*

To the memory of *Sokei-an*

総上他閑塵境

"You just go on clambering after the realm of worthless dust"

The Record of Linji

Contents

NOTES

BIBLIOGRAPHY

APPENDICES

Publisher's Note To The Quirin Press Revised Edition

The present publication in the Quirin Pinyin Updated Editions (QPUE) series updates and revises *Zen Dust* by Isshū Miura and Ruth Fuller Sasaki, which was originally published by Harcourt, Brace & World (New York) in 1967.

The revisions bring this title in line with current scholarship and practices. Apart from updating the older Wade-Giles transliteration of Chinese words to the current *pinyin* standard, the text has been fully re-set and any inconsistencies and typographical errors corrected; the only alteration being the reference to the Wade-Giles in the foreword which has been removed and replaced by "*pinyin*."

For the sake of consistency Chinese names in bibliographic entries have been updated to *pinyin*, even though any Wade-Giles transliterations in English language titles have been retained. The index has been fully revised and expanded to include Chinese characters where appropriate. Chinese characters have also been added to the text where appropriate, save for any characters that could not be established from original sources with absolute certainty.

For the parts they have played in the production and publication of this revised edition of Ruth Fuller Sasaki's unique work, we are indebted to a number of people and organizations. Our thanks go to Joan Watts, Anne Watts, and Michael Gamer for permission to re-issue this title; and to Cheryl Hutty for proofing the work and implementing the extensive *pinyin* updating and checking of all the Chinese and Japanese characters.

Quirin Press
Melbourne, 2015

Foreword

The First Zen Institute of America, founded in New York City in 1930 by the late Sasaki Sōkei-an 佐々木曹渓庵 Rōshi for the purpose of instructing American students of Zen in the traditional manner, celebrated its twenty-fifth anniversary on February 15, 1955. To commemorate that event it invited Miura Isshū 三浦一舟 Rōshi of the Kōon-ji 廣園寺, a monastery belonging to the Nanzen-ji 南禪寺 branch of Rinzai Zen and situated not far from Tokyo, to come to New York and give a series of talks at the Institute on the subject of koan study, the study which is basic for monks and laymen in traditional, transmitted Rinzai Zen.

Isshū Rōshi, though he spoke no English, was well qualified to deliver such a series of talks. At the age of ten he had become the personal disciple of Seigo Hōgaku 棲梧寶嶽, one of the heirs of the famous Zen master Shaku Sōen 釋宗演 of the Engaku-ji 圓覺寺, Kamakura. At the age of twenty he entered the monastery connected with the Rinzai Zen temple of Tenryū-ji 天龍寺 on the outskirts of Kyoto, then a short time later transferred to the monastery of Nanzen-ji within Kyoto itself. For twelve years he studied and practiced there under the stern stick of Nanshinken 南針軒 Rōshi. On the death of his master, he followed Nakamura Taiyū 中村泰祐 Rōshi, Nanshinken's heir, to the Kōon-ji. Two years later he completed his Zen study under Taiyū Rōshi. During the nine years that followed, he successively held the position of priest of two important Zen temples then, at the request of

Taiyū Rōshi who was retiring, he returned to the Kōon-ji to become master of that monastery. Isshū Rōshi's visit to New York in 1955 to give the series of lectures mentioned above was followed by two more short visits, one in 1956 and the other in 1959. In 1960 he returned to New York to teach.

The series of eight talks which Isshū Rōshi gave in New York in the late winter of 1955 had as its subject the system of koan study at present in use in all the Rinzai monasteries in Japan. This system was originated by Hakuin Ekaku 白隠慧鶴 (1686–1769), the reorganizer and revivifier of Japanese Rinzai Zen, and further developed by his immediate disciples. Isshū Rōshi delivered these talks in Japanese; at the conclusion of each, an English translation was read which had been made by myself from the Rōshi's previously prepared manuscript.

The success of the talks and the fact that a like treatment of the subject had never appeared in print in any western language led to plans being undertaken to publish an English translation of the series. *Zen Dust* was chosen by Isshū Rōshi as the title for the projected book, all words about Zen being but dust to be gotten rid of, or, from a deeper standpoint, having no real existence at all.

Further consideration made clear the fact that considerable background material would be needed to make Isshū Rōshi's text understandable to the general reader and really useful to the Zen student.

The work now consists of three distinct sections: an essay on the history of the koan, Isshū Rōshi's text, and selections from *Zenrin kushū* 禪林句集, a phrase anthology used in koan study.

With very few exceptions, the books that have appeared on Zen thus far, when they have made any mention at all of the koan, have handled this important Zen teaching device superficially or mistakenly. The time now seems to have come for at least a preliminary survey of the koan, its origin, history, and use. "The History of The Koan in Rinzai (Linji) Zen" which comprises the first section of *Zen Dust*, is an attempt to provide western readers with such a study. The deficiencies and inadequacies of this survey will be immediately apparent, as will the tentative nature of many of the statements in it. In spite of the mass of existing Chinese and Japanese Zen literature, there is little specific source material available on which to draw for such a study, and no modern Japanese or Chinese writer has thus far treated the koan from this standpoint. Particularly difficult to answer satisfactorily is the question of how the koan was used throughout the history of Zen, up to and even including the time of Hakuin and his disciples. The Zen masters have all remained disappointingly silent on this point, and we have only scattered hints in their writings to rely on. I am grateful indeed to SHIBAYAMA Zenkei 柴山全慶, Chief Abbot of the Nanzen-ji monastery, for the helpful suggestions he has given me on this subject in a private conversation.

The reader may find some difficulty in making the transition from the English style of "The History of The Koan" to that of the translation of Isshū Rōshi's text. The differences in style are due, in part at least, to the different standpoints from which koan study is approached. "The History of The Koan" aims at being an objective, factual approach; Isshū Rōshi's approach is that of one who is within the actual practice itself. For the westerner who either is studying Zen or hopes to study it, the second, or "feeling approach," is of the utmost importance. While we are standing outside Zen we must look at it clearly and coolly, as a fact in history; when we are in Zen we must give ourselves over to it completely if we are to experience what Zen is concerned with. The two standpoints should not be confused; rather, they must be carefully differentiated.

Isshū Rōshi's talks have been subjected to a minimum of editing; only such passages have been deleted as were related to the occasion on which they were given and thus had no bearing on the subject itself. An attempt has been made to reproduce in English the simplicity of the Rōshi's Japanese style, so that western readers might become acquainted with the flavor of a Zen master's talks as they might be given to a Japanese audience. The quotations, some of considerable length, are quite consistent with Far Eastern literary traditions. Writers and speakers, through custom and modesty, have always been prone to offer their own views through the words of old and accepted authorities.

No attention has previously, I believe, been given to the use of *jakugo* 著語 or "capping phrases" in Rinzai Zen koan study. Their purpose is explained in "The History of The Koan." Part Three of *Zen Dust* is devoted to translated excerpts from the anthology of quotations in which the majority of accepted jakugo are to be found. Since the Japanese reading of the Chinese text of these phrases is often special for Zen, these readings and the Chinese character text have been included for the interest they may have to students.

No apology is made for the length of the majority of the notes for Part One and Part Two. They are not intended as footnotes; rather, they are intended to provide western students of Zen Buddhism, who have little or no access to such information as they contain, with adequate background for the persons and subjects taken up in the texts. Except in a few instances, reference has not been made to the numerous and varied authorities consulted. Japanese scholars have carried out meticulous research in the field of Buddhist studies, and their works—histories, essays, encyclopedias, chronologies, etc.—have been an invaluable source of information. Nor have the works of western scholars been neglected where competent material exists on a given subject.

It is, however, to the old Chinese and Japanese biographical texts that we must return again and again. Fortunately or unfortunately, these are less concerned with historical fact than with traditional accounts of doctrinal lineage, religious practices, enlightenment experiences, and anecdotes. But it is essential that the informed Zen student be acquainted with the traditions also. In addition, much for these notes has been derived from personal contacts with living Japanese Zen masters and scholars during many years devoted to traditional Zen practice.

The Bibliography has been arranged with the idea of distinguishing clearly between Chinese and Japanese works. Only the more important books referred to in "The History of The Koan," Isshū Rōshi's text, and the Notes have been included. There has been no intention to make of it a comprehensive bibliography of Zen literature. On the other hand, rather full descriptions are given for the more important titles, in order that those readers who are interested in Zen literature may know something about the history of the book and the kind of material it contains. Biographies of the authors, when not included in the description of the book, will be found in the Notes. The General Index provides a quick reference to their position there when needed.

Since the subject proper of *Zen Dust* is Hakuin Ekaku's system of koan study and since long quotations from his writings comprise a part of Isshū Rōshi's text, that great master is in a sense the hero of the book. No work in which Hakuin appears would be complete without some examples of his painting and calligraphy. Hakuin was not a painter in the professional sense of the term; he was a Zen master who used his great talent as an artist in teaching Zen, particularly to his lay followers. Thanks to the extreme kindness and courtesy of the Marquis Hosokawa Moritatsu 細川護立, who studied at the monastery of Daitoku-ji in his youth and whose interest in Zen has continued unfailingly through half a century, it has been possible to include in *Zen Dust* a number of Hakuin's paintings, all from the Marquis' famous collection.

Every writer on Japanese Zen is faced with the problem of how to deal with Chinese proper names and Chinese Buddhist (or Zen) technical terms, for no book on Japanese Zen can be written without constant reference to the old Chinese masters, the places where they lived, the books they wrote, or the special words they used. Unfortunate though it may be, for the time at least, the study of Zen history and literature as well as the practice of Zen itself can best be pursued in Japan. Japanese Buddhist scholars, even when they are acquainted with Chinese, tend to use only Japanese pronunciations for Chinese names and terms; the Japanese Zen masters use nothing else. Westerners studying in Japan must of necessity conform to the Japanese custom in speaking, but accuracy demands that, in writing, names and terms (when not translated) be rendered in the language of their origin. Thus the western student has no alternative but to familiarize himself thoroughly with both pronunciations.

Probably no method of handling this problem of dual pronunciation is totally satisfactory. The present book makes no claim to have offered a solution of the problem or even to have been consistent throughout in the method used. Rather, the primary intention has been to give the Chinese names for Chinese people, places, and so forth, and to make a clear differentiation between these and the Japanese pronunciations for them. Therefore, when a name (or word) with the Chinese characters for it is immediately followed by another name (or word) within parentheses, the former may be assumed to be originally Chinese, the latter, its Japanese equivalent. When a name (or word) with Chinese characters is not followed by a parenthesis, it may be assumed that its origin is Japanese. An exception to this rule has been made in Isshū Rōshi's text. There, the Japanese pronunciation has been used throughout for all names and terms, regardless of whether they were originally Chinese or Japanese. This has been done in order not to disturb the sense of participating in a Japanese roshi's lecture or interrupt the flow of the text. In every case, the Notes will be found to supply the Chinese characters and pronunciations lacking in the text itself. On the other hand, the Bibliography and the General Index list all entries under their original pronunciations; Japanese equivalents for Chinese names or words appear, but are referred to the Chinese originals.

One more point must be mentioned regarding the Chinese and Japanese pronunciation of Chinese characters in Zen. Zen, as a whole, has always been somewhat arbitrary in the matter of pronunciation for names and terms. Particularly in Japan, the Sōtō and Rinzai schools, and even the different teaching lines in the latter, have tenaciously clung to their own traditional renderings. An attempt has been made throughout this work to give the pronunciation preferred in the line to which the person under discussion belongs, but consistency in pronunciation or conformity to modern dictionary standardization is neither desirable nor possible. In romanization, the [*pinyin*] system has been used for Chinese; for Japanese, the modified Hepburn system has been followed, except where it does not reproduce pronunciations current in Japanese Rinzai Zen. In all but a few cases, the names of Japanese and Chinese persons are given with the family name first and the personal name following; capitalization clearly establishes the order. The names of Chinese and Japanese Buddhist priests are given in the order most usually accepted in Japanese Buddhism.

The problem of the anglicization of words also presents itself. The word "Zen" has now become all but standard English for the name of this school of Buddhism as a whole, and is so used here. The Chinese equivalent "Chan," has, however, been employed when a subject is being handled from the Chinese standpoint specifically, or to make a clear distinction between the Chinese and Japanese schools. There are, in addition, a number of other words, such as *rōshi*, *sōdō*, *kenshō*, which it seems advisable to anglicize eventually in their Japanese pronunciation, since the English language provides no exact equivalent for them and since these words must be an integral part of the daily vocabulary of the Zen scholar or the practicing Zen student. When these first appear in this text they are given in italics in Japanese romanized form with proper markings; thereafter they are used as English words.

Two technical terms of great importance in Zen have also been used as English words in *Zen Dust*. The Chinese word *dao* 道, in Japanese *dō*, is one of several terms which the early Chinese Buddhists took over from Daoism. In Chinese Buddhism the term *dao* sometimes means "the Way," that is, the Eightfold Path of the Buddha, or the "way" leading to enlightenment; sometimes it means enlightenment itself, sometimes Nirvana. In Zen, however, its meaning is more closely akin to that in Daoism; it is the Absolute, the Ultimate Principle, Truth, Reason, the indescribable source of all existence and all manifested phenomena. Since western philosophical and religious thought has not developed the concepts embedded within and clinging to this Chinese word, no equivalent term exists in the English language. Moreover, to translate it by a single English word, though that might be appropriate in a given context, is to permit western associative concepts to blot out the original Chinese overtones. Therefore, it would seem preferable to treat the word "Dao" as an adopted word in English, thus permitting it gradually to acquire for the English reader the meanings and shades of meaning rightfully belonging to it. The word has thus been used wherever it appears in this text, leaving to the reader to feel into it what the context implies.

The Sanskrit word *dharma*, in Chinese *fa* 法, and in Japanese pronounced *hō*, also is the product of the specific culture and thought of the country of its origin, and no one word in any European language can contain its many and varied meanings. It is now an accepted word in English and has found a place in recent English dictionaries. As a technical term in Hinduism, the meanings of the word "dharma" vary greatly from those it has acquired as a Buddhist technical term. In this later usage, which alone concerns us, it has two distinct meanings: firstly, Law, Truth, religion, the doctrines and teachings of the Buddha, Buddhism; secondly, the elements of existence, things, phenomena. In order not to confuse the reader, it would seem helpful to write the term "Dharma" when it is used with any one of the meanings in the first group; when it is used with any one of the meanings in the second group, to write it "dharma" or "dharmas." This rule has been used throughout in *Zen Dust*. A few other Buddhist terms will be found in their original Sanskrit forms, but when these appear they are treated in the Notes.

Though only the names of Isshū Rōshi and myself appear on the title page of *Zen Dust*, the book as it now stands is actually the work of a happy collaboration in which a number of persons have joined. The first expression of gratitude belongs to Isshū Rōshi for providing western readers with so intimate and sympathetic a text. Thanks are next offered to Gotō Zuigan 後藤瑞巖 Rōshi, former Chief Abbot of Myōshin-ji and of Daitoku-ji, for his guidance in the rendering of the Japanese readings of the *Zenrin kushū* excerpts and his painstaking explanation of the meanings read into them in Zen, from which certain of the English translations have profited. To all the members of the Research Staff of the First Zen Institute of America in Japan we are particularly indebted for their devoted cooperation: To Professor Yoshitaka Iriya, Head of the Department of Chinese Literature, Nagoya University, and our Director of Research, who has been our instructor and guiding hand throughout; to Professor Seizan Yanagida, Department of Buddhist Philosophy, Hanazono University, whose broad knowledge of Zen history and literature has contributed much to the Notes and Bibliography; to Professor Hisao Kanaseki, Department of English Literature, Kobe University, and Professor Teruo Oka, Liberal Arts Faculty, Kyoto University, for English translations of Japanese background material; to Mr. Philip Yampolsky and Dr. Burton Watson, former members of the Staff, who were of great assistance while they were with us; to Mr. Kenneth Walden, who typed the final manuscript; to Mr. Kazuhiro Furuta, who had the tedious task of writing the Chinese characters in the manuscript; and finally to Mr. Kikutarō Saitō, who designed *Zen Dust* and has personally supervised every phase of its production with the utmost patience and care. However, all errors of fact or interpretation, as well as inaccuracies in the English rendering of translated material are my own.

In conclusion, the First Zen Institute of America in Japan wishes to express its gratitude to the Bollingen Foundation, New York, for its generous grant toward the preparation and publication of *Zen Dust*.

Ruth Fuller Sasaki

Ryōsen-an
Daitoku-ji,

June 1, 1965

PART ONE

The History of the Koan in Rinzai (Linji) Zen

I. The Koan in Chinese Zen

The living heart of all Buddhism is enlightenment or satori, and it is upon satori that Zen Buddhism is based. But Zen is not satori, nor is satori Zen. Satori is the goal of Zen. Moreover, the satori that is the goal of Zen is not merely the satori experience; it is the satori experience deepened through training and directed to a definite end.

The state of satori is outside of time. The training before and after satori is within time. The masters who devised the methods of training used in Zen were men living in given environments in given periods of history; their personalities and those of their students, to say nothing of their attitudes, actions, and speech, were in part determined by the times and the cultures in which they lived. The teaching methods of the earliest days have undergone much modification through the centuries. In the future, in Japan as well as in the West—when and if real Zen does go West—the present forms of the traditional methods will undoubtedly be still further modified. The principles and aims of the Zen masters cannot be said to have changed, however. When these are changed, there will no longer be any Zen.

Zen makes use of three kinds of training in bringing its followers to the experience of satori and maturing that experience: meditation or zazen, the study of koans, and daily life. The Zen manner of employing meditation and daily life is distinctive, but the koan and the methods of using it are unique and to be found in Zen alone. It is with a short survey of the koan and its use as they developed in history, particularly with reference to the school of Zen known in China as the Linji 臨濟, and in Japan as the Rinzai,[1] that we shall be concerned here.

There is no need to consider the misinformation being spread about the koan by those professed exponents of Zen in the West who have never studied koans themselves. The Zen masters have stated quite clearly what a koan is and for what purpose it is used. One of the best of these statements is to be found in the *Zhongfeng heshang guanglu*,[2] the "record" of the Linji master Zhongfeng Mingben 中峰明本 (Chūhō Myōhon, 1263–1323),[3] who lived during the Yuan 元 (Gen) dynasty (1260–1368). When he was asked why the teachings of the buddhas and patriarchs were called "public records," that is, koans, he replied:

> The koans may be compared to the case records of the public law court. Whether or not the ruler succeeds in bringing order to his realm depends in essence upon the existence of law. *Gong* 公 (*kō*), or "public," is the single track followed by all sages and worthy men alike, the highest principle which serves as a road for the whole world. *An* 案 (*an*), or "records," are the orthodox writings which record what the sages and worthy men regard as principles. There have never been rulers who did not have public law courts, and there have never been public law courts that did not have case records which are to be used as precedents of laws in order to stamp out injustice in the world. When these public case records (koans) are used, then principles and laws will come into effect; when these come into effect, the world will become upright; when the world is upright, the Kingly Way will be well ordered.
>
> Now, when we use the word "koan" to refer to the teachings of the buddhas and patriarchs, we mean the same thing. The koans do not represent the private opinion of a single man, but rather the highest principle, received alike by us and by the hundreds and thousands of bodhisattvas of the three realms and the ten directions. This principle accords with the spiritual source, tallies with the mysterious meaning, destroys birth-and-death, and transcends the passions. It cannot be understood by logic; it cannot be

transmitted in words; it cannot be explained in writing; it cannot be measured by reason. It is like the poisoned drum[4] that kills all who hear it, or like a great fire that consumes all who come near it. What is called the "special transmission of the Vulture Peak"[5] was the transmission of this; what is called the "direct pointing of Bodhidharma at Shaolinsi"[6] was a pointing at this.

....

From the time long ago when the lotus flower was held up on the Vulture Peak until today, how can there have been only seventeen hundred koans?[7] Yet the koans are something that can be used only by men with enlightened minds who wish to prove their understanding. They are certainly not intended to be used merely to increase one's lore and provide topics for idle discussion.

The so-called venerable masters of Zen are the chief officials of the public law courts of the monastic community, as it were, and their words on the transmission of Zen and their collections of sayings are the case records of points that have been vigorously advocated. Occasionally men of former times, in the intervals when they were not teaching, in spare moments when their doors were closed, would take up these case records and arrange them, give their judgment on them, compose verses of praise on them, and write their own answers to them. Surely they did not do this just to show off their erudition and contradict the worthy men of old. Rather, they did it because they could not bear to think that the Great Dharma might become corrupt. Therefore they stooped to using expedients in order to open up the Wisdom Eye of the men of later generations, hoping thereby to make it possible for them to attain the understanding of the Great Dharma for themselves in the same way. That is all.

The word *gong*, or "public," means that the koans put a stop to private understanding; the word *an*, or "case records," means that they are guaranteed to accord with the buddhas and patriarchs. When these koans are understood and accepted, then there will be an end to feeling and discrimination; when there is an end to feeling and discrimination, birth-and-death will become empty; when birth-and-death becomes empty, the Buddha-way will be ordered.

What do I mean by according with the buddhas and patriarchs? The buddhas and patriarchs have been greatly sorrowed to

> see that sentient beings bind themselves to the realm of birth-and-death and sensual delusion, so that, through the countless kalpas of the past down to the present, none have been able to free themselves. Therefore they displayed words in the midst of wordlessness and handed down forms in the midst of formlessness. But once the bonds of delusion have been loosed, how can there be any words and forms left to discuss?
>
> If an ordinary man has some matter which he is not able to settle by himself, he will go to the public law court to seek a decision, and there the officials will look up the case records and, on the basis of them, settle the matter for him. In the same way, if a student has that in his understanding of his enlightenment which he cannot settle for himself, he will ask his teacher about it, and the teacher, on the basis of the koans, will settle it for him.
>
> The koan is a torch of wisdom that lights up the darkness of feeling and discrimination, a golden scraper that cuts away the film clouding the eye, a sharp ax that severs the root of birth-and-death, a divine mirror that reflects the original face of both the sacred and the secular. Through it the intention of the patriarchs is made abundantly clear, the Buddha-mind is laid open and revealed. For the essentials of complete transcendence, final emancipation, total penetration, and identical attainment, nothing can surpass the koan.[8]

The origin of the koan and the method of using it lie in the nature of Zen itself. The masters of earliest Zen discerned that the source of the dynamic power of Buddhism was not in the sutras and the voluminous commentaries upon them, but in the enlightenment of Shakyamuni and in his teaching that every man has the potentiality of attaining this enlightenment for himself. Supported by faith in this teaching, these early masters forged ahead with indomitable courage to gain this realization for themselves through the method Shakyamuni had used and advocated, that is, meditation. Having attained the realization and comprehended its deepest meaning as well as its implications for human life, out of the compassionate heart born of their enlightenment they sought ways and means of assisting others to achieve the same experience. Meditation certainly remained the basic practice. Though methods of meditation were developed in Zen that differed from those in other Buddhist sects, whether of Indian or

Chinese origin, we have no evidence that meditation itself was ever abandoned or even neglected. Nor is it neglected today. The different schools of Zen developed somewhat different ways of handling the mind during meditation, but in all schools the main road to the attainment of satori is still that of practicing meditation in the posture in which Shakyamuni Buddha was sitting when he attained his enlightenment.

The earliest Chinese masters seem to have attained their enlightenment with little instruction. The histories of their lives indicate that most had been Buddhist monks, many from a young age, and as such were steeped in the doctrines of the Buddhist scriptures. Many had studied the classics of Confucianism and Daoism as well. Their inability to attain the enlightenment they sought through the study of written words caused them to seek out meditation masters. When these monks had reached some profound insight through their meditation practice they went to the master to have their insight verified by his. Or, if they were beset by doubts, they went to him to have these doubts resolved. Many times the master's one word at this point brought them to satori. If the master seemed to be *their* master, they remained with him for a number of years; if not, they went on to other masters until they found the one they recognized to be their own. When their enlightenment had been attested to and confirmed, they retired to the mountains to spend long years in ripening it. Only gradually did other seekers find them out and come to live with or near them. From such a group a new temple might arise, or, if the master's fame had reached the capital, a command might come to take charge of one already established.

The satori or enlightenment that the old masters experienced was ineffable and incommunicable. It had not come about as the result of thinking or reasoning. It was, indeed, an experience beyond and above the intellect. Understanding this only too well, they did not, on the whole, attempt to describe their experiences in words. They knew that verbal explanations were useless as a means of leading their students to the realization itself. They had to devise other means.

In the mountain monasteries where they preferred to live, the early Chinese masters were in intimate contact with their disciples, sharing all phases of their daily life and work. While master and monks were picking tea, planting trees, or sitting around the fire together, the master, by means of a seemingly simple question about something in the immediate situation, would indicate to the disciple some aspect of the immutable Principle, bringing him to a deeper realization, or test the depth of understanding he had already achieved.

From time to time the masters took the high seat in the main hall of the monastery and gave lectures to the assembly of monks. On such occasions they did not expound the sutras or scriptures as did the clerics of other sects of Buddhism. Though, on the whole, Zen masters were conversant with the teachings of other schools—and many of these teachings undoubtedly underlie Zen thought and doctrines——from the first Zen had prided itself on *not* being founded on any scripture. Zen was concerned only with Absolute Mind. Absolute Mind was the masters' one theme, pure, original, basic Mind, and their every word and action was a pointing to and a manifesting of Absolute Mind. In energetic and vivid language, much of it the colloquial idiom of the time, interspersed with quotations from the sutras and other Buddhist writings, the old masters relentlessly drove their message home. When they gave their own views, these were apt to be expressed in cryptic statements and formulas. At such times members of the community and any visiting monks and laymen who might be present were free to ask the master for further elucidation. They were also free to ask him questions of their own, or to bring up one of the numerous stereotyped questions that Zen adherents seemed always to have at hand when they had nothing else to inquire about.

The master took advantage of all such opportunities to demonstrate the Principle, to awaken the questioner to deeper levels of understanding, or to destroy his pretensions. The answer the master gave, whether in word or in action, though always pointing to the Principle, was invariably adapted to the particular occasion. Thus it often came about that at different times the same master gave different answers to the same question. Furthermore, since these early masters were men of great originality and creative ability, their ways of demonstrating the profound Principle, their questions, and even their answers to the stock questions asked them, invariably bore the stamp of their own individual genius.

As the number of students around the famous masters grew larger, the personal contacts of the earlier days could not be maintained except with immediate disciples. Then a master might give to a number of students a certain question that he had already found effectual.

Though the question originally had arisen in response to an immediate situation and Was the immediate and personal problem of the individual disciple to whom it had been addressed, since the principle the master was making manifest through it was the immutable Principle and therefore valid for all men, the question also was valid for other students. Such questions performed the function of koans, and there is some evidence that by the end of Tang (618–907) the masters themselves were referring to them as koans.[9] But they were not koans in the full sense of the word, for they were questions being used by the masters who had originally created them. However, when Nanyuan Huiyong 南院慧顒 (Nan'in Egyō, *d.* 930),[10] a descendant of Linji Yixuan 臨濟義玄 (Rinzai Gigen, *d.* 866)[11] in the 3rd generation, questioned a disciple about certain of Linji's formulas,[12] Koan Zen, or the use of the words of earlier masters in a fixed and systematized form to instruct or test a student, may be said to have truly begun.

From that time on, the most illustrious masters, though they did not entirely cease creating their own koans, depended in large part on the "words of the ancients" in instructing their students, and the less talented masters relied upon them entirely. We may suppose that there were at least two reasons for this: the decline in the high level of creative genius with which the earlier masters had been endowed, and the great increase in the number, with a corresponding decrease in the quality, of the monks and lay students who were now flocking to individual monasteries by the hundreds, even thousands, to be instructed by the more reputable masters.

What were the "words of the ancients" now being used as "public records" or koans? Briefly, they consisted of questions the early masters had asked individual students, together with the answers given by the students; questions put to the masters by students in personal talks or in the course of the masters' lectures, together with the masters' answers; statements of formulas in which the masters had pointed to the profound Principle; anecdotes from the daily life of the masters in which their attitudes or actions illustrated the functioning of the Principle; and occasionally a phrase from a sutra in which the Principle or some aspect of it was crystallized in words. By presenting a student with one or another of these koans and observing his reaction to it, the degree or depth of his realization could be judged. The koans were the criteria of attainment.

Thus a unique method had been evolved for assisting men to attain religious awakening, a method of teaching in which there was no stated creed to be believed or precepts to be followed, no instruction in doctrines or discussions about them, no wordy descriptions of the stages on the way to enlightenment. Nor did the masters examine their students by asking them to state their views and beliefs in words. The koan was the examination. If the student had attained the understanding of the Principle as embodied in the koan, he would reply in such a fashion as clearly to indicate this. If not, then he must take the koan and wrestle with it, in the meditation hall and in the course of carrying out his daily tasks, until such time as he and it became one. The master gave him no further help or instruction.

But there was one serious weakness in this system that early began to be apparent. When the master picked up something right before the student's eye and used it to instruct him, the realization of this very thing as the manifestation or functioning of the Principle was the disciple's own and immediate problem. There was neither time nor opportunity to consider. Here stood the master towering above him demanding right then and there an immediate response. Of course the student might, and often did, fail to respond satisfactorily. But even then the problem remained his own, personal, immediate, and vital problem to solve, and to solve as quickly as possible if he was to have any peace of mind. But when many koans had been written down and he could read them at his leisure, or he had heard them stated many times and their possible or probable meanings discussed, the immediacy to him of even one koan, let alone hundreds, became difficult to feel. It became easy to give in to thinking about them, to comparing those of one master with those of another, to considering them in their historical setting, to enjoying them as literary curiosities. This tendency to handle the koan intellectually has been a persistent problem throughout the history of Koan Zen, and still remains one today.

Collections of "old cases," as the koans were sometimes called, as well as attempts to put the koans into a fixed form and to systematize them to some extent, were already being made by the middle of the 10th century. We also find a few masters giving their own alternate answers to some of the old koans and occasionally appending verses to them. In many cases these "alternate answers" and verses ultimately became attached to the original koans and were handled as koans supplementary to them.

The Linji master Fenyang Shanzhao 汾陽善昭 (Fun'yō Zenshō, 947–1024)[13] was the first to employ all these various trends. His "record," the *Fenyang Wude chanshi yulu*, includes three collections of one hundred koans each. The first collection consists of old koans, for each of which Fenyang wrote a verse epitomizing the import of the koan in poetical language; the second consists of koans he himself had made and for which he provided his own answers; the third is made up of old koans, together with Fenyang's alternate answers to them. These three collections became the models for later literary productions of a similar kind.

The most important of the collections of koans with attached verses was that made by Xuedou Chongxian 雪竇重顯 (Setchō Jūken, 980–1052),[14] a master of the Yunmen 雲門 (Ummon) School, which was later absorbed by the Linji School. Xuedou's *Baize songgu* contained one hundred "old cases" favored in his teaching line, and included eighteen original koans by the famous founder, of the school, Yunmen Wenyan 雲門文偃 (Ummon Bun'en, 862/4–949).[15] Xuedou was not only an outstanding Zen master but a distinguished poet of the time.

A century later the Linji master Yuanwu Keqin 圜悟克勤 (Engo Kokugon, 1063–1135)[16] used Xuedou's collection as the basis for a series of lectures in which he commented not only upon the one hundred koans Xuedou had selected but on Xuedou's verses as well. Yuanwu's lectures, recorded and compiled by his disciples, were soon issued under the title *Biyan lu*.

In Yuanwu's time the intellectualistic tendencies in Koan Zen were already widespread. Men were reasoning and theorizing about the koans, comparing and memorizing them and their answers in large numbers, and writing verses and explanatory statements about them. Though Yuanwu himself engaged in considerable literary activity, he was keenly aware of the dangers inherent in this trend, and spoke out sharply against it. He insisted, as had other masters before him from Yunmen on, that it was through penetration into a few koans, or even into only one, that the attainment of true insight into Absolute Mind is achieved. "If you understand a single koan right now, you can clearly understand all the teachings of the ancients as well as those of the men of today," he stated.

It was during the lifetime of Yuanwu's successor Dahui Zonggao 大慧宗杲 (Daie Sōkō, 1089–1163)[17] that Koan Zen entered its determinative period. Dahui was a true heir of Yuanwu. He vigorously opposed the literary and intellectual approach to the koan, and even went so far as to take violent measures to have his master's *Biyan lu* destroyed, feeling that the study of it was injurious to true Zen attainment. On the other hand, Dahui just as firmly advocated the right use of the old koans. The method he ceaselessly urged on his students was concentrated introspection of the koan, introspection into which not the slightest deliberation or intellectualization entered. The koan was to be introspected only, introspected deeper and deeper until its full content was revealed.

By Dahui's time, with the exception of the Caodong 曹洞 (Sōtō) School,[18] the various teaching lines of Zen that had originally stemmed from the disciples of the Sixth Patriarch[19] had virtually all been absorbed into the Linji School. The masters of the Caodong School, while they used koans and made the usual collections of selected koans with verses and commentaries attached, tended to place more emphasis upon the practice of meditation. Now a famous controversy arose between Dahui and Hongzhi Zhengjue 宏智正覺 (Wanshi Shōgaku, 1091–1157),[20] a leading master of the Caodong School. Dahui upheld the introspection of the koan as the superior method for attaining satori, while Hongzhi advocated that satori be attained through sitting quietly and bringing the mind to a state of complete tranquillity and emptiness. Dahui was not against the correct practice of meditation or zazen, in fact he was strongly in favor of it. It was primarily in zazen that the koan was to be introspected. What Dahui was against was the adherence to a quietistic type of sitting that he felt could only result in passivity and lifelessness, never in the dynamic experience of true satori. And Hongzhi, however strongly he may have championed "silent-illumination" meditation, did not himself dispense with the koan.[21] From this time on the Zen of the Linji School came to be known as *kanhua chan* 看話禪 (*kanna zen*), or "introspecting-the-koan Zen," and the Zen of the Caodong School as *mozhao chan* 默照禪 (*mokushō zen*), or "silent-illumination Zen." Perhaps the controversy between the two masters was not so heated as it was later made to appear. Dahui and Hongzhi seem always to have been friends, and before his death Hongzhi entrusted the disposition of his affairs to Dahui. Nevertheless, later generations of adherents in both schools continued the argument with a fervor not always so free from rancor and virulence as it had originally been.

Throughout the Yuan dynasty and into the Ming (1368–1644), the masters of both schools carried on their literary activities uninterruptedly. It is ironic indeed that a school which was founded upon an experience above all words should have produced the vast amount of literature that Zen produced in China and later in Japan. But at no time in the history of Zen were the masters unaware of their basic aim or of the problems that faced them in accomplishing it. Whether the method they advocated for the attainment of satori was the introspection of koans or the practice of zazen only, the masters had but one sole purpose, that of assisting men to realize Absolute Mind for themselves. And their writings, voluminous as they undeniably were, were attempts to urge men on to this goal.

In what way the later Chinese masters instructed their students in the koans is not clear. Certainly they gave numerous lectures in commentary on the koans, and their disciples seem to have recorded these lectures more or less meticulously. But whether the masters used koans to question their students during or at the conclusion of their lectures, whether the students in groups or individually came to the masters freely or at stated times, whether the master gave the student the koan or whether the student chose a koan for himself and then went to the master to have his insight tested, we do not know with any certainty. In Dahui's writings we find some disparaging remarks about the "transmission in the secret room," but he gives us no clue as to what the "secret room" was. After the great influx of monks and lay students into the monasteries at the end of Tang and the beginning of Song (960–1279), the numbers of followers slowly decreased, but there must always have been large groups of disciples around the important masters. Presumably the masters continued to be in close contact with their immediate disciples and to use the opportunities offered in daily life to question and instruct them. This is as much as can at present be said about this aspect of koan study. Perhaps the future will see it further clarified.

The development of the koan method reached its apogee in China in the Song dynasty. The masters of the Yuan still displayed some of the old virility, but by then Zen had already begun its long decline in

China. During Ming, the Linji School absorbed not only the Caodong School, but all other schools of Chinese Buddhism as well, to say nothing of elements from Tibetan Tantric Buddhism, popular Daoism, and the native folk religion. Fully accepted in the Chan of the Ming dynasty were the *nianfo* 念沸 (*nembutsu*)[22] practices of the Pure Land School, which, having had a few advocates for a short period in the early days of Chan, from the beginning of the Yuan dynasty had been gradually infiltrating it again. Though certain teachers in the direct lines of transmission from the masters of Song and Yuan continued the traditional ways of teaching, they did so only with many adaptations to the new accretions and the changing times.

Modern Chinese Chan, about which we are only now beginning to know something, seems to be a development from the Chan of the Ming and Qing (1644–1912) dynasties. Japanese Zen, as we shall see, had its roots in the Zen of Song and early Yuan. The one line of Ming Zen that came to Japan had little or no direct influence upon the teaching or teaching methods already firmly established there in the Rinzai and Sōtō schools. In Japan today, therefore, in order to make a clear differentiation, Japanese Zen is often referred to as "Song Zen," and modern Chinese Chan as "Ming Zen."

II. The Koan in Japanese Zen

Zen was introduced into Japan at a very early date, but five centuries were to pass before conditions were ripe for it to take root. The first known meditation teacher in Japan was the Japanese monk Dōshō 道昭 (629–700), who went to China in 653 to study under the famous Buddhist scholar Xuanzang 玄奘 (Genjō, 600?–664), and on his return to Japan taught meditation at a temple in Nara. In 736 the Chinese Commandment Master Daoxuan Lüshi 道璿律師 (Dōsen Risshi, 702–760) arrived in Nara. There he propagated not only the teachings of the Commandment or Vinaya Sect (Risshū 律宗 Lüzong)[23] but also those of the Kegon Sect 華嚴宗 (Huayanzong)[24] and those of the Northern School of Zen[25] as well. Daoxuan's Japanese heir Gyōhyō 行表 (722–797) is said to have taught the meditation of this school of Zen to the Japanese Tendai 天台 monk Saichō 最澄 (767–822). Later, Saichō went to China and studied at Tiantaishan 天台山 (Tendaizan).[26] While he was there he was given the Tiantai (Tendai) ordination and, in addition, received instruction from Vinaya, Chan (Zen), and Zhenyan 眞言 (Shingon)[27] masters. After he had returned to Japan and founded the Japanese Tendai Sect on Mount Hiei 比叡山 near Kyoto, Dengyō Daishi 傳教大師, the posthumous title by which Saichō is better known, included the practices of all these schools in his teaching. The last of the early Zen teachers was Yikong 義空 (Gikū, *n.d.*), a master of the Southern School of Zen[28] who came to Kyoto in the middle of the 9th century at the invitation of the Empress-Consort Danrin 檀林 (787–851). Although Yikong was under the patronage of the Court, his teaching had little success, and a few years later he returned to China. For the next three centuries the power of the Tendai and Shingon sects was such that no other Buddhist school could gain a foothold in Japan.

Over three hundred years later the Tendai monk Myōan Eisai 明庵榮西 (1141–1215),[29] during his second trip to China, studied under a Linji master and received the Seal of Transmission.[30] After his return to Kyoto, he founded there in 1202 the temple known as the Kennin-ji 建仁寺,[31] the first Zen temple to be established in Kyoto. Eisai introduced the teaching of Rinzai Zen at the Kennin-ji, but even at this late period he found it necessary to include with it Shingon and Tendai practices.

Eisai's successor at the Kennin-ji was Ryōnen Myōzen 了然明全 (1184–1225). Among Myōzen's students was a young monk, Dōgen Kigen 道元希玄 (1200–1253), who had become discouraged with his Tendai studies on Mount Hiei. Dōgen was eager to go to China, and urged Myōzen to accompany him. In 1223 master and disciple set forth on their voyage. During their stay in China Myōzen died, but Dōgen remained on, continuing his Zen practice under the Sōtō 曹洞 (Caodong) master Tiantong Rujing 天童如淨 (Tendō Nyojō, 1163–1228) until he had received the Seal of Transmission. Tiantong, though he is known to have used certain koans in his teaching, was one of the most outspoken opponents of the Kanna Zen ("introspecting-the-koan Zen") of the Linji School. His attitude in this respect and its influence upon his Japanese disciple was a determining factor in the course that Sōtō Zen was to follow in Japan through all the long years to come.

Dōgen returned to Japan in 1227. Though an aristocrat by birth, from the first he avoided any contact with either the Imperial Court at Kyoto or the Shogunate in Kamakura. He had no wish to found a school; he desired only to live quietly in a small temple, devoting himself to the realization of the truths of Buddhism through meditation and daily life. But students, both monks and laymen, were soon coming to him. As their numbers increased, he moved from one country temple to another. In 1245 the great monastery of Eihei-ji 永平寺, built for him by his disciples in the mountains of Echizen 越前, in present-day Fukui Prefecture, was completed. Dōgen had now become the deeply revered founder of the sect of Japanese Sōtō Zen.

Dōgen's Zen was centered in zazen. The meditation practice which he vigorously affirmed was that known as *shikan taza* 祇管打坐, "zazen only." "Zazen is the Buddha-dharma and the Buddha-dharma is zazen," he wrote in his great work *Shōbōgenzō*. Nevertheless Dōgen did not reject koans;[32] like his master before him, he seems to have used them in instructing his immediate disciples. Under Keizan Jōkin 瑩山紹瑾 (1268–1325), fourth patriarch of the sect, the koan was completely discarded, in theory at least, and zealous efforts were made to give Japanese Sōtō Zen a widespread and popular appeal. Nevertheless, the study of koans and of the koan collections of the Sōtō masters of Song has continued to play an important part in Sōtō training, though undoubtedly the masters of the sect have handled this teaching device in a somewhat different manner than have the masters of Japanese Rinzai Zen.

Only two Chinese Sōtō masters, descendants of Hongzhi Zhengjue in the 6th and 7th generations, are recorded to have journeyed to Japan, one in 1309 and the other in 1351.[33] Both taught their style of Zen at various Rinzai temples in Japan, and both founded teaching lines that soon became extinct. They seem to have made no contact with the Japanese branch of their own sect. Japanese Sōtō Zen, despite the adaptations to Japanese life and culture made in it by its later patriarchs, has always been and still is preeminently Dōgen's Zen.

The history of Japanese Rinzai Zen is quite different. During a period of one hundred and seventy-five years after the return of Eisai from China, twenty lines of Rinzai Zen teaching were brought to Japan and established there either by Chinese masters, many of them fleeing the disturbed political conditions in China, or by Japanese monks who had gone to China to study with Chinese masters and had received the Seal of Transmission from them. One of the more notable of the Japanese pilgrim monks was Shinchi Kakushin 心地覺心 (1207–1298),[34] who studied under Wumen Huikai 無門慧開 (Mumon Ekai, 1183–1260).[35] Kakushin returned to Japan in 1254, bringing with him his master's famous koan collection *Wumenguan* (*Mumonkan*). Another pilgrim monk was Nampo Jōmyō 南浦紹明 (1235–1309),[36] better known by his Imperially bestowed title Daiō Kokushi 大應國師. He went to China in 1259 and took his training under the Chinese Linji master Xutang Zhiyu 虛堂智愚 (Kidō Chigu, 1185–1269),[37] returning to Kyoto in 1267. The last of the Rinzai teaching lines was that founded by the Japanese monk Daisetsu Sonō 大拙祖能 (1313–1377),[38] who left for China in 1344 and returned in 1358. Thereafter, while the intercourse between Chinese and Japanese Zen did not cease, it gradually diminished. No outstanding master appeared and no new teaching line was established for another three hundred years.

The Kamakura period (1185–1333) saw the rapid rise to prominence of Japanese Rinzai Zen. Great headquarter temples were erected at Kamakura and Kyoto, and branch temples established throughout the country under the aegis of emperors, shoguns, and feudal lords. This illustrious patronage, to which was added that of artists, intellectuals, warriors, and wealthy merchants, continued on through the Ashikaga period (1338–1573). During this period Rinzai temples became the centers of inspiration for an aesthetic flowering that has, correctly or incorrectly, made Zen and Japanese culture almost synonymous words. Rinzai Zen, now completely adapted to its new environment, settled down into comfortable complacency.

All the Chinese and Japanese monks who had brought Rinzai Zen to Japan could trace their lineage directly back to the founder Linji Yixuan (Rinzai Gigen). All had brought with them the texts as well as the koans handed down to them by their teachers, and continued to use these in instructing their disciples. Whatever differences there may have been in their teaching were due to traditions in their teaching lines or to personal preferences, not to differences in basic principles.

The Japanese genius for the preservation of tradition fostered the continued transmission of the koans and their answers in the forms in which they had originally been handed down. Little attempt at innovation seems to have been made. Only a very few new koans were created by Japanese masters, and in their commentaries upon texts these masters followed closely the commentaries traditional in their own teaching lines. One thing should, perhaps, be mentioned here, however. The monks who came to Japan in the Kamakura period had brought with them, in addition to Zen texts, works on the Neo-Confucianism of Song, and were the first to introduce these to Japan. With many Zen priests, the study of these Neo-Confucian texts became a new and added interest. Though it cannot be said that Japanese Rinzai

Zen was influenced by Confucianism, a tinge of it can occasionally be discerned in the writings of later Rinzai Zen men.

We have little specific information about the way in which the Japanese masters instructed their students in koans during these centuries. On the whole, the manner of transmission was probably as traditional as were the koans transmitted. But one difference is apparent. While the Chinese masters may have earlier begun to instruct some of their disciples individually in their private rooms, the coming of Japanese students encouraged this practice. Few, if any, Japanese monks were acquainted with spoken Chinese when they first arrived in China, but all could write Chinese. From the first the Chinese masters apparently received their Japanese disciples individually in their rooms, and instructed them through an exchange of written questions and answers. When the Japanese monks returned home to become masters themselves, though there was no barrier of language between them and their disciples, they continued the practice of giving koan instruction in private, and this practice seems to have become generally accepted in Japan.

The stagnation into which Rinzai Zen had sunk by the beginning of the Tokugawa era (1603–1867) was disturbed in the middle of the 17th century by the arrival at Nagasaki in 1654 of Yinyuan Longqi 隱元隆琦 (Ingen Ryūki, 1592–1673). Ingen, to give him the Japanese name by which he was later always known, came to Japan as a refugee from the Manchus. He was a master of the Linji School, and had at one time resided at the Huangboshan 黃檗山 (Ōbakuzan)[39] in Fujian Province. The Zen which Ingen brought with him was late Ming dynasty Zen with all its accretions. Neither the Rinzai nor Sōtō sects of Japanese Zen received Ingen with much cordiality. Eventually the reigning emperor granted him land at Uji, near Kyoto, where, with the help of craftsmen and artisans who had accompanied him from China, he built an imposing monastery and temple in late Ming style, which he named the Mampuku-ji 萬福寺 after the original temple at Huangboshan. The fresh ideas in art, architecture, literary studies, and monastic organization introduced by Ingen had a direct influence that was far reaching in many fields. The new teaching and teaching methods he brought with him, however, though they may have had some indirect influence on later Rinzai Zen, were openly adopted only within the walls of the temples of the Ōbaku Sect which he founded.

Ingen's coming marked the beginning of the end of the long lethargy into which the world of Rinzai Zen had sunk. Less than fifty years later Hakuin Ekaku 白隱慧鶴 appeared and shook that world to its foundations,

SUGIYAMA Iwajirō 杉山岩次郎 was born January 19, 1686, in the village of Hara, situated at the foot of Mount Fuji on the Tōkaidō, the main road between Edo (Tokyo) and the old capital Kyoto. The name Hakuin Ekaku, by which he has always been known, is a combination of his two religious names. The temple priest who shaved his head as a youth gave him the name Ekaku; he himself adopted the name Hakuin in his early thirties. The *gō* or literary name he took was Kokurin 鵠林. His father was a samurai and his mother the daughter of the owner of a post station in the village.

As the youngest of five children, Hakuin was much with his mother, a devotee of the Nichiren 日蓮 Sect,[40] and her religious nature had a deep influence upon him. He was a highly sensitive boy and gifted with a remarkable memory. At four he is said to have known by heart over three hundred of the local songs. When he was eight years old, after attending a service at which a section of the Lotus Sutra was chanted, he returned home and recited it exactly as he had heard it. At another time, a sermon on the Eight Hot Hells so stimulated the child's naturally excitable imagination that for a long time he lived in constant fear of experiencing their torments.

At the age of fifteen he gained his parents' consent to become a monk at the Shōin-ji 松蔭寺, a small Zen temple in his native village. Not long afterwards the temple priest became ill, and Hakuin went to live at the monastery of Daishō-ji 大聖寺 in the nearby town of Numazu. There he continued his training for several years. In 1705, when he was nineteen, he went through a mental crisis which plunged him into deep despair and led him to set out on a pilgrimage that took him from temple to temple in various parts of the country.

One fine summer day, the abbot of the Zuiun-ji 瑞雲寺, a temple in present Gifu Prefecture where Hakuin was then staying, put his library containing books on Buddhism, Confucianism, and Daoism, out to air. Seeing them, Hakuin, who was still uncertain of the path he wished to pursue in life, determined to settle the matter by picking up one of the volumes at random and letting it decide his fate. The book he chose chanced to be a famous collection of anecdotes from the lives of the old Chinese Zen masters. When he read in it the story of how Shishuang Chuyuan 石霜楚圓 (Sekisō Soen, 986–1039)[41] kept himself awake during his long meditation vigils by sticking himself in the thigh with a gimlet, young Hakuin resolved to continue his training until he, too, had attained enlightenment.

Hakuin then set out again on his pilgrimage. In 1708 he settled down for a time at the Eigan-ji 英巖寺 in Niigata Prefecture and devoted himself to zazen and koan study. Early one morning, after a night spent in meditation, he had his first glimpse of satori. For him the experience was so overwhelming that he was certain no one in hundreds of years had had so deep a satori as he. When the master of Eigan-ji refused to approve his enlightenment, Hakuin visited a number of other masters, hoping to get their recognition. No one agreed with him. Finally, his pride decidedly humbled, he came to Dōkyō Etan 道鏡慧端 (1642–1721)[42] of the Shōju-an 正受庵 in Nagano Prefecture. This stern master subjected Hakuin to the hardest possible discipline, and, though he stayed with Etan only eight months—he was recalled to Numazu by the illness of his former teacher at the Daishō-ji—Hakuin succeeded in attaining his first real satori and his master's acknowledgment of it. Hakuin had previously had a number of teachers and later was to have others as well, but Shōju Rōjin 正受老人, as Etan was popularly known, was his real master. Throughout his entire life Hakuin never ceased being grateful to the old man.

In 1710 Hakuin was back in the Shōin-ji, the little temple in Hara where he had first been a novice. That same year, as the result of the strenuous practices he had subjected himself to, he had a severe nervous breakdown. After consulting several medical men and receiving no help from them, he finally sought out Hakuyūshi 白幽子,[43] a hermit living in the mountains northeast of Kyoto. Through certain curious methods taught him by Hakuyūshi, Hakuin was able to cure himself completely.

Hakuin gave his first sermon two years later at the Shōin-ji. He was then twenty-six. But he soon resumed his wanderings, studying koans with various masters in different parts of the country. His satori experiences increased in frequency and depth. The death of his father in 1716—his mother had died some years earlier—again brought him back to Hara and the Shōin-ji. There he began to preach and teach. In 1718 he went to Kyoto and resided for a short time at the headquarters temple of Myōshin-ji 妙心寺.[44] Upon his return to Hara he settled down in the Shōin-ji, never again to leave it for long.

Hakuin's fame now began to spread through the country, and disciples and lay followers came to him in ever increasing numbers. For the rest of his long life he taught and lectured continuously. Over the years he discoursed and commentated upon all the important Zen koan collections, many of the works of the Chinese Zen masters, and a few of the Buddhist sutras. He was a voluminous writer. His writings on Zen, for the most part in Chinese style, are rough, vigorous, and full of vivid imagery and picturesque expressions. For his lay followers, many of them the simple people of the neighboring farms and villages, he wrote in Japanese, using the Japanese syllabary which they could easily read. These writings, in which above all he stressed morality, obedience, and a virtuous life, were often punctuated with charming songs and verses of his own making.

Hakuin trained his disciples severely in traditional methods, exhorting them to zazen practice and further and further study of koans. His own experience of koan study under many different masters had given him a familiarity with the koans and the methods then in use in different teaching lines. He systematized these koans and methods to some extent himself, and this systematization was completed later by the most able of his many heirs. Furthermore, he created a considerable number of new koans, the most famous of which is that known as "The Sound of the Single Hand."

Hakuin's own deep and repeated satori experiences led him to encourage his students to strive for the same profound penetration as he had attained. Like his great Chinese predecessor Dahui, he insisted upon satori above everything else. But unlike Dahui, who had urged deeper and deeper satori through the continuously deeper introspection of a koan or koans but had made no attempt at any systematization of study, Hakuin considered that, after satori had once really been experienced, this satori should be gradually deepened and deepened by means of a systematized after-satori training. He divided Zen training into two parts: satori, and training after satori. The system originated by him and completed by his disciples is explained in detail by Isshū Rōshi in Part Two of this book.

But teaching, lecturing, and writing exhausted neither Hakuin's talents nor his tremendous energy. He encouraged and supervised the reprinting of the *Hannya shingyō* and the *Kannon gyō* 觀音經. He restored at least one temple in addition to his own Shōin-ji, and was instrumental in the rebuilding of two more, one of them the beautiful mountain monastery of Ryūtaku-ji 龍澤寺 in nearby Mishima, where he installed his great disciple Tōrei Enji 東嶺圓慈 (1721–1792).[45] Moreover, Hakuin was a brilliant painter and calligrapher in the true Zen style. A thousand or more examples of his work have come down to us, and his genius in this field is only now being fully recognized. He is also said to have carved the wooden statue of himself in the possession of the Shōin-ji, a statue that shows him in full robes, grasping a long and menacing stick, eyes sharply penetrating, and the whole figure alive with restrained power. If this was the master his disciples faced in their koan interviews with him, their hearts must indeed have quailed and cold sweat run down their bodies.

But Hakuin had a warm and human side as well. Due to his own "meditation illness" in his youth, he showed much concern for the health of his disciples and often instructed them in the practices he had learned from the old hermit Hakuyūshi. Also, Hakuin was much beloved by the more humble among his lay followers. They came to him constantly for advice on the problems facing them in their daily life, a life which at that time was particularly bitter for the peasantry. Hakuin's kindness and helpfulness never failed. In his religious instruction to them he was always broad-minded, often recommending the teachings and practices of other schools of Buddhism when he felt that these answered their simple needs better than the austere practices of Rinzai Zen. Where his Zen students were concerned, however, Hakuin was opposed to any way but that of the traditional Rinzai School. He often spoke out harshly against the "silent-illumination" meditation of the Sōtō Sect and the *nembutsu* practice followed by adherents of the Pure Land sects.

Hakuin's teaching to his own disciples and to all Zen students may be summed up simply in this way: Men must realize Absolute Mind through their zazen practice and their koan study; through continued zazen practice, koan study, and daily life that realization must be ever deepened so that it may be made visible in every thought, word, and act, whatsoever these may be. Morality is the foundation stone of practice; without morality there can be no true practice and therefore no true attainment. And, finally, health of body must be preserved in order to carry the practice on to its completion.

Hakuin Ekaku died quietly in his sleep at the Shōin-ji, January 18, 1769, at the age of eighty-three.

And now the whole world of Japanese Rinzai Zen began to awake. Monks' Halls or *sōdō* 僧堂 were gradually established in connection with those headquarter temples that did not already have them, and at some of the sub-temples as well. The masters or *rōshi* 老師 in charge of these sodos were all Hakuin's disciples—he is said to have had ninety odd—or their direct heirs. Changes were made in the arrangement of the meditation halls and the monks' living quarters, some of these following the style Ingen had earlier introduced at the Mampuku-ji. All aspects of daily life were strictly regulated, and a curriculum of study instituted that consisted of zazen, koan study, daily labor, begging, and sutra chanting. The year was divided into spring and autumn terms of three months each when the monks lived and studied in the sodo; each term was followed by a vacation period of three months during which the monks were free to return to their home temples in other parts of the country.

The system of koan instruction originated by Hakuin now replaced all previous methods of instruction. This system was developed and refined by his disciples, including his direct heir Gasan Jitō 峨山慈棹 (1727–1797).[46] But it was Gasan's two heirs, Inzan Ien 隱山惟琰 (1751–1814)[47] and Takujū Kosen 卓洲胡僊 (1760–1833),[48] who finally fixed "Hakuin Zen" in the two teaching styles current today.[49] Neither Hakuin nor his disciples compiled any collections of koans, at least none that were ever published. (The koans that Hakuin created are still transmitted only by word of mouth to the student in the master's room.) Except for Hakuin's koans, generally given in the earlier stages of koan study, the masters took their koans from the old Chinese collections, *Wumenguan* (*Mumonkan*), *Biyan lu* (*Hekigan roku*), *Linji lu* (*Rinzai roku*), and *Xutang lu daibie* (*Kidō roku daibetsu*), and from a collection made in Japan shortly before Hakuin's time known as *Kattō shū*. In the Inzan and Takujū lines, the answers to the koans were more or less standardized for each line respectively.

Another innovation that seems to have been instituted either by Hakuin or his disciples was the use of *jakugo* 著語 or "capping phrases" in koan study. Long before, Fenyang Shanzhao had appended his own verses, epitomizing the import of the koan in poetical language, to each of the hundred koans that comprised one of his collections, and Zen men had been writing such verses on koans ever since. Now, when the student had satisfied the master as to his understanding of a koan, he was asked to bring to the master a line or two in verse or prose which, as with Fenyang's verses, summarized the import of the koan. In this case, however, the capping phrase was not to be original with the student; it was to be a quotation taken from the literature, preferably secular, of any period. *Zenrin kushū*, an anthology of quotations from Chinese and Japanese sources compiled shortly before Hakuin's time, with which he is said to have become acquainted in his youth, was the principal source for these jakugo. A detailed description of this anthology constitutes PART THREE of this work. Masters of the Inzan line used jakugo for most, but not all, of the koans; those of the Takujū School used jakugo for all koans, often demanding several successively for a single koan. As with the answers to the koans, the jakugo for each koan seems to have been more or less standardized in each of these two teaching lines.

In the curriculum of the monastery, koan study unquestionably held first place. Every monk studied koans under the personal supervision of the master of the monastery. When a monk entered the sodo the master gave him his first koan; he did not choose it himself, as would seem to have been the general custom previously. On this koan the monk meditated until he had attained a satori deep enough to satisfy the master that he was ready to begin his "practice after satori." The attainment of the first satori, or *kenshō* 見性,[50] was expected to take two or three years, the full training after satori, from ten to fifteen years more.

The master or roshi met his student-monks individually at stated times for a private interview called *sanzen* 參禪. This might take place several times a day during the weeks especially devoted to meditation and known as *sesshin* 接(攝)心, or only once or twice a day at other times. The etiquette for such an interview was definitely prescribed and extremely formal. The monk entered the master's room after a series of deep bows outside and inside the entrance to it, sat down facing the master, stated his koan immediately, and gave the answer he had arrived at. If the master was convinced that the student's insight tallied with the koan, he might accept the answer, then ask him to bring a jakugo for it at the next regular time for sanzen. If not, the master might give the student a word of encouragement or drop a hint to let him know that he was on the wrong path. Most often, however, the master did not utter a single word; he merely rang a little bell at his right hand, indicating that the interview was over and he was ready to receive the next student. Etiquette demanded that the monk leave the room at once after making the usual bows. Thus there was little or no opportunity for the student to ask a question or even to open his mouth after his first words.

On certain fixed days the roshi gave a *teishō* 提唱, or lecture, to the monks. For this lecture he took a high seat facing the altar in the center of the main hall of the monastery, and discoursed, in the fashion set by Hakuin, on one of the old koan collections, taking up one "case" or a part of a case at each lecture successively until he had covered the entire collection.

Such is the manner of koan study that has prevailed in Japanese Rinzai Zen from the time of Hakuin and his disciples to the present day. Many of the forms and ceremonies still observed in Zen temple life can be traced back to customs current in China during the Song and Yuan dynasties and in Japan during the Kamakura and Ashikaga periods. Certain definitely feudalistic elements are discernible in the method of koan instruction which Hakuin originated. The period in which he lived was the middle of the Tokugawa era, an era when all aspects of Japanese life were frozen in a rigid feudalistic pattern. It is only natural, therefore, that the changes Hakuin made, revolutionary though many of them must have seemed in his own day, should have conformed, in externals at least, to the period of history in which he lived. And the Japanese reverence for tradition where form is concerned has preserved these externals punctiliously.

The upsurge of vitality in Rinzai Zen to which Hakuin gave the impetus was dealt a heavy blow in the first years of the Meiji era (1868–1912), when the government withdrew its support from all Buddhist temples and monasteries, deprived many of them of their holdings in land, and for a short time even openly persecuted them. But before many years had passed, despite the government's continued official support of Shintō, the various Buddhist sects, including those of Rinzai and Sōtō Zen, regained much of their earlier vigor. In the Rinzai monasteries of Kamakura and Kyoto several powerful Rinzai masters appeared who attracted to themselves talented disciples and lay adherents of importance in governmental, educational, and financial circles.[51]

The strong spirit of nationalism which, fostered by the government, began to take root in Japan in the last years of the 19th century, was accompanied by a mounting national pride in the great periods of the country's history. The stern martial code of the samurai of the Kamakura era was glorified and held up as the ideal way of conduct for citizen and soldier alike; the artistic creations of the Ashikaga era were reappraised and introduced to the western world as a flowering in the field of the arts that could only have been produced by the Japanese genius. Japanese Zen was credited with having been the source of those unique spiritual qualities with which the best in Japanese culture was now seen to be infused. The use of religion as a legitimate political expedient had been accepted throughout Japanese history, and it was accepted again. The military faction, fast rising to absolute power, saw in certain Zen practices a possible tool for the accomplishment of their ends. They now openly solicited assistance from Rinzai Zen in stimulating and sustaining the people's ardor. They were not refused.

The end of the last war found Rinzai Zen in a state of spiritual and physical exhaustion. The new land redistribution laws took away from the temples all but the last of their acres, and, with supporters reduced to the few who were still faithful believers, the priests in many cases were forced to find outside employment in order to keep their temple roofs in repair and themselves in daily necessities. The attention of the nation was completely concentrated on reconstruction and the regaining of material prosperity.

The Japanese Zen masters of today are trying faithfully to carry on their teaching against tremendous odds. Furthermore, they are bound by a traditional system which, as regards many of its forms, is a relic of the feudal age. All are aware of this, but the great problem facing them is how to adapt to modern life and thought without losing the very essence of Zen itself. The West's, to them, unanticipated interest in Zen and the slightly reviving interest of Japanese laymen may help to point a way. Zen has always made the same teaching available to laymen as to monks. The masters who have transmitted traditional Zen have, with few exceptions, always been temple men, but from the earliest times laymen have been among their more distinguished disciples.

Enlightenment, the personal experience of Reality, is man's ultimate experience. The quest for this experience is the most difficult quest upon which he can embark. It demands of him faith, determination, sacrifice, and, above all, passion. Without the sustained sense of urgency which passion imparts, the goal cannot be achieved. All the great men of Zen have understood this. The koans were in part devised to keep the sense of urgency sustained during the intervals when the heat of passion subsided. The seemingly unsolvable problem goads the disciple on mercilessly; when at last it is solved, the assurance that the insight attained tallies with the insight of enlightened men before him renews the disciple's faith in himself and his determination to press on. The koans are indeed peerless aids in the quest for the experience of enlightenment.[52]

PART TWO

Koan Study In Rinzai Zen

I. The Four Vows

Zen is "without words, without explanations, without instruction, without knowledge." Zen is self-awakening only. Yet if we want to communicate something about it to others, we are forced to fall back upon words.

I am only a practicing Zen monk. I have no scholarly learning and no literary accomplishments. However, using my own experience as the basis, in the following pages I shall try to tell you something about the course of study and practice followed by Zen monks during the years they spend in the training hall.

But first I should like to introduce you to the Four Vows. Every Buddhist not only recites the Four Vows morning and evening, but tries to keep them always in mind and to carry them out to the best of his ability throughout the course of his entire lifetime. For Zen monks, especially, these are the most important of all vows:

> Sentient beings are numberless;
> I take a vow to save them.
> The deluding passions are inexhaustible;
> I take a vow to destroy them.
> The Gates of Dharma are manifold;
> I take a vow to enter them.
> The Buddha-way is supreme;
> I take a vow to complete it.[1]

This is *the* Vow. Various karmic relations played a part in my going to New York in the spring of 1955 to give the talks on which this book is based, but this Vow was the fundamental cause. If you will firmly establish the Four Vows in your heart, my purpose will be more than fulfilled.

II. Seeing Into One's Own Nature (1)

When we Zen students enter the zendo, needless to say our first aim is to attain the state of *kenshō*,[2] that is, "to attain insight into our own real nature." If you ask me the question, "What is kensho—what is this 'seeing into one's own real nature'?" I am afraid I can give you no other answer than to say: "Kensho is just kensho, nothing more."

Our great masters of olden times have described the experience in various ways. One master said that kensho is just like coming back to life again after having lost your hold on the edge of a precipice and fallen to your death. Another master has said that kensho is the moment when you die the Great Death. And another has spoken of it as the state in which Great Life clearly manifests itself.

Though there are many ways of describing this state of seeing into one's own nature, all are merely something our old masters have said *about* it. The actual experience of true kensho can be attained only by yourself through your own self-awakening in your own body. There is no other way. In order to reach this state of seeing into our own nature, we Zen monks labor diligently and painstakingly day and night. A Zen monk without kensho is not worth a penny.

The experience of kensho has been handed down directly from Shakyamuni Buddha through successive generations of patriarchs to men of the present by means of the "transmission of Mind by mind."[3] As long as the direct experience of kensho continues to be thus transmitted from generation to generation, Zen will not disappear, regardless of whether great temples and religious establishments exist or not.

Daitō Kokushi,[4] founder of the Daitoku-ji,[5] in his last admonition spoke emphatically about the importance of kensho for Zen monks. His words are something like this:

"Some of you may preside over large and flourishing temples with Buddha-shrines and rolls of scripture gorgeously decorated with gold and silver, you may recite the sutras, practice meditation, and even lead your daily lives in strict accordance with the precepts, but if you carry on these activities without having the eye of kensho, every one of you belongs to the tribe of evil spirits.

"On the other hand, if you carry on your activities with the eye of kensho, though you pass your days living in a solitary hut in the wilderness, wear a tattered robe, and eat only boiled roots, you are the man who meets me face to face every day and requites my kindness."[6]

Seeing into our own real nature is the first principle for Zen monks. Therefore, always keeping foremost in our minds the koan we have been given, we never cease seeking kensho day and night, night and day. In order that you may know with what seriousness we seek it, I shall tell you about Eka Daishi,[7] the second patriarch of our Zen Sect in China. This will afford a better example than anything I could tell you from my own experience.

Long ago Bodhidharma[8] was staying at a small temple called Shōrin-ji, practicing the zazen we call wall-gazing.[9] At that time there was a lofty-minded man, Jinkō by name, who had lived a long time near the Yi and Luo rivers in Henan. He had read widely and deeply. He paid no attention to gaining a livelihood, but loved to roam among the lakes and mountains. He used to say: "Alas, the teachings of Confucius and Laozi are concerned only with propriety and conduct; the *Zhuangzi* and the *Book of Changes* fall far short of exhausting the Marvelous Principle."[10]

One day he said to himself: "I have heard that Bodhidharma, the Great Teacher, is now living at the Shōrin-ji. The sage is not far away; I must go to that mysterious place."

So he went to the Shōrin-ji. But, since the Master constantly sat erect and silent facing the wall, Jinkō heard from him no words of instruction or encouragement. Then Jinkō thought to himself: "In their search for Dao, the men of olden times crushed their bones and took out the marrow,[11] or cut their veins and drained their blood to appease the hunger of others;[12] they spread their hair upon the muddy road for a buddha to walk upon;[13] they threw themselves from the top of a cliff to feed the starving tigers below.[14] The men of olden times did this. Am I not also a man?"

On the ninth night of the twelfth month there was a violent storm of wind and snow, and the cold pierced to the bone. Jinkō stood motionless through it all. When dawn broke, the snow reached above his waist. Seeing this, the Master was filled with pity. "You have been standing in the snow for a long time," he said. "What do you seek?"

With his voice choked with tears, Jinkō replied: "My only request is that the Master, in his mercy, may deign to open the Gate of Sweet Dew[15] and save all sentient beings."

"The incomparable Marvelous Dao of all the Buddhas," replied the Master, "is attained only by long diligence in a practice difficult to practice, and by long endurance of that which it is difficult to endure. Why should you, with your shallow mind and arrogant heart, beg me for the True Vehicle[16] and suffer such hardships in vain?"

Upon hearing these words, Jinkō drew his sword from under his robe, cut off his left arm at the elbow, and placed it before the Master. At this, the Master knew Jinkō to be a vessel of Dharma.[17] He said: "All the Buddhas, when they seek Dao, forget their bodies for the sake of Dharma. You have cut off your arm. Now you, also, are capable of seeking."

"May I hear from you about the Dharma Seal of All the Buddhas?"[18] Jinkō asked.

"The Dharma Seal of All the Buddhas is not obtained from another," the Master said.

"Your disciple's mind is as yet without repose," said Jinkō. "I beg you, Master, let me have repose of mind."

"Bring me your mind and I will repose it for you," the Master replied.

"Though I seek for my mind, I cannot get it," said Jinkō.

"I have reposed your mind for you," said the Master.

At these words Jinkō attained satori.[19]

In such ways as this our patriarchs strove at the risk of their lives to attain kensho—to attain insight into their own real nature. If it was for the sake of Dharma, they did not hesitate to sacrifice their bodies or lay down their lives. Following their example, we also sit and practice meditation. Of course we do not go to the extreme of cutting off our arms. If we were to imitate Jinkō, however many arms we might have they would not suffice. Nevertheless we do such things as practicing zazen stark naked in mid-winter.

Nanshinken,[20] the late Rōshi of the Nanzen-ji Sodo,[21] in his day had the reputation of being the most severe of all the sodo roshis in Japan. Whenever he found any of us negligent in our practice, he would wield his *nyoi*[22] ruthlessly, and, every O Sesshin, many of us would bear the resultant bumps on our heads. I am still deeply grateful for Nanshinken's nyoi.

I am told that a pearl is produced only through the pearl-oyster's enduring the pain of having a grain of sand bore into its flesh, fighting against it, and protecting itself against it. We, also, by fighting all kinds of difficulties and overcoming them, strive to develop the jewel of spiritual cultivation.

III. Seeing Into One's Own Nature (2)

Because the experience of kensho—seeing into one's own real nature—is the pivot of Zen, and because the attainment of this experience is the fundamental aim of our Zen practice, our patriarchs have spoken and written many stimulating and encouraging words in order to urge their students on to more strenuous efforts. The great Japanese Zen Master Hakuin is one of those who have much to say on kensho, and in his *Sokkō roku kaien fusetsu* explains kindly and with scrupulous care the preparatory attitude of mind necessary for this experience. He says:

> If you wish to seek Buddha, you must first have insight into your own real nature. Without this insight, what benefit will you derive from reciting the Nembutsu or chanting the sutras? The word "Buddha" means "Awakened." When you awaken, it is your own mind that is Buddha. If somewhere else than in your own mind you seek a Buddha having a tangible form, you are a foolish fellow. It is like a man who is seeking for fish. He must first of all look in the water because, since fish are the product of water, outside water there are no fish.[23] Just so, he who wishes to seek Buddha must first of all look into his own mind because, since Buddha is the product of mind, outside mind there is no Buddha.

You may ask: "If, as you say, there is no Buddha outside mind, how can one awaken one's own mind and get to the bottom of it?"

I reply: "Is it mind that asks this question? Is it nature? Do you call it spirit, or do you call it soul? Does it reside on the inside, on the outside, or in the middle? Is it blue or yellow, red or white? You yourself must examine closely. When you are standing, examine closely; when you are sitting, examine closely. While you are eating your rice, while you are drinking your tea, while you are speaking, while you are silent, carry on this investigation intently and earnestly. Under no circumstances search among the teachings of the sutras or in written words. Never ask your teachers to explain. But when your activity of mind is exhausted and your capacity for feeling comes to a dead end, if something should take place not unlike the cat springing upon the mouse or the mother hen hatching her eggs, then in a flash great livingness surges up. This is the moment when the phoenix escapes from the golden net, when the crane breaks the bars of its cage. But, though you spend twenty or thirty years of your life in fruitless effort, and even up to the moment of death fail to break through, you must vow never even for a moment to think that the tales of any decrepit old man or woman can be of benefit to you in any way. If you do, their words will cling to your bones and stick to your skin, and you will never be able to rid yourself of them, to say nothing of achieving the ultimate aim of the patriarchs.

That is why a man of old said: "For the study of Zen there are three essential requirements."[24] What are these three essential requirements? The first is a great root of faith; the second is a great ball of doubt;[25] the third is great tenacity of purpose. A man who lacks any one of these is like a three-legged kettle with one broken leg.[26]

What is a root of faith? It is nothing less than the belief that every man possesses his own intrinsic nature into which he can attain insight, and that there is a Fundamental Principle[27] which can be completely penetrated. Just this. But, even though he has sincere faith, if a man does not bring concentrated doubt to bear upon the koans that are difficult to pass through,[28] he cannot get to the bottom of them and penetrate them completely. And, though this ball of doubt be firmly solidified, if it is not succeeded by great tenacity of purpose, it will not be shattered. Therefore it is said that, for slothful sentient beings, Nirvana endures for three asaṁkhyeya kalpas,[29] for intrepid sentient beings, the attainment of Buddhahood takes place in an instant of thought. You must always be ardent.

The study of Zen is like boring wood to get fire. The wisest course is to forge straight ahead without stopping. If you rest at the first sign of heat, and then again as soon as the first wisp of smoke arises, even though you bore for three asaṁkhyeya kalpas, you will never see a spark of fire. My native place is close to the seashore, barely a few hundred paces from the beach. Suppose a man of my village is concerned because he does not know the flavor of sea water, and wants to go and taste it for himself. If he turns back after having taken only a few steps, or even if he returns after having taken a hundred steps, in either case when will he ever know the ocean's bitter salty taste? But, though a man comes from as far as the mountains of Kōshū or Shinshu, Hida or Mino,[30] if he goes straight ahead without stopping, within a few days he will reach the shore, and, the moment he dips the tip of one finger into the sea and licks it, he will instantly know the taste of the waters of the distant oceans and the nearby seas, of the southern beaches and the northern shores, in fact of all the sea water in the world.[31]

Thus Hakuin Zenji painstakingly explains the matter for the sake of those of us who are studying Zen. Although he tells us not to search in the sutras and other writings, not to be led astray by the words of men, this is very difficult indeed. However, our patriarchs have not left us without assistance. I said previously that, in our ceaseless seeking for kensho, we Zen monks always keep foremost in our minds the koan we have been given. What is the koan we are given when we first enter the monastery and begin our Zen study? Our teacher usually selects one of these three:

The Sixth Patriarch[32] asked the head monk Myō: "Thinking neither of good nor of evil, at this very moment what was your original aspect before your father and mother were born?"[33]

A monk asked Master Jōshū:[34] "Has the dog Buddha-nature or not?"

Jōshū answered: "Mu!"[35]

Hakuin Zenji used to say to his disciples: "Listen to the sound of the Single Hand!"[36]

In the first line of his *Zazen wasan*,[37] Hakuin Zenji says: "Sentient beings are intrinsically Buddha." When Shakyamuni was sitting under the Bodhi Tree and, on catching a glimpse of the morning star, came to his Great Awakening, he also exclaimed: "How wonderful! Every sentient creature is endowed with the intrinsic wisdom and virtuous characteristics of Tathāgata."[38]

All the phenomena that are unfolding before our eyes, all, without any exception, just as they are, are the reality we see when we attain insight into our own real nature. All are Tathāgata. All sounds are the profound and exquisitely subtle voice of Dharma. Why is it impossible for us to receive them as they are? Shakyamuni Buddha, Hakuin, and all the patriarchs of the past have proclaimed: "Sentient beings are intrinsically Buddha," or, "Every sentient creature is endowed with the intrinsic wisdom and virtuous characteristics of Tathāgata." But though these sounds are correctly broadcasted, our receiving instruments emit only a confusion of noise, and, constantly engrossed in things as we are, we cannot distinguish the precious and subtle sounds lost in the interference. To say this does not mean that our receiving instruments are inferior. Such is not at all the case. Each one of us has exactly the same remarkable receiving instrument as the Buddha had. What is essential is to know how to adjust it.

When we enter the sodo, the first instruction we receive is, "Give up your life!" It is easy to pronounce the words "Give up your life!" but to do so is a difficult matter. However, if we do not put an end once and for all to that which is called "self" by cutting it off and throwing it away, we can never accomplish our practice. When we do, a strange world reveals itself to us, a world surpassing our reckoning, where he who has cast away his self gains everything, and he who grasps for everything with his illusory concepts in the end loses everything, even himself.

Of course, what I have been saying all this while is just a part of the confusion of sounds of which the world is so full. But I hope that every one of you, with your wonderful receiving instruments, may correctly catch the exquisite voice of Dharma and attain Shakyamuni's so-called "True Dharma Eye," "Marvelous Mind of Nirvana," and

"True Form of the Formless."[39] Whenever the din becomes unbearable, I beg you to practice zazen. Zazen is the peerless method of adjusting our receiving instruments.

IV. The Hosshin and Kikan Koans

Though I have already spoken at some length on the subject of kensho or seeing into one's own true nature, I shall say a little more about it. Since kensho is the foundation of Zen, however much we may think about it, we still do not know it, and, however many times we may speak about it, we can never speak too often.

Hakuin Zenji, in his *Sokkō roku kaien fusetsu*, which I have previously quoted, has this further to say:

> My humble advice to you distinguished persons who study the profound mystery of the Buddha-dharma is this: Your close examination of yourself must be as urgent as saving your own head were it ablaze; your efforts to penetrate into your own original nature must be as tireless as the pursuit of an indispensable thing; your attitude toward the verbal teachings of the buddhas and patriarchs must be as hostile as that toward a deadly enemy.[40]
>
> In Zen, he who does not bring strong doubt to bear upon the koans is a dissolute, knavish good-for-nothing. Therefore it is said: "Underlying great doubt there is great satori; where there is thorough questioning there will be a thoroughgoing experience of awakening."[41]
>
> Do not say: "Since my worldly duties are many and troublesome, I cannot spare time to solidify my doubt firmly," or, "Since

> my thoughts are always flying about in confusion, I lack the power to apply myself to genuine concentration on my koan."
>
> Suppose that, among the dense crowds of people in the hurly-burly of the market place, a man accidentally loses two or three pieces of gold. You will never find anyone who, because the place is noisy and bustling or because he has dropped his pieces of gold in the dirt, will not turn back to look for them. He pushes any number of people about, stirs up a lot of dust, and, weeping copious tears, rushes around searching for his gold. If he doesn't get it back into his own two hands, he will never regain his peace of mind. Do you consider the priceless jewel worn in the hair,[42] your own inherent marvelous Dao, of less value than two or three pieces of gold?[43]

On hearing Hakuin Zenji's kind words of admonition, any person of resolute purpose will certainly have his mettle aroused. But for one who is without aspiration, of course they will be but the recitation of the Nembutsu in a horse's ear.[44] Treasuring such words of admonition in our hearts, and bearing always in mind the conduct of the patriarchs in their daily activities, we face squarely to the koan we have been given, study it faithfully, and work wholeheartedly. We pass beyond time, are not swayed by all kinds of external circumstances, keep our inner mind calm and composed, and make this mind firm and hard as an iron wall. If this concentrated reflection[45] is built up continuously over one year, two years, three years, insight into one's own true nature will inevitably take place.

The realm which is revealed to us once we see into our own true nature is none other than that known in Sanskrit as the *Dharmakāya*, and, in Japanese, the *hosshin*.[46] Since the Dharmakāya has been explained backward and forward in the works of the various schools that depend upon the scriptures and their commentaries, I shall not take it up from the scholastic point of view. In *Rinzai roku*, the Zen Master Rinzai speaks about the Dharmakāya this way: "The pure light in each instant of thought is the Dharmakāya Buddha within your own house."[47]

With the aid of our first koan we attain our first glimpse into the undifferentiated realm of the Dharmakāya. To deepen our insight into this realm, to become acquainted intimately with this, our original home, and to make it our constant dwelling place, we study many koans known as Dharmakāya koans, or, in Japanese, *hosshin* koans. Let me give you a few examples:

> A monk asked Kassan Oshō:[48] "What is the Dharmakāya?" "The Dharmakāya is without form," Kassan replied.[49]

> A monk once said to Dairyō Oshō:[50] "The physical body decomposes. What is the indestructible Dharmakāya?"
> Dairyō answered with this verse:
> "Blooming mountain flowers
> Are like golden brocade;
> Brimming mountain waters
> Are blue as indigo."[51]

> When Ummon[52] was asked, " What is the pure Dharmakāya?" he replied: "The flowering hedge [surrounding the privy]."[53]

> To Jun Oshō's[54] verse on the Dharmakāya was this:
> When the cows of Eshū are well fed with grain,
> The horses of Ekishū have full stomachs.[55]

This is like saying that, when an American sneezes, an Englishman catches cold.

Fu Daishi[56] composed the following verse on the Dharmakāya:

> Empty-handed, yet holding a hoe;
> Walking, yet riding a water buffalo.[57]

If, on coming upon expressions such as these, you feel as if you were meeting a close relative face to face at a busy crossroad and recognizing him beyond a question of a doubt, then you can be said to understand the Dharmakāya. But, if you use common sense to conjecture about it, or run hither and thither trying to follow the words of others, you will never know the Dharmakāya. An old master has said: "There are many intelligent men, but few who have attained insight into their own real nature." Truly this one thing—seeing into one's own real nature—is the eternal eye of Zen.

But now that we have once achieved kensho, if we stop here and do not go forward another step, we cannot experience the patriarchs' marvelous realm of differentiation.[58] To save ourselves from this misfortune, it is necessary to pass through many intricate koans having to do with differentiation. The Zen term for the complex interlockings of differentiation is *kikan*,[59] and the koans that have been devised to aid us in successfully dealing with these interlockings are called *kikan* koans.

In the *Hekigan roku* there is a passage that reads:

> Jade is tested by fire, gold is tested by a touchstone, a sword is tested by a hair, water is tested by a stick. In our school, one word or one phrase, one action or one state, one entrance or one departure, one "Hello!" or one "How are you!" is used to judge the depth of the student's understanding, to observe whether he is facing forward or facing backward. If he is a fellow with blood in his veins, he will immediately go off, shaking his sleeves behind him, and, though you shout after him, he will not come back.[60]

With the help of the *kikan* koans we release ourselves from the bonds that hold us fast, get out of the sticky morass in which we are floundering, and return to the unfettered freedom of the open fields. Some people may say: "If I have gained insight into my real nature once, that is enough. Why should I go further and study many *kikan* koans?" The old masters lashed out at such persons, calling them "earthworms living in the mud of self-accredited enlightenment." "We awaken to Reality suddenly, and are perceiving phenomena right now." As we master the interlockings of differentiation one by one, and our understanding becomes clearer and clearer, Reality becomes increasingly distinct.

The following are some of the koans used to enable us to manipulate these interlockings freely:

> Tosotsu Etsu Oshō[61] devised three barriers as tests for his students:
>
> 1. You pull out the weeds and study the profound mystery only in order to see into your original nature. Where is your original nature at this moment?

2. One who has realized his own original nature escapes from birth-and-death. When the light of your eyes falls to the ground, how will you escape?

3. One who has escaped from birth-and-death knows whither he goes. When the Four Great Elements that compose your body separate, where will you go?[62]

A monk asked Master Jōshū: "What is the meaning of Bodhidharma's coming from the West?"

"The cypress tree in the garden," Jōshū replied.[63]

Three times the National Teacher Chū[64] called to his attendant, and three times the attendant answered him. The National Teacher said: "I always used to think that I was beholden to you, but all along it was really you who were beholden to me."[65]

We must make our way through the mass of complex interlockings that comprise the realm of differentiation, and enter the inner sanctuary of the patriarchs. To accomplish this, we must train ourselves by concentrated reflection on our koans over and over again. Daie Oshō[66] used to say to people: "I have experienced great satori eighteen times, and lost count of the number of small satoris I have had."[67] If even the old masters had to train themselves thus, surely we haven't a moment to waste.

When the power of kensho—the power of seeing into our own true nature—is weak, we cannot alter the karma clinging to us from the past that hinders our attainment. If the wisdom that comprehends differentiation is not completely bright, we cannot benefit sentient beings. But to make this differentiation-wisdom bright is a difficult undertaking indeed.

V. The Gonsen Koans

I have spoken at some length about the Dharmakāya or *hosshin* koans and about the *kikan* koans. The next type of koan we take up in our Zen study is that known as the *gonsen* koan.[68] *Gonsen* means literally "the study and investigation of words." *Gonsen* koans are those words and phrases of the patriarchs that are difficult to understand. Now that we have succeeded in entering the Dharmakāya (*hosshin*), and in making our way through the interlockings of differentiation (*kikan*), we must devote our efforts to penetrating into the innermost meaning of words and phrases.

We often hear it said: "In our sect (i.e. the Zen Sect) there are no written letters to be set down, no words and phrases to be made known, no delusions to be freed from, no enlightenment to be attained." But, if we were to sit down right here in what an old master has called "the deep pit of emancipation," we should, after all, be violating the true meaning of the Buddha-dharma. Hence, for us students of Zen, beneath a single phrase there exists life and there exists death, within a single response there lies release and there lies capture, upon a single expression rests the realm of the myriad transformations which it is impossible for any man to know, whosoever he may be. This is why we must know the many subtle meanings within a single word.

Ummon Zenji said: "Men of immeasurable greatness are tossed about in the ebb and flow of words."[69] If you can penetrate directly into words and understand them thoroughly, everything, from vicious words to the inane disputations of the world, will be transformed into ghee of the finest flavor.[70]

Hakuin Zenji put it thus: "Dancing and singing are the voice of the Dharma."[71]

An old master has said: "In our sect there are no words or phrases; there is not a single thing to give to men." But for the very reason that there are no words and phrases, words and phrases are the more wonderful. Because the hidden valley is without partiality, it echoes the footsteps of whomsoever enters it. For the very reason that there is not a single thing, the ten thousand things are the more mysterious. Because the great bell is of itself soundless, when it is struck by the bell-beam it reverberates with a flood of sound. Penetrating into the Fundamental Principle and penetrating into the teachings on it are not different from this. The four propositions of logic are abandoned and the hundred negations wiped out.[72] Then, in whatsoever way or however freely you may speak, you can instantly "cut off the tongue of every man on earth."[73] But if, because you desire the emancipation of only your own one body, you do not pass through the *gonsen* koans, how are you going to save sentient beings?

In the *Laṅkāvatāra-sūtra* we find this passage: "To penetrate into the Fundamental Principle and not to penetrate into the teachings on it is like opening your eyes in the dark. To penetrate into the teachings and not into the Fundamental Principle is like shutting your eyes in the daylight. To penetrate into both the Fundamental Principle and the teachings on it is like opening your eyes in the clear light of day."[74] Perhaps by now you have come to realize the importance of these *gonsen* koans, these koans that are concerned with the study and investigation of words.

Long ago Bodhidharma described his teaching as: "A special transmission outside the scriptures; not founded upon words and letters; by pointing directly to man's own mind, it lets him see into his own true nature and thus attain Buddhahood." Frequently, as the result of misunderstanding this statement, people do not read the scriptures and the writings of the patriarchs, or they consider verbal teachings to be of minor importance. That so many of our own sect have today abandoned these studies is a matter for regret. When a teaching outside the scriptures is clearly understood, the teaching within the scriptures should not interfere with it. If a teaching outside the scriptures does not admit the teaching within the scriptures, then it is not a true teaching. When the insight into both is clear, there is no prejudice against either.

To illumine one's mind with old learning at a bright window during the day and to deepen one's discernment of the Principle by meditation in the Monks' Hall during the night, this is, indeed, to illumine one's own nature with the teachings and to illumine the teachings with one's own nature. Inside and outside are one, this and that are transcended. It is just like two mirrors mutually reflecting one another with no shadow between them.

But, though written words and spoken phrases can be the source of emancipation, they can be the source of bondage as well. Depending upon the way they are used, they become the finest ghee or the most vicious poison.

Now let me show you a few of the koans through the study of which we attain insight into the mystery of words:

> A monk once said to Fuketsu Oshō:[75] "Speech and silence tend toward separation [from It] or concealment [of It]. How shall we proceed so as not to violate It?"
>
> Fuketsu replied with the following verse:
>
> "I always remember Kōnan in the spring,
> The partridges crying and flowers spilling their fragrance."[76]

> A monk asked Nansen:[77] "Is there a truth that has not been preached to men?"
>
> "There is," said Nansen.
>
> "What is this truth?" asked the monk.
>
> Nansen answered: "This is not mind, this is not Buddha, this is not a thing."[78]

> A monk asked Master Jōshū: "What is Jōshū?"
>
> "East gate, west gate, south gate, north gate," Jōshū replied.[79]

> One day Chōsha Oshō[80] went for a ramble in the mountains. On his return to the monastery, the head monk said to him: "Oshō, where have you been?"

"I have come from a ramble in the mountains," Chōsha replied.

"Where did you go, Oshō?" the head monk inquired.

"Going, I followed the fragrant grasses; returning, I pursued the falling blossoms," answered Chōsha.

"How very springlike the feeling!" exclaimed the head monk.

"Still better is the dripping of autumn dew from the full-blown lotus flowers," returned Chōsha,

Setchō's *jakugo* was: "I am grateful to you for your answer."[81]

We also study Haryō Oshō's[82] "Three Pivotal Words":

1. A monk asked Haryō Oshō, "What is the Daiba Sect?"
   "Filling a silver bowl with snow," Haryō replied.
2. "What is the Blown Hair Sword?"
   "The tip of each branch of coral supports the moon."
3. "What is Dao?"
   "A bright-eyed man falls into a well."[83]

Commenting upon these three questions and answers, Ummon said: "At some anniversary of my death, if you recite these 'Three Pivotal Words,' that will suffice to requite my kindness."

Such is the high regard in which we hold a phrase. But let me warn you, and this is the important point, if you are caught in the entanglement of words, you will lose your freedom.

When Shakyamuni was about to enter Nirvana, Mañjuśrī[84] addressed him, saying: "I entreat the World Honored One to turn the Wheel of Dharma for the last time."

The World-Honored One upbraided Mañjuśrī, saying: "From the day I entered the Deer Garden until I came here to the bank of the Hiraṇyavatī River, I have never uttered a single word."[85]

Is this turning the Wheel of Dharma or not? It is difficult indeed fully to exhaust the mystery of words.

VI. The Nantō Koans

The next type of koan we study is that known as the *nantō* koan.[86] *Nantō* means "difficult to pass through," so the *nantō* koans are the koans most difficult to pass through. Even though we have smashed the tub of black lacquer[87] with the help of the *hosshin* koans, moved through the multifold interlockings of the *kikan* koans, and, through the study of many *gonsen* koans, completed our investigation of those words of the patriarchs that are difficult to understand, to our regret we find that the dwelling place of the patriarchs is still as far away as the distant horizon. When we look up at it, it seems higher and higher; when we enter it, it seems deeper and deeper. Even for the patriarchs what formidable difficulties there were! This is the place called *nantō*, the place difficult to pass through. Not until we have penetrated these *nantō* koans one by one can we be said to be true monks.

In his *Sokkō roku kaien fusetsu*, Hakuin Zenji says:

> My advice to you eminent persons who study this profound teaching is this: You resolute men must dauntlessly display your spirit and attain insight into your real nature once. But, the moment your insight into your own nature has become perfectly clear, discard the insight you have attained, and settle these *nantō* koans. Then you will understand beyond the question of a doubt the words of the *Nirvana Sutra* when it says: "All the Buddhas and

> World Honored Ones see their Buddha-nature with their own eyes as clearly as they see the mango fruit lying in the palms of their hands."[88]
>
> Furthermore, you will penetrate into the patriarchs' final experience. Then, for the first time, grasping in your two hands the talons and teeth from the cave of Dharma[89] and wearing the supernatural talisman that wrests life from death,[90] you can enter the realms of the Buddhas and sport in the world of the Maras;[91] you can pull out the nails and wrench out the wedges,[92] spread the cloud of Great Compassion,[93] practice the almsgiving of the Great Dharma,[94] and abundantly benefit those who come to you from all directions; yet all the while you are only an old monk with two horizontal eyes and a perpendicular nose, who, having nothing further to do, enjoys the greatest ease.
>
> This is what is called being a true descendant of the patriarchs and a man who requites the kindness he has received. Now you may pass your days in tranquillity, drinking tea when there is tea, eating rice when there is rice. If there is nothing further to do, that is all right; if there is something to do, that is all right. The patriarchs cannot lay their hands on you, and you can spend ten thousand ounces of gold.[95]

Until a Zen monk has reached this point he cannot be at ease even when drinking a cup of tea.

Nanshinken, my former teacher, often used to speak about this in his talks to the monks. "The practice of Zen," he would say, "is just like making a fine sword. The raw iron must be heated until it becomes red hot; then it must be beaten into shape, then put in the fire again, then thrust into cold water, then beaten into shape again—tempered and polished over and over and over again to bring it to completion. Then you will have a truly fine sword. There will be nothing it touches that such a sword does not cut through. On the other hand, if the tempering is insufficient, the blade will be defective or blunt. It won't cut the head off even a turnip."

For this reason, the more satoris you have attained the more you must experience, the clearer your understanding becomes the more you must study.

As examples of these *nantō* koans, let me show you these:

When the Taifu Riku Kō[96] and Nansen were talking one day, Riku Kō said: "The Dharma Master Jō[97] has said: 'Heaven-and-Earth and I have one and the same source; the ten thousand things and I have one and the same body.' Is this not extraordinary?"

Pointing to a flower in the garden, Nansen said to the Taifu: "When men of today look at this flower, it seems to them like a dream."[98]

The poet Setchō wrote the following verse in commentary upon Nansen's remark:

Hearing, seeing, understanding, knowing—
Each of these is not separate.
For him, mountains and rivers
Do not appear in the mirror.
When the frosty heaven's moon has set
And midnight nears,
Whose shadow with mine
Will the clear pool reflect, cold?[99]

Goso Hōen Zenji[100] said: "It is like a water buffalo's passing through a window-lattice. Its head, horns, and four hoofs have all passed through. Why can't its tail pass through?"[101]

And another koan known as Sozan's Memorial Tower:

Once, when the monk who was director of affairs in the monastery came to talk with Sozan Nin Zenji[102] about the construction of the Master's memorial tower, the Zenji said: "How much money will you give the builder?"

"That rests with you, Oshō," the monk replied.

"Is it better to give the builder three cash, or better to give him two cash, or better to give him one cash?" asked Sozan. "However, if you can speak, build the tower for me yourself."

The monk was dumbfounded.

At that time Rasan[103] was living in a hermitage on the Daiyu Peak.[104] One day a monk who came to the mountain to see him recounted this conversation between Sozan and the director of affairs at the monastery.

"Has anyone been able to speak?" asked Rasan.

"As yet, no one," replied the monk.

"Then go back to Sozan," said Rasan, "and tell him this: if you give the builder three cash, you won't get a memorial tower in your entire lifetime; if you give him two cash, you and he together will be a single hand; if you give him one cash, you will do him such injury that his eyebrows and hair will fall out."

The monk returned and gave the message to Sozan. The Zenji assumed a dignified manner and, gazing far off toward the Daiyu Peak, bowed and said: "I had thought there was no man who could speak, but on the Daiyu Peak is an old Buddha who emits dazzling shafts of light reaching even to this distance. Nonetheless, he is a lotus blooming in midwinter."

Upon hearing of Sozan's words, Rasan said: "By my speaking thus, the tail hairs of the tortoise have suddenly grown several feet longer."[105]

Addressing the assembly at the end of the summer sojourn, Suigan[106] said: "My brothers, since the beginning of the summer I have done a lot of talking. Look, have I any eyebrows left?"

Hōfuku[107] said: "The robber has a coward's heart."

Chōkei[108] said: "Growing!"

Ummon said: "*Kan*!"[109]

And then there is the koan known as Enkan's Rhinoceros-horn Fan:

One day Enkan Oshō[110] called to his attendant and said: "Fetch me my rhinoceros-horn fan."

"The fan has been broken," said the attendant.

"If the fan has been broken, then bring me the rhinoceros itself," Enkan returned.

The attendant had no reply.[111]

Setchō's verse on this reads:

> The rhinoceros-horn fan
> Has long been in use,

But when a question is asked,
No one knows in truth what it is.
The boundless fresh breeze
And the horn on the head,
Just as rain clouds that have passed,
Are difficult to pursue.[112]

When you have succeeded in passing through these and many other *nantō* koans without any hesitation and without any doubt —these koans that are difficult to believe, difficult to explain, difficult to enter into, difficult to penetrate—you will have made an exhaustive study of the *jiji muge hokkai*,[113] the Dharma-world where each thing interpenetrates and harmonizes perfectly with every other thing without any hindrance whatsoever, the realm of complete effortlessness.

VII. The Goi Koans

We are now approaching the summit of our formal study of Zen. Though we have penetrated many koans, including those difficult to pass through, the patriarchs want us to make a still deeper study of the doctrines of our sect. To that end they would have us take up the *Tōzan goi*,[114] the "Five Ranks" devised by Tōzan Ryōkai Zenji.[115]

The Five Ranks has sometimes been called the philosophy of Zen. However, without the insight we have gained as the result of passing through many previous koans, we would not be prepared to grasp the profound meaning of the Five Ranks. Intellectual ability has no part in the comprehension of the wisdom of the patriarchs. The study of the Five Ranks is more nearly like a severe and final examination, for he who undertakes this study will be called upon not only to review all that he has previously come to understand, but to clarify, correlate, and deepen still further the insight he has attained. He will have to polish again each facet of his spiritual jewel, which he has cut so laboriously and painstakingly. But, in doing so, he will see for the first time the total inclusiveness, perfect symmetry, and matchless beauty to which it has been brought under the training devised by the old masters.

Hakuin Zenji has given a penetrating commentary upon the Five Ranks in his *Keisō dokuzui*, I shall let him speak in my place. Perhaps after reading his words you will understand why we value the *goi* koans so highly.

The Five Ranks of The Apparent and The Real: The Orally Transmitted Secret Teachings of the [Monk] Who Lived on Mount Tō[116]

We do not know by whom the *Jeweled-mirror Samādhi*[117] was composed. From Sekitō Oshō,[118] Yakusan Oshō,[119] and Ungan Oshō,[120] it was transmitted from master to master and handed down within the secret room. Never have [its teachings] been willingly disclosed until now. After it had been transmitted to Tōzan Oshō, he made clear the gradations of the Five Ranks within it, and composed a verse for each rank, in order to bring out the main principle of Buddhism. Surely the Five Ranks is a torch on the midnight road, a ferry-boat at the riverside when one has lost one's way!

But alas! The Zen gardens of recent times are desolate and barren. "Directly-pointing-to-the-ultimate"[121] Zen is regarded as nothing but benightedness and foolishness; and that supreme treasure of the Mahayana, the *Jeweled-mirror Samādhi*'s Five Ranks of the Apparent and the Real, is considered to be only the old and broken vessel of an antiquated house. No one pays any attention to it.

[Today's students] are like blind men who have thrown away their staffs, calling them useless baggage. Of themselves they stumble and fall into the mud of heterodox views and cannot get out until death overtakes them. They never know that the Five Ranks is the ship that carries them across the poisonous sea surrounding the rank of the Real, the precious wheel that demolishes the impregnable prison-house of the two voids.[122] They do not know the important road of progressive practice; they are not versed in the secret meaning within this teaching. Therefore they sink into the stagnant water of śrāvaka-hood[123] or pratyeka-buddhahood.[124] They fall into the black pit of withered sprouts and decayed seeds. Even the hand of Buddha would find it difficult to save them.

That into which I was initiated forty years ago in the room of Shōju[125] I shall now dispense as the alms-giving of Dharma. When I find a superior person who is studying the true and profound teaching and has experienced the Great Death,[126] I shall give this secret transmission to him, since it was not designed for men of medium and lesser ability. Take heed and do not treat it lightly!

How vast is the expanse of the sea of the doctrine, how manifold are the gates of the teaching! Among these, to be sure, are a number of doctrines and orally transmitted secret teachings, yet never have I seen anything to equal the perversion of the Five Ranks, the carping criticism, the tortuous explanations, the adding of branch to branch, the piling up of entanglement upon entanglement. The truth is that the teachers who are guilty of this do not know for what principle the Five Ranks was instituted. Hence they confuse and bewilder their students to the point that even a Śāriputra or an Ānanda[127] would find it difficult to judge correctly.

Or, could it be that our patriarchs delivered themselves of these absurdities in order to harass their posterity unnecessarily? For a long time I wondered about this. But, when I came to enter the room of Shōju, the rhinoceros of my previous doubt suddenly fell down dead... Do not look with suspicion upon the Five Ranks, saying that it is not the directly transmitted oral teaching of the Tōzan line. You should know that it was only after he had completed his investigation of *Tōzan's Verses*[128] that Shōju gave his acknowledgment to the Five Ranks.

After I had entered Shōju's room and received the transmission from him, I was quite satisfied. But, though I was satisfied, I still regretted that all teachers had not yet clearly explained the meaning of "the reciprocal interpenetration of the Apparent and the Real."[129] They seemed to have discarded the words "reciprocal interpenetration," and to pay no attention whatsoever to them. Thereupon the rhinoceros of doubt once more raised its head.

In the summer of the first year of the Kan'en era (1748–1751), in the midst of my meditation, suddenly the mystery of "the reciprocal interpenetration of the Apparent and the Real" became perfectly clear. It was just like looking at the palm of my own hand. The rhinoceros of doubt instantly fell down dead, and I could scarcely bear the joy of it. Though I wished to hand it on to others, I was ashamed to squeeze out my old woman's stinking milk and soil the monks' mouths with it.

All of you who wish to plumb this deep source must make the investigation in secret with your entire body. My own toil has extended over these thirty years. Do not take this to be an easy task! Even if you should happen to break up the family and scatter the household, do not consider this enough. You must vow to pass through seven, or eight, or even nine thickets of brambles. And, when you have passed through the thickets of brambles, still do not consider this to be enough. Vow to investigate the secret teachings of the Five Ranks to the end.

For the past eight or nine years or more, I have been trying to incite all of you who boil your daily gruel over the same fire with me to study this great matter thoroughly, but more often than not you have taken it to be the doctrine of another house,[130] and remained indifferent to it. Only a few among you have attained understanding of it. How deeply this grieves me! Have you never heard: "The Gates of Dharma are manifold; I vow to enter them all?"[131] How much the more should this be true for the main principle of Buddhism and the essential road of sanzen!

Shōju Rōjin has said: "In order to provide a means whereby students might directly experience the Four Wisdoms, the patriarchs, in their compassion and with their skill in devising expedients, first instituted the Five Ranks." What are the so-called Four Wisdoms? They are the Great Perfect Mirror Wisdom, the Universal Nature Wisdom, the Marvelous Observing Wisdom, and the Perfecting-of-Action Wisdom.[132]

Followers of the Way, even though you may have pursued your studies in the Threefold Learning[133] continuously through many kalpas, if you have not directly experienced the Four Wisdoms, you are not permitted to call yourselves true sons of Buddha. Followers of the Way, if your investigation has been correct and complete, at the moment you smash open the dark cave of the eighth or Ālaya consciousness,[134] the precious light of the Great Perfect Mirror Wisdom instantly shines forth. But, strange to say, the light of the Great Perfect Mirror Wisdom is black like lacquer. This is what is called the rank of "The Apparent within the Real."[135]

Having attained the Great Perfect Mirror Wisdom, you now enter the rank of "The Real within the Apparent."[136] When you have accomplished your long practice of the Jeweled-mirror Samādhi, you directly realize the Universal Nature Wisdom and for the first time enter the state of the unobstructed interpenetration of Noumenon and phenomena.[137]

But the disciple must not be satisfied here. He himself must enter into intimate acquaintance with the rank of "The Coming from within the Real."[138] After that, by depending upon the rank of "The Arrival at Mutual Integration,"[139] he will completely prove the Marvelous Observing Wisdom and the Perfecting-of-Action Wisdom. At last he reaches the rank of "Unity Attained,"[140] and, "after all, comes back to sit among the coals and ashes."

Do you know why? Pure gold that has gone through a thousand smeltings does not become ore a second time. My only fear is that a little gain will suffice you. How priceless is the merit gained through the step-by-step practice of the Five Ranks of the Apparent and the Real! By this practice you not only attain the Four Wisdoms, but you personally prove that the Three Bodies[141] also are wholly embraced within your own body. Have you not read in the *Daijō shōgongyō ron*: "When the eight consciousnesses are inverted, the Four Wisdoms are produced; when the Four Wisdoms are bound together, the Three Bodies are perfected?"[142] Therefore Sōkei Daishi[143] composed this verse:

> Your own nature is provided
> With the Three Bodies;
> When its brightness is manifested,
> The Four Wisdoms are attained.[144]

He also said: "The pure Dharmakāya is your nature; the perfect Sambhogakāya is your wisdom; the myriad Nirmāṇakāyas are your activities."[145]

Tōzan Ryōkai's Verses on the Five Ranks

> The Apparent within the Real:
> In the third watch of the night
> Before the moon appears,
> No wonder when we meet
> There is no recognition!
> Still cherished in my heart
> Is the beauty of earlier days.[146]

The rank of "The Apparent within the Real" denotes the rank

of the Absolute, the rank in which one experiences the Great Death, shouts "KA!"[147] sees Dao, and enters into the Principle. When the true practitioner, filled with power from his secret study, meritorious achievements, and hidden practices, suddenly bursts through into this rank, "the empty sky vanishes and the iron mountain crumbles."[148] "Above, there is not a tile to cover his head; below, there is not an inch of ground for him to stand on."[149] The delusive passions are non-existent, enlightenment is non-existent, Samsara[150] is non-existent, Nirvana is non-existent. This is the state of total empty solidity, without sound and without odor, like a bottomless clear pool. It is as if every fleck of cloud had been wiped from the vast sky.

Too often the disciple, considering that his attainment of this rank is the end of the Great Matter[151] and his discernment of the Buddha-way complete, clings to it to the death and will not let go of it. Such as this is called "stagnant water"[152] Zen; such a man is called "an evil spirit who keeps watch over the corpse in the coffin."[153] Even though he remains absorbed in this state for thirty or forty years, he will never get out of the cave of the self-complacency and inferior fruits of pratyeka-buddhahood. Therefore it is said: "He whose activity does not leave this rank sinks into the poisonous sea."[154] He is the man whom Buddha called "the fool who gets his realization in the rank of the Real."[155]

Therefore, though as long as he remains in this hiding place of quietude, passivity and vacantness, inside and outside are transparent and his understanding perfectly clear, the moment the bright insight [he has thus far gained through his practice] comes into contact with differentiation's defiling conditions of turmoil and confusion, agitation and vexation, love and hate, he will find himself utterly helpless before them, and all the miseries of existence will press in upon him. It was in order to save him from this serious illness that the rank of "The Real within the Apparent" was established as an expedient.

The Real within the Apparent:
A sleepy-eyed grandam
Encounters herself in an old mirror.
Clearly she sees a face,
But it doesn't resemble hers at all.

Too bad, with a muddled head,
She tries to recognize her reflection![156]

If the disciple had remained in the rank of "The Apparent within the Real," his judgment would always have been vacillating and his view prejudiced. Therefore, the bodhisattva of superior capacity invariably leads his daily life in the realm of the [six] dusts,[157] the realm of all kinds of ever-changing differentiation. All the myriad phenomena before his eyes—the old and the young, the honorable and the base, halls and pavilions, verandahs and corridors, plants and trees, mountains and rivers—he regards as his own original, true, and pure aspect. It is just like looking into a bright mirror and seeing his own face in it. If he continues for a long time to observe everything everywhere with this radiant insight, all appearances of themselves become the jeweled mirror of his own house, and he becomes the jeweled mirror of their houses as well. Eihei[158] has said: "The experiencing of the manifold dharmas through using oneself is delusion; the experiencing of oneself through the coming of the manifold dharmas is satori."[159] This is just what I have been saying. This is the state of "mind and body discarded, discarded mind and body."[160] It is like two mirrors mutually reflecting one another without even the shadow of an image between. Mind and the objects of mind are one and the same; things and oneself are not two. "A white horse enters the reed flowers"; "snow is piled up in a silver bowl."[161]

This is what is known as the Jeweled-mirror Samādhi.[162] This is what the *Nirvana Sutra* is speaking about when it says: "The Tathāgata sees the Buddha-nature with his own eyes."[163] When you have entered this samādhi, "though you push the great white ox, he does not go away";[164] the Universal Nature Wisdom manifests itself before your very eyes. This is what is meant by the expressions, "There exists only one Vehicle," "the Middle Path," "the True Form," "the Supreme Truth."[165]

But, if the student, having reached this state, were to be satisfied with it, then, as before, he would be living in the deep pit of "fixation in a lesser rank of bodhisattva-hood."[166] Why is this so? Because he is neither conversant with the deportment of the bodhisattva, nor does he understand the causal conditions for a

Buddha-land.[167] Although he has a clear understanding of the Universal and True Wisdom, he cannot cause to shine forth the Marvelous Wisdom that comprehends the unobstructed interpenetration of the manifold dharmas.[168] The patriarchs, in order to save him from this calamity, have provided the rank of "The Coming from within the Real."

The Coming from within the Real:
Within nothingness there is a path
Leading away from the dusts of the world.
Even if you observe the taboo
On the present emperor's name,
You will surpass that eloquent one of yore
Who silenced every tongue.[169]

In this rank, the Mahayana bodhisattva does not remain in the state of attainment that he has realized, but from the midst of the sea of effortlessness he lets his great uncaused compassion shine forth. Standing upon the four pure and great Universal Vows, he lashes forward the Dharma-wheel[170] of "seeking Bodhi above and saving sentient beings below."[171] This is the so-called "coming-from within the going-to, the going-to within the coming-from."[172] Moreover, he must know the moment of [the meeting of] the paired opposites, brightness and darkness. Therefore the rank of "The Arrival at Mutual Integration" has been set up.

The Arrival at Mutual Integration:
When two blades cross points,
There's no need to withdraw.
The master swordsman
Is like the lotus blooming in the fire.
Such a man has in and of himself
A heaven-soaring spirit.[173]

In this rank, the bodhisattva of indomitable spirit turns the Dharma-wheel of the non-duality of brightness and darkness. He stands in the midst of the filth of the world, "his head covered with dust and his face streaked with dirt."[174] He moves through the confusion of sound and sensual pleasure, buffeted this way and buffeted that. He is like the fire-blooming lotus,[175] that, on encountering the flames, becomes still brighter in color and purer in fragrance. "He enters the market place with empty hands,"[176] yet others receive benefit from him. This is what is called "to be on the road, yet not to have left the house; to have left the house, yet not to be on the road."[177] Is he an ordinary man? Is he a sage? The evil ones and the heretics cannot discern him. Even the buddhas and the patriarchs cannot lay their hands upon him. Were anyone to try to indicate his mind, [it would be no more there than] the horns of a rabbit or the hairs of a tortoise[178] that have gone beyond the farthest mountain.

Still, he must not consider this state to be his final resting place. Therefore it is said, "Such a man has in and of himself a heaven-soaring spirit." What must he do in the end? He must know that there is one more rank, the rank of "Unity Attained."

Unity Attained:
Who dares to equal him
Who falls into neither being nor non-being!
All men want to leave
The current of ordinary life,
But he, after all, comes back
To sit among the coals and ashes.[179]

The Master's verse-comment says:[180]

How many times has Tokuun, the idle old gimlet,
Not come down from the Marvelous Peak!
He hires foolish wise men to bring snow,
And he and they together fill up the well.[181]

The student who wishes to pass through Tōzan's rank of "Unity Attained" should first study this verse.[182]

It is of the utmost importance to study and pass through the Five Ranks, to attain penetrating insight into them, and to be totally without fixation or hesitation. But, though your own personal study of the Five Ranks comes to an end, the Buddha-way stretches endlessly and there are no tarrying places on it. The Gates of Dharma are manifold.

VIII. The Commandments

With the completion of the *goi* koans, our study of the Buddha-dharma as it has been traditionally handed down in the Zen Sect comes to an end. Only one more important question remains to be answered: How are we to conduct ourselves in our daily life so as never to violate the Buddha-dharma? When we have fully penetrated the last of the Five Ranks we make our own the fundamental attitude of mind from which all the activities of the patriarchs have stemmed. But to live this attitude from morning to evening and from evening to morning is the ultimate aim of Zen practice. To this end we must pass through the Ten Commandments, scrutinizing them over and over, going from refinement to refinement, from minute detail to minute detail. In our daily activities, our feet walk on the real earth; in the environment surrounding us, we meet that which it is our destiny to meet; we are the master, we are the embodiment of the doctrine.

As for the Ten Commandments, they are the traditional commandments handed down from the time of Shakyamuni Buddha:[183]

> Do not destroy life.
> Do not steal.
> Do not commit an unchaste act.
> Do not lie.
> Do not take intoxicating liquor.

Do not report the wrong-doing of anyone
among the four groups.[184]
Do not slander another by praising yourself.
Do not covet.
Do not be stirred to anger.
Do not revile the Three Treasures.[185]

However many times we may have heard these commandments, or even recited them ourselves, it is not until we observe them in sanzen with our fully opened Zen eye that we come to understand their grandeur. To live in accordance with their words is difficult enough; to live in accordance with their deepest meaning is an undertaking such as only our previous long practice could prepare us for.

How magnificent our religion is! How profound the Truth we follow! When we obtain it, mastering it is difficult; when we master it, exhausting it is difficult. When we have mastered and exhausted it, its wondrousness is still difficult to fathom. There is still progress to be made to reach the ultimate goal. What is this ultimate goal? Daitō Kokushi devoted the twenty years he lived among the beggars under Gojō Bridge in Kyoto to the long cultivation of his spiritual body. Kanzan Kokushi,[186] founder of the Myōshin-ji, after he had gained the essence of Daitō Kokushi's Dharma, went deep into the mountainous district of Ibuka, and cultivated himself for many years. In the daytime he worked as a hired laborer; at night he went into his cliff dwelling and sat in quietude. When we bring ourselves to think about the accomplishments of the patriarchs, and see ourselves as we are today, we cannot but feel alarmed.

In the *Hōkyō zammai* of Tōzan Ryōkai, it is said: "Hidden practice and secret activity seem stupid and foolish, but when you have succeeded to your inheritance you are called a master among masters."[187] How many words there are that penetrate to the very marrow of our bones!

In the monasteries of the Rinzai Sect of Zen, at the beginning and middle of the summer and winter terms, and on the night before Rōhatsu Ō Sesshin,[188] the masters read to their monks the *Kikan*,[189] or "Admonitions," handed down through generations in each monastery. These Admonitions are important guiding principles for the monks, and words of encouragement to them in their practice. Though they are intended for monks living in a monastery, and certain of them do not apply to laymen, the underlying principles for laymen and monks are not different. The spirit in which both must undertake and carry through their practice is exactly the same; the goal toward which all are striving is the same goal. Let me select a few passages from the *Admonitions* of my monastery, Kōon-ji:[190]

> All you worthy Zen students, confronting the realm where understanding through reason does not exist, each and every one of you must summon up the koan which is his own to study, and investigate it to the limit, backward and forward. No matter what confusion and what difficulties you may encounter, you must never give up.
>
> Do not take sanzen like a blind man. Do not haphazardly point to this and that, saying, "This is Zen," "That is satori." Explaining a thing does not hit the pivot. By real sanzen you must attain the true proof. If you do not experience satori, what are you good for?
>
> Do not build your house upon the sand. Make your true mind the basic ground; make your resolute vows the foundation stones; make your genuine satori the measuring line; make your zazen practice the beams and the ridgepole. If you diligently and steadfastly carry on your quest with your entire being, never stopping for a moment, the day will surely come when you will attain that bright vision which is the result of your long and strenuous effort.
>
> Be apprehensive, take heed! Exert yourselves, be on your guard!

I have spoken about the essential points in the course we students traverse in our Zen practice. Though I am sure many remain obscure and difficult for you to understand, the essence of Zen is simple. It is freedom, it is actuality, it is action, it is daily life.

For those of us who follow this religion, our journey has no end, for, though our formal practice may be completed, its final step is a rededication to the accomplishment of the Four Vows, a task continuing into eternity.

PART THREE

Selections From A Zen Phrase Anthology (Zenrin Kushū)

A Zen Phrase Anthology

Zenrin kushū 禪林句集 A Zen Phrase Anthology, is a collection of phrases and verses well known to all students of Zen, whether they be monks or laymen.

The original of the work, entitled *Ku zōshi* 句雙紙 A Phrase Book, was compiled sometime toward the end of the 15th century by Tōyō Eichō Zenji 東陽英朝禪師 (1429–1504), a descendant in the 7th generation of Kanzan Egen, founder of the Myōshin-ji. It consisted of some 5,000 quotations taken from Buddhist sutras, the records of Chinese Zen patriarchs, Confucian texts, Daoist writings, and the works of Chinese poets. These quotations were arranged in sections according to the number of Chinese characters in each, beginning with entries of a single character, and progressing numerically through those of two, three, four characters, five characters and parallel five-character phrases, six characters and parallel six-character phrases, seven characters and parallel seven-character phrases, to those of eight characters and parallel eight-character phrases.

The collection seems to have remained in manuscript form until the latter half of the 17th century, when a person who styled himself Ijūshi 已十子, and about whom nothing is known, undertook to edit it. Ijūshi states in his postscript to the book that he was originally a Confucianist, but in middle life became a monk and carried on some Zen practice. Later, however, "due to an unfortunate circumstance," he had to return to Confucianism. Because of his desire to repay the debt of gratitude he felt toward his Zen friends, he decided to edit Eichō's work, which he believed would be useful to beginners in Zen study. To each section Ijūshi added an appendix of additional quotations, bringing the total to about 6,000 entries. Furthermore, except in the case of the few quotations whose sources he could not trace, he appended to each entry the title and section of the original work from which it had been taken. The collection was finally published in 1688 under its present title, *Zenrin kushū*.

In the two hundred and fifty odd years since the book first appeared, numerous editions have been printed, some with explanatory notes for each entry in addition to source references. A number of abbreviated versions have also been published, as well as other anthologies based upon it or resembling it and bearing similar titles. Even a kind of phrase dictionary has appeared, containing entries not included in the original work, though lacking many others. Copies of any edition of Ijūshi's text are difficult to find today, even at second hand. The most easily available of the similar works are the abridged version, *Zenrin kushū*, edited by SHIBAYAMA Zenkei, and published by Kichūdō 其中堂 in Kyoto in 1952, and the section entitled "Kushū" 句集 in *Zudokko* (*Zokuhen*), pp. 173–301.

Today *Zenrin kushū*, or its equivalent, is still the constant companion of every Japanese student of sanzen, for within its thousands of phrases he must find the particular traditional *jakugo* or "capping phrase"—sometimes two or three—for the koan he is studying, and present it to his teacher as the final step in his study of the koan. Day by day and week by week, thumbing through this work, usually printed in small type on thin paper in a size convenient for the pocket or the sleeve, the student memorizes a word here and a phrase there, until his mind gradually becomes a repository for many of the famous and beautiful lines from Chinese literature.

No translation of the complete *Zenrin kushū* in any European language has as yet been published. However, English translations of a number of the verses are to be found throughout the various English writings of D.T. SUZUKI. *Zen in English Literature*, and *Haiku*, Vol. I, both by R. H. BLYTH, also contain English translations of some of the phrases. Others by the Zen Master Sokei-an are scattered through *Cat's Yawn*.

The selections that follow have been chosen by Isshū Rōshi from each of the twelve sections of the anthology, and illustrate the wide variation in content and literary form to be found in it. Sources, and, except in a few cases, explanatory notes, have been omitted.

ONE-CHARACTER PHRASES

1 是
Ze!
Yes! Good! Right! Correct! All right! That's it!

2 了
Ryō!
Understood! Clear! Finished! Done!

3. 點
Ten!
There! That's it! Just so! Check!

4. 參
San!
Reflect further! Think more deeply! Investigate more thoroughly.
Ask! Enquire!
This second usage is encountered occasionally when a master, in the course of a lecture, asks his audience to question him further.

5. 錯
Shaku!
Error! Wrong! Mistake! It doesn't hit the mark!

6. 囗
Ka! or *Ga!*
Ha! Ho!
This character is found only in Zen literature, where it is most

often used to indicate a spontaneous cry made at the moment of attaining satori, and thus, by inference, satori itself. It is an exclamation giving the impression of great power.

It is also a loud cry shouted rhythmically and in unison by a group of men engaged in some heavy labor, for instance, fishermen dragging their boat up onto the shore.

7. 無

Mu!

Mu!

As an exclamation, this word should not be translated. It was made famous by Jōshū Jūshin 趙州從諗 (Zhaozhou Congshen). When used as a negative it means: without, has not, …-less; nothing, none.

8. 關

Kan!

Kan!

An untranslatable exclamation made famous by Ummon Bun'en 雲門文偃 (Yunmen Wenyan), and known as one of his "One Word Barriers" (*ichijikan* 一字關 *yiziguan*). The literal meaning is: a frontier pass, a barrier which is difficult to pass through.

9. 瞎

Katsu!

Blind! Dumbell! Dunce! Ignoramus!

Used in its literal meaning, this word refers to a stupid or ignorant man. In Zen, however, it is often a complimentary term for a completely enlightened man who, to those who have no eye to see, appears to be just an everyday person with no smell of Zen about him.

10. 喝

Katsu!

Katsu!

An untranslatable exclamatory shout first given by Baso Dōitsu 馬祖道一 (Mazu Daoyi), but later made famous by Rinzai Gigen 臨濟義玄 (Linji Yixuan) and the Rinzai School of Zen.

TWO-CHARACTER PHRASES

11. 如是
Nyoze.
Thus; like this; in this way. Just so!

12. 看看
Miyo, miyo!
Look, look! Watch out, watch out!

13. 不識
Fushiki.
[I] don't know.

14. 不會
Fue.
[I] don't understand. [I] can't understand.

15. 未在
Mizai.
Not yet. Not at all. Never.

16. 會也
E seri.
E su ya?
[I] understand. [I] have understood.
Do you understand? Have you understood?

17. 恁麼
Immo.
Thus; like this; like that; in this (or that) way.

18. 蹉過
Saka or *shaka.*
To pass by without recognition. To miss a person, or a chance. To slip from the right way.

19. 珍重
Chinchō!
Farewell! Good-bye! Take care of yourself!
A phrase used at parting.

20. 休去
Kyū shisaru.
To have been silenced; to have been caused to cease (speaking). Not to continue further.
The implication always inherent in this phrase is that the person who ceases speaking agrees with, or is forced to accept, what has just been said by the other.

THREE-CHARACTER PHRASES

21. 鐵酸餡
Tessan'an.
Iron sour-stuffing.
Something you can't get your teeth into. Also a term of abuse.

22. 看脚下
Kyakka o miyo!
Look where you're going! Watch where you step!

23. 野狐精
Yakozei.
A wild fox spirit.
Used as a term of abuse.

24. 露堂堂
Rodōdō.
Apparent; perfectly clear. Revealed!

25. 惺惺著
Seiseijaku!
Be clever! Be astute! Be alert!

26. 是什麼
Kore nanzo?
What's this?

    An expression usually employed when referring to a thing. When used for a person it is a term of abuse.

27. 信不及
Shinfugyū.
To lack self-reliance; to lack faith in oneself. To be unable to believe.

28. 可惜許
Kashakko!
Too bad! What a pity! What a shame! Regrettable!

29. 喫茶去
Kissako!
Go drink your tea!

30. 莫妄想
Maku mōzō!
Don't be deluded!

FOUR-CHARACTER PHRASES

31. 柳綠花紅
Yanagi wa midori, hana wa kurenai.
The willows are green, the flowers are red.

32. 獨步丹霄
Tanshō ni doppo su.
I alone walk in the red heavens.

33. 失錢遭罪
Shissen sōzai.
To lose one's money and incur punishment as well.

34. 再犯不容
Saibon yurusazu.
A second offense is not permitted.

35. 識法者懼
Hō o shiru mono wa osoru.
He who knows the law fears it.

36. 自領出去
Zuryō shukko.
To take what's coming to you and get out.

37. 知而故犯
Shitte kotosara ni okasu.
To know, yet deliberately to transgress.

38. 活潑潑地
Kappatsupatsuji or *kappappatchi.*
Briskly and spiritedly.

39. 認賊爲子
Zoku o mitomete ko to nasu.
To acknowledge a thief as one's child.

40. 掩耳偷鈴
Mimi o ōte suzu o nusumu.
To cover one's ears and steal the bell.

41. 言語道斷
Gongo dōdan.
Words fail.

42. 笑裏藏鋒
Shōri ni hokosaki o zō su.
To hide a spear within a smile.

43. 呑吐不下
Dondo fuge.
It can't be swallowed, it can't be spit out.

44. 龍頭蛇尾
Ryūtō dabi.
A dragon's head and a snake's tail.
That is, a good beginning and a poor ending.

45. 靈龜曳尾
Reiki o o hiku.
The sacred tortoise drags its tail.

46. 破家散宅
Hake santaku.
The family is broken up, the house destroyed.

47. 癩兒牽伴
Raiji han o hiku.
The leper drags his friends along with him.

48. 勞而無功
Rō shite kō nashi.
To work hard and accomplish nothing.

49. 落草不少
Rakusō sukunakarazu.
He's fallen deep in the weeds.

50. 賓主歷然
Hinju rekinen.
Guest and host are clearly distinguishable.

FIVE-CHARACTER PHRASES

51. 溪梅一朵香
Keibai ichida kambashi.
Fragrant, the valley's single plum flower.

52. 歩歩清風起
Hoho seifū okoru.
At every step the pure wind rises.

53. 好事不如無
Kōzu mo naki ni wa shikazu.
Even a good thing isn't so good as nothing.

54. 自屎不覺臭
Jishi kusaki o oboezu.
He doesn't recognize the smell of his own dung.

55. 憐兒不覺醜
Ji o awarende minikuki o oboezu.
A beloved son is not ugly.

56. 剜好肉作瘡
Kōniku o egutte kizu to nasu.
To gouge out healthy flesh and make a wound.

57. 能使得爺錢
Yoku yasen o tsukai etari.
He made good use of his father's money.

58. 壺中日月長
Kochū jitsugetsu nagashi.
In the pot sun and moon shine eternally.

Once upon a time there was a hermit who always carried about with him a pot that could hold a peck of rice. At night he slept in the pot. Sometimes the pot changed into the universe with the sun and moon in it. He named the pot "Pot Heaven," and he himself was known as Mr. Pot.

59. 鑊湯無冷處
Kakutō ni reisho nashi.
There's no cool spot in a cauldron of boiling water.

60. 蝦跳不出斗

Ka odoredomo, tō o idezu.
Though the frog leaps, it can't get out of the bushel.

61. 貧兒思舊債
Hinji kyūsai o omou.
The poor man thinks about his unpaid debts.

62. 泥裏洗土塊
Deiri ni dokai o arau.
To wash a clod of earth in the mud.

63. 室内一盞燈
Shitsunai issan no tō.
The single-saucer lamp within the room.

64. 好語不說盡
Kōgo tokitsukusazare.
In a good talk, don't explain everything.

65. 按牛頭喫草
Gozu o anjite kusa o kisseshimu.
Pushing down the ox's head, he makes it eat grass.

66. 巧匠不留跡
Kōshō ato o todomezu.
A skillful craftsman leaves no traces.

67. 地肥茄子大
Chi koete nasubi dai nari.
When the earth is fertile, the eggplants are large.

68. 特地一場愁
Tokuji ichijō no urei.
The extremity of grief.

69. 聖朝無棄物
Seichō ni kibutsu nashi.
There is no waste in the Imperial Court.

70. 白雲抱幽石
Hakuun yūseki o idaku.
White clouds hold lonely rocks in their embrace.

PARALLEL FIVE-CHARACTER PHRASES

71. 掬水月在手
弄花香满衣
Mizu o kiku sureba, tsuki te ni ari;
Hana o rō sureba, ka e ni mitsu.
Scoop up water, and the moon is in your hands;
Toy with flowers, and their fragrance scents your garments.

72. 泣露千般草
吟風一様松
Tsuyu ni naku sempan no kusa,
Kaze ni ginzu ichiyō no matsu.
A thousand grasses weep tears of dew,
A single pine tree murmurs in the breeze.

73. 覓火和烟得
擔泉帶月歸
Hi o motomete wa kemuri ni washite e;
Izumi o ninatte wa tsuki o obite kaeru.
Seeking fire, you find it with smoke;
Carrying spring-water, you bring it back with the moon.

74. 林下十年夢
湖邊一笑新
Rinka jūnen no yume!
Kohen isshō arata nari.
Ten years of dreams in the forest!
Now on the lake's edge laughing,
Laughing a new laugh.

75. 十方無壁落
四面又無門
Jippō hekiraku naku,
Shimen mata mon nashi.
The ten directions are without walls,
The four quarters are without gates.

76. 誰知遠烟浪
別有好思量
Tare ka shiru tōki enrō ni
Betsu ni kōshiryō aru koto o?
Who can know that far off in the misty waves
Another yet more excellent realm of thought exists?

77. 十年歸不得
忘却來時道
Jūnen kaeru koto o ezu,
Raiji no michi o bōkyaku su.
For ten years I couldn't return;
Now I've forgotten the road by which I came.

78. 只可自怡悦
不堪持贈君
Tada mizukara ietsu subeshi,
Ji shite kimi ni okuru ni taezu.
Only I myself can enjoy it;
It is not suitable to present to you.

79. 泉聲中夜後
山色夕陽時
Sensei chūya no nochi,
Sanshoku sekiyō no toki.
The murmuring of the spring as the night deepens,
The coloring of the hills as the sun goes down.

80. 陰陽不到處
一片好風光

In'yō futō no tokoro
Ippen no kōfūkō.
Where the sun and moon do not reach,
There is marvelous scenery indeed!

81. 高捲吟中箔
濃煎睡後茶
Takaku ginchū no sudare o maite;
Komayaka ni suigo no cha o senzu.
Singing his poem, he rolls the bamboo blind high;
Having finished his nap, he parches the tea leaves dark.

82. 枯木裏龍吟
髑髏裏眼睛
Kobokuri no ryūgin,
Dokurori no gansei.
The dragon-hum in the dead tree,
The eyeball in the dry skull.

83. 幽鳥語喃喃
辭雲入亂峯
Yūchō go nannan,
Kumo o ji shite rampō ni iru.
A hidden bird twitters "Nam, nam."
Taking leave of the clouds, I enter the scattered peaks.

84. 秋風吹渭水
落葉滿長安
Shūfū Isui o fukeba,
Rakuyō Chōan ni mitsu.
Autumn wind, blowing over the waters of the Wei,
Covers all Chang'an with falling leaves.

85. 微風吹幽松
近聽聲愈好
Bifū yūshō o fuki,
Chikaku kikeba, koe iyo-iyo yoshi.
A light breeze stirs the lonely pine,
The sound is more pleasant heard from close by.

86. 皮膚脱落盡
唯有一眞實
Hifu datsuraku shitsukushite
Tada ichi shinjitsu nomi ari.
Now that I've shed my skin completely,
One true reality alone exists.

87. 能爲萬象主
不逐四時凋
Yoku banzō no shu to natte,
Shiji o otte shibomazu.
When you're really master of the myriad forms,
Throughout the four seasons there's no withering, no decay.

88. 相逢相不識
共語不知名
Aiōte aishirazu,
Tomo ni katatte na o shirazu.
I meet him, but know not who he is;
I converse with him, but do not know his name.

89. 隨流認得性
無喜亦無憂
Nagare ni shitagatte shō o nintoku sureba,
Ki mo naku mata yū mo nashi.
When you recognize [Mind's] nature while according with its flow,
There's no more joy, nor is there any sorrow.

90. 一華開五葉
結果自然成
Ikka goyō hiraite
Kekka ji'nen ni naru.
The five petals of the one flower open,
And the fruit of itself is ripe.

SIX-CHARACTER PHRASES

91. 前三三後三三
Zen sansan, go sansan.
Before, three times three,
Behind, three times three.

92. 痴兀兀兀兀痴
Chi gotsugotsu, gotsugotsu chi.
Stupidly steadfast, steadfastly stupid.

93. 懸羊頭賣狗肉
Yōtō o kakete kuniku o uru.
He displays a sheep's head but sells dog flesh.

94. 井覷驢驢覷井
Sei ro o mi, ro sei o miru.
The well looks at the ass,
The ass looks at the well.

95. 倒騎牛入佛殿
Sakashima ni ushi ni notte butsuden ni iru.
Riding backwards on an ox,
I enter the Buddha-hall.

96. 好兒不使爺錢
Kōji yasen o tsukawazu.
A good son doesn't use his father's money.

97. 面赤不如語直
Men no akakaran yori wa, go no naokaran ni wa shikazu.
Honest speech is better than a red face.

98. 嗔拳不打笑面
Shinken shōmen o da sezu.
An angry fist does not strike a smiling face.

99. 鉢裏飯桶裏水
Hatsurikan, tsūrisui.
Rice in the bowl, water in the bucket.

100. 無孔笛最難吹
Mukuteki mottomo fukigatashi.
The flute without holes is the most difficult to blow.

101. 三人證龜作鼈
Sannin kame o shō shite betsu to nasu.
Three men testified about the tortoise, so that makes it a turtle.

A wise man once said: "If a man told you he had seen a tiger in the street, you wouldn't believe him. If a second man said the same thing, you wouldn't believe him either. But if a third man said he also had seen one, you'd believe that there had been a tiger in the street."

102. 臂膊不向外曲
Hihaku soto ni mukatte magarazu.
The arm doesn't bend outward.

103. 入地獄如箭射
Jigoku ni iru koto ya no iru ga gotoshi.
Going to hell with the speed of an arrow.

104. 聞名不如見面
Na o kikan yori wa omote o min ni wa shikazu.
Better to see the face than to hear the name.

105. 烟霞不遮梅香
Enka baikō o saegirazu.
The hazy mist does not stay
The plum flower's fragrance.

106. 家醜莫向外揚
Kashū soto ni mukatte aguru koto nakare.
Don't display the family skeletons in public.

107. 跨瞎驢追猛虎
Katsuro ni notte mōko o ou.
Astride a blind ass he pursues a fierce tiger.

108. 急水上打毬子
Kyūsuijō ni kyūsu o da su.
He's hitting at a ball on swift-flowing water.

109. 良賈深藏如虛
Ryōko wa fukaku zō shite munashiki ga gotoshi.
The good merchant hides his possessions well and appears to have nothing.

110. 藏頭白海頭黑
Zōzu haku, Kaizu koku.
Mr. Zang's head is white, Mr. Hai's head is black.

PARALLEL SIX-CHARACTER PHRASES

111. 認箇照照靈靈
落在驢前馬後
Kono shōshō reirei o mitomete,
Rozen bago ni rakuzai su.
Believing this to be radiance and spirituality, he is content to run in front of asses and follow after horses.

112. 寒時寒殺闍梨
熱時熱殺闍梨
Kanji wa jari o kansatsu shi,
Netsuji wa jari o nessatsu su.
The cold kills you with cold, the heat kills you with heat.

113. 上無片瓦蓋頭
下無寸土立足
Kami henga no kōbe o ōu naku,
Shimo sundo no ashi o rissuru nashi.

Above, there isn't a piece of tile to cover his head; below there isn't an inch of earth for him to stand on.

114. 口欲談而辭喪
心欲緣而慮忘
Kuchi danzen to hosshite ji sō shi;
Kokoro enzen to hosshite ryo bōzu.
When the mouth wants to speak about it, words fail; when the mind seeks affinity with it, thought vanishes.

115. 日月照臨不到
天地蓋覆不盡
Jitsugetsu mo shōrin shi itarazu;
Tenchi mo gaifuku shitsukusazu.
Sun and moon cannot illumine it completely; heaven and earth cannot cover it entirely,

116. 雖與我同條生
不與我同條死
Ware to dōjō ni shōzu to iedomo,
Ware to dōjō ni shi sezu.
Though we're born of the same lineage, we don't die of the same lineage.

117. 相罵饒你接觜
相唾饒你潑水
Ainonoshiru koto wa nanji ni yurusu kuchibashi o tsuge;
Aida suru koto wa nanji ni yurusu mizu o sosoge.
When we're reviling one another, you may give me tit for tat; when we're spitting at one another, you may spew me with slobber.

118. 逐鹿者不見山
攫金者不見人
Shika o ou mono wa yama o mizu,
Kin o tsukamu mono wa hito o mizu.
The deer-hunter doesn't see the mountains, the miser doesn't see men.

119. 達磨不來東土
二祖不往西天
Daruma Tōdo ni kitarazu,
Niso Seiten ni yukazu.
Bodhidharma didn't come to China, the Second Patriarch didn't go to India.

120. 入息不居陰界
出息不涉萬緣
Nissoku onkai ni kyo sezu,
Shussoku ban'en ni watarazu.
Breathing in, he does not stay in the realm of the skandhas; breathing out, he is not concerned with the myriad things.

121. 去年貧未是貧
今年貧始是貧
Kyonen no hin wa imada kore hin narazu,
Konnen no hin wa hajimete kore hin.
Last year's poverty was not real poverty,
But this year's poverty is poverty indeed.

122. 諸天捧花無路
外道潛覷不見
Shoten hana o sasaguru ni michi naku,
Gedō hisoka ni miru ni miezu.
The devas find no path on which to strew flowers; the heretics secretly spying find nothing to see.

123. 離婁不辨正色
師曠豈識玄絲
Ri Rō shōshiki o benzezu;
Shi Kō ani genshi o shiran ya?
Even Li Lou cannot discern the true form;
How, then, can Shi Kuang distinguish the subtle tune?

Li Lou (Ri Rō) and Shi Kuang (Shi Kō) were both men of ancient times. The former was famous for his sharp eyesight, the latter for his sharp hearing.

124. 去年梅今歳柳
顏色馨香依舊
Kyonen no ume konsai no yanagi—
Ganshoku keikō kyū ni yoru.
Last year's plum and this year's willow—
Their color and fragrance are as of old.

125. 坐斷毘盧頂𩕳
曾不見有佛祖
Biru chōnei o zadan shite
Katsute busso aru koto o mizu.
Having cut off the top of Vairocana's head, I don't know that any buddha or patriarch ever existed.

126. 天際日上月下
檻前山深水寒
Tensai hi nobori tsuki kudaru,
Kanzen yama fukaku mizu samushi.
At the limits of heaven the sun rises and the moon sets,
Beyond the balustrade the mountains deepen and the waters become chill.

127. 只見渓回路轉
不知身在桃源
Tada kei meguri michi tenzuru o mite,
Shirazu mi no tōgen ni aru koto o.
He sees only the winding of the stream and the twisting of the path,
He does not know that already he is in the land of the immortals.

128. 欲識佛性義理
當觀時節因緣
Busshō no giri o shiran to hosseba
Masa ni jisetsu innen o kanzu beshi.
He who would understand the meaning of Buddha-nature
Must watch for the season and the causal relations.

129. 一切聲是佛聲
一切色是佛色
Issai no koe wa kore busshō,
Issai no iro wa kore busshiki.
Every voice is the voice of Buddha, every form is the Buddha-form.

130. 雁無遺蹤之意
水無沈影之心
Kari ni ishō no i naku,
Mizu ni chin'ei no kokoro nashi.
The wild goose has no intention of leaving traces, the water has no thought of engulfing reflections.

SEVEN-CHARACTER PHRASES

131. 説似一物即不中
Setsuji ichimotsu soku fuchū.
The instant you speak about a thing you miss the mark.

132. 燕雀何知鴻鵠志
Enjaku nanzo kōkō no kokorozashi o shiran ya?
How can the mountain-finch know the wild swan's aspiring?

133. 八角磨盤空裏走
Hakkaku no maban kūri ni washiru.
The eight-cornered mortar rushes across the sky.

134. 狸奴白牯放毫光
Ri'nu byakko gōkō o hanatsu.
The badger and the white bull emit a glorious radiance.

135. 一鳥不鳴山更幽
Itchō nakazu yama sara ni yū nari.

With no bird singing
The mountain is yet more still.

136. 枯木花開劫外春
Koboku hana hiraku gōgai no haru.
In the spring beyond time
The withered tree flowers.

137. 鷺鷥立雪非同色
Roji yuki ni tatsu, dōshoku ni arazu.
When the snowy heron stands in the snow, the colors are not the same.

138. 再來不直半文錢
Sairai hammonsen ni atarazu.
A second try is not worth half a cash.

139. 兩箇猢猻探水月
Ryōko no koson suigetsu o saguru.
A pair of monkeys are reaching
For the moon in the water.

140. 爲君幾下蒼龍窟
Kimi ga tame ni ikutabi ka sōryōkutsu ni kudaru.
How many times for your sake
Have I not gone down into the blue dragon's cave!

141. 入火眞金色轉鮮
Hi ni itte shinkin iro utata azayaka nari.
When pure gold enters the fire,
Its color becomes still brighter.

142. 遠山無限碧層層
Enzan kagiri naku hekisōsō.
Endlessly rise the distant mountains,
Blue heaped upon blue.

143. 明月蘆花君自看
Meigetsu roka kimi mizukara miyo.

You must see for yourself
The reed-flowers drenched in moonlight.

144. 星在秤兮不在盤
Hoshi wa shō ni atte ban ni arazu.
The marks are on the balance-arm,
Not on the scale-pan.

145. 自笑一聲天地驚
Jishō isshō tenchi odoroku.
My single peal of laughter
Startles heaven and earth.

146. 針鋒頭上翻筋斗
Shimpō tōjō ni kinto o hirugaesu.
To turn a somersault on a needle's point.

147. 多口阿師難下觜
Taku no ashi kuchibashi o kudashi gatashi.
The garrulous reverend can't open his trap.

148. 一回擧著一回新
Ikkai kojaku sureba, ikkai arata nari.
Each time you bring it up,
Each time it is new.

149. 鼠入錢筒伎已窮
Nezumi sentō ni itte gi sude ni kiwamaru.
The rat that entered the money box is at its wit's end.

In old China, a bamboo tube, open only at one end and its diameter that of the coins to be stored in it, was used for a money box.

150. 千古萬古與人看
Senko banko hito no tame ni misu.
Eternally and everlastingly
It is revealing itself to men.

PARALLEL SEVEN-CHARACTER PHRASES

151. 泉州白家酒三盞
喫了猶言未沾唇
Senshū Hakke no sake sansan,
Kisshi owatte nao iu, imada kuchibiru o uruosazu to.
You've drunk three cups of wine
At the house of Bai in Quanzhou,
And yet you still declare,
"My lips aren't even moistened."

152. 水自竹邊流出冷
風從花裏過來香
Mizu wa chikuhen yori ryūshutsu shite hiyayaka ni,
Kaze wa kari yori sugikitatte kambashi.
Water from the edge of the bamboos
Flows out refreshing,
Breeze from the heart of the flowers
Passes by fragrant.

153. 湘潭雲盡暮山出
巴蜀雪消春水來
Shōtan kumo tsukite bozan ide,
Hashoku yuki kiete shunsui kitaru.
When Xiangtan's clouds disperse,
The evening mountains appear;
When Bashu's snows vanish,
The spring waters flow.

154. 鴛鴦繡出從君看
莫把金針度與人
En'ō o nuiidashite kimi ga miru ni makasu,
Kinshin o totte hito ni doyo suru koto nakare.
The mandarin ducks I've embroidered
I give you leave to look at,
But the golden needle that made them
Do not pass on to men.

155. 三級浪高魚化龍
痴人猶戽夜塘水
Sankyū nami takō shite uo ryū ni ke su,
Chijin nao kumu yatō no mizu.
Waves at the Yu Gate have risen
And the fish become dragons,
Yet fools still scoop out
The embankment's dank water.

In ancient times King Yu 禹 of the Xia 夏 dynasty cut a three-tiered sluice through the Longmen 龍門 mountains on the border between Shaanxi and Shanxi provinces to open up a passage for the Yellow River. This was known as the Gate of Yu or the Dragon Gate. There is an old legend that, on the third day of the third month, when the peach trees are in flower, vigorous carp that could scale this three-tiered waterfall would become dragons.

156. 江上晩來堪畫處
漁人披得一蓑歸
Kōjō banrai egaku ni taetaru tokoro;
Gyojin issa o hi shiete kaeru.
Evening near the riverside—
A scene for a painter.
Throwing on his straw raincoat,
The fisherman returns home.

157. 尋常一樣窓前月
纔有梅花便不同
Yonotsune ichiyō sōzen no tsuki,
Wazuka ni baika areba, sunawachi onajikarazu.
The moon outside my window
Is usually the same moon,
But as soon as there are plum flowers
It becomes a different moon.

158. 安禪不必須山水
滅却心頭火自涼
Anzen wa kanarazu shimo sansui o mochiizu;

Shintō mekkyaku sureba, hi mo onozukara suzushi.
No need at all of hills and streams
For quiet meditation;
When the mind has been extinguished,
Even fire is refreshing.

159. 猿抱子歸青嶂後
鳥啣花落碧岩前
Saru ko o idaite seishō no ushiro ni kaeri;
Tori hana o fukunde hekigan no mae ni otsu.
The monkeys, clasping their young to their breasts,
Return behind the blue peaks;
A bird, holding a flower in its beak,
Alights before the green grotto.

160. 榔𣗪横擔不顧人
直入千峯萬峯去
Sokuritsu ō ni ninatte hito o kaerimizu,
Jiki ni sempō bampō ni irisaru.
With his staff across his back,
He pays no heed to men;
Quickly entering the myriad peaks,
He goes upon his way.

161. 只見落紅風拂盡
豈知庭樹綠陰多
Tada rakkō kaze no haraitsukusu o miru;
Ani teiju ryokuin no ōki koto o shiran ya?
I saw merely fallen petals
Blown away by the wind;
How could I know that the garden trees'
Green shadows are many?

162. 凛凛孤風不自誇
端居寰海定龍蛇
Rinrin taru kofū mizukara hokorazu;
Kankai ni tango shite ryōda o sadamu.
Fearsome and solitary in mien,

He does not boast of himself;
But, dwelling gravely in his domain,
Decides who is snake, who is dragon.

163. 江國春風吹不起
鷓鴣啼在深花裏
Kōkoku no shumpū fukitatazu.
Shako naite shinka no uchi ni ari.
Over the river country
Spring winds are not stirring,
From within the deep flowers
The partridges cry.

164. 有意氣時添意氣
不風流處也風流
Iki aru toki iki o soe;
Fūryū narazaru tokoro mata fūryū.
When your spirit is high,
Augment your spirit.
Where there is no style,
There is also some style.

165. 白鷺下田千點雪
黄鶯上樹一枝花
Hakuro ta ni kudaru senten no yuki;
Kōō ki ni noboru isshi no hana.
Snowy herons alighting in a field—
Thousands of snowflakes!
Yellow nightingales perching in a tree—
A flower-decked bough.

166. 約臂黄金寛一寸
逢人猶道不相思
Hiji ni yaku suru ōgon yuruki koto issun,
Hito ni ōte wa nao iu aiomowazu to.
The golden bracelet on her arm
Is too loose by an inch,

Yet on meeting one she merely says:
"No, I'm not in love."

167. 荷葉團團團似鏡
菱角尖尖尖似錐
Kayō dandan to shite kagami yori mo madoka ni,
Ryōkaku sensen to shite kiri yori mo surudoshi.
Lotus leaves are round,
Rounder even than a mirror;
Water-chestnut horns are sharp,
Sharper even than a gimlet.

168. 沒底藍兒盛白月
無心椀子貯清風
Mottei ranji ni byakugetsu o mori,
Mushin wansu ni seifū o takuwau.
In the bottomless bamboo basket
I put the white moon;
In the bowl of mindlessness
I store the pure breeze.

169. 自携瓶去沽村酒
却著衫來作主人
Mizukara hei o tazusaesatte sonshu o kai;
Kaette san o tsukekitatte shujin to naru.
He himself took the jar
And bought the village wine;
Now he dons a robe
And makes himself the host.

170. 竹影掃堦塵不動
月穿潭底水無痕
Chikuei kai o haratte chiri ugokazu,
Tsuki tantei o ugatte mizu ni ato nashi.
Bamboo shadows sweep the stairs,
Yet not a mote of dust is stirred;
Moonbeams pierce to the bottom of the pool,
Yet in the water not a trace remains.

EIGHT-CHARACTER PHRASES

171. 金屑雖貴落眼成翳
Kinsetsu tattoshi to iedomo, manako ni ochite ei to naru.
Though gold-dust is precious, in the eyes it obscures the vision.

172. 朝打三千暮打八百
Chōda sanzen, boda happyaku.
Three thousand blows in the morning, eight hundred blows in the evening.

173. 好雪片片不落別處
Kōsetsu hempen, bessho ni ochizu.
Lovely snowflakes, they fall nowhere else!

174. 龜上覓毛兎邊求角
Kijō ni ke o motome, tohen ni tsuno o motomu.
To look for hair on the back of a tortoise or seek for horns on the head of a rabbit.

175. 石人點頭露柱拍手
Sekijin tentō sureba, rochū te o haku su.
When the stone man nods his head, the wooden pillar claps its hands.

176. 針頭削鐵鷺股割肉
Shintō ni tetsu o kezuri, roko ni niku o saku.
To shave iron from a needle-point; to hack flesh from a heron's leg.

177. 垂絲千尺意在深潭
Suishi senjaku, i shintan ni ari.
When I drop the line down a thousand feet, my objective lies in the depths of the pool.

178. 鷄寒上樹鴨寒下水
Niwatori samū shite ki ni nobori, kamo samū shite mizu ni

kudaru.
When chickens are cold they roost in a tree; when ducks are cold they dive into the water.

179. 眞不掩僞曲不藏直
Shin gi o ōwazu, kyoku choku o kakusazu.
The true does not conceal the false, the bent does not hide the straight.

180. 快人一言快馬一鞭
Kaijin ichigen, kaiba ichiben.
To the intelligent man, one word; to the fleet horse, one flick of the whip.

181. 弄泥團漢有什麼限
Deidan o rō suru no kan, nan no kagiri ka aran?
When will the fellow who plays with dirt ever have done!

182. 凡聖同居龍蛇混雜
Bonshō dōgo, ryōda konzatsu.
Laymen and holy men dwell together, dragons and snakes intermingle.

183. 官不容針私通車馬
Kan ni wa hari mo irezu, watakushi ni wa shaba o tsūzu.
Officially, a needle is not permitted to pass; unofficially, carriages can get through.

184. 蚌含明月兎子懷胎
Bō meigetsu o fukumi, toshi kaitai su.
The oyster holds a moonbeam in its mouth, the rabbit cherishes a child in its womb.

In ancient China it was believed that pearls are created by the entrance of a moonbeam into the aperture in an oyster's shell, and that a rabbit becomes pregnant when it looks at the full moon.

185. 入火不燒入水不溺
Hi ni itte mo yakezu, mizu ni itte mo oborezu.

Entering fire he is not burned, entering water he is not drowned.

186. 朝到西天暮歸東土
Ashita ni wa Seiten ni itari, kure ni wa Tōdo ni kaeru.
In the morning he reaches India,
In the evening he returns to China.

187. 呑舟魚不遊數仞谷
Donshū no uo wa sūjin no tani ni asobazu.
A fish that can swallow a boat doesn't swim around in a valley stream.

188. 巣父飲牛許由洗耳
Sōfu ushi ni mizukai, Kyo Yū mimi o arau.
Chaofu waters his ox, Xu You washes his ears.

Chaofu (Sōfu) and Xu You (Kyo Yū) were two men of ancient China, famous for their spotless integrity. When the Emperor Yao 堯 (*trad.* 2357 BCE) offered his throne to Xu You, the latter is said to have hurried off to wash his ears in the stream in order to cleanse them of defilement. Chaofu, hearing of this, led his ox upstream to drink so that it would not be contaminated by the water in which Xu You had washed his ears.

189. 不慕諸聖不重己靈
Shoshō o shitawazu, korei o omonzezu.
I do not emulate the sages; I do not esteem my own spirit.

190. 天上天下唯我獨尊
Tenjō tenge yuiga dokuson.
In heaven and on earth, I alone am to be revered.

PARALLEL EIGHT-CHARACTER PHRASES

191. 劍輪飛處日月沈輝
寶杖敲時乾坤失色

Kenrin tobu tokoro, jitsugetsu hikari o shizume;
Hōjō teki suru toki, kenkon iro o shissu.
When the sword-disc flies,
Sun and moon darken;
When the jewel-staff strikes,
Heaven and earth pale.

192. 爐鞴之所鈍鐵猶多
良醫之門病者愈甚
Rohai no tokoro dontetsu nao ōku,
Ryōi no mon byōsha iyo-iyo hanahadashi.
In the blacksmith's shop there are still piles of blunt iron; at the good physician's gate more and more sick men wait.

193. 孤峰頂上目視雲霄
古渡頭邊和泥合水
Kohō chōjō manako ni unshō o mi,
Koto tōhen wadei gassui.
From the top of the solitary peak,
I gaze at the clouds;
Close by the old ferry landing,
I am splashed with mire.

194. 冬至月頭賣被買牛
冬至月尾賣牛買被
Tōji gettō ni aru toki, hi o utte ushi o kai;
Tōji getsubi ni aru toki, ushi o utte hi o kau.
On the first day of winter
I sell my quilt and buy an ox;
On the last day of winter
I sell my ox and buy a quilt.

195. 追大鵬於藕絲竅中
納須彌於蟭螟眼裏
Taihō o gūshi kyōchū ni oi;
Shumi o shōmei ganri ni iru.
To pursue the Great Roc into the tube of a lotus stem; to put Mount Sumeru into the eye of a midge.

196. 姑蘇臺畔不語春秋
納僧面前豈論玄妙
Koso daihan shunjū o katarazu;
Nōsō menzen ani gemmyō o ronzen ya?
On the Gusu Terrace
We do not speak of *The Spring and Autumn*,
In front of my face
How can you discuss the profoundly mysterious!

The terrace was a pleasure pavilion built by King Fucha of Wu 吳夫差 for his beautiful concubine Xishi 西施. Its ruins were used in Chinese poetry as a metaphor for the inevitable fall of pomp and power. *The Spring and Autumn* is an historical work traditionally said to have been edited by Confucius in such a way as to pass moral judgment on the men and events recorded in it.

197. 欲能其詩先能其心
欲能其畫先能其容
Sono shi o yoku sen to hosseba, mazu sono kokoro o yoku shi;
Sono ga o yoku sen to hosseba, mazu sono yō o yoku seyo.
If you want to write such a poem, you must first be capable of such a mind; if you want to paint such a picture, you must first be capable of grasping such a form.

198. 漁歌烟浦咸稱富貴
樵唱雲樹共樂昇平
Gyo wa empo ni utatte, mina fūki to shō shi,
Shō wa unju ni tonaete, tomo ni shōhei o tanoshimu.
The fishermen singing on the misty shore
All extol good fortune and honor;
The woodcutters chanting among the lofty trees
Together rejoice in the era of peace.

199. 若也會得入鄉隨俗
若也不會餓死首陽
Moshi mata etoku seba, kyō ni itte zoku ni shitagau;
Moshi mata e sezumba, Shuyō ni gashi sen.
If you can understand, you will return to your village and

become a rustic; if you cannot understand, you will starve on Shouyang.

> When King Wu of Zhou 周武王 overthrew the Yin 殷 dynasty, the two brothers Bai Yi 伯夷 and Shu Qi 叔齊, heirs to a feudal kingdom under the Yin, condemned him as a rebel and, refusing to "eat the grain of Zhou," withdrew to a mountain called Shouyang (Shuyō), where, with only ferns for food, they eventually starved to death.

200. 孤峯頂上嘯月眠雲
大洋海中翻波走浪
Kohō chōjō tsuki ni usobuki kumo ni nemuru;
Taiyō kaichū nami o hirugaeshi nami o hashirasu.
On the top of the solitary peak,
He whistles at the moon and sleeps in the clouds;
Within the vast ocean,
He overturns the waves and rouses the breakers.

201. 天與不取反受其咎
時至不行反受其殃
Ten no atauru o torazareba, kaette sono toga o uku;
Toki itatte okonawazareba, kaette sono wazawai o uku.
Not to take what Heaven gives is to incur Heaven's calamity; not to act when the moment comes is to incur Heaven's misfortune.

202. 白雲堆裏不見白雲
流水聲裏不聞流水
Hakuun tairi hakuun o mizu;
Ryūsui seiri ryūsui o kikazu.
Enwrapped in billows of white clouds, I do not see the white clouds; absorbed in the sound of flowing water, I do not hear the flowing water.

203. 堯風蕩蕩野老謳歌
舜日熙熙漁人鼓棹
Gyōfū tōtō to shite yarō ōka shi;
Shunjitsu kiki to shite gyojin sao o ko su.

When Yao's influence spread throughout the land,
The peasants sang their songs;
When Shun's radiance shone o'er his vast domain,
The fishermen drummed with their oars.

Yao (Gyō) and Shun were Sage Emperors in the golden age of China.

204. 以盲爲明以聾爲聰
以危爲安以吉爲凶
Mō o motte myō to nashi, rō o motte sō to nashi;
Ki o motte an to nashi, kitsu o motte kyō to nasu.
I take blindness as vision, deafness as hearing;
I take danger as safety and prosperity as misfortune.

205. 隔山見煙便知是火
隔墻見角便知是牛
Yama o hedatete kemuri o mireba, sunawachi kore hi naru koto o shiri;
Kaki o hedatete tsuno o mireba, sunawachi kore ushi naru koto o shiru.
When I see smoke beyond the mountain I know there's a fire; when I see horns beyond the fence I know there's an ox.

206. 欲透塵勞須知要徑
將施妙藥先候病原
Jinrō o tōran to hosseba, subekaraku yōkei o shiru beshi;
Masa ni myōyaku o hodokosan to seba, mazu byōgen o ukagau.
To pass through the dusty turmoil of the world you must know the main road; to dispense healing medicine you must first enquire into the source of the illness.

207. 凡夫若知即是聖人
聖人若會即是凡夫
Bompu moshi shiraba, sunawachi kore seijin;
Seijin moshi e seba, sunawachi kore bompu.
When an ordinary man attains knowledge he is a sage; when a sage attains understanding he is an ordinary man.

208. 鸚鵡能言不離飛鳥
猩猩能言不離禽獸
Ōmu yoku mono iu mo, hichō o hanarezu;
Shōjō yoku mono iu mo, kinjū o hanarezu.
Though a cockatoo can talk,
It is still just a bird;
Though an orang-outang can speak,
It is still just a beast.

In ancient China the *xingxing*, nowadays translated as "orang-outang," was considered to be a fabulous animal that could speak and also understand men's thoughts and intentions.

209. 非規矩不能定方圓
非準繩不能正曲直
Kiku ni arazumba, hōen o sadamuru koto atawazu;
Junjō ni arazumba, kyokuchoku o tadasu koto atawazu.
But for the rule and the compass, the square and the circle could not be determined; but for the plumb-line, the straight and the bent could not be rectified.

210. 不萠枝上金鳳翱翔
無影樹邊玉象圍繞
Fubō shijō kimpō kōshō,
Muyō juhen gyokuzō inyō.
Above the budless branches
The golden phoenix soars,
Around the shadowless tree
The jade elephant circumambulates.

Drawings by Hakuin Ekaku

Hakuin Zenji, Self-Portrait

醜上添醜又一層
者般醜惡破瞎秀
鏖近代斷無瞎僧
挫今時默照邪黨
爲群魔僧
群魔隊裏
爲千佛嫌
千佛場中

Sembutsu jōchū
Sembutsu ni kiraware;
    Gumma tairi
    Gumma ni nikumaru.
Konji mokushō no jatō o kujiki,
Kindai dammu no kassō o minagoroshi ni su.
    Shahan shūaku no hakattoku
    Shūjō shū o sou mata issō.

In the realm of the thousand buddhas
He is hated by the thousand buddhas;
    Among the crowd of demons
    He is detested by the crowd of demons.
He crushes the silent-illumination heretics of today,
And massacres the heterodox blind monks of this generation.
    This filthy blind old shavepate
    Adds more foulness still to foulness.

Plum and Sparrow

寒梅
的的
西來
意

Kambai
tekiteki
sairai
no i

The winter plum—
clearly
the meaning
of the coming from the West

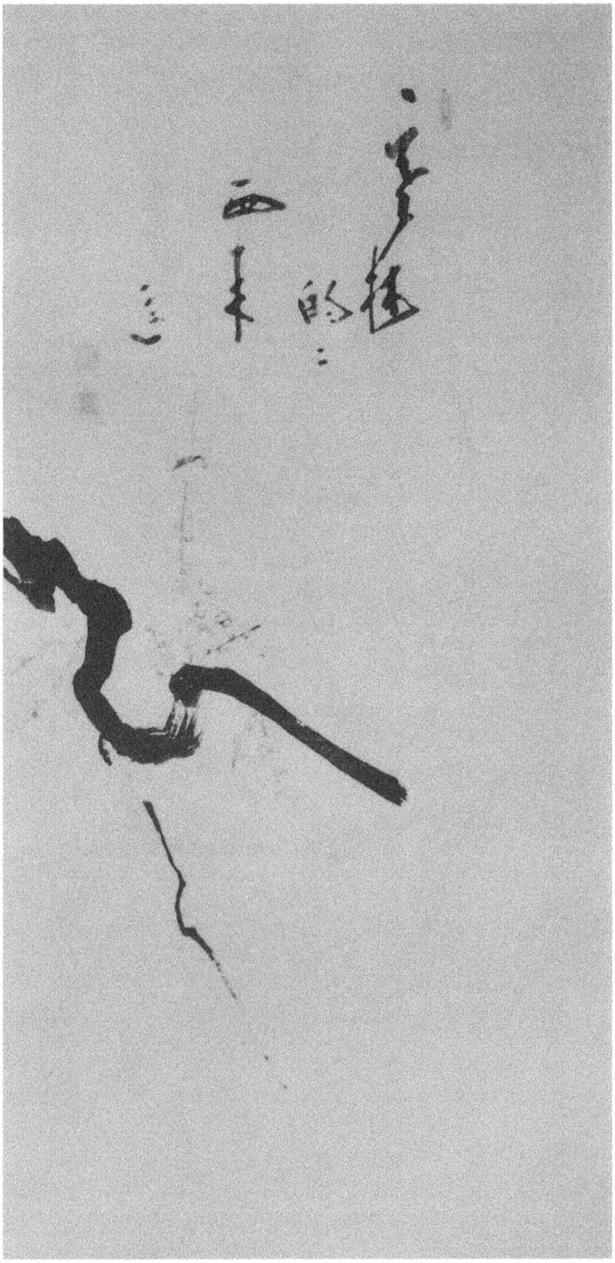

Chrysanthemums

悠然
見
南山

Yūzen to shite
nanzan o
miru

Quietly
gazing
at the distant southern hills

The Bridge of Mama*

世の中の
人のうへにも
かけて見よ
誰か心の
まゝの
つぎは
し

Yo no naka no hito no ue ni mo,
kakete miyo
Tare ka kokoro no
Mama no tsugihashi.

Who has the jointed bridge of Mama
in his heart,
Him would I have throw it
across the world of men

* A famous bridge at Katsushika 葛飾, northeast of old Tokyo, and mentioned in several love songs in the *Man'yōshū*.

The Monkey

獼猴探水月
到死不休歇
放手沒深泉
十方光皓潔

Mikō suigetsu o saguri,
Shi ni itaru made kyūketsu sezu.
Hōshu shinsen ni mossureba,
Jippō hikari kōketsu.

The monkey is reaching for the moon in the water,
Until death overtakes him he'll never give up.
If he'd let go the branch and disappear in the deep pool,
The whole world would shine with dazzling pureness.

Zazen

おぼう　今日は

奇特に　坐禅と

出かけて　じゃの

おうよ

"O bō! kyō wa
kidoku ni zazen to
dekakete ja no!"
"Ō yo!"

"Hey, bonze!
Wonder of wonders
you're doing zazen today."

"Sure!"

Bodhidharma

直指人心見性成佛

沙羅樹下八十三歳老衲
白隠叟目鏡なしに書

Jikishi
Ninshin
Kenshō
Jōbutsu

Sharajuge hachijūsansai rōnō,
Hakuin sō megane nashi ni sho su.

Directly points
To man's mind.
He sees into his own nature
And attains Buddhahood.

The eighty-three year old Buddhist monk
Hakuin drew this without his spectacles.

Death

死

若人見徹

名眞

大丈夫

SHI

Moshi hito kentetsu sureba
Shin no
daijōbu
to nazuku

DEATH

He whose insight penetrates here
is a truly great man.

Daitō Kokushi as a Beggar

乞者隊裏被席
依貪甜瓜見生擒
手なしに瓜をひきやるなら
成程足なして参り申さふ

Kossha tairi ni seki o kōmuri,
Tenka o musaboru ni yotte shōkin seraru.
"Te nashi ni uri o hikyaru nara,
Naruhodo ashi nashi de mairi mōsō."

Wearing a straw mat among the crowd of beggars,
Through his greed for sweet melons he's been taken alive.
"If You give me the fruit without using Your hands,
Of course I'll enter Your presence without using my feet."

Kannon

慈眼視衆生
福寿
海無量

沙羅樹下八十三歳
老衲書

Jigen ji shujō
Fukuju
kai muryō

Sharajuge hachijūsansai
rōnō shosu

The Eye of Compassion watches over sentient beings,
The Sea of Blessings
is beyond measure.

The eighty-three year old Buddhist monk drew this.

Notes

Notes, Part One

1. In order to indicate how the Rinzai Sect of Zen has come to be one of the two main streams of transmitted Zen teaching in Japan, and what tributary streams have contributed to its present comprehensiveness, a bare outline of the transmission through the past fourteen hundred years may be found useful.

   Chan 禪 (Zen), as a sect, may be said to begin with its first Chinese patriarch, the Brahmin monk known as Bodhidharma, who is traditionally said to have arrived in southern China from India about 520 (or 527) CE. Though teachers of various types of Buddhist meditation had preceded Bodhidharma, none succeeded in establishing a school or line of disciples. According to the tradition, Bodhidharma transmitted his Dharma to Huike 慧可 (Eka, 487–593), the Second Patriarch; Huike transmitted his Dharma to Sengcan 僧璨 (Sōsan, *d.* 606), the Third Patriarch; and Sengcan transmitted his Dharma to Daoxin 道信 (Dōshin, 580–651), the Fourth Patriarch. Thus far Chinese Chan may be said to have been one undifferentiated teaching. After the Fourth Patriarch, however, the first diverging line appears. Daoxin's disciple Hongren 弘忍 (Gunin, 601–674) became his successor in the orthodox patriarchal line; but a second heir, Farong 法融 (Hōyū, 594–657), established himself on the Niutoushan 牛頭山 (Gozuzan), in the southwestern part of present Jiangsu, and founded a line of Chan known as the Ox-head (Niutou 牛頭 Gozu) School, which continued independently for some eight or nine generations.

The Fifth Patriarch Hongren handed on the orthodox patriarchal transmission to Huineng 慧能 (Enō, 638–713), the Sixth Patriarch, but also gave the Seal of Transmission to Shenxiu 神秀 (Jinshū, 605?–706). This disciple founded his own line of Chan, later known as the Northern School, which, though important in its day, did not survive beyond five or six generations.

The patriarchate, as such, came to an end with Huineng. Three of his heirs carried on his teachings in three distinct lines. Heze Shenhui 荷澤神會 (Kataku Jinne, 670–762) founded the Heze 荷澤 (Kataku) School, which died out after five or six generations; Qingyuan Xingsi 青原行思 (Seigen Gyōshi, *d.* 740) and Nanyue Huairang 南嶽懷讓 (Nangaku Ejō, 677–744) became founders of the two individual lines which have formed the main streams of Zen through the centuries.

Within one hundred and fifty years after the death of Qingyuan Xingsi, three outstanding masters in his line had developed their own distinctive schools of Zen: the Caodong 曹洞 (Sōtō), founded by Dongshan Liangjie 洞山良价 (Tōzan Ryōkai, 807–869); the Yunmen 雲門 (Ummon), founded by Yunmen Wenyan 雲門文偃 (Ummon Bun'en, 862/4–949); and the Fayan 法眼 (Hōgen), founded by Fayan Wenyi 法眼文益 (Hōgen Bun'eki, 885–958). In the course of the same period, two distinctive schools developed in the line of Nanyue Huairang: the Guiyang 潙仰 (Igyō), founded by Guishan Lingyou 潙山靈祐 (Isan Reiyū, 771–853), and the Linji 臨濟 (Rinzai), founded by Linji Yixuan 臨濟義玄 (Rinzai Gigen, *d.* 866). Together, these five schools were known as the Five Houses (*wujia* 五家 *goke*) of Chan.

About one hundred years later, the direct heir of Linji Yixuan in the 7th generation left two distinguished heirs, each of whom established his own line of Linji teaching: Yangqi Fanghui 楊岐方會 (Yōgi Hōe, 992–1049) established the Yangqi 楊岐 (Yōgi) line, and Huanglong Huinan 黃龍慧南 (Ōryō E'nan, 1002–1069) established the Huanglong 黃龍 (Ōryō) line. These two lines together with the Five Houses mentioned above are known as the Seven Schools or Sects (*qizong* 七宗 *shichishū*) of Chan.

Among the Five Houses, the Caodong School, though it borrowed koans from other houses and schools, continued as an individual stream of Chan in China until the Ming 明 dynasty 1368–1644), when it was finally absorbed into the Linji School. In the 13th century, however, it was brought to Japan, and there, as the Japanese Sōtō Sect, has continued to keep its individual identity both in teaching and organization.

The Linji School did not at first flourish widely. Its syncretistic tendencies, however, were already apparent by the end of the 10th century, when a 6th generation descendant of the founder introduced certain Caodong doctrines into the body of his own teaching. By the time the Yangqi and Huanglong lines were well established, the teachings of the Guiyang and Fayan schools, both of which had lasted only six generations, had already been taken into these Linji lines; a hundred years later, those of the Yunmen School, after flourishing for ten generations, were also to be absorbed. The Huanglong line never succeeded in producing men of the stature of those in the Yangqi line. The Japanese heir of an 8th generation master brought the teachings of the Huanglong school to Japan in the 12th century, but neither in China nor in Japan did the school survive much longer.

Meanwhile the Yangqi line had been steadily rising in power and importance. With the disappearance of the Huanglong line, the teachings of which it took over, the Yangqi line now represented all the previously separate schools of Chan teaching that had arisen after the Sixth Patriarch, with the exception of the Caodong School, though, as we have seen, even some of the teachings of this school had become a part of its inheritance. The koans which had been created by masters in each of these individual schools were now being given by Yangqi masters to their disciples, together with such koans as these masters themselves were newly creating. In a word, Yangqi Chan and Linji Chan had become synonymous.

In the 13th and 14th centuries a number of eminent Yangqi men brought the teachings of this school to Japan. Among these men were twenty representative masters who founded their own Japanese lines between 1235 and 1358. Eleven of the twenty were Chinese masters, nine were Japanese monks who had studied in China and received the Seal of Transmission from Yangqi masters there. Some of these lines endured for many generations, some for relatively few. By the end of the 17th century all the Zen masters in Japan represented the Yōgi (Yangqi) line of Rinzai Zen, with the exception of those in the independent Sōtō (Caodong) Sect and those in a line of Ming Chan that had come to Japan in the middle of the 17th century.

At the beginning of the 18th century, the Japanese monk Hakuin Ekaku 白隠慧鶴 (1686–1769)—a direct descendant of the Japanese priest Nampo Jōmyō 南浦紹明 (1235–1309) who had brought Yangqi teachings to Japan in 1267—after studying koans with a number of masters in various parts of the country, consolidated the teachings of those Yōgi lines still existing in Japan. The Japanese Rinzai Zen masters of today are all descendants of the ninety-odd heirs to whom Hakuin Zenji gave the Seal of Transmission during his lifetime. Thus, through Hakuin, present-day masters trace their lineage back through Yangqi Fanghui, Linji Yixuan, and Nanyue Huairang, to the Sixth Patriarch, and thence to the founder of Zen, Bodhidharma himself.

2. See the BIBLIOGRAPHY for all books mentioned in this work where, as in the present case, the title is not followed by the Chinese characters for it.

3. Zhongfeng Mingben 中峰明本 (Chūhō Myōhon, 1263–1323) was a native of Hangzhou 杭州 (Kōshū), and his family name was SUN 孫 (SON). At an early age he left his home and became a monk. While on a pilgrimage he visited Gaofeng Yuanmiao 高峰原妙 (Kōhō Gemmyō, 1238–1295), a Linji (Rinzai) master of the Yangqi (Yōgi) line, who was living on Tianmushan 天目山 (Temmokuzan) in Zhejiang 浙江 (Sekkō), and remained to serve that master diligently. It is said that Mingben once became so disturbed at his lack of progress that he beat his head against a pillar. His first glimpse of understanding came on reading the following passage in the *Diamond Sutra*: "All those [who cherish, recite, and disseminate this sutra] will carry the Tathāgata's Highest Perfect Awakening." [*T* 8: 750c.17*f*] At twenty-four, Mingben attained satori while watching the flowing water of a spring. Eventually he received the Transmission of Dharma from Yuanmiao.

After taking leave of his master, Mingben had no fixed residence, but lived sometimes in one or another of the huts on the Middle Peak (Zhongfeng 中峰 Chūhō) of Mount Tianmu, sometimes aboard river boats. The Yuan emperor Renzong 仁宗 (Jinsō, *r.* 1312–1320) invited Mingben, now known as Zhongfeng, to the Court. Though the Master declined the Imperial invitation, the Emperor presented him with a robe and conferred upon him the title Foci Yuanzhao Guanghui Chanshi 佛慈圓照廣慧禪師 (Butsuji Enshō Kōe Zenji). Emperor Yingzong 英宗 (Eisō, *r.* 1321–1323) also held the Master in great respect. Zhongfeng's students included princes and commoners as well as a number of Japanese monks. Seven years after the Master's death at the age of sixty, Emperor Wenzong 文宗 (Bunsō, *r.* 1330–1331) bestowed upon him posthumously the titles Zhijue Chanshi 智覺禪師 (Chikaku Zenji) and Puying Guoshi 普應國師 (Fuō Kokushi).

Zhungfeng's writings and recorded sermons are contained in the *Tianmu Zhongfeng heshang guanglu* and the *Tianmu Mingben chanshi zalu*. He is also the author of the *Puying guoshi Huanzhu'an qinggui*.

4. A reference to the following passage in the Nirvana Sutra:

> Suppose a man takes various kinds of poisons and paints a large drum with them, then strikes it in the midst of a group of people. Though these people may have no desire to listen to it, yet all who hear the sound of the drum will die. [*T* 12: 420a.8]

5. Apocryphal tradition attributes the origin of the Zen Sect to the following incident: One day the Buddha was preaching to the assembly on the Vulture Peak. During the sermon he held up a golden lotus flower. No one among the assembly understood his meaning except his senior disciple Mahākāśyapa, who looked at the Buddha and smiled. Thereupon the Buddha said, "I have the True Dharma Eye, the Marvelous Mind of Nirvana. This I now transmit to you, Mahākāśyapa." On the basis of this tradition Mahākāśyapa is considered to be the first in the line of the Indian patriarchs of Zen.

The *Tiansheng guangdeng lu*, a collection of biographies of Indian and Chinese Zen monks compiled in 1036, contains in its section devoted to Mahākāśyapa [*ZZ* 2乙: 8.4.306b–d] what seems to be the earliest appearance of this story. In the *Rentian yanmu*, a work compiled about 150 years later, a question is asked [*T* 48: 325b.5] as to the source of the story, and the reply made that it is contained in the 3 *juan* work *Dafantianwang wenfo jueyi jing* 大梵天王問佛決疑經 (*Daibontennō mombutsu ketsugi kyō*). The name of such a sutra does not appear in any Chinese catalogue of sutras. Did it really ever exist? Had it been lost before it could be included in a catalogue? We do not know.

However, two sutras bearing this title do exist, one in 2 *juan* [*ZZ* 87: 4.302c–325b] and one in 1 *juan* [*ibid.*, 325c–339a]. The story of the Buddha's holding up the flower appears in both, but the versions differ somewhat, the latter substantially following the *Tiansheng guangdeng lu* version. The origin of these two sutras is obscure. On the basis of internal textual evidence it seems probable that they were composed in Japan, perhaps toward the end of the Kamakura 鎌倉 era (1185–1333), in order to provide a bona fide basis for the tradition of the origin of the Zen Sect. Thus the actual source of this lovely legend, so profound in its meaning, still eludes us. The Zen koan based upon the legend will be found in *Wumenguan* 6 [*T* 48: 293b.12].

The Vulture Peak (*Skr.* Gṛdhrakūṭa), a mountain outside the city of Rājagṛha, was probably so named because it was shaped like a vulture's head or because flocks of vultures lived on it. Its caves and caverns were a favorite haunt of ascetics. The early scriptures record that Shakyamuni Buddha preached many of his sermons there. A mythical Vulture Peak is the setting of the present story, as well as of the preaching of various Mahayana scriptures.

6. A reference to the phrase "it points directly to man's own mind" in the statement describing the principles of the Zen Sect and traditionally attributed to Bodhidharma. For a discussion of this statement, *see* Part Two, Note 2. The Shaolinsi 少林寺 (Shōrin-ji) was the temple where Bodhidharma remained sitting in meditation for nine years.

7. Even today the statement is often made that there are 1700 Zen koans. Actually many more exist, though many less are in general use. The round figure 1700 was arrived at in early days by attributing one koan to each of the 1701 Zen masters whose names appear in the 11th century biographical collection known as the *Jingde chuandeng lu*. A great many anecdotes and *mondō* 問答 (*wenda*), exchanges of question and answer, from which koans derived, are, indeed, found in the biographies contained in this work, but as a matter of fact actual biographies are given for only about 960 masters. The remaining 700-odd masters are mentioned by name only.

8. From the "Shanfang yehua" 山房夜話 (Sambō yawa) "Evening Talks in a Mountain Hut," in *juan* 11 of the *Zhongfeng heshang guanglu* [*KZ* 31: 7.606a.18–c.10].

9. There are two passages in which Huangbo Xiyun 黃蘗希運 (Ōbaku Kiun, *d. ca.* 850) is recorded to have used the word "koan." In *juan* 1 of the *Wujia zhengzong zan*, a text compiled at the end of Song, there is a story about a meeting between Huangbo and six monks who came to see him. The ensuing mondo between the Master and one of the monks came to an end with the Master's apparent acceptance of the monk's position. The next day, however, when Huangbo had taken the high seat to give a sermon,

he said: "Will the monk who was seeking the antelope come forward?" The monk who had previously questioned the Master stepped out from the assembly. Huangbo said: "Yesterday's *koan* had not been completed when I desisted…" [*ZZ* 2乙: 8.5.458a.2]. Also, in one of the Ming versions of the *Wanling lu*, Huangbo is recorded as saying: "If you fellows of character observe this *koan*: A monk asked Zhaozhou (Jōshū), 'Has the dog Buddha-nature or not?'…" [*T* 48: 387b.3] Since the section in which this statement appears is lacking in both the Song and the other Ming version of the same text, not too much weight can be given to this example.

With the following, however, we are on firmer ground. In the *Chuandeng lu* biography of Huangbo's heir Chen Zunsu 陳尊宿 (Chin Sonshuku, 780?–877?) is the following: "When the Master saw a monk approaching he said, 'As an immediately present (*xiancheng* 現成 *genjō*) *koan* I spare you from thirty blows.'" [*T* 51: 291b.17]

10. Nanyuan Huiyong 南院慧顒 (Nan'in Egyō, *d.* 930), also known as Baoying Heshang 寶應和尚 (Hōō Oshō), was an heir of Xinghua Cunjiang 興化存獎 (Kōke Zonshō, 830–888), one of the most important of the heirs of Linji Yixuan (Rinzai Gigen). He lived at the Baoyingyuan 寶應院 (Hōō-in), which was either an alternate name for or one of the buildings within the Nanyuan 南院 (Nan-in), a temple situated in Ruzhou 汝州 (Joshū), a part of modern Henan. The section on him in the *Chuandeng lu* [*T* 51: 298b.21–c.20] contains merely a few of his sermons and some mondos in which he takes part. Recent research has established the date of his death as given above, but no further biographical information seems to be available. Through Nanyuan's only heir, Fengxue Yanzhao 風穴延沼 (Fuketsu Enshō, 896–973), the transmission of the Linji (Rinzai) School was continued and further developed.

11. Linji Yixuan 臨濟義玄 (Rinzai Gigen, *d.* 866) was the founder of the Linji (Rinzai) School of Zen. Though there is no evidence that in his lifetime Linji intended to found a school, his personality and the manner and content of his teaching were so outstanding as to provide naturally the foundation for a distinctive style of Zen.

Yixuan's family name was Jing 邢 (Kei), and he was a native of the village of Nanhua 南華 (Nanka) in Cao 曹 (Sō), a prefecture south of the Yellow River in modern Shandong. Though the date of his birth is not known, modern scholars place it between 810 and 815. Nor do we know how old Yixuan was when he became a monk, though again we may surmise that he was about twenty, the usual age at that period. Thereafter he devoted himself to studying the Vinaya (Discipline) and other Mahayana schools and doctrines and familiarizing himself with numerous sutras and commentaries.

Some five or six years later, having become dissatisfied with these studies, Yixuan journeyed south to Jiangxi 江西 (Kōzei). There he entered the monastery of the Chan master Huangbo Xiyun (Ōbaku Kiun) with the purpose of devoting himself to meditation. After three years had gone by without achieving any results from his practice, Yixuan was induced by the head monk of the monastery to approach Huangbo with the question, "What is the cardinal principle of Buddha-dharma?" The Master's answer was a sharp blow. Twice more he asked Huangbo the same question, and twice more received only a blow in reply. Thoroughly discouraged, Yixuan prepared to leave the monastery. But the Master persuaded him to go first to see the old monk Dayu 大愚 (Daigu, *n.d.*), who was living not far away. The story of Yixuan's subsequent enlightenment under Dayu and his return to Huangbo's monastery for ten years of further practice is too well known to need repetition here.

After receiving the Transmission of Dharma from Huangbo, Yixuan went on a long pilgrimage, in the course of which he visited a number of masters. Eventually, perhaps about 849 or 850, he settled in a small temple just inside the capital city of Zhenzhou 鎮州 (Chinshū) in the northern part of the province of Hebei 河北 (Kahoku). Since the temple was situated on the bank of the river Hutuo 滹沱 (Koda) near a river-crossing, it was called the Linjiyuan 臨濟院 (Rinzai-in), or "Temple Overlooking the Ford." There the Master remained for some ten years, preaching and teaching the Dharma his master Huangbo had transmitted to him.

About 861 or 862, Linji, as the Master is more popularly called, left Zhenzhou, and, after a short journey southward, took up his residence in a temple in Weifu 魏府 (Gifu), in southern Hebei. There he spent the remainder of his life in retirement, attended always by his devoted disciple Xinghua Cunjiang (Kōke Zonshō). His last conversation, in which his disciple Sansheng Huiran 三聖慧然 (Sanshō Enen, *n.d.*) figures prominently, is a striking example of the Zen style of using abusive words in giving praise:

> When the Master was about to pass away he seated himself and said, "After I die, do not let my True Dharma Eye disap-

> pear." Sansheng came forward and said, "How could we let your True Dharma Eye disappear!" "Later on, when someone asks you about it, what will you say?" asked the Master. Sansheng gave a "*He!*" "Who would have thought that my True Dharma Eye would disappear when it reached this blind ass!" said Linji. After he had spoken these words, the Master, sitting erect, revealed his Nirvana. [*Linji lu*; *T* 47: 506c.3–7]

There is some disagreement as to the date of the Master's death, perhaps due to a copyist's error, but the weight of evidence places it on May 27, 866. His Imperially conferred posthumous title was Huizhao Chanshi 慧照禪師 (Eshō Zenji). The *Zhenzhou Linji Huizhao chanshi yulu* is the record of the Master's sermons, sayings, and certain episodes in his life, compiled after his death by his disciples.

Linji Yixuan was in the 6th generation in the line of direct transmission from the Sixth Patriarch, through Nanyue (Nangaku), Mazu 馬祖 (Baso, 709–788), Baizhang 百丈 (Hyakujō, 720–814), and Huangbo (Ōbaku). He is recorded to have left twenty-two heirs, but only the line of Xinghua Cunjiang (Kōke Zonshō) continued and flourished, eventually forming the Linji School.

Linji is famous in Zen history for his free use of the stick (*bang* 棒 *bō*) and his shouting "*He!*" 喝 ("*Katsu!*"). Both actions were teaching devices. He used the stick to arouse students or to demonstrate the dynamic nature of the Principle. He explained the meaning behind his "*He!*" in one of his so-called formulas (*see below*, Note 12). Shouting the "*He!*" was not original with Linji, however. The first recorded "*He!*" was that shouted by Mazu during an interview with his great disciple Baizhang. So mighty was Mazu's voice, Baizhang later told his disciples, that he was deaf for three days afterwards. The use of the stick and the shout became one of the characteristic features of the Linji School, and the masters of the Rinzai Sect in Japan still employ both in their teaching.

12. The *Linji lu* contains several groups of short, cryptic statements made by Linji Yixuan (Rinzai Gigen) in order to demonstrate the Principle and instruct his disciples. Within three or four generations his descendants had named each of these grouped statements or formulas, and were giving them as fixed problems, or koans, to their students. In a few other cases, later masters made formulas from material in Linji's sermons and gave names to them. All of these eventually came to be known as Linji (Rinzai) Koans.

Among the most famous of Linji's own grouped statements are the following:

Sihe 四喝 (*Shikatsu*) The Four *He*:

In some instances the "*He!*" is like the jeweled sword of the Vajra King; in some instances the "*He!*" is like the golden-haired lion crouching on the ground; in some instances the "*He!*" is like a grass-tipped pole for decoying fishes; in some instances the "*He!*" does not function as a "*He!*" [*T* 47: 504a.26–28]

Siliaojian 四料簡 (*Shiryōken*) The Four Positions of Subject and Object:

Sometimes I take away man and do not take away the surroundings; sometimes I take away the surroundings and do not take away man; sometimes I take away both man and the surroundings; sometimes I take away neither man nor the surroundings. [*Ibid.*, 497a.22–24]

Sanju 三句 (*Sanku*) The Three Phrases:

Linji took the high seat.

A monk asked: "What is the First Phrase?" The Master said: "When the Seal of the Three Essentials is revealed, the vermilion dots are seen to be merged, and yet, without resort to discussion, host and guest are distinct."

"What is the Second Phrase?" The Master said: "How could Miaojie permit Wuzhuo to question him? How can skill in the use of expedients go against the power to cut through the myriad streams [of notions]?"

"What is the Third Phrase?" The Master said: "Look at the puppets playing on the stage! All their jumps and jerks depend upon the man behind." [*Ibid.*, 497*a*.15–19]

As H. Dumoulin says: "With all such formulas the technical terms must be understood as symbols. We are concerned with a logical or metaphysical dialectic regarding the relationship of subject and object, relative and Absolute, appearance and Reality." [*DCZ*, p. 23] For a similar formula developed in the Caodong (Sōtō) School, that of the Five Ranks (*wuwei* 五位 *goi*), *see* Part Two, Chapter VII, "The *Goi* Koans."

13. Fenyang Shanzhao 汾陽善昭 (Fun'yō Zenshō, 947–1024), in the 6th generation of the Linji (Rinzai) School, was one of the several heirs of Shoushan

Shengnian 首山省念 (Shuzan Shōnen, 926–993). It is recorded that Shanzhao visited seventy-one teachers before he came to Shoushan, and had rather inclined toward the teachings of the Caodong (Sōtō) School. After receiving the Seal of Transmission from Shoushan, he went to live at the Taiziyuan 太子院 (Taishi-in) in Fenzhou 汾州 (Funshū), in modern Shanxi, where he remained for the rest of his life. As a teacher Fenyang was active and original. He was the first of the Linji masters to make use of the Five Ranks (*wuwei* 五位 *goi*) of the Caodong School. Through his heir Shishuang Chuyuan 石霜楚圓 (Sekisō Soen, 986–1039), the main stream of Linji Zen was continued. Fenyang's posthumous title was Wude Chanshi 無德禪師 (Mutoku Zenji). His writings and sayings are recorded in the *Fenyang Wude chanshi yulu*.

The *Xu chuandeng lu* gives the following account of the Master's death:

> A messenger came from the Governor to invite Fenyang to become the chief priest of a certain temple. He said that, as a result of the Master's refusing the Governor's three previous requests, he, the messenger, had been severely punished each time on his return. "If you do not accept this time," he said, "there is nothing left for me but to die." The Master laughed. "Old age and illness have prevented me from leaving the mountain," he said. "However, if I go, I'd like to decide the time of my going myself. There's no need to go with you." "If only you will accept, you are free to choose the time," replied the messenger.
>
> The Master then ordered food to be brought for a farewell meal, and put on his travelling garb. "I'm going ahead," he said to his monks. "Who can come with me?" A monk came forward and said, "I can go." "How far can you walk in a day?" the Master asked. "Fifty *li*," the monk replied. "You can't follow me," said Fenyang. Another monk volunteered. "How far can you go?" the Master asked. "Seventy *li*," the monk replied. "You can't go either," said the Master. The Master's attendant now came forward. "I can go with you," he said. "I can accompany you wherever you go." "You can follow me," said Fenyang. Turning to the messenger the Master said, "I'm going ahead." Then, putting down his chopsticks, he quietly died. [*T* 51: 470b.3–14.]

14. Xuedou Chongxian 雪竇重顯 (Setchō Jūken, 980–1052) was a master in the 4th generation of the Yunmen (Ummon) School of Zen. He was a na-

tive of Suizhou 遂州 (Suishū), in modern Sichuan, and his family name was Li 李 (Ri). At the age of eighteen, after the sudden death of his mother, he decided to become a monk. He took the full commandments at a temple in Yizhou 益州 (Ekishū), also in Sichuan; then, becoming interested in the teachings of the Zen Sect, he visited several of its masters successively. Finally he travelled to Suizhou 隋州 (Zuishū), in modern Hubei, where he met the Yunmen master Zhimen Guangzuo 智門光祚 (Chimon Kōso, *d.* 1031). He became Guangzuo's disciple, attained enlightenment under him, and eventually became his heir.

After receiving the transmission, Chongxian lived for a time on the Cuifengshan 翠峰山 (Suihōzan) in Suzhou 蘇州 (Soshū), in modern Jiangsu. Later he removed to the Zishengsi 資聖寺 (Shishō-ji) on Mount Xuedou 雪竇山 (Setchōzan), in present-day Zhejiang. There for thirty years he actively engaged in teaching and writing, doing much to revive the Yunmen School, which at that period had suffered something of a decline. Xuedou, as he was known in his later years, died at the age of seventy-two, leaving seventeen heirs. His posthumous title, conferred by the Song emperor Renzong 仁宗 (Jinsō, *r.* 1022–1062), was Mingjue Dashi 明覺大師 (Myōkaku Daishi).

Xuedou Chongxian was a famous poet and writer of his time. His collection of one hundred koans with appended verse commentaries, the *Xuedou baize songgu*—originally a part of his "Record," the *Mingjue chanshi yulu*—and numerous other writings, rank among the finest works of Zen literature.

15. Yunmen Wenyan 雲門文偃 (Ummon Bun'en, 862/4–949) was the founder of the Yunmen (Ummon) School, which flourished widely for some three hundred years before it was absorbed into the Linji (Rinzai) School toward the end of the Southern Song (Nansong 南宋 Nansō, 1127–1279).

Wenyan was a native of Jiaxing 嘉興 (Kakō) in Suzhou 蘇州 (Soshū), in modern Jiangsu, and his family name was Zhang 張 (Chō). He became a monk under a commandment master in his native place, and studied the Vinaya diligently. Dissatisfied with his understanding, he went to see Chen Zunsu 陳尊宿 (Chin Sonshuku, 780?–877?), earlier a fellow-disciple of Linji under Huangbo (Ōbaku). Three times Wenyan had to pound on Chen Zunsu's gate before the Master, an eccentric recluse, opened it a crack. As Wenyan pushed his foot into the opening, the Master seized him by his robe and cried, "Speak, speak!" Then, before the young monk could reply, he bawled, "You good-for-nothing!" and slammed the heavy gate shut on Wenyan's leg. Wenyan let out a yell of pain, but in that instant attained satori. His leg was crippled for the remainder of his life.

Following the advice of Chen Zunsu, now nearing the age of one hundred, Wenyan went to Xuefeng Yicun 雪峰義存 (Seppō Gison, 822–908), an important master in the line of Qingyuan Xingsi (Seigen Gyōshi), then living in Fuzhou 福州 (Fukushū), in modern Fujian. After some years of practice under Xuefeng, he eventually received the Transmission of Dharma. Thereafter he made a pilgrimage to the tomb of the Sixth Patriarch in Shaozhou 韶州 (Shōshū), in modern Guangdong. While in Shaozhou, Wenyan joined the assembly of Rumin Chanshi 如敏禪師 (Nyobin Zenji, *d.* 918), a master in the 5th generation of the line of Nanyue Huairang (Nangaku Ejō), and upon Min Chanshi's death succeeded him as priest of the Lingshuyuan 靈樹院 (Reiju-in). Later, under the patronage of the powerful LIU 劉 (RYŪ) family—during the Five Dynasties (Wudai 五代 Godai, 907–960) the rulers of the kingdom of Nanhan 南漢 (Nankan), of which Shaozhou was a part—the Master founded the Guangtai chanyuan 光泰禪院 (Kōtai zen'in) on Mount Yunmen 雲門山 (Ummonzan), in modern Guangdong. There he remained until his death, teaching his highly individual style of Zen to the hundreds of students who crowded around him.

One day in his eighty-fifth year, Yunmen wrote a farewell letter to the King of Nanhan and gave a last sermon to his eighty monks. Then, despite his crippled leg, he seated himself in the full lotus posture and passed away. During the Master's lifetime the King of Nanhan had bestowed upon him a purple robe and the title Kuangzhen Chanshi 匡眞禪師 (Kyōshin Zenji). Seventeen years after his death, the then reigning king conferred upon him the posthumous title Hongming Chanshi 弘明禪師 (Kōmyō Zenji).

In his later years the Master was known for his short and clear answers to his disciples' questions. Many of these were answers of one syllable only, and came to be known as Yunmen's "One Word Barriers" (*yiziguan* 一字關 *ichijikan*). The hundreds of koans he originated, together with his sermons and sayings, compose the *Yunmen Kuangzhen chanshi guanglu*. Eighteen of his most famous koans will be found in the *Biyan lu* (*Hekigan roku*), and five in the *Wumenguan* (*Mumonkan*).

16. Yuanwu Keqin 圜悟克勤 (Engo Kokugon, 1063–1135) was in the 4th generation of the Yangqi (Yōgi) line of the Linji (Rinzai) School. He was

a native of Pengzhou 彭州 (Hōshū), in modern Sichuan, and his family, whose name was Luo 駱 (Raku), had long been Confucianists. As a child he had an exceptional memory, and it is said that he could memorize a passage of a thousand characters in a single day. While on a visit to a temple in his late teens, he was looking through some Buddhist books when the feeling came over him that he had a deep relationship with Buddhism, stemming from a previous existence. After thinking the matter over carefully, he left home and became a monk.

For several years he visited one Zen master after another. Finally he came to see Wuzu Fayan 五祖法演 (Goso Hōen, 1024?–1104), a famous master of the Yangqi line. When Fayan would not sanction his views, Keqin took his leave in anger. But during a subsequent illness he recalled the Master's parting words, "Remember me when you are ill with the fever," and, as soon as he had recovered, he returned to Fayan, who was now living on Wuzushan 五祖山 (Gosozan) in Qizhou 蘄州 (Kishū), in modern Hubei. This was the famous Yellow Plum Mountain where the Fifth Patriarch Wuzu Hongren 五祖弘忍 (Goso Gunin, 601–674) had lived, and which had thereafter been called the "Fifth Patriarch's Mountain" in his memory. There Keqin devoted himself diligently to religious practices, attained satori, and became one of Fayan's heirs.

The illness of his mother in 1102 recalled Keqin to Sichuan. At the request of the Prefect of Chengdu 成都 (Seito), in the same province, he took up his residence at the Zhaojuesi 昭覺寺 (Shōkaku-ji), remaining there for eight years. Later, he was officially invited to live at the Lingquanyuan 靈泉院 (Reisen-in) on Jiashan 夾山 (Kassan) in Lizhou 澧川 (Reishū), in present-day Hunan, and it was at this temple that the Master gave the lectures later compiled and published by his disciples under the title *Biyan lu* (*Hekigan roku*).

Keqin's fame as a Zen master now spread far and wide, and his many students included both monks and laymen, not a few of the latter being high government officials. A purple robe and the title Foguo Chanshi 佛果禪師 (Bukka Zenji) were bestowed upon him by Emperor Huizong 徽宗 (Kisō, *r.* 1100–1125). By Imperial command he resided at several famous temples in the north, and, after the exodus of the Court to Hangzhou, in the south. Emperor Gaozong 高宗 (Kōsō, *r.* 1127–1162) of the Southern Song now conferred upon him the title Yuanwu Chanshi 圜悟禪師 (Engo Zenji), by which he was thereafter generally known.

In 1130 Yuanwu returned to his old temple in Chengdu. On an early autumn day in 1135, feeling a little indisposed, the Master seated himself in the meditation posture, wrote a farewell verse to his disciples, threw down his writing brush, and passed away. The following year the posthumous title Zhenjue Chanshi 眞覺禪師 (Shinkaku Zenji) was conferred upon him by Imperial decree.

Yuanwu left sixteen heirs, among whom the most important were Dahui Zonggao 大慧宗杲 (Daie Sōkō, 1089–1163) and Huqiu Shaolong 虎丘紹隆 (Kukyū Jōryū, 1077–1136). In later generations a number of Shaolong's descendants became founders of Japanese Zen lines. In addition to the famous *Biyan lu*, the Master's sermons, discourses, writings, and letters are contained in the *Yuanwu Foguo chanshi yulu* and the *Yuanwu xinyao.*

17. Dahui Zonggao 大慧宗杲 (Daie Sōkō, 1089–1163) was a master in the 5th generation of the Yangqi (Yōgi) line. His family name was Xi 奚 (Kei), and he was a native of Xuancheng 宣城 (Senjō), in modern Anhui. As a youth he studied Confucianism but at seventeen he had his head shaved and became a monk. On reading the *Yunmen guanglu* he was deeply moved by a sense of close relationship with the old master Yunmen Wenyan (Ummon Bun'en), and this feeling remained with him throughout his life. In accordance with the practice of the time, Zonggao set out on a long pilgrimage. At first he visited all the important Caodong (Sōtō) masters. Then he joined the assembly of Zhantang Wenzhun 湛堂文準 (Tandō Bunjun, 1061–1115) of the Huanglong (Ōryō) line of Linji (Rinzai) Zen.

After that master's death, Zonggao went to stay at the Tianning Wanshousi 天寧萬壽寺 (Tennei Manju-ji), one of the great temples in the Northern Song capital Bianliang 汴梁 (Benryō), modern Kaifeng. At that time Yuanwu Keqin (Engo Kokugon) was chief abbot of the temple. One day when Yuanwu had taken the high seat in the lecture hall, he said: "A monk asked Yunmen: 'From whence come all the buddhas?' Yunmen answered: 'The East Mountain walks over the water.' But if I were asked, I would not answer that way. 'From whence come all the buddhas?' A fragrant breeze comes of itself from the south, and in the palace pavilion a refreshing coolness stirs." [*Dahui lu* 17; *T* 47: 883a.15–18] At these words Zonggao suddenly attained enlightenment. Perhaps it was at this time that he took for his *zi* 字 (*azana*) the name Dahui, or "Great Wisdom." At any rate, he continued his practice under the Master's stern stick, was guided by him to complete understanding, and eventually acknowledged as one of his heirs.

Thereafter, Dahui was appointed to increasingly important positions in the temple, until eventually he took Yuanwu's place on the high seat and in the sanzen room. He was held in the highest esteem among the religious community, and his fame spread even through the capital itself. In 1126 the Prime Minister of the Right, Lǚ Shun 呂舜 (Ryo Shun, *n.d.*), presented him with a purple robe and the title Fori 佛日 (Butsunichi).

When the invading Jurchen brought the Northern Song (Bei-Song 北宋 Hokusō) dynasty (960–1127) to an end, Dahui fled south. For a time he stayed with his master, Yuanwu, who, in obedience to Imperial command, was then living at the Zhenruyuan 眞如院 (Shinnyo-in) on Yunjushan 雲居山 (Ungozan), in present-day Jiangxi. Hongzhi Zhengjue 宏智正覺 (Wanshi Shōgaku) visited Yuanwu there, and it is possible that Dahui at that time met this Caodong master with whom he was later to carry on so long and vigorous a controversy. When Yuanwu returned to Sichuan in 1130, Dahui built a hermitage for himself on the site of an old Yunmen temple at the back of the mountain. There he attracted many followers. Soon, however, he journeyed farther south and took up his residence at the Yunmen'an 雲門庵 (Ummon-an) at Xiaoxi 小溪 (Shōkei), in modern Fujian. In 1137 he was invited by Yuanwu's former disciple Zhang Jun 張浚 (Chō Shun, 1086–1154), now Prime Minister, to live at Jingshan 徑山 (Kinzan) in Lin'an 臨安 (Rin'an), near the Southern Song capital, Hangzhou. There the Master's religious activities flourished greatly, and over two thousand students gathered to study under him.

In the early summer of 1141, as a result of becoming involved in a serious political affair, Dahui was deprived of his authorization to wear the robe of a priest. He now went into retirement at Hengyang 衡陽 (Kōyō), in modern Hunan, where he remained for nearly ten years. It was during this period that he wrote his *Zhengfayanzang.*

In 1150 the Master moved to Meiyang 梅陽 (Baiyō), in modern Guangdong. At that time the district of Mei was suffering from a plague, and over half the hundred-odd disciples who had accompanied the Master there died. During this period Dahui devoted all his efforts to helping and converting the populace, and, though he received his pardon in 1155 and was again permitted to wear his robe, he remained in Meiyang, refusing all the invitations that were now heaped upon him.

An Imperial command came in 1158 for the Master to return to his former temple at Jingshan. There some seventeen hundred disciples gathered around him. He was treated with great favor by Emperor Xiaozong 孝宗

(Kōsō, *r.* 1162–1189), who presented the Master with a plaque on which he had inscribed with his own hand the three characters Miaoxi'an 妙喜庵 (Myōki-an), or "Hermitage of Marvelous Joy." In 1161 the Master retired, but he continued to receive Imperial patronage until his death on September 5, 1163, at the age of seventy-five. The posthumous title Pujue Chanshi 普覺禪師 (Fukaku Zenji) was conferred upon him by Imperial decree.

Dahui left ninety-four heirs. In later generations two lines of Japanese Zen stemmed directly from him. He was most famous for his lifelong opposition to the quietistic meditation of the Caodong (Sōtō) School, which he contemptuously characterized as "silent-illumination heterodox Zen" (*mozhao xiechan* 默照邪禪 *mokushō jazen*), and his vigorous championing of Yuanwu's views on the koan as a necessary means to enlightenment. Under Dahui the systematic and dynamic koan practice known as "introspecting-the-koan Zen" (*kanhua chan* 看話禪 *kanna zen*) became the definitive method of the Linji School, in contrast to the "silent-illumination Zen" (*mozhao chan* 默照禪 *mokushō zen*) of the Caodong School.

In addition to the *Zhengfayanzang*, the only literary work from Dahui's own hand, the Master's sermons and voluminous writings compiled by his disciples will be found in the *Dahui Pujue chanshi yulu*, the *Dahui Pujue chanshi zongmen wuku*, and the *Dahui Jue chanshi pushuo*.

18. The Caodong 曹洞 (Sōtō) School was founded by Dongshan Liangjie 洞山良价 (Tōzan Ryōkai, 807–869), a 5th generation heir of Qingyuan Xingsi (Seigen Gyōshi), one of the direct disciples of the Sixth Patriarch. The origin of the sect's name has long been in question. One opinion is that it derives from the first character of both Dongshan's name and that of his heir Caoshan Benji 曹山本寂 (Sōzan Honjaku, 840–901). Another opinion is that the first character *cao* refers to Caoxi 曹溪 (Sōkei), where the Sixth Patriarch passed most of his teaching years, and was appropriated in order to establish the direct descent of the sect from Huineng and thus prove its masters to be his authentic successors.

Dongshan transmitted to his disciple Caoshan the "secret" teaching which he himself had received from his teacher Yunyan Tansheng 雲巖曇晟 (Ungan Donjō, 780?–841), and which Dongshan had incorporated in a poem entitled *Baojing sanmei*, "The Jeweled-mirror Samadhi." This was the teaching known as the Five Ranks (*wuwei* 五位 *goi*). Caoshan systematized and developed this doctrine of the Five Ranks and made it the characteristic teaching of his line. This line died out after four or five generations.

A second teaching line in the Caodong School stemmed from another of Dongshan's heirs, Yunju Daoying 雲居道膺 (Ungo Dōyō, *d.* 902). Daoying is said to have received the true essence of Dongshan's Dharma, but not his teaching on the Five Ranks. Sometime during the Xiantong 咸通 (Kantsū) era (859–873) of Tang, Daoying built a temple on Yunjushan 雲居山 (Ungozan), in modern Jiangxi. There he lived for thirty years, surrounded by a group of never less than fifteen hundred disciples, so it is said. After the line of Caoshan Benji had died out, that of Yunju Daoying became the accepted Caodong line. At first its masters seem to have had little if any interest in the doctrine of the Five Ranks. By the beginning of Southern Song (1127–1279), however, attention had again turned to these abstruse teachings, and many commentaries were being written on them by Caodong masters.

The teachings of Yunju's line were brought to Japan in 1227 by the Japanese priest Dōgen Kigen 道元希玄 (1200–1253), in the 13th generation after Yunju. Dōgen radically altered the doctrines and practices after his return from China, and his successors made further changes in them, with the result that present-day Japanese Sōtō Zen differs considerably from the Chinese school out of which it originally developed.

19. There are a number of old biographies of the Sixth Patriarch, all differing from one another on various points. The following story of his life is based upon the account in *juan* 5 of the *Chuandeng lu* [*T* 51: 235b.10–237a.12].

Huineng 慧能 (Enō, 638–713) was the thirty-third patriarch of Zen, and the sixth patriarch of Chinese Zen. His family name was Lu 盧 (Ro), and his forebears had been natives of Fanyang 范陽 (Han'yō), in modern Hebei. In the Wude 武德 (Butoku) era of Tang (618–626), his father had been degraded in official rank and sent to Nanhai 南海 (Nankai), in present Guangdong. Later the family moved to Xinzhou 新州 (Shinshū), in the same province.

When the boy was three years old his father died, and he was reared by his mother. As he grew up, the family became more and more poverty-stricken, and young Lu supported his mother by gathering and selling firewood. One day he went into the city carrying a load of wood on his back. There he heard a stranger reciting a sutra. At the line, "Without abiding anywhere [the bodhisattva] should produce this mind," a tremor ran through the youth's body. Timidly he asked, "What teaching is this, and from whom did you receive it?" The stranger replied that he had been reciting the *Diamond Sutra*, and that he had received it from Hongren of Huangmei 黄梅弘忍 (Ōbai Gunin, 601–674). The youth told his mother of the encounter, then said that he wanted to leave home and seek a master who could instruct him in this Dharma.

At first Lu went to nearby Shaozhou 韶州 (Shōshū). There he made many friends among the people. Being much impressed with his religious understanding, they restored the Baolinsi 寶林寺 (Hōrin-ji), an old temple at neighboring Caoxi 曹溪 (Sōkei), and asked him to live there. One day he said to himself: "I seek the Great Dharma. Why should I be satisfied with a middling state of understanding?" Thereupon he set out on his way. On reaching the stone grotto of Xishan 西山 (Seizan) in Lechang 樂昌 (Rakushō), in modern Guangdong, he met the meditation teacher Zhiyuan 智遠 (Chion, *n.d.*) who advised him to go immediately to Huangmeishan 黄梅山 (Ōbaizan), the "Yellow Plum Mountain," in modern Hubei, to see the Fifth Patriarch Hongren. This Lu did, arriving at the mountain in 671, The story of his eight months as a laborer in the rice-hulling shed of the temple, of the verse he wrote to express his understanding of enlightenment, of Hongren's midnight transmission to him of the Dharma Seal as well as Bodhidharma's robe and bowl, and of his secret flight and subsequent years of hiding, are too well known for repetition.

On January 28, 676, the layman (*jushi* 居士 *koji*) Lu appeared at the Faxingsi 法性寺 (Hōshō-ji) in Nanhai and was given lodging at the temple. At that time the Dharma Master (*fashi* 法師 *hōshi*) Yinzong 印宗 (Inshū, 627–713) was lecturing there on the *Nirvana Sutra*. He immediately recognized Lu's remarkable understanding of Dharma, and questioned him about his earlier experiences. Two weeks later Lu's head was shaved by Yinzong, and on February 26th, as Huineng (Enō), he received the full commandments.

On March 16, 677, escorted by Yinzong, who had now become his disciple, and some thousand monks and nuns, Huineng returned to the old Baolinsi at Caoxi. The Prefect of Shaozhou requested the Master to preach at the Dafansi 大梵寺 (Daibon-ji). The sermons Huineng gave there, recorded and gathered together by his disciples, form about half of the work known as *The Sixth Patriarch's Platform Sutra*. The Master then returned again to the Baolinsi, and there for a period of some thirty-five years promulgated his teaching of Sudden Awakening (*dunwu* 頓悟 *tongo*).

In 705 Emperor Zhongzong 中宗 (Chūsō, *r.* 705–710) invited the Master to take up his residence at the capital, Chang'an 長安 (Chōan), but

Huineng declined. On his return, the Imperial messenger explained the Master's teaching in a memorial to the Throne. The Emperor, much impressed, then bestowed upon Huineng five hundred pieces of silk, a robe of rare material, and a crystal bowl. On January 8, 706, the name of the Baolinsi was changed by Imperial decree to Zhongxingsi 中興寺 (Chūkō-ji). The end of the following year the Prefect of Shao was ordered by Imperial decree to beautify the temple further and again to change its name, this time to Faquansi 法泉寺 (Hōsen-ji). He was also ordered to convert the Master's old home in Xinzhou into the Guo'ensi 國恩寺 (Kokuon-ji).

One day in 712 the Master gave a sermon to his disciples which concluded with this verse:

> The soil of mind embraces every kind of seed;
> With the falling of the universal rain, one and
> all put forth sprouts.
> When the flower of sudden awakening bursts
> into bloom,
> The fruit of enlightenment ripens of itself.

His sermon ended, the Master dismissed all but his immediate disciples for the last time, saying, "Each, according to your individual circumstances, depart and go your way."

On August 12, 712, the Master directed some of his disciples to proceed ahead of him to the Guo'ensi in Xinzhou, and there build a pagoda. On July 27, 713, he called for a boat and travelled down the river to the temple that had originally been his old home. On August 28 of the same year, after he had finished bathing, the Master seated himself in the lotus posture and died. The old books say that the room was filled with a strange fragrance, and a white rainbow stretched across the sky. Huineng was seventy-six years old. The posthumous title Dajian Chanshi 大鑑禪師 (Daikan Zenji) was bestowed upon him by Emperor Xianzong 憲宗 (Kensō, *r.* 806–820).

When the Fifth Patriarch Hongren handed Bodhidharma's robe and bowl to Huineng, he is said to have instructed him not to transmit them again, as they would only become the cause of contention. There are many tales about what happened to these insignia of the transmission, but it seems probable that they were long kept in the Baolinsi—later the Faquansi—at Caoxi.

The *Chuandeng lu* gives the names of forty-three direct heirs of the Sixth Patriarch. Among these, three were of great importance for the future development of Chinese Zen: Heze Shenhui 荷澤神會 (Kataku Jinne, 670–762), founder of the Heze 荷澤 (Kataku) School, which continued for five generations, then came to an end with Guifeng Zongmi 圭峰宗密 (Keihō Shūmitsu, 780–841), also the fifth and last patriarch of the Huayan 華嚴 (Kegon) Sect; and Qingyuan Xingsi (Seigen Gyōshi) and Nanyue Huairang (Nangaku Ejō), from whom the Five Houses and Seven Schools stemmed.

20. Hongzhi Zhengjue 宏智正覺 (Wanshi Shōgaku, 1091–1157) was a famous master of the Caodong (Sōtō) School in the 9th generation of the Yunju 雲居 (Ungo) line. Zhengjue's family name was Li 李 (Ri), and he was a native of Xizhou 隰州 (Shūshū), in present-day Shanxi. As a child he was exceedingly intelligent, and he is said to have memorized several thousand characters before he had reached the age seven. He left home to become a monk when he was eleven; at fourteen he received the full commandments.

In his eighteenth year Zhengjue went to study under the Caodong master Kumu Facheng 枯木法成 (Komoku Hōjō, *n.d.*) who was living in Ruzhou 汝州 (Joshū), in modern Henan. A few years later Facheng sent him to Danxia Zichun 丹霞子淳 (Tanka Shijun, *d.* 1119), the heir of one of Facheng's Dharma-brothers, who was living at Danxiashan 丹霞山 (Tankazan) in nearby Dengzhou 鄧州 (Tōshū). Zhengjue spent four years under Danxia, and before the Master's death received the Seal of Transmission. Thereafter he lived successively at several temples, and instructed a number of disciples.

In 1129, when he was thirty-nine, Zhengjue went to live at the Jingdesi 景德寺 (Keitoku-ji) on Tiantongshan 天童山 (Tendōzan) in Mingzhou 明州 (Meishū), in present Zhejiang. There he remained until his death, refusing all invitations to leave the mountain. The Jingdesi had been a small and dilapidated temple when the Master first came to live in it, but under his supervision it was reconstructed on a grand scale. Its huge meditation hall was said to have been large enough to accommodate at one time the twelve hundred students who gathered around him.

One day in the autumn of 1157, when he was in his sixty-seventh year, Zhengjue put on his travelling garb and journeyed down the mountain for the first time in nearly thirty years. He visited the commander of the army, the government officials in the district, and the patrons of the temple, thanking them all for their kindness during the years, and saying good-bye. On the 10th of November the Master returned to the Jingdesi. The following morning, after bathing and changing his robes, he sat down in the formal position and gave a farewell talk to his assembled monks. Then, turning to his attendant, he called for a brush. First he inscribed a letter to Dahui Zonggao (Daie Sōkō), with whom he had been engaged in controversy so many years, asking him to take charge of his affairs after his death. Then, still holding his brush, he wrote:

Illusory dreams, phantom flowers—
Sixty-seven years.
A white bird vanishes in the mist,
Autumn waters merge with the sky,

[*Xu chuandeng lu* 7; *T* 51: 579c.23f]

Six months later the Southern Song emperor Gaozong conferred upon him the posthumous title Hongzhi Chanshi 宏智禪師 (Wanshi Zenji).

Hongzhi's sermons and writings, compiled by his disciples, are to be found in the *Hongzhi chanshi guanglu*. Included in this work are the two collections, each of one hundred old koans, which the Master had compiled. One of these, the *Songgu baize* 頌古百則 *Juko hyakusoku*) Verse Comments on One Hundred Old Koans, has appended verses in the style made famous a hundred years earlier by the Yunmen master Xuedou Chongxian (Setchō Jūken). It contains several koans that appear in Xuedou's work, as well as a number of Linji (Rinzai) koans.

21. Prior to the time of Hongzhi Zhengjue 宏智正覺 (Wanshi Shōgaku), the masters of the Yunju (Ungo) line of the Caodong (Sōtō) School, to which Hongzhi belonged, do not seem to have taken a position against the koan and its use. Touzi Yiqing 投子義青 (Tōsu Gisei, 1032–1083), three generations earlier than Hongzhi, had compiled a collection of one hundred koans with appended verses, as had Hongzhi's own teacher, Danxia Zichun (Tanka Shijun). Hongzhi was therefore only following the tradition of his line when he made his own two collections, the *Songgu baize* 頌古百則 (*Juko hyakusoku*) and the *Niangu baize* 拈古百則 (*Nenko hyakusoku*).

In his preface to Hongzhi's *Songgu* and *Niangu*, Hongzhi's disciple Wen'an Sizong 聞庵嗣宗 (Mon'an Shishū, *n.d.*) says: "The venerable master [Hongzhi] collected two hundred koans of the virtuous men of old. He made their import known by means of verses; he made clear their main principles by indicating their essential points." [*T* 48: 18b.12*f*] And in one of his informal talks to his disciples, after having spoken at length about a certain koan, Hongzhi himself says: "If you have even a little Buddhist theory, then all kinds of concepts, illusions, and mixed-up thoughts will be produced in profusion. The koan is manifest right here before you. Penetrate it to the root; penetrate it to the source!" [*Ibid.*, 67a.18–20]

22. The term *nianfo* 念佛 (*nembutsu*) means literally "to think about Buddha." In actual usage, however, it means to recollect Amituofo 阿彌陀佛 (Amida Butsu) in the heart or mind, and to recite his name with the mouth. There are two Sanskrit names for this Buddha: Amitābha, meaning "Boundless Light," and Amitāyus, meaning "Boundless Life."

The worship of Amituo and the *nianfo* practices that derive from it depend upon the Chinese translations of three (?) Sanskrit Mahayana "Pure Land" sutras. These scriptures deal with Amituo Buddha and his "Land of Bliss" (Skr. *Sukhāvatī*) situated in a world to the west of this one. The Chinese translation of the name of this paradise is Jingtu 淨土 (Jōdo), or "Pure Land," and the Chinese and Japanese Buddhist sects that depend upon these scriptures are known as the Pure Land sects. There are some differences between the existing Sanskrit sutras and the Chinese translations considered authentic in the Pure Land sects, but these are minor and need not concern us here.

In the first of these Chinese translations, the *Wuliangshou jing* (Larger Sukhāvatī Sūtra), Shakyamuni Buddha is represented as telling how, in ages past, the monk Fazang 法藏 (Hōzō; Skr. Dharmākara) requested instruction from the Buddha of that period on the practices necessary to become a buddha and to make a buddha-land. When he had heard the requirements, Fazang decided to undertake the quest, but vowed in forty-eight vows that he would not enter into Buddhahood until, through his austerities and religious practices, he had made a buddha-land in which could be fulfilled the conditions he had made in his vows. These conditions were, in general, that he could transfer the merit he had acquired through his practices to such other beings as he wished, until they, too, had attained Nirvana. In the course of aeons of time Fazang became Amituo (Amida) Buddha, and created in the Western Heaven the buddha-land known as the Pure Land. The most important of his forty-eight vows were the eighteenth, nineteenth, and twentieth. The eighteenth vow stated that, with the exception of those who have committed the five deadly sins or spoken badly of the Buddha-dharma, all beings anywhere who have faith in Amituo Buddha and wish to be born in his paradise will be born there if they repeat his name at least ten times. The nineteenth vow stated that, at the moment of death, Amituo Buddha will appear before all those who have heard his name and meditated upon him with serene thoughts, and will conduct them to his Pure Land. The twentieth vow stated that those beings who, after they have heard Amituo's name, direct their thoughts toward his land, mature a stock of merit through their serene thoughts, and wish to be born in his heaven, will achieve their desire.

The second Chinese scripture, the *Amituo jing* (Smaller Sukhāvatī Sūtra), is given over largely to a description of the Pure Land, but makes the requirement for entrance into it not merit or good works, but the hearing and bearing in mind of Amituo's name for from one to seven nights.

The third scripture, the *Guan wuliangshoufo jing* (Dhyāna Sūtra), describes a number of meditations on Amituo which it recommends to those who wish to enter his heaven, but further states that an evil man, even one who has committed the five deadly sins, also will be reborn in the Pure Land if, on his deathbed, he thinks of Amituo and repeats ten times the formula "Adoration to Amitābha Buddha" (*Namo Amituofo* 南無 [or 那麻] 阿彌陀佛 *Namu Amida Butsu*).

The *Larger Sukhāvati* was first translated into Chinese between 167 and 186 CE, the *Smaller Sukhāvati* in 402, and the Dhyāna Sūtra between 424 and 432. From the beginning of the 3rd century on, the Pure Land doctrines were being promulgated in China, at first largely through the efforts of the Indian monks who had translated them and were proficient in the practices, and later by their Chinese disciples. Presenting, as it did, an easy way of salvation, the worship of Amituo Buddha was quickly accepted by the majority of early Chinese Buddhists in both the north and the south. The first organized group to practice the *nianfo* seems to have been the White Lotus Society founded by Huiyuan 慧遠 (Eon, 334–416) at the Lushan 廬山 (Rōzan), in present Jiangxi; thus, Huiyuan may be considered the nominal founder of the Chinese Pure Land School. However, another line, stemming from the Indian monk Bodhiruci, who reached the eastern capital Luoyang 洛陽 (Rakuyō) in 508 and worked there until between 534 and 537, was carried on by Tanluan 曇鸞 (Donran, 476–542), Daochuo 道綽 (Dōshaku, 562–645), and Shandao 善導 (Zendō, 613–681). This is the line which the Japanese Pure Land schools recognize as authentic.

The Amituo doctrines and practices were not confined to the Pure Land schools only, however, but penetrated into all the other Chinese Buddhist sects. The Tiantai 天台 (Tendai) and Zhenyan 眞言 (Shingon) sects included Pure Land practices and doctrines side by side with their own; and the Zen Sect, in its early days, did likewise, as we shall presently see.

By the 7th century, the *nianfo* (*nembutsu*) practices were of four types: "invocation of the name" (*chengming* 稱名 *shōmyō*); "contemplation of the figure of Amituo Buddha" (*guanxiang* 觀像 *kanzō*); "contemplation of the characteristic marks and virtues of the Buddha" (*guanxiang* 觀想 *kansō*); and "contemplation of the Dharma-body of the Buddha" (*shixiang* 實想 *jissō*).

The invocation of the name, or repetition of the phrase *Namo Amituo fo*, was the most widespread and popular of the *nianfo* practices. The Pure Land School of Tanluan, Daochuo, and Shandao taught this oral nianfo, explaining that "thought and voice are one" (*niancheng shiyi* 念稱是一 *nenshō zeichi*). The other types of *nianfo* were, of course, meditations on Amituo, and seem to have been carried on with and without the invocation of the name.

All the *nianfo* practices, but particularly the contemplation practices, entered into early Zen through three disciples of the Fifth Patriarch Hongren (Gunin), and their followers and descendants. Fachi 法持 (Hōji, 635–702) and his disciple Zhiwei 智威 (Chii, 646–722), after receiving the Seal of Transmission from Hongren, returned to the Niutoushan 牛頭山 (Gozuzan), in modern Jiangsu, where they had originally lived, and became the fourth and fifth patriarchs respectively of the Ox-head (Niutou 牛頭 Gozu) School, a minor line of Zen originally founded by Farong 法融 (Hōyū, 594–657), one of the heirs of the fourth patriarch of the orthodox Zen line, Daoxin 道信 (Dōshin, 580–651). In his later years Fachi became a Pure Land devotee, and is said to have practiced the *guanxiang*, or meditation upon the figure of the Buddha, in all the activities of his daily life. Still another of Hongren's disciples, Zhishen 智詵 (Chisen, 609–702), had some connection with the *nianfo*. The Ox-head School gradually died out, and, with the spread of the Sixth Patriarch's teaching of Sudden Enlightenment, the Amituo practices were all but abandoned in the Zen schools.

We do not hear of them again until the beginning of the 10th century, when the famous and enthusiastic syncretist Yongming Yanshou 永明延壽 (Yōmyō Enju, 904–975), of the Fayan 法眼 (Hōgen) School of Zen, favored the combining of Zen and the *nianfo*. Yongming's view was that the surest way to attain realization was to follow both methods at the same time.

From Yongming's time on, these practices began little by little again to filter into the various lines of Chinese Chan, until by the beginning of the 14th century they had spread through all the monasteries. Some of the masters took a decided stand against the *nianfo*; some were more lenient, and held the position that either path would do, though attempting to walk both at the same time would only end in confusion; still others held that there was no difference between the practices of Zen and those of the Pure Land School. It should be noted, however, that in the Zen schools the emphasis seems to have been more upon the contemplation types of the Amituo practice, with and without the invocation of the name, than upon the invocation alone.

By the early years of the Ming 明 dynasty (1368–1644), the Pure Land schools had been completely combined with Chinese Chan, and everywhere Amituo practices were being carried out side by side with those of Zen. These practices were an integral part of the teaching of the Huangbo 黃檗 (Ōbaku) School brought to Japan in the middle of the 17th century by Yinyuan Longqi 隱元隆琦 (Ingen Ryūki, 1592–1673). This school of Zen, however, did not take a strong hold in Japan. On the other hand, the Japanese Rinzai and Sōtō sects, stemming as they did from the masters of the late Song and early Yuan periods, have never sanctioned the *nembutsu* practices in their monasteries.

> (A detailed study of the relation of the Amituo practices to early Chinese Chan is to be found in Ui Hakuju's *Zenshūshi kenkyū*, Vol. I, pp. 169–194; D.T. Suzuki, in his *Essays in Zen Buddhism*, Second Series, pp. 135–188, takes up these practices and their penetration into Chinese Chan from the middle of the Yuan dynasty on.)

23. The Vinaya Sect (Lüzong 律宗 Risshū) was the Chinese (and later, Japanese) Buddhist sect which based its teachings and practices upon the Vinaya, the collection of rules of life to be observed by members of the order of Buddhist monks. The original Vinaya is said to have been compiled by Shakyamuni's disciple Upāli after the Buddha's death. Later, with the growth of the Order and its division into a number of sects, each sect established its own individual Vinaya or code of rules. Among the complete Vinayas now extant is that known as the *Vinaya-piṭaka* of the Pali Canon, the code of monastic regulations observed by the Theravāda School today.

Monastic rules were probably brought into China by the earliest Buddhist missionaries. The Indian monk Dharmakāla (*n.d.*), when he visited Luoyang in 250, made a Chinese version of a portion of the Vinaya of the Hinayana Mahāsāṅghika Sect, and administered the commandments to Chinese postulants. Dharmakāla was later regarded as the founder of the Chinese Commandment or Vinaya Sect (Lüzong).

The monastic rules that reached China during the early centuries were all incomplete. The Chinese monks were deeply concerned about this lack of a full code of regulations, and kept searching for a complete Vinaya, in the meanwhile formulating such rules and regulations of their own as they found necessary. By the beginning of the 5th century, however, their hopes were fulfilled with the arrival in China of the complete Vinaya of the Hinayana Sarvāstivādins. This was translated into Chinese at Chang'an during the years 404–409 by Kumārajīva (350–*ca.* 409), Puṇyatāra (*n.d.*), and others. A second complete Hinayana Vinaya, that of the Dharmagupta School, was brought to Chang'an a few years later. It was translated into Chinese by Buddhayaśas (*n.d.*) and others between 410 and 412, and was known as the "Four-section Vinaya" (*Sifen lü* 四分律 *Shibun ritsu*). Translations of the complete monastic rules of two other Indian Hinayana schools followed within the next twelve years. About two hundred and fifty years later the Chinese pilgrim monk Yijing 義淨 (Gijō, 635–713) brought back from India still another Hinayana Vinaya, that of the Mūlasarvāstivādin School.

Though many Chinese Buddhist scholars studied the different Vinayas as they were translated, the majority devoted their attention to the Four-section Vinaya. However, it was Daoxuan 道宣 (Dōsen, 596–667), in the 8th generation of the Commandment Sect after Dharmakāla, who first founded an independent Chinese Vinaya school based upon the *Sifen lü*. Since he lived on the Zhongnanshan 終南山 (Shūnanzan) to the south of Chang'an, Daoxuan was also called Nanshan Lüshi 南山律師 (Nanzan Risshi), the "Commandment Master of Nanshan." His sect, correctly the Sifen Lüzong, was more generally known as the Nanshan Vinaya Sect (Nanshan Lüzong 南山律宗 Nanzan Risshū). The teachings of the Nanshan Sect were not limited to those in the *Sifen lü*, however. Daoxuan, who had studied Tiantai (Tendai) doctrines as well as those of the "Representation Only" (*Skr.* Vijñaptimātrata; Faxiang 法相 Hossō) School under Xuanzang 玄奘 (Genjō, 600?–664), included in his important commentary on the *Sifen lü* certain Mahayana elements which had their origin in the somewhat questionable Brahma-net Sutra (*Fanwang jing* 梵網經 *Bommō kyō*) [*T* 24: 997–1010a]. This sutra had been translated into Chinese by Kumārajīva in 406, and contained what was purported to be Mahayana Bodhisattva Commandments. Though several of Daoxuan's contemporaries founded commandment schools of their own based upon the *Sifen lü*, none of these schools continued for long. Nor was Yijing, some decades later, any more successful in his attempt to found an independent Vinaya school.

The Nanshan Vinaya Sect was first introduced into Japan by Daoxuan Lüshi 道璿律師 (Dōsen Risshi, 702–760) of Chang'an, who had come to Nara 奈良 in 736 at the request of two Japanese monks. In addition to being a commandment master (*lüshi* 律師 *risshi*), Daoxuan was the Dharma-heir of Puji 普寂 (Fujaku 651–739) of the Northern School of Zen, and was well-versed in the Huayan (Kegon) doctrines as well.

However, Daoxuan Lüshi was not considered the founder of the Japanese Commandment Sect (Risshū). This honor was reserved for Jianzhen 鑑眞 (Ganjin, 688–763), a 3rd generation disciple of the Daoxuan 道宣 (Dōsen) who had founded the Nanshan Vinaya Sect. Jianzhen had been the recipient of an invitation from the Japanese emperor Shōmu 聖武 (*r.* 724–749) to come to the island country and establish his sect there. Five times he attempted to cross the sea, and five times met with disaster; but his determination did not weaken. Blind, and having lost most of his disciples, Jianzhen finally made a sixth attempt to reach Japan, and this time was successful. In February 754, from the commandment platform (*kaidan* 戒壇) before the great Vairocana Buddha at the Tōdai-ji 東大寺 in Nara, Ganjin—to give Jianzhen his Japanese name—administered the commandments to the now retired Emperor Shōmu, the reigning Empress Kōken 孝謙 (*r.* 749–758), and more than four hundred noblemen. This was the first formal Buddhist ordination ceremony to take place in Japan. By Imperial order Ganjin later founded two other commandment platforms in the Nara area, and for nearly a century thereafter almost all Japanese monks took the commandments before one of these altars in accordance with the rites of the Nanzan Risshū.

In 822, however, soon after the death of its founder Dengyō Daishi 傳教大師 (767–822), the Japanese Tendai 天台 Sect succeeded in establishing a commandment platform on Mount Hiei 比叡山 near Kyoto. There the Tendai Mahayana commandments, which were based upon the *Lotus Sutra* and known as the "Complete and Immediate Commandments"

(*Endon-kai* 圓頓戒) were administered. From that time on the Nanzan Sect of Nara gradually declined.

24. The Huayanzong 華嚴宗 (Kegon-shū) was one of the most important of the Buddhist sects to be established in China. Its doctrines, based upon the Indian Mahayana *Avataṁsaka-sūtra* (*Huayan jing* 華嚴經 *Kegon kyō*), represent the final development of Buddhist philosophy in China.

Though the first Chinese translation of the sutra, that in 60 *juan*, was not made until between 418 and 420, several individual sections from it had been rendered into Chinese considerably earlier. One of these sections in particular, that known as The Sutra of the Ten Stages [of the Bodhisattva] (Skr. *Daśabhūmika-sūtra*; *Shidi jing* 十地經 *Jūji kyō*), from the first had attracted the attention of Chinese Buddhist scholars. In the early part of the 6th century, by which time not only the sutra itself but also the commentaries on its *Daśabhūmika* section by such famous Indian masters as Nāgārjuna and Vasubandhu had been translated into Chinese, a school known as the Dilun 地論 (Jiron) School developed, which was concerned with the study of these related texts, and thus may be considered a precursor of the Chinese Huayan School.

By the end of the 6th century, however, other Chinese Buddhist scholars were interesting themselves in the contents of the *Huayan jing* as a whole. Among these, the Meditation Master Du Shun 杜順禪師 (To Jun Zenji, 557–640), whose religious name was Fashun 法順 (Hōjun), was the first to establish a school based upon the doctrines set forth in the sutra. Du Shun was a learned monk of Chang'an (Chōan) who, after long practice under a meditation teacher, had retired to the Zhongnanshan (Shūnanzan), the mountain south of Chang'an where the founder of the Chinese Commandment Sect, Daoxuan (Dōsen), was then living also. There for a long period of years Du Shun devoted himself to an intensive study of the *Huayan jing*. As the best scholars from the Dilun School joined the large group of students around the Master, this earlier school was gradually absorbed into the rising Huayan School. Du Shun is considered to be the first patriarch of the Huayan Sect. For a more detailed study of Du Shun, *see* Part Two, Note 54.

During his lifetime Du Shun, to whom many miracles were attributed, was believed to be an incarnation of the Bodhisattva Mañjuśrī (Wenshu 文殊 Monju). The sutra makes special mention of Mañjuśrī, and the Chinese translation states that the Bodhisattva is living on the Qingliang

Mountain 清凉山 (Shōryō-zan), where he is continually proclaiming the Dharma. This mountain was early identified with Wutaishan 五臺山 (Godai-zan) in North China, and the great Huayansi 華嚴寺 (Kegon-ji) established there was the center of the cult of Mañjuśrī.

Under the second patriarch of the school, Du Shun's disciple Zhiyan 智儼 (Chigon, 602–668), the doctrinal foundations of the school were further elaborated and strengthened. Zhiyan, whose title was Zhixiang Dashi 至相大師 (Shisō Daishi), also lived and worked on the Zhongnanshan. He wrote several important works based upon his master's teachings, and his Korean disciple Yixiang 義湘 (Gishō, 625–702) founded the first Huayan school in Korea in 668.

But it was the third patriarch of the Huayan Sect, Zhiyan's disciple Fazang 法藏 (Hōzō, 643–712), who brought the school to its full flowering. The period was that of the height of the Tang culture, when, under the patronage of the Court and the aristocracy, Buddhist studies, particularly those of the more profound philosophies, reached their ultimate development.

Fazang was born in Chang'an in a family originally from Sogdiana in Chinese Turkestan. For a short period after he had become a monk he was a member of the translation office of the great Xuanzang (Genjō), but later he resigned from that position due to differences of opinion with the Master. From that time on he turned to the study of the *Huayan jing*, devoting himself to completing and systematizing the doctrines of his two predecessors, Du Shun and Zhiyan. When the Khotanese monk Śikṣānanda (652–710) brought the long version of the *Avataṁsaka-sūtra* to Chang'an at the request of Empress Wu of Tang 唐武后 (Tō no Bukō, *r.* 685–704), and translated it into Chinese between 695 and 699, Fazang was among those who assisted him in making the "New Translation," as it was known. Toward the end of his life Fazang also helped Yijing (Gijō), who, after returning from his travels, worked on translations in Chang'an between 700 and 712. But such translation work was a minor part of Fazang's literary activity. His commentaries and writings of various types are said to have numbered more than 100 Chinese volumes.

Fazang's exposition of the *Huayan jing* was of the greatest profundity. Though he had assisted in the translation of the "new" version, he seems always to have preferred the "old," and his lectures on it combined brilliance and wit with the deepest philosophical insight. One of his most famous lectures was that which he gave in 699 before Empress Wu. Since the

Empress and members of the Court who had gathered to hear him found the Huayan philosophy difficult to comprehend, Fazang used the image of a golden lion in the palace to illustrate his doctrines. This discourse in written form is known as the "Essay on the Golden Lion" (*Jinshizi zhang* 金師子章 *Konjishi shō*). It will be found imbedded in two commentaries [*T* 45: 663a–667a and 667a–670c], each by a Song scholar in the Huayan line.

> (For translations of this work, see: *A History of Chinese Philosophy*, by Fung Yu-lan, translated by Derk Bodde, Vol. II, pp. 341–359; *Sources of Chinese Tradition*, compiled by Wm. Theodore de Bary, Wing-tsit Chan, and Burton Watson, pp, 369–373; and *The Essence of Buddhism*, by D. T. Suzuki, pp. 54–60.)

On another occasion, when Fazang wanted to demonstrate to his students the Huayan doctrine of the mutual and unhindered interpenetration of all existences with each other, known as Indra's Net, the Master set up in the center of a hall a Buddha-image illumined by a torch, and so arranged ten mirrors around it that they were all facing one another. Each of the mirrors was then seen to reflect not only the central image but the reflection in each of the other mirrors and the reflection of the reflections *ad infinitum*.

Fazang is also known as Xianshou Dashi 賢首大師 (Genju Daishi) and Guoyi Fashi 國一法師 (Kokuichi Hōshi), the latter being a title conferred upon him by Emperor Zhongzong of Tang.

The Huayan philosophy, brought to its full development by Fazang, is known as the Perfect Teaching of the One Vehicle (*yicheng yuanjiao* 一乘圓教 *ichijō engyō*). Its basic tenet may be stated as "The all are the One and the One is the all." That is, phenomena are Ultimate Reality and Ultimate Reality is phenomena. The "One," or Ultimate Reality, in this school is termed the Realm of the Principle (Skr. *dharmadhātu*; *lifajie* 理法界 *rihokkai*). But the term *dharmadhātu* in its other aspect is interpreted as the Realm of All Dharmas (phenomenal existences), in which case it is called the *shifajie* 事法界 (*jihokkai*), that is, "the all." The universe is said to exist as a result of the Universal Causation of the Dharmadhātu (*fajie yuanqi* 法界緣起 *hokkai engi*), or otherwise stated, in the words of J. Takakusu, "the universe is universally co-relative, generally interdependent, and mutually originating, having no single being existing independently." [*The Essentials of Buddhist Philosophy*, p. 114] This theory of universal causation is elaborated and explained in the Ten Mysterious Gates (*shixuanmen* 十玄門 *jūgemmon*) and the Sixfold Characteristics [of All Dharmas] (*liuxiang* 六相 *rokusō*), doctrines first stated by Du Shun, but revised and completed by Fazang.

The *Huayan jing* purports to have been spoken by Shakyamuni immediately after his great enlightenment and to disclose the total content of this experience. Since included in the content of the experience were all the teachings which the Buddha was to promulgate during his lifetime, the sutra embraces all the truths which he revealed later by gradual stages, adapting them to the occasion and the capacity of his listeners. The Huayan School, therefore, admits the relative truth of all prior teachings, and arranges them in an unbroken sequence of five graded stages, so that each represents one aspect of the total truth. This doctrine, known as the Five Teachings (*wujiao* 五教 *gokyō*), sets forth, in order, the Hinayana, Quasi-Mahayana, Completed Mahayana, and Sudden Teaching, then culminates in the Perfect Teaching of the One Vehicle, that is, the Huayan.

This is but a fragmentary glimpse of the magnificent structure of Huayan philosophy. The basic truth on which this structure was erected was stated simply and directly by Fazang himself when he said:

> Because sentient beings are deluded they think they should discard the illusory and enter the real. But once enlightenment is attained, the illusory is itself the real. There is no other real to enter.
>
> [*Xiu Huayan aozhi wangjin huanyuan guan* 修華嚴奧旨妄盡還源觀 (*Shū Kegon ōshi mōjin gengen kan*) The Practice of the Contemplation of the Abstruse Meaning of the Avataṁsaka for Bringing an End to Illusion and Returning to the Origin; *T* 45: 639b.9*f*]

After Fazang, the Huayan patriarchal line was temporarily suspended. Fazang's heir Huiyuan 慧苑 (Eon, *n.d.*), because he advanced teachings contrary to those of his great master, was never recognized by the sect. The line was revived two or three generations later, however, by Chengguan 澄觀 (Chōkan, 737–838), also known as Qingliang Dashi 清涼大師 (Shōryō Daishi). Chengguan first studied Zen under the Niutou (Gozu) master Huizhong 慧忠 (Echū, 683–769), then under Jingshan Daoqin 徑山道欽 (Kinzan Dōkin, 714–792) of the same school. Later he went to Wutai Wuming 五臺無名 (Godai Mumyō, 722–793), a direct disciple of Heze Shenhui (Kataku Jinne). After Chengguan had settled on the

Zhongnanshan, he instituted a new Huayan school, uniting within it such diverse elements as the teachings of the lay-scholar Li Tongxuan 李通玄 (Ri Tsūgen, 639–734), an advocate of the "New Translation" of the *Huayan jing*, and doctrines from both the Niutou and the Heze schools of Zen, and, it would seem, from Tiantai (Tendai) as well. Because Chengguan refuted the heresies spread earlier by Huiyuan and restored the Huayan doctrines to their original purity, he is honored as the fourth patriarch of the sect.

Chengguan was the author of a number of treatises on the "New Translation" of the sutra. To him may also be attributed the formulation of the important Huayan doctrine of the Four Dharmadhātu (*sifajie* 四法界 *shihokkai*): the "realm" of phenomena (*shifajie* 事法界 *jihokkai*); the "realm" of noumenon (*lifajie* 理法界 *rihokkai*); the "realm" of the unhindered mutual interpenetration of noumenon and phenomena (*lishi wu'ai fajie* 理事無礙法界 *riji muge hokkai*); and the "realm" of the unhindered mutual interpenetration of phenomena and phenomena (*shishi wu'ai fajie* 事事無礙法界 *jiji muge hokkai*). Though Chengguan asserted that the *Huayan jing* speaks of the four *dharmadhātu*, and though the doctrine is certainly implicit in Fazang's teachings, it is Chengguan who must be credited with the definitive statement of a concept which was to be of great importance to Zen.

The fifth patriarch of the sect was the famous Guifeng Zongmi 圭峰宗密 (Keihō Shūmitsu, 780–841). Zongmi was originally a Confucian scholar. In his twenty-eighth year, when he was on his way to take the official examinations in his native province, present Sichuan, he happened to meet Suizhou Daoyuan 遂州道圓 (Suishū Dōen, *n.d.*), fourth patriarch of the Heze School of Zen, The young man seems to have immediately discarded his political ambitions. He took the tonsure, became Daoyuan's disciple, and eventually his successor as fifth patriarch of the Heze Sect. Later he went to Chang'an, where he studied Huayan doctrines under Chengguan, and, on that master's death, succeeded him as fifth patriarch of the Huayan Sect as well. Zongmi was a brilliant writer and philosopher; a number of his treatises on both Huayan and Chan remain to us.

With Zongmi the Huayan Sect as a sect came to an end. Though the Sanskrit *Gaṇḍavyūha-sūtra*, an extended version of certain Chapters of the *Avataṁsaka-sūtra*, had been translated into Chinese by the Kashmirian monk Prajña (*n.d.*) between 796 and 798, and individual scholars were to continue to study the sutra and the commentaries on it written by the earlier patriarchs, the political confusion of the later Tang was now such that the organized study and propagation of such profound teachings as those of the Huayan School could no longer be carried on. This era saw the rise to prominence of the Chan Sect. The teachings of Chan were simpler and more direct, and it placed emphasis on practice above all else.

While the Huayan School was being influenced to some extent by the earlier schools of Chan, certain Huayan doctrines had already been infiltrating into Chan. Shenxiu (Jinshū, 605?–706), founder of the Northern School of Zen and a noted scholar of other Buddhist schools, is said to have had deep insight into the teachings of the *Huayan jing*. Two commentaries on the sutra are attributed to him, the *Huayanjing su* 華嚴經疏 (*Kegon-kyō sho*), in 30 *juan*, and the *Miaoli yuanchengguan* 妙理圓成觀 (*Myōri enjōkan*), in 3 *juan*. Unfortunately only the titles of these works remain today. Shenxiu's heir Puji (Fujaku) seems also to have had close connections with the Huayan School for he was known as the Venerable Master of Huayan (Huayan Zunzhe 華嚴尊者 Kegon Sonja).

It was the Huayan doctrines of identity and mutual interpenetration, however, which seem to have been of special interest to the Chan masters in the traditional lines. In the poem "In Praise of Identity" (*Cantongqi* 參同契 *Sandōkai*) by Shitou Xiqian 石頭希遷 (Sekitō Kisen, 700–790), the direct heir of Qingyuan Xingsi, distinct traces of the influence of this doctrine can be seen. These are still more apparent in the "Jeweled-mirror Samadhi" (*Baojing sanmei*), a long poem by Dongshan Liangjie (Tōzan Ryōkai, 807–869), founder of the Caodong (Sōtō) Sect, and also in the Five Ranks as stated by Caoshan Benji (Sōzan Honjaku), Dongshan's heir. Certainly Linji Yixuan's "Four Positions of Subject and Object" owe much to this Huayan doctrine. And Fayan Wenyi 法眼文益 (Hōgen Bun'eki, 885–958), founder of the Fayan (Hōgen) School of Zen, is said to have had his students study the writings of both Du Shun and Fazang.

The Huayan (Kegon) teachings were introduced to Japan in 736 by Daoxuan 道璿 (Dōsen, 702–760). In addition to being a master in the Vinaya (Commandment) School, Daoxuan was a disciple of Puji of the Northern School of Zen, who, as has been noted above, was known as the Venerable Master of Huayan. Thus, Daoxuan was also learned in Zen and Kegon. He was the first to introduce the Vinaya and Kegon teachings to Japan, and he is said to have lectured on Zen as well. Daoxuan was followed in 740 by the Korean monk Shenxiang 審祥 (Shinshō, *d.* 742), a disciple and heir of the third Huayan patriarch, Fazang (Hōzō). The Japanese monk Rōben 良辨 (689–773), who seems to have been a disciple of Shenxiang, taught the doctrines of Kegon to Emperor Shōmu (*r.* 724–749), and was one of the founders of the Tōdai-ji, the great Kegon temple in Nara. The figure of Mahāvairocana Buddha, the Great Sun Buddha, who symbolizes the ideals and doctrines of the Huayan, was enshrined in the Tōdai-ji by Emperor Shōmu, with the hope of making this temple not only the center of Buddhism in Japan but the heart of an ideal land which he dreamed of creating through the enlightened doctrines of Kegon.

25. The Northern School of Zen (Beizong 北宗 Hokushū) was founded by Shenxiu 神秀 (Jinshū, 605?–706), one of the heirs of the Fifth Patriarch Hongren 弘忍 (Gunin, 601–674). The name "Northern School" was applied to the Zen of Shenxiu and his disciples, who taught in the area north of the Yellow River and in the two capitals of Luoyang (Rakuyō) and Chang'an (Chōan), at the time that the proponents of the Zen of Huineng were attempting to discredit Shenxiu's doctrines and to establish the Sixth Patriarch's teaching line, which they termed the "Southern School," as the only authentic line of Zen transmission.

As a youth Shenxiu had studied the classics of Confucianism and Daoism. He was ordained as a monk at twenty, but it was not until 656, when he was already fifty, that he came to the Yellow Plum Mountain (Huangmeishan 黃梅山 Ōbaizan) and joined the Fifth Patriarch's assembly. There he soon held the "first seat" because of his outstanding intellectual attainments. He remained with Hongren for six years, and in 662 received the Master's Dharma Seal. (Modern historians on the whole agree with the *Chuandeng lu* in giving 671 as the date of the arrival of the layman Lu, later Huineng, at the Yellow Plum Mountain. Others hold that he did not reach there until early in 674, the year of the Fifth Patriarch's death, since Lu remained on the mountain only eight months and the Fifth Patriarch died shortly after transmitting the robe to him. Thus the traditional story of the verses on Bodhi, which Shenxiu and Huineng are said to have written to prove their worthiness for the transmission, is rudely removed from the realm of historical fact.)

After he left the Fifth Patriarch, Shenxiu went into retirement and spent some fifteen or sixteen years in ascetic practices. Later he settled at the Yuquansi 玉泉寺 (Gyokusen-ji) on Mount Dangyang 當陽山 (Tōyōzan) in Jiangling 江陵 (Kōryō), in modern Hubei. There he gradually began to propagate his style of Zen. His fame spread, and in 700, when he was ninety-four, he was summoned to the capital, where he spent the remaining six years of his life. Empress Wu of Tang was one of Shenxiu's devoted adherents. The Master died full of honors at the age of one hundred and one. The posthumous title Datong Chanshi 大通禪師 (Daitsū Zenji) was almost immediately conferred upon him by Emperor Zhongzong 中宗 (Chūsō, *r.* 705–710). According to the tomb inscription written for him by the famous Confucian scholar ZHANG Yue 張説 (CHŌ Etsu, *d.* 730), on the day of the Master's burial "the Imperial chariot, coming to take leave of him, went as far as the Wu Bridge, and the princes and nobles, bidding him a sad farewell, went as far as the waters of the Yi." [*Fozu lidai tongzai* 佛祖歷代通載 (*Busso rekidai tsūsai*), *juan* 12; *T* 49: 586c.28*f*]

Shenxiu's Zen style was known as the "Gradual Teaching" (*jianjiao* 漸教 *zenkyō*), in contradistinction to the "Sudden Teaching" or "Abrupt Teaching" (*dunjiao* 頓教 *tongyō*) of Huineng and the Southern School. Both schools recognized that the Buddha-nature was basically inherent in all beings, but the Gradual School taught that the delusions and passions were substantially existent, that only little by little were they eradicated, and that final realization was reached through gradual practice. Shenxiu held in particular reverence the teachings of the *Laṅkāvātara-sūtra*, a text which, from the time it is said to have been handed to the Second Patriarch by Bodhidharma, had been the favorite scripture in all Zen schools.

In spite of the attacks made upon it by Heze Shenhui 荷澤神會 (Kataku Jinne, 670–762), the vigorous propagandist of the Southern School, the Northern School continued to flourish under Shenxiu's immediate disciples, who, like himself, were distinguished scholars as well as Zen men of attainment. After their deaths, however, due to the lack of capable heirs, the continued denunciations of Heze Shenhui and his followers, and the rise of outstanding masters in the Sixth Patriarch's line, the Northern School began to decline, and, some five generations after Shenxiu, died out entirely.

26. Tiantaishan 天台山 (Tendaizan), the "Heavenly Terrace," is a mountain in Zhejiang Province, about one hundred and eighty miles southeast of Hangzhou. It is shaped like an inverted eight-petaled lotus, with eight great ridges, eight valleys, and innumerable peaks. From the time of the Former Han (Qian-Han 前漢 Zenkan, 206 BCE–25 CE) its thick forests and deep ravines afforded a retreat to hermits, Daoists, and retired

scholars. In the Chiwu 赤烏 (Sekiu) era (238–251) of the Wu 吳 (Go) dynasty (222–280), the first Buddhist temples were built on the mountain, and thereafter priests of all Buddhist sects came there to live, including *dhyāna*, or meditation, masters.

In 575 there arrived on the mountain a man, who, through his profound scholarship and religious genius, was to establish Tiantaishan as the greatest of all Chinese Buddhist centers. Zhiyi 智顗 (Chigi, 538–597) originally had been a follower of Bodhidharma's teachings. But, feeling that meditation was insufficient and having great veneration for the *Lotus Sutra*, he went to see Huisi 慧思 (Eshi, 515–577), who as the heir of Huiwen 慧文 (Emon, *n.d.*), the actual founder of the Lotus School, was an accomplished scholar in the doctrines of the *Lotus Sutra*. After being instructed by Huisi in the Lotus Meditation, Zhiyi, then thirty-eight, went with a large company of monks to Tiantaishan, where, according to tradition, they were further instructed in all branches of Buddhism by a certain Dingguang 定光 (Jōkō, *n.d.*), a monk who had lived for some forty years on the mountain.

During the nine years of his stay on Tiantaishan, Zhiyi completed his organization of the doctrines and practices of his school, and founded the great monastery of Guoqingsi 國清寺 (Kokusei-ji), which accommodated some four thousand monks. Thereafter he travelled extensively. He lectured before the last of the Chen 陳 (Chin) dynasty (557–589) emperors, spent some time on the Lushan 廬山 (Rōzan), received the title of Zhizhe Dashi 智者大師 (Chisha Daishi) from Emperor Wendi 文帝 (Buntei, *r.* 589–604) of the Sui 隋 (Zui) dynasty (581–618), and in 593 founded the Yuquansi 玉泉寺 (Gyokusen-ji) on Mount Dangyang 當陽山 (Tōyōzan), in modern Hubei, where Shenxiu, founder of the Northern School of Zen, lived and taught ninety years later. One day in his fifty-ninth year, Zhizhe Dashi set out for the capital in answer to the summons of his friend the Heir Apparent—later Emperor Yangdi 煬帝 (Yōdai, *r.* 604–617)—but was suddenly stricken just as he was passing through the west gate of Tiantaishan. He died shortly afterwards in the nearby Shichengsi 石城寺 (Sekijō-ji).

The basis of the Master's teachings was the synthesis and conciliation of all Buddhist doctrines and schools. He gave equal emphasis to ceremonial, discipline, meditation, and the study and recitation of the sutras. His famous system of meditation, termed *zhiguan* 止觀 (*shikan*), in Sanskrit *śamatha-vipaśyanā*, consisted of methods for calming and concentrating the mind in order that it might have clear insight into truth. Though the classifications into which he organized Buddhist doctrines were inclusive of all types of scriptures, teachings, and methods, for him the *Lotus Sutra* contained the complete, final, and perfect teaching. It was the crowing glory of Buddhism.

Despite the fact that Zhizhe Dashi was actually third in succession in his line of the Lotus School, he was honored by being made the founder of the school, renamed the Tiantai after the mountain which was its home. The Master's voluminous teachings and writings were recorded and compiled by his able disciple Guanding 灌頂 (Kanjō, 561–632), second patriarch of the Tiantai Sect. The seventh patriarch, Daosui 道邃 (Dōsui, *n.d.*) was the teacher of Saichō 最澄 (767–822), founder of the Japanese Tendai Sect.

27. The Zhenyan 眞言 (Shingon) or "True Word" Sect, also known as the Mijiao 密教 (Mikkyō), or "Esoteric Teaching," derives from the Indian Yogācāra School of Mahayana Buddhism, and has close resemblances to Indian Tantrayāna and Mantrayāna, as well as to Tibetan Buddhism. Its chief object of worship is Mahāvairocana Buddha (Dari rulai 大日如來 Dainichi Nyorai), the Great Sun Buddha. Its basic doctrine teaches that the entire cosmos is the body of Vairocana, and all existences in it manifestations or emanations from him. Thoughts, words, and actions, in their essential nature, are likewise his. Thus, through prescribed ritual practices, that is, the use of words (Skr. *mantra*; *mandala* 漫怛攞 *mantara*), manual movements and signs (Skr. *mudrā*; *miyin* 密印 *mitsuin*), and concentrated thought (Skr. *yoga*; *yuqie* 瑜伽 *yuga*), perfect communion between the devotee and Buddha can be attained. The sect's esoteric doctrines are depicted and in large part taught through *maṇḍala* (*mantuoluo* 曼陀羅 *mandara*), schematic diagrams composed of arrangements of related buddhas, bodhisattvas, and deities, or Sanskrit letters representing them.

The first to promulgate the mystic teachings in China was Śubhākarasiṁha (Shanwuwei 善無畏 Zemmui, 637–735), who had earlier been king of a small Indian state. He had studied at the great Buddhist university of Nālandā and was versed in all phases of the esoteric teaching. He reached Chang'an (Chōan) in 716, and eight years later went on to Luoyang (Rakuyō), where he died is his ninety-ninth year. He translated several Sanskrit works of his school into Chinese, and in 725, with the aid of Yixing 一行 (Ichigyō, 683–727), a Chinese monk of the Northern School of Zen, translated the basic text of the sect, the *Mahāvairocana-*

sūtra (*Dapiluzhena jing* 大毘盧遮那經 *Daibirushana kyō*), usually known as the *Dari jing* 大日經 (*Dainichi kyō*) Great Sun Scripture, in 7 *juan* [*T* 18: 1–55a], Śubhākarasiṁha is considered the first patriarch of the Chinese Zhenyan School.

The second patriarch was Vajrabodhi (Zhigangzhi 金剛智 Kongōchi, 671–741), the son of a Central Indian king. He had taken orders in Nālandā in 680, then travelled widely through India, Malaya, and Ceylon, studying under masters of several different schools, but especially under adepts in the mystic teachings. He reached Luoyang in 720, having come to China by sea. Some twenty-five of his translations into Chinese are included in the present Chinese Tripiṭaka. He died in Luoyang at the age of seventy-one.

The third patriarch of the sect was the famous Indian monk Amoghavajra (705–774), known in China both as Zhizaṇg 智藏 (Chizō) and Bukong 不空 (Fukū). Amoghavajra seems to have been born in Ceylon, and in his teens to have come to China by sea with his uncle. There he soon became the disciple of Vajrabodhi. On the death of his teacher, Amoghavajra visited Ceylon and India, returning to China in 746. After staying in several different places he eventually took up his residence in Chang'an in 756, and remained there until his death. Amoghavajra was immensely popular with the Imperial family. He baptized Emperor Xuanzong 玄宗 (Gensō, *r.* 712–756), and instructed the two succeeding emperors, Suzong 肅宗 (Shukusō, *r.* 756–762) and Daizong 代宗 (Daisō, *r.* 762–779). He was also famous for his ability at both making rain and stilling storms. One hundred and sixty-nine works translated by him are contained in the present Tripiṭaka.

The fourth patriarch of the Zhenyan Sect was Huiguo 惠果 (Keika, 746–805), a Chinese disciple of Amoghavajra. The Japanese monk Kūkai 空海 (774–835) better known by his posthumous title Kōbō Daishi 弘法大師, studied under Huiguo when he came to China in 804. A year later, after the death of his teacher, Kūkai went back to Japan to become the founder of the Japanese Shingon Sect.

With the death of the fourth patriarch, the importance of the Zhenyan Sect in China declined, until it became little more than a system of popular superstition implemented by spells, charms, and magic incantations.

28. The Southern School (Nanzong 南宗 Nanshū) of Zen is so called because the Sixth Patriarch Huineng 慧能 (Enō, 638–713), who is considered its

founder, lived and taught in the south, and in order to differentiate its teaching and teaching line from that of Shenxiu 神秀 (Jinshū, 605?–706), who for the greater part of his life lived and taught in the north.

While Shenxiu's Zen was known as the "Gradual Teaching" (*jianjiao* 漸教 *zengyō*), Huineng's was known as the *dunjiao* 頓教 (*tongyō*), the "Sudden Teaching" or "Abrupt Teaching." This latter was based upon the view that delusions and passions are substantially non-existent, and that therefore there is nothing to eliminate gradually. Total realization can be attained suddenly, in an instantaneous and immediate perception of reality. The dhyana—or meditation—practice of this school, termed "Patriarchal Dhyana" (*zushichan* 祖師禪 *soshi-zen*), was a practice leading to the immediate intuitive experience. It was called "patriarchal" because the practice was held to have been that taught by Bodhidharma and handed down through the patriarchs who succeeded him.

"Sudden" as well as "gradual" realization is mentioned in the *Laṅkāvatāra-sūtra*, a scripture that had had close connection with Zen from Bodhidharma's time. The Sixth Patriarch, however, seems to have preferred the *Diamond Sutra*, perhaps because he attained his first enlightenment on hearing a line from it, perhaps because its teaching of the voidness of all dharmas afforded a better doctrinal foundation for his own teaching. At any rate, after his time interest in the *Laṅkāvatāra* declined and the *Diamond Sutra* became the favored text in Chinese Zen.

But the division of Zen into a "gradual" school, equated with the teachings of Shenxiu in the North, and a "sudden" school, equated with those of Huineng in the South, seems to have come about during the lifetime of Heze Shenhui 荷澤神會 (Kataku Jinne, 670–762) and to have been in large part due to his efforts. (Modern scholars are divided in their opinions as to the historical validity of a number of the conflicting statements about Shenhui's life and activities contained in the old biographies and records. The following account is based upon Ui Hakuju's essay "Katakushū no seisui" 荷澤宗の盛衰 "The Rise and Fall of the Kataku School," in his *Zenshūshi kenkyū*, Vol. I, pp. 195–268.)

Little is known of Shenhui's early years. When he was in his late twenties, that is, about 699, he seems to have become the disciple of Shenxiu, founder of the "Northern School," and to have remained with him until that Master was summoned to the Court in Luoyang (Rakuyō) in 701. Then, following his master's instructions, Shenhui went south to Caoxi 曹溪 (Sōkei), where he became a member of Huineng's assembly. After remaining there for three or four years he made a long pilgrimage, during which he visited various famous places. In 709 he returned to Caoxi, and thereafter remained constantly at Huineng's side until the Patriarch's death in 713. Shortly before Huineng entered his final Nirvana, he transmitted his Dharma to Shenhui.

The records are silent regarding Shenhui's life for the next few years. In 720, however, an Imperial decree ordered him to take up his residence at the Longxingsi 龍興寺 (Ryūkō-ji) in Nanyang 南陽 (Nan'yō), not far south of Luoyang. At this time Puji (Fujaku) and Yifu 義福 (Gifuku, 658–736), both heirs of the "Northern School" founder Shenxiu, were enjoying the greatest success at the capital, and were to continue to do so for another ten years. Shenhui, who seems to have gone from time to time to the capital to preach, now began to attack the orthodoxy of the "Northern School," asserting that to Huineng alone belonged the title of Sixth Patriarch and that his teaching of "Sudden Enlightenment" alone was the orthodox Dharma transmitted in the patriarchal line. These attacks culminated in the famous assembly which Shenhui organized in 734 at the Dayunsi 大雲寺 (Daiun-ji) in Huatai 滑台 (Katsudai), a place in Henan somewhat to the north of present Kaifeng 開封 (Kaihō). At this assembly Shenhui is recorded to have said:

> "No one else in the world understands Bodhidharma's Southern School. If there were anyone else, I would no longer preach. The purpose of today's address is to distinguish the true from the false and to determine the correct views for students of the Way throughout the Empire."
>
> [From the preface by DUGU Pei 獨孤沛 (DOKKO Hai) to the "Putidamo nanzong ding shifei lun" 菩提達摩南宗定是非論 (Bodaidaruma nanshū tei zehi ron), known as "The Treatise Establishing the True and the False," in the *Shenhui heshang yiji*, p. 162.2–4].

From that day on the distinction between Shenxiu's style of Zen and that of Huineng was fixed, and the Northern and Southern schools differentiated.

In 745 Shenhui was invited to live at the Hezesi 荷澤寺 (Kataku-ji) in Luoyang, the temple from which his name derives. There he continued his attacks on the Northern School, and held monthly meetings at which he advocated the "sudden" doctrine of Huineng. Interest in the Southern School began to grow.

In spite of the fact that most of Shenxiu's direct disciples had now died, the Northern School was still active. For a number of years the attacks upon it by Shenhui and his followers seem to have gone unnoticed, or to have been met with indifference. Various charges were hurled against adherents of the Northern School, such as the monstrous ones of attempting to steal Bodhidharma's robe from Caoxi, to mutilate the stele on which the succession of the transmission was recorded, and to sever the head of the Sixth Patriarch from his mummified body, but none seem to have had any foundation in fact. However, as time went on and the influence of Shenhui and his followers increased, animosity grew. In 753 a minor official, who was an adherent of the Northern School, brought a charge against Shenhui of gathering people together for seditious purposes. Though the charge was patently false, it resulted in Shenhui's banishment.

This banishment lasted for a period of three years. In 756, when the An Lushan 安祿山 (An Rokusan) rebellion had laid waste the two capitals of Luoyang and Chang'an (Chōan), the central government found itself in serious financial difficulties. To gain funds for the support of the army, ordination platforms were set up at various local centers of government, and monks ordained for a sum. Shenhui was now recalled to Luoyang to take charge of the ordination platform there. In spite of his age —he was now eighty-six—his success was so overwhelming that he was summoned to the Court and favored in a number of ways by Emperor Suzong 肅宗 (Shukusō). From then until his death in 762 at the age of ninety-three, Shenhui enjoyed Imperial favor, and the Southern School flourished increasingly.

Thirty-four years after Shenhui's death, Emperor Dezong 德宗 (Tokusō, *r.* 779–805) called together a group of Zen masters to determine orthodoxy and heterodoxy. At this assembly the Southern School was pronounced the orthodox school, and Shenhui named its seventh patriarch. Thus, in 796, the division between the Northern and Southern schools and the "Gradual" and "Sudden" teachings was permanently confirmed. But Shenhui's line, known as the Heze 荷澤 (Kataku) Sect, was not to carry on long the teachings which he had championed so vigorously. It survived its founder by only five generations, and came to an end almost simultaneously with the Northern School. It was the lines of Qingyuan Xingsi (Seigen Gyōshi) and Nanyue Huairang (Nangaku Ejō), two other disciples of Huineng, that were destined to transmit the Sixth Patriarch's Zen even as far as today.

Several of Shenhui's sermons have been found in manuscript in the caves of Dunhuang 敦煌 (Tonkō), in modern Gansu Province. Four of these have been edited and published by Hu Shi 胡適 under the title *Shenhui heshang yiji.*

29. Myōan Eisai 明菴榮西 (1141–1215) was a native of Bitchū 備中, in modern Okayama Prefecture, and his surname was Kaya 加陽. He began his study of Buddhism at the age of eight under his father's direction, and at fourteen went to the Tendai headquarters on Mount Hiei 比叡山 near Kyoto, where he was ordained and took the commandments. There he underwent the severe discipline of the Tendai Sect and made a thorough study of its doctrines, among which at that time the esoteric teachings held a place of great importance. In 1168 he set sail for China. On arriving there he visited Tiantaishan (Tendaizan) and other Buddhist places, returning to Kyoto in the autumn of the same year.

Eisai brought back with him from China a number of Tiantai texts. In the course of studying these and the works of early Japanese Tendai masters, he noticed frequent mention of the Zen Sect and its meditation practices. He determined to return to China and concentrate on Zen studies, and also to make a pilgrimage to India. Eisai embarked a second time for China in 1186. On his arrival, finding that the political situation was such as to make a trip to India impossible, he again went to Tiantaishan. There he became the disciple of Xu'an Huaichang 虛庵懷敞 (Kian Eshọ̄, *n.d.*), a master in the 8th generation of the Huanglong (Ōryō) line of Linji (Rinzai) Zen. When Huaichang later took up his residence at Tiantongshan 天童山 (Tendōzan) in Mingzhou 明州 (Meishū), in present Zhejiang, Eisai accompanied him, and eventually received the transmission of the Dharma of the Linji line from him. In the summer of 1191, as Eisai was preparing to leave China, the Master presented him with a robe, a bowl, a staff, a kneeling cloth (*zuoju* 坐具 *zagu*), a whisk (*fuzi* 拂子 *hossu*), and a certificate (*yinzheng* 印證 *inshō*), visible evidences of the validity of the transmission.

After landing in Japan in the autumn of 1191, Eisai spent some time in Kyūshū 九州, then went on to Kyoto with the intention of establishing a Zen temple in the capital. His plans were frustrated, however, by the opposition of the priests of the esoteric sects. In 1194 he returned to Kyūshū, and at Hakata 博多 founded the Shōfuku-ji 聖福寺, the first Zen temple to be established in Japan, and today an active monastery belonging to the Myōshin-ji 妙心寺. As the opposition of the Tendai and Shingon sects still continued, Eisai wrote his famous tract *Kōzen gokoku ron* 興禪護國論 The Propagation of Zen for the Protection of the Country, in 3 *kan* [*T* 80: 1a–17b], in which he declared that Zen was not a new religion, and cited many eminent Japanese Buddhist teachers who in the past had advocated meditation practice.

Eisai now took up his residence in Kamakura 鎌倉, where he soon gained the favor of the Shogunate. In 1200 he was invited to become the founder of the Jufuku-ji 壽福寺 there. In 1202 the Shogun, MINAMOTO Yoriie 源頼家 1202–1203), requested Eisai to become chief abbot of the Kennin-ji 建仁寺, which he had just established in Kyoto. Though the Kennin-ji was nominally a Zen temple—the first of the sect to be built in the capital—the power of the esoteric sects was still great enough to have a decree passed that their doctrines and practice, as well as those of Zen, should be taught and studied there. Eisai continued to be favored by the Shogunate, and held a number of positions of high rank and importance in Nara, Kyoto, and Kamakura. He died in Kamakura at the Jufuku-ji in August, 1215.

Eisai left a large number of disciples, and later came to be considered the founder of Zen in Japan. He is also famous for having introduced the tea plant to Japan. He enthusiastically advocated tea as a drink in his essay entitled *Kissa yōjō ki* 喫茶養生記 Tea-drinking as a Means of Prolonging Life. [*Dainihon bukkyō zensho*, *Yūhōden sōsho*, pp. 505–518]

30. The Seal of the Transmission of Dharma (*chuanfayin* 傳法印 *dembōin*), or, simply, the Seal of Transmission, is the acknowledgment by a Zen master that his disciple has attained the same insight into Truth as that which the master himself had previously attained, and which had been acknowledged by his master before him. This acknowledgment implies the recognition of the disciple as an authentic heir not only of the Dharma of his master and his master's line but of the Dharma of the continuous line of Zen teachers reaching back to Bodhidharma, and thence to Shakyamuni. Furthermore, the disciple who has received this acknowledgment is thereby qualified to hand on the transmission to his disciple or disciples. There are various expressions for the act of transmission or the recognition of attainment. The most usual term in Japanese Zen today is "to give *inka*," *inka* 印可 meaning "seal of approval." The master usually gives this acknowledgment to the disciple privately. However, it is

often accompanied by some visible evidence of the recognition, as when the Fifth Patriarch handed Bodhidharma's robe and bowl to Huineng as proof of the transmission of the patriarchate to him. From Song times on it became customary for the master to give the disciple, as a token of the transmission, a painting of or by himself on which he had inscribed a verse hinting at this transmission, one of this own robes, or a written certificate. Sometimes all three were given. This custom is still followed in large part in Japan today.

31. The Kennin-ji 建仁寺, head temple of the Kennin-ji line of the Japanese Rinzai Sect, is situated in Gion 祇園, a district in the east-central part of Kyoto. The temple was originally established by the Kamakura Shogun MINAMOTO Yoriie 源頼家 (*r.* 1202–1203) for the Rinzai priest Myōan Eisai 明菴榮西 (1141–1215). Construction of the buildings, which were in Song style and modeled after those at Baizhangshan 百丈山 (Hyakujōzan) in China, was started in 1202, the second year of the Kennin 建仁 era (1201–1203), and completed three years later. The name Kennin-ji was given to the temple by the Emperor Tsuchimikado 土御門 (*r.* 1198–1210) to commemorate the era in which it was built.

Since the monks of the Enryaku-ji 延暦寺, the main temple of the powerful Tendai Sect on Mount Hiei, were hostile to Eisai's intention of establishing in the capital a temple devoted to the teachings of the Zen Sect, a potential rival, Eisai found it expedient to have constructed within the Kennin-ji compound two special temples, the Shingon-in 眞言院 and the Shikan-in 止觀院. At the former the esoteric doctrines and practices of Tendai were taught, at the latter its specific meditation practices. Eisai called his own school of Zen the *Yōjō taimitsu* 葉上台密, the "Yōjō Line of Tendai Mysticism," naming it for the Yōjō Valley on Mount Hiei.

For some time subsequent to Eisai's death his disciples presided as abbots at the Kennin-ji. After two fires, one in 1246 and one in 1256, had all but destroyed the temple, Enni Ben'en 圓爾辨圓 (1201–1280) became its chief abbot. Ben'en was a Japanese priest who, after journeying to China and receiving there the transmission of the Yangqi (Yōgi) line, had returned to found the Zen headquarters temple of Tōfuku-ji 東福寺 in Kyoto. Ben'en was followed by the Chinese priest Lanxi Daolong 蘭溪道隆 (Rankei Dōryū, 1213–1278), also of the Yangqi line, who had arrived in Japan in 1247, and in 1253 had become the founder of the Kenchō-ji 建長寺, the Rinzai Sect headquarters in Kamakura. During Rankei's tenure of office the Kennin-ji was reorganized as a center for Rinzai Zen studies only, and, for a time, renamed the Kennei-ji 建寧寺.

During the period known as the Northern and Southern Dynasties (Nambokuchō 南北朝 1332–1392), many eminent Chinese and Japanese monks resided at the Kennin-ji. But as other monastic establishments, built for Zen clerics favored by the Court and the Shogunate, rose in prestige and power in the Muromachi 室町 era (1338–1573), the importance of the Kennin-ji gradually diminished. Nevertheless it has always been honored as the oldest Rinzai Zen headquarters temple in Kyoto, and continues to be so today.

32. In 1766, Honkō Katsudō 本光瞎堂 (*n. d.*), a priest of the Japanese Sōtō Sect, published a three-volume work in *kambun* 漢文 (Chinese characters), entitled *Nempyō sambyakusoku funō go* 拈評三百則不能語 Comments on Three Hundred Koans in Unutterable Words, and consisting of three hundred old koans, each with a short commentary by his teacher Ein Shigetsu 慧印指月 (*d.* 1764). Katsudō claimed that the koans in the work were those composing a collection that Shigetsu Oshō had earlier discovered, and that this collection was one which had originally been compiled by Dōgen Kigen 道元希玄 (1200–1253), the founder of Japanese Sōtō Zen. In a preface printed in Katsudō's publication, a preface alleged to have been written by Dōgen himself for his original compilation, the title of the collection is given as *Shōbōgenzō* 正法眼藏 Treasury of the True Dharma Eye. Sōtō Sect adherents insisted that Dōgen did not use koans, and that Katsudō's work was spurious. Therefore the book has never been included in the various collections of Sōtō works.

About 1935, however, Volume II of a three-volume work written in *kambun* and bearing the title *Shōbōgenzō* was discovered in the Kanazawa Bunko 金澤文庫, the library of the Shōmyō-ji 稱名寺, presently a Shingon-Risshū 眞言律宗 Sect temple, in Kanagawa Prefecture. This has been definitely identified as a work by Dōgen, although the writing is not in his hand. It corresponds with the second volume of the work published by Katsudō more than one hundred and fifty years earlier, proving that this latter was not a forgery. The presumption now is that Katsudō's publication was indeed based upon a koan collection compiled by Dōgen for the use of his disciples, and that the original title of Dōgen's compilation was *Shōbōgenzō*. Furthermore, the *Shōbōgenzō* in general use in the Sōtō Sect today, which, is written in Japanese, is now considered to be a collection of Dōgen's explanatory discourses on the koans of his original collection. It would also seem that the term "*shōbōgenzō*" was used by Dōgen with the meaning of "koan collection."

33. The first of these Chinese Sōtō masters was Dongming Huiri 東明惠日 (Tōmei E'nichi, 1272–1340), in the 6th generation after Hongzhi Zhengjue (Wanshi Shōgaku, 1091–1157). He reached Japan in 1309 and taught Sōtō Zen at the Rinzai temples of Kenchō-ji and Engaku-ji 圓覺寺, both in Kamakura. He was 18th abbot of the Kenchō-ji and 10th abbot of the Engaku-ji. His line, known as the Tōmei line, soon became extinct.

The second Chinese Sōtō master to come to Japan was Dongling Yongyu 東陵永璵 (Tōryō Eiyo, *d.* 1365), in the 7th generation after Hongzhi Zhengjue. After his arrival in 1351 he resided for a time at the Tenryū-ji 天龍寺, then at the Nanzen-ji 南禪寺, teaching Sōtō doctrines and practices at both these Rinzai headquarter temples in Kyoto. He was the 23rd abbot of the Nanzen-ji. The Tōryō teaching line which he founded also soon became extinct.

34. Shinchi Kakushin 心地覺心 (1207–1298) was born in the village of Kambayashi 神林 in Shinano 信濃, present Nagano Prefecture. His family name was Tsunezumi 常澄; the name Shinchi was a *gō* 號 which he took for himself. At the age of fifteen he began his study of Buddhism at the local *jingū-ji* 神宮寺. (Until the Meiji 明治 era [1868–1912], Buddhist schools using buildings within the precincts of a Shintō shrine were called *jingū-ji*.) At nineteen, Shinchi received the tonsure, and we may surmise that at this time he was given the name Kakushin. At twenty-nine he took the full commandments from Chūgaku Risshi 忠學律師 (*n. d.*) before the commandment platform of the Tōdai-ji in Nara.

The same year (1235), Kakushin went to the Shingon 眞言 center established by Kōbō Daishi (774–835) on Mount Kōya 高野山, in present Wakayama Prefecture. There he was initiated into the esoteric practices of the Shingon Sect and studied its doctrines. At that time Gyōyū Zenji 行勇禪師 (1163–1241), an heir of Myōan Eisai, founder of the Kennin-ji, was living at Kōyasan and teaching Rinzai Zen meditation. Kakushin met Gyōyū, became interested in Zen, and began his Zen practice under that master. When Gyōyū went to Kamakura in 1239 to take up his residence at the Jufuku-ji, Kakushin accompanied him, and assisted him with the temple administration until the Master's death in 1241. Kakushin subsequently went to see the Japanese Sōtō master Dōgen Kigen, who was then living at Fukakusa 深草, not far from Kyoto, and from Dōgen received the Bodhisattva Commandments. Thereafter he visited a number of Zen masters, studying for a time with each, but meanwhile making plans for a journey to China.

In 1249 Kakushin succeeded in getting passage to China on a commercial ship. On his arrival there he made his way directly to Jingshan 徑山 (Kinzan), in modern Zhejiang Province, only to find that the Yangqi (Yōgi) line master Wuzhun Shifan 無準師範 (Bushun Shihan, 1177–1249), with whom he had hoped to study, had unfortunately died earlier the same year. Greatly disappointed, Kakushin then set out on a pilgrimage which took him during the next few years to most of the important Buddhist centers in China. In 1253 he heard from a Japanese monk whom he happened to meet that the greatest Zen teacher in China was then Wumen Huikai 無門慧開 (Mumon Ekai, 1183–1260). Kakushin immediately hastened to the Huguo Renwangsi 護國仁王寺 (Gokoku Ninnō-ji), near Hangzhou in modern Zhejiang, where Huikai was then living.

At their first meeting a deep relationship was established between the Japanese monk and the Chinese master. Huikai said, "There is no gate to my place. From where did you enter?" "I entered from no-gate [*wumen*]," replied Kakushin. "What is your name?" "My name is Kakushin [Enlightened Mind]." The Master immediately composed a verse:

> Mind, just this is Buddha;
> Buddha, just this is Mind.
> Mind and Buddha, thus, thus,
> In the past and now.

[*Emmyō kokushi gyōjitsu nempu; Zoku Gunsho ruijū* 9上: 351*b*.13*f*]

Six months later Kakushin received the Seal of Transmission. It is recorded that when he was about to take leave of the Master in 1254, Huikai presented him with a robe, a portrait of himself, and a copy of his famous koan collection *Wumenguan* (*Mumonkan*), which he had written with his own hand.

In 1256 Kakushin is said to have dispatched a letter from Japan to his old master in China, together with a crystal rosary and a block of gold. Four years later he received from Huikai a robe, a scroll painting of portraits with the seven Zen masters in their mutual line, from Wuzu Fayan (Goso Hōen *d.* 1104) through Huikai and including Kakushin himself.

These and other gifts were accompanied by a letter in which the Master said that he would not live much longer. He died the same year.

Meanwhile Kakushin had been asked to become founder of the Saihō-ji 西方寺, a temple at Yura 由良 in Wakayama Prefecture. This temple, later renamed the Kōkoku-ji 興國寺, was the Master's home for the next forty years. In 1281 the retired Emperor Kameyama 龜山 (*r.* 1259–1274) induced the Master to come to Kyoto and live for a short time in the Zenrin-ji 禪林寺, a former Imperial villa on Higashiyama 東山, which he had converted into a temple. Kakushin was again induced in 1285 to leave the hills of Yura, which he dearly loved, to become the founder of the Myōkō-ji 妙光寺, a temple to the west of Kyoto, which Prime Minister Fujiwara Morotsugu 藤原師繼 (*n. d.*) had built in memory of his deceased son. But again Kakushin soon returned to the Saihō-ji. During these visits the Master was often invited to lecture before the retired Emperor Kameyama and the reigning Emperor Go-Uda 後宇多 (*r.* 1274–1287) at the detached palace in Saga 嵯峨, to the west of Kyoto. Kakushin died in the autumn of 1298 in his ninety-second year. During the Master's lifetime, the retired Emperor Kameyama had given him the title Hottō (*var.* Hattō) Zenji 法燈禪師, and, after his death, the retired Emperor Go-Daigo 後醍醐 (*r.* 1318–1339) bestowed upon him the posthumous title of Emmyō 圓明. In the records of the Zen Sect his name is generally given as Hottō Emmyō Kokushi 法燈圓明國師.

Kakushin was one of the most distinguished and influential of the early Japanese Zen priests. He had many students, both monks and laymen. He made "Jōshū's *Mu*" (*Chaozhou wuzi* 趙州無字 *Jōshū no muji*), the first koan in his master's collection *Mumonkan*, the basis of his teaching, and it is said that he never failed to talk about it to the large audiences who gathered to hear him speak. But, though he was preeminently a Zen man, he never entirely gave up his interest in the Shingon teaching in which he had been instructed early in his Buddhist life. Many interesting tales are told about mysterious and miraculous supernatural events in which he figured.

Furthermore, he was the founder of the Japanese Fuke 普化 Sect. This sect employed the music of the long bamboo flute known as the *shakuhachi* 尺八 as a means to enlightenment. Its members, for the most part laymen, were called *komusō* 虛無僧, "Monks of Nothingness." There is no historical evidence for the existence of this sect in China, but, according to the tradition handed down in the Japanese sect, it was founded by the eccentric Tang dynasty monk Puhua 普化 (Fuke, *n. d.*), a friend of Linji Yixuan (Rinzai Gigen). Its active propagator in China is reputed to have been Puhua's disciple, the layman Zhang Bo 張伯 (Chō Haku, *n. d.*) of Henan 河南 (Kanan). Shinchi Kakushin is said to have received instruction in the secrets and old airs of the sect from a fellow student under Wumen Huikai, a certain Zhang Can 張參 (Chō San, *n. d.*), in the 16th generation from Puhua.

When Kakushin returned to Japan he was accompanied by four Chinese lay disciples of Zhang Can, and after he had taken up his residence at the Saihō-ji he built a hermitage for them there called the Fuke-an 普化庵. Years later the samurai Yoritake Ryōen 寄竹了圓 (*d.* 1298), while resting on a beach after a battle, attained some degree of enlightenment on hearing the music of a shakuhachi drifting in from a boat on the foggy sea. He eventually found his way to the Myōkō-ji, where Kakushin was then living, and the Master instructed him in the practices of the Fuke Sect and those of Zen as well. Thereafter, as Kochiku Zenji 虛竹禪師, Yoritake actively propagated the Fuke Sect in Japan. During the Tokugawa 德川 era (1603–1867) many masterless samurai, or *rōnin* 浪人, became members of the Fuke Sect. The lawless ones among them often used its costume, a conspicuous feature of which was a large openwork bamboo basket-hat covering the face, as a disguise while thieving, plundering, and killing. As a result the sect was outlawed by the Meiji Government and officially has never been revived.

35. Wumen Huikai 無門慧開 (1183–1260) was an heir of the Yangqi (Yōgi) line master Yuelin Shiguan 月林師觀 (Gatsurin Shikan, 1143–1217). He was in the 8th generation of the Yangqi line and in the 15th generation of direct descent from Linji Yixuan (Rinzai Gigen). His family name was Liang 梁 (Ryō), and he was a native of Liangzhu 良渚 (Ryōsho) in Hangzhou 杭州 (Kōshū), in modern Zhejiang Province.

Huikai's first teacher was a certain Gong Heshang 肱和尚 (Kō Oshō) of the Tianlongsi 天龍寺 (Tenryū-ji) in his home district. From there he went on to Suzhou 蘇州 (Soshū), in present Jiangsu, and placed himself under Yuelin Shiguan at the Wanshousi 萬壽寺 (Manju-ji). Yuelin's monastery was an extremely austere establishment where the discipline was arduous, severe, and long. Huikai was given Yuelin's favorite koan, "Jōshū's *Mu*." For six years he strugged with it in vain. To keep himself awake he would walk the corridors and butt his head on the pillars; finally he vowed that he would burn his body if he ever fell asleep. Then, according to the *Yantong* [ZZ 2乙: 12.5.481c.17–d.2], one day as he was standing in the Buddha Hall near the Sumeru Seat—the name given to the dais for the Buddha-image—he heard the sound of the drum and experienced satori. He immediately composed the following verse:

> From the azure heaven bright with the noon-day sun,
> A sudden crash of thunder!
> All living beings on the Great Earth
> Open wide their eyes,
> Everything in the entire universe
> In a like manner bows the head,
> And Sumeru, leaping up,
> Dances a merry *santai.*

The following day Huikai entered the Master's room to tell him of his attainment. Instantly Yuelin said, "What spirits and devils have bewitched you?" Huikai shouted "*He!*" The Master shouted "*He!*" Huikai again shouted "*He!*" From that time on he was called Wumen, or "No-gate."

Huikai began his teaching career at the age of thirty-six. During the next twenty-odd years he moved from temple to temple, instructing many monks and preaching to large groups of people. His famous koan collection *Wumenguan* (*Mumonkan*) was compiled in 1228, during his forty-sixth year. In 1246, when he was sixty-four, he was ordered by Imperial decree to establish the important monastery of Huguo Renwangsi (Gokoku Ninnō-ji) near Hangzhou. It was there that the Japanese monk Shinchi Kakushin visited him in 1253.

Toward the end of his life the Master retired to a small temple on the beautiful West Lake (Xihu 西湖 Seiko) in the vicinity of Hangzhou. He was temporarily recalled to the capital by Emperor Lizong 理宗 (Risō, *r.* 1224–1264) of the Southern Song to conduct a ceremony to relieve the severe drought from which the country was then suffering. Even while the Master was delivering his discourse the heavens suddenly opened and rain fell in torrents. The Emperor thereupon conferred on Huikai the honorary title of Foyan Chanshi 佛眼禪師 (Butsugen Zenji), and presented him with a gold brocade shoulder-robe (*jiasha* 袈裟 *kesa*).

Throughout his life Huikai was simple and direct in his conduct and plain in his speech. Even when he had been given his first important appointment as head of the Baoyin Youcisi 報因祐慈寺 (Hōin Yūji-ji), a monastery near Hangzhou, he continued to wear a soiled robe, carry his own slops, and do manual labor. In his old age he remained simple and jovial. He is said to have become very thin, even emaciated; his robe was always old and worn, his long hair always dishevelled. He died on May 15, 1260, in his seventy-eighth year.

In addition to the *Wumenguan*, we have the *Wumen heshang yulu* 無門和尚語錄 (*Mumon oshō goroku*) [*ZZ* 2: 25.3.250d–264c], a collection of the Master's sermons, talks, and verse, compiled by Pujing 普敬 (Fukei, *n. d.*) and other disciples, with biographical items added by each.

36. Nampo Jōmyō 南浦紹明 (1235–1309) was a native of the country district of Abe 安倍 in Suruga 駿河, present Shizuoka Prefecture, and his family name was Fujiwara 藤原. At fifteen he took the commandments at a local temple, then at eighteen went to the Kenchō-ji in Kamakura to study under its founder, the Chinese priest Rankei Dōryū (Lanxi Daolong) of the Yōgi line of Rinzai Zen.

In 1259 Jōmyō set out for China. There he went to Xuedoushan 雪竇山 (Setchōzan), in modern Zhejiang, to study under Xutang Zhiyu 虛堂智愚 (Kidō Chigu, 1185–1269), who, like Jōmyō's former teacher, was in the 10th generation of the Yangqi (Yōgi) line. When Zhiyu moved to the Jingcisi 淨慈寺 (Jinzu-ji), and later to Jingshan (Kinzan), Jōmyō accompanied him. In the late summer of 1265 he attained satori and received the Seal of Transmission from the Master. On returning to Japan in 1267 he went immediately to Kamakura, and there remained for two or three years with his former teacher, Dōryū.

Jōmyō was appointed abbot of the Kōtoku-ji 興德寺, at Fukuoka 福岡 in Kyushu, in 1270. Three years later he moved to the nearby temple of Sōfuku-ji 崇福寺, where he remained for the next thirty years. (Sōfuku-ji is today one of the monasteries belonging to the Rinzai headquarters of Daitoku-ji.) In 1304 Jōmyō was called to Kyoto, and in the following year became abbot of the Manju-ji 萬壽寺. During his stay in the capital, the retired Emperor Go-Uda gave him the sanction to build a Zen temple on Higashiyama, to be called the Kagen-ji 嘉元寺, but in spite of the retired Emperor's support the power of the Tendai monks on Mount Hiei was still great enough to defeat Jōmyō's plan.

A little later he was called to Kamakura by the Hōjō 北條 Government to assume the position of chief abbot at the Kenchō-ji. In his discourse at the installation ceremony, he is recorded to have said: "On the twenty-ninth day of the twelfth month of this year, my coming is coming from nowhere. On the twenty-ninth day of the twelfth month of next year, my going will be going to nowhere." [*Daiō goroku*; *T* 80: 127b.19–21] He died exactly one year later on the day he had predicted, February 8, 1309 by western chronology. As his teacher Zhiyu had done before him, Jōmyō left a death verse:

> I rebuke the wind and revile the rain,
> I do not know the buddhas and patriarchs;
> My single activity turns in the twinkling of an eye,
> Swifter even than a lightning flash.
>
> [*Ibid.*, 23*f*]

By Imperial decree Jōmyō was given the posthumous title Enzū Daiō Kokushi 圓通大應國師, and the Ryōshō-ji 龍翔寺 built in the western outskirts of Kyoto to enshrine his ashes. Early in the 16th century the Ryōshō-ji was moved to within the precincts of the Daitoku-ji 大德寺, founded in Kyoto by Jōmyō's disciple Daitō Kokushi 大燈國師 (1282–1338). Some forty years ago the Ryōshō-ji was rebuilt and enlarged, and it now serves as the main monastery of the Daitoku-ji.

Daiō Kokushi 大應國師, to give the Master the name by which he is best known, left a large number of eminent heirs. The lines which they and their descendants founded have formed the main streams of Japanese Rinzai Zen throughout the past six hundred and fifty years. The Master's teachings are recorded in the *Enzū Daiō kokushi goroku*.

37. Xutang Zhiyu 虛堂智愚 (Kidō Chigu, 1185–1269) was a native of Siming-xiangshan 四明象山 (Shimei-zōzan), a village in present-day Zhejiang Province, and his family name was Chen 陳 (Chin). At sixteen he had his head shaved and took the commandments at a local temple. Then he set out on a long pilgrimage, eventually coming to Jingshan 徑山 (Kinzan), northwest of the then capital city of Hangzhou. At Jingshan he became the disciple of Yun'an Puyan 運庵普巖 (Un'an Fugan, 1156–1226), in the 9th generation of the Yangqi (Yōgi) line of Linji (Rinzai) Zen, and after some years received the Seal of Transmission from this master.

After Puyan's death, Zhiyu travelled widely. He was closely connected with the Imperial Court, and during his lifetime was the superior of more than ten different temples, most of them important government-sponsored establishments. In 1258, when he was serving as chief abbot at Ayuwangshan 阿育王山 (Aikuōzan), in present Zhejiang, he became involved in difficulties with the government and was forced to retire. He was soon reinstated, but after a short time chose to retire to the Xuedoushan (Setchōzan), where the poet-priest Xuedou Chongxian (Setchō Jūken) had lived some two hundred years earlier. It was during this period that the Japanese monk Nampo Jōmyō came to study with him. Zhiyu's voluntary retirement soon came to an end when he was appointed by Imperial decree first to the Jingcisi 淨慈寺 (Jinzu-ji) and then to the temple at Jingshan where he had long lived as a monk. Shortly before his death at Jingshan in 1269 at the age of eighty-five, he wrote the following verse:

> During eighty-five years
> I've had no acquaintance with buddhas and patriarchs.
> With arms akimbo I stride along,
> The Great Void extinguishing utterly my footprints.
>
> [*Xutang lu*; *T* 47: 1063b.15*f*]

Among the few heirs whom Zhiyu left, the most distinguished was his Japanese disciple Nampo Jōmyō, afterwards known as Daiō Kokushi. As Jōmyō's teacher, Zhiyu is still honored in Japan. On the anniversary of the death of Daitō Kokushi, Daiō Kokushi's heir, three portraits are always hung side by side in the main hall of the Daitoku-ji, those of Kidō Chigu (Xutang Zhiyu), Daiō Kokushi, and Daitō Kokushi.

Zhiyu's teachings are recorded in the *Xutang heshang yulu*. The Daibie 代別 (Daibetsu) section of this work, consisting of a collection of one hundred koans, is still used in advanced koan study in Japanese Rinzai Zen.

38. Daisetsu Sonō 大拙祖能 (1313–1377) was a native of Kamakura, and his family name was FUJIWARA 藤原. At fourteen he took the tonsure and the full commandments at the Tendai headquarters on Mount Hiei; at seventeen he entered the Zen headquarters temple of Tōfuku-ji in Kyoto. From there he went on to study with various masters, including the Chinese Sōtō (Caodong) priest Dongming Huiri (Tōmei E'nichi), who was then teaching at the Rinzai headquarters of Kenchō-ji and Engaku-ji in Kamakura. For a brief period Sonō also took sanzen from Musō Soseki 夢窓疎石 (1275–1351), founder of the Rinzai headquarters temple of Tenryū-ji in Saga, to the west of Kyoto.

Sonō now determined to go to China for further study. In 1344 he joined a large group sailing from Hakata, in Kyushu, and reached the continent the same year. After a short time spent in visiting various temples, he came to the Shengshousi 聖壽寺 (Shōju-ji) in Wuzhou 務州 (Bushū), in modern

Zhejiang, where he became the disciple of Qianyan Yuanchang 千巖元長 (Sengan Genchō, 1284–1357). Yuanchang was an heir of Zhongfeng Mingben (cf. Part One, Note 3), and in the 14th generation of the Yangqi (Yōgi) line of Linji (Rinzai) Zen. Two years later Yuanchang called his Japanese disciple into his room and presented him with Zhongfeng's robe as a sign of the Transmission of Dharma to him.

For the next ten years Sonō travelled about China, then in 1358 returned to Japan. From that time on he was continuously engaged in constructing and serving as chief abbot of various temples in Kyushu and the Kantō 關東 (present Tokyo) area, meanwhile instructing many disciples. For short periods of time he was head of the Kenchō-ji and the Engaku-ji in Kamakura. It is said of him that, when the Shogun Ashikaga Yoshimitsu 足利義滿 (*r.* 1368–1394) called him to be chief abbot of the Kenchō-ji, Sonō, not wishing to accept the position but not being able to refuse, assumed it for merely ten days, then took his departure for the north country. He rebuilt and became the Restoring Founder (*chū kaisan* 中開山) of the Ryōgon-ji 楞嚴寺 in Hitachi 常陸, present Ibaraki Prefecture. In 1376, the year before his death, a great monks' hall was added to the Ryōgon-ji to accommodate the three thousand students who had flocked there to study with him. The same year he was again summoned to Kamakura, and the following year died at the Engaku-ji. Sonō's posthumous title was Kōen Myōkan Zenji 廣圓明鑑禪師.

Daisetsu Sonō was the last of the Japanese priests who, after going to China for study, brought back the teachings of the Yōgi line of Rinzai Zen and established their own lines of descent in Japan. Sonō's line, the Daisetsu-ha 大拙派, flourished for a number of generations after the founder's death.

39. There are two mountains in China bearing the name Huangboshan 黃檗山 (Ōbakuzan) that are important in Zen history. The first is near the southeast coast of China, not far from the present city of Fuzhou in Fujian Province. In 789, a monk in the Sixth Patriarch's line, Zhenggan 正幹 (Shōkan, *n. d.*) by name, built a hut on this mountain and called it the Boretang 般若堂 (Hannya-dō). Some eight years later the building was enlarged and the name changed to Jianfusi 建福寺 (Kempuku-ji). During the Song period the temple was abandoned and became only a haunt for crows. In 1614, however, the Prime Minister She Wenzhong 葉文忠 (Shō Bunchū, *n. d.*) built on the site of the old ruins a magnificent temple called

the Wanfusi 萬福寺 (Mampuku-ji). It was at this temple that Yinyuan Longqi (Ingen Ryūki, 1592–1673) lived before he came to Japan, and it was for this Ōbakuzan and this Mampuku-ji that he named the Ōbaku Sect (Ōbaku-shū 黃蘗宗) headquarters which he built near Uji 宇治, to the southwest of Kyoto.

The second Huangboshan is south of the Yangzi River in central China. At the end of the 8th century a young monk named Xiyun 希運 (Kiun) took his vows at the Jianfusi on the Huangboshan in Fujian. He then went north, studied under the Zen master Baizhang Huaihai 百丈懷海 (Hyakujō Ekai, 720–814), and became Baizhang's most important heir. After Xiyun had become master of his own assembly of monks, his most ardent lay disciple, the eminent official Pei Xiu 裴休 (Hai Kyū, 797–870), built a temple for him in the mountains of what is now western Jiangxi. Because of Xiyun's fondness for the mountain where he had lived as a youth, he named the mountain on which the new temple was built Huangboshan, and the temple itself the Huangbosi 黃蘗寺 (Ōbaku-ji). It was here that Xiyun's most famous disciple, Linji Yixuan (Rinzai Gigen), studied under him, and here that the Master, best known in Zen history as Huangbo Xiyun (Ōbaku Kiun), died about 850. The exact location of this Huangboshan is not known today.

40. The Nichiren 日蓮 Sect is the only major Buddhist sect to have its origin in Japan and to bear the name of its founder. The man who was later to call himself Nichiren was born in 1222 in the family of a fisherman of Kominato 小湊, a village on the southeast coast of Bōshū 房州, present Chiba Prefecture. His childhood name was Zennichimaro 善日麿. At eleven the boy was sent to the nearby monastery of Kiyozumi 清澄, and at fifteen was ordained and given the Buddhist name Renchō 蓮長. He was early obsessed by the question: What was the Truth taught by the Buddha? Finding no answer through the Nembutsu 念佛 practice—recitation of the name of Amida Buddha—he had been ordered to follow, he prayed to the Bodhisattva Ākāśagarbha (Kokūzō Bosatsu 虛空藏菩薩), the guardian of all wisdom and achievement, that he might become the wisest man in Japan. To this end he decided to study the doctrines of all schools of Buddhism. He visited various temples throughout the country, then spent ten years (1243–1253) studying the *Lotus Sutra* at the Tendai headquarters on Mount Hiei. He concluded that the *Lotus Sutra* contained the true teaching, but that the Tendai doctrines as originally taught by the founder

Dengyō Daishi should be revised and adapted to the times. Returning to his old monastery of Kiyozumi, on May 17, 1253, in his thirty-second year, he proclaimed his new Lotus Sutra Doctrine and the invocation *Namu myōhō renge kyō* 南無妙法蓮華經 "Hail to the Lotus of the Marvelous Dharma," the repetition of which was to save the world. At this time, also, he announced that he had taken Nichiren as his name.

Nichiren now became an itinerant preacher, and, as no temple welcomed him, he preached on street corners and along the roadsides. This was a time of great unrest in Japan. The political situation was precarious, and the country suffering from earthquake, famine, and plague. Nichiren found ready listeners for the violent attacks he began to launch upon every sect of Buddhism, for he claimed that these disasters had all been brought on through the heretical teachings of the clergy. In 1260, while staying at Kamakura in a hermitage he had built for himself, he wrote and presented to the Hōjō Regent Nagatoki 長時 (*r.* 1256–1264) a tract in which he stated that religious life and national life were one, that the government should destroy by the sword all those who taught heretical doctrines, and that peace and prosperity could be attained only through the unification of Buddhism under the true teachings of the *Lotus Sutra*, that is, his own. He was tried and banished in 1261, and again in 1271, but each time returned after three years to continue his violent attacks on government officials and members of the clergy, both individually and collectively.

Nichiren now considered himelf to be an incarnation of the Bodhisattva Viśiṣṭacāritra (Jōgyō Bosatsu 上行菩薩), the "Bodhisattva of Distinguished Action," who, the *Lotus Sutra* had prophesied, would come into the world to preach the Truth in the age of the "destruction of the Dharma" (*mappō* 末法). He said of himself in one of his tracts: "I will be the pillar of Japan, I will be the eyes of Japan, I will be the great vessel of Japan." Many converts flocked to him. Though the ruling government officials urged him to modify the viciousness of his utterances, he consistently refused. In the summer of 1274 Nichiren retired to a small temple he had built at Minobu 身延, on the western slope of Mount Fuji, and there disciples gradually gathered around him. Eight years later, in the autumn of 1282, he journeyed from Minobu to a temple he had earlier founded in Ikegami 池上, near the center of present Tokyo. There, a month later, he died, reciting lines from the *Lotus Sutra* with his last breath.

Nichiren's views on the *Lotus* differed from those of Dengyō Daishi in that Nichiren placed emphasis not on philosophical doctrines but on the practices of the Buddha. The true devotee of the *Lotus*, he held, is one who carries on the practices the Buddha practiced. All practices are summed up in the invocation *Namu myōhō renge kyō*, and only through the repetition of this formula can the individual attain immediate Buddhahood in this body, and the salvation of the world be realized. The founder's pugnacious, militant, and violently nationlistic spirit has characterized his followers throughout the centuries and continues to do so even today.

41. Shishuang Chuyuan 石霜楚圓 (Sekisō Soen, 986–1039) was a native of Quanzhou 全州 (Zenshū), in modern Guangxi Province, and his family name was Li 李 (Ri). In his early twenties he became a monk, and, on hearing of the fame of Fenyang Shanzhao (Fun'yō Zenshō), a 6th generation descendant of Linji Yixuan (Rinzai Gigen), went to Fenzhou 汾州 (Funshū), in modern Shanxi, to study under him. Fenyang immediately recognized the exceptional ability of the new disciple, and devoted special attention to his training. For two years Chuyuan was denied access to the Master's room. Every time he appeared there he was cursed and abused. One night the disciple began to complain of the treatment he was receiving, but, before he could finish speaking, Fenyang scolded him roundly and beat him with his stick. Chuyuan started to call for mercy, but the Master clapped his hand over the disciple's mouth. At this moment Chuyuan was enlightened. He remained some years longer with Fenyang, and eventually received inka from him.

Thereafter Chuyuan lived in turn at several different temples in Sichuan, Jiangxi, and Henan. His connection with government officials and the Imperial Court became increasingly close. Eventually he went to the Shishuangsi 石霜寺 (Sekisō-ji) in Tanzhou 潭州 (Tanshū), in modern Hunan Province. This temple had been built on Mount Shishuang 石霜山 (Sekisōzan) in late Tang by Shishuang Qingzhu 石霜慶諸 (Sekisō Keisho, *d.* 888), in the 5th generation of the Qingyuan Xingsi (Seigen Gyōshi) line. Chuyuan subsequently resided at several other temples, but returned to Mount Shishuang shortly before his death in his fifty-fourth year.

The Master's posthumous title was Ciming Chanshi 慈明禪師 (Jimyō Zenji). He is also known as Shishuang Ciming 石霜慈明 (Sekisō Jimyō) and Ciming Chuyuan 慈明楚圓 (Jimyō Soen). His teachings are recorded in the *Ciming chanshi wuhui zhuchi yulu*.

Though Chuyuan's life was relatively short, he is extremely important for the Linji (Rinzai) School of Zen. Among the fifty-odd heirs whom he left were his two outstanding disciples Yangqi Fanghui 楊岐方會 (Yōgi Hōe, 992–1049) and Huanglong Huinan 黃龍慧南 (Ōryō E'nan, 1002–1069). With these two masters, the Linji School became divided into two teaching lines, the Yangqi (Yōgi) and the Huanglong (Ōryō). It was the descendants in these lines who carried the Linji teachings in two streams down through the ensuing centuries,

42. Dōkyō Etan 道鏡慧端 (1642–1721) was a native of Iiyama 飯山 in Shinano 信濃, present Nagano Prefecture. He was the son by a concubine of a samurai with the family name of Sanada 眞田 in the service of the lord of Matsushiro 松代 of Shinano. "Dōkyō" was a *gō* 號 which he took for himself; another name by which he often called himself was Saishōō 栽松翁, "Old Pine Planter."

Though the boy was brought up in the household of Lord Matsudaira 松平 of Iiyama, he early had the desire to become a monk. At nineteen he was in the retinue of Lord Matsudaira when that daimyo went to visit the Shogun in Edo 江戸, modern Tokyo. While in the Eastern Capital the youth heard the name of Shidō Bu'nan 至道無難 (1603–1676), a Zen priest in the 17th generation of the line of Nampo Jōmyō (Daiō Kokushi), and immediately went to see him at his hermitage, the Shidō-an 至道庵, in the Azabu 麻布 district of Edo. Bu'nan shaved the youth's head, and, after subjecting him to severe training for a year, gave him inka. Dōkyō Etan, as he was now known, then made a long pilgrimage to various temples in northeastern Japan. When he returned four years later to see his old master, Bu'nan ordered him to become his successor at the Shidō-an, but Etan refused and went back to his native Iiyama.

There, following the example of the eccentric Tang dynasty monk Chen Zunsu (Chin Sonshuku) (cf. Part One, Note 15), whom he greatly admired, Etan cut himself off from the world and retired with his mother to a hermitage in the village of Taruzawa 樽澤 in the mountains of Shinano. His way of life there was austere in the extreme; his robes were always tattered and his hair long and unkempt. To keep his samadhi power undiminished he used to sit through the night in a deserted graveyard, unmindful of the pack of wolves that sniffed at his throat. In 1676 the lord of Iiyama, who often invited the Master to his castle, but whose invitations were invariably refused, bestowed upon Etan's hermitage the name Shōju-an 正受庵, and thereafter the Master was usually referred to as Shōju Rōjin 正受老人, "the old man of the Shōju [Hermitage]." He seldom accepted a student, and, when he did, subjected him to the severest discipline.

Etan's character, which was both harsh and compassionate, is clearly brought out in the account of his relations with his famous heir, Hakuin Ekaku 白隱慧鶴 (1686–1769). One day in the spring of 1710, Dōju Sōkaku 道樹宗覺 (1679–1730), Etan's only disciple at the time and later one of his heirs, came to the Shōju-an accompanied by Hakuin, then in his twenty-fourth year. The old man was cutting firewood when they arrived, and only after considerable urging on Sōkaku's part agreed to return to the hermitage and receive the visitor. Hakuin, who had prepared himself in advance for the meeting, immediately presented the old man with a written statement of his understanding of Zen. Etan crushed the paper in his left hand without looking at it. "This is something you've learned," he said. Then, thrusting out his right hand, he continued, "But what have you seen?" "If I'd seen something I could present to you, I'd spit it out," returned Hakuin, making a pretense of vomiting. The old man came closer. "How do you understand Jōshū's *Mu*?" he asked. "In Jōshū's *Mu* there's no place to put hands or feet," said Hakuin. The old man grabbed the end of Hakuin's nose with his fingers. "Yah! Here's some place to put hands and feet," he bawled. Hakuin's entire body broke out in sweat and he threw himself on the ground before Etan. The old man roared with laughter. "You dead shavepate in a ghost cave!" he shouted.

After eight months of desperate effort, Hakuin finally received from Etan the secrets of Tōzan's Five Ranks (*Dongshan wuwei* 洞山五位 *Tōsan no goi*) and acknowledgment as his heir. When Hakuin was leaving, the Master, now in his sixty-eighth year, accompanied him part way through the mountain pass. His farewell words to his disciple were: "Do your best to breed a few genuine monks. Don't seek for many. Making great vessels of Dharma is difficult. If there's one man or only half a man who is genuine, he may be able to revive our Rinzai Zen, which is in such a sad state of decline."

Etan died in his eightieth year. Tradition has it that, at the end, he seated himself in the meditation posture and composed the following verse:

> In the frantic hurry [of dying]
> It's difficult to utter the last word.
> If I were to speak the wordless word,
> I wouldn't speak, I wouldn't speak!

[*Shōju rōjin shū*, p. 35]

Then, laying down his brush and laughing heartily, he passed away.

Though Etan had spent almost all of his life in seclusion in the mountains of Iiyama, his Zen was transmitted to later generations through the efforts of his disciple Hakuin. For a time after his death the Shōju-an was a *dōjō* 道場, or training hall, for laymen, under Dōju Sōkaku, but after a generation or two it became merely another poor mountain temple, and remains so today. In 1781, sixty years after Shōju Rōjin's death, Hakuin's distinguished disciple Tōrei Enji 東嶺圓慈 (1721–1792) visited the Shōju-an and restored Etan's tomb. He gave it the name *Saishōtō* 栽松塔, "Tomb of the Pine Planter," and had engraved on it an inscription which he had written extolling the virtues of his master's master.

No records of Etan's teachings remain other than such as may be found here and there in Hakuin's writings. The verses he jotted down on odd pieces of paper during his lifetime were long kept bundled together in the Shōju-an. Some twenty-five years ago these were taken out and published under the title *Shōju rōjin shū*. This work also includes Tōrei's biography of Etan, the *Shōju Dōkyō Etan anju anroku*.

43. Until recent years there has been some question as to whether Hakuyūshi 白幽子 was a real person or merely a figure about whom innumerable legends had grown. It is true that Hakuin Zenji, in his *Yasen kanna* 夜船閑話, wrote in detail of his visit to Hakuyūshi in the mountains of Kita-Shirakawa 北白川 on the outskirts of Kyoto, and of the practices in which the hermit instructed him. How much of Hakuin's story is an old man's cloudy reminiscence of an event that took place in his youth, and how much pure invention for the benefit of his students, has never been clear. As Hakuin tells it, he was suffering from a nervous malady called "Zen sickness," the result, perhaps, of too intense and continued meditation practice. Since the usual medical remedies were ineffective, he sought out the hermit and was taught by him an unusual type of introspection of the body called *Nanso no hō* 輭酥の法, "Butter Method." Hakuyūshi's instructions, as recorded by Hakuin, would seem to have stemmed from Yijing 易經 (Eki kyō) and Daoist teachings. After three years of this practice Hakuin was entirely cured.

(Cf. "Yasen Kanna" 夜船閑話 "A Chat on a Boat in the Evening," translated by R.D.M. Shaw and Wilhelm Schiffer, S.J., *Monumenta Nipponica*, Vol. XIII, Nos. 1–2 (1956), pp. 101–127.)

The recent researches of Itō Kazuo 伊藤和男 have proved that the hermit Hakuyūshi was an actual person. His real name was Ishikawa Jishun 石川慈俊, and he was born in 1646 in Kanazawa 金澤, near present-day Yokohama. He was the youngest disciple of Ishikawa Jōzan 石川丈山 (1583–1672), a samurai who had become an eminent Confucian scholar and poet, and who devoted the last forty years of his life to writing in his villa Shisendō 詩仙堂 on the slopes of Mount Hiei in Kyoto.

At the age of sixteen, Jishun left Ishikawa Jōzan and disappeared into the mountains on the outskirts of Kyoto. There he lived forty-eight years, changing his dwelling place from time to time. He died in the mountains near Kita-Shirakawa in 1709 as the result of an accidental fall from a cliff. He was buried to the north of the Shinnyo-dō 眞如堂, a Tendai temple on Kurodani 黑谷 in Kyoto. The stone that had long marked his grave was stolen in 1901, but two years later another was erected in its place by the famous Meiji era painter Tomioka Tessai 富岡鐵齋 (1836–1924).

Several pieces of Hakuyūshi's calligraphy exist. A short writing by him inscribed in his own hand and entitled *Kinshi-sen* 謹志箴 "Precepts for Myself," was recently found in the Kansai University Library 關西大學研究室 in Osaka Prefecture. It is dated Genroku 元祿 12, third month, third day (April 3, 1699), and reads as follows:

> Having long dwelt in cloudy ravines and under green pines, I know nothing of roaming abroad or seeing the world, but have the defect of being stupid and limited in learning and experience. Quietly I regret the shortness of my life. Usually I enjoy reading books, but without plumbing their meaning too deeply. I search out the paths of sages without desiring fame or benefit. I am content with poverty, and do not hide from the wind or the sun. With one piece of cloth and a gourd often empty, I do not grieve for today, but await the decree of Heaven.

(For more on this strange figure, *see* "Hakuyūshi no hito to sho" 白幽子の人と書 "Hakuyūshi, the Man and his Calligraphy," by Itō Kazuo 伊藤和男, *Zenbunka*, Vol. II, No. 6 [Nov. 1956], pp. 40–48.)

44. The Rinzai Zen headquarters temple of Myōshin-ji 妙心寺 was originally established in 1337 by the cloistered Emperor Hanazono 花園 (*r.* 1308–1318). Having taken the tonsure in 1335, two years later Hanazono converted a part of his country residence to the west of Kyoto into a retreat

for Zen study and meditation, and there spent much of his time until his death in 1348. (The building used by him as a retreat, now called the Gyokuhō-in 玉鳳院 "Jade Phoenix Hall," still exists in approximately its original form at the Myōshin-ji.) Hanazono was an ardent student-disciple of the Zen priest Shūhō Myōchō 宗峰妙超 (1282–1338), founder of the Daitoku-ji and better known under his title Daitō Kokushi 大燈國師. When the Kokushi (National Teacher) was in failing health the last year of his life, Hanazono asked him to recommend someone to become the first abbot of the small religious establishment he had set up. The Kokushi suggested his heir Kanzan Egen 關山慧玄 (1277–1360), who was then living in seclusion in the mountains of Ibuka 伊深, in present Gifu Prefecture. Following the Kokushi's advice, Hanazono summoned Kanzan to Kyoto and installed him as founder of the temple, to which the cloistered Emperor had given the name Myōshin-ji, "Temple of the Marvellous Mind."

The original Myōshin-ji was an unpretentious establishment with few buildings. Kanzan lived a life of the utmost frugality, avoiding anything that had even a touch of luxury. He wore tattered clothes, raised his own vegetables, allowed the buildings to fall into disrepair and the roofs to leak. Musō Soseki, founder of the Tenryū-ji 天龍寺 and an intimate of emperors and shoguns, happened one day to pass by the Myōshin-ji on his way to Kyoto and stopped to visit Kanzan. Drawing a couple of coins from his sleeve, Kanzan ordered an attendant to go and buy some bean cakes at a shop in front of the temple. Then, as he had no tray, he served the tea on the cover of his ink-stone box. Musō Soseki was much impressed with the extreme simplicity of Kanzan's life and is said to have stated later that Kanzan's line would eventually take precedence over his own.

Over the years the Myōshin-ji was gradually enlarged by additional buildings, but during the Ōnin War 應仁の亂 (Ōnin no ran, 1467–1477) the temple was destroyed by fire. In the late 15th century, Emperor Go-Tsuchimikado 後土御門 (*r.* 1465–1500) assisted in its restoration, and various feudal lords contributed to its further expansion. The Tokugawa era (1603–1867) saw the Myōshin-ji at its most flourishing. At that time many samurai became monks or studied there as laymen, with the result that not a few of the particular customs and manners still traditional at this temple bear the imprint of their samurai origin.

Today the Myōshin-ji is the largest of the headquarter temples of the Japanese Rinzai Sect. It is located in Hanazono 花園, now a western suburb of Kyoto. In addition to its *Semmon Dōjō* 專門道場 or Training Hall for Monks (i.e. monastery), it has several affiliated monasteries and over three thousand dependent temples in various parts of Japan. It also maintains the Hanazono Daigaku 花園大學 in Hanazono, a university specializing in Buddhist and Zen studies.

45. Tōrei Enji 東嶺圓慈 (1721–1792) was a native of Kanzaki 神崎, in present Shiga Prefecture, and his family name was NAKAMURA 中村. His mother came from a Shintō family of some importance, and throughout his life Enji continued to have close connections with Shintō and Shintō thought. At the age of nine the boy was taken to a local temple to become a monk. In his seventeenth year he went to the Daikō-ji 大光寺, in present Miyazaki Prefecture, and there three years later took the commandments from Kogetsu Zensai 古月禪材 (1667–1751), an important Rinzai priest of the time. In 1743, while on a visit to his home in Shiga, he heard of Hakuin Zenji and immediately went to the village of Hara 原, in present Shizuoka Prefecture, where Hakuin's temple, the Shōin-ji 松蔭寺, was located.

Enji had not been long under Hakuin when the illness of his mother recalled him to his home village and kept him there for nearly two years. Then, in 1746, he set out for Kyoto. He seems to have had at least a first satori experience while with Hakuin, and now wanted to devote himself to a period of "after satori" (*gogo* 悟後) practice. In a retreat he found for himself to the east of the Kamo 加茂 River in the old capital, he subjected himself to severe and solitary meditation practice for one hundred and fifty days. This period culminated in a profound experience, about which he at once wrote to Hakuin. But Enji was forced to remain in Kyoto, for as a result of this arduous discipline he developed tuberculosis, an illness from which he suffered more or less continuously throughout the remainder of his life. His enforced idleness in Kyoto during the early part of the illness gave him an opportunity to read and study a number of Zen texts. The foundations for his later career as a Zen scholar were undoubtedly laid at this time.

It was during this stay in Kyoto that Enji wrote one of his most notable books, the *Shūmon mujintō ron*. The work was completed in 1748 and immediately sent to Hakuin. The following year Enji received a letter from his old master expressing admiration for the work. Shortly after this, his health much improved, Enji was able to leave Kyoto and return to the Shōin-ji. Hakuin then made him one of his heirs and presented him with his own robe. Enji was now invited to become the abbot of several different temples, but he consistently refused, preferring to devote himself to writing and lecturing on Zen texts in Edo and Kyoto. In 1755 he took for himself the *gō* Tōrei, and it is by this name that he is generally known.

Hakuin, who seems to have been particularly attached to Tōrei, during the latter part of his life purchased for his disciple the Ryūtaku-ji 龍澤寺, an old temple on the lower slopes of Mount Fuji at Mishima 三島, not far from Hara. At that time the Tokugawa government was attempting to force smaller temples to merge with larger establishments, and, when this could not be accomplished, was confiscating those that had no active priest. In order to save such temples from destruction, it was not unusual for priests who could raise sufficient funds to buy and restore one. When the Shidō-an in Edo was placed on sale a little later, it also was purchased by Hakuin; thereafter this former home of Shidō Bu'nan, the teacher of Hakuin's teacher Shōju Rōjin, was used by Tōrei as his residence whenever he was in Edo lecturing.

After Hakuin's death early in 1769, Tōrei devoted himself to rebuilding the Ryūtaku-ji, honoring his master by making him its founder. Tōrei remained at the Ryūtaku-ji for twenty years. His *Goke sanshō yōro mon* is one of the main literary products of this period of his life. So also were his monographs on the lives of Shidō Bu'nan (*Kaisan Shidō Bu'nan anju zenji anroku*), of Shōju Rōjin (*Shōju Dōkyō Etan anju anroku*), and of Hakuin (*Ryūtaku kaiso Jinki Dokumyō zenji nempu*), all basic works for the history of the Hakuin School of Zen. The Master was a famous calligrapher and an excellent painter in the style currently known as *zenga* 禪畫. Many of his paintings and calligraphic writings, as well as his literary works, clearly show evidence of his continued interest in Shintō.

In 1791 Tōrei, now in his early seventies, moved to the Zuisen-ji 瑞泉寺, near Nagoya, but the following year retired to a small temple in his native village, where he passed away a few months later. The Master's posthumous title was Butsugo Jinshō Zenji 佛護神照禪師.

46. Gasan Jitō 峨山慈棹 (1727–1797) was a native of Ōshū 奥州 in northeastern Japan. As a youth he became a monk under Gessen Zen'e 月船禪慧 (1702–1781) at the Kōken-in 高乾院 in Miharu 三春, present Miyagi Prefecture. Gessen was an heir of Kogetsu Zensai 古月禪材, under whom Tōrei Enji 東嶺圓慈 had first studied. Kogetsu, like his contemporary, Hakuin, had practiced under many different Zen masters in his youth, and later founded a teaching line of his own known as the Kogetsu Line

古月派 (*Kogetsu-ha*). During Kogetsu's lifetime, and for several generations afterwards, considerable rivalry seems to have existed between the Kogetsu and Hakuin teaching lines.

At sixteen, Jitō left Gessen, and, as appears to have been the fashion at that time, visited some thirty different masters in various parts of Japan. He was about thirty years old when he returned to Gessen, who was now living at the Tōki-an 東輝菴 in Nagata 永田, near Edo. As a result of his extensive studies, Jitō had become supremely confident of his own Zen understanding and felt that there was no one who could teach him anything further. One day he mentioned to Gessen that he had as yet had no experience with Hakuin's Zen, and it might be well if he went down to Hara and tested the old master out. Gessen was able to dissuade him from this course of action for a time, but somewhat later, on being told that Hakuin was giving *teishō* 提唱 (Zen lectures) in Edo, Jitō went to hear him. What he heard led him to leave at once for Hara and the Shōin-ji. Some four years of severe discipline had to pass before Hakuin acknowledged him as one of his heirs.

After Hakuin's death in 1769, Jitō, or Gasan, as he was now usually called, spent some time with his former teacher Gessen at the Tōki-an in Nagata, then moved to the Rinshō-in 麟祥院 in Edo, where he is said to have had some five hundred disciples. When Gessen died in 1781, Gasan again returned to the Tōki-an, but continued his contact with the Rinshō-in by giving teisho there from time to time. In addition, he served for short periods as abbot of several other temples, including the Shōin-ji at Hara. He died on New Year's Day, 1797, at the hot spring resort of Atami.

Gasan left a number of heirs, among whom the most famous were Inzan Ien 隱山惟琰 (1751–1814) and Takujū Kosen 卓洲胡僊 (1760–1833).

47. Inzan Ien 隱山惟琰 (1751–1814) was born in Echizen 越前, modern Fukui Prefecture, and his family name was SUGIMOTO 杉本. He was taken to the Kōtoku-ji 興德寺 in Mino 美濃, present Gifu Prefecture, at the age of nine, and became a monk under Rōzan Oshō 老山和尚 (*d.* 1781). At sixteen he began his Zen study under Bankoku Oshō 萬國和尚 (*n. d.*), a priest who was promulgating the teachings of Bankei Yōtaku 盤珪永琢 (1622–1693), one of the more important and individualistic Zen teachers just prior to Hakuin's time. After three years with Bankoku Oshō, Ien went to the more orthodox Rinzai master Gessen Zen'e, who was then living at the Tōki-an in Nagata, near Edo. Gessen had been the first teacher

of Gasan Jitō, whose heir Ien was later to become. Gessen was renowned for his strictness, and only after seven days of insistent pleading was Ien admitted to his monastery. After seven years of practice under Gessen, Ien joined a group of other monks on a pilgrimage to the temples of the Kantō (Tokyo) and Kansai 關西 (Kyoto-Osaka) districts. Somewhat later he went to the Baisen-ji 梅泉寺 in Mino, where his first teacher Rōzan Oshō was now living. After the old teacher's death in 1781, Ien continued to live at the Baisen-ji for nine years longer.

Then, hearing of the success Gasan Jitō was now having as a teacher of Hakuin's Zen at the Tōki-an, Ien went there to see him. He remained to study under Gasan for two years, and finally, in 1791, when he was thirty-nine, he received the Transmission of Dharma from the Master and was named one of his heirs.

Thereafter for a number of years, Ien, or Inzan, as he is usually known from the "style" (*azana* 字) he had taken for himself, moved about from temple to temple in the Gifu area teaching Hakuin-style Zen. He was a powerful teacher and extremely successful in instructing both monks and laymen. In 1806 he rebuilt the Zuiryō-ji 瑞龍寺, now within the city of Gifu, adding to it a large Monks' Hall (*sōdō* 僧堂). In 1808 he was called to assume the position of abbot of the Myōshin-ji in Kyoto, and in that capacity presided at the ceremonies held for the 450th aniversary of the death of its founder, Kanzan Egen. He soon returned to the Zuiryō-ji, however, and died there in his sixty-fourth year. Inzan's posthumous title was Shōtō Enshō Zenji 正燈圓照禪師. The record of his teachings will be found in the *Inzan roku*.

For the Inzan School, *see* Note 49, below.

48. Takujū Kosen 卓洲胡僊 (1760–1833) was born in Tsushima 津島, a village on the outskirts of present Nagoya City, and his family name was Suzuki 鈴木. At fifteen the youth took the commandments at the Sōken-ji 總見寺 in Nagoya. This temple, built in 1583, was one of several of the same name erected in memory of the famous Oda Nobunaga 織田信長 (1534–1582) by his son Oda Nobuo 織田信雄 (1558–1630). At nineteen Kosen went on a pilgrimage, visiting various teachers. The following year he heard Hakuin Zenji's heir Gasan Jitō lecture at the Tōki-an in Nagata, near Edo, and decided to join his assembly. Gasan gave the young monk "Jōshū's *Mu*" as a first koan. Kosen studied diligently, but found that his duties in the monastery interfered with his meditation practice. He asked permission

to use a special room in which he could constantly sit without any thought of food or sleep. His request was granted, and at the end of ninety days he completed his first koan. Kosen then resumed his usual monastic life. After remaining for fourteen years with Gasan, he received the Transmission of Dharma and was acknowledged by the Master as one of his heirs.

Takujū, as Kosen is more generally known, now returned to the Sōken-ji, and quietly devoted himself to his own studies for nearly twenty years. In 1813 he was appointed abbot of the Myōshin-ji, and presented with a purple robe. Thereafter he soon began to attract disciples. Many monks came to take instruction from him in koan study and to hear his lectures; the feudal lord of Owari 尾張 and members of prominent and powerful families numbered among his numerous lay disciples and followers. He was especially successful as a lecturer and gave teisho on all the major Zen literary works, both Chinese and Japanese.

To accommodate the large numbers of students who were now flocking to him, Takujū rebuilt the Monks' Hall at the Sōken-ji in 1820. He also lectured and taught at various temples in the Kansai and Nagoya areas. In 1832, when he was seventy-two, he retired to the Tōrin-in 東林院, a small temple within the Sōken-ji compound. He died there the following year. Takujū's posthumous title was Daidō Enkan Zenji 大道圓鑑禪師.

For the Takujū School, *see* Note 49, below.

49. All the present-day teaching lines of Rinzai Zen in Japan stem from either Inzan Ien or Takujū Kosen. The teaching and teaching methods in both lines or schools are almost identical, but both still bear to some extent the characteristics of their respective founders, men of quite different temperaments. Inzan Zen may be characterized as sharp, vigorous, and dynamic; Takujū Zen as quiet, meticulous, and detailed. It may be of interest to note that among the various monasteries in Japan today presided over by masters of the Inzan line are those of the Myōshin-ji, Daitoku-ji, Shōkoku-ji 相國寺, Tenryū-ji, and Tōfuku-ji in Kyoto and the Engaku-ji in Kamakura; among the monasteries under masters of the Takujū line are those of the Nanzen-ji and Kennin-ji in Kyoto, and the Kenchō-ji in Kamakura.

50. For *kenshō* 見性, *see* Part Two, Chapters II and III.

51. Among these Rinzai Zen masters of the Meiji era, the one who was to be the most important for Zen in the West was Kōsen Sōon 洪川宗温 (1816–

1892). As a young man Kōsen had studied Confucianism, but at twenty-five he became a monk under Daisetsu Jōen 大拙承演 (1807–1855), in the 3rd generation of the Inzan line, then teaching at the Shōkoku-ji in Kyoto. At Daisetsu's suggestion, Kōsen later went to his master's fellow-disciple Gisan Zenrai 儀山善來 (1802–1878) of the Sōgen-ji 曹源寺 in Okayama Prefecture. Some time after he had completed his Zen study and become Gisan's heir, Kōsen was appointed abbot of the Eikō-ji 永興寺 in Yamaguchi Perfecture, and there taught Zen to the feudal lord of Iwakuni 岩國 and many of his samurai retainers. His well-known work *Zenkai ichiran* 禪海一瀾 One Wave on the Sea of Zen, written in 1862, was a commentary on Confucian terms from the Zen standpoint, and is still considered an important text for study in Kōsen's line of Zen.

In 1875 Kōsen was appointed head of the Religious and Educational Bureau of the new Meiji government, and the same year also became Chief Abbot (*kanchō* 管長)—a new official title, instituted in the early years of the Meiji era—of the Engaku-ji in Kamakura. Kōsen was particularly interested in instructing lay students in Zen, and was the first Rinzai Zen master to stress the importance of modern university study for Zen monks.

Kōsen's most important heir was Kōgaku Sōen 洪嶽宗演 (1859–1919), better known as SHAKU Sōen 釋宗演. Kōsen, early realizing that his disciple had an extraordinarily brilliant mind, sent him to the Keiō Gijuku 慶應義塾, later Keiō University, so that he might have an education requisite for the times. When he was twenty-nine, his Zen study completed, Sōen was sent to Ceylon to study Hinayana Buddhism. He remained there over two years, returning to Japan via Siam and China. After Kōsen's death in 1892, Sōen became Kancho and Roshi of the Engaku-ji. The following year he attended the World Conference of Religions held in Chicago during the summer of 1893, Sōen Zenji was the first Rinzai Zen master to travel to the West. He made two subsequent visits to the United States, and on the latter of these continued on around the world.

Sōen Zenji's senior heir and adopted son was Tetsuō Sōkatsu 輟翁宗活 (1870–1954), usually called Shaku Sōkatsu 釋宗活. As a young layman Sōkatsu studied under Kōsen Zenji. After his master's death he took the tonsure and became a disciple of Kōsen's heir Sōen. When he had completed his Zen study and received inka from Sōen Zenji, Sōkatsu made a long pilgrimage through Japan, then on to Burma and Siam, wearing his monk's robes and carrying a begging bowl. On his return to Japan, at his master's suggestion Sōkatsu revived the Ryōmō Kyōkai 兩忘協會, a layman's group for Zen practice originally founded by Kōsen Zenji. Sōkatsu Roshi devoted his entire life to teaching laymen, particularly university professors and students. With a group of his disciples he went to California in 1906, intending to establish a Zen center there, but after remaining for four years he returned to Japan, feeling that the time was still not ripe for spreading Zen to the West. Two of his four heirs became priests after receiving the Transmission of Dharma from him. The first was GOTŌ Zuigan 後藤瑞巖 (1879–1965), later Kancho of the Myōshin-ji and of the Daitoku-ji. The second was SASAKI Shigetsu 佐々木指月 (1882–1945), whose name in the line of Daitoku-ji priests is Sōshin Taikō 宗岑大綱. As Sōkei-an Rōshi, to give him his better-known teaching name, he founded The First Zen Institute of America in New York in 1931.

Two other disciples of Sōen Zenji are also of great importance for the introduction of Japanese Rinzai Zen to the West. The distinguished Buddhist scholar SUZUKI Daisetsu 鈴木大拙 (1870–) began his Zen studies under Kōsen Zenji while a university student in Tokyo, then, after Kōsen's death, became Sōen Zenji's disciple. In 1897, at the recommendation of his master, the young SUZUKI went to the United States to study western philosophy and culture. He acted as interpreter for Sōen Zenji on the latter's second and third visits to America, but remained several years longer to continue his studies, returning to Japan only in 1909, His subsequent career as one of the foremost living authorities on Zen Buddhism is too well known to need further comment.

The second of these two disciples of Sōen Zenji was the monk SENZAKI Nyogen 千崎如幻 (1876–1958), who taught Zen for many years in San Francisco and Los Angeles.

52. The following articles or sections of longer works have provided helpful material on the history of the development of the koan:

"Kōan no rekishiteki hatten keitai ni okeru shinrisei no mondai" 公案の歴史的發展形態における眞理性の問題 "The Problem of Truth in the Historical Development of the Koan," by FURUTA Shōkin 古田紹欽 [*Bukkyō no kompon shinri*, pp. 807–840].

"Hakuinkei kanna no ichikanken" 白隱系看話の一管見 "An Interpretation of the Koan in the Hakuin School," by SHIBAYAMA Zenkei 柴山全慶 [*Zengaku kenkyū*, No. 38 (Dec. 1943), pp. 1–30].

"The Zen Master Dōgen," *A History of Zen Buddhism*, by H. DUMOULIN,

S.J., pp. 151–174.

"The Zen Mysticism of Hakuin," *ibid.*, pp. 242–268.

"The Koan Exercise," *Essays in Zen Buddhism*, Second Series, by D.T. Suzuki, pp. 17–189.

"The Koan," *An Introduction to Zen Buddhism*, by D.T. Suzuki, pp. 99–117.

Notes, Part Two

1. *Shi guseigan* 四弘誓願 (*Si hongshiyuan*) The Four Universal Vows:
衆生無邊誓願度 *Shujō muhen seigan do;*
煩惱無盡誓願斷 *Bonnō mujin seigan dan;*
法門無量誓願學 *Hōmon muryō seigan gaku;*
佛道無上誓願成 *Butsudō mujō seigan jō.*

The Four Universal Vows, which every follower of Mahayana Buddhism takes in one form or another, has a long history. Originally the vows were closely related to the Four Noble Truths, and expressed the intention of the follower to make these Truths known to all men who were ignorant of them, in order that, through their realization of the Truths, they might attain final Nirvana. With the passage of time the theories regarding the meaning and import of the vows changed somewhat, as did the wording of them, but in no school were they discarded. The various sects of Chinese Buddhism each developed its own formulas and interpretations. The Shingon 眞言 (Zhenyan) Sect has five vows; the Jōdo 淨土 (Jingtu) Sect has six vows; the Tendai 天台 (Tiantai) and Zen 禪 (Chan) sects each have four.

The earliest Zen text containing the formula of the Four Vows in approximately the wording used today seems to be the Tonkō 敦煌 (Dunhuang) version of the *Sixth Patriarch's Sutra* [*T* 48: 337–345b]. There [*ibid.*, 339b.14–16] the Sixth Patriarch explains these Four Universal Vows and exhorts his disciples to recite them three times successively, a practice still carried on by Japanese Zen followers.

The objection is sometimes raised that it is illogical to vow to save numberless sentient beings before one has saved oneself. But when Shakyamuni first determined to seek an answer to the problem of suffering, his aim was not to solve this problem for himself alone, but for all other beings as well. Hinayana Buddhism, stressing the more obvious aspects of the Buddha's enlightenment, set up as its ideal the Arhat, who seeks primarily his own enlightenment. Mahayana Buddhism, however, grasping the full import of Shakyamuni's experience and his subsequent life, found its ideal in the Bodhisattva, whose own enlightenment is but the first step in his career of helping others to attain theirs. For the Mahayana Buddhist, with the true awakening of the desire for enlightenment spontaneously arises the awakening of "the compassionate heart," that is, the desire to share this enlightenment with others. Zen Buddhism is Mahayana Buddhism, and the vow which the Zen follower takes is the Mahayana vow. The vows to destroy the deluding passions, to enter all the Dharma-gates, and to complete the path of Buddhahood, are taken in order to fulfill the first vow, the vow to share with all fellow sentient beings the fruits of the practice, whether they be few or many. Only when the first vow has been fully taken is the Zen follower ready to begin the practice.

2. *Kenshō* 見性 (*jianxing*), "seeing into one's own nature," is one of the most important terms in Zen. It is, of course, an approximate synonym for satori, enlightenment, or awakening. The nature we are here urged to see into is the Buddha-nature that every sentient being is believed to possess intrinsically. The doctrine that the Buddha-nature is the ground of being of every existing thing is basic for the Zen Sect; however, it neither originated in the Zen Sect nor is exclusive with it.

Though almost all schools of Mahayana Buddhism accept this doctrine, it was not known in China until early in the 5th century. When Dōshō 道生 (Daosheng, 355–434), a disciple of the great Kumārajīva (350-*ca.*409), first promulgated the view that even the *icchantika*, those completely abandoned to sensuality, possessed the Buddha-nature and therefore would eventually attain Buddhahood, he was severely censured. Some twenty years later, however, with the arrival in China of the complete text of the *Mahāparinirvāṇa-sūtra*, the sutra was found to set forth this very doctrine, and Dōshō was completely vindicated.

Nor did the phrase so often found in Zen texts, "*kenshō jōbutsu*" 見性成佛 (*jianxing chengfo*), "to see into your own nature and attain Buddhahood," originate in the Zen Sect. The earliest text in which it seems to have appeared is the *Daihatsu nehan gyō shūge* 大般涅槃經集解 (*Daboniepan jing jijie*) [*T* 37: 377–611], a commentary on the *Nirvana Sutra*. In *kan* 33 of this text we find the statement: "Sōryō says: 'Seeing into our own nature and becoming Buddha denotes that our own nature is Buddha,'" 僧亮曰。見性成佛，即性爲佛也。[*Ibid.*, 490c. 26] Sōryō 僧亮 (Sengliang, *n. d.*) was a monk belonging to the Nirvana School, a school composed largely of scholars interested in interpreting the *Nirvana Sutra*. The School flourished for a time in South China, but was later incorporated into the Tendai 天台 (Tiantai) School. Sōryō is known to have been a contemporary and friend of the compiler of the above-named commentary, the Dharma Master Hōryō 寶亮法師 (Baoliang Fashi, 444–509), who was also of the Nirvana School.

The most famous and widely quoted passage in which the phrase *kenshō jōbutsu* is to be found is the following passage describing the principles of the Zen Sect as distinguished from those of other schools of Buddhism:

> A special transmission outside the scriptures, not founded upon words and letters; by pointing directly to man's [own] mind, it lets him see into [his own true] nature and [thus] attain Buddhahood. 教外別傳，不立文字，直指人心，見性成佛。*Kyōge betsuden, furyū monji; jikishi ninshin, kenshō jōbutsu.*

Though tradition has erroneously ascribed the authorship of these lines to Bodhidharma, it must be acknowledged that they embody the "special message" of Chinese Zen from the time of Bodhidharma, the traditional founder, on through the centuries. Individual phrases of this passage are to be found alone, or in combinations of two or three together, in several early Zen texts, but as a set formula it appears first in the *Sotei jion* 祖庭事苑 (*Zuting shiyuan*) A Collection from the Halls of the Patriarchs [*ZZ* 2: 18.1], a work compiled by Bokuan Zenkyō 睦菴善卿 (Mu'an Shanqing, *n. d.*), dated 1108, and consisting of extracts from the records of various Zen masters with commentary by the compiler. In *kan* 5 of this work appears the following:

> In transmitting Dharma, all the patriarchs in the beginning used the doctrines of the Tripiṭaka together with the practice. Later, however, the founder Bodhidharma transmitted the Seal of Mind only, destroying dependence on [the Tripiṭaka] and clarifying our Cardinal Doctrine. This is what we mean when we say: "A special transmission…." [*Ibid.*, 66c. 10*ff*]

3. *Ishin denshin* 以心傳心 (*yixin chuanxin*), here translated as the "transmission of Mind by mind," is a statement of one of the basic principles of the Zen Sect, and undoubtedly is of very early origin. In Zen circles, Bodhidharma is traditionally considered to have been the first to formulate the statement, since the "*Ketsumyaku ron*" or "On Relationships," one of the six treatises attributed to Bodhidharma and collected under the title *Shōshitsu rokumon shū*, has as its opening line: "The three worlds arise from and all return to the One Mind. From Buddha to Buddha, Mind is transmitted by mind." 三界興起，同歸一心，前佛後佛，以心傳心. [*T* 48: 373b.13] Though we cannot accept the view that Bodhidharma was the author of either this treatise or these lines, both probably date from the Tō 唐 (Tang) dynasty (618–907), perhaps even from its early years.

   The phrase may sometimes be rendered as "to transmit from mind to mind." An example of this usage is to be found in another early text, the Tonkō (Dunhuang) version of the *Sixth Patriarch's Sutra*. There, the Fifth Patriarch, after handing the patriarchal robe to Enō 慧能 (Huineng, 638–713), is represented as saying: "As for the Dharma, it is to be transmitted from mind to mind." 法以心傳心。 [*T* 48: 338a.17]

   The phrase states the pivot of the Zen teaching method, a method which demands that the teacher have a student as much as that the student have a teacher. At the moment the disciple's mind reaches the same state of intuitive understanding as that of the master, a fusion of minds takes place, and the understanding of the disciple becomes one with that of the master, or, in the traditional words, the master "transmits" his mind to the disciple. No words are employed in this transmission, which, in Zen, is considered to be the only method by which the ultimate truth of Buddhism can be correctly handed down from generation to generation.

   How much is demanded of the student may be judged from the following: When Hyakujō Ekai 百丈懷海 (Baizhang Huaihai, 720–814) transmitted his Dharma to his great disciple Ōbaku Kiun 黃蘗希運 (Huangbo Xiyun, *d. ca.* 860), it was with these words: "When [the disciple's] insight is identical with that of the master, the master's power is diminished by half. When [the disciple's] insight surpasses that of the master, then he is worthy of receiving the transmission." [*Keitoku dentō roku* 6; *T* 51: 249c.17, n. 27]

4. Daitō Kokushi 大燈國師 (1282–1338) was born in the province of Harima 播磨, near present-day Osaka. His family name was Kɪ 紀, and his

religious name Shūhō Myōchō 宗峰妙超. He entered temple life as a boy of eleven, took the commandments, and studied Tendai doctrines. In 1301 he went to the Manju-ji 萬壽寺, a Zen temple in Kamakura, and there practiced under Kōhō Kennichi 高峰顯日 (1241–1316). In 1304, hearing by chance that Nampo Jōmyō 南浦紹明 (1235–1309)—usually known by his posthumous title Daiō Kokushi 大應國師—had been called to Kyoto by Emperor Go-Uda 後宇多 (*r.* 1274–1287), Shūhō hastened to the capital to become a disciple of this famous master.

When the Kokushi was appointed abbot of the Kenchō-ji 建長寺 in Kamakura in 1308, Shūhō followed him there. Daiō had previously given his disciple "Ummon's Barrier" (*Ummon no kanji* 雲門關字 *Yunmen guanzi*) as a koan. Shūhō had been in Kamakura only ten days, when, according to the statement in his biography, the *Daitō kokushi gyōjō*:

> [The following day] he suddenly smashed through the "Barrier," and reached the state of the complete harmonization of opposites, the boundless and absolute Truth, where the Great Dharma manifested itself before his very eyes. Sweat drenched his body. He ran directly to the Master's study. "Almost the same path!" he cried. The Kokushi, greatly startled, said, "Last night in my dreams I saw Ummon enter my room. Now today you have passed through the Barrier. You must be a second Ummon!" Covering his ears Shūhō ran out.
>
> The next day he presented the Master with two verses:
>
> Having once penetrated the Cloud Barrier,
> The living road opens out north, east, south and west.
> In the evening resting, in the morning roaming, neither
> host nor guest.
> At every step the pure wind rises.
>
> Having penetrated the Cloud Barrier, there is
> no old road,
> The azure heaven and the bright sun, these are my native
> place.
> The wheel of free activity constantly changing is difficult
> to reach.
> Even the golden-hued monk (Kāśyapa) bows
> respectfully and returns.
>
> …When the Master had read these lines he picked up his brush

> and wrote [beside them]: "You have already cast away brightness and joined yourself to darkness. I am not like you. Now that my line has reached to you, it is firmly established. But for twenty years you must ripen your spiritual understanding." [*T* 81: 223a.22–b.4]

This was the proof of the Transmission of Dharma (*inka* 印可) from Nampo to Shūhō. The document is still kept as one of the treasures of the Daitoku-ji 大德寺,

On the death of the Kokushi a few months later, Shūhō returned to Kyoto. A number of legends grew up around his "twenty years of silence," as they are popularly known. It is said that he really spent them living among the beggars under Gojō Bridge in Kyoto, quite indistinguishable from his ragged associates. Eventually, so the story has it, Emperor Hanazono 花園 (*r.* 1308–1318) heard of him, and wished to invite him to preach at his palace. Having also heard that this unusual beggar was fond of a certain melon known as *makuwa-uri*, the Emperor went to Gojō Bridge in disguise carrying a large basket of the fruit. There he handed the melons to the beggars one by one, carefully scanning each face as he did so. Noticing one with unusually brilliant eyes, the Emperor said, as he offered the melon, "Take this without using your hands." The immediate response was, "Give it to me without using your hands."

The historical facts are not so romantic, however. After his return to Kyoto in 1309, Shūhō went to live at the Ungo-ji 雲居寺, a small temple on Higashiyama. Six years later he built for himself a hermitage in the district to the northwest of Kyoto known as Murasakino 紫野, Purple Fields, from the purple field flowers that grew there in abundance. To this hermitage he gave the name "Daitoku" 大德, Great Virtue. The following year, the hermitage was enlarged with the help of a relative of influence at the Court. The same year (1316), Shūhō was called to the palace to lecture before Emperor Hanazono. (This interview, and another that followed a few days later, are described at some length in *The Essence of Buddhism*, by D. T. Suzuki, pp. 18–20.)

Shūhō's fame now began to spread. After Emperor Go-Daigo 後醍醐 (*r.* 1318–1339) had ascended the throne, the Master was again called to the palace. (This interview, also, is described in Suzuki, *ibid.*, p. 27*f*). In 1324, land in the Murasakino district was given the Master for a large temple, and funds for the building were gathered by a group of important persons headed by Gen'e 玄惠 (*d.* 1350), a Tendai monk attached to the Court and famous as a Confucian scholar. The opening ceremony of the Daitoku-ji was held on February 9, 1327, under the patronage of both the reigning Emperor and the retired Emperor Hanazono, the latter of whom had now become Shūhō's personal disciple. For the remainder of his life the Master lived in the Daitoku-ji, except for a visit of one hundred days to the Sōfuku-ji 崇福寺, the temple of his master, Daiō Kokushi, in Fukuoka, Kyushu, In 1334 Shūhō received the title Kōzen Daitō Kokushi 興禪大燈國師 from the retired Emperor, and the same year Emperor Go-Daigo conferred upon him the title Kōshō Shōtō Kokushi 高照正燈國師.

Because of a crippled leg, Daitō Kokushi had for many years been unable to sit in the full lotus position for meditation. On January 21, 1338, feeling his death approaching, he seated himself on his meditation seat, broke his crippled leg with his own strength, and assumed the full lotus posture. Then, in spite of agonizing pain, he seized his powerful brush and wrote his final words, as had his teacher Daiō before him, and Daiō's teacher Kidō:

> I have cut off buddhas and patriarchs;
> The Blown Hair [Sword] is always burnished;
> When the wheel of free activity turns,
> The empty void gnashes its teeth.

With the last stroke, his brush fell from his hand, and he died. At the Daitoku-ji his blood-stained hemp robe and his last writing are brought out each year on the anniversary of his death, and reverence paid to them.

The Kokushi was fifty-six when he died. He left fifteen eminent disciples, among them Kanzan Egen 關山慧玄 (1277–1360), who was later to become the founder of the Rinzai Zen temple of Myōshin-ji 妙心寺, in the suburbs of Kyoto, and Tettō Gikō 徹翁義亨 (1295–1369), who succeeded Daitō Kokushi as second abbot of the Daitoku-ji. The Master's teachings are contained in the *Daitō kokushi goroku* and the *Daitō kokushi hōgo.*

5. The Daitoku-ji 大德寺, Temple of Great Virtue, is one of the seven headquarter temples of the Rinzai Sect of Zen in Kyoto. It was founded in 1327 by Shūhō Myōchō 宗峰妙超 (1282–1338), better known as Daitō Kokushi 大燈國師, under the patronage of the retired Emperor Hanazono and the reigning Emperor Go-Daigo, both of whom designated the temple their official place of worship. Under continued Court patronage the Daitoku-ji flourished greatly, and numerous sub-temples were erected within the main compound. In 1453 the temple suffered a disastrous fire, and in 1468

it was completely destroyed during the war then ravaging Kyoto. Reconstruction was begun in 1473, again under Imperial patronage, and with the aid of substantial contributions from several rich Sakai merchants. Oda Nobunaga 織田信長 (1534–1582), Toyotomi Hideyoshi 豊臣秀吉 (1536–1598), and the Tokugawa Shogunate, as well as many feudal lords, warriors, and merchant princes, have been among the temple's adherents and patrons through the centuries. During the five-year persecution of Buddhism that followed the Meiji Restoration in 1868, a number of the sub-temples were either destoyed or greatly reduced in size. The Daitoku-ji is still, however, one of the most important of the Rinzai headquarters, with branch temples in various parts of Japan. It supports two training halls for monks, one within the main temple precincts in Kyoto and one at the Sōfuku-ji 崇福寺, in Fukuoka, Kyushu.

The main temple (*honzan* 本山) and its immediately surrounding sub-temples are virtual storehouses of art treasures, in large part paintings and ceramics, presented as gifts by adherents, many of whom were wealthy merchants engaged in the China trade in the 16th and 17th centuries. The more important of these treasures, together with a number of buildings and gardens in the style favored by the aesthete tea masters of the Ashikaga 足利 (1338–1573) and Momoyama 桃山 (1573–1603) eras, are classified as National Treasures, or Important Cultural Properties. The Daitoku-ji has always been the center of the Tea Cult, and, in the tea rooms of several of its sub-temples Sen no Rikyū 千利休 (1522–1591), Kobori Enshū 小堀遠州 (1579–1647), and other famous tea masters, brought the tea ceremony to a perfection that, in form at least, it continues to exhibit to this day.

The Ryōshō-ji 龍翔寺, a temple originally built in the western suburbs of Kyoto by order of the retired Emperor Go-Uda to enshrine the ashes of Daiō Kokushi, the teacher of Daitō Kokushi, was removed to the Daitoku-ji precincts between 1532 and 1534. When the Ryōshō-ji was rebuilt some forty years ago, it was enlarged to serve as the new quarters of the main Daitoku-ji monastery (*Semmon Dōjō* 専門道場 Training Hall for Monks).

6. This is a paraphrase of a part of the *Kōzen Daitō kokushi yuikai*, The Last Admonitions of Kōzen Daitō Kokushi. Originally these "Admonitions" were recited before a roshi's *teishō* 提唱, or Zen lecture, by the monks of temples or monasteries related to the Daitoku-ji teaching line. It is probably only since Hakuin's time that this practice has become common to all Japanese Rinzai monasteries.

7. Eka Daishi 慧可大師 (Huike Dashi, 487–593). The name Eka was given to the Second Patriarch by Bodhidharma. Previous to their meeting, Eka had called himself Jinkō 神光 (Shenguang).

8. Most readers are undoubtedly acquainted with some of the many legends that have gathered around the name of Bodhidharma (Bodaidaruma 菩提達磨 Putidamo), the Indian monk who is traditionally said to have reached China in 520, and to have been the founder of Chinese Zen. Modern scholars of Zen history, discarding the traditions, admit only that Bodhidharma was probably a Brahmin who came from India by sea, arriving in South China toward the end of the Sō 宋 (Song) dynasty (420–479); that he wandered northward, finally reaching the kingdom of Gi 魏 (Wei); that he remained there for a considerable time promulgating meditation practices; and that he had two or three Chinese disciples, including Eka 慧可 (Huike).

 The only authentic non-Buddhist reference to Bodhidharma is that in the *Rakuyō garan ki* 洛陽伽藍記 (*Luoyang qielan ji*) History of the Buddhist Temples of Luoyang [*T* 51: 999a–1022b], written in 547. There the author Yō Genshi 楊衒之 (Yang Xuanzhi, *n. d.*), an official of the time, states that when he was visiting the Einei-ji 永寧寺 (Yongningsi), one of the famous temples in Rakuyō (Luoyang), he came upon Bodhidharma, the monk from the western land, sitting in quiet admiration before the beauty of the shrines and pagodas. The old monk said that he was one hundred and fifty years old, and had come from far away, travelling over many lands. [*Ibid.*, 1000b.19–21] From the known history of the temple, it would seem that this encounter took place sometime between 516 and 526. Where and when Bodhidharma died, no one actually knows.

9. Zen tradition has it that, when Bodhidharma had reached the country of Gi (Wei), he retired to the Shōrin-ji 少林寺 (Shaolinsi), a temple on Mount Sū 嵩山 (Songshan) not far from the capital city Rakuyō 洛陽 (Luoyang). His own hermitage there, built on a peak of the mountain known as the Shōshitsu 少室 (Shaoshi), was called the Mempeki-an 面壁庵 (Mianbi'an), "Wall-gazing Hermitage." Here the Master is said to have sat for nine years in silent meditation, facing the sheer wall of the cliff that rose up in front of his hut. From this derives the practice known as "wall-gazing" (*hekikan* 壁觀 *biguan*), or meditation facing a blank wall. Today, in memory of Bodhidharma's long meditation, young Zen monks, when they have been

accepted for entrance into a monastery, must first sit in an isolated room facing a blank wall, and practice zazen alone and in silence for three days.

10. Marvelous Principle (*myōri* 妙理 *miaoli*): Truth, the Ultimate Principle, the Absolute.

11. This refers to the story of the Bodhisattva Sadāpralapa (Sattabarin 薩陀波崙 Satuobolun) as related in the "Ever-bewailing Bodhisattva Chapter" (*Jōtai bosatsu bon* 常啼菩薩品 *Changti pusa pin*) of the Chinese versions of the *Mahāprajñāpāramitā-sūtra* (*Daihannya haramitta kyo* 大般若波羅蜜多經 *Dabore bolomiduo jing*). The chapter was included in several early Chinese renderings of sections of the sutra, as well as in Kumārajīva's 30 *kan* version of it, made between 400 and 409. It is Chapter 77 [*T* 6: 1059a–1067b] of the complete translation of the sutra in 600 *kan* made by Genjō 玄奘 (Xuanzang) in 659. The story that follows is based upon Genjō's translation.

The Bodhisattva Sadāpralapa, "Ever-bewailing Bodhisattva" (Jōtai Bosatsu 常啼菩薩 Changti Pusa)—so called because he continually sorrowed over the sufferings of sentient beings in the world—desired to attain the Great Perfection of Wisdom. Being advised to seek out the Bodhisattva Dharmodgata (Hōyū Bosatsu 法涌菩薩 Fayong Pusa), who dwelt in the City of Marvelous Fragrance (Myōkōjō 妙香城 Miaoxiangcheng), he immediately set out on his quest. Before long, his funds were exhausted. In order to have the means to continue his journey, he determined to sell his body. Wicked demons, who wanted to thwart him in accomplishing his purpose, caused the ears of men to become so deaf that no one could hear him calling out the sale of his body. They failed to deafen the ears of only one person, the young daughter of a certain rich man.

Meanwhile, the great god Indra (Taishakuten 帝釋天 Dishitian) changed himself into a young Brahmin, and offered to purchase Sadāpralapa's blood, marrow, and heart. Sadāpralapa thereupon caused his blood to stream from his body, crushed his bones and took the marrow from them, and was about to tear out his heart when the rich man's daughter heard his voice crying. She informed her parents, and they brought the Bodhisattva to the City of Marvelous Fragrance, where at last he met Dharmodgata Bodhisattva.

12. This is a reference to the story that appears in Chapter 13, the "King Compassionate Power Bestows His Blood Chapter" (*Jirikiō kesshi bon* 慈力王

血施品 *Ciliwang xueshi pin*) [*T* 4: 360b.8–c.13] of the Chinese translation of the *Damamūka-sūtra* (*Kengu kyō* 賢愚經 *Xianyu jing*) Sutra on the Wise and the Foolish. This sutra, probably a Hinayana work, was translated into Chinese in 445 by the Chinese monk Ekaku 慧覺 (Huijue, *n. d.*) and others, while Ekaku was working in Kōshō 高昌 (Gaochang), a city in what is now the Turfan area.

According to the sutra, when Shakyamuni was once staying in Śrāvastī he related the following story to his assembled monks: Aeons ago there lived a great and good king called Maitrībala (Jirikiō 慈力王 Ziliwang), who assiduously practiced the ten virtues. Since all his people followed their king's example and also practiced the ten virtues, the yakṣas—malignant demons who lived on human flesh—dared not attack them, and were thus famished for food. One day five of the yakṣas came before the King and recounted their plight. In compassion, King Maitrībala shed his own blood and let them eat their fill. Then the King said to the yakṣas: "If, as I hope, I become a buddha in the future, I will give the food of Dharma to you five yakṣas first of all." Shakyamuni then told his monks that King Maitrībala was none other than himself in an earlier existence, and that the five ascetics, to whom he gave his first sermon after he had attained enlightenment and who became his first disciples, had been these same yakṣas.

13. This refers to the opening episode [*T* 3: 472c–473b.11] in the *Taishi zuiō hongi kyo* 太子瑞應本起經 (*Taizi ruiying benqi jing*) Sutra on the Origin of the Glorious Appearance of the Crown Prince, a life of Shakyamuni translated into Chinese by the Sino-Scythian layman Shi Ken 支謙 (Zhi Qian, *n. d.*) who worked in Nanjing between 223 and 253.

Ages ago, when Dīpaṁkara (Jōkō 定光 Dingguang) was the Buddha, there lived a young hermit, by name Māṇavaka (Judō 儒童 Rutong), who was engaged in severe ascetic practices. Hearing that Dīpaṁkara Buddha was approaching the capital city of the kingdom, he hastened there. As the Buddha passed, Māṇavaka offered him five lotus flowers, and spread his long hair on the muddy road for the Buddha to walk upon. Dīpaṁkara stopped, and, addressing the young ascetic, prophesied that in the far distant future Māṇavaka would become the Buddha Shakyamuni.

14. In the *Shashin bon* 捨身品 (*Sheshen pin*) "Chapter on Sacrificing the Body" [*T* 16: 353c.21–356c.21], Chapter 17 of the *Konkōmyō kyō*, Shakyamuni is

represented as relating the following account of an event which took place during one of his earlier existences as a bodhisattva.

There was once a king named Mahārata (Makarada 摩訶羅陀 Moheluotuo) who had three sons, the youngest of whom was Mahāsattva (Makasatta 摩訶薩埵 Mohesatuo). One day the youth was playing on the edge of a cliff in the bamboo forest when he saw below him a tigress with seven cubs, all about to die of starvation. As he looked at the emaciated beasts, Mahāsattva thought to himself: "In the past I have thrown away my life many times because of my desire to save sentient beings. Why do I not sacrifice my life again?" Whereupon he pierced his neck with a sharp-pointed bamboo stick, and, as the blood streamed from the wound, threw himself over the cliff to the starving tigers below. The beasts devoured his body ravenously until only the bones remained.

15. Gate of Sweet Dew (*kanromon* 甘露門 *ganlumen*) is a Buddhist term meaning the "Gate of Immortality," that is, the gate leading to Nirvana. It derives from the Sanskrit *amṛta* (*kanro* 甘露 *ganlu*), the "nectar of immortality."

16. True Vehicle (*shinjō* 眞乘 *zhencheng*), the true teaching or true doctrine. "Vehicle" is a metaphor much used in Buddhism for the teaching which carries men to salvation.

17. Vessel of Dharma (*hōki* 法器 *faqi*) is a metaphor used in Zen for a person with the nature and capacity to receive the true Dharma and to transmit it to others.

18. Dharma Seal of All the Buddhas (*shobutsu hōin* 諸佛法印 *zhufo fayin*) is a technical term for the immutable truth of the Buddha-dharma. It is called a "seal" because, like the seal of a ruler, it is recognized everywhere. By it the validity of a doctrine can be verified, regardless of time or place. Hinayana Buddhism recognizes three Dharma Seals—impermanence, non-ego, and Nirvana—as criteria of the validity of a sutra or a teaching. Mahayana Buddhism recognizes only a single criterion, the One Dharma Seal (*ichihōin* 一法印 *yifayin*) also known as the *jissōin* 實相印 (*shixiangyin*), a term which may be translated as "Seal of the True Form [of the Dharmas]," or "Seal of Reality." It was the Mahayana Dharma Seal that the Second Patriarch was asking about.

19. This is the story most often told about Eka 慧可 (Huike), and, for the transmission of Zen, the most important. But all the versions of his life to be found in the old biographical collections make it clear that he did not come totally unprepared to Bodhidharma, and all have considerable to say regarding his life after he received the Transmission. Though the biographies in such collections contain many stories that cannot stand the light of modern historical criticism, Zen students should be acquainted with them as part of the traditional background of Zen. Following are two excerpts from the section devoted to Eka in *kan* 2 of the *Keitoku dentō roku*:

> The twenty-ninth patriarch,[a] Eka Daishi, was a native of Burō 武牢 (Wulao), [in modern Henan]. His family name was Ki 姬 (Ji). His father Seki 寂 (Ji) had never had a child. Voicing his thoughts, he said, "Our house reverences virtue. How is it that we are childless?" And he made supplication for a long time. One night he became aware that the room was filled with a strange light, whereupon his wife conceived a child. Later, because of the auspicious omen of the bright room, he named his son Kō 光 (Guang), "Light."
>
> In his youth the boy was extraordinarily ambitious. He read widely in the Book of Odes and the Book of Documents; he was still better versed in the principles of Daoism. He paid no attention to family matters, but loved to roam among the hills and lakes. Later he studied some Buddhist writings, and came to understand their inner meaning by himself. Thereupon he went to Mount Kō at Ryūmon 龍門香山 (Longmen Xiangshan) [northwest of Luoyang], where he was ordained a monk by the Meditation Master[b] Hōjō 寶靜禪師 (Baojing Chanshi). He received the full commandments at the Eiboku-ji 永穆寺 (Yongmusi) [in Luoyang]. He went from lecture to lecture and discussion to discussion; he studied the meaning of the Hinayana and the Mahayana everywhere. When he was thirty-two years of age, he returned to Mount Kō, and there spent his days in quiet sitting for a period of eight years.
>
> One day, in the midst of his meditation, he suddenly saw a spirit, who addressed him thus: "You desire to attain the fruit. Why do you stay here? The Great Dao is not far off. You must go to the South." Kō understood this to be spiritual advice, and

> for that reason changed his name to Jinkō 神光 (Shenguang), "Spiritual Light." The following morning he awakened with a severe pain in his head, and felt as though a thorn were piercing his brain. His teacher was undertaking to treat him, when a voice was heard from the sky, saying: "This is not an ordinary illness. It has to do with a great change in character and disposition." Kō finally told his teacher about his vision. The teacher, on observing the top of Kō's head, saw that a protuberance resembling five peaks had arisen on it.[c] Thereupon he said: "This phrenological sign is an auspicious omen; it is a proof that you will attain the fruits. The spirit ordered you to go to the South. Undoubtedly this means that Bodhidharma of the Shōrin-ji is your teacher." Having received these instructions, Kō went at once to the Shōshitsu. [*T* 51: 220b.26–c.12]

Then follows Jinkō's meeting with Bodhidharma as described by Isshū Rōshi. Jinkō was forty when he met the First Patriarch. He is said to have remained with the Master five or six years. After he had received the Master's robe and bowl—the visible signs of the transmission—and, according to some texts, a copy of the four-volume *Laṅkāvatāra-sūtra*, Eka is said to have wandered from place to place. In 551 he came one day upon a layman, who questioned him about the Dharma. Eka immediately recognized the man's deep innate understanding, and, after some instruction, shaved his head and gave him the name Sōsan 僧璨 (Sengcan). He then transmitted his Dharma to Sōsan and handed him Bodhidharma's robe and bowl, thus acknowledging him as his successor and the third patriarch of Zen in China.

> When the Daishi had handed on the Transmission he went to the capital, Gyō 鄴 (Ye), [in modern Henan], and there expounded the Dharma, adapting his words to the occasion. The single sound [of the Dharma] permeated far and wide, and monks and nuns, lay men and lay women took the Three Refuges.[d] Thirty-four years passed in this way. Then, hiding his light, obscuring his traces, and changing his appearance, he sometimes entered the wine houses, sometimes went into the butcher shops, sometimes consorted with menials. When people questioned him, saying, "You are a man of Dao. Why do you go on like this?" he would answer, "I myself make my mind harmonious. What concern is this of yours?"

Also, in front of the main gate of the Kyōkyū-ji 匡救寺 (Kuangjiusi) in the Kanjō 筦城 (Guancheng) district, [also in Henan], he spoke about the Supreme Dao. His listeners were as numerous as the trees of the forest. At that time the Dharma Master Benwa 辨和法師 (Bianhe Fashi) was lecturing within the temple on the *Nirvana Sutra*. His students, upon hearing the Daishi expounding the Dharma, left their teacher one by one. Benwa could not restrain his anger. He brought slanderous accusations against the Daishi before the district magistrate Teki Chūkan 翟仲侃 (Di Zhongkan). Chūkan, deceived by the evil words, charged the Daishi with violating the law. The Master willingly gave himself up. Those who understood the truth said that this was repayment of a past debt.[e] The Daishi's age at this time was one hundred and seven years. [*Ibid.*, 221a.6–16]

a. According to the traditional patriarchal lineage, beginning with Shakyamuni, Bodhidharma was the twenty-eighth Indian patriarch of Zen. In the line of Chinese patriarchs, Bodhidharma was, of course, the first, and Eka the second.

b. At this time Buddhist monks who gave instruction in meditation were known as *zenji* 禪師 (*chanshi*), or Meditation Masters; those who studied and lectured on the scriptures were called *hōshi* 法師 (*fashi*) or Dharma Masters. Later, the title "Zenji," with the meaning "Zen Master," was limited to eminent monks of the Zen Sect.

c. A reference to the fact that Mount Sū 嵩山 (Songshan), where Bodhidharma was living, was one of the famous "Five Peaks" of China.

d. A formula recited by all Buddhists when they enter the Buddhist life: "I take my refuge in Buddha; I take my refuge in Dharma; I take my refuge in Sangha."

e. The Daishi had earlier stated to his heir Sōsan that he had a debt from a previous existence to repay. Of course he was put to death for his alleged crime.

20. Nanshinken 南針軒 was the teaching name of Kōno Mukai 河野霧海 (1864–1935), an outstanding Zen master of modern times. He became a novice at the age of nine. At seventeen he entered the monastery of the Shōgen-ji 正眼寺, a temple near Gifu belonging to the Myōshin-ji branch

of Rinzai Zen. Three years later he went to Kyoto, and there studied for two years at the Hanazono Daikyō-in 花園大教院, now Hanazono University 花園大學, attached to the Myōshin-ji. In 1884 Mukai entered the Kokeizan 虎溪山, a monastery in the mountains near Nagoya belonging to the Nanzen-ji 南禪寺 branch of Rinzai Zen. Here, under Dokutan Sōsan 毒湛匝三 (1840–1917), a famous master in the 5th generation of the Takujū 卓洲 line, he devoted himself to koan study with exceptional zeal. The story is often told of his walking into the lotus pond of the temple while in deep concentration on the koan "Mu" 無 (*Wu*), and of having to be dragged out by his fellow monks. After ten years of practice he received his inka.

Two years of study under an eminent Confucian scholar in Tokyo now followed, then several years as a temple priest. In 1903 he was called to the Nanzen-ji in Kyoto to succeed his former master, Dokutan, as Rōshi of the Nanzen-ji Sodo. Six years later he was elected Chief Abbot (*kanchō* 管長) of the Nanzen-ji, and held that office for twenty years. But Nanshinken was essentially a Zen master, and his greatest talent lay in training monks. Through these years he did not give up his position in the monastery, but taught there continuously until his death in 1935.

Nanshinken was admired throughout the world of Rinzai Zen for the strict, even severe, training he gave his monks, as well as for his own frugal way of life. He had a number of heirs, but during his lifetime never divulged their names. After Nanshinken's death, several of his older monks went to his heir NAKAMURA Taiyū 中村泰祐 (1886–1954), then Rōshi of the Kōon-ji 廣園寺, a branch Sodo of the Nanzen-ji near Tokyo, and eventually received their inkas from him. Thus Isshū Rōshi, though under Nanshinken for many years, is Taiyū Rōshi's heir.

21. Nanzen-ji 南禪寺, The Temple of Southern Zen, is situated on a wooded slope of the Higashiyama 東山, mountains forming the eastern boundary of the old capital of Kyoto. It is one of the largest and most important of the Rinzai Zen headquarter temples in Japan.

After his retirement, Emperor Kameyama 龜山 (*r.* 1259–1274) erected a magnificent detached palace on Higashiyama. The story has it that before long the palace became haunted by ghosts and demons. To exorcise these apparitions, the retired Emperor called in a famous priest from the Tōdai-ji 東大寺 in Nara. Incantations and invocations were carried on for ninety days, but to no avail. Finally the retired Emperor consulted the Zen priest

Mukan Fumon 無關普門 (1212–1291), an heir of Enni Ben'en 圓爾辨圓 (1201–1280), founder of the Tōfuku-ji 東福寺. Fumon answered, "Even in the Analects of Confucius, a secular book to us, it is written that a demon cannot get the better of a man of complete virtue." The retired Emperor, much impressed with these words, then ordered Fumon to rid the palace of its unwanted occupants. Accompanied by numerous monks and disciples, Fumon moved into the palace. They chanted no sutras and recited no incantations, only sat day and night in meditation. Not a demon or an apparition was ever seen again. In gratitude, the retired Emperor made the palace into a Zen temple, and appointed Fumon as its first abbot, later bestowing upon him the title Daimin Kokushi 大明國師.

Under the continued patronage of the retired Emperor, and later that of the reigning emperor Go-Daigo, the Nanzen-ji grew in grandeur and power. It was reduced to ashes during the Ōnin War 應仁の亂 (1467–1477), and all attempts at restoration failed for more than a hundred years afterwards. In 1606, however, Toyotomi Hideyori 豐臣秀頼 (1593–1615), the son of Toyotomi Hideyoshi, re-erected the Buddha Hall, and, during the early years of the Tokugawa Shogunate (1603–1867), other buildings were gradually constructed, until the temple regained something of its former glory and prestige. Since the Meiji Restoration (1868), together with all Buddhist temples, particularly those of Rinzai Zen, the fortunes of the Nanzen-ji have suffered a decline. In the Rinzai Sect today, however, it stands second only to the Myōshin-ji in the number of temples belonging to it in various parts of the country, as well as in the number of its adherents.

Like the Daitoku-ji, the Nanzen-ji also contains several famous buildings and gardens, and owns numerous works of art. Its large training hall for monks is housed in a sub-temple within the precincts of the main temple. This was rebuilt by Nanshinken Rōshi in 1928, and renamed by him the Sembukurin-ji 薝蔔林寺. The Nanzen-ji also has several detached monasteries in other parts of Japan.

22. *Nyoi* 如意 (*ruyi*), a short curved stick of wood or bamboo, sometimes flexible—the literal meaning of the word is "at will, freely"—which is one of the ceremonial religious implements used by high-ranking Zen priests. During sanzen 參禪—the private interview with a disciple who is studying koans—the roshi usually has his *nyoi* lying just in front of him, within easy reach to apply to the lazy or erring student.

23. In Hakuin's time people believed that fish were spontaneously generated by water.

24. Hakuin is here referring to a passage in the *Kōhō oshō zen'yō* 高峰和尚禪要 (*Gaofeng heshang chanyao*) The Zen Monk Gaofeng's Essentials of Zen [*ZZ* 2: 27.4.352b–362a]. Kōhō Oshō was Kōhō Gemmyō 高峰原妙 (Gaofeng Yuanmiao, 1238–1295), of the Yōgi 楊岐 (Yangqi) line of Rinzai Zen, and the teacher of Chūhō Myōhon 中峰明本 (Zhongfeng Mingben). The original passage is as follows:

    There are three essentials which are absolutely necessary for the real study of Zen. The first is to have a great root of faith (*daishinkon* 大信根 *daxin'gen*). When you know this thoroughly, it is as if your steadfastness were that of Mount Sumeru. The second is a great tenacity of purpose (*daifunshi* 大憤志 *dafenzhi*). It is like the passion that possesses you when, on meeting the enemy who slew your father, you instantly want to cut him in two with your sword. The third is a great feeling of doubt (*daigijō* 大疑情 *dayiqing*). This is like the anxiety you experience when, having committed a heinous crime in secret, you are in suspense as to whether you will be found out or not. If you possess these three essentials through every hour of the day, I promise you that you will soon achieve success. You need not fear that the turtle will escape from the earthen jar. But if you lack even one of these essentials, you will be like a three-legged caldron with a broken leg. In the end you will become a useless vessel. [*Ibid.*, 357c.17–d.4]

25. The vivid expression "ball of doubt" (*gidan* 疑團 *yituan*) is an old one in Zen. Perhaps the earliest usage of it is that in the enlightenment poem of Rakan Keijin 羅漢桂琛 (Luohan Guichen, 867–928), a monk in the 8th generation of the line of Seigen Gyōshi 青原行思 (Qingyuan Xingsi, *d.* 740), through Tokusan Senkan 德山宣鑑 (Deshan Xuanjian, 780/2–865). Rakan Keijin's Dharma-heir was Hōgen Bun'eki 法眼文益 (Fayan Wenyi, 885–958), founder of the Hōgen 法眼 (Fayan) School of Zen. The poem is as follows:

    In the seventh year of Xiantong,
    I began my study of the Way.

Everywhere I went I met with words,
But I couldn't understand them.
The ball of doubt within my heart
Was as big as a big wicker basket.
For three springs I found no joy
In the quietude of woods and streams.
Then unexpectedly I chanced to meet
A King of Dharma seated on his mat of felt.
Marshalling up my doubts,
I laid them all before him.
The Master, from his mat of felt,
Rose up just like a dragon,
And, baring his right arm,
Struck my chest a single blow.
My ball of doubt, fright-shattered,
Fell to the ground with a crash!
When I raised my head to look about me,
I saw that the sun from the first had been round.
After that I went wandering—
Clump, clump, clack, clack~
And from that day to this
Have always been joyous.
Hearing now that my belly
Is replete to distention,
I no longer go hither and thither
Carrying my bowl in my hand.

[*Keitoku dentō roku* 11; *T* 51: 288c.19–25]

26. A popular saying, still in use today, deriving from the *Book of Changes* (*Eki kyō*) under the 50th hexagram, "Three-legged caldron" (*tei* 鼎 *ding*), fourth place: "The legs of the caldron are broken, spilling the lord's porridge and soiling his person. Misfortune." 鼎折足，覆公餗，其形渥。凶。

27. The word *shūshi* 宗旨 (*zongzhi*), here translated as Fundamental Principle, is a Zen term usually meaning the essential doctrine of a specific text or school. In this instance, however, it is used by Hakuin to mean Absolute Reality.

28. *Nantō watō* 難透話頭 (*nantou huatou*), the term here used by Hakuin refers to those koans which later were classified as *Nantō* Koans (cf. PART TWO, Chapter VI). In Japanese Rinzai Zen the word *watō* is a synonym for koan.

29. Three asaṁkhyeya kalpas (*san'asōgi kō* 三阿僧祇劫 *san'asengqijie*), sometimes abbreviated as *sangi* 三祇 (*sanqi*). A kalpa is a period of time consisting of years without number. "Three asaṁkhyeya kalpas" is a Buddhist technical term meaning the incalculable aeons of time neccessary for a bodhisattva to become a buddha.

30. In the Tokugawa era these were provinces in central Japan. They now form parts of Nagano, Yamanashi, and Gifu prefectures.

31. *Hakuin oshō zenshū*, Vol. 2, pp. 411.11–413.8.

32. For the biography of the Sixth Patriarch, *see* PART ONE, Note 19.

33. *So iwaku: "Fushizen fushiaku, shō yomo no toki, nako ka kore jōza ga fubo mishō izen no honrai no memmoku?"* 祖云。不思善，不思惡，正與麼時，那箇是上座父母未生已前本來面目。[*Kattō shū* 1, 2] The traditional background of this koan, as given in the *Sixth Patriarch's Sutra* and elsewhere, is as follows:

After the Fifth Patriarch in the dead of the night had transmitted his Dharma and Bodhidharma's robe and bowl to the layman RO (LU), thereafter to be known as the Sixth Patriarch Enō (Huineng), he ordered him to flee immediately from the Yellow Plum Mountain in order to escape the antagonism of the assembly when it should learn that the transmission had been given to one who appeared to be only an ignorant laborer. The next morning, when Enō's departure was discovered, a band of several hundred monks set out in pursuit of him. For two months their search was unsuccessful. Then one day, when Enō had reached the Daiyurei 大庾嶺 (Dayuling), a mountain range forming the border between present Jiangxi and Guangdong provinces, he was overtaken by the head monk Myō (Myō *jōza* 明上座 Ming *shangzuo*). When he saw Myō approaching, Enō placed the robe and bowl on a rock, saying, "These are the expression of faith. How can they be taken by physical force?" Coming forward, Myō tried to lift them, but they were as immovable as a mountain. He hesitated, trembling with fear. Then he said, "I have come seeking the Dharma, not the robe and the bowl. I beg of you, Anja, to explain the Dharma to me." Whereupon Enō said, "Thinking neither of good nor of evil, at this very moment what was your original aspect before your father and mother were born?" At these words Myō attained satori.

34. Jōshū Jūshin 趙州從諗 (Zhaozhou Congshen, 778–897), one of the great figures of Chinese Zen in the latter part of the Tang dynasty, was the heir of Nansen Fugan 南泉普願 (Nanquan Puyuan, 748–835), and thus in the 4th generation of the line of Nangaku Ejō 南嶽懷讓 (Nanyue Huairang).

Jūshin was born in the village of Kaku 郝 (Hao) in Sōshū 曹州 (Caozhou), in present Shandong, and his family name was Kaku 郝 (Hao). As a young boy he entered a temple in his native district, then at eighteen went to Nansenzan 南泉山 (Nanquan shan) in Chishū 池州 (Chizhou), in modern Anhui, where he joined the assembly of the Zen master Fugan. After he had attained satori under Fugan, he went to Mount Sū 嵩山 (Songshan), in present Henan, and took the full commandments at the commandment platform there. Thereafter he returned to Mount Nansen, and remained with Fugan until the Master's death.

Now in his late fifties, Jūshin set out on a pilgrimage that took him over the greater part of China and during which he visited all the eminent Zen masters of the time. He is said to have remarked: "I will ask a child of seven to instruct me if his understanding is greater than mine; I will instruct a man of one hundred if his understanding is less than mine." He had reached an advanced age—eighty, it is said—when he was invited to reside at the old Kannon-in 觀音院 (Guanyinyuan) in the eastern suburbs of the city of Jōshū 趙州 (Zhaozhou), in modern Hebei. There he remained until his death some forty years later at the remarkable age of one hundred and twenty, his temple continuously thronged with monks, eminent officials, and military men.

In the later years of his life, one of Jōshū's devoted adherents was Ō Yō 王鎔 (Wang Rong, 873–921), who as a lad of ten had succeeded his father as Governor of Jōshū. When the young Governor first came to visit the Master, Jōshū did not go to the gate to meet him, but received him sitting on his meditation seat. Later, however, when one of Ō's officers came to see him, the Master hastened to greet him at the entrance to the temple. The monks were puzzled by this unusual behavior, and questioned Jōshū about it. "I make it my rule," he replied, "to receive my most eminent guests sitting on my meditation chair; I descend from my chair to receive my next most eminent guests; and my least eminent guests I receive in front of the temple gate." When he heard this remark, the Governor was much impressed, and, from then on until the Master's death, a close relationship existed between them. Though the Governor offered Jōshū financial assistance, the Master, a man of the simplest habits, invariably refused it. When the broken-down walls of his meditation hall let in the harsh winter winds of North China, and when his preaching platform collapsed from rot and decay, he merely patched them up with old planks and pieces of rope.

Shortly before his death, Jōshū presented the Governor with his whisk (*hossu* 拂子 *fuzi*), saying, "This is something I have not finished using in my lifetime." And when his disciples, gathering around him for the last time, questioned the Master about his real age, Jōshū replied, "No one can count the number of beads on the thread of a rosary."

Jōshū employed neither the stick (*bō* 棒 *bang*) nor the shout (*katsu* 喝 *he*), as did other Zen masters of his time, but his terse comments are said to have been equally fear-inspiring. "Jōshū's lips flash light," Zen students of the time said of him. Though his Dharma line did not belong to any of the Five Houses, and perished a few generations after him, the light that flashed from his lips provided later generations with innumerable koans, and continues to illumine the Zen of today. The *Hekigan roku* includes twelve koans deriving from him, the *Mumonkan*, five; many others originating with him are given to students to ponder over in the course of their Zen study. The Master's famous "*Mu*" koan is still regarded as the first gate that every Zen student must pass through.

Jōshū's posthumous title was Shinsai Zenji 眞際禪師 (Zhenji Chanshi). The record of his life and teachings is to be found in the *Jōshū Shinsai zenji goroku*.

35. *Jōshū Oshō, chinami ni sō tou: "Kusu ni kaette busshō ari ya mata inaya?" Shū iwaku: "Mu!"* 趙州和尚因僧問，狗子還有佛性也無。州云，無。 [*Mumonkan* 1; *T* 48: 292c.22] The circumstances under which this famous mondo took place are unknown.

36. *Ika naru ka kore sekishu no onjō?* 如何是隻手音聲。 This koan, originated by Hakuin Zenji, does not appear in any koan collection, though it is mentioned several times in the Master's writings.

37. *Zazen wasan* 坐禪和讃 "Song of Zazen," a poem by Hakuin Zenji written in Japanese, is to be found in all handbooks used for sutra chanting in the Rinzai Sect of Zen. It is invariably recited when a group of laymen gather to practice zazen or to listen to a lecture by a roshi or eminent priest. Since it is a poem all Zen students should know by heart, an English translation follows:

Sentient beings are intrinsically Buddha.
It is just as it is with ice and water—
Apart from water there is no ice,
Apart from sentient beings there is no Buddha.
They do not know how near at hand He is;
How vain their seeking in far distant places!
They are like one who cries, "I thirst!"
Whilst standing in the midst of water;
Or like the child of a rich household
Who goes astray in some poor village.
The cause of their endlessly traversing the Six Ways
Is the dark road of their own ignorance.
Treading one dark pathway, then another,
When can they ever leave Samsara!

O the Samadhi of the Mahayana,
There are no words with which to praise it!
Alms-giving, commandments, and the other Paramitas,
Nembutsu, repentance, and religious practice,
These and good deeds countless in variety,
All are embraced within it.
Even he who achieves the merit of but one sitting
Wipes out his immeasurable accumulation of
transgressions.
Where can he find the evil ways?
Indeed the Pure Land is not far distant.
When graciously this truth vouchsafes
To touch his ear but once,
He who offers praise and adoration
Will thereby gain illimitable blessings.

How much the more, then, if you turn and enter in it,

And directly prove your own true nature!
Your own true nature, being no-nature,
Already is far removed from wanton words.
The gate of the oneness of cause and effect opens,
The non-dual, non-triple road lies straight ahead.
The formless form now being your form,
Going or returning you go not elsewhere;
The thoughtless thought now being your thought,
Singing and dancing are the voice of the Dharma.
How vast and unobstructed the empty sky of Samadhi!
How perfect and bright the moon of the Four Wisdoms!
At this moment, what is there more for you to seek,
With Nirvana itself manifest before you?
This very place, this is the Lotus Land;
This very body, this is Buddha.

38. The story of Shakyamuni's enlightenment as given here is limited to Zen literature and is the orthodox Zen account of this great event. That it differs from the traditional version found in Indian Buddhist literature is immediately apparent. Two distinct traditions are present in the story as we have it today, that regarding the occasion of the enlightenment and that regarding the words Shakyamuni spoke immediately after his enlightenment. It is interesting to speculate on the development of this story, since it presents an example of the evolution of a legend into an acknowledged doctrine of considerable importance. The steps noted below suggest the course this development would appear to have taken over the centuries.

The first mention of the "morning star" seems to have been in the *Fuyō kyō*, a Chinese work alleged to be a translation of the Sanskrit *Lalitavistara*, a legendary life of the Buddha dating from the 3rd or 2nd century B.C.E. The text [ed. Vaidya, p. 253.15] states that Shakyamuni attained his enlightenment "at dawn" (*aruṇa*). But in *kan* 6 of the *Fuyō kyō*, where this event is described, the Sanskrit *aruṇa* is rendered as "when the morning star appeared." The text reads: "When the morning star appeared, the clear, all-embracing Great Awakening took place; he attained the supreme and true Dao, and completed the highest perfect enlightenment." 明星出時，廓然大悟，得無上正眞道，爲最正覺。 [*T* 3: 522b. 13*f*]

That Shakyamuni first *saw* the morning star, then attained his awakening, appears to have been a development in the story for which the masters of the Zen Sect were responsible. In the *Zemmon nenju shū*, a Zen koan collection printed in Korea about 1226, these words appear: "When the World-Honored One *saw* the morning star he awakened to Dao." 世尊見明星，悟道。 [*Kan* 1; 7b.9] This statement is followed by four comments upon it, one by a Zen master of the Tang and three by masters of early Song. The comments of two of the Song masters also contain the phrase "when the World Honored One *saw* the morning star." So we may surmise that this part of the story had already assumed its present form by the early part of the Sō 宋 (Song) dynasty (960–1279).

For the words which, according to Zen tradition, Shakyamuni uttered immediately after his enlightenment, and which differ so greatly from those the Indian tradition credits him with saying, we must go back in time to another source, to the *Kegon kyō* (*Huayan jing*) in 80 *kan*, the Chinese translation of the Sanskrit *Avataṁsaka-sūtra* made between 695 and 699. There, in *kan* 51, we find the following: "At that time, [that is, immediately after his enlightenment] the Tathāgata, with his unobstructed Wisdom Eye, gazed universally upon all the sentient beings in the Dharmadhātu, then spoke these words: 'Wonderful, wonderful! How can it be that all sentient beings are endowed with the intrinsic wisdom of the Tathāgata?'" 爾時如來，以無障礙清淨智眼，普觀法界一切衆生，而作是言，奇哉，奇哉，此諸衆生，云何具有如來智慧。 [*T* 10: 272c.25–27]

However, it is in a 12th century history of Buddhism which puts special emphasis upon Zen that we find the exact statement of Shakyamuni's words as they are given today. In *kan* 21 of the *Ryūkō bukkyō hennen tsūron*, it is recorded that Emperor Kensō 憲宗 (Xianzong, *r.* 806–820) of Tang questioned Chōkan Kokushi 澄觀國師 (Chengguan Guoshi, 737–838), fourth patriarch of the Kegon 華嚴 (Huayan) Sect, about the Kegon teachings on the Dharmadhātu, the ground and cause of all things. Chōkan, who was the acknowledged authority of the time on the *Kegon kyō* (*Avataṁsaka-sūtra*), was obviously referring to the above quoted line from the sutra itself when, after describing the Dharmadhātu in some detail to the Emperor, he said: "Therefore the World Honored One, as soon as he had attained his True Awakening, exclaimed: 'How wonderful! I now universally observe that all sentient beings are endowed with the Tathāgata's intrinsic wisdom and virtuous characteristics.'" 故世尊初成正覺，歎曰，奇哉，我今普見一切衆生，具有如來智慧德相。[*ZZ* 2 乙: 3.4.313d.9–11] Chōkan Kokushi was the teacher of Keihō Shūmitsu

圭峰宗密 (Guifeng Zongmi, 780–841), fifth patriarch of both the Kegon Sect and the Kataku 荷澤 (Heze) School of Zen. Did the words of Chōkan become the common property of Zen men through his disciple Shūmitsu?

And finally, in the early part of the 12th century, Daie Sōkō 大慧宗杲 (Dahui Zonggao, 1089–1163), having taken the high seat, said to his assembled monks: "Old Shakya, when he was at the foot of the Mountain of True Awakening, on lifting up his head and seeing the morning star appear, suddenly awakened to Dao. Thereupon he said with surprise, 'How wonderful! All sentient beings are endowed with the intrinsic wisdom and virtuous characteristics of the Tathāgata. Only because they cling to their deluded thinking they are not able to prove this.'" 釋迦老子，初在正覺山前，舉頭見明星出現，忽然悟道，遂乃歎曰，奇哉一切衆生具有如來智慧德相，但以妄想執著而不證得。 [*Daie goroku* 16; *T* 47: 878b.19–21] In this completed form the story continues to be an important doctrinal statement in the Zen Sect today.

39. True Dharma Eye (*shōbō genzō* 正法眼藏 *zhengfa yanzang*); Marvelous Mind of Nirvana (*nehan myōshin* 涅槃妙心 *niepan miaoxin*); True Form of the Formless (*jissō musō* 實相無相 *shixiang wuxiang*). These are words supposedly spoken by Shakyamuni when he transmitted his Dharma to his disciple Mahākāśyapa (cf. Part One, Note 5). The earliest account of this transmission, as has already been stated, appears in *kan* 2 of the *Tenshō kōtō roku* (1036): "The World Honored One addressed the assembly saying: 'I have the True Dharma Eye, the Marvelous Mind of Nirvana. This I entrust to you, Mahākāśyapa.'" 世尊告衆曰，吾有正法眼藏，涅槃妙心，付囑摩訶迦葉。 [*ZZ* 2 乙: 8.4.306c.2*f*] By the time this story was retold about one hundred and fifty years later in *kan* 1 of the *Rentō eyō* (1183), it had been expanded to read as follows: "The World Honored One said: 'I have the True Dharma Eye, the Marvelous Mind of Nirvana, the True Form of the Formless, the Subtle Dharma Gate, which does not set up words and phrases, and is a separate transmission outside the scriptures. This I entrust to you Mahākāśyapa.'" 世尊云，吾有正法眼藏，涅槃妙心，實相無相，微妙法門，不立文字，教外別傳。付囑摩訶迦葉。 [*ZZ* 2乙: 9.3.221a.1*f*] This expanded version of the words attributed to Shakyamuni when he transmitted his Dharma has been handed down through the centuries in the Zen schools of both China and Japan, and has been of great importance for Zen doctrine.

40. Hakuin's statement here accords with the view current in Zen from early times. In the *Keitoku dentō roku* biography of Ryūge Koton 龍牙居遁 (Longya Judun, 835–923), a direct heir of Tōzan Ryōkai 洞山良价 (Dongshan Liangjie, 807–869), Ryūge is recorded as quoting the following words of his master: "Only when you regard the teachings of the patriarchs and the buddhas as you would a newly-made enemy of your house are you qualified to be a student." 祖教佛教似生怨家，始有學分。[*T* 51: 337b.17*f*] The meaning is, of course, that, if a student closely familiarizes himself with words or verbal teachings, he will become attached to them and never attain the direct realization of the Truth of which they are but the shadow. Since hatred toward an enemy of long standing tends to diminish, the simile "newly-made enemy" is used to indicate the extreme hostility the student should feel toward words. He should shun them as perils to his life.

41. Hakuin Zenji is here paraphrasing a passage in the *Kōhō oshō zen'yō* (cf. Part Two, Note 24): "Where there is complete faith there is complete doubt; when you attain complete doubt, you attain complete satori." 信有十分，疑有十分。疑得十分，悟得十分。[*ZZ* 2: 27.4.356b.15]

42. A metaphor taken from the parable in the *Lotus Sutra* [Kern, *op. cit.*, pp. 274–277: Soothill, *op. cit.*, pp. 186–189] in which the sutra is called the crown-jewel of the Tathāgata and compared with the most precious treasure of a mighty monarch, the jewel of jewels worn in his hair.

43. *Hakuin oshō zenshū*, Vol. 2, pp. 413.11–414.6.

44. *Uma no mimi ni nembutsu* 馬の耳に念佛。 A popular expression meaning useless advice.

45. "Concentrated reflection" is a tentative English translation of the word *kufū* 工夫 or 功夫 (*gongfu*). The Japanese student of koans never speaks of "meditating upon" a koan. He "kufus" a koan, literally "works on," "considers," "inquires into," "looks intently into" it, knowing that its solution lies within the koan itself and can be realized only when he and the koan have become completely one. The term is a very old one. Its earliest known usage is that in a poem entitled *Rakudō ka* 樂道歌 (*Ledao ge*) Song of Delighting in the Way, by Nangaku Myōsan 南嶽明瓚 (Nanyue

Mingzan, *n. d.*), a disciple of Fujaku 普寂 (Puji, 651–739) of the Northern School of Zen. In the poem Myōsan says:

> To try to concentrate (*kufū*) on something outside,
> This is indeed to be a stupid fool.
> 向外覓工夫 *Hoka ni mukatte kufū o motomu,*
> 總是癡頑漢 *Sō ni kore chigan no kan.*
> [*Keitoku detō roku* 30; *T* 51: 461b. 18*f*]

46. The *Dharmakāya* (*hosshin* 法身 *fashen*) means literally "Dharma-body," "Law-body," "Truth-body." It is interpreted as the "embodiment of Truth," the "essential body of Buddha," the "spiritual body," the "essence of being." True kensho is the attaining of this state, the seeing into it, for the absolute state of our own essential being is none other than the Dharmakāya.

47. *Nanji ga ichinenshinjō no shōjōkō, kore nanji ga okuri no hosshimbutsu nari.* 你一念心上清淨光，是你屋裏法身佛。 [*Rinzai roku*; *T* 47: 497b.17*f*]

48. Kassan Zenne 夾山善會 (Jiashan Shanhui, 805–881) was a monk in the 5th generation of the line of Seigen Gyōshi (Qingyuan Xingsi). He was born in Kentei 峴亭 (Xianting) in Kōshū 廣州 (Guangzhou), in the southern part of modern Guangdong, and his family name was Ryō 寥 (Liao). He was a boy of nine when he entered a temple on Mount Ryūge 龍牙山 (Longyashan) in Tanshū 潭州 (Tanzhou), in modern Hunan. In his twenties he went to Kōryō 江陵 (Jiangling), in modern Hubei, where he took the commandments, studied the Tripiṭaka, and became a lecture-master (*zasu* 坐主 *zuozhu*). He also joined a meditation assembly and practiced earnestly.

Later he went to live at Keikō 京口 (Jingkou), in present Jiangsu. One night when he was lecturing, a monk asked him, "What is the Dharmakāya?" "The Dharmakāya is without form," Zenne replied. "What is the Dharma Eye?" "The Dharma Eye is without flaw," the Master said. Then he continued, "In front of the eyes there are no dharmas. The meaning exists in front of the eyes, but it is not to be reached by the eyes or the ears."

At this point a visiting monk in the audience laughed. Zenne was disconcerted and asked, "Why do you laugh?" "Though you're a regular monk, you haven't a master," said the visitor. "You should go to Katei and see the Boatman Monk." "Will my going be advantageous?" Zenne asked. "As for that teacher, above he hasn't a piece of tile to cover his head; below he hasn't a gimlet point of earth to stand on," the monk replied.

The visiting monk was Dōgo Enchi 道吾圓智 (Daowu Yuanzhi, 769–835), an heir of Yakusan Igen 藥山惟儼 (Yueshan Weiyan, 745–828), and the Boatman Monk was Sensu Tokujō 船子德誠 (Chuanzi Decheng, *n. d.*), Dōgo's fellow-disciple under Yakusan. Tokujō was at that time living as a ferryman, and people familiarly called him Sensu Oshō 船子和尚 (Chuanzi Heshang), the Boatman Monk.

Zenne put on his travelling garb and went straightway to Katei 華亭 (Huating), in the present district of Suzhou. He found the Boatman Monk plying his skiff on the river. They understood each other at a glance. Sensu Oshō transmitted his Dharma to Zenne, then, so it is said, disappeared, never to be seen again.

Zenne, following his master's instructions, now retired from the world for more than thirty years. In 870 he built a small hermitage on Kassan 夾山 (Jiashan) in Reishū 澧州 (Lizhou), in present Hunan. Gradually students gathered around him. At first they built their own little huts; later, however, the populace erected a temple for the Master and called it the Reisen-in 靈泉院 (Lingquanyuan).

One of Zenne's most famous verses is that he gave as an answer to the monk who asked him, "What is the state of Kassan?"—"state" (*kyō* 境 *jing*) superficially meaning the physical environment, but, more profoundly, the state of consciousness, and "Kassan," of course, referring to the mountain and the Master as well:

> The monkeys, clasping their young to their breasts,
> Have returned behind the blue peaks;
> A bird, holding a flower in its beak,
> Alights before the green grotto.
>
> [*Keitoku dentō roku* 15; *T* 51: 324b.21*f*]

The final phrase of this verse, "green grotto" (*hekigan* 碧巖 *biyan*), became the name of the abbot's quarters (*hōjō* 方丈 *fangzhang*) at the Reisen-in. It was there, over two hundred years later, that Engo Kokugon 圜悟克勤 (Yuanwu Keqin, 1063–1135) gave the series of lectures that were published subsequently under the title *Hekigan roku* (*Biyan lu*).

49. *Sō tou, "Ika naru ka kore hosshin?" Shi (Kassan Zenne) iwaku: "Hosshin musō."* 僧問，如何是法身。師「夾山善會」曰。法身無相。 [*Keitoku*

dentō roku 15; *T* 51: 323c.24*f*]

50. Dairyo Chikō 大龍智洪 (Dalong Zhihong, *n. d.*) was a monk in the 8th generation of the Seigen Gyōshi (Qingyuan Xingsi) line, through Tokusan Senkan (Deshan Xuanjian). Nothing is known about his life except that he was an heir of Hakuchō Shien 白兆志圓 (Baizhao Zhiyuan, *n. d.*), and that he lived on the Dairyōzan 大龍山 (Dalongshan), a mountain in Rōshū 朗州 (Langzhou), in present Hunan. That Chikō was essentially a poet, and that the beauty of the environment in which he lived on Mount Dairyō was a source of inspiration to him, may be gathered from another of his verses given in response to a question by one of his monks:

A monk asked Dairyō, "What is the Mysterious?" The Master replied:

"The breeze brings the water's voice
Close to my pillow;
The moon carries the mountain's shadow
Near to my couch."

[*Keitoku dentō roku* 23; *T* 51: 394a.15*f*]

51. *Sō Dairyō ni tou: "Shikishin wa haie su, ika naru ka kore kengo hosshin?" Ryō iwaku: "Sanka hiraite nishiki ni nitari; kansui tataete ai no gotoshi."* 僧問大龍，色身敗壞，如何是堅固法身。龍云，山花開似錦，澗水湛如藍。 [*Hekigan roku* 82; *T* 48: 208a.27*f*]

52. For Ummon's biography, see Part One, Note 15.

53. *Sō Ummon ni tou: "Ika naru ka kore shōjō hosshin?" Mon iwaku: "Kayakuran."* 僧問雲門，如何是清淨法身。門云，花藥欄。 [*Hekigan roku* 39; *T* 48: 177b.14] The usual translation of the phrase "*kayakuran*" 花藥欄 (Huayaolan), a favorite in Chinese poetry, is "peony-flower hedge." The translation in the text is the Japanese Rinzai Zen rendering of the phrase as given to koan students today.

54. To Jun 杜順 (Du Shun, 557–640), a famous monk of early Tang, was the founder of the Kegon (Huayan) School, and its first patriarch. He was born in Mannen 萬年 (Wannian) in the Chōan 長安 (Chang'an) district. His family name was To 杜 (Du), and his religious name Hōjun 法順 (Fashun), but he is generally known as To Jun.

At the age of eighteen he became a monk. He studied meditation under the Meditation Master Sōchin 僧珍禪師 (Sengzhen Chanshi, *n. d.*) of the Inshō-ji 因聖寺 (Yinshengsi), in the city of Chōan. Then he went to live at Mount Shūnan 終南山 (Zhongnanshan), to the south of Chōan. There he devoted himself for many years to the study of the *Avataṁsaka-sūtra* (*Kegon kyō* 華嚴經 *Huayan jing*). Many monks gathered around him at the Shūnanzan to be instructed in the teachings of the sutra and the meditation practices in which To Jun was very proficient. Later, the Master went on a pilgrimage throughout the country, converting people and promulgating the doctrines related to Samantabhadra (Fugen 普賢 Puxian), the Bodhisattva of Universal Virtue, who has a position of special importance in the *Kegon kyō*.

To Jun was particularly adept in performing miracles. Once when he was staying in the mountains with his disciples and followers, they were plagued by hordes of ants. The Master drew a circle around himself and the others with his staff, and by the following day all the ants had disappeared. On another occasion the Master came to a river in full flood. Suddenly the waters receded, leaving a stretch of dry river bottom. When To Jun had crossed to the other side, the waters flowed back again. In the later years of his life, the Master's fame as a miracle worker and holy man reached the ears of Emperor Taisō 太宗 (Taizong, *r.* 627–649) of Tang, and he was summoned to the Imperial Court. There he preached before the Imperial family and members of the nobility. He died at the Gizen-ji 義善寺 (Yishansi) in Chōan at the age of eighty-three.

Under To Jun the Kegon 華嚴 (Huayan) School first took definite form. As has already been mentioned, the Master was extremely well-versed in contemplation and meditation practices, and these, together with his other teachings, he handed on to his disciple Chigon 智儼 (Zhiyan, 602–668), who succeeded him as the second patriarch of the school. Two short writings are attributed to To Jun: the *Kegon gokyō shikan* 華儼五教止觀 (*Huayan wujiao zhiguan*) The Five Ways of Contemplation according to the Avataṁsaka School, in 1 *kan* [*T* 45: 509a–514a], and the *Kegon ichijō jūgemmon* 華嚴一乘十玄門 (*Huayan yicheng shixuanmen*) The Ten Mysterious Gates of the One Vehicle according to the Avataṁsaka School, also in 1 *kan* [*T* 45: 514a–518c].

Even during his lifetime, To Jun seems to have been regarded as an incarnation of Mañjuśrī (Monju 文殊 Wenshu), the Bodhisattva of Intrinsic Wisdom. The following legend concerning him has for centuries been handed down in the Zen Sect: A certain monk who had been studying the *Kegon kyō* under To Jun for thirty years set out on a pilgrimage to Godaizan 五臺山 (Wutaishan), in modern Shanxi. Since this mountain had long been reputed to be the dwelling-place of Mañjuśrī, he hoped to see the Bodhisattva there and worship him. On the way the monk met an old man, who said to him, "Mañjuśrī does not live on Godaizan. Mañjuśrī is none other than the Meditation Master To Jun who lives on Mount Shūnan." The monk was much surprised to hear this, and told the old man that he had been studying for thirty years with this same To Jun. The old man, replied, "You have been foolish not to worship him during these thirty years. But you'll be able to see and worship Mañjuśrī if you hurry back to Shūnanzan this evening. Otherwise you'll never have the opportunity again." When the monk reached Shūnanzan he learned that the Master had died the previous night. Then he realized that the old man he had met on the way was none other than To Jun himself, the incarnation of Mañjuśrī.

55. *Eshū no ushi ka o kissureba, Ekishū no uma hara fukuru.* 懷州牛喫禾，益州馬腹脹。 [*Sekisō Soen zenji goroku*; *ZZ* 2: 25.1.93a.6]

56. Fu Daishi 傅大士 (Fu Dashi, 497–569) is one of the most popular and interesting figures of early Chinese Buddhism. So many marvelous stories and legends have grown up around him that it is difficult to separate fact from fancy. The following story of his life is based upon his traditional biography.

He is said to have been born in the village of Keiteiri 稽停里 (Qitingli), in present Zhejiang. His family name was Fu 傅 (Fu), and his given name Kyū 翕 (Xi). As a youth Fu Kyū was a kind and simple fellow, who devoted his time largely to fishing. When he had filled his basket with fish he would put it into the deep part of the river, saying, "Those who want to go, go; those who want to stay, stay." The people of his village naturally thought him somewhat daft. At sixteen he married, and he and his wife had two sons, Fuken 普建 (Pujian) and Fusei 普成 (Pucheng). In his twenty-fourth year Fu Kyū was sitting one day on the river bank fishing, when a foreign mendicant monk came along and spoke to him about the teachings of the Buddha. Fu Kyū was deeply moved and immediately threw away all his fishing implements.

He now built a little hut for himself and his family under a pair of sāla trees at the foot of nearby Pine Mountain (Shōzan 松山 Songshan). When he had attained some degree of enlightenment as the result of his ascetic practices he took the religious name of Sōrin Juge Tōrai Gedatsu Zenne Daishi 雙林樹下當來解脱善慧大士 (Shuanglin Shuxia Danglai Jietuo Shanhui Dashi), the "Bodhisattva Zenne Who Will Attain Emancipation under the Twin [Sāla] Trees." During the day he and his wife worked in their fields raising vegetables, or hired themselves out as manual laborers; at night Fu Daishi talked about the Buddha-dharma to anyone who cared to come and join him. After subjecting himself to severe ascetic discipline for seven years, he had visions in which three buddhas appeared to him. But the district official thought him possessed of a demon, and locked him up in prison. Ten days later, when the official went to see the Daishi, he found him well and in good spirits, though he had had no food during the entire interval. Conscience-stricken, the official released him and told him to return home.

Shortly after this, the Daishi announced to the many students who now gathered around him that he had come from the Tuṣita Heaven (Tosotsuten 兜率天 Doushuaitian)—the heaven where the future Buddha Maitreya (Miroku 彌勒 Mile) waits to be born—to expound the highest truth, which up to this time had been hidden, but was now about to be revealed.

During the Daitsū 大通 (Datong) era (527–529) of the Ryō 梁 (Liang) dynasty (502–557), the district was stricken with famine. The Daishi sold his house and fields, and with the money obtained food to feed the starving villagers. He also persuaded his wife and sons, as well as a number of other persons, to be sold as slaves in order to raise money for the same purpose. A few months later, however, all the women, including the Daishi's wife, were freed by the landowner who had bought them.

In 534 the Daishi dispatched a disciple with a letter setting forth his religious views to Ryō no Butei 梁武帝 (Liang Wudi, *r.* 502–549). This was the emperor with whom, tradition says, Bodhidharma had had an interview soon after his arrival in China. Somewhat later the same year, the Emperor commanded the Daishi to appear at Court for an audience. He was much impressed with the Daishi and ordered him to live at the Jōrin-in 定林院 (Dinglinyuan) at Shōzan 鐘山 (Zhongshan), near the capital, present Nanjing. Many eminent monks now came to the Daishi's gate, and the Emperor summoned him for several more audiences. In 535, however, he returned to his old home and built a Buddha Hall and a pagoda under the sāla trees there.

In the early spring of 548, the Daishi gave away all his fields and estates to the people. The following month he told his followers that he was going to go without food in order to purify his mind and body, and that on the eighth day of the fourth month he would immolate himself by fire as an offering to the Three Treasures—Buddha, Dharma, and Sangha—for the benefit of all living creatures on earth. He hoped thus to bring to an end the suffering the people were undergoing as the result of the military disasters at the end of the Ryō dynasty. When the day for his immolation came, nineteen of his disciples wanted to burn themselves in his place; a hundred or more burned their fingers, cut off their ears, or sold themselves as slaves; and others engaged in extreme ascetic practices, in order to persuade the Daishi not to carry out his intention. He finally yielded to their pleas.

Some years later, when famine again stalked the land, the Daishi worked in the fields with his followers, gathering grass and acorns for gruel. Everything he had he gave to the poor and the starving. In 555 he preached on non-attachment to the physical body, and as a result three of his followers burned themselves to death on the top of Sōrinzan 雙林山 (Shuanglinshan). During the years that followed, the Daishi continued his ministrations to the poor, held great religious meetings regularly to exorcise evil spirits and prevent misfortunes, and continued to purify his mind and body by extreme ascetic practices, hoping thus to bring peace and ease to all beings.

Fu Daishi died May 25, 569, at the age of seventy-three. His body was cremated on the top of the Sōrinzan. Everyone considered him to have been an incarnation of Maitreya. He had never taken orders, but remained a layman during his entire life. He was often portrayed in painting and sculpture with his wife and two boys, a tall figure with a long beard, wearing a Confucian hat, a Buddhist robe, and Daoist shoes. He is credited with the invention of the revolving bookcase for holding scriptures, which, like the prayer-wheel, can assist those who turn it to attain salvation, no matter how ignorant they may be.

The *Zenne daishi goroku* contains the prose writings and poems attributed to him.

57. *Kūshu ni shite jotō o tori, hokō shite suigyū ni noru.* 空手把鋤頭，步行騎水牛。 [*Zenne daishi goroku* 3; *ZZ* 2: 25.1.13a.15]

58. *Busso shabetsu no myōsho* 佛祖差別妙處, that is, the phenomenal world as seen with the enlightened eye.

59. *Kikan* 機關 (*jiguan*).

60. From the Introductory Statement (*suiji* 垂示 *chuishi*) to Case 23 of the *Hekigan roku*. [*T* 48: 164a.25–27]

61. Tosotsu Jūetsu 兜率從悦 (Doushuai Congyue, 1044–1091) was a monk in the 3rd generation of the Ōryō 黃龍 (Huanglong) line of Linji (Rinzai) Zen. He was born in Kenshū 虔州 (Qianzhou), in modern Jiangxi, and his family name was Yu 熊 (Xiong). At the age of fifteen he became a monk. He studied under several masters consecutively, for, though he had a brilliant mind, his self-conceit made it difficult for him to accept authority. Finally, however, the sharp criticism given him by Ungai Shuchi 雲蓋守智 (Yungai Shouzhi, 1025–1115), a direct disciple of Ōryō E'nan 黃龍慧南 (Huanglong Huinan, 1002–1069), founder of the Ōryō line, caused Jūetsu to reconsider his attitude. He then went to Hōbō Kokumon 寶峰克文 (Baofeng Kewen, 1025–1102), another of Ōryō's direct heirs, and remained with him until he had received the Transmission of Dharma.

Thereafter Jūetsu went to Rokuonzan 鹿苑山 (Luyuanshan) in Tanshū 潭州 (Tanzhou), in present Hunan, where a number of disciples gathered around him. One day an old monk named Shōso 清素 (Qingsu, *n. d.*) came to the mountain. Shōso was over eighty years old, and had been a personal disciple of Sekiso Sōen 石霜楚圓 (Shishuang Chuyuan, 986–1039), the master of Ōryō E'nan. The old monk told Jūetsu that, though he had been under Sekisō for thirteen years and had reached his present advanced age, he would not dare teach others. He severely criticised Ōryō, saying that his followers too quickly left their teacher and set themselves up in the world as masters before their learning or practice were sufficient. The old monk's remarks struck home, and after some reflection Jūetsu asked permission to become his disciple. Under Shōso, Jūetsu now devoted himself again to practice, later receiving inka from the old monk.

In 1089 Jūetsu was invited by the governor of Kōshū 洪州 (Hongzhou), in modern Jiangxi, to lecture at Mount Tosotsu 兜率山 (Doushuaishan), a mountain named for the Tuṣita Heaven where the future Buddha Maitreya dwells. The Master died there two years later in his forty-eighth year.

Among Tosotsu's lay students during these last years was the official—later Prime Minister—Chō Shōei 張商英 (Zhang Shangying, 1043–1121), whose Buddhist name was Mujin Koji 無盡居士 (Wujin Jushi). After Tosotsu's death, Chō Shōei built a tower in the Master's memory, and on his petition the posthumous title Shinjaku Zenji 眞寂禪師 (Zhenji Chanshi) was conferred upon Tosotsu by Imperial decree. Some of the Master's sayings will be found in a short work entitled *Tosotsu Etsu zenji go* 兜率悦禪師語 (*Doushuai Yue chanshi yu*) The Words of the Zen Master Etsu of Tosotsu, compiled by his disciple Shinjō 眞淨 (Zhenjing, *n. d.*), in the *Zokkai kosonshuku goyō*, kan 1 [*ZZ* 2: 23.5.433c–434b].

62. Tosotsu's Three Barriers (*Tosotsu sankan* 兜率三關 *Doushuai sanguan*):

1. *Hassō sangen wa tada kenshō o hakaru; sakkon shōnin no shō izure no tokoro ni ka aru?* 撥草參玄，只圖見性，即今上人，性在甚處。

2. *Jishō o shikitoku sureba, masa ni shōji o dassu; gankō otsuru toki, somosan ka dassen?* 識得自性，方脱生死，眼光落時，作麼生脱。

3. *Shōji o dattoku sureba, sunawachi kyosho o shiru; shidai bunri shite, izure no tokoro ni mukatte ka saru?* 脱得生死，便知去處，四大分離，向甚處去。

[*Mumonkan* 47; *T* 48: 298c.21–24]

63. *Jōshū chinami ni sō tou: "Ika naru ka kore soshi seiraii?" Shū iwaku: "Teizen no hakujushi."* 趙州因僧問，如何是祖師西來意。州云，庭前柏樹子。 [*Mumonkan* 37; *T* 48: 297c.5*f*]

64. Chū Kokushi 忠國師 (Zhong Guoshi) was the Imperially bestowed title of Nan'yō Echū 南陽慧忠 (Nanyang Huizhong, *d.* 776). Echū was born in Esshū 越州 (Yuezhou), in present Zhejiang. At the age of sixteen he went south to Sōkei 曹溪 (Caoxi), in modern Guangdong, and became a monk under the Sixth Patriarch Enō 惠能 (Huineng). After he had received the Transmission of Dharma from Enō, he retired to Mount Hakugai 白崖山 (Baiyaishan) in Nan'yō 南陽 (Nanyang), in modern Henan. There he lived and practiced for forty years without ever leaving the mountain.

In 761 Emperor Shukusō 肅宗 (Suzong, *r.* 756–762) of Tang summoned Echū to the capital, Chōan (Chang'an). There the Master lived in the Seizen-in 西禪院 (Xichanyuan) of the Sempuku-ji 千福寺 (Qianfusi), and from time to time preached before the Emperor and the Court. In the Master's later years, Emperor Daisō 代宗 (Daizong, *r.* 762–779) presented him with the Kōtaku-ji 光宅寺 (Guangzhaisi) for his residence in the capital, and conferred upon him the title "National Teacher of Two Emperors" (Ryōtei Kokushi 兩帝國師 Liangdi Guoshi).

> When the Kokushi became aware that his death was approaching he went to pay a farewell visit to Emperor Daisō. The Emperor said, "After your Nirvana what can I, your disciple, do to honor your memory?" "I ask you to build for me a seamless tower," replied the Kokushi. "Please tell me, my Master, after what design you wish it to be built," said the Emperor. The Kokushi was silent for a little, then asked, "Do you understand?" "No, I do not understand," replied the Emperor. "After this humble monk has gone," said the Kokushi, "my attendant Ōshin will know this matter well."
>
> On January 4, 776, the ninth day of the twelfth month of the tenth year of the Daireki 大暦 (Dali) era (766–779), the Kokushi lay down on his right side, and passed away. His disciples carried out the funeral ceremonies and built a tower in his memory. By Imperial decree, the posthumous title Daishō Zenji 大證禪師 (Dacheng Chanshi) was bestowed upon the Master.
>
> Later, Emperor Daisō summoned Ōshin to Court and questioned him about his earlier conversation with the National Teacher. Ōshin was silent for a little while, then asked, "Do you understand?" "No, I do not understand," replied the Emperor. Ōshin then recited a verse:
>
> "South of the Xiang
> And north of the Tan
> Is a country abounding in gold.
> Under a shadowless tree, a ferry-boat,
> In the Emerald Pavilion, no one who knows."
>
> Ōshin later went to live at Mount Tangen 耽源山 (Danyuanshan) in Kisshū 吉州 (Jizhou), in modern Jiangxi, and was thereafter called Tangen Ōshin 耽源應眞 (Danyuan Yingzhen, *n. d.*).

The above version of this story, known as "Chū Kokushi's Seamless Tower" (*Chū kokushi muhōtō* 忠國師無縫塔 *Zhong guoshi wufengta*), has been taken from *kan* 5 of the *Keitoku dentō roku* [*T* 51: 245a.3–14]. As a koan, the story will be found in the *Hekigan roku* 18 [*T* 48: 157c.18–158a.4].

65. *Kokushi Sankan: Kokushi mitabi jisha o yobu. Jisha mitabi ō zu. Kokushi iwaku: "Masa ni omoeri, ware nanji ni kobu su to, ganrai kaette kore nanji ware ni kobu su."* 國師三喚：國師三喚侍者。侍者三應。國師云，將謂吾辜負汝，元來却是汝辜負吾。 [*Mumonkan* 17; *T* 48: 295a.23*f*]

66. For the biography of Daie Oshō, *see* PART ONE, Note 17.

67. Isshū Rōshi is here quoting from the *Shūmon mujintō ron* by Tōrei Enji: 大慧日。大悟十八度。小悟不知其數。 [*T* 81: 587c.1*f*]

68. *Gonsen* 言詮 (*yanquan*).

69. *Botsuryō no taijin, gomyakuri ni tenkyaku seraru.* 沒量大人，被語脈裏轉却。 [*Ummon kōroku* 2; *T* 47: 556c.6]

70. Ghee (*daigo* 醍醐 *tihu*), the rich oil skimmed from boiled butter, and used principally for ceremonial purposes in India. In Buddhism "ghee" is a metaphor for the perfect Buddha-truth.

71. A line from Hakuin's *Zazen wasan*. For an English translation of the entire poem, *see* PART TWO, Note 37.

72. Indian schools of Buddhist philosophy developed a system of related formulas based upon principles of logic, the purpose of which was to destroy men's delusive thinking about Reality through dialectical reasoning carried to the limits of human logic. The basic terms in this system were the "four propositions" (*shiku* 四句 *siju*) and the "hundred negations" (*hyappi* 百非 *baifei*). In the system as it is usually referred to in Zen writings, the four propositions are: "one" (*ichi* 一 *yi*), "the other" (*i* 異 *yi*), "being" (*yū* 有 *you*), and "non-being" (*mu* 無 *wu*). The hundred negations are developed from the four propositions by the following process:

"One" is considered as "one" (*ichi* 一 *yi*), as "not-one" (*hiichi* 非一 *feiyi*), as "both one and not-one" (*yaku-ichi yaku-hiichi* 亦一亦非一 *yiyi yifeiyi*), and as "neither one nor not-one" (*hiichi hi-hiichi* 非一非非一 *feiyi feifeiyi*). This method of consideration is used for each of the four propositions in turn, thus making, in all, sixteen statements or "negations." These sixteen statements are now each considered in terms of the past, present, and future, thus becoming forty-eight statements. These forty-eight statements are next considered in terms of the two states, that of "having already arisen" (*iki* 已起 *yiqi*) and that of "not yet having arisen" (*miki* 未起 *weiqi*), thus making ninety-six statements. To these ninety-six the original four propositions are now added to make the full one hundred statements, or "negations."

This is how Zen handles the matter:

> A monk once said to Baso (Mazu), "Your Reverence, abandoning the four propositions and wiping out the hundred negations, please point out to me directly the meaning of [Bodhidharma's] coming from the West." Baso said, "I don't feel like explaining to you today. Go and ask Chizō." The monk then went and asked Zō. Zō said, "Why don't you ask the Master?" The monk said, "The Master told me to ask you." Rubbing his head with his hand, Zō said, "I've got a headache today. Go and ask Brother Kai." The monk asked Kai. Kai said, "Since coming here I don't know." The monk now returned and told Baso what had taken place. Baso said, "Zō's head is white, Kai's head is black." [*Keitoku dentō roku* 7; *T* 51: 252a.23–29]

73. When Rinzai Gigen (Linji Yixuan) was taking leave of his teacher Ōbaku Kiun (Huangbo Xiyun) for the last time, Ōbaku called to his attendant, "Bring the back-rest and the arm-rest of my deceased teacher Hyakujō (Baizhang)." "Attendant, bring fire!" cried Rinzai. "That's all right," said Ōbaku, "but take them with you anyway. In the future you'll cut off the tongue of every man on earth." [*Rinzai roku*; *T* 47: 505c.2–7] In such a way Ōbaku acknowledged Rinzai's complete understanding and the Transmission of Dharma to his disciple.

74. Isshū Rōshi has here quoted from page 67 of the *Muji myō kyō* 無字妙經 The Wondrous Sutra of *Mu*, a work by his personal teacher Seigo Hōgaku 棲梧寶嶽. Hōgaku Rōshi did not state in which Chinese translation of the *Laṅkāvatāra-sūtra* this passage appears. It would seem, rather, to be the commentary of some Zen master on two important terms appearing in *kan* 3 of Guṇabhadra's version of the sutra, the *Ryōga abattara hō kyō*, namely, "to penetrate into the teachings" (*settsū* 說通 *shuotong*) and "to penetrate into the Fundamental Principle" (*shūtsū* 宗通 *zongtong*). These terms are treated at some length in Guṇabhadra's text. [*T* 16: 499b.23–c.7 and 503a.19–b.1].

75. Fuketsu Enshō 風穴延沼 (Fengxue Yanzhao, 896–973) was the sole heir of Nan'in Egyō 南院慧顒 (Nanyuan Huiyong, *d.* 930), and in the 4th generation of the Rinzai (Linji) line of Zen. Fuketsu was a decisive figure for the Rinzai School, since through him alone Rinzai's teachings were preserved and transmitted to later generations.

Enshō was born in Yokō 餘杭 (Yuhang), present Hangzhou, and his family name was Ryū 劉 (Liu). After becoming a monk, he first studied the doctrines and texts of the Tendai (Tiantai) School. Then he visited a number of Zen masters. Finally, becoming interested in the Rinzai style of Zen, he travelled north to Jōshū 汝州 (Ruzhou), in present Henan, to study under Nan'in Egyō. Nan'in, also known as Hōō Oshō 寶應和尙 (Baoying Heshang), was the heir of Rinzai's direct disciple Kōke Zonshō 興化存獎 (Xinghua Cunjiang, 830–888). If we may believe the old records, Nan'in instructed Enshō thoroughly in Rinzai's teachings, including the founder's various grouped statements, and finally transmitted to him the Dharma Seal.

After Nan'in's death, Enshō in his wanderings came one day to a deserted building on Mount Fuketsu 風穴山 (Fengxueshan) in Jōshū. The walls had crumbled and the rafters of the roof collapsed. On inquiring of an old peasant, Enshō found that these were the ruins of the former Fuketsu-ji. A group of monks who followed the Vinaya School had once lived there, but, when they became old and food was scarce because of bad harvests, they had abandoned the building, leaving behind a Buddha-statue, a drum, and a bell. When Enshō asked if he might stay there, the old peasant replied that he was welcome to. Thereafter, the Master lived a solitary life in this ruined old temple. During the day he begged his food in the nearby villages; at night he sat in meditation with burning pine resin his only light. This was a period of political turmoil in the district, and for nearly ten years no one came to seek him out.

Then gradually a few students gathered. The Prefect of Jōshū, hearing of him, visited him and became his follower. In 951, with the aid of the Prefect, Fuketsu—as he was now always called—founded the Kōe-ji 廣慧寺 (Guanghuisi) in the city of Jōshū, and began spreading the teachings of Rinzai.

One day in his seventy-eighth year, Fuketsu wrote farewell letters to his adherents. Early the following morning he took his seat in the hall, and recited the following verse to his assembled monks:

> Truth, availing itself of the flow of time,
> Must of necessity save all beings.

Remote from it though they who long for it may be,
Step by step they will approach it.
In years to come, should there be an old man
Whose feelings resemble mine,
Day after day the incense smoke will rise,
Night after night the lighted lamp will burn.
[*Fengxue chanshi yulu*; *ZZ* 2; 23.2.121d.3–4]

Then, taking the full lotus posture, he passed away.

Fuketsu left several heirs. Shuzan Shōnen 首山省念 (Shoushan Shengnian, 926–993) was the most important of these, and through him the main Rinzai line was continued. The record of Fuketsu's life and teachings is to be found in the *Fuketsu zenji goroku* 風穴禪師語錄 (*Fengxue chanshi yulu*) [*Kosonshuku goroku*, kan 7; *ZZ* 2: 23.2.120c–121d].

76. *Fuketsu Oshō chinami ni sō tou: "Go moku wa, ribi ni wataru, ikan ga fubon o tsū zen?" Ketsu iwaku: "Tokoshinae ni omou, Kōnan sangetsu no uchi, shako naku tokoro hyakka kambashi."* 風穴和尚因僧問：語默涉離微，如何通不犯。穴云，長懷江南三月裏，鷓鴣啼處百花香。 [*Mumonkan* 24; *T* 48: 296a.12–14]

77. Nansen Fugan 南泉普願 (Nanquan Puyuan, 748–835), one of the great figures of Chinese Zen of the Tang period, was in the 3rd generation of the line of Nangaku Ejō (Nanyue Huairang). He was a native of Shintei 新鄭 (Xinzheng) in Teishū 鄭州 (Zhengzhou), in modern Henan, and his family name was Ō 王 (Wang). In his later years, Nansen often referred to himself as "old man Ō," or "old teacher Ō."

When he was nine years old the boy's head was shaved by Daie Zenji 大慧禪師 (Dahui Chanshi, *n. d.*) at Daikaizan 大隗山 (Daweishan), in his native province. At thirty he took the full commandments at Mount Sū (Songshan), and thereafter gave himself up to Buddhist studies. At first he investigated the texts of the Vinaya schools. Then he frequented the preaching halls and listened to lectures on the *Laṅkāvatāra* and *Avataṁsaka* sutras. Next he devoted himself to the Sanron 三論 (Sanlun) School, a school based upon the works of Nāgārjuna and his disciples. Finally, Fugan knocked at the door of the great Zen master Baso Dōitsu 馬祖道一 (Mazu Daoyi, 709–788), the heir of Nangaku Ejō. According to the old texts, Fugan now forgot all that he had previously learned, and attained the absolute freedom of the Samādhi of Play (*yuge zammai* 遊戲

三昧 *yuxi sanmei*).

Fugan was in his forty-seventh year when, in 795, he went to Mount Nansen 南泉山 (Nanquanshan) in Chishū 池州 (Chizhou), in modern Anhui Province. There he built a retreat for himself with his own hands, and did not come down from the mountain for thirty years. In 828 Riku Kō 陸亘 (Lu Geng, 764–834), the Governor of Senjō 宣城 (Xuancheng) in the same province, heard of the Master's style of Zen, and invited him to come to the city to spread his teachings. Students now gathered around Nansen in large numbers, and his renown quickly spread far and wide.

From time to time thereafter, the Master left his mountain temple, the Nansen-in 南泉院 (Nanquanyuan), to mingle with people in the world. Once, so the story goes, he decided to visit a certain manor house. That very night the local God of the Soil informed the lord of the manor that Nansen would come the following morning, so he made preparations for the Master's visit. When Nansen arrived he asked, "How did you know I was coming?" The lord of the manor said, "Last night the local God of the Soil informed me of your Reverence's impending visit." Nansen said, "Because old Ō's practice has no power, he is spied upon by gods and demons." Thereupon, a monk who had accompanied the Master said, "Your Reverence, you are already such a good teacher, why should you be spied upon by gods and demons?" "Put another portion of food before the local God of the Soil," was Nansen's reply.

The Master also occasionally visited Governor Riku Kō in the city of Senjō. Their friendship deepened into a master-disciple relationship, and eventually Riku Kō received the Transmission of Dharma from Nansen. The Master had several other heirs, among them Chōsha Keijin 長沙景岑 (Changsha Jingcen, *n. d.*) and the famous Jōshū Jūshin (Zhaozhou Congshen). Ōbaku Kiun (Huangbo Xiyun), the teacher of Rinzai Gigen (Linji Yixuan), also spent some time as a member of Nansen's assembly, though he later became the heir of Hyakujō Ekai 百丈懷海 (Baizhang Huaihai, 720–814). The old records of Nansen's life contain a wealth of interesting anecdotes and mondos, many of which in later times became koans. The *Hekigan roku* contains six Nansen koans, and the *Mumonkan*, four.

The *Keitoku dentō roku*, kan 8, gives the following account of Nansen's last days:

> When the Master was about to die, the head monk asked him, "Your Reverence, a hundred years from now where will you be?"

> "I shall be a water buffalo at the foot of the hill," said the Master.
> "Will it be all right for me to follow you?" asked the head monk.
> "If you follow me, you must hold a stalk of grass in your mouth," was Nansen's reply.
>
> At daybreak on the morning of the 27th of January, 835, the Master said to his disciples, "The star has been fading and the lamp growing dim for a long time. Do not say that I came or went." His words ceased, and he passed away. He was in his eighty-seventh year. [*T* 51: 259a.26–b.3]

The recorded sermons of the Master are to be found in the *Chishū Nansen Fugan zenji goyō* 池州南泉普願禪師語要 (*Chizhou Nanquan Puyuan Chanshi yuyao*), in *Kosonshuku goroku* 12 [*ZZ* 2: 23.2.145c–150c].

78. *Nansen Oshō chinami ni sō toute iwaku: "Kaette hito no tame ni tokazaru tei no hō ariya?" Sen iwaku: "Ari." Sō iwaku: "Ika naru ka kore hito no tame ni tokazaru tei no hō?" Sen iwaku: "Fuzeshin, fuzebutsu, fuzemotsu."* 南泉和尚因僧問云，還有不與人説底法麼。泉云，有。僧云，如何是不與人説底法。泉云，不是心，不是佛，不是物。 [*Mumonkan* 27; *T* 48: 296b.10–13]

79. *Sō Jōshū ni tou: "Ika naru ka kore Jōshū?" Shū iwaku: "Tōmon, saimon, nammon, hokumon."* 僧問趙州，如何是趙州。州云，東門，西門，南門，北門。 [*Hekigan roku* 9; *T* 48: 149a.19*f*]

80. Chōsha Keijin 長沙景岑 (Changsha Jingcen, *n. d.*) was an heir of Nansen Fugan (Nanquan Puyuan, 748–835), and thus in the 4th generation of the line of Nangaku Ejō (Nanyue Huairang). Nothing is known of Keijin's life before he joined Nansen's assembly at the Nansen-in in Chishū (Chizhou), in modern Anhui Province. After receiving the Seal of Transmission from Nansen, Keijin went to Tanshū 潭州 (Tanzhou), in present Hunan, where he founded the Rokuon-in 鹿苑院 (Luyuanyuan). Later he left this temple, and wandered over the Chōsha 長沙 (Changsha) district to the south of Lake Dōtei 洞庭湖 (Dongtinghu), in the same province.

No further details of the Master's life are known, but a few excerpts from his sermons, as well as several poems and anecdotes, have been handed down. He left two heirs, Setchō Jōtsū 雪竇常通 (Xuedou Changtong, *n. d.*) and Kinka Genrei 金華嚴靈 (Jinhua Yanling, *n. d.*). Chōsha's posthumous title was Shōken Daishi 招賢大師 (Zhaoxian Dashi).

Once Chōsha was visiting Kyōzan Ejaku 仰山慧寂 (Yangshan Huiji, 807–883), the disciple of Isan Reiyū 潙山靈祐 (Guishan Lingyou, 771–853) and co-founder with him of the Igyō (Guiyang) School of Zen. During the evening, while they were enjoying the full moon, Kyōzan said, "All men without exception have THIS, but they cannot use it." "How true," replied Chōsha. "Now won't you please use it?" "How do you use it?" countered Kyōzan. Chōsha seized him by the chest, threw him down on the ground, and trampled on him. As he got to his feet, Kyōzan said, "You're just like a tiger." Thereafter Chōsha was popularly known as "Jin, the Tiger" (Jin Daichū 岑大蟲 Cen Dachong).

In one of his sermons Chōsha is recorded to have said to his monks:

> "The entire universe is your eye; the entire universe is your complete body; the entire universe is your own luminance; the entire universe is within your own luminance. In the entire universe there is no one who is not your own self. I repeat what I am continually saying to you: All the Buddhas of the Three Worlds (past, present, and future) and all the sentient beings in the Dharmadhātu, these are the light of Great Intrinsic Wisdom (*Mahāprajñā*)." [*Keitoku dentō roku* 10; *T* 51: 274a.12–16]

The following short poem by Chōsha has been much quoted in the Zen Sect through the centuries:

> Those who study the Way
> Do not know the real,
> Because from the first they recognize
> Only the perceiving mind.
> That which from the beginningless beginning
> Has been the source of birth and death,
> This it is that stupid men
> Call the original body.
>
> [*Ibid.*, 274b.17*f*]

81. *Chōsha ichijitsu yusan shite, kaette monshu ni itaru. Shuso tou: "Oshō izure no tokoro ni ka korai su?" Sha iwaku: "Yusan shi kitaru." Shuso iwaku: "Izure no tokoro ni ka itari kitaru?" Sha iwaru: "Hajime wa hōsō ni shitagatte sari, mata rakka o oute kaeru." So iwaku: "Ōi ni shun'i ni nitari." Sha iwaru: "Mata shūro no fukyo ni shitataru ni masareri." Setchō jakugo shite iwaru: "Tōwa o sha su."* 長沙，一日遊山，歸至門首。首座問，和尚什麽處去來。沙云，遊山來。首座云，到什麽處來。沙云，始隨

芳草去。又逐落花回。座云，大似春意。沙云，也勝秋露滴芙蕖。雪竇著語云，謝答話。 [*Hekigan roku* 36; *T* 48: 174b.3–10]

82. Haryō Kōkan 巴陵顥鑒 (Baling Haojian, *n. d.*) was a monk who lived during the Five Dynasties (Godai 五代 Wudai, 907–960) and early Song. Few details of his life are known.

When he first became a member of the assembly of Ummon Bun'en, Ummon said to him, "Seppō [i.e., Ummon's teacher, Seppō Gison 雪峰義存 (Xuefeng Yicun, 822–908)] once said to me, 'Open up the gate, Bodhidharma is coming!' What do you think about that?" "He smashed your nose," Kōkan replied. Ummon said, "The King of the Asuras got angry and hit Mount Sumeru a blow. Then he leapt up into the Brahma Heaven and told Indra about it. Is that why you're hiding your body in Japan?" "You'd better not act like that," Kōkan said. "Tell me," returned Ummon, "when your nose is smashed, what then?" Kōkan was silent. Then, according to some stories, Ummon continued, "Now I see clearly that from the first your Zen has been only lip Zen."

After that the monks called Kōkan "Chattering Kan" (Kan Takō 鑒多口 Jian Duokou). He seems to have been a somewhat eccentric man, and was noted for always carrying around with him a patched kneeling cloth (*zagu* 坐具 *zuoju*). He was regarded as unusually brilliant, however, and under Ummon attained a deep realization. When the time came, he did not write the usual composition setting forth his understanding of the profound principles of Dharma. (From the end of the Tang such a composition was required of every Zen student before he received his master's official acknowledgment of the Transmission, and, in some form or other, it is still required in Japanese Rinzai Zen today.) In place of this composition, Kōkan presented Ummon with his "Three Pivotal Words." The Master was extremely pleased with them, and is recorded to have said: "Some day, on the anniversary of my death, just recite these three pivotal words. That will be sufficient to requite my kindness."

Later, Kōkan lived at the Shinkai-in 新開院 (Xinkaiyuan) in Haryō 巴陵 (Baling) to the east of Lake Dōtei (Dongtinghu). It is from this place that his name Haryō derives. It is said that Haryō never performed the customary ceremonies on the anniversary of Ummon's death, but, following his master's instructions, merely recited the "Three Pivotal Words."

83. Haryō Oshō's Three Pivotal Words (*Haryō oshō no santengo* 巴陵和尚三

轉語 *Baling heshang sanzhuanyu*):

1. *Ika naru ka kore dō? Myōgen no hito i ni otsu.*
如何是道。明眼人落井。
2. *Ika naru ka kore suimō no ken? Sango shishi tsuki o tōjaku su.* 如何是吹毛劍。珊瑚枝枝撐著月。
3. *Sō Haryō ni tou: Ika naru ka kore Daiba shū? Ryō iwaku: Ginwanri ni yuki o moru.* 僧問巴陵，如何是提婆宗。
陵云，銀盌裏盛雪。

[*Hekigan roku* 13 (*Hyōshō* section); *T* 48: 154a.29–b.2]

The order of these three questions and answers, sometimes called Haryō's "Three Phrases" (*sanku* 三句 *sanju*), will be found to vary in different texts. Isshū Rōshi reverses the order as given in the above *Taishō* reference.

84. Mañjuśrī (Monju 文殊 Wenshu) is the bodhisattva who represents the quality of Intrinsic Wisdom (Skr. *prajñā*; *chie* 智慧 *zhihui*). He is often shown standing on Shakyamuni's left as the Guardian of Wisdom, with Samantabhadra (Fugen 拽賢 Puxian), the Bodhisattva of Universal Virtue, standing to the right in his role of guardian of Law (*ri* 理 *li*). Mañjuśrī is usually portrayed as a beautiful youth. His hair is arranged in five tufts, representing the Five Wisdoms (*gochi* 五智 *wuzhi*); in one hand he holds a sutra and in the other the sword of wisdom which cuts off all delusions; and he rides upon a lion, the symbol of power and majesty.

85. This apocryphal episode, said to have taken place just before Shakyamuni passed into his final Nirvana, seems to be another legend with doctrinal implications which was developed and given wide currency in the Chinese Zen Sect. Its origin has thus far not been traced, but as it is given here it is a combination of two stories appearing in the *Zemmon nenju shū*:

When the World Honored One was about to pass into Nirvana, Mañjuśrī requested him to turn the Wheel of Dharma a second time. The World Honored One replied: "Mañjuśrī, I have lived in the world for forty-nine years and have not yet spoken a word. You ask me to turn the Wheel of Dharma a second time. Have I ever turned the Wheel of Dharma?" [*Kan* 1: 86.10–12]

When he was about to pass into Nirvana, the World Honored One addressed the assembly, saying: "From the time I entered the Deer Garden until I finally reached the banks on the

Hiraṇyavatī River' in this entire interval of time I have not spoken a single word." [*Kan* 1: 87.2–3]

When, or by whom, these two stories were combined into their present form, we do not know.

86. *Nantō* 難透 (*nantou*).

87. *Shittsū o daha su* 打破漆桶 (*dapo qitong*), "Tub of black lacquer," is an old Zen metaphor for the mass of delusions and passions in which human beings are caught. "To smash the tub of black lacquer" is to destroy these delusions and attain satori.

88. A famous quotation from *kan* 27 of the *Daihatsu nehan gyō*: 諸佛世尊眼見佛性，如於掌中觀阿摩勒果。 [*T* 12: 527c.29*f*]

89. *Hokkutsu no sōge* 法窟爪牙. "Cave of Dharma" is another name for the training-hall (*dōjō* 道場 *daochang*) or zendo. "Talons and teeth" are the spiritual powers, such as energy, determination, faith, concentration, and the understanding that results from the experience of satori, which are gained through long Zen practice. All of these have aided the student in destroying his own delusive thinking; now armed with them, he is prepared to assist others toward the goal of enlightenment.

90. *Datsumyō no shimpu* 奪命神符. A metaphor for the spiritual power attained after the experience of the Great Death.

91. *Makai* 魔界 (*mojie*), the world of evil. The king of this world is (Skr.) Māra, the Destroyer, the arch-enemy of all ascetics and holy men. When Shakyamuni sat in meditation under the Bodhi Tree, Māra attempted by every possible means to deflect him from his purpose, himself assuming frightening and monstrous forms, and, when this failed, sending his beautiful daughters to seduce the Buddha-to-Be. The world of Māra is inhabited by Māra's cohorts—lust maras, passion maras, sin-inspiring maras, evil-thought-inspiring maras—all of whom assist their ruler in waging the unceasing war of evil against good.

92. *Kugi o nuki, ketsu o ubau* 拔釘奪楔, that is, to assist others in their efforts to release themselves from the bondage of ignorance and delusion.

93. *Daijiun* 大慈雲 (*daciyun*). The great overspreading cloud from which the rain of mercy and compassion falls universally upon all sentient beings, fecundating the seeds of incipient Buddhahood.

94. *Daihōse* 大法施 (*dafashi*). There are two general categories of almsgiving (Skr. *dāna*), the almsgiving of material things and the almsgiving of the Buddha-dharma. To give others the true teaching is considered the highest form of charity in Mahayana Buddhism.

95. *Hakuin oshō zenshū*, Vol. 2, pp. 389. 3–8.

96. Riku Kō 陸亘 (Lu Geng, 764–834) was a prominent official of the middle Tang. He was a native of the district of Go 呉 (Wu) in Soshū 蘇州 (Suzhou), in modern Jiangsu. His "style" (*tzu* 字 *azana*) was Keizan 景山 (Jingshan). After passing the government examinations in 808, he was successively appointed to a number of different provincial posts. In the later years of his life he held the office of Prefect (*shishi* 刺史 *cishi*), or Governor, of Senshū 宣州 (Xuanzhou) and Kyūshū 歙州 (Xizhou), both districts in modern Anhui, and concurrently that of Head of the Bureau of Censors. It was while he was residing in Senshū that Riku Kō met the Zen master Nansen Fugan (Nanquan Puyuan), became his devoted disciple, and, later, one of the Master's Dharma-heirs. Riku Kō died in office a few months before Nansen passed away.

Several interesting conversations between Nansen and "His Honor" (*taifu* 大夫 *dafu*) Riku Kō have been handed down:

> [On an early visit to the Master], Riku Kō said, "In olden days there was a man who raised a goose in a bottle. As the goose grew bigger, it became impossible to get it out. Now, the man did not want to break the bottle, and did not want to hurt the goose. Your Reverence, how would you get the goose out?" Nansen called out, "Taifu!" "Yes, sir," Riku Kō responded. "Now it's out!" said Nansen. At this the Taifu attained some understanding. [*Keitoku dentō roku* 10; *T* 51: 279b.1–4]
>
> [One day] the Taifu said, "In your disciple's house is a stone. Sometimes it sits, sometimes it lies down. Now I'm trying to carve it into a Buddha. Is it possible?" "Possible," replied Nansen. "It is not impossible?" queried the Taifu. "Impossible, impossible," said Nansen. [*Ibid.*, 8; *T* 51: 258b.21–23]

> Riku Kō was taking leave of the Master to return to the government office at Senjō. "When you are there, with what will you regulate the people?" asked Nansen. "I shall regulate them with wisdom," said the Taifu. "If that's so, then every living soul will suffer great misery," was the Master's response. [*Ibid.*, c.23–25]

97. The Dharma Master Jō 肇法師 (Zhao Fashi), better known as Sōjō 僧肇 (Sengzhao, 374–414), was one of the most distinguished of the early Chinese Buddhist scholar-monks. He was a native of Chōan 長安 (Chang'an). Since his family was extremely poor, when he was a small boy he began earning his living as a copyist, and thus from an early age had the opportunity to acquaint himself with classical learning and literary style. He was particularly drawn to the *Rōshi* 老子 (*Laozi*) and the *Sōji* 莊子 (*Zhuangzi*). But one day he happened to read the old translation of the *Vimalakīrti-nirdeśa*, and instantly realized that this was a more profound work than any he had hitherto encountered. He now left his home, became a monk, and devoted himself to the study of Buddhist texts, both Hinayana and Mahayana. By the time he was twenty he was famous in the capital Chōan for his brilliance in metaphysical discussion.

A few years later, hearing that the famous Kuchan monk Kumārajīva (350–*ca.* 409) was being held captive in Kozō 姑臧 (Guzang), then the capital of the kingdom of Ryō 涼 (Liang), in what is now Gansu Province, Sōjō journeyed to this city in the far west and became the Master's disciple. When Kumārajīva was brought to Chōan in January, 402, by Yō Kō 姚興 (Yao Xing, *r.* 394–416) of the Later Qin (Goshin 後秦 Houqin 384–417), Sōjō accompanied him to the capital, and was appointed one of the large group of distinguished scholars and monks gathered to assist Kumārajīva in his translation work.

When Kumārajīva had completed his translation of the *Vimalakīrti-nirdeśa* (*Yuimakitsu shosetsu kyō*) Sōjō immediately compiled the *Chū Yuimakitsu kyō* 注維摩詰經 (*Zhu Weimojie jing*) [*T* 38: 327a–420a]. This was a work consisting of the lectures on the sutra given by Kumārajīva to his disciples during the course of the translation work, and interpretations of the sutra by Sōjō and his fellow disciple Dōshō 道生 (Daosheng, 355–434).

Shortly after the appearance in 404 of Kumārajīva's translation in 27 *kan* of the *Mahāprajñāpāramitā-sūtra* (*Makahannya haramitsu kyō* 摩訶般若波羅蜜經 *Mohobore boluomi jing*) [*T* 8: 217–424], Sōjō wrote his first original work, a treatise entitled "Prajñā Is without Knowledge" (*Hannya muchi ron* 般若無知論 *Bore wuzhi lun*). The Master is said to have praised his disciple's work highly, and it was thereafter sent to several noted Buddhist clerics living in other parts of the country, all of whom replied with letters of admiration and requests for further clarification of difficult points. Sōjō's famous *Jōron* is a compilation comprised of this treatise, together with two letters relating to it, and three other treatises written somewhat later.

In addition to the *Chū Yuimakitsu kyō* and the *Jōron*, the only works definitely known to be from Sōjō's hand are two prefaces. The first [*T* 1: 1a–b] is a preface to the translation of the *Dīrghāgama* (*Jō agon kyō* 長阿含經 *Chang ahan jing*) by Buddhayaśas (*n. d.*) and Jiku Butsunen 竺佛念 (Zhu Fonian, *n. d.*); the other [*T* 30: 167c–168a], a preface to Kumārajīva's translation of the *Śata-śāstra* (*Hyaku ron* 百論 *Bailun*). There are still extant several other prefaces, a commentary on the *Diamond Sutra*, and a treatise entitled *Hōzō ron* 寶藏論 (*Baozang lun*) [*T* 45: 143b–150a] which are attributed to him, but it seems likely that these were written at the beginning of Tang or earlier by some scholar-monk or monks who appropriated Sōjō's name.

According to an old tradition in the Zen Sect, a tradition for which there are no substantial grounds, a few years after Kumārajīva's death Sōjō incurred the displeasure of the Shin ruler Yō Kō, and was ordered to kill himself. He begged for a reprieve of seven days, and during that time wrote the above-mentioned *Hōzō ron*. The same tradition holds that, just before killing himself, Sōjō wrote the following poem:

> The four great elements
> From the first have been masterless;
> The five accumulations of shadows
> In their origin are empty.
> Laying one's head down
> On the naked blade of a sword
> Is not one whit different
> From cutting through the spring breeze.
>
> [*Keitoku dentō roku* 27; *T* 51: 435b.1*f*]

Several koans, popular since Tang times, contain what are believed to be phrases taken from the *Hōzō ron*, for example, the first part of the Ummon koan in Case 62 of the *Hekigan roku* [*T* 48: 193c.22–25].

(The dates for Kumārajīva and Sōjō given here and elsewhere throughout this work are those proposed by TSUKAMOTO Zenryū 塚本善隆 in his "Dates of Kumārajīva 鳩摩羅什 and Sengzhao 僧肇 Reexamined," in the *Silver Jubilee Volume of the Zinbun Kagaku Kenkyusyo*, pp. 568–584.)

98. *Riku Kō taifu, Nansen to gowa suru tsuide, Riku iwaku: "Jō Hōshi iwaku, 'Tenchi to ware to dōkon; bambutsu ware to ittai.' Mata hanahada kikai nari." Nansen teizen no hana o sashite, taifu o meshite iwaku: "Toki no hito kono isshu no hana o miru koto, yume no gotoku ni ainitari."* 陸亘大夫與南泉語話次，陸云，肇法師道，天地與我同根，萬物與我一體。也甚奇怪。南泉指庭前花，召大夫云，時人見此一株花，如夢相似。 [*Hekigan roku* 40; *T* 48: 178a.3–7] RIKU Kō was quoting from Sōjō's "*Nehan mumyō ron*." [*T* 45: 159b.28*f*]

99. *Monken kakuchi ichiichi ni arazu, sanga wa kyōchū ni atte mizu. Sōten tsuki ochite yo masa ni nakaba naran to su. Tare ka chōtan to tomo ni kage o terashite samukaran?* 聞見覺知非一一，山河不在鏡中觀。霜天月落夜將半，誰共澄潭照影寒。 [*Hekigan roku* 40; *T* 48: 178b.18–21]

100. Goso Hōen 五祖法演 (Wuzu Fayan, 1024?–1104) was an important master in the 3rd generation of the Yōgi (Yangqi) line of Rinzai (Linji) Zen. He was a native of Hasei 巴西 (Baxi) in Menshū 綿州 (Mianzhou), in present Sichuan, and his family name was Tō 鄧 (DENG). He had already reached the age of thirty-five before he left his home to become a monk. After taking the commandments, he first studied the "Consciousness Only" (*yuishiki* 唯識 *weishi*) doctrines at the provincial capital of Seito 成都 (Chengdu). But becoming dissatisfied with these studies, he journeyed to Kōnan 江南 (Jiangnan), the district south of the Yangzi River, in present Jiangsu and Anhui, to seek a teacher in the sect that "transmits the Buddha-mind."

Eventually he came to Enkan Hōen 圓鑑法遠 (Yuanjian Fayuan, 991–1067), in the 7th generation of the Rinzai line, who was living on Mount Fu 浮山 (Fushan) in Jōshū 舒州 (Shuzhou), north of the river in present Anhui. The first time he met Enkan, the old master said to him: "The Tathāgata had a secret word, but Mahākāśyapa could not keep it hidden." Hōen pondered on this statement for about a year. Then the Master told him that since he, Enkan, was becoming aged, it would be better for Hōen to go to Shutan Zenji 守端禪師 (Shouduan Chanshi, 1025–1072), a direct heir of Yōgi Hoe (Yangqi Fanghui), who was then living at Hakuunzan

白雲山 (Baiyunshan) in the same district. Hōen followed the old master's advice, and, after a number of years of practice, became Shutan's most outstanding heir.

After Shutan's death, Hōen spent some time at Mount Shimen 四面山 (Simianshan), a part of Mount Hakuun. Then he journeyed to Kishū 蘄州 (Qizhou), in modern Hubei, and took up his residence on the famous Yellow Plum Mountain (Ōbaizan 黃梅山 Huangmeishan), where the Fifth Patriarch Gunin (Hongren) had lived four hundred years earlier. This mountain, also known as "East Mountain" (Tōzan 東山 Dongshan), after Gunin's death had been given the name "Fifth Patriarch's Mountain" (Gosozan 五祖山 Wuzushan) in the Patriarch's memory. It is from the fact that Hōen lived for over thirty years on this mountain that his name Goso Hōen derives.

Hōen was a straightforward, unassuming man, well-known for the plain, even colloquial, style of his lectures. He used to refer to himself as "Uncle Tō of West River" (Seisen Tōshiha 西川鄧師波 Xichuan Dengshibo), or "the fellow who lives somewhere-or-other at the foot of East Mountain" (Tōzanka sahentei 東山下左邊底 Dongshanxia zuobiandi). At his monastery he trained many students and developed a number of important heirs, the most famous among whom was Engo Kokugon (Yuanwu Keqin). (Cf. Part One, Note 16.)

The *Katai futō roku* in *kan* 8 gives the following account of the end of Hōen's life:

> One day, looking at his disciples, the Master said, "After my death how will you students carry on my teaching?" Bukkan said, "The brilliantly colored phoenix dances in the red heaven." Butsugen said, "The iron snake lies across the old road." Raising his leg, Bukka (Engo) said, "Look at my uplifted foot!" "He who will destroy my sect is Kokugon," the Master said.
>
> In the early summer of 1104, Hōen took the high seat and said farewell to his disciples in these words: "Jōshū Oshō had a last phrase. How do you understand it? Let someone step forward and speak. If you can understand, there will be no hindrance to your freedom and joy. If perchance you cannot, how shall I explain this good thing to you?" The Master sat quietly for a time, then continued "My explanation is ended. But not every one knows it. Do you want to understand? For the rich man a thousand mouths are too few; for the poor man one body is too much. Farewell!"

> At that time the main gate of the temple was under construction. The Master now went personally to inspect the work. [To the workmen] he said, "All of you must exert yourselves. I shall not come again." Then he returned to his own rooms, washed his hair, and bathed his body. The next morning at dawn he quietly passed away, sitting in the full lotus posture.
>
> That night, mountains were demolished and rocks came hurtling down. For forty *li* around, the cliffs and valleys shook and roared. The ashes from his funeral pyre were as abundant as rain. His memorial tower was constructed on the south side of East Mountain. The Master's years were more than eighty. [*ZZ* 2 乙: 10.1.68 d.13–69a.5]

The record of the Master's teachings, compiled by several of his disciples, will be found in the *Hōen zenji goroku* 法演禪師語錄 (Fayan chanshi yulu) [*T* 47: 649a–669a].

101. *Goso iwaku: "Tatoeba suikogyū no sōrei o suguru ga gotoshi; zukaku shitei subete sugiowaru, nani ni yotte ka biha suguru koto o ezaru."* 五祖曰，譬如水牯牛過窓櫺，頭角四蹄都過了，因甚麼尾巴過不得。[*Mumonkan* 38: *T* 48: 297c.12–14]

102. Sozan Kōnin 疎山光仁 (Sushan Guangren, 837–909) was a monk in the 2nd generation of the Chinese Sōtō (Caodong) School. He was a native of Shinkan 新淦 (Xin'gan) in Kisshū 吉州 (Jizhou), in present Jiangxi. At first he listened to lectures and studied Buddhist doctrines at the Tōrinji 東林寺 (Donglinsi) on the Rōzan 廬山 (Lushan). But he soon became dissatisfied and exclaimed, "[This is just] investigating line by line and counting rows of black letters. Words aren't so good as silence. [This is] rejecting oneself and looking to others for assistance. The false isn't so good as the true." Whereupon he tucked up his robes and began his wanderings. [*Rentō eyō* 22; *ZZ* 2 乙: 9.5.401b.13*f*]

After visiting a number of famous Zen masters, including Isan Reiyū (Guishan Lingyou), Ummon Bun'en (Yunmen Wenyan), Kassan Zenne (Jiashan Shanhui), and others, Kōnin finally went to Tōzan 洞山 (Dongshan) in Inshū 筠州 (Yunzhou), in modern Jiangxi, where he joined the assembly of Tōzan Ryōkai (Dongshan Liangjie), one of the founders of the Chinese Sōtō Sect. After Tōzan's death, Kōnin went to live on Mount So 疎山 (Sushan) in Bushū 撫州 (Fuzhou), also in Jiangxi, and there spent the remainder of his life promulgating the Sōtō teachings. He left four heirs.

Nin Zenji, as the Master is usually called, was an ugly man of very short stature, and inclined to be sickly. He was often referred to somewhat contemptuously as "Uncle Dwarf," or the "Bantam Teacher." On the other hand, he was mentally very alert. Among his fellow-monks he was the cleverest and sharpest in argument. When he was a member of Tōzan's assembly, it was said of him that "his innate power in displaying the innermost mystery was that of a man who could chew the iron tip of an arrow. Everyone considered him an expert in estimating men's characters, and when it came to all kinds of samadhi, they said: 'We've only to ask Uncle Dwarf.'" [*Keitoku dentō roku* 17; *T* 51: 339c.12–21]

But the old records consistently speak of Nin Zenji disparagingly. The *Zenrin sōbō den* 禪林憎寶傳 (*Chanlin sengbao zhuan*), a 12th century biographical collection, recounts the following unpleasant story about him:

> Knowing that [Tōzan Ryōkai] was about to transmit his Dharma to his disciple [Sōzan Honjaku], Uncle Dwarf secretly crawled under the Master's rope-bottomed chair and lay down on his stomach. Ryōkai was unaware of this. At midnight the Master handed to his disciple [Sōzan] the Jeweled-mirror Samadhi, the Secret of the Five Ranks, and the Three Kinds of Leakage, previously given him by his master Ungan. When the transmission was completed, Sōzan bowed twice and hurried out. Uncle Dwarf now stuck out his head and bawled, "Tōzan's Zen is in the palm of my hand!" Ryōkai was greatly astonished, and said, "Stealing the Dharma by using the dirtiest of means will avail you nothing." Later everything turned out just as he had said. [*ZZ* 2 乙: 10.3.222b.8–11]

(In the Chinese, Ryōkai's rebuke contains a double-entendre referring to Kōnin's inability to keep from vomiting whenever he wanted to speak about the Dharma. The biographer's concluding remark undoubtedly refers to this, since the illness continued many years. In spite of the episode quoted above, Kōnin seems eventually to have received inka from Ryōkai, as he is everywhere listed as one of that master's heirs.)

Nin Zenji seems to have had some literary bent for he is said to have left a treatise on Kegon (Huayan) doctrines, and a series of poems, but these are no longer extant. Just before he died, he wrote the following verse:

> My path lies beyond the blue sky,
> Where white clouds have no resting place.

In the world there is a rootless tree,
Its withered leaves, escorted by the wind, return.
[*Keitoku dentō roku* 17; *T* 51: 340a.11*f*]

103. Rasan Dōkan 羅山道閑 (Luoshan Daoxian, *n. d.*), a monk in the 7th generation of the line of Seigen Gyōshi (Qingyuan Xingsi), lived from the end of the Tang into the early years of the Five Dynasties (Godai 五代 Wudai, 907–960). His family name was Chin 陳 (Chen), and he was a native of Chōkei 長溪 (Changxi) in Fukushū 福州 (Fuzhou), in present Fujian Province. After becoming a monk and taking the full commandments, he travelled about visiting many Zen masters, but found none who fully satisfied him. Finally he went to the Gantōzan 巖頭山 (Yantoushan), to the east of Lake Dōtei (Dongtinghu) in present Hunan, where Gantō Zenkatsu 巖頭全奯 (Yantou Quanhuo, 828–887), an heir of Tokusan Senkan (Deshan Xuanjian), was living. Dōkan joined Gantō's assembly, and eventually received the Seal of Transmission from him.

After he had left the Gantōzan, Dōkan went on a long pilgrimage which took him to Godaizan (Wutaishan) in the far north. He remained several years on this mountain sacred to the Bodhisattva Mañjuśrī. After he had returned to the south, he was invited by Ō Shinchi 王審知 (Wang Shenzhi, 862–925), Prince of the State of Bin 閩 (Min), in present Fujian, to live at the Rasan 羅山 (Luoshan). Although Ō Shinchi bestowed upon him the title Hōbō Daishi 法寶大師 (Fabao Dashi), the Master was usually referred to as Rasan. According to Rasan's biography in *kan* 17 of the *Keitoku dentō roku*:

> On the day when the Master was to give his first sermon, he had no more than taken the high seat in the hall when he arranged his robes as for leave-taking, and said, "Farewell!" He remained sitting in silence for a little while, then continued, "If there is anyone who has not yet understood, let him come forward." A certain monk stepped out from the assembly and bowed. Raising his voice, the Master cried, "How pitiful!" The monk tried to ask a question, but the Master shouted, "Get out!" … …
>
> When Rasan felt that his death was approaching, he took the high seat to give a last sermon to his assembled monks. He sat quietly for a little, then extended his left hand. The monk in charge of temple affairs (*shuji* 主事 *zhushi*) did not fathom the Master's meaning and had the monks on the east side step

back. When the Master extended his right hand, the *shuji* had the monks on the west side step back. Then the Master said to the assembly, "If you want to requite the kindness of Buddha, the best way is to spread the great teaching. I am going home, I am going home. Farewell!" As the Master's words ended, a smile came over his face and he passed away. [*T* 51: 341a.25–b.26]

104. The Daiyurei 大庾嶺 (Dayuling) is a range of peaks on the boundary between present Guangdong and Jiangxi provinces. It is here that the Sixth Patriarch hid himself for a number of years after receiving the Transmission. The biographies of Rasan Dōkan do not mention his staying here, but since, in the koan, he is said to have been living in a hermitage on the mountain, perhaps this episode took place before he went to live at Rasan.

105. *Bushū Sozan Nin Zenji, chinami ni shuji no sō shi no tame ni jutō o tsukuri owari, kitatte shi ni mōsu. Shi iwaku: "Nanji ikusen o motte ka shōnin ni atau?"*

Sō iwaku: "Issai oshō ni ari."

Shi iwaku: "Sammon o motte shōnin ni atauru o yoshi to nasan ka? Ryōmon o motte shōnin ni atauru o yoshi to nasan ka? Ichimon o motte shōnin ni atauru o yoshi to nasan ka? Moshi iieba, waga tame ni shitashiku jutō o tsukure."

Sono sō bōzen tari.

Rasan toki ni Daiyurei ni atte jūan su. Nochi ni sō atte Dairei ni itari, zenna o koji su. Rei iwaku: "Kaette hito no iiuru ari ya?"

Sō iwaku: "Imada hito no iiuru arazu."

Rei iwaku: "Nanji kaette Sozan ni koji shite ie: 'Moshi sammon o motte shōnin ni ataeba, oshō kono shō ketsujō shite tō o eji; moshi ryōmon o motte shōnin ni ataeba, oshō to shōnin to tomo ni issekishu o idasan; moshi ichimon o motte shōnin ni ataeba, shōnin o tairui shite, bishu daraku sen.'"

Sō kaette Sozan ni koji su. Shi igi o gu shi, haruka ni Dairei o nozonde raihai shi, santan shite iwaku: "Masa ni omoeri hito nashi to, Daiyurei ni kobutsu ari. Hikari o hanatte, ite sukan ni itaru. Shikari to iedomo, mata kore rōgetsuri no renge."

Dairei kikiete iwaku: "Ware yomo ni iu, hayaku kore kimō nagaki koto sūshaku."

撫州疎山仁禪師因主事僧爲師造壽塔了，來白師。師曰，汝將幾錢與匠人。僧云，一切在和尙。師云，爲將三文與匠人好，爲將兩文與匠人好，爲將一文與匠人好，若道得，與吾親造壽塔。其僧茫然。羅山時在大庾嶺住庵。後有僧到大嶺，擧似前話。嶺云，還有人道得麼。僧云，未有人道得。嶺云，你歸擧似疎山道，若將三文與匠人，和尙此生決定不得塔。若將兩文與匠人，和尙與匠人共出一隻手。若將一文與匠人，帶累匠人眉鬚墮落。僧回擧似疎山。師具威儀，遙望大嶺禮拜，讃歎云，將謂無人，大庾嶺有古佛，放光射至此間，雖然，也是臘月裡蓮花。大嶺聞得云，我與麼道，早是龜毛長數尺。 [*Kattō shū*, 2, 5]

106. Suigan Reisan 翠巖令參 (Cuiyan Lingcan, *n. d.*), a monk who lived during the Five Dynasties (907–960), was in the 7th generation of the line of Seigen Gyōshi (Qingyuan Xingsi). Reisan was a native of Koshū 湖州 (Huzhou), in modern Zhejiang. After visiting a number of Zen masters in various parts of the country, he came to Seppōzan 雪峰山 (Xuefengshan), in present Fujian Province, and joined the assembly of the famous Seppō Gison 雪峰義存 (Xuefeng Yicun, 822–908), an heir of Tokusan Senkan (Deshan Xuanjian). After Reisan had received the Transmission from Seppō he went to live on Suiganzan 翠巖山 (Cuiyanshan) in Meishū 明州 (Mingzhou), in present Zhejiang. There he remained for nearly thirty years.

In his later life, Suigan was invited by the King of Go-Etsu 吳越 (Wu-Yue), Sen Kōshuku 錢弘俶 (Qian Hongchu, 929–988), to take up his residence at the Ryūsaku-ji 龍冊寺 (Longcesi), a temple within the capital city of Go-Etsu, present-day Hangzhou. Here, under royal patronage, the Master seems to have spent his remaining years propagating Zen with considerable success.

Though few details regarding Suigan's life have been transmitted, a verse which he seems to have written for his students has come down to us:

How pitiful, how very pitiful!
To search for dry ashes in the waves of the sea.
If you would only withdraw your hands,
At that very moment IT would come.

[*Sodō shū* 10: Vol. 3, p. 57.8*f*]

107. Hofuku Jūten 保福從展 (Baofu Congzhan, *d.* 928) was a monk in the 7th generation of the line of Seigen Gyōshi (Qingyuan Xingsi). His family

name was CHIN 陳 (CHEN) and he was a native of Fukushū 福州 (Fuzhou), modern Fujian. At the age of fifteen he became a monk and a disciple of the great Zen master Seppō Gison (Xuefeng Yicun), who lived on Seppōzan (Xuefengshan) in Fukushū. After three years of practice, Jūten went on a long pilgrimage, during the course of which he took the full commandments at the Daichū-ji 大中寺 (Dazhongsi), in the same province, and visited many masters. Thereafter he rejoined his former master's assembly on Seppōzan, remaining there for many years and becoming one of Seppō Zenji's several distinguished heirs.

Among the many monks who thronged around Seppō in those days were Ummon Bun'en 雲門文偃 (Yunmen Wenyan, 862/4–949), Chōkei Eryō 長慶慧稜 (Changqing Huileng, 854–932), Gensha Shibi 玄沙師備 (Xuansha Shibei, 835–908), and Kuzan Jin'an 鼓山神晏 (Gushan Shenyan, 863–929). All, including Jūten, were close friends, and all are said to have constantly discussed together various problems relating to koans. Undoubtedly this early interchange of views and experiences between men who were to become leading Zen masters in their generation had much to do with the form which koans and the methods of koan study took from that time on.

In 918, Ō Empin 王延彬 (WANG Yanbin, *n. d.*), Prefect (*shishi* 刺史 *cishi*) of Senshū 泉州 (Quanzhou), in present Fujian, became Jūten's disciple, and assisted the Master in founding the Hofuku-in 保福院 (Baofuyuan) in that city. There Hofuku, as Jūten was now generally known, spent the rest of his life vigorously promulgating the style of Zen made famous by his master Seppō Gison.

According to the biography of Hofuku in *kan* 19 of the *Keitoku dentō roku*:

> One day in the third year of the Tensei 天成 (Tiancheng) era (926–929) of Tang, the Master seemed slightly indisposed. When a monk entered his room to inquire how he was feeling, the Master said, "You and I are intimate friends of long standing. Have you any remedy for me?" "Yes," said the monk, "I have many remedies, but I hear that you can't practice abstinence."
>
> To the assembly of monks the Master said, "For the past ten days my strength has been failing. This merely means that my time has come." A monk asked, "Should it be, Master, that your time has really come, which would you prefer, to go or to stay?" "Dao!" replied Hofuku. "In that case," replied the monk, "I won't

disturb you further." "Ah, losing one's money and incurring punishment as well," said the Master. Then, sitting quietly in the lotus posture, he passed away. This was the third month and the eleventh day (April 4, 928). [*T* 51: 355b.29–c.7]

108. Chōkei Eryō 長慶慧稜 (Changqing Huileng, 854–932) was a monk in the 7th generation of the line of Seigen Gyōshi (Qingyuan Xingsi). His family name was Son 孫 (Sun), and he was a native of Enkan 鹽官 (Yanguan), in present Zhejiang Province. At the age of thirteen he went to Soshū 蘇州 (Suzhou), in Jiangsu, and there at the Tsūgen-ji 通玄寺 (Tongxuansi) had his head shaved and took the full commandments. In 878 he journeyed south to the country of Bin 閩 (Min), where he visited the Sai-in 西院 (Xiyuan) in Chōraku 長樂 (Changle), in present Fujian, and had an interview with Reiun Shigon 靈雲志勤 (Lingyun Zhiqin, *n. d.*), an heir of Isan Reiyū (Guishan Lingyou). Reiun had attained satori when he saw the peach flowers in bloom, and his verse written at the time is famous in Zen:

> Some thirty years I sought an expert swordsman.
> How many times leaves fell, how many times branches
> burst into bud!
> But from the instant I saw the peach flowers blooming,
> From that moment to this I have had no doubts.
> [*Keitoku dentō roku* 11; *T* 51: 285a.25*f*]

But Eryō presently went on to Fukushū (Fuzhou) to join the assembly of Seppō Gison (Xuefeng Yicun).

Seppō soon discerned that Eryō was an exceptionally earnest student. (Tradition has it that during his twenty-odd years of practice he wore out seven sitting cushions.) According to the story as it is given in *kan* 10 of the *Sodō shū* [Vol. 3, pp. 66–67], the Master said to Eryō one day, "I'm going to give you the same treatment a horse doctor uses in restoring a dead horse to life. Can you take it?" "Whatever you say I'll do," replied the young monk. "Well," continued Seppō, "you don't need to come to me for sanzan three or four times a day. Just keep your mind and body as still as a charred tree stump in the mountains. Then, if you're slow, you'll hit on something after ten years; if you're middling, after seven; or if you're fast, after three."

For two and a half years Eryō practiced zazen diligently. Then one night, while sitting in the meditation hall, he felt restless and disturbed.

He left the hall, and walked two or three times around the tea garden. Suddenly overcome by an irresistible desire to sleep, he lay down on the bare ground. When he awoke sometime later he got up and returned to the meditation hall. As he was rolling up the bamboo screen in the entrance, a beam of light from the lantern within the hall struck his eye, and in that moment he attained satori. Eryō went immediately to the Master's quarters, but, finding that Seppō was asleep, stood outside leaning on a pillar. Suddenly a laugh escaped him. The Master, hearing it, came to the entrance. "What are you doing here in the middle of the night?" he asked. In reply, Eryō recited the following verse:

"How strange! How strange!
When the screen is rolled up, all under Heaven is complete.
Were someone to ask me what I've seen,
I'd pick up my whisk and hit him on the mouth."

When Seppō heard these words he was greatly pleased. "I've had seventeen hundred disciples since I came to live in this temple," he said, "and now at last I've found half a holy man."

The following morning, when Seppō had taken the high seat in the hall, he asked Eryō to step forward. "The assembly is doubtful about what happened to you last night. They seem to think that you and I staged the whole affair. Now, since you've attained some insight, speak a word." Thereupon Eryō recited these lines:

"Within the ten thousand forms, one naked body;
Only he who himself affirms it can be intimate with it;
Until yesterday I was mistakenly pursuing it halfway;
Today I clearly see the ice within the fire."

Thereafter, for over twenty years, Eryō went back and forth between Seppōzan, the Sai-in in Chōraku, and other temples. Finally, in 906, Ō Empin (Wang Yanbin), the Prefect of Senshū (Quanzhou), became the Master's disciple, and built for him the Shōkei-in 招慶院 (Zhaoqingyuan) in the city of Senshū. Some years later, Eryō was invited by Empin's uncle, Ō Shinchi (Wang Shenzhi), Prince of Bin, to live at the Sai-in. When an Imperial tablet inscribed with the characters 長慶院, "Chōkei-in" (Changqingyuan), was bestowed upon the temple, its name was changed to accord with the inscription, and Eryō was thereafter known as Chōkei Oshō 長慶和尚 (Changqing Heshang).

Since this was a period of great political disorder and resultant wars, many monks and laymen came to Fukushū from the north and took refuge in the temples there. It is said that, during the remainder of the Master's life, there were never less than fifteen hundred people living in the Chōkei-in. After the Master's death, the royal family of Bin bestowed upon him the posthumous title of Chōkaku Zenji 超覺禪師 (Chaojue Chanshi).

(*The Empire of Min*, by Edward H. SCHAFER, contains interesting material on the WANG family, including details regarding their relationship to various Zen monks.)

109. *Suigan gematsu ni shu ni shimeshite iwaku: Ichige irai, hindei no tame ni setsuwa su. Miyo, Suigan ga bimō ari ya?" Hofuku iwaku: "Zoku to naru hito kokoro kyo nari." Chōkei iwaku: "Shō zeri." Ummon iwaku: "Kan."* 翠巖夏末示衆云，一夏以 來，爲兄弟説話。看。翠巖眉毛在麼。保福云，作賊人心虛。長慶云，生也。雲門云，關。 [*Hekigan roku* 8; *T* 48: 148b.1–4]

110. Enkan Saian 鹽官齊安 (Yanguan Qi'an, 750?–842) was a monk in the 3rd generation of the line of Nangaku Ejō (Nanyue Huairang). His family name was RI 李 (LI), and he was a native of Kaimon 海門 (Haimen) in Yōshū 揚州 (Yangzhou), in modern Jiangsu. After becoming a monk he spent some time in the study of the Vinaya. Then, hearing of Baso Dōitsu (Mazu Daoyi), who was living on the Kyōkōzan 龔公山 (Gonggongshan) in Kōshū 洪州 (Hongzhou), in modern Jiangxi, he went to visit that great master, became his disciple, and, eventually, one of his many heirs.

For thirty years after Baso's death Saian wandered from place to place. Finally, when he was over seventy, he settled for a time at the Hōraku-ji 法樂寺 (Falesi) on Shōzan 蕭山 (Xiaoshan) in Esshū 越州 (Yuezhou), in present Zhejiang. Sometime later he was invited to reside at the Chinkoku Kaishō-in 鎮國海昌院 (Zhenguo Haichangyuan), a temple in Enkan 鹽宫 (Yanguan), now the Hangzhou district. From this place derives the name by which he is most often called. In his early nineties, the Master suddenly passed away one day while attending a feast.

Enkan's family was distantly related to the ruling house of the Tang. At the time that RI Chin 李忱 (LI Chen) was being pursued by his nephew, Emperor Busō 武宗 (Wuzong, *r.* 841–846), Chin, disguised as a Buddhist layman named Yūkō 有光 (Youguang), took refuge in Enkan's temple. When, on Busō's death, RI Chin ascended the throne as Emperor Sensō 宣宗 (Xuanzong, *r.* 846–860), he did not forget Enkan's kindness.

He immediately put an end to the widespread persecution of Buddhism which had taken place during his predecessor's reign, and did much to restore to that faith some of its former power and prestige.

After Enkan's death, the Emperor bestowed upon him the posthumous title Gokū Zenji 悟空禪師 (Wukong Chanshi). The memorial stupa which he built for Enkan is said to have been the most magnificent constructed for a Buddhist monk up to that time.

It was Enkan's disciple Gikū 義空 (Yikong, *n. d.*) who was the first to bring to Japan the Sixth Patriarch's Zen, that is, the Zen of the Southern School. The famous Japanese Shingon priest Kōbō Daishi 弘法大師 (774–835), the year before he died, suggested to Empress Danrin 壇林 (787–851), consort of Emperor Saga 嵯峨 (*r.* 810–823), that an Imperial messenger be sent to China to invite a Zen monk to Japan. When the messenger returned some fifteen years later he was accompanied by Giku. On the occasion of her first meeting with the Chinese monk, the Empress is said to have composed the following verse:

> Clouds rising over the mountains of Tang
> Are smoke from fires burning in our land.

Giku's mission was not successful, however, and after a few years he returned to China, leaving, so tradition has it, only a stone inscription near the Rashōmon in Kyoto to bear witness to his attempt to propagate Zen in the eastern land.

111. *Enkan ichijitsu jisha o yobu: "Waga tame ni saigyū no sensu o mochikitare." Jisha iwaku: "Sensu yaburenu." Kan iwaku: "Sensu sude ni yaburenaba, ware ni saigyūji o kaeshi kitare." Jisha tai nashi.* 鹽官一日喚侍者，與我將犀牛扇子來。侍者云，扇子破也。宫云，扇子既破，還我犀牛兒來。侍者無對。 [*Hekigan roku* 91; *T* 48: 215c.1–4]

112. *Saigyū no sensu mochiuru koto taji, monjaku sureba ganrai sō ni shirazu. Kagiri naki seifū to zukaku to, kotogotoku un'u no satte oigataki ni onaji.* 犀牛扇子用多時。問着元來總不知。無限清風與頭角。盡同雲雨去難追。 [*Hekigan roku* 91; *T* 48: 216a.12–15]

113. *Jiji muge hokkai* 事事無礙法界, the fourth of the Four Dharmadhātu of the Kegon (Huayan) School. Cf. Part One, Note 24.

114. *Tōzan goi* 洞山五位 (*Dongshan wuwei*).

115. Tōzan Ryōkai 洞山良价 (Dongshan Liangjie, 807–869) was the heir of Ungan Donjō 雲巖曇晟 (Yunyan Tansheng, 780?–841), and thus in the 5th generation of the line of Seigen Gyōshi (Qingyuan Xingsi). He was born in Kaikei 會稽 (Kuaiqi), in present Zhejiang Province, and his family name was Yu 俞 (Yu). While still a boy, he was put under a teacher at a country temple. One day he was told by his teacher to recite the *Hannya shingyō* (Heart Sutra). When he came to the passage "there is no eye, no ear, no nose, no tongue, no thought," he stopped and quickly ran his hand over his face. Then he said to his teacher, "I have eyes and ears, a nose and a tongue. Why does the sutra say I haven't?" The teacher, astonished at the boy's unusual remark, said, "I am not your teacher," and sent him to Reimoku Zenji 靈默禪師 (Lingmo Chanshi, 747–818), one of the many heirs of Baso Dōitsu (Mazu Daoyi).

Later, Ryōkai visited Nansen Fugan (Nanquan Puyuan), another of Baso's heirs, and after that, Isan Reiyū (Guishan Lingyou), in the 3rd generation of Baso's line. In the course of a conversation with Isan, Ryōkai asked the Master to explain to him the meaning of "the preaching of Dharma by the sentientless" (*mujō seppō* 無情說法 (*muqing shuofa*), a famous phrase originating with Nan'yō Echū 南陽慧忠 (Nanyang Huizhong), one of the Sixth Patriarch's heirs. Though Ryōkai could not comprehend Isan's answer, the Master recognized the young monk's abilities, and advised him to visit Ungan Donjō, an heir of Yakusan Igen 藥山惟儼 (Yueshan Weiyan, 745–828).

Ryōkai went straightway to Mount Ungan 雲巖山 (Yunyanshan) in Tanshū 潭州 (Tanzhou), in modern Hunan.

> [After he had explained to Ungan the circumstances of his coming] Ryōkai asked: "Who can hear the preaching of the Dharma by the sentientless?" "The sentientless can hear it," replied Ungan. "Your Reverence, do you hear it?" asked Ryōkai. "If I were to hear it, you would not hear my preaching," the Master answered. "Why do I not hear it?" Ryōkai asked. Raising his whisk, Ungan asked, "Do you hear it?" "No," replied Ryōkai. "When you don't hear even my preaching how can you hear that of the sentientless?" said the Master. "On what work is the phrase 'the preaching of Dharma by the sentientless' based?" Ryōkai now asked. Ungan said, "Have you not seen the passage in the *Amida kyō* which says: 'The streams, the birds, the trees, the groves, all chant the name of Buddha, all chant the name of Dharma'?" At these words Ryōkai

attained some understanding. He recited the following verse:

> "How wonderful, how very wonderful!
> The preaching of the sentientless is inconceivable!
> Listening with the ear, it is difficult to understand,
> Hearing with the eye, then you know it."
>
> [*Tōzan goroku*; *T* 47: 507c.4–13]

Ungan transmitted to Ryōkai the "secret teaching" he had received from his master Yakusan, though the disciple seems not to have fully comprehended it until after Ungan's death. (For their last conversation and Ryōkai's subsequent full enlightenment, *see* Note 120 below.) After he had left Ungan, Ryōkai spent some years visiting different masters. When the persecution of Buddhism which had been taking place during the reign of Emperor Busō came to an end with the Emperor's death in 846, Ryōkai went to live on Mount Shimpo 新豐山 (Xinfengshan) in Kōshū 洪州 (Hongzhou), in present Jiangxi. Later he moved to the Furi-in 普利院 (Puliyuan) on Tōzan 洞山 (Dongshan) in Inshū 筠州 (Yunzhou), also in present Jiangxi. There he spent the remainder of his life instructing a large company of disciples in his distinctive teachings, teachings which clearly bore the imprint of the Master's philosophically inclined mind. According to the *Tōzan goroku*:

> On the first day of the third month of the tenth year of the Kantsū 咸通 (Xiantong) era (860–874), early in the morning the Master ordered his head to be shaved, his body to be bathed, and a fresh robe brought. Then, after striking the bell, he said farewell to the assembly, and gravely passed away. All the monks wailed bitterly, and for a long time could not control their lamentations.
>
> Suddenly the Master opened his eyes and said, "The hearts of men who go forth into the homeless life should not be dependent upon things. This is true practice. What use is there in grieving when troublesome life comes to rest in death?" Then he called the monk in charge of temple affairs and ordered him to prepare a "Fools, Feast" for everyone, intending thus to rebuke the assembly for their attachment to him. When their demonstrations of affection still did not cease, the Master postponed his going for seven days. When the food had been provided and everything was ready, the Master also partook of the feast. Finally he said, "Why do all you monks behave so rudely? Why do you make such a disturbance when I am on the point of departure?"

> On the eighth day, after he had bathed, sitting erect the Master set out on his long journey. His age was sixty-three. He had been a monk for forty-two years. His Imperially bestowed posthumous title was Gohon Daishi 悟本大師 (Wuben Dashi). [*Ibid.*, 515a.6–14]

Tōzan Ryōkai was a poet of distinction, and incorporated much of his teaching in his considerable body of verse. His most famous poem is the *Hōkyō zammai*, though of no less importance are his "Verses on the Five Ranks" (*Goi no ju* 五位頌 *Wuwei song*). The doctrines obscurely set forth in these two works were further developed and systematized by Tōzan's heir Sōzan Honjaku 曹山本寂 (Caoshan Benji, 840–901), and became the basic teachings of the Chinese Sōtō 曹洞 (Caodong) School, of which master and disciple are considered the co-founders. (For more on the Chinese Sōtō Sect, *see* Part One, Note 19.) Tōzan left many heirs, the most important of whom, after Sōzan, was Ungo Dōyō 雲居道膺 (Yunju Daoying, *d.* 902). The record of the Master's life and teachings is to be found in the *Inshū Tōzan Gohon zenji goroku*.

116. *Tōjō goi henshō kuketsu* 洞上五位偏正口訣 [*Keisō dokuzui* 3; *Hakuin oshō zenshū*, Vol. 2, pp. 81–88]. The text which follows under this title is, with the exception of a few minor deletions, a complete English translation of Hakuin's treatise on the Five Ranks (*goi* 五位 *wuwei*). The English rendering of many of the Buddhist and Zen technical terms to be found in the work is tentative, since western languages are, for the most part, not provided with a vocabulary which can adequately express the more subtle eastern philosophical and metaphysical concepts, particularly those based upon direct experience. What the Five Ranks is concerned with is states of realization which are beyond words and beyond intellectual comprehension. True understanding of the Five Ranks can be reached only under a Zen master and through the method of study known as sanzen. Those who wish to grasp the full import of Tōzan's teaching must, perforce, study it this way.

As for the English rendering of the title of Hakuin's treatise, the term here translated as "ranks" (*i* 位 *wei*) should be understood as "steps" or "positions" in a series, designated as such for the purpose of setting forth the doctrine. "The Apparent" translates *hen* 偏 (*pian*)—literally "the bent," "the inclined," "the partial"—a term indicating that which is differentiated, manifested in form, or, in other words, phenomena. It is the equivalent of *ji* 事 (*shi*) in the Kegon (Huayan) teaching (cf. PART ONE, Note 24). In the Five Ranks it is represented by a solid white circle ○ symbolizing "brightness." "The Real" translates *shō* 正 (*zheng*)—literally "the straight," "the correct," "the true"—a term indicating that which is undifferentiated, unmanifested, or, Noumenon. It is the equivalent of *ri* 理 (*li*) in Kegon. In the Five Ranks it is represented by a solid black circle ● symbolizing "darkness." The [Monk] Who Lived on Mount Tō" is, of course, Tōzan Ryōkai (Dongshan Liangjie).

117. *Hōkyō zammai* 寶鏡三昧 (*Baojing sanmei*), the long poem attributed to Tōzan Ryōkai in which the doctrine of the Five Ranks is set forth in highly enigmatic language.

118. Sekitō Kisen 石頭希遷 (Shitou Xiqian, 700–790) was one of the great figures in early Chinese Zen. He was a native of Kōyō 高要 (Gaoyao) in Tanshū 端州 (Duanzhou), in what is now Guangdong, and his family name was CHIN 陳 (CHEN). The old biographies speak of him as an unusually intelligent child, with a calmness and self-assurance far beyond his years. The district in which he was born was at that time quite uncivilized, and the natives, many of whom lived in caves, were in the habit of building shrines to malevolent deities and making sacrifices of wine and oxen to them. It is said that the boy used to go out and destroy these shrines, then return leading the oxen.

When he was twelve or thirteen years old, young CHIN went to visit the Sixth Patriarch at Sōkei 曹溪 (Caoxi), a place not very far distant from his home. Enō (Huineng), struck by the youth's perspicacity, kept him with him, and gave him some instruction. A year or two later (713), he was among the disciples who surrounded the Patriarch on his deathbed. Little is known of his life during the years that followed, until, in 728, he took the full commandments at the Rafuzan 羅浮山 (Luofushan), in the northern part of present Guangdong.

Shortly thereafter, Kisen—to give him his Buddhist name—went to see Seigen Gyōshi (Qingyuan Xingsi), one of the most important of the Sixth Patriarch's Dharma-heirs, who was then instructing many disciples on the Seigenzan 青原山 (Qingyuanshan) in Kisshū 吉州 (Jizhou), in modern Jiangxi. At their first interview Seigen made the famous remark about his new disciple: "I have many horned animals in my assembly, but one unicorn will suffice." [*Keitoku dentō roku* 5; *T* 51: 240b.10] (In China the unicorn [*rin* 麟 *lin*] was a fabulous animal, the appearance of which presaged some extraordinary and auspicious event.) Kisen spent several years under Seigen Gyōshi, and inherited his Dharma.

In 742 Kisen went to the Nangaku 南嶽 (Nanyue), in the southeastern part of present-day Hunan. There, on a large flat rock a little to the east of an old temple known as the Nan-ji 南寺 (Nansi), he built a hut for himself. From this, people called him Sekitō Oshō 石頭和尚 (Shitou Heshang), the "priest [who lives] on top of the stone." At that time three other Zen masters were also living on the "Southern Peak" (Nangaku): the Sixth Patriarch's heirs Nangaku Ejō 南嶽懷讓 (Nanyue Huairang) and Nangaku Kengo 南嶽堅固 (Nanyue Jiangu), and a disciple of Fujaku 普寂 (Puji) of the Northern School of Zen. Since these men spoke in the highest terms of Sekitō's understanding, many of their disciples came to study with him.

For twenty-three years the Master remained on the Nangaku. His teaching and his teaching method may be clearly discerned in the following:

> One day when the Master had taken the high seat in the hall, he said: "My Dharma has been transmitted to me by a preceding Buddha. It is of no matter whether it be by meditation or by zealous religious practice; the important thing is to attain the Buddha-wisdom. This very Mind, just this is Buddha. Mind, Buddha and sentient beings, perfect wisdom and the defiling passions—these are but different names for one and the same substance.
>
> "All of you must know your own Mind-essence, know that its substance is apart from extinction and permanence, and that its nature is neither stained nor pure; know that it is absolutely still and completely whole, and that [in it] secular and sacred are exactly the same; know that its responding to circumstances is limitless, and that it is apart from mind and consciousness. The Three Worlds and the Six Ways [of Transmigration] are only appearances [produced by] your own mind, like reflections of the moon in water, or images seen in a mirror. How can [this Mind] be subject to birth and death? If you know this well, you will lack for nothing."
>
> The disciple Dōgo asked, "Who obtained the essential teaching of Sōkei?"
>
> The Master said, "He who understands Buddha-dharma obtained it."
>
> "Did you obtain it, Master?" Dōgo asked.

"I don't understand Buddha-dharma," Sekitō replied.
"What about emancipation?" asked another monk.
"Who binds you?" said the Master.
"What about the Pure Land?"
"Who defiles you?" was the reply.
"What about Nirvana?"
"Who puts you in Samsara (birth-and-death)," was Sekitō's reply. [*Keitoku dentō roku* 14; *T* 51: 309b.12–22]

In 764, at the request of some of his disciples, Sekitō went to Ryōtan 梁端 (Liangduan) in Tanshū 潭州 (Tanzhou), near present Changsha. There his fame as a Zen master came to equal that of the great Baso Dōitsu (Mazu Daoyi). Though the records are not clear, it seems probable that Sekitō returned to the Nangaku after a stay of some ten years in Tanshū. He died there in his ninety-first year.

Sekitō left a number of Dharma-heirs, among whom Yakusan Igen 藥山惟儼 (Yueshan Weiyan, 745–828) and Tennō Dōgo 天皇道悟 (Tianhuang Daowu, 748–807) became the most famous. During the Chōkei 長慶 (Changqing) era (821–824), the Tang emperor Bokusō 穆宗 (Muzong *r.* 820–824) bestowed upon the Master the posthumous title Musai Daishi 無際大師 (Wuji Dashi).

Two famous poems from Sekitō's hand have come down to us, the *Sandōkai* 參同契 (*Cantongqi*) In Praise of Identity [*Keitoku dentō roku* 30; *T* 51: 459b.7–21], and the *Sōanka* 草庵歌 (Cao'ange) Song of the Grass Hut [*ibid.*, 461c.8–21]. Neither has been translated into a western language. In the *Sandōkai*, traces may be discerned of Daoistic thought, of certain ideas from the *Jōron* (*Zhao lun*), and of the Kegon (Huayan) doctrine of the Four Dharmadhātu (*shihokkai* 四法界 *sifajie*) (cf. Part One, Note 24). This short poem was particularly important for both Sōtō (Caodong) and Rinzai (Linji) Zen, since within it lay the rudiments of the doctrine of the Five Ranks, later fully developed by Sekitō's descendants, Tōzan Ryōkai (Dongshan Liangjie) and Sōzan Honjaku (Caoshan Benji), founders of the Chinese Sōtō Sect.

(The dates given above for Sekitō and his disciples are those proposed by Ui Hakuju, *Zenshūshi kenkyū*, Vol. I, pp. 396–411.)

119. Yakusan Igen 藥山惟儼 (Yueshan Weiyan, 745–828) was a monk in the 3rd generation of the line of Seigen Gyōshi (Qingyuan Xingsi). He was

born in Kōshū 絳州 (Jiangzhou), in modern Shanxi, but while he was still a child the family, whose name was Kan 韓 (Han), moved to Shimpō 信豐 (Xinfeng) in Nankō 南康 (Nankang), in what is now Jiangxi. At seventeen the youth's head was shaved by Eshō Zenji 慧照禪師 (Huizhao Chanshi, *n. d.*), a disciple of Nangaku Ejō (Nanyue Huairang). From that time on until the age of twenty-nine, when he took the full commandments, he seems to have devoted himself to the study of the Vinaya and the sutras.

In 773 Igen visited the famous Zen master Sekitō Kisen (Shitou Xiqian), who at that time seems to have been again living at the Nangaku (Nanyue). According to late accounts, on Sekitō's advice Igen went to Baso Dōitsu (Mazu Daoyi), who was then teaching at the Kaigen-ji 開元寺 (Kaiyuansi) in Kōshū 洪州 (Hongzhou), in modern Jiangxi, and remained with that master for a number of years. Even if this be true, it is nevertheless clear that Igen later returned to the Nangaku to serve Sekitō and to receive the Transmission of Dharma from him.

Sometime before Sekitō's death in 790, Igen left the Nangaku and went to the Yakusan 藥山 (Yueshan) in Reishū 澧州 (Lizhou), to the west of Lake Dōtei 洞庭湖 (Dongtinghu) in present Hunan. It is said that, when he first arrived on the mountain, Igen asked the village headman to give him a cowshed as quarters for himself and, presumably, a few disciples who were accompanying him. Later, when the group of disciples numbered forty or fifty, a hut was built for the Master on the mountainside nearby. There, for many years, he seems to have spent much of his time in studying the sutras, particularly the *Avataṁsaka*, the *Mahāparinirvāṇa*, and the *Saddharma-puṇḍarīka*, But Yakusan, as he is generally called from the mountain on which he lived, seems to have thoroughly disapproved of sutra study for his monks.

In the summer of 820, Ri Kō 李翺 (Li Ao, *n. d.*), the Prefect of nearby Rōshū 朗州 (Langzhou), came to pay his respects to Yakusan. According to *Keitoku dentō roku* 14:

> [When Ri Kō entered the Master's room] the Master was holding a volume of sutras in his hand, and did not look up. His attendant addressed him, saying, "The Prefect is here." Kō, who was a quick-tempered man, said, "To hear the name is better than to see the face." "Prefect!" exclaimed the Master. "Yes, Your Reverence," responded Kō. "How dare you esteem the ear and scorn the eye!" demanded the Master. Kō saluted with folded

hands, and offered, his apologies.

Then Kō asked, "What is that which is Dao?" The Master pointed above and below with his hand. "Do you understand?" "No," said Kō, "I do not understand." "The clouds are in the heaven, the water is in the jar," said the Master. Kō was delighted with these words. Bowing deeply, he offered this verse:

"He has trained his body to resemble that of a crane.
Beneath a thousand old pine trees are two boxes of sutras.
I came to ask about Dao; there were only these words:
'The clouds are in the heaven, the water is in the jar.'"

"What are commandments, meditation, and wisdom?" Kō then asked. "My room is without such useless furnishings," replied the Master. Kō could not fathom the profound meaning of these words. "Prefect," said the Master, "if you wish to take on this thing, you must at once sit down upon the summit of the mountain—high, high—and walk upon the bottom of the sea—deep, deep. [*T* 51: 312b.10–21]

Thereafter, during the period he held office in Roshu, Ri Ko came often to visit Yakusan.

One evening the Master walked to the top of the mountain. As the clouds suddenly parted and the moon appeared, Yakusan laughed a great laugh. The sound of the laugh echoed as far as Reiyō, some ninety *ri* to the east. The inhabitants of the district thought it had come from a house to the east. The following morning they set out to investigate the matter, and soon came to Mount Yaku. The monks said, "Oh, last night the Master laughed a great laugh on the top of the mountain." Ri Kō later presented the Master with the following poem:

He has chosen a lonely dwelling, and is content
 with the rustic life;
Year after year he goes to greet no one, he sees no one off.
Once he climbed straight to the top of a lone peak,
And, as the moon broke through the clouds,
 laughed a great laugh.

[*Ibid.*, 22–27]

When Yakusan was about to die he called out in a loud voice, "The Dharma-hall is falling down! The Dharma Hall is falling down!" All the monks rushed to hold up the pillars. The Master clapped his hands and laughed loudly. "You don't understand my meaning," he cried, and thereupon passed away. He was in his eighty-fourth year. Later, the posthumous title of Kōdō Daishi 弘道大師 (Hongdao Dashi) was bestowed upon him by Imperial decree. He left two important heirs, the brothers Ungan Donjō 雲巖曇晟 (Yunyan Tansheng, 780?–841) and Dōgo Enchi 道吾圓智 (Daowu Yuanzhi, 769–835).

(The dates given above for Yakusan and his disciples are those proposed by Ui Hakuju, *Zenshūshi kenkyū*, Vol. II, pp. 425–457.)

120. Ungan Donjō 雲巖曇晟 (Yunyan Tansheng, 780?–841) was a monk in the 4th generation of the line of Seigen Gyōshi (Qingyuan Xingsi). He was a native of Kenshō 建昌 (Jianchang) in Shōryō 鍾陵 (Zhongling), in present Jiangxi, and his family name was Ō 王 (Wang). Because he was born covered with the placenta, his name was often associated with that of Ānanda's disciple Śaṇavāsa, third in the traditional lineage of Indian patriarchs of Zen, who is reputed to have been born in the same manner.

After becoming a monk at the age of sixteen, Donjō went to the Sekimonzan 石門山 (Shimenshan) in Kōshū 洪州 (Hongzhou), also in modern Jiangxi, where he entered the assembly of Hyakujō Ekai 百丈懷海 (Baizhang Huaihai), an heir of the famous Baso Dōitsu (Mazu Daoyi). Donjō served Hyakujō faithfully for nearly twenty years. After Hyakujō's death, on the advice of his elder brother Dōgo Enchi (Daowu Yuanzhi), Donjō went to Mount Yaku (Yueshan) in Reishū (Lizhou). There he joined the group of monks under Yakusan Igen, a group of which his brother Enchi was already a member. Eventually the brothers became Yakusan's two most important heirs.

Donjō now made a pilgrimage, visiting various masters and engaging with them in mondo, many of which became famous in Zen. Finally he retired to a stone cave on Mount Ungan 雲巖山 (Yunyanshan) in Tanshū 潭州 (Tanzhou), in modern Hunan, and there seems to have remained for the rest of his life. The name Ungan, by which he was thereafter generally known, derives, of course, from that of the mountain.

Many travelling monks visited Ungan, staying with him for a time, then continuing on their way. Among these was one named Ryōkai, later to be known as Tōzan Ryōkai (Dongshan Liangjie). The last conversation between the Master and Ryōkai is recorded in *Keitoku dentō roku* 15:

When Ryōkai came to say farewell to the Master, Ungan asked,

"Where are you going?" "Though I'm leaving Your Reverence, I haven't yet decided where I shall go," replied Ryōkai. "Aren't you going to Konan?" asked the Master. "No," said Ryōkai. "Aren't you going to your native place?" "No," said Ryōkai. "When will you return here?" asked Ungan. "When Your Reverence has a dwelling place, then I'll come." "Once you have gone it will be difficult for us to meet," said the Master. "It will be difficult not to meet," returned Ryōkai.

Then Ryōkai said, "Your Reverence, a hundred years from now, if someone were to ask me, 'Can you draw a portrait of your master?' how should I reply?" "Only answer him, 'Just *this* it is'," said Ungan. Ryōkai remained silent for a time. Then Ungan said, "In undertaking this matter you must investigate minutely." Ryōkai still had some doubts.

Later, when Ryōkai was crossing a stream, he saw his reflection in the water, and [at that moment] completely realized the meaning of [Ungan's] earlier words. He composed this verse:

Seeking it from others is forbidden.
For thus it becomes farther and farther estranged.
Now that I go my way entirely alone,
There is nowhere I cannot meet it.
Now it is just what I am,
Now I am not what it is.
Thus must one understand,
Then one accords with the Truly So.

[*T* 51: 321c.12–24]

The *Keitoku dentō roku* 14 speaks of Ungan's death as follows:

In the tenth month of the first year of the Kaishō 會昌 (Huichang) era (841–846), the Master was taken ill. On the 26th day, after he had bathed, he called the monk in charge of temple affairs, and ordered him to prepare a feast for a certain elder monk (*jōza* 上坐 *shangzuo*) who was departing the next day. But on the following day no one left, and during the night the Master died. He was sixty years old. When his body was cremated, more than a thousand grains of ashes remained. These were put in a stone tomb. The title Mujū Daishi 無住大師 (Wuzhu Dashi) was bestowed upon him by Imperial decree. His memorial bore the inscription "Jōshō" 淨勝 (Jingsheng). [*T* 51: 315b.14–18]

Ungan Donjō had four Dharma-heirs, Tōzan Ryōkai, mentioned above, and three other men of lesser importance for the history of Zen. Neither he nor his teacher Yakusan before him left any writings.

121. *Kōjō jikishi* 向上直指 (*xiangshang zhizhi*), a technical term characterizing the primary aim of Zen, that is, the direct leap into the Absolute State without any previous or gradual stages of approach.

122. *Nikū* 二空 (*erkong*) is a reference to the doctrine that "both men and dharmas [phenomenal existences] are devoid of any essential or permanent nature" (*ninkū hōkū* 人空法空 *renkong fakong*), or, in other words, that men have no permanent ego or soul, and that the very things that make up existence have in themselves no substantial reality. In developed Mahayana Buddhism this doctrine is held to be a relative truth, and to remain attached to it, or any part of it, is considered a primary hindrance to progress on the path toward enlightenment.

123. *Śrāvaka*, a Sanskrit term meaning "hearer," originally referred to Shakyamuni's disciples, that is, "those who heard [the Buddha's] voice." The usual Chinese translation of the term is *shengwen* 聲聞 (*shōmon*), literally "voice-hearer." Later, "śrāvaka" came to mean a disciple in the initial Hinayana stage of the Path. Since the śrāvaka's understanding does not go beyond the Four Truths (Skr. *catvāry āryasatyāni*; *sishengdi* 四聖諦 *shishōtai*) and the Egolessness of Man and the Insubstantiality of Dharmas (cf. above, Note 122), though he may succeed in reaching arhatship and Nirvana, his attainment is of an inferior grade.

124. *Pratyeka-buddha* is a Sanskrit word meaning literally "individually awakened." Originally, pratyeka-buddha was the name given to one who attains enlightenment in an age when there is no buddha, or, one who, living alone and in solitude, reaches arhatship and Nirvana through his own efforts, independently of a teacher. Somewhat later, however, perhaps through linguistic confusion, the term pratyeka-buddha was held to designate a disciple in the second stage of the Hinayana Path, one whose understanding has progressed beyond that of the śrāvaka to include the Twelve-fold Chain of Causation (*dvādaśāṅga-pratītyasamūtpada*; *shi'er yinyuan* 十二因緣 *jūni innen*). The earliest Chinese term for pratyeka-buddha, *yuanjue* 緣覺 (*engaku*) "enlightened [as a result of pondering

upon] the Chain of Causation," expressed this second Indian concept. But Xuanzang 玄奘 (Genjō, 600?–664), with his excellent knowledge of Sanskrit, realizing what the primary meaning of the term pratyeka-buddha had been, translated it as *dujue* 獨覺 (*dokkaku*), "individually enlightened," thus conveying its original meaning exactly. Still another Chinese term, *bishifo* 辟支佛 (*byakushi-butsu*), a semi-phonetic rendering of *pratyeka-buddha*, is sometimes found. It is the latter term that Hakuin has used in this text. Since the pratyeka-buddha and the śrāvaka are concerned with their personal salvation alone, from the Mahayana standpoint the enlightenment of both is inferior to that of the bodhisattva, who undertakes his practice in order that eventually he may use it for the salvation of others.

125. Hakuin is here referring to his teacher Dōkyō Etan 道鏡慧端, familiarly known as Shōju Rōjin 正受老人. For Shōju's biography, *see* PART ONE, Note 42.

126. The "Great Death" (*daishi ichiban* 大死一番 *dasi yifan*) is a Zen expression referring to the experience of one who, having cast away all thoughts and conceptions and made his mind completely empty, penetrates into Absolute Mind. In this moment he reaches the ultimate point of self-negation, his personal ego is extinguished, and he is reborn into the "Great Life" (*daikatsu* 大活 *dahuo*).

In Case 41 of the *Hekigan roku* we find the following koan: Jōshū (Zhaozhou Congshen) asked Tōsu 投子 (Touzi), "When a man who has experienced the Great Death comes to life again, what then?" 大死底人却活時如何 *Daishitei no hito kaette kassuru toki ikan?* [*T* 48: 178c.16] In his comment on this koan, Engo (Yuanwu Keqin) says, "You must experience this Great Death, and then attain Life." 須是大死一番却活始得 *Subekaraku kore daishi ichiban shite kaette kasshite, hajimete u beshi.* [*Ibid.*, 179a.10*f*]

127. Śāriputra and Ānanda were two of Shakyamuni's great disciples.

128. "Tōzan's Verses" are The Verses on the Five Ranks (*Goi no ju* 五位頌 *Wuwei song*) [*Ninden gammoku* 3; *T* 48: 314c.8–18]. These are five stanzas attributed to Tōzan Ryōkai, in which the five successive steps in the doctrine of the Five Ranks are described one by one. The four-line verses are written in a folksong style popular with poets of middle and later Tang.

The first line of each verse, in three characters, gives the name of the individual rank. In every case this line defies translation, for the Chinese characters themselves do no more than indicate the intended meaning, they do not state it. The following three seven-character lines of each verse describe in metaphorical language the experience realized in the specific rank. Later in his treatise, Hakuin quotes the five verses and gives his commentary upon them.

129. "The reciprocal interpenetration of the Apparent and the Real" (*henshō ego* 偏正回互 *pianzheng huihu*) is a technical term taken from the *Hōkyō zammai* [*T* 47: 515a.25]. For an understanding of the Five Ranks doctrine it is important not to conceive of what is termed "reciprocal interpenetration" as something static, something that has taken place. Rather, it is a process continuously going on.

130. A reference to the fact that the doctrine of the Five Ranks originated in the Chinese Sōtō (Caodong) School of Zen. This teaching had already entered the Rinzai (Linji) School by the end of the 10th century, probably through Fun'yō Zenshō (Fenyang Shanzhao, 947–1024), and thereafter was considered to be an integral part of the teachings of the school. Tōzan Ryōkai's second heir, Ungo Dōyō 雲居道膺 (Yunju Daoying, *d.* 902), and Ungo's immediate successors, evinced little interest in the Five Ranks (cf. PART ONE, Note 18). But, by the middle of the 13th century, Chinese masters of the Sōtō School were again concerning themselves with this esoteric doctrine, and this interest continued well into Ming times.

Dōgen Kigen (1200–1253), founder of Japanese Sōtō Zen, appears to have been far from enthusiastic about the Five Ranks. But later Japanese Sōtō men became fascinated with it, and wrote many commentaries upon it, most of them, as Hakuin has put it, "adding branch to branch and piling entanglement upon entanglement."

In the Japanese Rinzai Sect, we hear nothing specific about the Five Ranks teaching until the time of Shōju Rōjin. The fact that Shōju Rōjin counted several Sōtō monks among his friends may have stimulated his interest in this teaching, and this interest he transmitted to his disciple Hakuin. Hakuin, as this treatise makes clear, was convinced not only of the importance of the doctrine, but of his own responsibility to clear away all the mistaken interpretations and nonsensical jargon that obscured its true meaning. From Hakuin's time on, the *Goi*, or Five Ranks, has had a place of the highest importance in Rinzai Zen koan study.

131. This is, of course, the third of the Four Universal Vows (cf. Part Two, Note 1).

132. The Four Wisdoms (Skr. *catvāri-jñānāni*; *shichi* 四智 *sizhi*) are:

1. Great Perfect Mirror Wisdom (Skr. *ādarça-jñānam*; *daienkyōchi* 大圓鏡智 *dayuanjingzhi*)
2. Universal Nature Wisdom (Skr. *samatā-jñānam*; *byōdōshōchi* 平等性智 *pingdengxingzhi*)
3. Marvelous Observing Wisdom (Skr. *pratyavekṣaṇā-jñānam*; *myōkansatchi* 妙觀察智 *miaoguanchazhi*)
4. Perfecting-of-Action Wisdom (Skr. *kṛityānusthāna-jñānam*; *jōshosachi* 成所作智 *chengsuozuozhi*).

133. The Threefold Learning (Skr. *trīṇi çikṣāṇi*; *sangaku* 三學 *sanxue*) comprises: the study of the rules of discipline (Skr. *adhiçīlam*; *kaigaku* 戒學 *jiexue*); the study of meditation (Skr. *adhicittam*; *jōgaku* 定學 *dingxue*); and intellectual study (Skr. *adhiprajñā*; *egaku* 慧學 *huixue*). The first is equated with the Vinaya texts, the second with the sutras, the third with the śāstras (*ron* 論 *lun*) and commentaries on the sutras.

134. The Consciousness Only (Skr. *vijñānamātra*; *yuishiki* 唯識 *weishi*) School posits eight kinds of cognition, or consciousness (Skr. *aṣṭa-vijñānāni*; *hasshiki* 八識 *bashi*) as follows:

1. Visual Cognition (Skr. *cakṣur-vijñāna*; *genshiki* 眼識 *yan-shi*)
2. Auditory Cognition (Skr. *śrotra-vijñāna*; *nishiki* 耳識 *er-shi*)
3. Olfactory Cognition (Skr. *ghrāṇa-vijñāna*; *bishiki* 鼻識 *bi-shi*)
4. Gustatory Cognition (Skr. *jihvā-vijñāna*; *zesshiki* 舌識 *sheshi*)
5. Tactile Cognition (Skr. *kāya-vijñāna*; *shinshiki* 身識 *shen-shi*)
6. Mental Cognition (Skr. *mano-vijñāna*; *ishiki* 意識 *yishi*)
7. Individuating Consciousness (Skr. *kliṣṭa-mano-vijñāna*;

manashiki 末那識 *monashi*), or “Holding-on-to” Consciousness (Skr. *ādāna-vijñāna*; *adanashiki* 阿陀那識 *atuonashi*)

8. Storing Consciousness (Skr. *ālaya-vijñāna*; *arayashiki* 阿賴耶識 *alaiyeshi*).

From early times Zen has accepted this analysis of the structure of man’s mind and, within the tradition, continues to do so today.

135. “The Apparent within the Real” (*shōchūhen* 正中偏 *zhengzhongpian*), the first of the Five Ranks, is symbolically represented by a half-black, half-white circle ◓. (This circle and the circles for the four ranks that follow are those given in the *Ninden gammoku* [*T* 48: 316b.20–25].)

136. “The Real within the Apparent” (*henchūshō* 偏中正 *pianzhongzheng*), the second of the Five Ranks, is represented by a half-white, half-black circle ◒.

137. “The state of the unobstructed interpenetration of Noumenon and phenomena” 理事無礙法界 *riji muge hokkai*, is the third of the Four Dharmadhātu of the Kegon (Huayan) School (cf. Part One, Note 24). Here Hakuin equates the Universal Nature Wisdom with this state.

138. “The Coming from within the Real” (*shōchūrai* 正中來 *zhengzhonglai*), the third of the Five Ranks, is represented by a white circle enclosing a black dot ◉.

139. “The Arrival at Mutual Integration” (*kenchūshi* 兼中至 *jianzhongzhi*), the fourth of the Five Ranks, is represented by a solid white circle ○.

140. “Unity Attained” (*kenchūtō* 兼中到 *jianzhongdao*), the last of the Five Ranks, is represented by a solid black circle ●.

141. The Three Bodies (Skr. *trikāya*; *sanshin* 三身 *sanshen*) are the three aspects under which, according to Mahayana doctrine, Buddha may be considered, namely: *Dharmakāya* (*hosshin* 法身 *fashen*); *Sambhogakāya* (*hōjin* 報身 *baoshen*); *Nirmāṇakāya* (*keshin* 化身 *huashen*).

The Dharmakāya, sometimes translated as “Truth-body” or “Law-body,” is the eternal, absolute state of Buddha, beyond words to describe or thought to conceive. It is Buddha as Ultimate Reality, Ultimate Truth. Regardless of whether a buddha exists in the world or not, Buddha in the Dharmakāya state remains eternally immutable and immobile, the essential and sole Reality.

The Sambhogakāya—"Bliss-body" or "Reward-body"—is interpreted as the body received as a reward for the countless merits gained as a bodhisattva. It is the guise under which Buddha reveals himself to the bodhisattvas. The Sambhogakāya is the supernatural and glorious form Buddha manifests when he addresses the great assemblies, as recorded in the Lotus and other sutras of the same type.

The Nirmāṇakāya, literally "Transformation-body," is the physical form which Buddha assumes when he reveals himself on earth to save sentient beings. Shakyamuni Buddha, who was born and lived as a man, attained enlightenment, taught the doctrine of salvation, and at death entered final Nirvana, was a manifestation of Buddha's Nirmāṇakāya.

All buddhas are endowed with these three bodies, which are both distinct and at the same time aspects of one body. Since all men possess the Buddha-nature, they are potential buddhas, and therefore also intrinsically endowed with the three bodies.

142. This is, in part, a reference to the following lines in Chapter 10, the "Chapter on Awakening" (*Bodai bon* 菩提品 *Puti pin*), of the *Daijō shōgongyō ron*, the Chinese translation of a 4th century Sanskrit text composed by Asaṅga (Mujaku 無著 Wuzhuo), one of the founders of the Indian Mahayana Yogācāra (*Yuga* 瑜伽 *Yujia*), or Consciousness Only (Yuishiki), School:

> All the Buddhas have four kinds of wisdom. The first is the Mirror Wisdom, the second is the Universal Wisdom, the third the Observing Wisdom, the fourth the Perfecting-of-Action Wisdom.... When the eighth vijñāna is inverted, the Mirror Wisdom is attained; when the seventh vijñāna is inverted, the Universal Wisdom is attained; when the sixth vijñāna is inverted, the Observing Wisdom is attained; when the remaining five vijñānas are inverted, the Perfecting-of-Action Wisdom is attained. [*T* 31: 606c.25–607a.2]

By the 9th century, the Yuishiki doctrine of the relation between the Three Bodies, the Four Wisdoms, and the Eight Consciousnesses had been fully accepted in Zen. We find it stated as a set formula in a question asked by an unnamed person of Daishu Ekai 大珠慧海 (Dazhu Huihai, *n. d.*), an heir of Baso Dōitsu (709–788), and recorded in Ekai's *Tongo nyūdō yōmon ron*:

> Someone asked: "[Regarding the statement] 'When the eight consciousnesses are inverted, the Four Wisdoms are completed; when the Four Wisdoms are bound together, the Three Bodies are completed,' which of the eight consciousnesses combine to make one wisdom, and which of them alone make one wisdom?" [*ZZ* 2: 15.5.424c.2*f*]

Ekai's answer to this question agrees exactly with the previously quoted statement in the *Shōgongyō ron*. The questioner continues further, however, and asks:

> "[Regarding the statement] 'when the Four Wisdoms are bound together, the Three Bodies are completed,' which of the wisdoms combine to make one body, and which of them alone make one body?"
>
> Ekai replied: "The Great Perfect Mirror Wisdom alone makes the Dharmakāya; the Universal Nature Wisdom alone makes the Sambhogakāya; the Marvelous Observing Wisdom and the Perfecting-of-Action Wisdom together make the Nirmāṇakāya. These three bodies are tentatively given names, and their differentiation in speech permits unenlightened persons to understand them. But once you have fully comprehended this principle, there will no longer be three bodies responding to needs." [*Ibid.*, 424c.11–15]

During the middle of the Tokugawa era there was considerable interest among Japanese scholar-monks in the doctrines of the Consciousness Only (Yuishiki) School, and a number of works were written on it. Since the second part of Hakuin's quotation—"when the Four Wisdoms are bound together, the Three Bodies are completed"—is not to be found in the *Shōgongyō ron*, and since in the *Tongo nyūdō yōmon ron* the source of the statement is not given, it seems probable that Hakuin was depending upon some commentary rather than personal acquaintance with either of these texts themselves.

143. Sōkei Daishi is the Sixth Patriarch Enō (Huineng). Sōkei (Caoxi) is the place where he lived during his teaching years.

144. *Jishō sanjin o gu su; hatsumei sureba shichi o nasu.* 自性具三身，發明成四智。 [*Rokuso dankyō*; *T* 48: 356b.3]

145. *Shōjō hosshin nanji no shō nari; emman hōjin nanji no chi nari; hyaku oku kesshin nanji no gyō nari.* 清淨法身儞之性，圓滿報身儞之智，百億化身儞之行。[*Ibid.*, 356a.28*f*]

It may be of interest to note what Rinzai Gigen (Linji Yixuan) said of the Three Bodies:

> The pure light in a single instant of your thought is the Dharmakāya Buddha within your own house; the non-discriminating light in a single instant of your thought is the Sambhogakāya Buddha within your own house; the non-differentiating light in a single instant of your thought is the Nirmāṇakāya Buddha within your own house. This threefold body is none other than you, who right now before my very eyes, stand listening to my sermon. [*Rinzai roku*; *T* 47: 497b.17–21]

146. The verse on the first rank, "The Apparent within the Real":

正中偏	*Shōchūhen*
三更初夜月明前	*Sankō shoya getsumei no mae*
莫怪相逢不相識	*Ayashimu koto nakare aiōte aishi razaru koto o*
隱隱猶懷舊日妍	*In'in to shite nao kyūjitsu no ken o idaku*

From this point on, Hakuin quotes Tōzan's verses on the Five Ranks one by one, and gives his commentary upon each in turn.

147. "Shouts 'KA!'" (*kaji ichige* 囫地一下 *gadi yixia*) is an expression used in Zen literature to indicate the spontaneous cry that escapes a person at the moment of satori (cf. Part Three, 6). The single word *ka* 囫 first came into this usage in late Tang, and from that time on was often employed by Zen masters. The use of *ka* in a four-character phrase soon followed. Sometimes we find the phrase as here used by Hakuin, sometimes it appears as *kaji issei* 囫地一聲 (*gadi yisheng*), literally "the sound of the *ka*." The latter expression concludes a passage from an informal talk by Hakuun Muryō 白雲無量 (Baiyun Wuliang, *n. d.*), a master in the 17th generation of the Yōgi (Yangqi) line of Rinzai Zen, who lived probably

during the first half of the 15th century. Since this passage, to be found in *Zenkan sakushin*, contains invaluable advice for koan students of today, it is quoted here in full:

> All through the twenty-four hours of the day, go with your koan, stay with your koan, sit with your koan, lie down with your koan. Let your mind be like a thorn bush, so that it can't be swallowed up by any [notions] of self or other, ignorance, the five passions, the three poisons, and such. Going, staying, sitting, lying, make your entire body a ball of doubt. But though doubt comes and doubt goes, yet all day long you remain as stupid and dumb as a wooden post. Then, upon hearing a sound or seeing a color, for a certainty you will shout "KA!" That is all. [*T* 48: 1100a.2–7]

148. *Kokū shōin shi, tetsuzan kudaku.* 虛空消殞，鐵山摧。The source of this phrase, much quoted in Zen, is unknown.

149. *Kami ni henga no kōbe ōu naku, shimo ni sundo no ashi o tatsuru nashi.* 上無片瓦蓋頭，下無寸土立足。 [*Keitoku dentō roku* 15; *T* 51: 324a.1*f*] This is the well-known line with which Dōgo Enchi (Daowu Yuanzhi) described his brother-disciple Sensu Tokusei (Chuanzi Decheng), known as the Boatman Monk. For the episode in which this line appears, *see* the biography of Kassan Zenne (Jiashan Shanhui), Part Two, Note 48.

150. The Sanskrit term *saṁsāra* (*shōji* 生死 *shengsi*) is a Buddhist technical term meaning the continuous succession of birth-death, birth-death. It is the exact opposite of the eternal stillness which is Nirvana.

151. "The Great Matter" (*daiji* 大事 *dashi*) is an expression often used in Zen for the ultimate truth of Buddhism. Here, Hakuin uses it with the meaning of "the complete practice for attaining the ultimate truth." This is an important term in Hakuin's Zen.

152. "Stagnant water" (*shisui* 死水 *sishui*) is an expression taken from the *jakugo* (verse-commentary) of Setchō Jūken (Xuedou Chongxian) to the koan in Case 20 of the *Hekigan roku*. The verse opens with the lines:

> The dragon on Dragon-tooth Mountain has no eye.
> Stagnant water has never stirred the wind of olden times.
> [*T* 48: 161a.29*f*]

153. "The evil spirit who keeps watch over the corpse in the coffin," 棺木裡守屍鬼 *kambokuri no shushiki*, is a vivid expression consisting of two phrases from late Tang works, which seem to have been combined by Hakuin. The first of the original phrases is from a poem by the Chinese poet Kanzan 寒山 (Hanshan), about whom nothing is known other than can be gleaned from the poems associated with his name, but who has tentatively been placed in the late 8th or early 9th century. Hakuin wrote a commentary on Kanzan's three hundred poems, which he entitled *Kanzan shi Sendai kimon* 寒山詩闡提記聞 Kanzan's Poems: The Record of What Sendai Has Heard [*Hakuin oshō zenshū*, Vol. IV, pp. 27–363]. "Sendai" was one of the several literary names that Hakuin took for himself. The line of the poem in which the above phrase appears is:

> Though you were to become an immortal
> You would be like the evil spirit who keeps watch over
> the corpse.
>
> [*Ibid.*, 256.11]

The second phrase of the expression is from a line in a sermon by Ummon Bun'en (Yunmen Wenyan, 862/4–949), in the *Ummon kōroku*: "[The dead man] in the coffin winks his eye." [*T* 47: 552a.5]

154. *Ki kurai o hanarezareba, dokkai ni dazai su.* 機不離位墮在毒海。 [*Tōzan goroku*; *T* 47: 513c.11]. These are words addressed to Sōzan Honjaku (Caoshan Benji) by Tōzan Ryōkai (Dongshan Liangjie) when the latter was transmitting his Dharma to his disciple.

155. The sentence which immediately follows in the original text has, in this translation, been transposed to the commentary on the second rank, "The Real within the Apparent," p. 70.

156. The verse on the second rank, "The Real within the Apparent":

偏中正	*Henchūshō*
失曉老婆逢古鏡	*Shitsugyō no rōba kokyō ni au*
分明覿面更無眞	*Fummyō ni tekimen sara ni shin nashi*
爭奈迷頭還認影	*Ikan sen kōbe ni mayōte kaette kage o mitomuru koto o*

157. "Dust" (*jin* 塵 *chen*) is the Chinese rendering of the Sanskrit *guṇa*, a term meaning a "quality" or "attribute" of matter which is apprehensible

by the senses. The Chinese interpreted the term to mean literally "minute particle" or "dust," i.e., that which defiles the pure mind. The "six dusts" are sight, sound, smell, taste, touch, and thought; the "realm of the six dusts" is the phenomenal world as known through sense-perception.

158. Hakuin is here speaking of Dōgen Kigen, giving him the name of the great temple Eihei-ji 永平寺, which Dōgen built in Fukui Prefecture.

159. *Jiko o hakobite mambō o shō suru wa mayoi nari; mambō kitatte jiko o shō suru wa satori nari.* 運自己證萬法迷也，萬法來證自己悟也。 [*T* 82: 23c.7–9] This is a quotation from the "*Genjō kōan*" 現成公案 section of Dōgen Kigen's famous work *Shōbōgenzō.*

160. *Shinjin datsuraku, datsuraku shinjin.* 心身脱落，脱落心身。 [*Denkō roku* 2; *T* 82: 405a.9*f*] It was upon hearing these words spoken by his Chinese master, Tendō Nyojō 天童如淨 (Tiantong Rujing, 1163–1228), that Dōgen Kigen is said to have attained satori.

161. *Hakuba roka ni iri, ginwan ni yuki o moru.* 白馬入蘆花，銀碗盛雪。 The first of these quotations—"a white horse enters the reed flowers"—is a comment by Engo Kokugon on the first sentence of the koan in Case 13 of the *Hekigan roku*: "A monk asked Haryō, 'What is the Daiba Sect?'" [*T* 48: 153c.20] The second quotation—"Snow is piled up in a silver bowl"—is Haryō's reply to the monk's question. This reply, which concludes the koan, is, in turn, a phrase taken from Tōzan Ryōkai poem *Hōkyō zammai* [*T* 47: 515a.17*f*]. *See also* Haryō Oshō's "Three Pivotal Words," PART TWO, Chapter 5, p. 50.

162. Here Hakuin is speaking about the state of realization extolled in Tōzan's poem, not the poem itself.

163. *Shobutsu seson wa manako ni busshō o miru.* 諸佛世尊眼見佛性。 [*Nehan gyō* 27; *T* 12: 527c.29*f*] Hakuin has substituted "Tathāgata" for the phrase "all the Buddhas and World Honored Ones" of the original text.

164. Hakuin is here referring to the story of Daian Zenji's Ox. Chōkei Daian 長慶大安 (Changqing Da'an, 793–883), a Dharma-heir of Hyakujō Ekai (Baizhang Huaihai) and brother-disciple of Isan Reiyū (Guishan Lingyou),

in the course of a sermon to his monks, once said:

> I lived with Isan more than thirty years. I ate Isan's food, I excreted Isan's excrement, but I did not study Isan's Zen. All I did was to look after an ox. If he got off the road, I dragged him back; if he trampled the flowering grain in others' fields, I trained him by flogging him with a whip. For a long time how pitiful he was, at the mercy of men's words! Now he has changed into the white ox on the bare ground, and always stays in front of my face. All day long he clearly reveals himself. Even though I chase him, he doesn't go away. [*Keitoku dentō roku* 9; *T* 51: 265c.6–10]

165. These four expressions—"there exists only One Vehicle" (*yui'u ichijō* 唯有一乘 *weiyou yicheng*), "the Middle Way" (*chūdō* 中道 *zhongdao*), "the True Form" (*jissō* 實相 *shixiang*), and "the Supreme Truth" (*daiichigitai* 第一義諦 *diyiyidi*)—are important terms in Mahayana Buddhism. The first is from *kan* 1 of the *Myōhō renge kyō*, Kumārajīva's translation of the *Lotus Sutra*, where we find the lines: "Within the Buddha-lands of the ten directions there exists only One Vehicle." [*T* 9: 8a.17] The other three are found in the *Myōhōrenge-kyō gengi* 妙法蓮華經玄義 (*Miaofalianhua jing xuanyi*) [*T* 33: 681–814], a commentary on the *Lotus Sutra* by Chisha Daishi 智者大師 (Zhizhe Dashi), founder of the Tendai (Tiantai) School, as recorded by his disciple Kanjō 灌頂 (Guanding). In *kan* 8 of this work [*ibid.*, 782c], these three terms are explained as different names for the one and only Reality.

166. "Fixation in a lesser rank of bodhisattvahood" is a rendering of *bosatsu chōda* 菩薩頂墮 (*pusa dingduo*), a Mahayana term with an opprobrious connotation, found in *kan* 27 of the *Daichido ron* 大智度論 (*Tazhidu lun*), Kumārajīva's great Chinese translation (?) in 100 *kan* of Nāgārjuna's *Mahāprajñāpāramitā-śāstra* [*T* 25: 57–756]. There [*ibid.*, 262b.10*f*], this term is defined as the state of a bodhisattva who, though having made considerable progress on the path, becomes attached to the rank he has attained and has no desire to progress further.

167. "Causal conditions for a buddha-realm" (*bukkokudo no innen* 佛國土因緣 *foguotu yinyuan*), in Sanskrit *buddhakṣetra hetupratyaya*. *Buddhakṣetra*, or "buddha-realm," is a Mahayana technical term for the permanent state of enlightenment attained by a buddha, a state which

is the final achievement of the bodhisattva practice. *Hetupratyaya*, or "causal conditions," also a technical term, means primary and secondary causes, the effects arising from which produce not only a buddha-realm, but any other state, condition, or event.

168. In the original Japanese text, this sentence appears in the commentary on the first rank, "The Apparent within the Real" (cf. above, Note 155).

In the phrase, "the Marvelous Wisdom that comprehends the unobstructed interpenetration of the manifold dharmas" (*mambō muge no myōchi* 萬法無礙妙智 *wanfa wu'ai miaozhi*), Hakuin is relating the third of the Four Wisdoms—the Marvelous Observing Wisdom—to the fourth of the Four Dharmadhātu of the Kegon (Huayan) School (cf. PART ONE, Note 24).

169. The verse on the third rank, "The Coming from within the Real":

正中來	*Shōchūrai*
無中有路出塵埃	*Muchū ni michi ari jin'ai o izu*
但能不觸當今諱	*Tada yoku tōkin no ki ni furezumba*
也勝前朝斷舌才	*Mata zenchō danzetsu no sai ni masareri*

170. "Dharma-wheel" (*hōrin* 法輪 *falun*), in Sanskrit *dharmaçakra*, is a metaphor for the Buddha-truth. Like the wheel of the great god Indra which, in battle, crushes everything before it, the wheel of the Buddha-dharma rolls on eternally, subduing all opposition and crushing all evil.

171. *Jōgu bodai geke shujō* 上求菩提，下化衆生 (*shangqiu puti, xiahua zhongsheng*). This is a quotation from the *Makashikan* 摩訶止觀 (*Mohezhiguan*) [*T* 46: 1–140], a treatise in 20 *kan* on Tendai (Tiantai) meditation practice and theory, by Chisha Daishi (Zhizhe Dashi), as recorded by his disciple Kanjō (Guanding). The entire passage reads: "This is called to manifest the enlightened mind by thrusting aside the Four Truths relating to birth and death, and seeking Bodhi above and saving sentient beings below." [*Ibid*., 6a.18*f*]

172. *Kōkyochū kyorai, kyoraichū kōkyo* 向去中卻來，卻來中向去 (*xiangquzhong quelai, quelaizhong xiangqu*). This phrase, key to the understanding of the Five Ranks, defies satisfactory translation. It indicates the

continuous movement of the Real toward interpenetration with the Apparent, and of the Apparent toward the Real. The source of the quotation has not been found.

173. The verse on the fourth rank, "The Arrival at Mutual Integration":

兼中至	*Kenchūshi*
兩刃交鋒不須避	*Ryōjin hokosaki o majiete sakuru koto o mochiizu*
好手還同火裡蓮	*Kōshu kaette kari no hachisu ni onaji*
宛然自有冲天氣	*Ennen to shite onozukara chūten no ki ari*

174. *Kaitō domen* 灰頭土面 (*huitou tumian*) is a phrase from the long commentary by Engo Kokugon (Yuanwu Keqin) on the verse by Setchō Jūken (Xuedou Chongxian) in Case 43 of the *Hekigan roku*. There Engo says: "If he goes out into the world, his head will be covered with dust and his face streaked with dirt" [*T* 48: 180c.2]

175. "Fire-blooming lotus" (*kari no renge* 火裡蓮花 *huoli lianhua*) is a metaphor taken from the *Yuimakitsu shosetsu kyō*, Kumārajīva's translation of the *Vimalakīrtī-nirdeśa*. There, in the verse section at the end of Chapter 8, we find: "The lotus blooming in the fire, what a rare occurrence this must be said to be." [*T* 14: 550b.4]

176. "He enters the market place with empty hands" (*nitten suishu* 入鄽垂手 *ruchan chuishou*) [*ZZ* 2: 18.5.460c.12] is the title of the tenth verse in the *Jūgyūzu ju* 十牛圖頌 (*Shiniutu song*) Verses on the Ten Oxherding Pictures [*ibid.*, 459a–460d] by Kakuan Shion 廓庵師遠 (Kuo'an Shiyuan, *n. d.*), a Zen master in the 3rd generation after Goso Hōen (Wuzu Fayan, 1024?–1014).

> (For complete English translation of these verses, see *Manual of Zen Buddhism*, by D. T. Suzuki, pp. 127–144, and *Zen Flesh, Zen Bones*, by Nyogen Senzaki and Paul Reps, pp. 165–187. For a German translation, see *Der Ochs und sein Hirte*, by K. Tsujimura and H. Buchner, pp. 13–50.)

177. *Tochū ni atte kasha o hanarezu; kasha o hanarete tochū ni arazu* 在途中不離家舍，離家舍不在途中 [*T* 47: 497a.12*f*] is a famous line from the *Rinzai roku*.

178. "The horns of a rabbit and the hairs of a tortoise" (*tokaku kimō* 兔角龜毛 *tujiao guimao*) is an old Buddhist metaphor for that which is non-existent, and thus, by extension, false notions and delusions.

179. The verse on the fifth rank, "Unity Attained":

兼中到	*Kenchūtō*
不落有無誰敢和	*Umu ni ochizu tare ka aete wa sen*
人人盡欲出常流	*Ninnin kotogotoku jōru o iden to hossu*
折合還歸炭裡坐	*Setsugō kaette tanri ni ki shite zasu*

180. The "Master" here mentioned is Hakuin Zenji himself. This line was obviously inserted by his disciple Zenjo, who edited the *Keisō dokuzui*.

181. Actually, this verse is not Hakuin's own, as the text seems to imply, but one by Setchō Jūken (Xuedou Chongxian), from *kan* 5 of the collection of his writings and verse known as the *Myōgaku zenji goroku*:

德雲閑古錐	*Tokuun no kankosui*
幾下妙峯頂	*Ikutabi ka myōbuchō o kudaru*
傭他癡聖人	*Ta no chiseijin o yatōte*
擔雪共塡井	*Yuki o ninatte tomo ni sei o uzumu*

[*T* 47: 702b.25*f*]

The "Tokuun" 德雲 (Deyun) of the poem was Meghaśrī Bhikṣu, the first of the fifty-three teachers whom Sudhana (Zenzai Dōji 善財童子 Shancai Tongzi), the young aspirant of the *Nyūhokkai bon* of the *Kegon kyō*, visited on his pilgrimage. Tokuun lived on the "Marvelous Peak," though it was on another mountain that Zenzai found him after a search of seven days. The story of their interview is given in all three versions of the *Kegon kyō*, but the most satisfactory account is that in *kan* 62 of the "New Translation" of the sutra [*T* 10: 334a.9–335a.4].

182. For other explanations of the Five Ranks, see *Zen Buddhism and Psychoanalysis*, by D. T. Suzuki, Erich Fromm, and Richard DeMartino, pp. 59–76; *A History of Zen Buddhism*, by Heinrich Dumoulin, S. J., pp. 112–118; and *Ch'an and Zen Teaching*, Second Series, by Charles Luk, pp. 149–154 and 159–161.

183. The Ten Commandments (*jūjū kinkai* 十重禁戒 *shichong jinjie*):

1. 不殺生戒	*Fusesshō kai*

2. 不偸盜戒	*Fuchūtō kai*
3. 不邪婬戒	*Fujain kai*
4. 不妄語戒	*Fumōgo kai*
5. 不飲酒戒	*Fuonju kai*
6. 不說四衆過罪戒	*Fusetsu shishu kazai kai*
7. 不自讚毀他戒	*Fujisan kita kai*
8. 不慳貪戒	*Fukendon kai*
9. 不瞋恚戒	*Fushin'i kai*
10. 不謗三寶戒	*Fubō sambō kai*

184. The "four groups" are monks, nuns, male lay-believers, and female lay-believers.

185. The Three Treasures are, of course, the Buddha, the Dharma and the Sangha, or community of believers.

186. Kanzan Egen 關山慧玄 (1277–1360) was born in Nakano 中野 in Shinshū 信州, present Nagano Prefecture, and his family name was Takanashi 高梨. He entered the monk's life as a youth, and studied under his uncle, Gekkoku Sōchū 月谷宗忠 (*n. d.*), a Dharma-heir of Daiō Kokushi (Nampo Jōmyō) (cf. Part One, Note 36). In 1308, when Daiō went to live at the Kenchō-ji in Kamakura, Gekkoku took his nephew there and introduced him to the Kokushi, who accepted him as a disciple and gave him the name Egen. The relationship did not continue long, however, for the following year the Kokushi died, and Egen returned to his native place, to remain there for nearly twenty years.

Egen had reached the age of fifty when, on a visit to Kamakura, he heard that Daiō Kokushi's heir, Shūhō Myōchō (cf. Part Two, Note 4), was teaching at the newly founded Daitoku-ji in Kyoto. He immediately went to the capital and became a disciple of that master. Shūhō, who had attained his final enlightenment through the koan known as "Ummon's Barrier" 雲門關字 (*Ummon no kanji*), now gave this same koan to Egen. After two years of struggle Egen succeeded in passing through the "barrier." In acknowledgment of his attainment, Shuhō presented him with the following lines:

Kanzan

Where the road is barred and difficult to pass through,
Cold clouds eternally girdle the green mountain peaks.

> Though Ummon's single "*Kan*" has concealed its activity
> The true eye discerns [it] far beyond the myriad mountains.

> I herewith present to the "custodian of books" Egen, the *gō* "Kanzan." Mid-spring, fourth year of Karyaku (1329), signed Shūhō Myōchō of the Dragon Peak Mountain.

(This writing, Kanzan's inka, is kept today as one of the treasures of the Myōshin-ji.)

The Master now instructed Kanzan to complete his Zen practice by living for a time in seclusion in the mountains at Ibuka 伊深, in the northern part of what is now Gifu Prefecture. There, for eight years, he worked as a hired laborer, tending cattle or tilling fields during the day, and sitting in meditation during the night. A narrow shelf, jutting out from the edge of a high cliff behind the present Shōgen-ji 正眼寺, still bears the name "Kanzan's Meditation Stone."

In 1337, on the recommendation of Shūhō—now Daitō Kokushi —the cloistered Emperor Hanazono summoned Kanzan to Kyoto to be the founder of the small temple, formerly a part of his summer residence, which he had established in a western suburb of the capital, and to which he had given the name Myōshin-ji (cf. PART ONE, Note 44).

Kanzan was a man of sixty when he came to live at the Myōshin-ji. Despite the fact that his position under the patronage of the cloistered Emperor was one of considerable eminence, he continued his simple and frugal way of life. He disliked any kind of self-display, and so refused to give the usual address on the occasion of his installation. He accepted only a few students, and these few he trained with extreme severity. Since he never lectured, he left no material that could be compiled into a record, or *goroku*. Among the few koans he used in instructing his students, his favorite was "For Egen, here there is no birth-and-death" (*Egen ga, shari ni shōji nashi* 慧玄，這裏無生死). In later years, when Ingen Ryūki 隱元隆琦 (Yinyuan Longqi, 1592–1673), the Chinese founder of the Japanese Ōbaku Sect of Zen, visited the Myōshin-ji and asked to see the Founder's *goroku*, he was told that none existed. Much impressed, he said, "This koan of 'no birth-and-death' is superior to ten thousand volumes of *goroku*."

On the day of his death, Kanzan entrusted his affairs to his sole Dharma-heir, the former courtier Juō Sōhitsu 授翁宗弼 (1296–1380), and dressed himself in his travelling clothes. Then he went out from the abbot's quarters, and, standing quietly and alone beside the "Wind and Water Pond" at the front gate of the temple, he passed away. No tomb was constructed for him, and, out of deference to his memory, no funeral ceremony has ever been performed for a chief priest of the Myōshin-ji.

In the centuries following his death, the posthumous title of "Kokushi" was bestowed upon Kanzan six times by six different emperors. The last posthumous title given him, and the one by which he is presently best known, is that of Musō Daishi 無相大師, bestowed by Emperor Meiji in 1909.

To commemorate the 300th anniversary of Kanzan's death, Daigoku Yuiichi 大極唯一 (1608–1682) built a great temple in the mountains of Ibuka, where the Founder had spent his years of retirement, and named it the Shōgen-ji 正眼寺. The famous phrase "the True Dharma Eye, the Marvelous Mind of Nirvana" (*shōbō genzō nehan myōshin* 正法眼藏涅槃妙心), which, according to Zen tradition, Shakyamuni pronounced in transmitting his Dharma to his disciple Kāśyapa, provided the name "*Shōgen*" for this temple, as it had earlier provided the "*Myōshin*" for the Myōshin-ji.

Though Kanzan Egen left but one heir, his line, which had stemmed from the Chinese Yōgi (Yangqi) line master Kidō Chigu (Xutang Zhiyu, 1185–1269) through Daiō Kokushi and Daitō Kokushi, flourished greatly, and became one of the most important of all the lines of Rinzai Zen in Japan. Hakuin Ekaku was in the 17th generation of Kanzan's line, and from Hakuin have descended the majority of eminent Rinzai Zen roshis in Japan today.

187. *Sengyō mitsuyū, gu no gotoku ro no gotoku, tada yoku sōzoku suru o, shuchū no shu to nazuku.* 潛行密用，如愚如魯，但能相續，名主中主。 [*T* 47: 515b.9*f*]

188. *Rōhatsu Ō Sesshin* 臘八大接心 "The Great Meditation Period of the Eighth Day of the Twelfth Month." This is the period of concentrated zazen practice held in Japanese Rinzai monasteries from the first day of the twelth month—December or January, according to whether the monastery follows the solar or the lunar calendar—and ending early on the morning of the eighth day, when Shakyamuni is believed to have attained his Great Awakening. The regulations for this meditation period or *sesshin*

are more severe than those for any of the other sesshins held during the year. In the past they forbade sleep for the entire seven days and nights.

189. *Kikan* 龜鑑, literally "tortoise mirror." Since the tortoise was believed to be able to foretell the future and the mirror to reveal it, the phrase originally meant "magic mirror." Later it came to mean "example." The custom of reading *kikan* before any long period of meditation in a Zen monastery is an old one, dating perhaps from the Yuan dynasty, if not earlier. Originally the *kikan* consisted of famous stories of the strenuous, even painful, practices which monks of olden days had put themselves through in their efforts to attain satori, stories which were intended as examples to be emulated by the monks to whom they were read. From Hakuin's time on, in Japanese Zen the *kikan* more often took the form of a master's personal advice or admonitions to his students, and were usually read only before the sesshin periods. Today, in some monasteries, "admonitions" are read which have been handed down through several generations; in others, a roshi, in taking charge of a monastery, prepares his own.

190. Kōon-ji 廣園寺, an old and important Zen temple situated to the northwest of Tokyo on the outskirts of the town of Hachiōji 八王子, was founded in 1389 by Shun'ō Reizan 峻翁令山 (1344–1408), an heir in the 4th generation of Shinchi Kakushin 心地覺心 (1207–1298) (cf. Part One, Note 34). Shun'ō Reizan studied under a number of eminent Zen masters of his time, but received his inka from Bassui Tokushō 拔隊得勝 (1327–1387), third patriarch of the Shinchi line. After Bassui's death, Reizan became the abbot of his deceased master's temple, the Kōgaku-ji 向嶽寺, at Enzan 塩山 in Kōshū 甲州, present Yamanashi Prefecture. In the autumn of 1389 he was invited by Ōe Morochika 大江師親 (*d.* 1402), lord of Katakura 片倉城主, to become the founder of a temple which that feudal lord was erecting in his domain of Bushū 武州, now part of the Tokyo area. The new temple was called the Tosotsuzan Kōon-ji 兜率山廣園寺, "Kōon" being Ōe Morochika's Buddhist name, and "Tosotsuzan" deriving from Mount Tosotsu (Doushuaishan) in China, on which the Zen master Tosotsu Jūetsu (Doushuai Congyue, 1044–1091) had lived. (This master's "*Tosotsu sankan*" is the 47th koan in *Mumonkan*.)

After he had established himself at the Kōon-ji, Reizan became the most active propagator of Rinzai Zen in the Kantō area, particularly in the districts then known as Bushū and Yashū 野州. Though originally he had studied the teachings of several lines of Japanese Zen, he preferred to promulgate those which had been transmitted by the Chinese master Mumon Ekai (Wumen Huikai) (cf. PART ONE, Note 35) to his Japanese disciple Shinchi Kakushin, and handed down in Shinchi's line. Since the first Japanese printing of Ekai's famous koan collection, *Mumonkan*, contained many errors and was not widely known, Reizan undertook to produce a definitive edition of that work. The printing of this edition was completed at the Kōon-ji in 1405, and from that time on it has been the authoritative *Mumonkan* text in Japan.

In addition to his many disciples, Reizan had as devoted adherents several feudal lords, under whose aegis he founded eight or nine other important temples. The prestige of none of these, however, equaled that of the Kōon-ji. For a long time it was the secondary headquarters (*chūhonzan* 中本山) of the Shinchi line, with forty-nine sub-temples under its jurisdiction. The Kōon-ji's position was further enhanced when Emperor Shōkō 稱光 (*r.* 1412–1428) designated it as a "Hall for Imperial Worship" (*Chokugansho* 勅願所).

But even before Reizan's death the center of Zen Buddhism had begun to move from the Kantō area to Kyoto, where the Ashikaga Shogunate, now established in the capital, was showering its munificent patronage on Rinzai Zen temples and clerics. As the years passed, and the Kyoto temples reached still greater heights of eminence, in spite of the vigorous work of Reizan's line of disciples, the importance of the Kōon-ji declined. In 1590 a disastrous fire burned the temple to the ground, destroying all its records and treasures. In the early Edo period (1603–1867) the temple was partially rebuilt under the patronage of the Tokugawa Shogunate. Again laid waste by fire in 1702, it was once more rebuilt with help from the Shogunate, which had continued to support it. After the Meiji Restoration the Kōon-ji was taken over as a sub-temple by the Nanzen-ji Honzan in Kyoto. Some thirty-odd years ago it was designated a detached *Semmon dōjō* (Monks' Training Hall) of the Nanzen-ji, and so functions today. It was at the Kōon-ji Sōdō that Isshū Rōshi completed his Zen training, and it was to it that he returned fifteen years later to assume the position of roshi. This office he still holds, though *in absentia*.

Bibliography

Explanatory

The following treatment of the books and articles quoted from or mentioned throughout the MAIN TEXT and the NOTES of *Zen Dust* has been undertaken with the hope of broadening the western reader's acquaintance with Buddhist literature, especially Chinese and Japanese Buddhist works, and to make it easier for him to identify texts, their authors, and translators, not only in the present volume, but in other works as well.

The BIBLIOGRAPHY is divided into four sections. The first section lists the comprehensive Japanese collections in which the majority of the Chinese and Japanese texts mentioned are to be found, together with the abbreviations by which reference is made to them in this work.

The second section comprises selected titles, arranged in alphabetical sequence. Here, relatively detailed information will be found on each work—the various titles under which it is known, its origin, author and/or translator, textual organization, and contents. The literal English translations of titles appearing in this section are intended to provide the reader with no more than the bare meaning of the title. They are not given elsewhere.

The third section is an index to text translations in western languages and modern western and Japanese books and articles mentioned in this work, with full publication details.

The fourth section is an index to all the Sanskrit and Chinese titles mentioned throughout the work, and to the Japanese titles not appearing in the third section.

These two indexes render unnecessary the inclusion of book titles in the General Index of *Zen Dust*. Readers are asked to note that, though no book titles are listed in the General Index, the names of authors and translators will be found there.

Collections And Abbreviations

Dainihon bukkyō zensho 大日本佛教全書 Complete Collection of Japanese Buddhist Literature, in 150 vols., and 11 supplementary vols. [Tokyo: Bussho kankōkai, 1922]; *Yūhōden sōsho* 遊方傳叢書 "Records of the Travels of Eminent Monks" Section, vols. 113–116. Referred to by full title.

Dainihon kōtei zōkyō 大日本校訂藏經 Japanese Revised Buddhist Canon (Tokyo Edition), 40 cases 帙, 318 fasicules 冊 [Tokyo: Kōkyō shoin, 1880–1885]. Abbreviated as *SK*.

Dainihon kōtei zōkyō 大日本校訂藏經 Japanese Revised Buddhist Canon (Kyoto Edition), 36 cases 帙, 347 fasicules 冊 [Kyoto: Zōkyō shoin, 1902–1905]. Abbreviated as *KZ*.

Dainihon zokuzōkyō 大日本續藏經 Supplement to the Japanese Edition of the Buddhist Canon, 150 cases 帙, 750 fasicules 冊 [Kyoto: Zōkyō shoin, 1905–1912]. Abbreviated as *Zokuzōkyō* and *ZZ*.

Hakuin oshō zenshū 白隱和尚全集 Collected Works of Master Hakuin, edited by Gōtō Kōson 後藤光村, 8 vols. [Tokyo: Ryūginsha, 1935]. Referred to by full title.

Kokuhun tōhō bukkyō sōsho 國文東方佛教叢書 Library of Japanese Buddhism [Tokyo: Tōhō shoin, 1st Series, 10 vols., 1926; 2nd Series, 10 vols., 1931–1933]. Referred to by full title.

Kokuyaku zenshū sōsho 國譯禪宗叢書 Library of Zen Literature in Japanese Translation [Tokyo: Kokuyaku zenshū sōsho kankōkai, 1st Series, 12 vols., 1919–1921; 2nd Series, 10 vols., 1925–1931]. Referred to as *KZS*.

Taishō shinshū daizōkyō 大正新修大藏經 The Buddhist Canon Published in the Taishō Era, in 100 vols. [Tokyo: Taishō issaikyō kankōkai, 1924–1934]. Abbreviated as *Taishō* and *T*.

Zoku gunsho ruijū 續群書類從 Supplement to a Classified Collection of Miscellaneous Works, compiled by Hanawa Hokiichi 塙保已一 (1746–1822), 81 vols. [Tokyo: Zoku gunsho ruijū kanseikai, 1959]. Referred to by full title.

Descriptive Bibliography

AVALOKITEŚVARA-SŪTRA, Chapter 24 of the *Saddharma-pundarīka-sūtra* or *Lotus Sutra*.

This short scripture is entirely devoted to the nature, activities, and powers of Avalokiteśvara Bodhisattva. The origin and meaning of the Sanskrit name Avalokiteśvara is not clearly known. KERN (cf., *op. cit.* below) has suggested that the word means either "Lord of View," or "Everywhere Present." The Chinese have translated Avalokiteśvara as "Observer of the Sounds (Cries) in the World," since the Bodhisattva hears the cries of suffering beings everywhere and protects them in their distress. Originally the Bodhisattva was conceived of as male, but later, particularly in China, where an important cult based upon the sutra developed, Avalokiteśvara was worshiped as female, and as such continues to be worshiped today throughout the Far East.

In the episode which forms the *Avalokiteśvara* chapter of the Sanskrit version of the *Lotus Sutra*, Shakyamuni, on being asked why Avalokiteśvara is so called, enumerates the various types of calamities from which the power of the Bodhisattva can save men, and describes the great accumulation of merit attained by those who perform but a single act of adoration to him. When Buddha is asked in what manner the Bodhisattva appears in the world of transmigration and how he preaches the Dharma, he replies that Avalokiteśvara assumes the form consonant with the person to be converted and preaches to him in a manner which accords with the listener's understanding. It is interesting to note that, though the name of Avalokiteśvara had appeared in a few sutras of earlier date than the *Lotus Sutra*, a description of the Bodhisattva's characteristics and activities is found for the first time in this chapter.

An English translation of the Sanskrit version of the sutra will be found in Chapter 24 of *The Saddharma-Pundarīka*, by H. KERN, pp. 406–418.

Guanshiyin pusa pumen pin 觀世音菩薩普門品 (*Kanzeon bosatsu fumon bon*) Chapter on the Universal Gate of the Bodhisattva Who Observes the Sounds in the World; also known as the *Guanyin jing* 觀音經 (*Kannon gyō*) The Guanyin Sutra [*T* 9: 56c. 2–58b. 7].

This, the best-known Chinese version of the *Avalokiteśvara-sūtra*, forms Chapter 25 of the *Miaofa lianhua jing* 妙法蓮華經 (*Myōhō renge kyō*), Kumārajīva's Chinese translation of the *Lotus Sutra*, q.v. This Chinese version is almost identical with the Sanskrit text. Originally the verse section with which the chapter concludes was not a part of Kumārajīva's text. During the Sui 隋 (Zui) dynasty (581–618), it was copied from the corresponding chapter, number 24, of the Chinese translation of the *Lotus Sutra* made by the Indian monks Jñānagupta (Shenajueduo 闍那崛多 Janakutta, 523–600) and Dharmagupta (Damojiduo 達磨笈多 Datsumagyūta, *d.* 619), and inserted in the Kumārajīva text.

A synopsis in English of Kumārajīva's Chinese version of the *Guanyin Sutra* will be found in Chapter 25 of *The Lotus of the Wonderful Law*, by W.E. Soothill, pp. 247–251. An early translation of the same text will be found in *A Catena of Buddhist Scriptures*, by Rev. S. Beal, pp. 389–396. A complete English translation is contained in *Manual of Zen Buddhism*, by D.T. Suzuki, pp. 30–38, entitled "The Kwannon Sutra."

The *Guanyin Sutra* is second only to the *Heart Sutra* in popularity among most Buddhist sects in China and Japan. In the Japanese Zen Sects it is chanted at almost every ceremony attended by lay men and women, and there are few Zen lay devotees who cannot recite it by heart.

Avataṁsaka-sūtra

This is the abbreviated Sanskrit title given to a Mahayana scripture of the "broad" or "comprehensive" (Skr. *mahāvai-pulya*; *dafangguang* 大方廣 *daihōkō*) class, the complete Sanskrit text of which is no longer extant, but Chinese translations of which were the basic texts of the great Huayan 華嚴 (Kegon) School of Chinese Buddhism. The full Sanskrit title of the sutra as rendered from the Chinese by B. Nanjio (A Catalogue of the Chinese Tripiṭaka, p. 34a) reads *Mahāvaipulya buddhāvataṁsaka-sūtra*, which may be translated into English as The Great Comprehensive Sutra on the Adornments of Buddha. However, since the Sanskrit word *avataṁsaka* means "garland" or "wreath" and the Chinese characters 華嚴 are considered to translate *avataṁsaka*, the work is often called in English the *Wreath Sutra*. The original Sanskrit text appears to have consisted in large part of a number of independent sutras of varying dates—some undoubtedly very early—but more or less related in subject matter. It was probably compiled in South India during the 4th century CE.

Though, as has been said above, no complete Sanskrit text of the sutra is extant, manuscript versions of the Sanskrit text of one of the more important sutras contained within the *Avataṁsaka-sūtra* do exist. This is the *Daśabhūmika-sūtra*, The Sutra on the Ten Stages [of the Bodhisattva]. Two printed Sanskrit versions based upon these manuscripts have been published: *Daśabhūmika-sūtra et Bodhisattvabhūmi*, edited by J. RAHDER, and *Daśabhūmiśvaro nāma Mahāyānasūtram*, edited by R. KONDŌ. Though the *Daśabhūmika* has not been translated into a western language, a description of the ten stages as given in it will be found in *The History of Buddhist Thought*, by Edward J. THOMAS, pp. 205–210. See also *The Bodhisattva Doctrine in Buddhist Sanskrit Literature*, by Har DAYAL.

Several of the independent sutras which came to make up the *Avataṁsaka-sūtra* were brought to China and individually translated into Chinese considerably earlier than was the complete text of the sutra. Among these, the *Daśabhūmika-sūtra* seems to have been one of the earliest to arrive and one of the most often translated. It is recorded that the first Chinese translation of this text, one in 8 *juan* was made as early as 70 CE by a monk whose name is unknown and whose work unfortunately is lost. Five excerpts from the *Avataṁsaka*, one of them the *Daśabhūmika*, were translated into Chinese by Dharmarakṣa (Zhu Fahu 竺法護 Jiku Hōgo, *n. d.*), a monk from the Dunhuang 敦煌 (Tonkō) district who worked in Chang'an 長安 (Chōan) between 265 and 313. And toward the end of his life the great Central Asian scholar Kumārajīva (Jiumoluoshi 鳩摩羅什 Kumarajū, 350–*ca.* 409), with the help of the Kashmirian monk Buddhayaśas (Fotuoyeshe 佛陀耶舍 Butsudayasha, *n. d.*), also translated the *Daśabhūmika* and another sutra of the *Avataṁsaka* group as well. Though translation of independent sections of the *Avataṁsaka-sūtra* continued to be made from time to time even after the complete text had been rendered into Chinese, we shall confine ourselves below to a description of the two translations of the complete sutra, and of the closely related *Gaṇḍavyūha-sūtra*.

The Sanskrit work known under the title *Gaṇḍavyūha-sūtra*, though related to the *Avataṁsaka-sūtra*, is not, as is sometimes mistakenly supposed, identical with it, and should not be confused with it. The relationship of the two sutras will be taken up below. A number of manuscript versions of the Sanskrit text of the *Gaṇḍavyūha-sūtra* exist. The *Gaṇḍavyūha-sūtra*, critically edited by D.T. SUZUKI and Hōkei IDUMI, is a Sanskrit text in *devanāgarī* script based upon a study and collation of six of these extant manuscripts. Neither the *Avataṁsaka* nor the *Gaṇḍavyūha* has been translated into a western language.

Dafangguang fohuayan jing 大方廣佛華嚴經 (*Daihōkō butsukegon kyō*) The Comprehensive Sutra on the Adornments of Buddha; also known as the *Huayan jing* 華嚴經 (*Kegon kyō*); *Wreath Sutra*. Translated by the Indian monk Buddhabhadra (Fotuobatuoluo 佛陀跋陀羅 Butsudabatsudara, 359–429) and others at Chang'an between 418 and 420; 34 chapters in 60 *juan* [*T* 9: 395–788].

This first Chinese translation of the *Avataṁsaka-sūtra*, popularly known both as the "Sixty-*juan* Huayan" and the "Old Translation" (*jiuyi* 舊譯 *kuyaku*), was the version studied by the first three patriarchs of the Huayan School in China, namely, Du Shun 杜順 (To Jun, 557–640), Zhiyan 智儼 (Chigon, 602–668), and Fazang 法藏 (Hōzō, 643–712), and was thus the scripture on which the fundamental doctrines of this school were based. The sutra purports to have been spoken by Shakyamuni during the three weeks immediately following his great enlightenment and while he was still in deep meditation. Its content was said to be of such profundity that those who listened to him could not comprehend his meaning. Therefore, in order to give his message to the world, he was compelled to preach afterward many other sutras, adapting his teaching to the degree of understanding of his hearers. Actually, in this sutra Buddha does not give any discourses himself, but merely sanctions and praises the statements of various great bodhisattvas in the vast company surrounding him, particularly Mañjuśrī (Wenshu 文殊 Monju) and Samantabhadra (Puxian 普賢 Fugen), and from time to time emits marvellous rays of light from his body.

Each of the thirty-four chapters comprising the work bears an individual title giving a clear indication of its contents. Chapter 2 is on Vairocana Buddha (Dari rulai 大日如來 Dainichi Nyorai), the form of Buddha which symbolizes the universe as conceived of in the sutra; chapter 22, in 5 *juan*, is the equivalent of the *Daśabhūmika-sūtra*; chapter 31 is devoted to the Bodhisattva Samantabhadra; and the final chapter, in 17 *juan*, entitled "Entering the Dharmadhātu" (*Rufajie pin* 入法界品 *Nyūhokkai bon*), takes up the pilgrimage of the youth Sudhana, who, under the guidance of Mañjuśrī, visits many teachers in his quest for complete enlightenment.

Idem. Translated by the Khotanese monk Śikṣānanda (Shichanantuo 實叉難陀 Jisshananda, 652–710) and others, at Chang'an between 695 and 699; 39 chapters in 80 *juan* [*T* 10: 1–444].

Empress Wu 武后 (Bukō, *r.* 685–704) of Tang was a patroness and devotee of Fazang, third patriarch of the Huayan School. Hearing that a more complete text of the *Avataṁsaka-sūtra* existed than that on which the "Old Translation" had been based, she sent an envoy to Khotan to procure it. This was brought to Chang'an in 695 by Śikṣānanda, and translated by him with the assistance of Fazang and others. The Empress took a great interest in the work, attending, and even participating in, some of the translation meetings, and writing a preface for it.

The contents of the "Eighty-*juan* Huayan" or "New Translation" (*xinyi* 新譯 *shin'yaku*), as this version is called, approximately parallel those of the "Old Translation," though some new material is included and several chapters have been considerably extended. On the basis of this "New Translation," the fourth patriarch of the Huayan Sect, Chengguan 澄觀 (Chōkan, 737–838), developed the "New" Huayan School.

Dafangguang fohuayan jing: Ru busiyi jiezuo jingjie; Puxian xingyuan pin 大方廣佛華嚴經：入不思議解脱境界；普賢行願品 (*Daihōkō butsukegon kyō: Nyū fushigi gedatsu kyōgai; Fugen gyōgan bon*) The Comprehensive Sutra on the Adornments of Buddha: Chapters on Entering the Realm of Ineffable Emancipation and on the Activities and Vows of Samantahadra. Also known as the *Huayan jing* (*Kegon kyō*). Translated into Chinese by the Kashmirian monk Prajña (Bore 般若 Hannya, *n. d.*) in Chang'an between 796 and 798, in 40 *juan* [*T* 10: 661–851c].

This is a Chinese translation of the text known in Sanskrit as the *Gaṇḍavyūha-sūtra*. The fact that this Chinese version has customarily been called either by its main title only—which is identical with the titles of the two complete translations of the *Avataṁsaka*—or by the title "Forty-*juan* Huayan," has often caused it to be taken as a third translation of the great sutra. The complete Chinese title, however, clearly states the contents of the work. Both the Sanskrit *Gaṇḍavyūha* and the Chinese translation based upon it are much expanded versions of two sections of the Avataṁsaka texts upon which the "Old" and "New" translations were based. These sections formed chapter 34 of the "Old" and its equivalent chapter 39 of the "New"—in both Chinese translations entitled "Chapter on Entering the Dharmadhātu" (*Rufajie pin* 入法界品 *Nyūhokkai bon*)—and chapter 31 of the "Old" and its corresponding chapter 36 of the "New," in the former entitled "Chapter on the Activities of the Bodhisattva Samantabhadra" (*Puxian pusa xing pin* 普賢菩薩行品 *Fugen bosatsu gyō bon*), and in the latter merely "Chapter on the Activities of Samantabhadra."

The first thirty-eight *juan* of this work, which might better be designated by the first part of the subtitle, "Entering the Realm of Ineffable

Emancipation," are devoted to Sudhana's search for enlightenment and his visits to fifty-three teachers, under the guidance of the Bodhisattva Mañjuśrī. This search terminates in the young pilgrim's meeting with Maitreya (Mile 彌勒 Miroku), the Buddha of the Future, who shows him the great Tower of Vairocana Buddha, and eventually deems him prepared to enter it. There Sudhana is at last able to see with his own eyes the total universe and all existences in it, the very body of Buddha itself complete with each and every one of its adornments.

The two final *juan* are concerned with Sudhana's meeting with the Bodhisattva Samantabhadra, who, by instructing him in all the activities and vows that have constituted his own life as a bodhisattva, brings Sudhana to a full realization of bodhisattvahood.

For a sympathetic study of the meaning and ideals of the *Avataṁsaka* and *Gaṇḍavyūha* sutras, the relation of their teachings to Zen, and English translations of several passages from the latter sutra, see *Essays in Zen Buddhism*, Third Series, by D.T. Suzuki, pp. 21–214, to which the foregoing is much in debt. For a short description of the doctrines of the Huayan Sect, see Part One, Note 24, of this work.

Baojing sanmei 寶鏡三昧 (*Hōkyō zammai*) "The Jeweled-mirror Samadhi." By Dongshan Liangjie 洞山良价 (Tōzan Ryōkai, 807–869) [*Inshū Tōzan Gohon zenji goroku*; *T* 47: 515a.16–b.10].

This long poem, consisting of 94 lines in the ancient style of four characters to a line, is one of the famous works in Zen literature. From early times there have been differences of opinion as to its authorship, and the poem has been variously attributed to Shitou Xiqian 石頭希遷 (Sekitō Kisen, 700–790), Yueshan Weiyan 藥山惟儼 (Yakusan Igen, 745–828), Yunyan Tansheng 雲巖曇晟 (Ungan Donjō, 780?–841), and Dongshan Liangjie. Undoubtedly the first intimations of the ideas expressed in the *Baojing sanmei* are to be found in Shitou's poem *Cantongqi* 參同契 (*Sandōkai*) "In Praise of Identity" [cf. Part Two, Note 118]. These ideas were probably orally transmitted by Shitou to his heir Yueshan, somewhat developed by Yueshan and transmitted to his heir Yunyan, and, after further development by this latter master, transmitted by him to his heir Dongshan, who put them into their final and literary form at the time he transmitted his Dharma to his heir Caoshan Benji 曹山本寂 (Sōzan Honjaku, 840–901).

The basic concept or doctrine set forth in the work is that of the eternal and ever-continuous mutual interpenetration of the Absolute

(Noumenon) and the relative (phenomena). The "Jeweled-mirror Samadhi" of the title refers to the state of realization in which one's self is all phenomenal existences, and all phenomenal existences are one's self, the state which, in Hakuin's words, "is like two mirrors reflecting one another without even the shadow of an image between." Actually, however, four other states of realization are hinted at in the poem, one prior to that of the "Jeweled-mirror Samadhi," and three subsequent to it, making a total of five distinct but consecutive states of realization, five steps, positions, or ranks (*wuwei* 五位 *goi*) through which the abstruse doctrine of continuous mutual interpenetration is to be comprehended in its entirety and in its several aspects. At one point, five possible positions of the *Yi jing* hexagram No. 30—*Li* 離 *Ri*—are used as symbolic illustrations of these five states. In addition, the poem gives instructions for students to whom the doctrine has already been conveyed. This doctrine has been more succinctly, if no less abstrusely, stated in five short poems generally attributed to Dongshan and known as the "Verses on the Five Ranks" (*Wuwei song* 五位頌 *Goi no ju*). (For English translations of these and Hakuin's commentary upon them, *see* Part Two, pp. 67–72.)

Through the centuries innumerable commentaries have been written on the *Baojing sanmei* and the *Wuwei song* by men of all schools of Zen in both China and Japan. Since Dongshan and his disciple Caoshan, who further clarified and fixed the doctrine of the Five Ranks, were considered co-founders of the Chinese Caodong (Sōtō) Sect, it is in this sect that special emphasis has been placed upon the study of the *Baojing sanmei*. In Japanese Sōtō Sect monasteries it is still recited at the daily sutra-chanting services.

An English translation of the *Baojing sanmei* by Lu K'uan Yü (Charles Luk) will be found in that author's *Chan and Zen Teaching*, Second Series, pp. 149–154. A translation of Dongshan's "Verses on the Five Ranks" will be found on p. 135*f* of the same work.

Changuan Cejin 禪關策進 (*Zenkan sakushin*) To Encourage Zealous Study of the Zen Barriers (i.e., Koans). Compiled and with a preface by Zhuhong 袾宏 (Shukō, 1535–1615), published in 1600 in 1 *juan* [*T* 48: 1097–1109a].

Zhuhong, like many Zen men of the late Ming, was interested in making a synthesis not only of Zen and Nembutsu but of Confucianism, Taoism, and Buddhism. His compilation contains excerpts from the sermons and talks of Song and early Ming Zen masters of various schools, accounts of satori experiences, and quotations relating to Zen study taken from the sutras, gathered together, as stated in the title, for the purpose of stimulating and encouraging monks and laymen engaged in Zen meditation practice and koan study. It was in this work that Hakuin Ekaku 白隱慧鶴 found the story of Shishuang Chuyuan 石霜楚圓 (Sekisō Soen, 986–1039), who had kept himself awake during long periods of meditation by sticking his thigh with a gimlet, a story which is said to have led to the young Hakuin's decision to become a Zen monk.

The work was first published in Japan in 1762 by Hakuin's heir Tōrei Enji 東嶺圓慈(1721–1792), who wrote an epilogue for this edition.

Chanzong Wumenguan 禪宗無門關 (*Zenshū mumonkan*) The Gateless Barrier of the Zen School; also known as *Wumenguan* 無門關 (*Mumonkan*) The Gateless Barrier. By Wumen Huikai 無門慧開 (Mumon Ekai, 1183–1260), and edited by Zongshao 宗紹 (Shūshō, *n. d.*), in 1 *juan*; completed in 1228 and published in 1229 [*T* 48: 292a–299c].

This work is the most popular and widely used of all Zen koan collections. The Zen Master Wumen Huikai of the Yangqi (Yōgi) line of Linji (Rinzai) Zen selected forty-eight important koans from the sayings of the old masters, adding to each his own commentary in prose and verse. The Master's material was compiled and edited by his disciple Zongshao. The year after the work was completed it was offered to Emperor Lizong 理宗 (Risō, *r.* 1224–1264) in commemoration of the fifth year of his accession to the throne, and immediately printed. No copies of this original edition remain.

Concerning the occasion of the work, Huikai writes in his preface: "In the summer of the first year of the Shaoding era [1228], I was in charge of the assembly at the Longxiang temple in Dongjia [東嘉龍翔寺, in modern Zhejiang]. At the request of the monks I gave them koans of the old masters to use, just as tiles are used to knock at the gate, and guided the students, each according to his ability. Without my being aware of it, the notes I made gradually became a collection consisting of forty-eight cases, but arranged in no systematic order. I call the collection the *Wumenguan*." [*Ibid.*, 292b.16–19]

As for the full name of the text, Huikai has this to say at the beginning of his prose comment on the first koan in the collection: "Tell me, what are the barriers of the patriarchs? Only this one letter *Wu* 無 (*Mu*). This is the single barrier to the gate of of our school. Therefore I have given this work the title *Chanzong wumenguan*." [*Ibid.*, 292c.27*f*]

In 1245 Huikai's lay disciple, the official Meng Gong 孟珙 (Mō Kō, *d.* 1246), also known as Wu'an Jushi 無安居士 (Muan Koji), published a second edition, to which a 49th koan with prose and verse commentary was added. Wu'an stated in his postface that this koan was selected and commented upon by Anwan 安晚 (Amban). Anwan was the Buddhist name of Zheng Qingzhi 鄭清之 (Tei Seishi, *d.* 1251), a Song official who was also a lay disciple of Huikai.

When the Japanese monk Shinchi Kakushin 心地覺心 (1207–1298) took leave of Huikai in 1254 to return to his own country, the Master is said to have presented him with a copy of the *Wumenguan*. The work reputedly was first printed in Japan at the Kōkoku-ji 興國寺, a temple in present Wakayama Prefecture originally founded by Kakushin. That edition is said to have contained many errors, and a corrected second edition was produced in 1405 at the Tosotsuzan Kōon-ji 兜率山廣園寺. The colophon to this second edition says: "As the old blocks have been defaced, we ordered cutters to carve the blocks anew and the work has just been completed. The blocks will be kept in the Tosotsuzan Kōon-ji, Bushū. October 13, the twelfth year of Ōei 應永 [1405]. The monk in charge, Jōboku 常牧." [*Ibid.*, 299c.23–25] The Tosotsuzan Kōon-ji is a temple at Hachiōji, not far from Tokyo, which was related to Kakushin's line of disciples, and of which Isshū Rōshi, though presently living in New York, remains the priest. All the texts of the *Wumenguan* currently in use in Japan are based upon the Kōon-ji edition.

Complete English translations of the text are as follows: "The Gateless Gate," in *Zen Flesh, Zen Bones*, transcribed by Nyogen Senzaki and Paul Reps, pp. 109–161; "The Mu Mon Kwan, " in *Zen for the West*, by Sōhaku Ogata, Appendix I, pp. 79–134. D.T. Suzuki, in his *Essays in Zen Buddhism*, Second Series, pp. 249–252, has translated the introduction to the work and the first koan.

A complete German translation has been made by Heinrich Dumoulin, S.J., under the title *Das Wu-men-kuan*. Free renderings in German of seventeen koans with their commentaries and verses will be found in *Zen, der lebendige Buddhismus in Japan*, by Ōhasama-Faust.

Chodang chip 祖堂集 (*Sodō shū*) A Collection from the Halls of the Patriarchs. Compiled in 952 by the two monks Jing 靜 (Jō, *n. d.*) and Yun 筠 (In, *n. d.*), in 20 *juan*; published in Korea in 1245.

This, the oldest extant history of Chinese Zen, is a collection of the biographies of 246 Zen patriarchs and monks, their teachings, questions and answers (*wenda* 問答 *mondō*), transmission verses, and miscellaneous writings. Material on the Seven Buddhas of the Past, the twenty-eight patriarchs of Zen in India, the six Chinese patriarchs, and masters in the lines of descent from these latter until the time of the disciples of Xuefeng Yicun 雪峰義存 (Seppō Gison, 822–908), is arranged chronologically and classified according to master-disciple relationship and the several schools.

Nothing is known about the compilers other than that they were disciples of Wendeng 文僜 (Buntō, *n. d.*), also known as Jingxiu Chanshi 淨修禪師 (Jōshū Zenji), in the 3rd generation of Xuefeng's (Seppō's) line, and that they lived with Wendeng at the Zhaoqingyuan 招慶院 (Shōkei-in) in Quanzhou 泉州 (Senshū), in present Fujian. (The Zhaoqingyuan was the temple which Wang Yanbin 王延彬 [Ō Empin, *n. d.*] had built in 906 for Changqing Huileng 長慶慧稜 [Chōkei Eryō, 854–932], one of Xuefeng's direct heirs. Cf., Part II, Note. 108.)

After the compilation had been completed it was taken to Korea. It was published in 1245 at the Haein-sa 海印寺 (Kaiin-ji), a famous temple in Kyŏngsang-namdo 慶尚南道 (Keishō-nandō), southern Korea. At that time the Korean edition of the Buddhist Canon was in the course of being printed (1236–1251) at the same temple, and the format used in printing the *Chodang chip*, including the character script, was the same as that used for the Tripiṭaka.

The *Chodang chip* seems never to have been either printed or read in China. The work is of great interest for early Zen history, however, since it contains considerable material not to be found in the traditional Chinese biographical collections such as the *Jingde chuandeng lu*, and on some points even contradicts these later compilations. Also included in it are the biographies of seven Korean monks who had studied under Zen masters in China, then returned to their native land. Whether these biographies were originally in the compilation or whether they were added after it reached Korea is nowhere stated.

The text now available, a mimeographed copy of an original Haein-sa text, was published in 1960 in 5 volumes by the Hanazono Daigaku 花園大學, Kyoto.

Ciming chanshi wuhui zhuchi yulu 慈明禪師五會住持語錄 (*Jimyō zenji goe jūji goroku*) The Record of the Zen Master Ciming, Head of Five

Assemblies; also known as the *Ciming heshang wuhui yulu* 慈明和尚五會語錄 (*Jimyō oshō goe goroku*) The Record of the Five Assemblies of Master Ciming; *Shishuang Chuyuan chanshi yulu* 石霜楚圓禪師語錄 (*Sekisō Soen zenji goroku*) The Record of the Zen Master Shishuang Chuyuan; and the *Ciming lu* 慈明錄 (*Jimyō roku*) The Record of Ciming. In 1 *juan* [*ZZ* 2: 25.1.81a–93c].

This is the record of the sayings of Shishuang Chuyuan 石霜楚圓 (Sekisō Soen, 986–1039), one of the most important of the Linji (Rinzai) School masters in early Song. Ciming Chanshi was the Master's posthumous title.

As the second of the two short prefaces to the present work is dated 1027, it seems probable that a first compilation was made during the Master's lifetime. Huanglong Huinan 黃龍慧南 (Ōryō E'nan, 1002–1069), one of Shishuang's most eminent heirs and founder of the Huanglong (Ōryō) line of the Linji School, is credited with reediting the first section of the work, that covering the sermons given by the Master while he was living at the Guangli Chanyuan 廣利禪院 (Kōri zenyin) on Nanyuanshan 南源山 (Nangenzan), in present Jiangxi Province. It is nowhere clear, however, who the compiler or compilers of the remainder of the work were, or when it was first published.

The first preface to the present text states that the compilation was republished in 1153 as the first section of the *Ciming sijia lu* 慈明四家錄 (*Jimyō shike roku*) The Record of the Four Houses of Ciming, the remaining three sections of this work being devoted respectively to the records of Shishuang's other distinguished heir Yangqi Fanghui 楊岐方會 (Yōgi Hōe, 992–1049), founder of the Yangqi line of the Linji School, Yangqi's heir Baiyun Shouduan 白雲守端 (Hakuun Shutan, 1025–1072), and Baiyun's heir Wuzu Fayan 五祖法演 (Goso Hōen, 1024?–1104).

The main body of the work contains five brief accounts of the formal sermons and informal talks given by Shishuang while he was residing successively at five different Zen temples, as well as the *wenda* 問答 (*mondō*), or exchanges of question and answer between himself and his students, that took place at each. It concludes with three additional sections, entitled respectively *Xinglu* 行錄 (*Anroku*), the record of the Master's pilgrimage; *Kanbian* 勘辨 (*Kamben*), short conversations with various monks and laymen; and *Jiesong* 渴頌 (*Geju*), religious verse. The *Xinglu* and *Kanbian* sections were obviously patterned upon the two sections of like name in the *Linji lu* (*Rinzai roku*).

Selections from this work were included in *juan* 1 of the *Xukai guzunsu yuyao* (1238) [*ZZ* 2: 23.5.422d–426d], and in *juan* 11 of the *Guzunsu yulu* (1267) [*ZZ* 2: 23.2.141b–145c].

Dahui Jue chanshi pushuo 大慧覺禪師普説 (*Daie Kaku zenji fusetsu*) The Discourses of the Zen Master Dahui Jue; also known as the *Dahui pushuo* 大慧普説 (*Daie fusetsu*) The Discourses of Dahui. Compiled by Zuqing 祖慶 (Sokei, *n. d.*), in 5 *juan* [*KZ* 31.5].

This work comprises the talks on Zen given to his many religious and lay disciples by Dahui Zonggao 大慧宗果 (Daie Sōkō, 1089–1163), a famous master in the 5th generation of the Yangqi (Yōgi) line of Linji (Rinzai) Zen. The Master's posthumous title was Pujue Chanshi 普覺禪師 (Fukaku Zenji). The work was compiled between 1188 and 1190 by the Master's disciple Zuqing. These same discourses, as compiled by another disciple, Yunwen 蘊聞 (Ummon, *n. d.*), constitute *juan* 13–18 of the *Dahui Pujue chanshi yulu*.

Zuqing says in his preface to the compilation that, just as Ānanda had been the longest in attendance upon Shakyamuni, so he had been longest near his master Dahui and had heard all his discourses. Zuqing's work covers the same material as is found in Yunwen's version, but the arrangement of the discourses is different and much additional material is included.

For an English translation of an excerpt from this work, see D.T. Suzuki, *Essays in Zen Buddhism*, Second Series, pp. 93–95.

Dahui Pujue chanshi yulu 大慧普覺禪師語錄 (*Daie Fukaku zenji goroku*) The Record of the Zen Master Dahui Pujue; also known as the *Dahui yulu* 大慧語錄 (*Daie goroku*) The Record of Dahui, and the *Dahui lu* 大慧錄 (*Daie roku*) Dahui's Record. Compiled by Yunwen 蘊聞 (Ummon, *n. d.*) and other disciples; published in 1172, in 30 *juan* [*T* 47: 811b–943b.4].

This is a comprehensive collection containing the larger part of the writings, sermons, talks, and verse of Dahui Zonggao (Daie Sōkō, 1089–1163), a famous master in the 5th generation of the Yangqi (Yōgi) line of Linji (Rinzai) Zen. The Master's posthumous title was Pujue Chanshi 普覺禪師 (Fukaku Zenji).

The first eight *juan* of the work consist of the Master's *shangtang* 上堂 (jōdō), formal sermons from the high seat. The first section of *juan* 9 contains the Master's *bingfu* 秉拂 (*himpotsu*). (This term means literally "to take hold of the whisk," but, since this was the first action of a master on taking the high seat, the word is used as a term for a sermon.) These *bingfu* were talks which Dahui gave in place of Yuanwu Keqin 圜悟克勤 (Engo Kokugon), while he was visiting his old master at Mount Yunju 雲居山 (Ungozan). The second section of *juan* 9 bears the title *Shizhong jiyuan* 室中機緣 (*Shitchū kien*) "Koans Given in the Inner Room." This consists of koans which Dahui gave to students when he took Yuanwu's place in the sanzen room at Mount Yunju. *Juan* 10–12 are devoted to the Master's poems and verse of various types; *juan* 13–18 contain the *Dahui pushuo* 大慧普説 (*Daie fusetsu*), Dahui's discourses to religious and lay students; *juan* 19–24 comprise his *fayu* 法語 (*hōgo*), instructions for study and practice written for individual disciples; and *juan* 25–30 contain the Master's letters.

The material included in the *Dahui pushuo* (*juan* 13–18), as augmented and compiled by Zuqing 祖慶 (Sokei, *n. d.*), another of the Master's disciples, was published later under the title *Dahui Jue chanshi pushuo*.

English translations of short extracts from the *Dahui yulu* (Record of Dahui) will be found here and there in D.T. Suzuki's *Essays in Zen Buddhism*, Second Series. In the same author's *Essays in Zen Buddhism*, Third Series, p. 279, will be found another extract.

Dahui Pujue chanshi zongmen wuku 大慧普覺禪師宗門武庫 (*Daie Fukaku zenji shūmon buko*) The Chan (Zen) Arsenal of Dahui Pujue Chanshi; also known as the *Dahui wuku* 大慧武庫 (*Daie buko*) Dahui's Arsenal. Compiled by Daoqian 道謙 (Dōken, *n. d.*), in 1 *juan*, with a preface dated 1186 [*T* 47: 943b.8–957c.1].

A collection of comments on old Chan masters, as well as on a few who were his contemporaies, by Dahui Zonggao 大慧宗杲 (Daie Sōkō, 1089–1163), a famous master in the 5th generation of the Yangqi (Yōgi) line of the Linji (Rinzai) School. Dahui's posthumous title was Pujue Chanshi 普覺禪師 (Fukaku Zenji). Daoqian, who was one of the Master's disciples, had recorded many of Dahui's sermons and talks, and from these selected such short remarks and comments as he thought would be useful to students. The text is particularly rich in anecdotes.

Daitō kokushi hōgo 大燈國師法語 The Religious Instructions of the National Teacher Daitō. Edited by Washio Junkyō 鷲尾順敬, in 1 *kan* [*Kokubun tōhō bukkyō sōsho*, Second Series, Vol. I, pp. 147–155].

This short work consists chiefly of two *hōgo* 法語—instructions for Zen practice and study written for individual students—by Shūhō Myōchō 宗峰妙超 (1282–1338), better known by his title Daitō Kokushi. The first of these was composed for the consort of the retired Emperor Hanazono 花園 (*r.* 1308–1318), Empress Senkōmon-in Tsuneko 宣光門院實子 (*d.* 1360), the second for an unnamed person of high rank, perhaps the Empress. In both, the Kokushi, writing in Japanese, explains in clear and simple language the essential principles of Zen, and emphasises the necessity for attaining *kenshō* 見性—insight into one's own nature—through the practice of zazen and the observance of koans, citing many illustrations from the old Chinese masters. A fragment of a third *hōgo* in the same vein concludes this little collection. As these *hōgo* were copied down by hand generation after generation, several different versions of them exist. However, the text mentioned above is the one most easily available today.

Denkō roku 傳光錄 The Record of the Transmission of the Light, by Keizan Jōkin 瑩山紹瑾 (1268–1325), fourth patriarch of the Japanese Sōtō Sect. Edited by one of his disciples; in 2 *kan*, first published in 1857 [*T* 82: 343–411].

This is a Japanese Sōtō Sect biographical compilation patterned after the *Keitoku dentō roku*. The work, written in Japanese with inserted passages of *kambun* 漢文, opens with a life of Shakyamuni and continues through the line of Indian and Chinese patriarchs accepted by the Japanese Sōtō School up to and including the 50th patriarch, the Chinese master Tiantong Rujing 天童如淨 (Tendō Nyojō, 1163–1228). It concludes with biographies of Dōgen Kigen 道元希玄 (1200–1253), founder of Japanese Sōtō, and his heir Koun Ejō 孤雲懷奘 (1198–1280), the 51st and 52nd patriarchs respectively. The preface, written for the edition published in 1857, includes a short biography of Keizan Jōkin.

The Dongshan Records

Though Dongshan Liangjie 洞山良价 (Tōzan Ryōkai, 807–869) was one of the great figures of Chinese Zen in the late Tang, and, with his disciple Caoshan Benji 曹山本寂 (Sōzan Honjaku, 840–901), was the founder of the Caodong 曹洞 (Sōtō) School of Zen, the first collection of his recorded sayings and writings was made in China only at the end of the Ming dynasty (1368–1644). Within the following hundred years, however, two other important collections of material relating to Dongshan had been compiled in Japan by Japanese Sōtō Sect monks. Since the relationship of these three texts to one another is somewhat involved, they will be treated below under separate headings.

Ruizhou Dongshan Liangjie chanshi yulu 瑞州洞山良价禪師語錄 (*Zuishū Tōzan Ryōkai zenji goroku*) The Record of the Zen Master Dongshan Liangjie of Ruizhou; also known as the *Dongshan yulu* 洞山語錄 (*Tōzan goroku*) The Record of Dongshan. Compiled by Yufeng Yuanxin 語風圓信 (Gofū Enshin, *n. d.*) and Guo Ningzhi 郭凝之 (Kaku Gyōshi, *n. d.*), in 1 *juan* published in 1630 [*T* 47: 519b–526b].

This Chinese compilation comprises biographical material, sermons, mondos, and the Master's famous poem *Baojing sanmei* 寶鏡三昧 (*Hōkyō zammai*) "Jeweled-mirror Samadhi." The *Dongshan yulu* formed the first part of the section in the *Wujia yulu* 五家語錄 (*Goke goroku*) Records of the Five Houses, devoted to the Dongcaozong (Tōsōshū), the second part of which comprised the record of Dongshan's disciple Caoshan Benji. The *Wujia yulu*, as has been stated elsewhere, was compiled by Yufeng Yuanxin, a monk in the 24th generation of the Yangqi (Yōgi) line of Linji (Rinzai) Zen, and the unknown layman Guo Ningzhi, while they were living at Jingshan 徑山 (Kinzan), in present Zhejiang, and was probably published in Hangzhou about 1632. The work was brought to Japan a short time later.

Tōzan Gohon zenji goroku 洞山悟本禪師語錄 The Record of the Zen Master Tōzan Gohon; also known as the *Tōzan goroku* 洞山語錄 The Record of Tōzan. Compiled in 1739 by Gimoku Genkai 宜默玄契 (*n. d.*), in 1 *juan* [*KZS*, Vol. 8: Japanese translation, followed by Chinese character text].

This second compilation of material on Dongshan Liangjie (Tōzan Ryōkai) was made by the Japanese Sōtō Sect scholar-monk Gimoku Genkai. Gohon Zenji 悟本禪師 (Wuben Chanshi) was Tōzan's posthumous title. From internal evidence it is clear that Gimoku was well acquainted with the Tōzan text in the *Wujia yulu*, mentioned above, since his *Tōzan goroku* was in part based upon material he had taken from this Chinese work and reedited. (Gimoku's acquaintance with the *Wujia yulu* is further substantiated by the fact that the material in *kan* 1 of his *Sōzan goroku* 曹山語錄 [*KZS*, Vol. 8], a companion volume to his *Tōzan goroku*, was copied directly from the Caoshan [Sōzan] section of that Chinese compilation.) Gimoku included in his work material from an earlier Japanese "Record of Tōzan," only the title of which is extant today, several of the

Master's poems, and his "Verses on the Five Ranks" *Goi no ju* 五位頌 *Wuwei song*), the latter of which Gimoku had taken from a Japanese edition of the *Tōzan goi kenketsu* (see below).

Some years later Gimoku discovered new manuscript material on Tōzan in the district of Izumo 出雲, present Shimane Prefecture. This he published as a supplement to his *Tōzan goroku* under the title *Tōzan goroku no yo* 洞山語錄之餘 Supplement to the Record of Tōzan [*T* 47: 517a.l4–518a.16]. (This text will also be found concluding both the Japanese translation and the Chinese character text in the *KZS* reference above. Though the *Taishō* refers to material in Gimoku's text in various footnotes to other Tōzan records, it does not print the main text itself.)

Inshū Tōzan Gohon zenji goroku 筠州洞山悟本禪師語錄 The Record of the Zen Master Tōzan Gohon of Inshū, also known as the *Tōzan daishi goroku* 洞山大師語錄 The Record of Master Tōzan, and the *Tōzan goroku* 洞山語錄 The Record of Tōzan. Compiled by Shigetsu Ein 指月慧印 (*d.* 1764), in 1 *kan*, published in 1761 [*T* 47: 507a–517a.10].

This is the most complete of all the records of Tōzan Ryokai, and is that usually referred to when the "Record of Tōzan" is spoken of. Its compiler, the mid-Tokugawa era Sōtō monk Shigetsu Ein, had no direct acquaintance with the Chinese Ming compilation, but based his work upon materials existing in Japan in his time. These consisted of the writings of Dōgen Kigen and other Japanese Sōtō masters, and the *Tōzan goroku* of Gimoku Genkai, mentioned above, which had been compiled some twenty years earlier. Shigetsu took over this latter work in its entirety, but reedited and rearranged its contents. He copied the *Tōzan goroku no yo* directly from Gimoku's work, appending it to his own, but attributing it to its original compiler. Shigetsu also included in his work a number of Tōzan's writings: his longer poems, such as the *Hōkyō zammai* "Jeweled-mirror Samadhi," the *Shimpōgin* 新豐吟 (*Xinfengyin*) "Song of [Mount] Shimpō," and the *Genchūmei* 玄中銘 (*Xuanzhongming*) "On the Innermost Mystery"; shorter verses; prose selections; admonitions to himself and his disciples; and letters exchanged between his mother and himself.

In addition to the *Tōzan goroku*, Shigetsu also compiled a record of Tōzan's disciple Sōzan Honjaku, the *Bushū Sōzan Genshō zenji goroku* 撫州曹山元證禪師語錄 The Record of the Zen Master Sōzan Genshō of Bushū, in 1 *kan* [*T* 47: 526b.27–535c.18]. This work contains the "Verses on the Five Ranks" usually ascribed to Tōzan, since Shigetsu believed them to have been actually written by Sōzan. It is for this reason that the verses are mentioned by title only in Shigetsu's *Tōzan goroku*. Shigetsu's two compilations have always been considered complementary, and together are given the name *Sōtō nishi roku* 曹洞二師錄 The Records of the Two Sōtō Masters.

Dongshan wuwei xianjue 洞山五位顯訣 (*Tōzan goi kenketsu*) Key to the Secrets of Dongshan's Five Ranks; also known as the *Wuwei xianjue* 五位顯訣 (*Goi kenketsu*) The Key to the Secrets of the Five Ranks. Originally compiled by Huixia 慧霞 (Eka, *n. d.*) and Guanghui 廣輝 (Kōki, *n. d.*), in 1 *juan* [*ZZ* 2: 16.2.114c–133d].

This is a compilation of various prose commentaries on Dongshan Liangjie's doctrine of the Five Ranks, written by Caoshan Benji and other Chinese Caodong School masters. Dongshan's "Verses on the Five Ranks" and the verses of other Caodong masters are quoted in order to illustrate the commentaries. The compilers of the work are believed to have been direct disciples of Caoshan, and thus to have lived at the beginning of the 10th century. The original text went through several revisions, and numerous commentaries were gradually added to it during the Song and Yuan dynasties. After the text had been brought to Japan it underwent one more revision at the hands of several scholar-monks of the Sōtō Sect, and was first published there in 1680.

Dunwu rudao yaomen lun 頓悟入道要門論 (*Tongo nyūdō yōmon ron*) On the Essentials for Entering Dao through Sudden Awakening; also known as the *Dunwu yaomen* 頓悟要門 (*Tongo yōmon*) The Essentials of Sudden Awakening. By Dazhu Huihai 大珠慧海 (Daishu Ekai, *n. d.*); edited by Miaoxie 妙叶 (Myōkyō, *n. d.*); first published in 1374, in 2 *juan* [*ZZ* 2: 15.5.420c–433a].

The author of this work, Dazhu Huihai, was born during the Tang in Jianzhou 建州 (Kenshū), in present Fujian Province, and his surname was Zhu 朱 (Shu). He first entered the Dayunsi 大雲寺 (Daiun-ji) in Yuezhou 越州 (Esshū), to the southeast of present Hangzhou, in Zhejiang Province, where his head was shaved by a certain Daozhi Chanshi 道智禪師 (Dōchi Zenji, *n. d.*). Later he joined the assembly of Mazu Daoyi 馬祖道一 (Baso Dōitsu, 709–788), and, after some six years under that famous master, was accorded the Transmission of Dharma and acknowledged as an heir. Huihai then went back to Yuezhou to care for his now aged teacher Daozhi. No further details are known about his life other than that the present work was written after his retirement.

It is believed that, after the *Dunwu yaomen* was completed, Huihai secretly gave the manuscript to one of his disciples, who, on a visit to Mazu, showed the work to that master. After looking it over, Mazu is said to have exclaimed, "In Yuezhou there is a Great Pearl (*dazhu* 大珠 *daishu*), the perfect and bright luminance of which penetrates everywhere without hindrance." *Dazhu*, or "Great Pearl," is a play of words on Huihai's surname, also pronounced *zhu*.) Thereafter Huihai was known as Dazhu Huihai.

The editor-compiler of the present text of the work, Miaoxie, was a Tiantai (Tendai) scholar-monk of early Ming. He tells us in his preface that, in 1369, the second year of the Hongwu 洪武 (Kōbu) era (1368–1398), he discovered the original text in a "broken case." From this "discovery" he compiled the first *juan* of the present text, under its original title *Dunwu rudao yaomen lun*. He then reedited the biographical material on Huihai in *juan* 6 of the *Chuandeng lu*, as well as the Master's sermons and mondos in *juan* 28 of the same work, making these into a second *juan* which he entitled *Zhufang menren canwen yulu* 諸方門人參問語錄 (*Shohō monjin sammon goroku*) "The Record of Questions Asked by Disciples from Everywhere." For some unexplained reason, Miaoxie concluded this *juan* with the *Anxin famen*, attributed to Bodhidharma. His complete compilation was published in 1374.

The first *juan* of the work is devoted to a detailed exposition of the sudden awakening doctrine as it was taught in the Southern School of Chinese Zen during the Tang. The literary form employed is that of questions and answers. Probably the questions were ones propounded by Huihai himself, rather than those put to him by inquiring students, for thus the Master was better able to express his complete view of the subject. The second *juan*, as indicated above, comprises various of the Master's sermons and his answers to questions asked by his disciples. An interesting feature of the work is its many references to and quotations from Buddhist scriptures, showing that even an exponent of the "Sudden School" of Zen was aware of the necessity for a thorough grounding in the basic doctrines of Mahayana Buddhism.

The work as it now stands opens with a preface by Fuzong Chongyu 扶宗崇裕 (Fushū Sūyū, 1304–1378) of the Ayuwangshan 阿育王山 (Aikuōzan), in present Zhejiang, and closes with two epilogues, one by the compiler Miaoxie, the other by the monk Wanjin 萬金 (Mankin, *n. d.*). A colophon at the end states that the text was reprinted in 1597, the

25th year of the Wanli 萬曆 (Manreki) era (1573–1620) of Ming, at the Xingsheng Wanshou chansi 興聖萬壽禪寺 (Kōshō Manju zen-ji), at Jingshan 徑山 (Kinzan), in modern Zhejiang.

John Blofeld, in *The Zen Teaching of Hui Hai on Sudden Illumination*, has given an English translation of *juan* 1 and 2. He has omitted the *Anxin famen*—this is omitted from the *Zokuzōkyō* reprint also—as well as the preface and the epilogues.

Enzū Daiō kokushi goroku 圓通大應國師語錄 The Record of the National Teacher Enzū Daiō; also known as the *Daiō goroku* 大應語錄 The Record of Daiō. In 2 *kan*, first printed in 1372 at the Ryōshō-ji 龍翔寺, Kyoto [*T* 80: 94a–128b].

This is the record of the eminent Japanese Rinzai priest Nampo Jōmyō 南浦紹明 (1235–1309), whose posthumous title was Enzū Daiō Kokushi. The work opens with a short introduction by the Chinese monk Zongle 宗泐 (Sōroku, 1318–1391), in the 6th generation of the line of Dahui Zonggao (Daie Sōkō). The first *kan*, compiled by the Master's disciple Soshō 祖照 (*n. d.*) and others, contains various sermons from the high seat (*jōdō* 上堂 *shangtang*) and informal talks (*shōsan* 小參 *xiaocan*) given by the Kokushi during the years he was living at the Kōtoku-ji 興德寺 and the Sōfuku-ji 崇福寺, both in Fukuoka, Kyushu. The second *kan*, compiled by his disciple Sōshin 宗心 (*d.* 1351) and others, comprises the Master's sermons at the Manju-ji 萬壽寺 in Kyoto and the Kenchō-ji 建長寺 in Kamakura, together with miscellaneous short writings and verse. The work concludes with the Kokushi's tomb inscription composed by the Chinese monk Tingjun 廷俊 (Teishun, 1299–1368), also in the 6th generation of the Dahui line, and four epilogues, one by a Chinese monk, two by two Chinese monks living in Japan, and one by the distinguished Daitoku-ji priest Takuan Sōhō 澤庵宗彭 (1573–1645).

Fenyang Wude chanshi yulu 汾陽無德禪師語錄 (*Fun'yō Mutoku zenji goroku*) The Record of the Zen Master Wude of Fenyang; also known as the *Fenyang lu* 扮陽錄 (*Fun'yō roku*) The Record of Fenyang. Compiled by Shishuang Chuyuan 石霜楚圓 (Sekisō Soen, 986–1039), in 3 *juan* [*T* 47: 594–629c].

This work contains the sermons, talks, poems, and miscellaneous writings of Fenyang Shanzhao 汾陽善昭 (Fun'yō Zenshō, 947–1024), in the 6th generation of the Linji (Rinzai) School, whose posthumous title was Wude Chanshi. The compiler was the Master's most important heir. It seems probable that part of the text was printed during Fenyang's lifetime, but the entire work did not appear until 1101. The present text follows that of an edition printed in 1311.

The *Fenyang lu* is interesting for its several original features. *Juan* 1 is composed of the usual *shangtang* 上堂 (*jōdō*), formal sermons from the high seat, and *xiaocan* 小參 (*shōsan*), occasional informal talks. In addition, however, this *juan* contains Fenyang's verses in comment upon the Five Ranks (*wuwei* 五位 *goi*) of Dongshan Liangjie 洞山良价 (Tōzan Ryōkai, 807–869), founder of the Caodong (Sōtō) School, the first mention of this formula in any literature of the Linji School [*ibid.*, 605b.9–c.17].

Juan 2 is of particular importance, since the three collections of koans which it comprises became models for later Zen literary productions of a similar type. The first of these collections consists of one hundred *songgu* 頌古 (*juko*), old koans to which the Master added his own comment in verse; the second consists of one hundred *jiewen* 詰問 (*kitsumon*), koans which he himself devised and to which he appended his own answers (*daiyu* 代語 *daigo*); the third, of one hundred old koans to which he gave his own answers in place of those previously appended to the koans (*bieyu* 別語 *betsugo*). The final *juan* is devoted to a considerable collection of the Master's poems and religious verse.

Foguo yuanwu chanshi biyan lu 佛果圜悟禪師碧巖錄 (*Bukka Engo zenji hekigan roku*) The Green Grotto Record of the Zen Master Foguo Yuanwu; also known as the *Biyan lu* 碧巖錄 (*Hekigan roku*) The Green Grotto Record. Compiled by Puzhao 普照 (Fushō, *n. d.*), and edited by Guan Wudang 關無黨 (Kan Mutō, *n. d.*), published in 1128, in 10 *juan* [*T* 48: 139–225].

This famous Zen work is composed of a series of one hundred lectures given by Yuanwu Keqin 圜悟克勤 (Engo Kokugon, 1063–1135), a famous master in the 4th generation of the Yangqi (Yōgi) line of Linji (Rinzai) Zen. Foguo Chanshi 佛果禪師 (Bukka Zenji) was one of Yuanwu's Imperially bestowed titles.

The lectures were given on the *Xuedou baize songgu* 雪竇百則頌古 (*Setchō hyakusoku juko*), the collection of one hundred representative koans compiled by Xuedou Chongxian 雪竇重顯 (Setchō Jūken, 980–1052), of the Yunmen (Ummon) School, to each of which the compiler, a poet of great distinction, had added his own commentary in verse.

Yuanwu's students took notes of the Master's lectures, and these notes were later gathered together and compiled by his disciple Puzhao and edited by his lay disciple Guan Wudang.

The title of the book derives from the name of Yuanwu's study at the Lingquanyuan 靈泉院 (Reisen-in), the former temple of Jiashan Shanhui 夾山善會 (Kassan Zenne, 805–881), in present Hunan, where Yuanwu was residing at the time he gave the lectures. The name of the study, the "Green Grotto," in its turn derives from a famous verse which Jiashan gave in answer to a monk who once asked him, "What is the state of Jiashan?"

> The monkeys, clasping their young to their breasts,
> Return behind the blue peaks;
> A bird, holding a flower in its beak,
> Alights before the green grotto.
>
> [*Chuandeng lu*, juan 15; *T* 51: 324b]

In the *Biyan lu*, the one hundred koans follow in the same order as that in which they appear in Xuedou's work, but Yuanwu's commentary is added in a unique manner. Each koan, with its commentary, is presented in four sections, usually prefaced by a *chuishi* 垂示 (*suiji*), short introduction. Under the title *benze* 本則 (*honsoku*), literally "original case," the koan is first stated, but broken up into sentences or phrases, each followed by a short pithy remark by the Master. The *pingchang* 評唱 (*hyōshō*), long commentary on the koan, now follows. This in turn is succeeded by Xuedou's original comment in verse (*song* 頌 *ju*), but, as in the case of the koan itself, the verse is broken up and interspersed with short remarks by Yuanwu. The concluding section, also called *pingchang*, consists of Yuanwu's long commentary on Xuedou's verse.

Soon after its publication the *Biyan lu* was in wide use. Yuanwu's great disciple, Dahui Zonggao 大慧宗杲 (Daie Sōkō, 1089–1163), however, feeling that it revealed too much and was therefore harmful to Zen students, had it burned. For nearly two hundred years thereafter little was heard of the work. Sometime after 1300 the layman Zhang Mingyuan 張明遠 (Chō Meien, *n. d.*), who had collected several manuscript copies of the work in various parts of the country, began collating and editing these, finally republishing the text in 1317. This version of the *Biyan lu* reached Japan toward the end of the Kamakura era 鎌倉 (1185–1333). It has since been continuously used in all schools of Zen, but is particularly favored in the Rinzai School.

Dōgen Kigen 道元希玄 (1200–1253), founder of the Japanese Sōtō 曹

洞 Sect, brought a handwritten copy of the *Biyan lu* to Japan in 1227 when he returned from his study in China. This copy has been kept hidden in the Daijō-ji 大乘寺, a Sōtō Zen temple in Kaga 加賀, Ishikawa Prefecture, because of the tradition that anyone who looked at it would immediately become blind. It has always been known as the "One Night Hekigan," due to another tradition that Dōgen Zenji had copied the entire text from a borrowed book on the night before he sailed for Japan. Some years ago, D.T. Suzuki obtained permission to examine this manuscript. He later edited it, and it was published under the title *Bukka hekigan hakan kyakusetsu* 佛果碧巖破關擊節. It is possible that this title, which may be more or less literally translated as "Revelation and Appreciation from Bukka's Green Grotto," was the original title of Yuanwu's series of lectures. In this text the koans are not given in the usual sequence, and the commentaries are shorter and somewhat different.

A well-intentioned, but inadequate and misleading, English rendering of the *Biyan lu* is *The Blue Cliff Records*, translated, edited, and with commentary by R.D.M. Shaw. An English translation of Case (Koan) 55 by D.T. Suzuki will be found in that author's *Essays in Zen Buddhism*, Second Series, pp. 239–249, and of Case 88, in *Manual of Zen Buddhism*, pp. 120–127. A careful and scholarly German translation of the first thirty-three cases is contained in the *Bi-yän-lu*, by Wilhelm Gundert.

Foguo Yuanwu Zhenjue chanshi xinyao 佛果圜悟眞覺禪師心要 (*Bukka Engo Shinkaku zenji shin'yō*) The Essential Principles of Mind [as Explained] by the Zen Master Foguo Yuanwu Zhenjue; also known as the Yuanwu xinyao 圜悟心要 (*Engo shin'yō*) The Essential Principles of Mind [as Explained] by Yuanwu. Compiled by Ziwen 子文 (Shimon, *n. d.*), in 4 *juan* [*ZZ* 2: 25.4.348c–395c].

This is a collection of one hundred and forty-two short statements giving basic hints for the study and practice of Zen, written for individual religious and lay disciples by Yuanwu Keqin 圜悟克勤 (Engo Kokugon, 1063–1135), a master of the Yangqi (Yōgi) line of Linji (Rinzai) Zen. Foguo and Zhenjue Chanshi were two of Yuanwu's several Imperially bestowed titles. The compiler, whose full name was Hongfu Ziwen 洪福子文 (Kōfuku Shimon), was one of the Master's Dharma heirs. The work is of interest as illustrating the methods of instruction used by Yuanwu.

Virtually the same material as that contained in this text, though with some omissions, will be found in the section entitled *Fayu* 法語 (*Hōgo*),

"Suggestions for Religious Practice," in the *Yuanwu yulu*, *juan* 14 through the first half of *juan* 16 [*T* 47: 775c–788c], a work compiled by Huqiu Shaolong 虎丘紹隆 (Kukyū Jōryū), another of the Master's disciples.

Goke sanshō yōro mon 五家參詳要路門 A Detailed Study of the Fundamental Principles of the Five Houses [of Zen], by Tōrei Enji 東嶺圓慈 (1721–1792). With a preface and two appendices by the author and an epilogue by Daikan Monju 大觀文殊 (1766–1842); first published in 1827, in 5 *kan* [*T* 81: 605c–617c].

Tōrei Enji was a disciple of the famous Japanese Zen master Hakuin Ekaku 白隱慧鶴 (1686–1769), and a distinguished Zen literary man and historian. This work was undertaken by Tōrei at the request of his fellow-disciples under Hakuin, Gasan Jitō 峨山慈棹 (1727–1797) and Tairei 太靈 (*d.* 1804), and is based upon material in the earlier Chinese Zen work entitled *Rentian yanmu*. It was completed in 1788, but not published until thirty-five years after Torei's death by his disciple Daikan Monju.

The book, as its title indicates, is a careful study of the Five Houses or five distinct schools of teaching that had developed in Chinese Zen by the end of the 10th century: the Linji 臨濟 (Rinzai), Yunmen 雲門 (Ummon), Caodong 曹洞 (Sōtō), Guiyang 偽仰 (Igyō), and Fayan 法眼 (Hōgen). It is divided into five sections, one section being devoted to each "House." By the use of stories relating to their enlightenment, quotations from their sermons, and anecdotes, Tōrei skillfully indicates the particular character of each of the respective founders of the Five Houses, and the individual method and "style" of teaching which each originated and handed down to his successors. At the same time he clearly shows that, varied as their styles of Zen may have been, the founders of the Five Houses had one single purpose, that of correctly transmitting the Great Matter (*daiji* 大事), i.e., the Buddha-dharma as handed down by Bodhidharma.

Two additional essays by Tōrei were included with the basic text when it was published. These are the *Rōhatsu jishū* 臘八示衆 Instructions for Rohatsu, and the *Kankin bō* 看經榜 Sutra-chanting Announcement Board. The former stresses the importance of the satori experience, explains the attitude of mind necessary to carry on the practice successfully, and offers words of encouragement to students for each day of the Rōhatsu Ō Sesshin 臘八大接心, the week of severe meditation practice held toward the end of the year to commemorate the enlightenment of Shakyamuni. The latter speaks particularly of the correct mental attitude with which the scriptures must be chanted in order to benefit from their daily recitation.

The Guzunsu Collections

Guzunsu yuyao 古尊宿語要 (*Kosonshuku goyō*) Essential Sayings of the Old Worthies. Compiled by Sengting Shouze 僧挺守賾 (Sōtei Shusaku, *n. d.*); published in 1144, in 4 *juan*. Table of Contents (*mulu* 目錄 *mokuroku*) alone reprinted [*ZZ* 2: 24.1.95c].

This is a collection of the records of twenty Chinese Zen masters of the Tang and early Song. The compiler Sengting Shouze was a disciple of Zhu'an Shigui 竹庵士珪 (Chikuan Shikei, 1083–1146), a master in the 4th generation of the Yangqi (Yōgi) line of Linji (Rinzai) Zen. Sengting lived on the Gushan 鼓山 (Kuzan) in Fuzhou 福州 (Fukushū), in present Fujian Province, and his work was published at the Gushansi 鼓山寺 (Kuzan-ji), then a famous center for the printing of Buddhist books.

The compilation itself is not contained in any modern collection, but from the *mulu*, which the *Zokuzōkyō* reprints, we may ascertain that the work opened with material relating to Nanquan Puyuan 南泉普願 (Nansen Fugan, 748–835), in the 3rd generation of the line of Nanyue Huairang 南嶽懷讓 (Nangaku Ejō), and concluded with that relating to Zhimen Guangzuo 智門光祚 (Chimon Kōso, *d.* 1031), a monk in the 3rd generation of the Yunmen (Ummon) School.

Xukai guzunsu yuyao 續開古尊宿語要 (*Zokkai kosonshuku goyō*) A Continuation of the Essential Sayings of the Old Worthies; also known as the *Xukan guzunsu yuyao* 續干古尊宿語要 (*Zokkan kosonshuku goyō*) A Supplementary Cutting of the Essential Sayings of the Old Worthies, and the *Xu guzunsu yuyao* 續古尊宿語要 (*Zoku kosonshuku goyō*) Supplement to the Essential Sayings of the Old Worthies. Compiled by Huishi Shiming 晦室師明 (Maishitsu Shimei, *n. d.*), published in 1238, in 6 *juan* [*ZZ* 2: 23.5 and 24.1a–95a]. Table of Contents [*ZZ* 2: 24.1.98d–101a].

This supplement to the *Guzunsu yuyao* was compiled by Huishi Shiming, another monk who lived on the Gushan. It contains the complete or partial records of eighty-two Zen masters, no one of whom was included in the earlier 1144 collection. The work opens with material on Linji Yixuan 臨濟義玄 (Rinzai Gigen, *d.* 866), which, in the original edition, consisted of the complete *Linji lu* 臨濟錄 (*Rinzai roku*), together with the famous preface to it by Ma Fang 馬防 (Ba Bō). (The *Zokuzōkyō*, for convenience, gives only this preface in its reprint of the "Supplement," and refers readers to the *Chongke guzunsu yulu*, described below, for the full *Linji lu* text.) The "Supplement" concludes with material on Huo'an Shiti 或菴師體 (Wakuan Shitai, 1108–1179), in the 6th generation of the Yangqi line through Yuanwu Keqin (Engo Kokugon).

Chongke guzunsu yulu 重刻古尊宿語錄 (*Jūkoku kosonshuku goroku*) A Reissue of Records of the Old Worthies; also known as the *Guzunsu yulu* 古尊宿語錄 (*Kosonshuku goroku*) Records of the Old Worthies. Compiled in 1267 by Juexin 覺心 (Kakushin, *n. d.*), in 48 *juan* [*SK* 騰: 4–6, and *ZZ* 2: 23.2–4]. Table of Contents [*ZZ* 2: 24.1.97a–98c].

This third "Old Worthies" collection was made by Juexin, who was a woman lay-disciple of Wuchu Daguan 物初大觀 (Busso Daikan, *n. d.*), a monk in the 8th generation of the Yangqi line through Dahui Zonggao (Daie Sōkō). The place of publication is not stated, but since Wuchu Daguan and the group of disciples around him are known to have lived in, or in the environs of, the Southern Song capital Hangzhou 杭州 (Kōshū), it seems probable that the printing was done there.

For her collection, Juexin selected the records of the most representative Zen masters appearing in the two earlier works, and to these added the records of a few other men. Altogether, her compilation contains the complete, or approximately complete, records of thirty-six Zen masters from the middle of the 8th to the end of the 12th century. Included is the entire text of the *Linji lu* (*Rinzai roku*), together with some additional material on Linji not found elsewhere. The work opens with the record of Nanyue Huairang (677–744), and concludes with that of Fozhao Deguang 佛照德光 (Busshō Tokkō, 1121–1203), a direct disciple of Dahui Zonggao. The compilation was included in the Ming Tripiṭaka, and has been reprinted in two modern collections, as noted above.

Hongzhi chanshi guanglu 宏智禪師廣錄 (*Wanshi zenji kōroku*) The Comprehensive Record of the Zen Master Hongzhi; also known as the *Hongzhi guanglu* 宏智廣錄 (*Wanshi kōroku*) The Comprehensive Record of Hongzhi, and the *Hongzhi lu* 宏智錄 (*Wanshi roku*) The Record of Hongzhi. Compiled and edited by various disciples; published in 1166, in 9 *juan* [*T* 48: 1–121a.15].

This is a collection of the sermons, writings, and verse of Hongzhi Zhengjue 宏智正覺 (Wanshi Shōgaku, 1091–1157) of the Yunju 雲居 (Ungo) line of the Caodong (Sōtō) School of Zen. Hongzhi Chanshi 宏智禪師 (Wanshi Zenji) was the Master's Imperially bestowed posthumous title.

The first *juan* contains formal sermons and informal talks given at various temples where the Master lived prior to 1129, when he went to the Jingdesi 景德寺 (Keitoku-ji) on Mount Tiantong 天童山 (Tendōzan), in modern Zhejiang. *Juan* 2 comprises the *Songgu baize* 頌古百則 (*Juko hyakusoku*), Zhengjue's famous collection of one hundred old koans with accompanying original verses, in the style originated a hundred years earlier by the Yunmen (Ummon) School master Xuedou Chongxian (Setchō Jūken). *Juan* 3 consists of the *Niangu baize* 拈古百則 (*Nenko hyakusoku*), another collection of one hundred old koans, each with a short prose comment. Both these collections were also made before the Master went to live at the Jingdesi. *Juan* 4 and 5 contain, respectively, the Master's formal sermons and informal talks at the Jingdesi; *juan* 6 comprises his *fayu* 法語 (*hōgo*), or instructions for religious practice written for individual students; *juan* 7 his *zhenzan* 眞贊 (*shinsan*), verses in praise of various old masters, and his *xiahuo* 下火 (*akō*), verses composed on the occasion of the cremation of disciples and friends; and *juan* 8 and 9 are made up of his *jiesong* 偈頌 (*geju*), religious verse, and his *zhenming* 箴銘 (*shimmei*), aphorisms.

The *Songgu baize* was commented upon in a series of lectures by a later Caodong master, Wansong Xingxiu 萬松行秀 (Banshō Gyōshū, 1166–1246). These lectures, compiled by Xingxiu's disciples, are entitled the *Wansong laoren pingchang Tiantong Jue heshang songgu Congrong'an lu*.

Huangbo duanji chanshi wanling lu 黃蘗斷際禪師宛陵錄 (*Ōbaku Dansai zenji Enryō roku*) The Wanling Record of the Zen Master Duanji of Huangbo; also known as the *Wanling lu* 宛陵錄 (*Enryō roku*) The Wanling Record. Compiled by Huangbo's disciples, in 1 *juan*. Song version: *Guzunsu yulu*, juan 3 [*ZZ* 2: 23.2.93b–99d.1]. Ming versions: *Taishō* 48: 384a.25–387b.14, and *Sijia yulu*, juan 5 [*ZZ* 2: 24.5.416d–423d].

A short compilation of sermons by Huangbo Xiyun 黃蘗希運 (Ōbaku Kiun, *d. ca.* 850), his answers to questions put to him by students, including those by the eminent official Pei Xiu 裴休 (Hai Kyū, 797–870), and anecdotes about him. The compilation of the work has traditionally been attributed to Pei Xiu, who, during the time he was governor of Wanling 宛陵 (Enryō) in Jiangxi 江西 (Kōzei), spent some time with the Master. From internal textual evidence, however, modern Japanese scholars now believe that the work was probably compiled by other students of the Master. No date is known for the work. Duanji Chanshi 斷際禪師 (Dansai

Zenji) is the posthumous title conferred upon Xiyun by the Tang emperor Xuanzong 宣宗 (Sensō, *r.* 846–859).

An English translation of the work will be found in *The Zen Teaching of Huang Po*, by John Blofeld (Zhu Chan), pp. 67–132.

Inzan roku 隱山錄 The Record of Inzan. Edited by Tsuji Tōzan 辻東山; first printed in 1942, in 1 *kan*.

The record of Inzan Ien 隱山惟琰 (1751–1814), a 3rd generation heir of Hakuin Ekaku and founder of the Inzan School of Rinzai Zen. The work contains the Master's sermons, informal talks, verse, and miscellaneous writings, together with detailed biographical material. It was edited and published under the supervision of Gotō Zuigan 後藤瑞巖 (1879–1965), then abbot of the Zuiryō-ji 瑞龍寺 in Gifu City, who also provided the work with an epilogue.

Jianzhong Jingguo xudeng lu 建中靖國續燈錄 (*Kenchū Seikoku zokutō roku*) The Jianzhong Jingguo [Era] Supplementary Record of the Lamp; also known as the *Xudeng lu* 續燈錄 (*Zokutō roku*) The Supplementary Lamp. Compiled by Foguo Weibai 佛國惟白 (Bukkoku Ibyaku, *n. d.*); completed in 1101, published in 1103; In 30 *juan*, with a Table of Contents (*mulu* 目錄 *mokuroku*) in 3 additional *juan* [*ZZ* 2乙: 9.1–2].

This important work is one of the five traditional histories, or "records of the transmission of the lamp," of Chinese Zen. It was intended as a continuation of the two earlier Zen histories, the *Jingde chuandeng lu* (1004) and the *Tiansheng guangdeng lu* (1036). The compiler Foguo Weibai was a distinguished scholar-monk in the 7th generation of the Yunmen (Ummon) School of Chinese Zen, who lived at the Fayun chansi 法雲禪寺 (Hōun zen-ji) in Dongjing 東京 (Tōkei), the capital of the Northern Song, present Kaifeng in Henan. The work, dedicated to the Northern Song Emperor Huizong 徽宗 (Kisō, *r.* 1100–1125), was presented to him upon its completion. The Emperor wrote a preface to it and ordered it included in the Tripiṭaka. It was published in the second year of the Chongning 崇寧 (Sūnei) era (1102–1106) at the Dengjue chanyuan 等覺禪院 (Tōgaku zen-in) in Fuzhou 福州 (Fukushū), in present Fujian. The "Jianzhong Jingguo" of the title commemorates the year in which the compilation was completed.

For the most part the *Xudeng lu* comprises brief biographies, episodes relating to the Transmission of Dharma, *wenda* 問答 (*mondō*), or questions and answers between a master and his monks, and the prose and verse comments and poetical works of Zen masters in the various teaching lines that developed within the Five Houses (*wujia* 五家 *goke*) during the Northern Song dynasty. The abundance of material gives clear evidence of the prosperity of these schools during this era.

Juan 1, bearing the title *Zhengzongmen* 正宗門 (*Shōjūmon*) "The True School," is introductory. It sets forth the Transmission of Dharma from Shakyamuni through the twenty-eight Indian patriarchs, the six Chinese patriarchs, and various masters in the lines of Nanyue Huairang (Nangaku Ejō) and Qingyuan Xingsi (Seigen Gyōshi) to and including the earlier masters of the Five Houses living in late Tang. The individual entries are brief, since more extensive information had already been provided by the two earlier histories. The body of the work, *juan* 2 through 26, is given the general title *Duiji* 對機 (*Taiki*), literally, "Answers Corresponding to the Understanding of the Questioners." Here the masters of Northern Song are treated individually under their lines of descent. *Juan* 27, as its title *Niangu* 拈古 (*Nenko*) indicates, consists of a collection of prose comments on old koans; *juan* 28, entitled *Songgu* 頌古 (*Juko*), comprises verse comments on old koans; and *juan* 29–30, entitled *Jiesong* 偈頌 (*Geju*), contain a collection of religious verse.

Jiatai pudeng lu 嘉泰普燈錄 (*Katai futō roku*) The Jiatai [Era] Comprehensive Record of the [Transmission of the] Lamp; also known as the *Pudeng lu* 普燈錄 (*Futō roku*) Comprehensive Record of the [Transmission of the] Lamp. Compiled by Lei'an Zhengshou 雷庵正受 (Raian Shōju, 1146–1208); in 30 *juan*, with 3 additional *juan* devoted to introductory material and a Table of Contents (*mulu* 目錄 *mokuroku*) [*ZZ* 2乙: 10.1–2].

The title of this work derives from the fact that it was completed in 1204, the fourth year of the Jiatai era (1201–1204) of Southern Song. The compiler, a monk in the 10th generation of the Yunmen 雲門 (Ummon) line of Zen, immediately presented his work to Emperor Ningzong 寧宗 (Neisō, *r.* 1195–1224). It seems probable that by Imperial decree it was published the same year as a part of the Tripiṭaka.

A brief synopsis of the contents of the *Pudeng lu* will show that it is indeed a "Comprehensive Record." *Juan* 1 through 21 contain the biographies of Zen monks, nuns, and laymen (*jushi* 居士 *koji*) of various schools and lines, beginning with Bodhidharma and concluding with Mi'an Xianjie 密庵咸傑 (Mittan Kanketsu, 1118–1186) of the Yangqi (Yōgi) line of

Linji (Rinzai) Zen. Where, as in a number of instances, actual biographies are omitted, reference is given to earlier works in which such information can be found. *Juan* 22 and 23 contain biographies of emperors and eminent statesmen who favored Zen; *juan* 24 contains those of wise and virtuous priests of schools other than Zen. The remaining six *juan* comprise miscellaneous writings by various Zen masters: *juan* 25 is devoted to a series of long sermons (*guangyu* 廣語 *kōgo*); *juan* 26 to a collection of old koans with prose comments (*niangu* 拈古 *nenko*); *juan* 27 and 28 to old koans with verse comments (*songgu* 頌古 *juko*); *juan* 29 to longer and shorter religious poems (*jiezan* 偈贊 *gesan*); and *juan* 30 to short prose writings (*zazhu* 雜著 *zatcho*).

Since the majority of persons whose biographies and writings appear in the *Pudeng lu* lived in the period between the beginning of Northern Song (960–1127) and the middle of Southern Song (1127–1279), this work supplements such earlier Zen "histories" as the *Chuandeng lu* (1004), *Guangdeng lu* (1036), *Xudeng lu* (1101), and *Liandeng huiyao* (1182), and is counted with them as one of the "Five Records of the Lamp" (*Wudeng lu* 五燈錄 *Gotō roku*).

Jingde chuandeng lu 景德傳燈錄 (*Keitoku dentō roku*) The Jingde [Era] Record of the Transmission of the Lamp; also known as the *Chuandeng lu* 傳燈錄 (*Dentō roku*) The Transmission of the Lamp. Compiled by Daoyuan 道原 (Dōgen, *n. d.*) and edited by Yang Yi 楊億 (Yō Oku, 968–1024); in 30 *juan* [*T* 51: 196b–467a].

This work is a chronologically arranged collection of biographies of Zen patriarchs and monks, beginning with the Seven Buddhas of the Past (*guoqu qifo* 過去七佛 *kako shichibutsu*), and concluding with men of Daoyuan's own time, that is, the end of the 10th century. The early compilers of the Zen lineage undoubtedly felt an urgent need to establish a firm foundation for the authenticity of the Zen patriarchal transmission, since other Chinese Buddhist schools had already set up, or were in the course of setting up, analogous lineages of the transmission of their doctrines. Moreover, Chinese historiographical tradition had established more than adequate precedent for the methods employed by these early compilers. The lineage of Zen as set forth in the *Baolin zhuan* 寶林傳 (*Hōrin den*), compiled about 801 by Zhi [or Hui]ju 智[慧]炬 (Chiko, or Eko, *n. d.*) became the accepted lineage. Daoyuan, in compiling the *Chuandeng lu*, drew freely upon the *Baolin zhuan*, as well as upon the writings of other early monks. Today we cannot accept the historicity of the traditional Zen transmission from the Seven Buddhas through Bodhidharma as presented by Daoyuan, but, in spite of this and other lapses from historical accuracy, the *Chuandeng lu* still remains the most important source for early Zen history.

Daoyuan was a disciple of Tiantai Deshao 天台德韶 (Tendai Tokushō, 891–972), an heir of Fayan Wenyi (Hōgen Bun'eki), founder of the Fayan (Hōgen) School of Zen. Daoyuan's dates are not known, but it is presumed that he lived from the middle of the 10th century until well into the 11th. The fact that he presented his work to the Northern Song emperor Zhenzong 眞宗 (Shinsō, *r.* 997–1022) in 1004, the first year of the Jingde 景德 (Keitoku) era (1004–1007), has led to this year often being taken as its publication date. Actually, however, it was not until 1011 that the work was finally published under Imperial patronage.

The postface by Zheng Ang 鄭昂 (Tei Kō, *n. d.*) to the second edition of the work, dated 1132, contains the story that a certain Gongchen 拱辰 (Kōshin, *n. d.*) was the real author of the compilation, that Gongchen's manuscript was stolen from him by an unnamed monk when he was on his way to the capital, and that this unnamed monk (presumably Daoyuan) then had the work published under his own name. *Juan* 9 of the *Xudeng lu*, compiled in 1101, and *juan* 12 of the *Wudeng huiyuan*, compiled in 1252, both state that Gongchen was the heir of Jinshan Tanying 金山曇穎 (Kinzan Don'ei, 985–1060). No dates are known for Gongchen, but since his teacher would have been only nineteen years old the year the *Chuandeng lu* was presented to the Emperor, it is not likely that the disciple was its compiler. As a matter of fact, Gongchen is elsewhere credited with being the compiler of a biographical collection in 30 *juan* entitled *Zuyuan tongyao* 祖源通要 (*Sogen tsūyō*), a work about which nothing is known but its name. The story of the stolen manuscript was evidently based upon a confusion between the two similar compilations, the latter of which, the *Zuyuan tongyao*, had already been lost by 1132.

The *Chuandeng lu* has traditionally been said to contain the biographies of 1701 Zen patriarchs and monks. Actually, however, Daoyuan has given biographies for only some nine hundred and sixty men, listing merely the names of the remaining seven hundred and forty-odd persons. The biographies of the patriarchs and masters as given in the work contain not only the histories of their lives but many of their sayings and verses as well. Within these latter may be found the material for the majority of

Chinese Zen koans that date from before the beginning of the 11th century. The first twenty-six *juan* of the work are devoted to biographies and lists of the names of the less important disciples in the various teaching lines; *juan* 27 and 28 contain additional material relating to outstanding figures already treated in the biographies; *juan* 29 and 30 are given over to miscellaneous short writings in prose and verse by various famous Zen monks.

The *Chuandeng lu* as a whole has not yet been translated into a western language, but many quotations from it will be found throughout all the works in English of D.T. SUZUKI. Several lengthy excerpts have also been translated into English by LU K'uan Yü (Charles LUK) in his *Chan and Zen Teaching*, Second Series.

KAIANKOKU GO 槐安國語 Tales from the Land of Locust-tree Tranquillity, by Hakuin Ekaku 白隱慧鶴 (1686–1769). Compiled by Ichidaku 一諾 (*n. d.*) and others of Hakuin's disciples; first published in 1750 under the supervision of Zen'ichi 全乙(*n. d.*), also one of Hakuin's disciples, in 7 *kan* [*T* 81: 511a–580a].

This is one of the major works of the famous Tokugawa era Rinzai Zen master Hakuin Ekaku. It consists of a series of Zen lectures (*teishō* 提唱) which the Master delivered in 1749 at the Shōin-ji 松蔭寺, his temple in Hara 原, in present Shizuoka Prefecture. The basic text for this series of *teishō* was the first two *kan* of the *Daitō roku*, the recorded writings and sayings of Daitō Kokushi 大燈國師 (1282–1338), founder of the Daitoku-ji 大德寺. These *kan* consist of the *Daitoku goroku* 大德語錄, the *Sōfuku goroku* 崇福語錄, *Juko* 頌古 (old koans with verse commentary), and *Nenko* 拈古 (old koans with prose commentary).

Kan 1–4 of the *Kaiankoku go* comprise the actual texts of the *Daitoku goroku* and the *Sōfuku goroku*, interspersed with Hakuin's copious commentary. *Kan* 5 and 6 are devoted to the collection of forty-eight *juko*, with extensive interlinear prose commentary by Hakuin in the form and style used by Yuanwu Keqin 圜悟克勤 (Engo Kokugon, 1063–1135) in his famous *Biyan lu* (*Hekigan roku*). *Kan* 7 treats the collection of eleven *nenko* in the same manner.

The text of the *Kaiankoku go* given in the *Taishō daizōkyō* follows a printing of the work dated 1885, and contains three prefaces, one by Hakuin and two by Zen masters of the Meiji 明治 era (1868–1912). It concludes with an epilogue by Hakuin, and two colophons, one by Zen'ichi, and one by Taikō 退耕 (1818–1895), then Kanchō of the Rinzai Zen headquaters of Shōkoku-ji 相國寺, in Kyoto.

The whimsical title of the work derives from an old Chinese tale entitled *Nankemeng* 南柯夢 (*Nanka no yume*) "Dream of the South Branch." According to the story, a certain CHUNYU Fen 淳于棼 (JUN'U Fun) of Tang fell asleep one day under a locust tree and dreamed that he visited a fabulous country called Huai'anguo 槐安國 (Kaiankoku). There he had many wonderful experiences, married the king's daughter, and became a great official. On waking he discovered that the country of his dream was an ant colony within the locust tree under the south branch of which he had been sleeping. In China and Japan the phrases "land of locust-tree tranquillity" and "dream of the south branch" have thus come to be figures of speech for empty dreams.

KAISAN SHIDŌ BU'NAN ANJU ZENJI ANROKU 開山至道無難菴主禪師行錄 The Biography of the Founder, the Hermitage-dwelling Zen Master Shido Bu'nan; by Tōrei Enji 東嶺圓慈 (1721–1792) [*Hakuin oshō zenshū*, Vol. I, pp. 369–379].

This is a short but basic biography of the Zen master Shidō Bu'nan (1603–1676), in the 16th generation of the line of Kanzan Egen 關山慧玄 (1277–1360) of the Myōshin-ji 妙心寺. Shidō Bu'nan was the teacher of Dōkyō Etan 道鏡慧端 (1642–1721), the most important of the masters under whom Hakuin Ekaku studied. The author, Tōrei Enji, was Hakuin's immediate disciple, and a Zen historian and literary man of eminence.

KEISŌ DOKUZUI 荊叢毒蘂 Poison Blossoms from Thorn Thickets, by Hakuin Ekaku 白隱慧鶴 (1686–1769). Edited by Zenjo 禪恕 (*n. d.*), published in 1758, in 9 *kan* [*Hakuin oshō zenshū*, Vol. II, pp. 1–302].

This is a collection of sermons and talks given by the great Japanese Zen master Hakuin, as recorded by various of his disciples (*kan* 1–2), and of literary material from the Master's own hand (*kan* 3–9). The individual items comprising the work are undated, but the collection as a whole spans the greater part of the Master's long life. A short laudatory preface dated August, 1758, by the nobleman SUGAWARA Tamenari 菅原爲成 (1716–1759), precedes the text proper, and an epilogue by KIDA Ganshō 木田元照 (*n. d.*), a lay disciple of Hakuin living in Osaka, concludes it.

KIDA tells us in his epilogue that in the winter of 1756 he visited the Shōin-ji 松蔭寺, Hakuin's temple at Hara in Shizuoka Prefecture. Though the Master, then in his 71st year, was ill in bed, KIDA was permitted to take sanzen during his short stay. Also, he had the opportunity to look through Hakuin's nine-volume record (*goroku* 語錄) entitled *Keisō dokuzui*, which the Master's disciple Zenjo had compiled and edited. KIDA, much impressed with the work, urged its early publication. When the matter was taken up with Hakuin, the old master objected strenuously. KIDA therefore hid the manuscript in a bag, and secretly carried it back to Osaka, where he had it published.

A glance at the Table of Contents (*mokuroku* 目錄) will to some extent indicate the range of literary forms in which Hakuin's enormous talents found expression: *Kan* 1: *Jishū* 示衆 Sermons and Instruction to Disciples. *Kan* 2: *Jishū; Fusetsu* 普說 General Talks; *Juko* 頌古 Verse Comments on Old Koans; *Koko* 擧古 Lectures on Old Koans. *Kan* 3: *Tōjō goi henshō kuketsu* 洞上五位偏正口訣 [Treatise on] the Five Ranks; *Hōgo* 法語 Instructions for Practice Written for Individual Students; *Shōbutsuji* 小佛事 Remarks at Anniversary and Funeral Services. *Kan* 4: *Ben* 辯 Essays. *Kan* 5: *Ki* 記 Jottings; *Setsu* 說 Explanations [of Obscure Points]. *Kan* 6: *Sho* 書 Letters. Kan 7: *Jo* 序 Prefaces; *Batsu* 跋 Epilogues; *Mei* 銘 Inscriptions. *Kan* 8: *San* 贊 Laudatory Verses. *Kan* 9: *Geju* 偈頌 Religious Poems.

A supplement to the *Keisō dokuzui* in one *kan*, entitled *Keisō dokuzui shūi* 荊叢毒蘂拾遺 Gleanings from the *Keisō dokuzui* [*Hakuin oshō zenshu*, Vol. II, pp. 303–364], also compiled by Zenjo, was published in 1759. It comprises Hakuin's famous *Dokugo shingyō* 毒語心經 "Poisonous Words on the Heart Sutra" [*ibid.*, pp. 305–328], a prose and verse commentary on the *Hannya shingyō*, together with miscellaneous writings, teachings, laudatory verses, and religious poems.

KŌZEN DAITŌ KOKUSHI YUIKAI 興禪大燈國師遺誡 The Last Admonitions of the National Teacher Kōzen Daitō.

This famous short writing by Shūhō Myōchō 宗峰妙超 (1282–1338), better known as Daitō Kokushi, is not included in either of the two works devoted to the Master's teachings, the *Daitō kokushi goroku* and the *Daitō kokushi hōgo*, but can be found in most of the popular handbooks used for sutra chanting in the Rinzai Sect of Zen. It is also in the collection of koans and short Zen writings entitled *Zudokko*, p. 3. An English translation of the complete text of the Admonitions is contained in D.T. SUZUKI's *Manual of Zen Buddhism*, p. 147*f.*

Lalitavistara, Extended Narrative of the Sport of the Buddha.

This early Mahayana work, written in hybrid Sanskrit and deriving originally from the Hinayana Sarvāstivādin School, recounts the legendary history of Shakyamuni's life, beginning with the period when, as a bodhisattva, he was living in the Tuṣita Heaven and made the great decision to be born upon earth, and ending with his enlightenment and subsequent determination to preach. The work is an anonymous compilation containing both old and later legends, ballads, and other materials of a like kind. No date can be assigned to it, though it seems probable that it was composed during, or soon after, the first century BCE. Two Sanskrit texts are extant. One of these has been rendered into French by P. Foucaux and published in *Annales du Musée Guimet.*

The *Lalitavistara* was translated into Chinese four times, but, by 730 the first and third translations had already been lost. The two remaining Chinese translations are as follows:

Puyao jing 普耀經 (*Fuyō kyō*) Sutra of Universal Brightness. Translated in 308 by Dharmarakṣa (Zhu Fahu 竺法護 Jiku Hōgo, *n. d.*), in 8 *juan* [*T* 3: 483–583a].

Dharmarakṣa is noteworthy for the fact that he was one of the extremely few translators of Buddhist texts who was proficient in writing Chinese, and who could therefore render Sanskrit texts into Chinese without the aid of intermediaries. He came from a family of Scythian origin who had settled in Dunhuang 敦煌 (Tonkō). With his Buddhist teacher, he made a long pilgrimage to the western countries, and, on his return to China, brought back with him a large number of Sanskrit texts, many of which he translated into Chinese at Chang'an (Chōan) between 265 and 313. His translations included parts of the *Avataṁsaka-sūtra* and a partial text of the *Mahāparinirvāṇa-sūtra.*

Fangguang dazhuangyan jing 方廣大莊嚴經 (*Hōkō daishōgon kyō*) The Comprehensive Sutra on the Great Adornments [of Buddha]; also known as the *Dazhuangyan jing* 大莊嚴經 (*Daishōgon kyō*) The Sutra on the Great Adornments [of Buddha]. Translated in 683 by Divākara (Dipoheluo 地婆訶羅 Jibakara, 613–687), in 12 *juan* [*T* 3: 539a–617b.11].

Divākara was a monk from Central India who arrived in Chang'an in 676 and worked there and in Luoyang (Rakuyō) until his death.

Laṅkāvatāra-sūtra

Though we have no definite knowledge as to when or where the earliest text of this Mahayana scripture originated, it is at present generally supposed that it was composed in Southern India during the second or third century CE. The late Dr. NANJIO Bunyiu 南條文雄 (1849–1927) edited and published in 1923 a Sanskrit text of the sutra under the title *Bombun nyū Ryōga kyō* 梵文入楞伽經 The Sanskrit Sutra on the Entry into Lanka. This text was based upon a copy Dr. NANJIO had made of a Nepalese manuscript in the possession of the London Asiatic Society. Dr. NANJIO's Sanskrit text has been translated into English by D. T. SUZUKI under the title *The Lankavatara Sutra*, and this same author has also published a related work entitled *Studies in the Lankavatara Sutra*. In this latter work, p. 3, SUZUKI suggests that *Laṅkāvatāra*, literally "entering Laṅkā," refers to the Buddha's coming to Laṅkā to preach.

The sutra purports to have been spoken by the Buddha while he was on a visit to Lanka, an island to the south of India popularly identified as Ceylon. The opening scene presents the Buddha, together with a large company of bodhisattvas and monks, in the Castle of Laṅkā, where he is requested by Rāvaṇa, Lord of Laṅkā, to preach the Dharma. The Bodhisattva Mahāmati thereupon proceeds to question the Buddha on various subjects, and the body of the sutra is composed of the dialogue between them. SUZUKI considers that the somewhat confused construction of the work may be attributed to its being an unsystematic compilation of miscellaneous notes on various points of Mahayana doctrine. The chapter headings in SUZUKI's English translation of the text give an excellent survey of the contents: I–Rāvaṇa, Lord of Laṅkā, Asks for Instruction; II–Collection of All the Dharmas; III–On Impermanency; IV–On Intuitive Understanding; V–On the Deduction of the Permanency of Tathagatahood; VI–Momentariness; VII–On Transformation; VIII–On Meat Eating; IX–The Dhāraṇīs (sequences of meaningless sounds believed to have magical power when recited); X–Sagāthakam (verses).

Four Chinese translations of the Scripture were made between approximately 420 and 704 CE. The earliest, now lost, was that in 4 *juan* made by the Indian monk Dharmakṣema (?) (Tanwuchan 曇無讖 Dommusen, 385–433?), who came to China in 412 and worked between 414 and 421 in Guzang 姑臧 (Kozō), the second capital of the Northern Liang (Beiliang 北涼 Hokuryō) dynasty (397–439). It is believed that Dharmakṣema (?) translated the *Laṅkāvatāra-sūtra* shortly after he had finished his translation of the complete *Nirvana Sutra*.

The remaining three translations are as follows;

Lengqie abaduoluo bao jing 楞伽阿跋多羅寶經 (*Ryōga abattara hō kyō*) The Lankavatara Treasure Sutra; also known as the *Lengqie jing* 楞伽經 (*Ryōga kyō*) Lanka Sutra. Translated into Chinese by Guṇabhadra (Qiunabatuoluo 求那跋陀羅 Gunabatsudara, 394–468), dated 443, in 4 *juan* [*T* 16: 479–514b].

This, the second Chinese translation of the scripture, was made by Guṇabhadra, a Brahmin monk from Central India, who arrived in Canton in 435, and worked in present Nanjing, then the capital of the Song (Sō) dynasty (420–479). Daoxuan 道宣 (Dōsen, 596–667), in his *Xu gaoseng zhuan* 續高僧專 (*Zoku kōsō den*) Further Biographies of Eminent Monks, states that Bodhidharma handed a copy of the *Lengqie jing* in 4 *juan* to his disciple Huike 慧可 (Eka, 487–593), later the second patriarch of Chinese Chan, with the words: "I have observed that in this land of China there is only this sutra. If you depend upon this sutra, you will be able to save the world." [*T* 50: 552b.20*f*] It is believed that Guṇabhadra's translation was the text referred to, and in later centuries, this, the shortest, though not the easiest text to understand, was that on which the majority of Chinese commentaries were based. From the time of the Second Patriarch until that of the Sixth Patriarch, the *Laṅkāvatāra-sūtra* was widely studied by Zen men. And though interest in the sutra declined after the Sixth Patriarch, Huineng 慧能 (Enō, 638–713), indicated his preference for the *Diamond Sutra*, it never entirely died out. For the Northern School of Zen, the *Lanka Sutra* remained the preferred text.

Ru Lengqie jing 入楞伽經 (*Nyū Ryōga kyō*) The Sutra on the Entry into Lanka. Translated into Chinese by Bodhiruci (Putiliuzhi 菩提流支 Bodairushi, *n. d.*), *ca.* 513, in 10 *juan* [*T* 16: 514c–586b].

This third Chinese translation of the scripture was made by Bodhiruci, a monk from Central India, who arrived in Luoyang (Rakuyō) in 508, and worked there from that time until between 534 and 537.

Dacheng ru Lengqie jing 大乘入楞伽經 (*Daijō nyū Ryōga kyō*) The Mahayana Sutra on the Entry into Lanka. Translated into Chinese by Śikṣānanda and others between 700 and 704, in 7 *juan* [*T* 16: 587–640c].

The fourth and last translation of the scripture was made at the command of Empress Wu 武后 (Bukō, *r.* 685–704) of Tang by the Khotanese monk Śikṣānanda (Shichanantuo 實叉難陀 Jisshananda, 652–710), with the assistance of several Chinese scholars, while he was working in Chang'an (Chōan) and Luoyang. The Empress herself wrote the preface for the work.

The greater length of the translations by Bodhiruci and Śikṣānanda is due to the fact that they, as well as the Sanskrit text mentioned above, contain three chapters not found in Guṇabhadra's translation. These are chapters I, IX, and X. It seems obvious that these three chapters were added to the text, or texts, of the scripture after Guṇabhadra's time. The famous chapter "On Meat Eating," which is present in all the extant translations, is also considered to be an addition to a text still earlier than that which Guṇabhadra used. No translation into a European language has has been made of any of the Chinese texts, though D. T. SUZUKI states that he constantly consulted the three existing ones in making his English translation from the Sanskrit.

LONGXING FOJIAO BIANNIAN TONGLUN 隆興佛教編年通論 (*Ryūkō bukkyō hennen tsūron*) A Chronologically Arranged Comprehensive Treatise on Buddhism [Compiled in the] Longxing [Era]; also known as the *Fojiao biannian tonglun* 沸教編年通論 (*Bukkyō hennen tsūron*) A Chronologically Arranged Comprehensive Treatise on Buddhism; the *Biannian tonglun* 編年通論 (*Hennen tsūron*) A Chronologically Arranged Comprehensive Treatise [on Buddhism]; the *Longxing foyun tonglun* 隆興佛運通論 (*Ryukō butsuun tsūron*) The Longxing [Era] Comprehensive Treatise on the Development of Buddhism; and the *Foyun tongji* 佛運通記 (*Butsuun tsūki*) Complete Record of the Development of Buddhism. Compiled by Shishi Zuxiu 石室祖琇 (Sekishitsu Soshū, *n. d.*), completed in 1164 in 29 *juan*, with an additional *juan* devoted to a detailed Table of Contents (*mulu* 目錄 *mokuroku*) [ZZ 2乙: 3.3–4].

This history of Buddhism in China was compiled during the early part of the Southern Song (Nansong 南宋 Nansō) dynasty (1127–1279) by Shishi Zuxiu, a monk in the 6th generation of the Yangqi (Yōgi) line of Linji (Rinzai) Zen who lived in Longxing 隆興 (Ryūkō), in modern Jiangxi. The "Longxing" of the title commemorates the fact that the compilation was completed in the second year of the Longxing era (1163–1164) of Southern Song.

The work opens with the traditional story of the arrival of Buddhism in China during the reign of Emperor Ming 明 (Mei, *r.* 57–75 CE) of the Later Han (Houhan 後漢 Gokan) era (25–220 CE), continues through the periods of the Three Kingdoms, Six Dynasties, Tang, and Five Dynasties, and concludes with the second year of the Qiande 乾德 (Kentoku) era (963–968) of the Northern Song (Beisong 北宋 Hokusō) dynasty (960–1127). The final *juan* is given over to four epilogues, written for four different Buddhist works, by the Northern Song emperors Taizong 太宗 (Taisō, *r.* 960–976), Zhenzong 眞宗 (Shinsō, *r.* 997–1022), Renzong 仁宗 (Jinsō, *r.* 1022–1063), and Huizong 徽宗 (Kisō, *r.* 1100–1125).

The compilation was modeled upon the style that, by early Song, had become definitive for secular historical works. The successive dynasties are treated in chronologically arranged sections, each section opening with a general statement regarding the Buddhism of the time. Under each dynasty, important events are then noted in chronological order and commented upon; important persons are discussed under the supposed dates of their deaths. Historical information is supplemented by contemporary stone inscriptions and records, and special studies and criticisms are added on debatable points.

As the *Zokuzōkyō* text has neither a preface nor an epilogue, we cannot determine the exact date of the original publication of the work, nor do we know when it was first brought to Japan. It is supposed, however, that the text included in the *Zokuzōkyō* is based upon one of the Gozan 五山 editions published in Japan during the Muromachi 室町 era (1338–1573).

Mahāparinirvāṇa-sūtra The Sutra of the Great Decease, or the *Nirvana Sutra*.

This is a Mahayana scripture of uncertain date, professing to be the sermon preached by the Buddha just before his death. It should not be confused with the Hinayana *Mahāparinibbāna-suttanta* of the Pāli Canon, which deals with the last days and death of Shakyamuni. In this Mahayana sutra, the Buddha is represented as expounding the complete Mahayana teaching, including the doctrines that the Dharmakāya is characterized by permanence, joy, personality, and purity (*chang, le, wo, jing* 常樂我淨 *jō, raku, ga, jō*), and that all sentient beings, even the *icchantika* (persons completely given over to sensual enjoyment, and heretofore considered as forever excluded from attaining Nirvana), possess the Buddha-nature, and are thus destined for eventual salvation. There appears to be no complete Sanskrit text of the sutra extant. A fragment of a Sanskrit text has been discovered in recent years in Central Asia, and another was found in 1916 in the Hōju-in 寶壽院 on Mount Kōya 高野山, the headquarters of the Japanese Shingon 眞言 Sect, in Wakayama Prefecture. It is surmised that the latter was brought to Japan by Kōbō Daishi 弘法大師 (774–835), founder of this sect, when he returned from China in 806.

Several Chinese translations were made of the *Mahāparinirvāṇa-*

sūtra. The most important of these are as follows:

Foshuo fangdeng boniyuan jing 佛說方等般泥洹經 (*Bussetsu hōdō hatsunaion gyō*) The Vaipulya Parinirvana Sutra Preached by Buddha. Translated by Dharmarakṣa (Zhu Fahu 竺法護 Jiku Hōgo, *n. d.*), in 2 *juan* [*T* 12: 912a–929c].

This, the earliest translation of the sutra, is of a partial text only. It was made in Chang'an (Chōan) between 265 and 313 by the Scythian monk Dharmarakṣa, who also translated portions of the *Avataṁsaka-sūtra*, and the earliest text of the *Lalitavistara*.

Daboniepan jing 大般涅槃經 (*Daihatsu nehan gyō*) The Sutra of the Great Decease; also known as the *Niepan jing* 涅槃經 (*Nehan gyō*) Nirvana Sutra. Translated by Dharmakṣema (?) (Tanwuchan 曇無讖 Dommusen, 385–433?), in 40 *juan* [*T* 12: 365a–604].

This first translation of the complete text of the sutra was made by Dharmakṣema (?), a monk from Central India, while he was working at Guzang 姑臧 (Kozō), the capital of Northern Liang, in present Gansu, between 414 and 421. It is known as the "Northern Text." A partial translation into English of *juan* 12 and 39 will be found in *A Catena of Buddhist Scriptures*, by Rev. S. Beal, pp. 160–188.

Idem, revised by Huiyan 慧嚴 (Egon, 363–443) and others, in 36 *juan* [*T* 12: 605–852].

This is a revised version of the "Northern Text," undertaken by the Chinese monk Huiyan, a disciple of Kumārajīva, while he was living in Nanjing. After Huiyan's death in 443, the work of revision was carried on by others, and completed in 453. This is known as the "Southern Text."

On the basis of the translation by Dharmakṣema (?), and Huiyan's revision of it, there developed a "Northern" and a "Southern" Nirvana School. These were composed largely of scholars interested in the interpretation of the various doctrines set forth in the respective texts. As schools they had little importance, but their theories and views regarding the Dharmakāya, the Buddha-nature, and Nirvana, had a tremendous influence upon all later Chinese Buddhist thought. Both schools were eventually absorbed into the Tiantai 天台 (Tendai) School.

Mahāyāna-sūtrālaṁkāra, The Mahayana Adornments of the Sutras.

This Sanskrit text is one of the basic treatises of the Mahayana Yogācāra School. The author, Asaṅga, was a Brahmin living in the Gandhara area of northwest India, probably during the 4th century CE. He and his equally famous younger brother, Vasubandhu, originally belonged to the Hinayana Sarvāstivādin Sect. After Asaṅga had become a Mahayanist he is said to have converted his brother to his views, and together they founded the Indian Yogācāra School.

Though the text contains frequent quotations from the Āgamas, the Sanskrit version of the Pāli Nikāyas, it is an authoritative exposition of various Mahayana doctrines, among them the Trikāya (Three Bodies), the Tathāgata-garbha (Tathāgata-womb, the source of all things), and the Ālaya-vijñāna (Storing Consciousness), and gives perhaps the first systematic presentation of the concept of a one and only reality. Both Sanskrit and Tibetan versions of the text are extant. The Sanskrit text has been edited and translated into French by Sylvain Lévi, under the title *Mahāyāna-sūtrālaṁkāra*.

The only Chinese translation of the sutra is the following:

Dacheng zhuangyanjing lun 大乘莊嚴經論 (*Daijō shōgongyō ron*) Treatise on the "Mahayana Adornments of the Sutras"; also knovm as the *Zhuangyanjing lun* 莊嚴經論 (*Shōgongyō ron*) Treatise on the "Adornments of the Sutras." Translated into Chinese by Prabhāmitra (Boluopomiduoluo 波羅頗蜜多羅 Harahamittara, 565–633), in 13 *juan* [*T* 31: 589b–661].

The translator of this work by Asaṅga (Wuzhuo 無著 Mujaku) was a monk from Maghada in Central India, who arrived in Chang'an (Chōan) in 627. The translation was probably made during the last three years of his life, that is, between 630 and 633.

Mingjue chanshi yulu 明覺禪師語錄 (*Myōgaku zenji goroku*) The Record of the Zen Master Mingjue; also known as the *Xuedou Chongxian yulu* 雪竇重顯語錄 (*Setchō Jūken goroku*) The Record of Xuedou Chongxian, and the *Xuedou lu* 雪竇錄 (*Setchō roku*) The Record of Xuedou. Compiled by Wei Gaizhu 惟蓋竺 (I Gaijiku, *n. d.*) and others, in 6 *juan* [*T* 47: 669a–713b].

This work contains the sermons, informal talks, comments on the koans of earlier Zen masters, eulogies of old masters, and poems of Xuedou Chongxian 雪竇重顯 (Setchō Jūken, 980–1052), a master in the 4th generation of the Yunmen 雲門 (Ummon) School of Zen, and a famous poet of his time. Mingjue Chanshi 明覺禪師 (Myōgaku Zenji) was the Master's posthumous title. Wei Gaizhu and the other compilers of the work were all disciples of Xuedou. A part of the "Record" was probably compiled between 1030 and 1032, during the Master's lifetime, but final compilation of the total text was not undertaken until after his death.

The first two *juan* of the work are devoted to sermons and talks given by Xuedou at various temples and at various times. *Juan* 3, entitled *Niangu* 拈古 (*Nenko*), consists of the Master's prose comments on one hundred old koans. *Juan* 4 consists in large part of sermons and talks, but also contains Xuedou's comments upon the famous poem by Shitou Xiqian 石頭希遷 (Sekitō Kisen, 700–790) entitled *Cantongqi* 參同契 (*Sandōkai*). *Juan* 5 and 6 comprise the Master's poems. The work concludes with Xuedou's tomb inscription written by the Prime Minister Lü Xiaqing 呂夏卿 (Ryo Kakei, *n. d.*), who was one of the Master's lay disciples. It is dated March 14, 1065.

Originally the work contained another section entitled *Songgu* 頌古 (*Juko*), Xuedou's verse comments on one hundred old koans. It was upon this collection that, about one hundred years later, Yuanwu Keqin 圜悟克勤 (Engo Kokugon, 1063–1135) based the lectures which comprise his famous *Biyan lu* (*Hekigan roku*). Sometime after the *Biyan lu* was in wide circulation, the *Songgu* section seems to have been dropped from the text of the *Xuedou lu*, and was never replaced. The present *Taishō* text, reproducing a Ming edition of the work, does not contain it.

Prajñāpāramitā-hṛdaya-sūtra, The Heart of the Perfection of Wisdom Sutra; also known as the *Hṛdaya-sūtra*, or *Heart Sutra*.

As its title indicates, this exceedingly brief sutra contains the "heart" or essence of the Mahayana Perfection of Wisdom teaching. The Sanskrit text was composed in India sometime before 400 CE. The sutra exists in two versions, a short one consisting of the body of the text only, and a longer version in which the main text is prefaced by a short introduction and concluded with a short epilogue. Edward Conze has aptly described the sutra as "one of the sublimest spiritual documents of mankind." In it the Bodhisattva Avalokiteśvara instructs Śāriputra on how, by means of the practice of the Great Perfection of Intrinsic Wisdom, the disciple is led to realize that all the basic assertions of classical Buddhism, that is, the Five Skandhas, the Eighteen Dhātu, the Twelve-fold Chain of Causation, the Four Noble Truths, and, finally, wisdom and enlightenment even, are all in themselves void. Only when everything has been totally negated is the ultimate state of Śunyatā (Emptiness, or the Void), which is beyond all affirmation and negation, attained. This state is "the Other Shore," the True Bodhi (Enlightenment), the True Nirvana which is eternal, everlasting existence.

English translations by F. Max Müller of both the larger and the smaller sutras will be found in *Buddhist Mahāyāna Texts*, Part II, pp. 145–154. The most recent translation into English of the short Sanskrit text is that by Edward Conze, *Buddhist Wisdom Books*, pp. 77–107.

Mohebore boluomi damingzhou jing 摩訶般若波羅蜜大明咒經 (*Makahannya haramitsu daimyōju kyō*) The Great Bright Mantra of the Great Perfection of Wisdom Sutra. Translated into Chinese in 402 by Kumārajīva, in 1 *juan* [*T* 8: 847c.8–29].

This, the first Chinese translation of the *Heart Sutra*, was made by the great Central Asian missionary-translator Kumārajīva (Jiumoluoshi 鳩摩羅什 Kumarajū, 350–*ca.* 409) while he was living in Chang'an (Chōan). This version is based upon the short Sanskrit text.

Bore boluomiduo xinjing 般若波羅蜜多心經 (*Hannya haramitta shingyō*) The Perfection of Wisdom Heart Sutra; also known as the *Bore xinjing* 般若心經 (*Hannya shingyō*) The Wisdom Heart Sutra, or merely as the *Xinjing* 心經 (*Shingyō*) Heart Sutra. Translated into Chinese in 648 by Xuanzang 玄奘 (Genjō, 600?–664), in 1 *juan* [*T* 8: 848c].

This, also, is a translation of the short version of the sutra, and contains only 268 characters. Though several translations of the long version were made in later years in China, Xuanzang's short version has remained the most popular, and is chanted on every possible occasion by Chinese and Japanese Zen devotees, as well as by those of almost every other Buddhist sect.

More translations into western languages have been made of the *Heart Sutra* than of any other Mahayana text. Among the English translations of Xuanzang's version is that by D. T. Suzuki, "English Translation of the Shingyo," in his *Manual of Zen Buddhism*, pp. 26–30, and "Translation of the *Prajna-paramita-hridaya* Sutra" in the same author's *Essays in Zen Buddhism*, Third Series, pp. 216–219. In this latter work will be found two interesting essays, one on the Prajñāpāramitā doctrines in general (pp. 270–307), and one on the *Heart Sutra* (pp. 202–219), both interpreted from the Zen standpoint.

"A Straight Talk on the Heart Sutra" in *Chan and Zen Teaching*, First Series, by Lu K'uan Yü (Charles Luk), pp. 207–223, is a translation of the *Bore boluomiduo xinjing zhishuo* 般若波羅蜜多心經直説 (*Hannya haramitta shingyō jikisetsu*), in 1 *juan* [*ZZ* 1: 41.5.421d–424b], the Xuanzang text with running commentary by the late Ming dynasty master Hanshan Deqing 憨山德清 (Kanzan Tokusei, 1546–1623).

The Pure Land Sutras

Sukhāvatī-vyūha, The [Larger Sutra] Describing the Paradise of Amitābha; also known as the *Larger Sukhāvatī*.

This is a Mahayana scripture, probably dating from the 1st century CE, in which the Buddha Shakyamuni is represented as preaching to a large assembly on the Vulture Peak at Rājagṛha. In answer to a question by his disciple Ānanda, the Buddha describes Amitābha's "Land of Bliss," explains how it came into being, and how men may gain entrance into it. F. Max Müller's English translation of the Sanskrit text will be found in *Buddhist Mahāyāna Texts*, Part II, pp. 1–75, under the title "The Larger Sukhāvatī-vyūha."

From information available in old catalogues of the Chinese Tripiṭaka, it would appear that twelve translations of the [*Larger*] *Sukhāvatī-vyūha* had been made by 1000 CE. Seven of these have been lost. The earliest version, one of those no longer extant, was that made by the Parthian prince known in China as An Shigao 安世高 (An Seikō, *n. d.*). On the death of his father, he is said to have ceded his kingdom to his uncle and become a Buddhist monk. An Shigao was one of the most active of the early Buddhist missionaries to China. He arrived in Luoyang (Rakuyō) about 147 CE, and worked there continuously until 170, translating a large number of Buddhist texts. Fifty-five of his works are included in the *Taishō*.

The most important of the five extant versions of the [*Larger*] *Sukhāvatī-vyūha* is the following:

Wuliangshou jing 無量壽經 (*Muryōju kyō*) The Sutra of Boundless Life. Translated into Chinese by Saṅghavarman, in 2 *juan* [*T* 12: 265c–279a].

This is the second earliest extant Chinese translation of the [*Larger*] *Sukhāvatī-vyūha*. It was made by the "foreign" monk Saṅghavarman (Kang Sengkai 康僧鎧 Kō Sōgai, *n. d.*), during his stay in Luoyang about 252. It is upon this translation that the Chinese and Japanese Pure Land sects place their dependence.

Sukhāvatī-vyūha, The [Smaller Sutra] Describing the Paradise of Amitābha; also known as the *Smaller Sukhāvatī*.

This is a short Mahayana scripture, also dating probably from the 1st century CE, in which the Buddha is represented as preaching to an assembly in the Jetavana at Śrāvastī. Here, in response to a question by his disciple Śāriputra, Shakyamuni vividly describes Amitābha's "Land of Bliss," and states that men are born in this paradise only through repetition of the name of Amitābha Buddha. F. Max MÜLLER's English translation of this Sanskrit text is to be found in *Buddhist Mahāyāna Texts*, Part II, pp. 87–103, under the title "The Smaller Sukhāvatī-vyūha."

Several Chinese translations of the "Small" scripture were made. One of the earliest, and the most important, is the following:

Amituo jing 阿彌陀經 (*Amida kyō*) The Amitābha Sutra. Translated into Chinese by Kumārajīva in 402, in 1 *juan* [*T* 12: 346b–348b].

This translation of the [*Smaller*] *Sukhāvatī-vyūha* was made by the great Central Asian Buddhist scholar Kumārajīva (Jiumoluoshi 鳩摩羅什 Kumarajū, 350–*ca.* 409) while he was living in Chang'an (Chōan). A number of important commentaries were later written on it by masters of the Chinese Pure Land School. This translation, also, is still one of the basic texts for the Pure Land schools of China and Japan. An incomplete English translation of the Chinese text is included in *A Catena of Buddhist Scriptures*, by Rev. S. BEAL, pp. 378–383.

Guan wuliangshoufo jing 觀無量壽佛經 (*Kan muryōjubutsu kyō*) Sutra of the Meditations on the Buddha of Boundless Life; also known in English as the *Dhyana Sutra*. Translated into Chinese by the Indian monk Kālayaśas, in 1 *juan* [*T* 12: 340c–346b].

No Sanskrit text has as yet been discovered for this, the third of the Mahayana sutras on which the Pure Land schools of China and Japan depend. The restored Sanskrit title *Amitāyur-dhyāna-sūtra* has been given it, but scholars tend to believe that it is a spurious sutra, which, though purporting to be the translation of a Sanskrit text, was, in fact, originally written in Chinese. The Central Asian monk Kālayaśas (Jiangliangyeshe 畺良耶舍 Kyōryōyasha, *n. d.*) is credited with having translated the sutra while he was working in the southern capital, present Nanjing, between 424 and 432 (*var.* 443).

In this sutra, Shakyamuni Buddha is represented as appearing before Queen Vaidehī, who, imprisoned in the palace by her son, the wicked prince Ajātaśatru, had prayed to the Buddha to aid her. When she questions him as to how she may be born into the heaven of Amitāyus (Amitābha), the Buddha instructs her on the meditations by means of which she will attain her desire.

Junjirō TAKAKUSU's English translation of the Chinese text is to be found in *Buddhist Mahāyāna Texts*, Part II, pp. 159–201, under the title "Amitāyur-Dhyāna-Sūtra."

Puying guoshi huanzhu'an qinggui 普應國師幻住庵清規 (*Fuō kokushi Genjū-an shingi*) The Huanzhu Hermitage Rules of the National Teacher Puying; also known as the *Huanzhu'an qinggui* 幻住庵清規 (*Genjū-an shingi*) The Huanzhu Hermitage Rules. By Zhongfeng Mingben 中峰明本 (Chōhō Myōhon, 1263–1323), in 1 *juan* [*ZZ* 2: 16.5.486c–506d].

A manual of rules for ordering the daily life of monks living in a small hermitage, and named for one of the huts on the "Middle Peak" (Zhongfeng 中峰 Chuhō) of Mount Tianmu 天目山 (Temmokuzan), in modern Zhejiang, in which Mingben often stayed. Puying Guoshi 普應國師 (Fuō Kokushi) was one of the Master's Imperially bestowed posthumous titles.

Rentian yanmu 人天眼目 (*Ninden gammoku*) The Eye of Gods and Men. Compiled by Huiyan Zhizhao 晦巖智昭 (Maigan Chishō, *n. d.*); preface dated 1188, in 6 *juan* [*T* 48: 300a–336a].

A collection of the principal teachings, important sayings, and verse of the leading figures of the Five Houses (*wujia* 五家 *goke*) of Chinese Zen. Zhizhao, who was a monk in the Yangqi (Yōgi) line of Linji (Rinzai) Zen, spent some twenty years in compiling the work. It was revised in 1258, and an epilogue by Wuchu Daguan 物初大觀 (Busso Daikan, *n. d.*) added. When a second revision took place in 1317, Tianfeng Zhiyou 天峰致祐 (Tempō Chiyū, *n. d.*) provided another epilogue. The work was first published in Japan in 1303.

Ryūhō kaisan tokushi Kōzen Daitō Kōshō Shōtō kokushi goroku 龍寶開山特賜興禪大燈高照正燈國師語錄 The Record of the Founder of the Dragon-jewel [Mountain], Whose Imperially Bestowed Titles Were Kōzen Daitō and Kōshō Kokushi; also known as the *Daitō kokushi goroku* 大燈國師語錄 Record of the National Teacher Daitō, the *Daitō roku* 大燈錄 Record of Daitō, and the *Ryūhō goroku* 龍寶語錄 The Dragon-jewel Record. Second edition in 3 *kan* published in 1621 by [Kōgetsu] Sōgan [江月] 宗玩 [*T* 81: 191a–242c].

This work consists of the recorded teachings and sayings of Shūhō Myōchō 宗峰妙超 (1282–1338), founder of the Rinzai Zen headquarters temple of Daitoku-ji 大德寺 in Kyoto. Ryūhō[zan] 龍寶[山] is the "mountain" name for the Daitoku-ji. (Though Japanese Zen city temples were not built on mountains as were many of the famous Zen temples of China, an honorary "mountain" name was given to the most important establishments. From this, the founders of these temples were called "Openers of the Mountain" [*kaisan* 開山 *kaishan*], a title applied in Japan to all temple founders.)

The material for the *Daitō roku* was originally recorded by several of the Master's immediate disciples. Neither the name of the original compiler of the work nor the date of its first publication are known, since these do not appear in the second edition, and no copies of the first edition are known to exist today.

The second edition, of which all later editions are reproductions, was made in 1621 by Kōgetsu Sōgari (1574–1643), founder of the Ryōkō-in 龍光院, one of the most important of the sub-temples within the Daitoku-ji compound. In his colophon to this edition, written in typical Zen style, Sōgan says:

> The publication of the *Daitō kokushi goroku* was undertaken in the past, but the woodblocks were burned to ashes during the Ōnin War. Therefore I, Sōgan, of the twelfth generation in the Master's line, one hundred and fifty years after their destruction, hereby venture out of my own purse to publish the work again in three *kan*. This Record isn't worth half a penny, and those who read it will surely say that I have exposed the unsightly inside of my house to the eyes of the world. Now, in the seventh month and seventh year of Genna [1621], I humbly contribute this work to the revered temple Ummon-an 雲門庵 of the Daitoku-ji.

(The Ummon-an is the hall in the main building of the Daitoku-ji in which is enshrined the statue of Daitō Kokushi, as well as the memorial tablets [*ihai* 位牌] of the Imperial founders, chief abbots, and important priests of the Daitoku-ji line.)

Kan 1 of the work, recorded by Shōchi 性智 (*n. d.*) contains the first part of the *Daitoku goroku* 大德語錄. This consists of formal sermons and informal talks given by the Master at the Daitoku-ji from the opening ceremony on February 9, 1327 until the spring of 1331.

Kan 2 comprises several items: the *Sōfuku goroku* 崇福語錄, recorded by Sōtei 宗貞 (*n. d.*), containing sermons and talks given at the Sōfuku-ji in Fukuoka, Kyushu, during the Master's hundred-day visit to this temple in the summer of 1331; the second part of the *Daitoku goroku*, recorded by the disciple Egen 惠眼 (*var.* for [Kanzan] Egen [關山]慧玄, 1277–1360), consisting of sermons and talks given at the Daitoku-ji from the time of the Master's return from Kyushu in the autumn of 1331 until his death in 1338; *Nenko* 拈古, a collection of eleven old koans from the records of the Chinese masters, to each of which the Kokushi attached a comment in prose; and *Juko* 頌古, a collection of forty-eight old koans to each of which the Master appended a comment in verse.

Kan 3 bears the general title *Daitō kokushi sanshō goyō* 大燈國師參詳語要 "Daitō Kokushi's Essential Words for Careful Study," and consists of the Master's lectures and commentary on the *Setchō roku* 雪竇錄 (*Xuedou lu*), the record of Setchō Jūken 雪竇重顯 (Xuedou Chongxian, 980–1052), of the Ummon 雲門 (Yunmen) School of Chinese Zen. This is followed by the *Daitō kokushi gyōjō* 大燈國師行狀 "Biography of Daitō Kokushi," written in 1426 by Zenkō 禪興 (*n. d.*) of the Tokuzen-ji 德禪寺, the most important of the sub-temples within the Daitoku-ji compound. Finally, the short colophon translated above concludes the work.

The sequence of the items in *kan* 2 and 3 of the *Taishō* text will be found to differ somewhat from that in the original woodblock text of the second edition, which latter has been followed in this analysis of the work. In the *Taishō* reprint the *Juko* precedes the *Nenko* section in *kan* 2, and the "Biography" and the colophon have been removed from *kan* 3 and inserted after the *Nenko* section in *kan* 2.

The *Daitō roku* is the most important of all the early Japanese Zen *goroku*. Its position in Japanese Rinzai Zen literature has been enhanced by the fact that *kan* 1 and 2 were used by Hakuin Ekaku (1686–1769) as the basic text for the series of lectures which compose his notable work *Kaiankoku go*.

Ryūtaku kaiso Jinki Dokumyō zenji nempu 龍澤開祖神機獨妙禪師年譜 A Chronological Biography of the Zen Master Jinki Dokumyō, Founder of the Ryūtaku [Temple]. By Tōrei Enji 東嶺圓慈 (1721–1792), in 2 *kan* [*Hakuin oshō zenshū*, Vol. I, pp. 1–78].

This is a record of the events in the life of Hakuin Ekaku 白隱慧鶴 (1686–1769), the great Japanese Zen master of the Tokugawa era, arranged under successive years, by his direct heir, the eminent Zen historian and literary man Tōrei Enji. Jinki Dokumyō 神機獨妙 was the posthumous title bestowed upon Hakuin by Imperial decree shortly after his death. This is a basic text for the study of Hakuin's life.

Saddharma-puṇḍarīka-sūtra, The Lotus of the True Dharma; also known as the *Lotus Sutra.*

This, the most famous and popular of all Mahayana scriptures, was presumably composed in North India shortly before, or about the beginning of, the Christian era. Nothing can be stated with any certainty about the origin of the work, though it seems probable that additions were later made to an original text. The sutra consists of twenty-seven chapters, written in prose and verse, all but seven concluding with a metrical recapitulation of the prose material. The language of the sutra is ornate, and its message conveyed through elaborate imagery, metaphor, allegory, parable, and prophecy.

The *Lotus Sutra* is a vast and magnificent apocalyptic drama. The scene opens with Shakyamuni seated on the Vulture Peak where the historical Buddha gave so many of his sermons. But this Vulture Peak is a glorified peak, and the Buddha not the human Shakyamuni but the Great Eternal Buddha. Before him is an audience composed of tens of thousands of disciples, bodhisattvas, devas, gods, and dragon and demon kings, all with their myriad followers. By means of the ray which he sends forth from his forehead, the Buddha reveals to this great gathering infinite numbers of worlds, each with its heavens and hells and living beings, and in each of which a buddha is preaching the Dharma to vast numbers of disciples.

The doctrines proclaimed in the course of this marvelous assembly are indeed radical. There is only one vehicle (*yāna*), one path of practice, by which to reach ultimate attainment. This is the *Ekayāna*, the "One Vehicle," the *Buddhayāna*. All previous teachings about the śrāvaka, pratyeka-buddha, and bodhisattva vehicles have been but expedient means of instructing those who were not yet prepared to comprehend the ultimate truth of the Mahayana, which is now being vouchsafed for the first time. The buddhas appear in the world, accepting birth-and-death and teaching for limited periods of time, only for the salvation of beings. Actually, however, all are manifestations of the Eternal Buddha, and thus beyond all limitations of time and space. Likewise, every manifested world, every manifested existence, is a flower of the Eternal Lotus. Furthermore, faith in the Eternal Buddha is not only superior to any pious works or practices, but through such faith alone can all men attain Buddhahood and final Nirvana, a Nirvana which is beyond either eternal extinction or eternal existence. The last half of Chapter 11 contains the story of the

Dragon King's daughter who attains Buddhahood in the twinkling of an eye, though not before assuming a male body! Though the story is probably a later interpolation, it is perhaps the first time that woman's capacity for Buddhahood is acknowledged, even in this grudging manner.

Several Sanskrit manuscript versions of the sutra found their way to Europe in the 19th century. A French translation of one of these was made in 1852 by Eugene BURNOUF, under the title *Le Lotus de la bonne loi*. A Sanskrit manuscript in the possession of Cambridge University Library was translated into English by H. KERN, and published in 1909 under the title The *Saddharma-Puṇḍarīka*.

The first Chinese translation of the sutra, a partial one now lost, was made about 235 CE. Five other translations followed, two of which also are no longer extant. Of the remaining three, the following is the most widely accepted in the Far East:

Miaofa lianhua jing 妙法蓮華經 (*Myōhō renge kyō*) Sutra of the Lotus of the Marvelous Dharma; also known as the *Fahua jing* 法華經 (*Hōge kyō*) The Dharma-flower Sutra, or Lotus Sutra. Translated into Chinese by Kumārajīva in 406, containing 28 chapters in 7 *juan* [*T* 9: 1–62a].

This translation by the great Central Asian scholar-monk Kumārajīva (Jiumoluoshi 鳩摩羅什 Kumarajū, 350–*ca.* 409) was made during the period when he was working in Chang'an (Chōan). Originally it seems to have contained only twenty-seven chapters. Later, a more complete text was brought from Khotan and translated into Chinese by Jñānagupta (Shenajueduo 闍那崛多 Janakutta, 523–600) and Dharmagupta (Damojiduo 達磨笈多 Datsumagyūta, *d.* 619). Certain sections of that translation, lacking in the Kumārajīva text, were now added to the latter. One of these, the final half of Chapter 11 of the Sanskrit version—the section on the Dragon King's daughter—was inserted as a separate chapter, Chapter 12, in the Kumārajīva text, thus bringing the total number of chapters in this translation to twenty-eight. Another addition was the entire verse section concluding the famous *Guanyin Sutra*, Chapter 24 in the Sanskrit version of the *Lotus Sutra* and Chapter 25 in the Kumārajīva text.

No complete English translation of any Chinese text has appeared. *The Lotus of the Wonderful Law*, by W. E. SOOTHILL, is a synopsis of the contents of the sutra chapter by chapter, interspersed with translated passages. It is based upon the Kumārajīva text.

The *Lotus Sutra* is the basic text for the Chinese Tiantai and Japanese Tendai sects, and also for the Japanese Nichiren 日蓮 Sect, but the teachings of the scripture have had a profound influence upon all the Pure Land schools and Tibetan Buddhism as well.

Shanhui dashi yulu 善慧大士語錄 (*Zenne daishi goroku*) The Record of the Eminent Layman Shanhui; also known as the *Fu dashi yulu* 傅大士語錄 (*Fu daishi goroku*) The Record of the Eminent Layman Fu. Compiled during the Tang by Lou Ying 樓穎 (Rō Ei, *n. d.*), in 8 *juan*; revised by Lou Zhao 樓炤 (Rō Shō, 1072–1144), and published in 1143, in 4 *juan* [*ZZ* 2: 25.1.1a–27b].

This short work is the record of the renowned and semi-legendary Buddhist layman Fu Dashi 傅大士 (Fu Daishi, 497–569), Shanhui Dashi 善慧大士 (Zenne Daishi) is the Buddhist name which the Dashi took for himself.

The original compilation was the work of Lou Ying, a government official of the Tang, who was a devout layman. Lou Ying made a pilgrimage to the temples of various old monks who had studied under Shanhui, in order to gather material about the Dashi. This he compiled into a work consisting of 8 *juan*, adding to it his own preface.

The distinguished Song scholar-official Lou Zhao later revised the original work, adding to it newly discovered material on Shanhui and rearranging the entire contents into 4 *juan*. The text in current use in Japan is a reprint of the Lou Zhao text, printed in Japan in 1694. Included in this text is an epilogue by another famous official and Buddhist layman Song Lian 宋濂 (Sō Ren, 1310–1381), who had republished the work early in the Ming dynasty, apparently using as the basis for his edition some text other than the revised text of Lou Zhao.

Juan 1 of the work as it now stands is devoted to a biography of Shanhui; *juan* 2 contains his collected sayings, sermons, and a few poems. *Juan* 3 comprises a collection of Shanhui's verse written in different styles, and two memorial inscriptions composed in his honor by eminent officials. From internal evidence, a number of the poems in this *juan* are believed to be spurious works produced toward the end of Tang. *Juan* 4 contains the biographies of four monks otherwise unknown, who may, perhaps, have been friends and contemporaries of Shanhui. The *Fu dashi zhuan* 傅大士傳 (*Fu daishi den*) "Biography of Fu Dashi," which concludes this fourth *juan* in the *Zokuzōkyō* edition, appears to be a rewriting of the material on Shanhui to be found in several different parts of the *Chuandeng lu*.

The Shenhui Sermons

Though from late Tang times the Zen tradition has known of Heze Shenhui 荷澤神會 (Kataku Jinne, 670–762) as a Dharma-heir of the Sixth Patriarch, an adversary of Shenxiu's Northern School, and founder of the Heze School of Chan, nevertheless his great importance for the rise of the Southern School with its doctrine of "sudden awakening" (*dunwu* 頓悟 *tongo*) has only come to be understood in recent years. Investigation and study by modern scholars of manuscripts discovered shortly after the turn of the century in the caves of Dunhuang 敦煌 (Tonkō), in modern Gansu, have brought to light much previously unknown material relating to Shenhui. The number of manuscripts and fragments of manuscripts relating to this master found in Dunhuang attest to the popularity and dissemination of Shenhui's teachings in northwestern China. The evidence of still another source seems to indicate that this dissemination reached as far to the west as the kingdom of Khotan in Central Asia. From various manuscripts so far identified as being records of the Master's sermons or mondos, four specific texts have emerged. A chronological record of the work accomplished on these manuscripts provides an interesting glimpse of the critical studies of modern scholars in this field.

Nanyang heshang wenda zazheng yi 南陽和尚問答雜徵義 (*Nan'yō oshō mondō zatchō gi*) The Monk of Nanyang's Examination through Question and Answer of Various Inquiries on Points of Doctrine.

An untitled and incomplete MS in the Bibliothèque Nationale, Paris, known as P. (Pelliot) 3047(a), as critically edited by Hu Shi 胡適 (Ko Teki), was published in 1930 in that author's *Shenhui heshang yiji* 神會和尚遺集 The Posthumous Collection of the Monk Shenhui, *juan* 1, pp. 91–152.

In 1932, a photographic reproduction of an untitled MS in the Sekisuiken Bunko 積翠軒文庫 of Ishii Mitsuo 石井光雄, Kamakura, was published by Suzuki Teitarō 鈴木貞太郎 (Suzuki Daisetz) under the title *Tonkō shutsudo Kataku Jinne zenji goroku* 燉煌出土荷澤神會禪師語錄 The Record of the Zen Master Kataku Jinne Found at Tonkō. This was followed in 1934 by the publication under the same title of a steel type edition of the Ishii manuscript, critically edited by Suzuki and Kōda Rentarō 公田連太郎, in which the editors clearly established that the Ishii text was another version, albeit with additional material, of the Paris manuscript P. 3047(a), earlier edited by Hu Shi.

Entretiens du Maître de Dhyâna Chen-houei du Ho-tsö, by Jacques Gernet, published in 1949, contains, pp. 5–80, a French translation of the Hu Shi text, with textual emendations and detailed notes by the translator.

In 1959, Professor IRIYA Yoshitaka 入矢義高, from a microfilm copy of a MS known as S. (Stein) 6557 in the British Museum Dunhuang collection, established that S. 6557 closely resembled the ISHII text and was related to P. 3047(a). In addition to a considerable body of text, S. 6557 contains a preface in which the name of the compiler is stated to be LIU Zheng 劉澄 (RYŪ Chō) and the original title of the work to be that given at the head of this entry. This title corresponds exactly with the title of a work in the list of books brought back from China in 847 by the Japanese Tendai monk Ennin 圓仁.

In his article entitled "Deux Documents de Touen-houang sur le Dhyâna chinois," contributed in 1961 to *Essays on the History of Buddhism Presented to Professor Zenryū Tsukamoto*, pp. 1–27, Paul DEMIÉVILLE has called attention to the fact that Ed. CHAVANNES, in his *Les documents chinois découverts par Aurel Stein dans les sables du Turkestan oriental* (1913), p. 203, No. 958, describes a manuscript fragment on paper found by STEIN in Khotan. DEMIÉVILLE has confirmed that the eight lines of this manuscript are to be found in slightly varying form in the Paris P. 3047(a), the ISHII manuscript, and the British Museum S. 6557.

Putidamo nanzong ding shifei lun 菩提達摩南宗定是非論 (*Bodaidaruma nanshū tei zehi ron*) Treatise Establishing the True and the False according to the Southern School of Bodhidharma.

The incomplete MS bearing this title is known as P. 3047(b), since it was originally attached to P. 3047(a), mentioned above. In addition to the title, it contains the statement that the work was recorded by DUGU Pei 獨孤沛 (DOKKO Hai), a preface by the recorder, and, at its conclusion, his eulogies on the text. This text, critically edited by Hu Shi, forms *juan* 2 of that scholar's *Shenhui heshang yiji*, pp. 159–167. *Juan* 3 of this same work by Hu Shi, pp. 175–186, contains a critically edited text of the untitled P. 3488, another MS in the Paris collection, which Dr. Hu at the time suggested might be related to P. 3047(b).

GERNET has given us a French translation of P. 3047(b) and P. 3488 as edited by Hu Shi and emended by himself, in his work mentioned above, pp. 81–91 and 92–105.

In an article published in the *Bulletin de l'École Française d'Extrême-Orient*, XLIV, 1954, pp. 453–458, and entitled "Complément aux Entretiens du Maitre de Dhyâna Chen-houei," GERNET called attention to the fact that a hitherto unstudied MS in the Paris collection, known as P. 2045(a), also bore the title at the head of this entry, and that this was another version of a text of which, as Hu Shi had earlier correctly suggested, P. 3047(b), and P. 3488 were related fragments.

The relation of these three MSs was further confirmed in 1958 with the publication of an article by Hu Shi in Chinese entitled "Two Newly Edited Texts of the Ch'an Master Shên-hui from the Pelliot Collection of Tun-huang Manuscripts at the Bibliothèque Nationale in Paris," *Studies Presented to Yuen Ren Chao on His Sixty-fifth Birthday: Academia Sinica, Bulletin of the Institute of History and Philology*, Vol. XXIX, Part II, pp. 827–882.

Nanyang heshang dunjiao jietuo chanmen zhiliaoxing tanyu 南陽和上頓教解脱禪門直了性壇語 (*Nan'yō oshō tongyō gedatsu zemmon jikiryōshō dango*) The Platform Sermon of the Monk of Nanyang on Direct Realization of the Innate Nature according to the Chan Doctrine of Emancipation through the Teaching of Sudden [Awakening].

In 1935, in a work entitled *Shōshitsu issho* 少室逸書 Lost Writings from Shōshitsu, Suzuki published, together with other material, a photographic reproduction of MS 寒 81 in the Beijing collection of Dunhuang manuscripts. MS 寒 81 bore a title identical with that at the head of this entry except that the first two characters 南陽 were lacking. In spite of this omission, Suzuki surmised that this was a Shenhui text. In 1936, the text of this same MS, edited and revised by Suzuki and Kōda, appeared as one of the items in *Kōkan Shōshitsu issho oyobi kaisetsu* 校刊少室逸書及解説 Revised Edition of Lost Writings from Shōshitsu with an Interpretation, pp. 57–71.

In 1953, there was published in *Asia Major*, New Series, Vol. III, Part 2, pp. 132–155, under the title "The Sermon of Shên-hui," an English translation by W. Liebenthal of a Paris MS designated as P. 2045(b). This MS bore the complete title given at the head of this entry, but Liebenthal questioned its correspondence to the Beijing MS published nearly twenty years earlier by Suzuki. However, in his article mentioned above and published the following year (1954) in *Bulletin de l'École Française d'Extrême-Orient*, Gernet definitively established that P. 2045(b) was another and better version of the Beijing MS 寒 81, thus verifying Suzuki's earlier surmise.

The article by Hu Shi appearing in 1958 in the Academia Sinica publication mentioned above, contains, pp. 828–836, an edited text of the Paris

MS P. 2045(b) and a comparison of it to the Beijing MS, but without reference to the LIEBENTHAL translation or GERNET's earlier findings.

In 1959, Professor IRIYA identified two other MS fragments in the British Museum Collection, S. 2492 and S. 6977, as parts of this same text.

Dunwu wusheng bore song 頓悟無生般若頌 (*Tongo mushō hannya ju*) Eulogy on the Wisdom by Which There Is Sudden Awakening to No-birth.

This text, S. 468 of the British Museum collection, as critically edited by Hu Shi, forms *juan* 4 in his *Shenhui heshang yiji*, pp. 194–199.

A French translation based upon the Hu Shi text is found in GERNET's *Entretiens du Maître de Dhyâna Chen-houei du Hotsö* (1949), pp. 106–110.

The British Museum manuscript S. 5619 is another version of this same text and bears the same title. It seems not yet to have been studied.

Still another version of the same text, under the title *Heze dashi xianzong ji* 荷澤大師顯宗記 (*Kataku daishi kenjū ki*) Heze Dashi's Revelation of the Doctrine, is contained in the 10th century *Jingde chuandeng lu*, juan 30 [*T* 51: 458c.25–459b.6]. Wing-tsit CHAN's English translation of the *Chuandeng lu* text, with emendations based upon Hu Shi's edition of the British Museum S. 468, was published in 1960 under the title "Elucidating the Doctrine," and will be found in *Sources of Chinese Tradition*, pp. 396–400.

There remains only to note that in the *Chuandeng lu*, juan 28 [*T* 51: 439b.20–440a.2], is another short sermon by Shenhui, followed by a series of questions and answers, entitled *Luojing Heze Shenhui dashi yu* 洛京荷澤神會大師語 (*Rakukei Kataku Jinne daishi no go*) The Words of Heze Shenhui Dashi of Luoyang. Several passages in this text are almost identical with passages to be found in the first and third texts discussed above, the *Zazheng yi* and the *Tanyu*.

SHŌBŌGENZŌ 正法眼藏 Treasury of the True Dharma Eye. The writings, lectures, and sermons of Dōgen Kigen 道元希玄 (1200–1253), recorded by his disciple Ejō 懷奘 (1198–1280) and others, in 95 *kan* [*T* 82: 7–309].

This is a collection of ninety-five prose compositions, written in Japanese, in which the founder of Japanese Sōtō Zen expounds the essentials of Zen Buddhism in his characteristic style. These writings range over a period of twenty-three years of the Master's life. The first, entitled *Bendōwa* 辨道話, or "Talk on Discerning the Way" [*ibid.*, 15a–22b], was written in 1231, five years after Dōgen's return from China and while he was living at Fukakusa 深草, near Kyoto. The last, *Hachidainingaku* 八大人覺, or "Eight Awarenesses that the Great Man Should Possess" [*ibid.*, 308a–309b], was a sermon given during 1253, the last year of the Master's life, at the great mountain monastery of Eihei-ji 永平寺, the headquarters of the Sōtō Sect in Fukui Prefecture.

There are several different texts of the work. Two of these are more important than the others: the *Shōbōgenzō goshō* 正法眼藏御抄 Commentary on the *Shōbōgenzō*, in 75 *kan*, edited by Ejō and Sen'e 詮慧 (*n. d.*), and annotated by Kyōgō 經豪 (*n. d.*); and the *Sōgō bon* 宋吾本 Sōgō Text, in 60 *kan*, which had been compiled by Giun 義雲 (1253–1333), in the 5th generation of the Eihei-ji, or orthodox, Japanese Sōtō line, but which at one time was in the hands of a Sōtō Sect monk by the name of Sōgo, from whom it derived its name. In the latter part of the Tokugawa era (1603–1867), Gentō Sokuchū 玄透即中 (*d.* 1807), in the 50th generation of the Eihei-ji line, ordered Ontatsu 穩達 (*n. d.*) and Shunryō 俊量 (*n. d.*) to make a definitive edition of the Shōbōgenzō based upon all existing editions. Thus the so-called *Honzamban* 本山版 "Headquarters Edition," in 95 *kan*, was compiled between 1795 and 1811. This is the edition now in general use. (*See also* Part One, Note 32.)

Only a few excerpts from the *Shōbōgenzō* have as yet been translated into European languages. Such English and German translations as have appeared are as follows: *The Sōtō Approach to Zen*, by Masunaga Reihō 增永靈鳳, contains English translations of *Uji*, pp. 81–90; *Shōji*, pp. 91–99; *Genjōkōan*, pp. 125–132; and *Bendōwa*, pp. 133–161. "Das Buch Genjōkōan 現成公案 aus dem *Shōbōgenzō* 正法眼藏 des Zen Meisters Dōgen 道元," a German translation by Heinrich Dumoulin, S. J., of the *Genjōkōan* section, with a long introduction and notes, will be found in *Monumenta Nipponica* Vol. XV, 3–4 (1959–1960), pp. 217–232.

Shōju Dōkyō Etan anju anroku 正受道鏡慧端庵主行錄 "The Biography of the Hermitage Master Shōju Dōkyō Etan." By Tōrei Enji 東嶺圓慈 (1721–1792), in the *Shōju Rōjin shū*, pp. 27–36.

This is the basic biography of the Zen master Dōkyō Etan 道鏡慧端 (1642–1721), popularly known as Shōju Rōjin 正受老人. He was the heir of Shidō Bu'nan 至道無難 (1603–1676) of the line of Kanzan Egen 關山慧玄 (1277–1360) of the Myōshin-ji 妙心寺, and the most important of the several teachers of Hakuin Ekaku 白隱慧鶴 (1686–1769), the great reformer of Japanese Rinzai Zen. The author, Tōrei Enji, was a distinguished heir of Hakuin.

Shōju Rōjin shū 正受老人集 The Shōju Rōjin Collection. Edited by the Shinano Kyōiku Kai; published in 1937, in 1 volume.

This is a collection comprising biographical material drawn from various sources and the miscellaneous verse left in rough draft by Dōkyō Etan 道鏡慧端 (1642–1721), the most important of the Zen masters under whom Hakuin Ekaku 白隠慧鶴 (1686–1769) studied. Shōju Rōjin was the name by which Dōkyō Etan was most often called in his later years. This volume also includes the *Shōju Dōkyō Etan anju anroku*, the biography of Etan written by Tōrei Enji 東嶺圓慈 (1721–1792), Hakuin Zenji's most distinguished heir.

Shōshitsu rokumon 小室六門 Bodhidharma's Six Gates. In 1 *kan* [*T* 48: 365a-377a.11]. The title is elsewhere more correctly written 少室六門集 *Shōshitsu rokumon shū.*

This is a collection of six treatises long attributed to Bodhidharma (Bodaidaruma 菩提達磨 Putidamo), the monk from Southern India who probably arrived in China about 470 CE and traditionally is considered to be the founder of Chinese Zen. "*Shōshitsu*" 少室 (*Shaoshi*) is often used in literary works as a designation for Bodhidharma, since it is the name of the peak on Mount Sū 嵩山 (Songshan), in modern Henan, where Bodhidharma's hermitage is said to have been located.

The collection as we now have it was made in Japan, probably at the beginning of the Tokugawa 徳川 era (1603–1867), since the earliest extant edition is dated 1647. Nothing is known of the circumstances under which the work was compiled. The individual treatises of which it is composed, however, were written in China during the Tang (618–907), perhaps even in early Tang. There is little or no evidence that Bodhidharma actually wrote these treatises, though authorship of the two entitled *Nishu'nyū* and *Anjin hōmon* has been ascribed to him from Tang times.

The six sections of the work were originally independent compositions, each with its own title. The first section is in verse and is entitled *Shingyō ju* 心經頌 (*Xinjing song*) "Verses on the Heart Sutra." The remaining five sections are in prose, and each concludes with a verse. They bear the following titles: *Hasō ron* 破相論 (*Poxiang lun*) "On Breaking through Form"; *Nishu'nyū* 二種入 (*Erzhongru*) "The Two Ways of Entrance"; *Anjin hōmon* 安心法門 (*Anxin famen*) "The Gate of Repose of Mind"; *Goshō ron* 悟性論 (*Wuxing lun*) "On the Awakened Nature"; *Ketsumyaku ron* 血脈論 (*Xuemo lun*) "On the Lineage of Mind."

Manuscript copies of the *Nishu'nyū* and the *Anjin hōmon* have been found at Dunhuang 敦煌 (Tonkō), and are now in the British Museum, London, and the National Library, Beijing. The *Nishu'nyū* is also included in three Tang compilations, as follows:

The biography of Bodhidharma in the *Zoku kōsō den* 續高僧傳 (*Xu gaoseng zhuan*) Further Biographies of Eminent Monks, by Dōsen 道宣 (Daoxuan, 596–667), concludes with an untitled and somewhat edited text of the *Nishu'nyū* [*T* 50: 551c8–26].

A text of the *Nishu'nyū*, identical with that in the *Shōshitsu rokumon*, follows the biography of Bodhidharma in another text found at Dunhuang, the *Ryōga shiji ki* 楞伽師資記 (*Lengqie shizi ji*) Record of the Lanka School, by Jōkaku 淨覺 (Jingjue, 683–*ca.* 760) [*T* 85: 1285a.11–b.15].

The *Keitoku dentō roku*, kan 30, contains a text of the *Nishu'nyū*, prefaced by a short biography of Bodhidharma by Donrin 曇琳 (Tanlin, *fl.* 6th cent.), under the title *Bodaidaruma ryakuben daijō nyūdō shigyō* 菩提達磨略辨大乘入道四行 (*Putidamo lüebian dacheng rudao sixing*) "Bodhidharma's Short Treatise on the Four Practices for Entering the Mahayana Way" [*T* 51: 458b.7–c.24].

In all these Tang works the concluding verses found in the Japanese *Shōshitsu rokumon* collection are lacking.

An English translation of the *Keitoku dentō roku* text of the *Nishu'nyū*, together with Donrin's introductory remarks, will be found under the title "Meditation on the Four Acts," in D. T. Suzuki's *Essays in Zen Buddhism*, First Series, pp. 179–183. A few passages from the *Ketsumyaku ron*, there entitled "Treatise on the Lineage of Faith," will be found in the same work, pp. 233–235.

Shūmon kattū shū 宗門葛藤集 A Zen Koan Collection; also known as the *Kattō shū* 葛藤集 A Koan Collection. In 2 *kan* [*Zudokko*, pp. 109–197].

This collection of 272 miscellaneous koans, all from Chinese sources with the exception of a few of Japanese origin, is a basic collection for koan study in Japanese Rinzai Zen today. The work was undoubtedly compiled in Japan, but the name of the original compiler and the date of the first publication are unknown. Copies of woodblock editions dated 1689 and 1692 exist. During the Tokugawa (1603–1867) and early Meiji (1868–1912) eras, a number of editions of the work appeared, but it is presently most conveniently found in the *Zudokko*.

Shūmon mujintō ron 宗門無盡燈論 On the Eternal Lamp of Zen; also known as the *Mujintō ron* 無盡燈論 On the Eternal Lamp, and the *Tōron* 燈論 On the Lamp [of Zen]. By Fufu-an Enji 不不庵圓慈, with a preface by the author dated 1751; first published in 1800 by Muin 霧隱 (*n. d.*), in 2 *kan* [*T* 81: 581a–605b].

This is a work by Tōrei Enji 東嶺圓慈 (1721–1792), the most important of the disciples of Hakuin Ekaku 白隱慧鶴 (1686–1769), under one of the literary names he took for himself. In the long preface written while he was in Edo 江戸 (Tokyo) in 1751, Tōrei explains how he came to write this book and what his purpose in doing so was. He had gone to Kyoto in 1746 for a period of intense "after satori" meditation. As a result of the severe discipline to which he had subjected himself, he became ill with tuberculosis. On hearing that his case was hopeless and that he could not live much longer, Tōrei's deepest regret, so he tells us, was that he would not be able to carry out his vow to assist in the salvation of other sentient beings. Then he recollected the old story of how Sōjō 僧肇 (Sengzhao, 374–414), when he had incurred the displeasure of the King of Shin 秦 (Qin) and been ordered to kill himself, had devoted the last week of his life to writing the *Hōzō ron* 寶藏論 (*Baozang lun*) On the Treasure Storehouse. Tōrei resolved to do likewise, and to write down the essentials of Zen as he had been taught them by Hakuin. The rough draft of the work was completed in thirty days. The title was taken from the passage in the Yuima kyō 維摩經 (*Weimo jing*) which says, "One lamp continuously divides into hundreds of lamps, and each lamp lights other lamps endlessly," for Tōrei hoped that his own satori would be the source of the satori experience for innumerable other people. In 1749 he was able to return to the Shōin-ji 松蔭寺 at Hara 原 in Suruga 駿河, present Shizuoka Prefecture, and resume his studies under Hakuin. After he had received inka from the Master, Tōrei wanted to burn the book, as he felt it no longer served any purpose, but he was dissuaded from this course by Hakuin and his fellow disciples.

The *Mujintō ron* was first published eight years after Tōrei's death by his disciple Muin. Since then it has been used as an introduction to

Hakuin's Zen, and republished many times.

The work is divided into ten sections, the titles of which give a synopsis of the progressive system of Zen study and practice formulated by Hakuin. They are as follows: *Shūyu* 宗由 "The Origin of the [Zen] School"; *Shinshū* 信修 "True Practice"; *Genkyō* 現境 "Illusory States of Mind"; *Jisshō* 實證 "Real Proof [of Satori]"; *Tōkan* 透關 "Passing through the [First] Barrier"; *Kōjō* 向上 "Toward the Ultimate"; *Rikiyū* 力用 "The Power and Functioning [of Satori]"; *Shijō* 師承 "The Master's Acknowledgment"; *Chōyō* 長養 "The Ripening [of Satori]"; and Ruzū 流通 "Dispensing [the Dharma]." There is a supplementary section, also by Tōrei, entitled *Gyōji ron* 行持論 "On the Practice in Daily Life." This was probably added at the time the work was published.

Sijia yulu 四家語錄 (*Shike goroku*) The Record of the Four Houses; also known as the *Mazu sijia lu* 馬祖四家錄 (*Baso shike roku*) The Record of Mazu's Four Houses, and the *Sijia lu* 四家錄 (*Shike roku*) Record of the Four Houses. In 6 *juan* [*ZZ* 2: 24.5.405a–424a].

This is a collection of the recorded sayings of four distinguished Zen masters of the Tang dynasty, all in the line of Nanyue Huairang (Nangaku Ejō), namely, Mazu Daoyi 馬祖道一 (Baso Dōitsu, 709–788), Baizhang Huaihai 百丈懷海 (Hyakujō Ekai, 720–814), Huangbo Xiyun 黃蘗希運 (Ōbaku Kiun, *d. ca.* 850), and Linji Yixuan 臨濟義玄 (Rinzai Gigen, *d.* 866).

We do not know the name of the compiler, the sources upon which he drew, or the date of the first publication, but the title of the work is mentioned in the *Suichutang shumu* 遂初堂書目 (*Suishodō shomoku*), an early Southern Song catalogue edited by the Confucian scholar Yu Mao 尤袤 (Yū Bō, 1127–1194). The *Sijia yulu* was reprinted in the Yuan dynasty, but no copies of this edition are known to exist. The work was reedited and published in 1607 by Jie Ning 解寧 (Kai Nei, *n. d.*), also known as Jingshan Jushi 靜山居士 (Seizan Koji), of Dong'an 東安 (Tōan), in present Zhejiang. It is upon this edition that the present text is based.

The work is reprinted only in part in the *Zokuzōkyō*. Through the courtesy of Komazawa University 駒澤大學, a microfilm of their copy of the complete 1607 edition has been made available. From a cursory study of this it would appear that the original compiler rearranged the material available to him from earlier texts, and, except in the case of the section on Linji (Rinzai), included within each section material taken from several of these sources, thus making each of the *Sijia lu* "records" somewhat longer than any one of the earlier texts.

An analysis of the 1607 edition of the text follows:

Juan 1: *Jiangxi Mazu Daoyi chanshi yulu* 江西馬祖道一禪師語錄 (*Kōzei Baso Dōitsu zenji goroku*) "The Record of the Zen Master Mazu Daoyi of Jiangxi" [*ZZ* 2: 24.5.405c.1–409a.1].

Juan 2: *Hongzhou Baizhangshan Dazhi chanshi yulu* 洪州百丈山大智禪師語錄 (*Kōshū Hyakujōzan Daichi zenji goroku*) "The Record of the Zen Master Dazhi of Mount Baizhang in Hongzhou" [*ibid*., 409b.1–410-d.16].

Juan 3: *Baizhang guanglu* 百丈廣錄 (*Hyakujō kōroku*) "The Comprehensive Record of Baizhang" [*ibid*., 411a.1–411d.8]. All but a small portion of this section of the original work has been omitted in the *Zokuzōkyō*.

Juan 4: *Yunzhou Huangboshan Duanji chanshi chuanxin fayao* 筠州黃蘗山斷際禪師傳心法要 (*Inshū Ōbakuzan Dansai zenji denshin hōyō*) "The Principles of the Transmission of Mind as set forth by the Zen Master Duanji of Mount Huangbo in Yunzhou" [*ibid*., 412a–416c.10].

Juan 5: *Huangbo Duanji chanshi Wanling lu* 黃蘗斷際禪師宛陵錄 (*Ōbaku Dansai zenji Enryō roku*) "The Wanling Record of the Zen Master Duanji of [Mount] Huangbo" [*ibid*., 416d–423d].

Juan 6: *Linji Huizhao chanshi yulu* 臨濟慧照禪師語錄 (*Rinzai Eshō zenji goroku*) "The Record of the Zen Master Linji Huizhao." This section of the original text is omitted entirely in the *Zokuzōkyō*.

Epilogue [*ibid*., 424a] by Jie Ning, editor of the Ming edition.

The Sixth Patriarch's Platform Sutra

This famous Zen work is the only such text to bear the title "Sutra," a designation otherwise limited to works devoted to the words spoken, or purported to be spoken, by Buddha. The work, as suggested by the title, consists of a sermon, or sermons, delivered by the Sixth Patriarch, Huineng 慧能 (Enō, 638–713), from the preaching platform at the Dafansi 大梵寺 (Daibon-ji) in the city of Shaozhou 韶州 (Shōshū), about one hundred miles to the north of present Guangzhou, in Guangdong Province. In this sermon, the first important one given by the Sixth Patriarch, he stated at length his decidedly radical views on Buddhism and on Zen—views based in large part on the *Diamond Sutra*—and enunciated the doctrine of Sudden Enlightenment, a doctrine later to become the outstanding feature of the Southern School of Zen, of which he was the founder. In the course of time much additional material became attached to the original sermon—later sermons, talks with disciples, biographical details, legends—to form numerous versions of what may be called the "record" of the Sixth Patriarch. The two most important extant versions are the following:

Nanzong dunjiao zuishang dacheng mohebore boluomi jing: Liuzu Huineng dashi yu Shaozhou Dafansi shifa tanjing 南宗頓教最上大乘摩訶般若波羅蜜經：六祖慧能大師於韶州大梵寺施法壇經 (*Nanshū tongyō saijō daijō makahannya haramitsu kyō: Rokuso Enō daishi Shōshu Daibon-ji ni oite sehō suru no dankyō*) The Supreme Mahayana Perfection of Wisdom Sutra on the Southern School's Doctrine of Sudden [Enlightenment]: The Platform Sutra Preached by the Sixth Patriarch, Huineng Dashi, at the Dafan Temple in Shaozhou. In 1 *juan* [*T* 48: 337a–345b].

This Tang dynasty text, the earliest extant version of the work, is a 9th century manuscript found in 1907 in the cave-temple at Dunhuang 敦爐 (Tonkō), in modern Gansu Province, and now No. 5475 of the Stein Collection in the British Museum, London. It is generally known as the "Dunhuang Text of the Platform Sutra." This relatively short work has no sub-divisions, and is without a preface or an epilogue. The Master's disciple Fahai 法海 (Hōkai) is given as recorder and compiler, but it is probable that he acted in this capacity only for the initial sermon, or sermons, at the Dafansi.

D. T. Suzuki and Kōda Rentarō have edited the text somewhat freely under the title *Tonkō shutsudo Rokuso dankyō*. It has also been edited by Ui Hakuju, and will be found in that author's *Zenshūshi kenkyū*, Vol. II. pp. 117–172, under the title *Dankyō*.

An English translation by Wing-tsit Chan of excerpts from the Dunhuang Text will be found in *Sources of Chinese Tradition*, pp. 390–396. The same author has recently published a translation of the complete text under the title *The Platform Scripture*. Passages from the text have also been translated by D. T. Suzuki, *Manual of Zen Buddhism*, pp. 82–89.

Liuzu dashi fabao tanjing 六祖大師法寶壇經 (*Rokuso daishi hōbō dankyō*) The Sixth Patriarch's Treasure of Dharma Platform Sutra; also known as the *Liuzu tanjing* 六祖壇經 (*Rokuso dankyō*) The Sixth Patriarch's Platform Sutra, and the *Tanjing* 壇經 (*Dankyō*) The Platform Sutra. Compiled by Zongbao 宗寶 (Shūhō, *n. d.*), in 1291, in 1 *juan* [*T* 48: 345b–365a].

This version of the *Platform Sutra*, usually designated the "Yuan Text" from the name of the dynasty in which it was compiled, has been continuously in use in the Zen schools of China and Japan since the 14th century. Nothing is known about the compiler Zongbao other than what may be gleaned from his own statements accompanying the text. He signs himself at the beginning of the work as "the abbot and heir of the patriarchs, the monk Zongbao of the Wind and Banner [Temple], the Bao'en Guangxiao chansi" [*ibid.*, 347c]. The Bao'en Guangxiao chansi 報恩光孝禪寺 (Hōon Kōkō zen-ji) was probably a late name for the Faxingsi 法性寺 (Hōshō-ji) in Nanhai 南海 (Nankai), the present city of Guangdong, where Huineng first appeared after his years of hiding in the mountains. In Zongbao's own epilogue, the sixth to the work as it now stands, he writes that he collated three early versions of the sutra, then expanded his collated text with such material as he felt would be useful. The text of this version, which is about twice the length of the Dunhuang text, nevertheless approximately parallels it.

The Yuan Text opens with a preface by the monk Deyi 德異 (Tokui, *n. d.*), and an essay in praise of the sutra by Qisong 契嵩 (Kaisū, 1007–1072), a renowned scholar-monk in the 5th generation of the Yunmen (Ummon) School. The work is divided into ten sections: "Autobiography" (*xingyou* 行由 *gyōyu*); "Intrinsic Wisdom" (*prajñā*; *bore* 般若 *hannya*); "Questions" (*yiwen* 疑問 *gimon*); "Samādhi and Prajñā" (*dinghui* 定慧 *jōe*); "Meditation" (*zuochan* 坐禪 *zazen*); "Repentance" (*chanhui* 懺悔 *zange*); "Relationship" (*jiyuan* 機緣 *kien*); "Sudden and Gradual [Enlightenment]" (*dunjian* 頓漸 *tonzen*); "Imperial Edict" (*xuanzhao* 宣詔 *senshō*); and "Final Instructions" (*fuzhu* 付囑 *fuzoku*). The work concludes with six epilogues. The first is by Fahai, the Sixth Patriarch's disciple who recorded the Master's Dafansi sermons; the second is by an unnamed Song writer; the third and fourth consist of tomb inscriptions written by Tang officials; the fifth is a record of happenings after Huineng's death, by Lingtao 令韜 (Ryōtō, *n. d.*), the guardian of the Sixth Patriarch's tomb; and the sixth is by the compiler Zongbao.

The main text of the work, together with the fifth epilogue, was translated into English in 1929 by Wong Mu-lam. As edited by Dwight Goddard, this translation is to be found in *A Buddhist Bible*, pp. 497–561, under the title "The Sutra Spoken by the Sixth Patriarch." Edited by Christmas Humphreys, the same translation has been published as *The Sutra of Wei-lang* [*or Hui-Neng*]. An English translation of the Yuan Text by Lu K'uan Yü (Charles Luk) will be found in that author's *Chan and Zen Teaching*, Third Series, pp. 15–102, under the title "The Altar Sutra of the

Sixth Patriarch." In the Luk translation, Fahai's epilogue is presented as a preface, and the fifth epilogue, that by Lingtao, concludes the work.

Sokkō roku kaien fusetsu 息耕錄開筵普說 Talks on Zen Introductory to Lectures on the *Record of Sokkō*; also known as the *Kaien fusetsu* 開筵普說 Introductory Lectures. By Hakuin Ekaku 白隱慧鶴 (1686–1769), recorded by Tōko 東胡 (*n. d.*), revised by Gen'yaku 原譯 (*n. d.*), with a preface by Zenso Tenkei 禪祚天敬 (*n. d.*), and an epilogue entitled *Sokkō roku hyōshō jōgo* 息耕錄評唱剩語 "Further Words in Criticism and Praise of the *Record of Sokkō*" First published by Genshoku 玄軾 (*n. d.*), in 1743, in 1 *kan* [*Hakuin oshō zenshū*, Vol. II, pp. 365–450].

This work comprises material contained in several general talks on Zen which Hakuin Zenji gave to his students in the spring of 1740, as an introduction to a series of *teishō* 提唱 (Zen lectures) on the *Kidō roku* 虛堂錄 (*Xutang lu*), the record of the Chinese Zen master Kidō Chigu 虛堂智愚 (Xutang Zhiyu, 1185–1269). Hakuin states in his work that "Sokkō" was Kidō Zenji's *go* 號 (*hao*), or literary name, and for this reason he called the *Kidō roku* the *Sokkō roku*. However, we have only Hakuin's word for this fact, as no mention of it is made elsewhere.

The *Kaien fusetsu* ranks among the most important of Hakuin's works. It criticises severely the *mokushō* 默照 (silent illumination) of the Sōtō Sect, as well as the *nembutsu* 念佛 (recitation of the name of Amida Buddha) practiced in the Pure Land sects. In it the Master exhorts his students to cut off the root of life and death and to return to the true teaching of the Zen School.

The recording, revising, compiling, authorship of the preface, and publishing of the work were all undertaken by disciples of Hakuin. The unsigned epilogue is attributed to the Master himself.

Sŏnmun yŏmsong chip 禪門拈頌集 (*Zemmon nenju shū*) A Collection of Zen Prose and Verse Comments [on Old Koans]; also known as the *Yŏmsong chip* 拈頌集 (*Nenju shū*) A Collection of Prose and Verse Comments [on Old Koans]. Compiled and edited by the Korean monk Yŏng'ŭl Hyesim 永乙慧諶 (Eiitsu Ejin, 1178–1234), in 30 fascicles, and printed in Korea.

This work is a collection of 1125 koans based upon episodes from the lives and sermons of various Zen patriarchs and masters, beginning with Shakyamuni and continuing on into the Song dynasty (960–1279).

In addition, it contains important prose and verse comments by Chinese Zen monks of Tang and Song arranged in order of transmission from master to disciple.

The compiler-editor Yŏng'ŭl Hyesim, who called himself Muŭija 無衣子 (Mueshi), was a direct heir of Chinul 智訥 (Chitotsu, 1158–1210), founder of the Chogye 曹溪 (Sōkei) School, an exclusively Korean school of Zen still existing in that country. Chinul was not related to any Chinese line of Zen. He was a Korean monk who had made a deep study of the teachings of the Sixth Patriarch and the writings of the Chinese Yangqi (Yōgi) line master Dahui Zonggao 大慧宗杲 (Daie Sōkō, 1089–1163), and upon the basis of his personal understanding established his own sect.

The *Yŏmsong chip* was completed in 1226, and, though the date of publication is nowhere stated in the work, it seems probable that it was almost immediately printed at the Haein-sa 海印寺 (Kaiin-ji), the famous temple in Kyŏngsang-namdo 慶尚南道 (Keishō-nandō), in southern Korea, where the great Korean edition of the Tripiṭaka was printed between 1236 and 1251. The collection, considered the scripture of the Chogye School, was widely read in Korea and reprinted there several times.

A mimeographed copy of an original Haein-sa text of the *Sŏnmun yŏmsong chip* in the possession of the library of Hanazono University 花園大學, Kyoto, has been published in 10 volumes.

Suvarṇa-prabhāsa-sūtra, The Sutra of Golden Splendor.

This was a Sanskrit sutra of the Mahayana Vaipulya (*fangguang* 方廣 hōkō), or "comprehensive" type. Nothing seems to be known of its origin or the original date of its composition. It seems to have been an extremely popular scripture, and was translated into Chinese, Tibetan, and several Central Asian languages. The various translations indicate that additions were gradually made to a basic text, and that some of the doctrines expounded in the earlier versions were later further developed. The sutra, throughout a non-scholastic exposition of Mahayana doctrines, comprises many separate elements, the various chapters showing little inner connection. There is some teaching on the Void, some on the character of the Tathāgata—this resembling teachings in the *Lotus Sutra*—some on the bodhisattva practices. Other chapters are devoted to stories of the lives and deeds of various bodhisattvas, to spells, and to incantations. Fragments of a Sanskrit text and of a translation into Uighur have been found in Turkestan.

The two most important Chinese versions of the sutra are as follows:

Jinguangming jing 金光明經 (*Konkōmyō kyō*) The Sutra of Golden Splendor. Translated into Chinese by Dharmakṣema (?) (Tanwuchan 曇無讖 Dommusen, 385–433?), in 4 *juan* [*T* 16: 335–359b].

This is an incomplete translation, or the translation of an incomplete text, made by the Indian monk Dharmakṣema while he was working in Guzang 姑臧 (Kozō), the second capital of the Northern Liang (Beiliang 北涼 Hokuryō) dynasty (397–439). Though only a partial translation, this has always remained the most popular version in China.

Jinguangming zuishengwang jing 金光明最勝王經 (*Konkōmyō saishō-ō kyō*) Sutra of the Victorious King of Golden Splendor; also known as the *Zuishengwang jing* 最勝王經 (*Saishō-ō kyō*) The Victorious King Sutra. Translated by Yijing 義淨 (Gijō, 635–713), in 10 *juan* [*T* 16: 403–456].

This complete translation of the sutra was made between 700 and 712 by the Chinese monk Yijing after he had returned from his long voyage to India and was working in Luoyang (Rakuyō).

A German translation of Yijing's Chinese text will be found in Volume I of the *Suvarṇaprabhāsottama-sūtra*, Das Goldglanz-sūtra, by Johannes Nobel.

Tianmu Mingben chanshi zalu 天目明本禪師雜錄 (*Temmoku Myōhon zenji zatsuroku*) The Miscellaneous Record of the Zen Master Mingben of [Mount] Tianmu; also known as the *Mingben chanshi zalu* 明本禪師雜錄 (*Myōhon zenji zatsuroku*) The Miscellaneous Record of the Zen Master Mingben, and the *Zhongfeng zalu* 中峰雜錄 (*Chūhō zatsuroku*) The Miscellaneous Record of Zhongfeng. In 3 *juan* [*ZZ* 2: 27.4.362c–401d].

This is a collection of sermons, talks, letters, and poems by Zhongfeng Mingben 中峰明本 (Chūhō Myōhon, 1263–1323), an important master of the Linji (Rinzai) School during the Yuan (Gen) dynasty. None of the material in this work is included in the Master's more comprehensive record, the *Zhongfeng guanglu*. Neither the name of the compiler nor the date of publication is known.

Tianmu Zhongfeng heshang guanglu 天目中峰和尙廣錄 (*Temmoku Chūhō oshō kōroku*) The Comprehensive Record of Master Zhongfeng of [Mount] Tianmu; also known as the *Zhongfeng heshang guanglu* 中峰和尙廣錄 (*Chūhō oshō kōroku*) The Comprehensive Record of Master Zhongfeng, and the *Zhongfeng guanglu* 中峰廣錄 (*Chūhō kōroku*) The

Comprehensive Record of Zhongfeng. Compiled by Beiting Ciji 北庭慈寂 (Hokutei Jijaku, *n. d.*), in 30 *juan* [*KZ* 31: 6–7].

This is a collection of the recorded sayings and writings of Zhongfeng Mingben 中峰明本 (Chūhō Myōhon, 1263–1323), a monk in the 12th generation of the Yangqi (Yōgi) line of Linji (Rinzai) Zen, gathered together and compiled by Boting Ciji and other disciples of the Master. In 1334 the work was presented to the last of the Yuan (Gen) dynasty emperors, Shundi 順帝 (Juntei, *r.* 1333–1368), who ordered it included in the Tripiṭaka. The following year priests of the Dapuningsi 大普寧寺 (Daifu'nei-ji) in Hangzhou supervised the cutting of the woodblocks for the work, but before printing and distribution could be completed the blocks were burned in a fire that destroyed the temple. Some years later blocks were cut a second time, and the work was published on the Buddha's Birthday in 1387. Various editions were later printed in Japan, including one in Kyoto in 1673.

The work includes sermons by Zhongfeng, his commentaries on several important Buddhist texts, conversations on various topics relating to Zen study, and poems, prefaces, and others of his literary works.

Tiansheng guangdeng lu 天聖廣燈錄 (*Tenshō kōtō roku*) The Tiansheng [Era] Record of the Widely Extending Lamp; also known as the *Guangdeng lu* 廣燈錄 (*Kōtō roku*) The Record of the Widely Extending Lamp. Compiled by Li Zunxu 李遵勗 (Ri Junkyoku, *d.* 1038); published in 1036, in 30 *juan* [*ZZ* 2乙: 8.4–5].

This is a chronologically arranged compilation of biographies, sermons, and sayings of Zen patriarchs and monks, beginning with Shakyamuni and concluding with men who were contemporaries of the compiler. Li Zunxu, an important official married to an Imperial princess, worked on this compilation during the Tiansheng era (1023–1031) of Northern Song. He was an enthusiastic student and supporter of the Linji (Rinzai) School, and in compiling his work he placed special emphasis upon the line of transmission from which that school derived, even going so far as to include the text of the *Linji lu* (*Rinzai roku*), in practically the form we have it today. On its completion, the work was presented to Emperor Renzong 仁宗 (Jinsō, *r.* 1022–1063), who wrote a preface for it and ordered it included in the Buddhist Canon.

Vajracchedikā-prajñāpāramitā-sūtra, The Scripture of the Perfection of Transcendental Wisdom That Cuts Through (or, Like a) Diamond;

also known as the *Vajracchedikā*, The Diamond Cutter Sutra, or the *Diamond Sutra*.

This is a famous short sutra belonging to the Mahayana Perfection of Transcendental Wisdom (*prajñāpāramitā*) literature, which is concerned with the doctrine of *śūnyatā*, or the Void, in all its ramifications. The original work in Sanskrit was produced in India some time before 400 CE. The sutra purports to be a sermon given by the Buddha in the Jetavana in Śrāvastī, in which he answers the questions of the disciple Subhūti relating to the attainment of the Highest Perfect Awakening. A number of translations of the Sanskrit text have been made into western languages, but the latest, a most scholarly one, with a commentary by the translator, will be found in *Buddhist Wisdom Books*, by Edward Conze, pp. 21–71, under the title "The Diamond Sutra."

Jingang bore boluomi jing 金剛般若波羅蜜經 (*Kongō hannya haramitsu kyō*) The Diamond Perfection of Wisdom Sutra; also known as the *Jingang jing* 金剛經 (*Kongō kyō*) The Diamond Sutra. Translated into Chinese in 402 by Kumārajīva, in 1 *juan* [*T* 8: 748c.17–752c.7].

This, the first Chinese translation of the *Diamond Sutra*, was made by the great Central Asian Buddhist scholar Kumārajīva (Jiumoluoshi 鳩摩羅什 Kumarajū, 350–*ca.* 409) while he was working in Chang'an (Chōan). Several other Chinese versions by later translators followed under slightly varying titles, but that made by Kumārajīva has remained the preferred version.

Among the several English translations of this Chinese text, the following are the most recent: "The Kongogyo or Diamond Sutra," a partial translation by D.T. Suzuki, in *Manual of Zen Buddhism*, pp. 38–50; *The Jewel of Transcendental Wisdom*, by A.F. Price; and "The Diamond Cutter of Doubts," in *Ch'an and Zen Teaching*, First Series, by Lu K'uan Yü (Charles Luk), pp. 149–206. The latter is a translation of the *Jingang jueyi* 金剛決疑 (*Kongō ketsugi*) [*ZZ* 1: 39.1.57a–70a], the Kumārajīva text with a commentary by Hanshan Deqing 憨山德清 (Kanzan Tokusei, 1546–1623), a Zen master of late Ming.

The *Diamond Sutra* has been a favorite scripture in the Zen Sect since the time of the Sixth Patriarch. The following passage from it is traditionally said to have opened the Patriarch's mind while he was still a seller of kindling wood:

> All the Bodhisattvas Mahasattvas should thus produce the pure mind. Not abiding in form, they should produce this mind; not abiding in sound, smell, taste, touch, or dharmas, they should

produce this mind. Abiding nowhere, they should produce this mind. [*T* 8: 749c.20–23]

Several phrases from the sutra are used as koans in Japanese Rinzai Zen today.

The oldest known printed book the date of which can be ascertained is the copy of Kumarajīva's translation of the *Diamond Sutra* found in the caves at Dunhuang 敦煌 (Tonkō) by Sir Aurel STEIN. It is a scroll sixteen feet long printed from wood blocks, with a frontispiece depicting the Buddha, seated on the Lotus Throne and surrounded by a company of bodhisattvas and disciples, about to begin instructing Subhūti, who kneels before him. It bears the date May 11, 868. [Cf. *The Invention of Printing in China*, by Thomas Francis CARTER, p. 56.]

VIMALAKĪRTI-NIRDEŚA, The Teaching of Vimalakīrti.

This is an important Mahayana scripture in which is set forth the doctrine that the devout layman, living the householder's life, may yet follow the way of the bodhisattva and attain emancipation. No Sanskrit text is extant.

The sutra opens with Buddha preaching the Dharma in the Āmrapālī Grove in Vaiśālī to a great assembly of bhikshus, bodhisattvas, gods, and other beings from the four quarters of the universe. To this gathering comes Ratnakūṭa, son of a wealthy merchant of Vaiśālī, accompanied by the sons of five hundred other wealthy merchants. After paying adoration to Buddha, Ratnakūṭa begs the Blessed One to preach on the way a bodhisattva ought to follow in order to reach the Pure Land. This Buddha does, concluding his sermon by manifesting the Pure Land to the assembly through his supernatural powers.

The scene now changes, and we are introduced to the rich householder and lay disciple of Buddha, Vimalakīrti—the name means "spotless fame"—who is lying ill at his home in Vaiśālī. Vimalakīrti's great virtues, including his surpassing eloquence, are extolled at length. He is the ideal Buddhist householder. He has brought on his own illness in order that he may use it as an opportunity to expound the Dharma to his many visitors—kings, ministers, high officials, householders, and laymen alike. Buddha now requests his disciples one by one to visit Vimalakīrti to inquire about his illness. One by one they excuse themselves as unworthy. They fear to face the great layman, since all have previously gone down to defeat before his critical eloquence. Finally the Bodhisattva

Mañjuśrī agrees to go. All in the great assembly accompany him, to the number of tens of thousands, and all, through Vimalakīrti's miraculous powers, are accommodated at the same time in the sick man's ten-foot square room.

Mañjuśrī now inquires about the householder's illness, and Vimalakīrti answers this and other questions in such a way as to describe fully the bodhisattva practices as they are carried out in the life of the devout householder. The climax of the interview is reached when Vimalakīrti, having asked various bodhisattvas present about how a bodhisattva can enter the gate of non-duality, at Mañjuśrī's request answers the question himself by his "Great Silence." Vimalakīrti now rises from his sickbed and, together with the great company, joins Buddha in the Āmrapālī Grove and pays reverence to the Blessed One. The way of the bodhisattva is further explained and extolled by Buddha, and further supernatural wonders are manifested.

The *Vimalakīrti-nirdeśa* became very popular in China, and at least six translations of it were made. The most important of these are as follows:

Foshuo Weimojie jing 佛説維摩詰經 (*Bussetsu Yuimakitsu kyō*) The Vimalakīrti Sutra Preached by Buddha. Translated by ZHI Qian 支謙 (SHI Ken, *n. d.*) between 222 and 229, in 2 *juan* [*T* 14: 519a–536c].

This is the earliest translation. The text upon which it was based was obviously an early one, since the translation lacks certain material to be found in the later Chinese versions of the work. The translator ZHI Qian came from a family of Scythian origin, long resident in China. A very learned monk who knew many languages, he originally resided in Luoyang (Rakuyō), but because of political troubles fled to the south in 220, where he became attached to the Wu 吳 (Go) Court at Nanjing. During the succeeding years he translated a large number of Buddhist texts into Chinese. In 253 he retired to the mountains, and there died at the age of sixty.

Weimojie suoshuo jing 維摩詰所説經 (*Yuimakitsu shosetsu kyō*) Sutra of the Discourse of Vimalakīrti; also known as the *Weimo jing* 維摩經 (*Yuima kyō*) The Vimalakīrti Sutra. Translated by Kumārajīva, in 3 *juan* [*T* 14: 537a–557b].

This translation, made by Kumārajīva (Jiumoluoshi 鳩摩羅什 Kumarajū, 350–*ca.* 409) while he was living in Chang'an (Chōan), has always been the preferred version of the sutra. This text was early brought to Japan, where it became a favorite of the Prince Regent Shōtoku Taishi 聖徳太子 (573–621). Shōtoku Taishi's commentary on it, the *Yuimagyō gisho* 維摩經義疏, traditionally held to have been written by his own hand in 613, is the earliest example of a Japanese calligraphic manuscript in existence today.

Shuo Wugoucheng jing 說無垢稱經 (*Setsu Mukushō kyō*) Sutra of the Discourse on "Spotless Fame"; also known as the *Wugoucheng jing* 無垢稱經 (*Mukushō kyō*) "Spotless Fame" Sutra. Translated by Xuanzang 玄奘 (Genjō, 600?–664) in 650, in 3 *juan* [*T* 14: 557c–588a].

An English translation of the Kumarajīva version, by Idumi Hōkei 泉芳璟, entitled "Vimalakīrti's Discourse on Emancipation," appeared in *The Eastern Buddhist*, Vols. II (1922), III (1924–1925), and IV (1926–1928).

Das Sūtra Vimalakīrti, by Jakob Fischer and Yokota Takezō 横田武三, published in Japan in 1944, is a German translation of a Japanese rendering of a Chinese text, presumably Kumarajīva's.

L'Enseignement de Vimalakīrti, translated and annotated by Étienne Lamotte and published in 1962, is a French translation based upon Xuanzang's text and that in the Tibetan Kanjur.

The Vinaya Texts

Vinaya-piṭaka, The Basket of the Discipline; also known as *The Vinaya*.

This is the division of the Pāli Tipiṭaka, the Canon of the Theravāda School of Buddhism, which contains the works treating of the rules to be observed by members of the Sangha, the Confessional (*Pātimokkha*), rules for admission to the Order, observance of fast days, and related material. The entire *Vinaya-piṭaka* has been translated into English by Isabel Horner under the title *The Book of the Discipline*.

A number of both partial and complete Vinaya texts were rendered into Chinese. None of these Chinese texts has as yet been translated into a European language. Among the Chinese versions of complete Vinaya texts made at a relatively early date are the following:

Shisong lü 十誦律 (*Jūju ritsu*) The Ten-Section Vinaya. Translated by the Kashmirian monk Puṇyatāra (Furuoduoluo 弗若多羅 Futsu'nyatara, *n. d.*), Kumārajīva (Jiumoluoshi 鳩摩羅什 Kumarajū, 350–*ca.* 409), and others, at Chang'an (Chōan), between 404 and 409, in 61 *juan* [*T* 23: 1–469]. This is a version of the *Sarvāstivāda-vinaya*, the Vinaya of the Indian Hinayana Sarvāstivāda School.

Sifen lü 四分律 (*Shibun ritsu*) The Four-Section Vinaya. Translated by the Kashmirian monk Buddhayaśas (Fotuoyeshe 佛陀耶舍 Butsudayasha, *n. d.*), the Chinese monk Zhu Fonian 竺佛念 (Jiku Butsunen, *n. d.*), and others, in Chang'an, between 410 and 412, in 60 *juan* [*T* 22: 567–1014]. This is a version of the *Dharmagupta-vinaya*, the Vinaya of the Indian Hinayana Dharmagupta School. (*See also* PART ONE, Note 23.)

Mohesengqi lü 摩訶僧祇律 (*Makasōgi ritsu*) The Mahāsāṅghika Vinaya. Translated by the Indian monk Buddhabhadra (Fotuobatuoluo 佛陀跋陀羅 Butsudabatsudara, 359–429) and the Chinese monk Faxian 法顯 (Hokken, *d.* 422?), between 416 and 418, in Jiankang 建康 (Kenkō), modern Nanjing, in 40 *juan* [*T* 22: 227–548]. This is a version of the *Mahāsāṅghika-vinaya*, the Vinaya of the Indian Hinayana Mahāsāṅghika School.

Mishasebu [*hexi*] *wufen lü* 彌沙塞部[和醯]五分律 (*Mishasokubu* [*wakei*] *gobun ritsu*) The Five-Section Vinaya of the Mahīśāsaka School; also known as the *Wufen lü* 五分律 (*Gobun ritsu*) The Five-Section Vinaya. Translated by the Kashmirian monk Buddhajīva (Fotuoshi 佛陀什 Butsudajū, *n. d.*), the Chinese monk Zhu Daosheng 竺道生 (Jiku Dōshō, 355–434), and others, at the Longguangsi 龍光寺 (Ryūkō-ji), on the outskirts of present Nanjing, between 423 and 424, in 30 *juan* [*T* 22: 1–193]. This is a version of the *Mahīśāsaka-vinaya*, the Vinaya of the Indian Hinayana Mahīśāsaka School.

WANSONG LAOREN PINGCHANG TIANTONG JUE HESHANG SONGGU CONGRONG'AN LU 萬松老人評唱天童覺和尚頌古從容庵錄 (*Banshō rōjin hyōshō Tendō Kaku oshō juko Shōyō-an roku*) The Congrong Hermitage Record of the Commentary [Given by] Old Wansong on the Koan and Verse Collection of the Monk Jue of [Mount] Tiantong; also known as the *Congrong lu* 從容錄 (*Shōyō roku*) The Record of [the Hermitage] of Ease. Compiled by various disciples; published 1224, in 6 *juan* [*T* 48: 226a–292a.22].

This work comprises a series of lectures by Wansong Xingxiu 萬松行秀 (Banshō Gyōshū, 1166–1246) on the *Songgu baize* 頌古百則 (*Juko hyakusoku*), or one hundred old koans with appended original verses, which had been compiled by the Caodong 曹洞 (Sōtō) master Hongzhi Zhengjue 宏智正覺 (Wanshi Shōgaku, 1091–1157). Xingxiu, like Hongzhi, was a Caodong master of the Yunju 雲居 (Ungo) line. Earlier in his life he had given a commentary on this text, but at the beginning of the

Mongol invasion—Xingxiu then lived in the north—the manuscript of his lectures, as compiled by his disciples at the time, was lost. In his later years, after he had retired to the Congrong'an 從容庵 (Shōyō-an), a small temple within the large ecclesiastical establishment known as the Bao'en Hongjisi 報恩洪濟寺 (Hōōn Kōsai-ji) in Yanjing 燕京 (Enkei), present Beijing, his disciples requested him to give a commentary upon the text a second time. This second series of lectures was also recorded by the Master's disciples, and published under the lengthy title given above. The name "Wansong Laoren" derives from the Wansong'an 萬松庵 (Banshō-an), a remote hermitage where Xingxiu had lived before he retired to the Congrong'an.

In format these lectures much resemble those which the Linji (Rinzai) master Yuanwu Keqin 圜悟克勤 (Engo Kokugon, 1063–1135) had given on the similar collection of koans and verses made by Xuedou Chongxian 雪竇重顯 (Setchō Jūken, 980–1052) of the Yunmen (Ummon) School, and which comprise the *Biyan lu* 碧巖錄 (*Hekigan roku*). The *Congrong lu* holds the same place of esteem in the Caodong School as that held by the *Biyan lu* in the Linji School.

Wudeng huiyuan 五燈會元 (*Gotō egen*) A Compendium of the Five Lamps; also known as the *Huiyuan* 會元 (*Egen*) A Compendium. Compiled by Dachuan Puji 大川普濟 (Daisen Fusai, 1179–1253). First published in 1253, in 20 *juan*; second edition published in 1364, with two additional *juan* devoted to a Table of Contents (*mulu* 目錄 *mokuroku*) [*ZZ* 10.5.455c–11.4.416b].

This work, perhaps the most comprehensive of the traditional histories of Zen, was compiled by Dachuan Puji, a monk in the 8th generation of the Yangqi (Yōgi) line of Linji (Rinzai) Zen through Dahui Zonggao (Daie Sōkō). The compiler based his work upon the five earlier Zen histories or "records of the transmission of the lamp": the *Jingde chuandeng lu* (1004), the *Tiansheng guangdeng lu* (1036), the *Jianzhong jingguo xudeng lu* (1101), the *Zongmen liandeng huiyao* (1183), and the *Jiatai pudeng lu* (1204), combining the accounts given in these traditional histories as well as adding new material. Dachuan completed his work in 1252, and it was published the following year.

The work opens with accounts of the Seven Buddhas of the Past and the twenty-eight Indian patriarchs. These, together with the accounts of the six Chinese patriarchs and their important descendants to the end of the Tang, follow the order found in the *Chuandeng lu*. The remainder of the work, from the Five Dynasties (Wudai 五代 Godai, 907–960) until the beginning of the 13th century, is arranged according to the Five Houses and Seven Schools (*wujia qizong* 五家七宗 *goke shichishū*).

The *Wudeng huiyuan* has had a wide circle of readers both in China and in Japan, and has frequently been reprinted. The original edition, in 20 *juan*, had no *mulu*. The editor of the Yuan edition (1364), however, removed the headings of the individual sections, making from them a detailed Table of Contents in two additional *juan*. The *Zokuzōkyō* text is a reprint of the Yuan edition. A photographic reprint based upon the original text of 1252 was published in Changsha 長沙 (Chōsha), China, in 1930.

In *Ch'an and Zen Teachings*, Second Series, by Lu K'uan Yü (Charles Luk), will be found English translations of material from the *Wudeng huiyuan* on Linji (Rinzai), pp. 84–126; Caoshan (Sōzan), pp. 158–180; and Yunmen (Ummon), pp. 181–214.

Wudeng yantong 五燈嚴統 (*Gotō gentō*) The Corrected Lineage of the Five Lamps; also known as the *Yantong* 嚴統 (Gentō) The Corrected Lineage. Compiled by Feiyin Tongrong 費隱通容 (Hiin Tsūyō, 1593–1661), assisted by Baichi Yuangong 百癡願公 (Hyakuchi Gankō, *n. d.*), in 25 *juan*, with a Table of Contents (*mulu* 目錄 *mokuroku*) in 2 additional *juan*; published in 1654 [*ZZ* 2乙: 12.1–5.522b].

The compiler of this work, Feiyin Tongrong, was a monk in the 25th generation of the Yangqi (Yōgi) line of Linji (Rinzai) Zen, who lived and worked at Jingshan 徑山 (Kinzan), in modern Zhejiang.

The work itself is a voluminous history of the transmission of Zen in both India and China, beginning with the Seven Buddhas of the Past, and continuing up to and including men of the compiler's own time, the last years of the Ming dynasty. It includes detailed accounts of the transmission of Dharma from master to disciple, many of the sermons of the Zen patriarchs, and their *jiyu* 機語 (*kigo*), that is, words by which they brought their disciples to satori. Special emphasis is put upon the formation of the Five Houses (*wujia* 五家 *goke*), since the compiler's primary aim was to correct what he considered to be the mistakes made in the earlier traditional Zen histories, such as the *Chuandeng lu*, the *Guangdeng lu*, the *Wudeng huiyuan*, and others, as regards the transmission of Dharma in the orthodox lines of the Five Houses. In particular he wished to clarify the transmission as it related to the line of Nanyue Huairang 南嶽懷讓 (Nangaku Ejō, 677–744) and the Linji School which derived from it. Hence the title of the work.

Feiyin asserted that the Yunmen 雲門 (Ummon) and the Fayan 法眼 (Hōgen) schools, which previously had been considered as stemming from the line of Qingyuan Xingsi 青原行思 (Seigen Gyōshi, *d.* 740), actually belonged to the line of Nanyue. He further contended that the Caodong (Sōtō) School, which, according to his view, alone stemmed from the Qingyuan line, virtually came to an end with Tiantong Rujing 天童如淨 (Tendō Nyojō, 1163–1228), the Chinese master of Dōgen Kigen 道元希玄, founder of the Japanese Sōtō Sect. At the beginning of his work, Feiyin introduced considerable evidence in support of his position, and criticised sharply other writings that presented the traditional views.

Men in the Caodong School quickly and vigorously challenged Feiyin's theories, and he as promptly retorted to his critics with a short work entitled *Wudeng yantong jiehuo lun* 五燈嚴統解惑論 (*Gotō gentō gewaku ron*) To Dispel Doubts on the Corrected Lineage of the Five Lamps [*ZZ* 2 乙: 12.5.522c–531c]. Modern scholars of Zen history do not agree with Feiyin's views, however, and on the whole consider the lineage as given in the traditional histories more or less correct.

One of Feiyin's Dharma-heirs was Yinyuan Longqi 隱元隆琦 (Ingen Ryūki, 1592–1673), founder of the Japanese Ōbaku 黃檗 Sect of Zen. Ingen, to give him his Japanese name, brought with him from China a copy of his master's work, the *Wudeng yantong*, and had it reprinted in 1657 at the Fumon Fukugen zen-ji 普門福元禪寺, a temple in Settsu 攝津, near present Osaka. It is this edition of the work that the *Zokuzōkyō* reprints.

Wujia yulu 五家語錄 (*Goke goroku*) The Record of the Five Houses; also known as the *Wuzong lu* 五宗錄 (*Goshū roku*) The Record of the Five Schools. Compiled by Yufeng Yuanxin 語風圓信 (Gofū Enshin, *n. d.*) and Guo Ningzhi 郭凝之 (Kaku Gyōshi, *n. d.*), in 5 *juan* and 3 prefaces; published about 1632, presumably at modern Hangzhou, and brought to Japan shortly afterwards.

This work is a collection of the recorded sayings of the founders of the Five Houses (*wujia* 五家 *goke*) of Chinese Zen. The compilers, Yufeng Yuanxin, a monk in the 24th generation of the Yangqi (Yōgi) line of Linji (Rinzai) Zen, and Guo Ningzhi, an unknown layman who styled himself Wudidi Zhuren Limei Jushi 無地地主人黎眉居士 (Mujichi Shujin

Reibi Koji), worked together at Jingshan 徑山 (Kinzan), near present-day Hangzhou, in the early part of the Chongchen 崇禎 (Sūtei) era (1628–1644) of Ming.

Neither the *Taishō* nor the *Zokuzōkyō* reprint the text as a whole. Through the courtesy of Komazawa University 駒澤大學 it has been possible to obtain a microfilm of their copy of the Qing 清 (Shin) dynasty reprint made from the original blocks of the Ming edition. From a cursory examination of this microfilm copy, it would appear that in most cases the *Wujia yulu* texts are shorter than the earlier texts upon which its compilers drew, that the material has been differently arranged, and that some new material has been added.

There is some variation in the arrangement of the text as given in the Qing reprint and as indicated or reprinted in the *Taishō* or the *Zokuzōkyō*. The following analysis of the material accords with the Qing reprint. For such sections of the work as appear in both the *Taishō* and the *Zokuzōkyō*, the *Taishō* reference only will be given; for such sections as appear only in the *Zokuzōkyō*, reference will be to that collection.

Prefaces:

I: By Yumi Fazang 於密法藏 (Omitsu Hōzō, 1573–1635), an heir of Miyun Yuanwu 密雲圓悟 (Mitsuun Engo, 1566–1642) [*ZZ* 2: 24.5.424c–425b.3].

II: By the compiler Yufeng Yuanxin [*ibid.*, 504a.9–c.8].

III: By Miyun Yuanwu, a fellow-disciple of the compiler Yufeng Yuanxin [*ibid.*, 503d.5–504a.7]. This is lacking in the Qing reprint.

Wuzong yuanliutu 五宗源流圖 (*Goshū genryūzu*) Chart of the Transmission of the Five Schools [*ibid.*, 425a–c].

Linji zongzhi 臨濟宗旨 (*Rinzai shūshi*) The Principles of the Linji School, by Juefan Huihong 覺範慧洪 (Kakuhan Ekō, 1071–1128), in the 3rd generation of the Huanglong 黃龍 (Ōryō) line of Linji Zen [*ZZ* 2: 16.1.86a–88b].

Linjizong 臨濟宗 (*Rinzaishū*) The Linji School: *Zhenzhou Linji Yixuan chanshi* 鎮州臨濟義玄禪師 (*Chinjū Rinzai Gigen zenji*). Omitted from both the *Taishō* and the *Zokuzōkyō*.

Guiyangzong 潙仰宗 (*Igyōshū*) The Guiyang School:

(a) *Tanzhou Guishan Lingyou chanshi* 潭州潙山靈祐禪師 (*Tanshū Isan Reiyū zenji*) [*T* 47: 577a–582a.6].

(b) *Yuanzhou Yangshan Huiji chanshi* 袁州仰山慧寂禪師 (*Enshū*

Kyōzan Ejaku zenji) [*ibid.*, 582a.10–588a.17].

Dongcaozong 洞曹宗 (*Tōsōshū*) The Dongcao, i.e. the Caodong, School:

(a) *Ruizhou Dongshan Liangjie chanshi* 瑞州洞山良价禪師 (*Zuishū Tōzan Ryōkai zenji*) [*ibid.*, 519b–526b].

(b) *Fuzhou Caoshan Benji chanshi* 撫州曹山本寂禪師 (*Bushū Sōzan Honjaku zenji*) [*ibid.*, 536c–540b].

Fayanzong 法眼宗 (*Hōgenshū*) The Fayan School: *Jinling Qingliangyuan Wenyi chanshi* 金陵清凉院文益禪師 (*Kinryō Shōryōin Bun'eki zenji*) [*ibid.*, 588a.21–594a].

Yunmenzong 雲門宗 (*Ummonshū*) The Yunmen School: *Shaozhou Yunmen Kuangzhen Wenyan chanshi* 韶州雲門匡眞文偃禪師 (*Shōshū Ummon Kyōshin Bun'en zenji*). This section is omitted from both the *Taishō* and the *Zokuzōkyō*.

Wujia zhengzong zan 五家正宗贊 (*Goke shōjū san*) In Praise of the Five Houses of the True School; also known as the *Zhengzong zan* 正宗贊 (*Shōjū san*) In Praise of the True School. Compiled by Xisou Shaotan 希叟紹曇 (Kisō Shōdon, *n. d.*), completed in 1254, in 4 *juan* [*ZZ* 2乙: 8.5.452a–498c].

A collection of 74 biographies of eminent Zen monks arranged as follows: twelve men in the direct line from Bodhidharma through Xuefeng Yicun 雪峰義存 (Seppō Gison, 822–908); twenty six men of the Linji 臨濟 (Rinzai) School; fourteen men of the Caodong 曹洞 (Sōtō) School; fourteen men of the Yunmen 雲門 (Ummon) School; five of the Guiyang 潙仰 (Igyō) School; and three of the Fayan 法眼 (Hōgen) School. Each biography concludes with a verse of praise by the compiler, which, according to his preface, is designed to make clear the particular merits of the men of each of the Five Houses of Chinese Zen. Shaotan was of the Yangqi 楊岐 (Yōgi) line of the Linji School.

By *zhengzong*, "True School," is meant the school that correctly transmits the true Dharma as handed down from Bodhidharma. Originally, as it is in this work, the name was applied to the Zen School as a whole. The earliest instance of it in this usage seems to have been in the title of a work by Qisong 契嵩 (Kaisū, 1007–1072), published in 1064, entitled the *Chuanfa zhengzong ji* 傳法正宗記 (*Dembō shōjū ki*) History of the Transmission of Dharma in the True School [*T* 51: 715a–768c.21]. Later, however, the term was conferred as a title upon the Linji School, according to tradition by the Southern Song emperor Gaozong 高宗 (Kōsō, *r.* 1127–1162). In the Yuan 元 (Gen) dynasty (1260–1368) the title was Imperially bestowed upon the Caodong School as well.

Xu chuandeng lu 續傳燈錄 (*Zoku dentō roku*) The Further Transmission of the Lamp. Compiled by Yuanji Juding 圓極居頂 (Enki Kochō, *d.* 1404), in 36 *juan* [*T* 51: 469–714].

A compilation of biographies of Chinese Zen priests and monks intended to supplement the *Jingde chuandeng lu*. The work opens with a biography of Fenyang Shanzhao 汾陽善昭 (Fun'yō Zenshō, 947–1024) of the Linji (Rinzai) School—his early life only had been treated in the *Chuandeng lu*—and ends with the disciples of Songyuan Chongyue 松源崇岳 (Shōgen Sūgaku, 1139–1209), in the 8th generation of the Yangqi (Yōgi) line of the Linji School. The compiler was also of the Yangqi line, in the 6th generation after Songyuan Chongyue. Though the work contains biographies of Zen monks of all schools, it differs from other compilations in that it does not separate the various lines of transmission, but lists all entries as descendants of Huineng 慧能 (Enō), the Sixth Patriarch, beginning with the 10th generation after him and continuing through the 20th. We have no definite date for the earliest publication of the work, but it seems probable that it was first printed in the latter part of the Ming Tripiṭaka, publication of which was begun in 1372 in Nanjing.

Xuedou baize songgu 雪竇百則頌古 (*Setchō hyakusoku juko*) Xuedou's Hundred Koans with Verse Comments; also known as the *Xuedou songgu* 雪竇頌古 (Setchō juko) Xuedou's Verse Comments. By Xuedou Chongxian 雪竇重顯 (Setchō Jūken, 980–1052), in 1 *juan* [*Zudokko*, pp. 51–108].

A collection of one hundred representative old koans to each of which the poet-compiler, a master in the 4th generation of the Yunmen (Ummon) School of Zen, has added an original verse (*song* 頌 *ju*) expressing the inner meaning of the koan. Biographies in the *Chuandeng lu* were the source for the majority of the koans comprising the collection, the only exceptions being eighteen taken from the *Yunmen guanglu*, the record of Yunmen Wenyan (Ummon Bun'en, 862/4–949), founder of the Yunmen School. The *Xuedou songgu* was used a century later by Yuanwu Keqin (Engo Kokugon, 1063–1135) as the basis for the lectures that comprise his famous *Biyan lu* (*Hekigan roku*). Today, Xuedou's text can be found only within the *Biyan lu*, or in small koan anthologies compiled for the special use of koan students, such as the *Zudokko*.

Xutang heshang yulu 虛堂和尚語錄 (*Kidō oshō goroku*) The Record of Master Xutang; also known as the *Xutang lu* 虛堂錄 (*Kidō roku*) The Record of Xutang. Compiled by Miaoyuan 妙源 (Myōgen, *n. d.*), first printed in 1269, in 10 *juan* [*T* 47: 984–1064].

This work comprises the sermons, discourses, comments, verse, and miscellaneous writings of Xutang Zhiyu of Jingshan 徑山虛堂智愚 (Kidō Chigu of Kinzan, 1185–1269), in the 10th generation of the Yangqi (Yōgi) line of Linji (Rinzai) Zen, recorded by his various disciples and compiled by his disciple Miaoyuan. The first seven *juan* of the work were published just before Xutang died; the remaining three *juan*, known as the *Xuji* 續輯 (*Zokushū*), or "Supplement," were published immediately after the Master's death.

A copy of the first seven *juan* is said to have been brought to Japan by Xutang's Japanese heir, Nampo Jōmyō 南浦紹明 (1235–1309), better known by his posthumous title Daiō Kokushi 大應國師. In accordance with a wish expressed by the Kokushi shortly before his death, his disciples published in 1313 a Japanese edition of the complete *Kidō roku* in 10 *kan*, adding a short epilogue which includes miscellaneous biographical and other material.

The first half of *juan* 6 bears the general title *Daibie* 代別 (*Daibetsu*). It consists of a collection of one hundred old koans, to fifty-three of which are appended answers known as *daiyu* 代語 (*daigo*), "offered in place of another," and to the remaining forty-seven of which are appended answers known as *bieyu* 別語 (*betsugo*), "offered as a different opinion." In the former case a master offers a reply of his own to a mondo which had concluded with the monk engaged in the exchange unable to answer his master's final statement, thus answering "in place of" the original monk. In the latter case, the master, not being in agreement with the final answer to a koan or mondo, offers a different answer conveying his own view. These methods of handling old koans originated with Yunmen Wenyan 雲門文偃 (Ummon Bun'en, 862/4–949), founder of the Yunmen (Ummon) School of Zen, and koans with both types of appended answers will be found scattered through his record, the *Yunmen guanglu*. Fenyang Shanzhao 汾陽善昭 (Fun'yō Zenshō, 947–1024) of the Linji School, however, was the first to make collections of one hundred examples of each type of koan and appended answer.

The *Daibie* (*Daibetsu*) of Xutang Heshang (Kidō Oshō) is now used for advanced students of koan study in the Takujū 卓洲 line of Japanese Rinzai Zen. As a separate publication it will be found in the *Zudokko*, pp. 263–294, under the title *Xutang lu: daibie* 虛堂錄代別 (*Kidō roku: daibetsu*).

Yi jing 易經 (*Eki kyō*) The Book of Changes; also known as the *Zhouyi* 周易 (*Shūeki*) The Changes of Zhou.

This is a short manual on divination, centering around 64 hexagrams, which was used as a handbook by official diviners in China from feudal times, and which is still used today by fortune-tellers throughout the Far East. It gives clues to the interpretation of the results of the divination practice in which stalks of the milfoil are used. The text itself is thought to date from the early Zhou 周 (Shū) dynasty (1112–255 BCE). Later, probably in the early years of the Former Han (Qianhan 前漢 Zenkan, 206 BCE–25 CE), the "wings" or appendices were added, expounding the philosophy of "the changes" which characterize the workings of the cosmos. Because sections of the *Yi jing* have been traditionally attributed to Confucius and other sages of antiquity, and because much of its language is obscure and open to a wide variety of interpretation, the work has been a favorite subject of study among Chinese philosophers, and has exerted a tremendous influence upon the development of Chinese metaphysical thought. The *Yi jing* is one of the Five Classics of Confucianism.

There are two English translations of the work: *The Yi King*, translated by James Legge, and *The I Ching or Book of Changes:* The Richard Wilhelm German Translation Rendered into English by Cary F. Baynes. *Change:* Eight Lectures on the *I Ching*, by Hellmut Wilhelm, is a modern commentary on the work.

Yuanwu Foguo chanshi yulu 圜悟佛果禪師語錄 (*Engo Bukka zenji goroku*) The Record of the Zen Master Yuanwu Foguo; also known as the *Yuanwu yulu* 圜悟語錄 (*Engo goroku*) The Record of Yuanwu, and the *Yuanwu lu* 圜悟錄 (*Engo roku*) Yuanwu's Record. Compiled by Huqiu Shaolong 虎丘紹隆 (Kukyū Jōryū, 1077–1136); first printed in 1134, in 20 *juan* [*T* 47: 713b.23–810c].

The sermons, discourses, verse, and prose writings of Yuanwu Keqin 圜悟克勤 (Engo Kokugon, 1063–1135), a famous master in the 4th generation of the Yangqi (Yōgi) line of Linji (Rinzai) Zen. Both Yuanwu and

Foguo Chanshi were titles conferred upon the Master during his lifetime. The work was compiled by Yuanwu's heir Shaolong, and contains prefaces by Geng Yanxi 耿延禧 (Kō Enki, *n. d.*) and Zhang Jun 張浚 (Chō Shun, 1086–1154), both important officials who were lay disciples of Yuanwu.

Juan 1 through the first half of *juan* 8 are devoted to formal sermons from the high seat (*shangtang* 上堂 *jōdō*); the second half of *juan* 8 through *juan* 13, to informal discourses (*xiaocan* 小參 *shōsan*). *Juan* 14 through the first half of *juan* 16 contain suggestions for religious practice written for individual students (*fayu* 法語 *hōgo*); the second half of *juan* 16 through the first half of *juan* 18, prose comments on old koans (*niangu* 拈古 *nenko*); the second half of *juan* 18 through *juan* 19, verse comments on old koans (*songgu* 頌古 *juko*); and *juan* 20, miscellaneous verse and prose writings.

An amplified version of the material entitled *Fayu* [*ibid.*, 775c–788-c.21], as compiled by Hongfu Ziwen 洪福子文 (Kōfuku Shimon, *n. d.*), another of the Master's disciples, comprises the *Yuanwu xinyao.*

Yunmen Kuangzhen chanshi guanglu 雲門匡眞禪師廣錄 (*Ummon Kyōshin zenji kōroku*) The Comprehensive Record of the Zen Master Kuangzhen of [Mount] Yunmen; also known as the *Yunmen heshang guanglu* 雲門和尚廣錄 (*Ummon oshō kōroku*) The Comprehensive Record of Master Yunmen; the *Yunmen guanglu* 雲門廣錄 (*Ummon kōroku*) The Comprehensive Record of Yunmen; and the Yunmen lu 雲門錄 (*Ummon roku*) The Record of Yunmen. Compiled by Shoujian 守堅 (Shuken, *n. d.*), in 3 *juan*; first published in 1076 [*T* 47: 544c.28–576c].

This is the complete collection of the sermons, sayings, and koans of Yunmen Wenyan 雲門文偃 (Ummon Bun'en, 862/4–949), founder of the Yunmen School of Chinese Zen, compiled by his disciple Shoujian. Kuangzhen Chanshi 匡眞禪師 (Kyōshin Zenji) was the title bestowed upon the Master during his lifetime by the King of Nanhan.

Juan 1 of the work is entitled *Duiji* 對機 (*Taiki*). *Duiji*, literally "answers to questions," refers specifically to the answers given by the Master to questions put to him on formal occasions, and thus differs somewhat from *mondō*, which are exchanges of question and answer that may take place at any time. This *juan* contains 320 *ze* 則 (*soku*), "cases," or examples of these answers. It concludes with Yunmen's poem, *Shi'ershi ge* 十二時歌 (*Jūniji ka*) "Song of the Twelve Hours," and a few of his religious verses (*jiesong* 揭頌 *geju*).

The first section of *juan* 2 is entitled *Shizhong yuyao* 室中語要

(*Shitchū goyō*) "Essential Words from the Inner Room," and comprises 185 short remarks by Yunmen, each eliciting from some monk a question which the Master promptly answers. The second section of the same *juan* is entitled Chuishi daiyu 垂示代語 (*Suiji daigo*) "Statements and Substitute Answers." This title is a technical term for a method of instructing whereby the master makes a statement that demands a reply, and, when no one answers, states his own answer, or, in some cases, gives his own reply immediately without waiting for a response from the assembly. This section contains 290 *ze* (cases).

The first section of *juan* 3, consisting of 165 short interviews between Yunmen and visiting or other monks, is entitled *Kanbian* 勘辨 (*Kamben*). This is followed by the record of the Master's pilgrimage, his last instructions to his disciples, and other short writings.

Zhaolun 肇論 (*Jōron*) The Treatises of Zhao, in 1 *juan* [*T* 45: 150a–161b], is a compilation of the original writings of the brilliant scholar-monk Sengzhao 僧肇 (Sōjō, 374–414), a disciple of the great Central Asian scholar Kumārajīva (Jiumoluoshi 鳩摩羅什 Kumarajū, 350–*ca.* 409).

The *Zhaolun* comprises the following items: a preface by Huida 慧達 (Etatsu, *n. d.*); an introductory chapter entitled "Fundamental Principles" (*Zongbenyi* 宗本義 *Shūhongi*), perhaps the work of the unknown compiler; "On the Immutability of Things" (*Wubuqian lun* 物不遷論 *Butsu fusen ron*); "On the Emptiness of the Unreal" (*Buzhenkong lun* 不眞空論 *Fushinkū ron*); "Prajñā Is without Knowledge" (*Bore wuzhi lun* 般若無知論 *Hannya muchi ron*); the letter from Liu Yimin 劉遺民 (Ryū Imin, *d.* 410) of the Lushan (Rozan), written after he had received a copy of the *Bore wuzhi lun*, together with Sengzhao's reply to his friend; and "Nirvana Is Nameless" (*Niepan wuming lun* 涅槃無名論 *Nehan mumyō ron*). The four essays and the correspondence were probably written between 404 and 414, while Sengzhao was living in Chang'an (Chōan) and working with Kumārajīva and his associates on translations of Buddhist texts. The date of the compilation itself is not known, nor is the name of the compiler. From the beginning of the 6th century the *Zhaolun* became an essential text in the Chinese "Three Treatises" (Sanlun 三論 Sanron) School, and it was highly esteemed in both the Huayan (Kegon) and Chan (Zen) schools as well.

The Book of Chao is an English translation of the complete text of the *Zhaolun*, with copious notes and appendices by Walter Liebenthal.

The *Jōron kenkyū* 肇論研究, Studies in the *Zhaolun*, is an important Japanese contribution to the study of the Buddhism of Sengzhao's time by scholars of the Zinbun Kagaku Kenkyusho 人文科學研究所 (The Research Institute of Humanistic Studies) of Kyoto University, compiled and edited by the distinguished Buddhist scholar Tsukamoto Zenryū 塚本善隆. It contains a revised text of the *Zhaolun*, and a Japanese translation with notes and indices; Dr. Tsukamoto and six other members of the Research Institute have each contributed a special article.

The dates given for Kumārajīva and Sengzhao are those established by Dr. Tsukamoto cf., "The Dates of Kumārajīva 鳩摩羅什 and Sengzhao 僧肇 Reexamined," by Tsukamoto Zenryū, translated from the Japanese by Leon Hurvitz, in the *Silver Jubilee Volume of The Zinbun Kagaku Kenkyusyo*, pp. 568–584.

Zhaozhou Zhenji chanshi yulu 趙州眞際禪師語錄 (*Jōshū Shinsai zenji goroku*) The Record of the Zen Master Zhenji of Zhaozhou; also known as the *Zhaozhou zushi yulu* 趙州祖師語錄 (*Jōshū soshi goroku*) The Record of the Patriarch of Zhaozhou; the *Zhaozhou heshang yulu* 趙州和尚語錄 (*Jōshū oshō goroku*) Master Chaozhou's Record; and the *Zhaozhou lu* 趙州錄 (*Jōshū roku*) The Record of Zhaozhou. In 2 *juan*, contained in the *Guzunsu yulu*, *juan* 13 and 14 [*ZZ* 2: 23.2.152c.–167d].

This is a collection of the sermons and mondos of Zhaozhou Congshen 趙州從諗 (Jōshū Jūshin, 778–897), one of the great Zen masters of the late Tang. Zhenji Chanshi 眞際禪師 (Shinsai Zenji) was the Master's posthumous title. The text proper is preceded by a short biography of the Master entitled *Zhaozhou Zhenji chanshi xingzhuang* 趙州眞際禪師行狀 (*Jōshū Shinsai zenji gyōjō*), which is said to have been dictated in 953 by Huitong 惠通 (Etsū) of the Dongyuan 東院 (Tō-in) in Dongdu 東都 (Tōto). At the end of *juan* 2 will be found Zhaozhou's well-known poem *Shi'ershi ge* 十二時歌 (*Jūniji ka*) "Verses on the Twelve Hours," four of his short poems, a verse for the Master's portrait by his great friend and patron, Governor Wang Rong 王鎔 (Ō Yō, 873–921), and two poems lamenting the Master's death by an unknown person, perhaps the same Governor Wang.

Nothing is known regarding the original compiler of the text or of the date of its original publication. But since the *Zokuzōkyō* edition of the text, referred to above, ends with a notation stating that it was re-edited by Chengshi 澄諟 (Chōshoku, *n. d.*) of the Xixianyuan 棲賢院

(Seiken-in) on the Lushan 廬山 (Rozan), who was a second-generation disciple of Fayan Wenyi 法眼文益 (Hōgen Bun'eki, 885–958), we may surmise that the original edition was already in circulation by the end of the 10th century.

The *Zhaozhou yulu* was included in the two great collections of records of Zen masters, the *Guzunsu yuyao*, published in 1144, and the *Chongke guzunsu yulu*, published in 1267. Some time during the Ming dynasty, Yunmen Yuancheng 雲門圓澄 (Ummon Enchō, 1561–1626), in the 27th generation of the Caodong (Sōtō) line, took the *Zhaozhou lu* of the *Guzunsu yulu*, wrote a preface for it, and had his disciples Mingsheng 明聲 (Myōshō, *n. d.*) and Yan Dacan 嚴大參 (Gen Daisan, *n. d.*) publish it as a separate work in 3 *juan* under the title *Zhaozhou heshang yulu*. In this edition the original compilation was mistakenly attributed to a certain Wenyuan 文遠 (Bun'en, *n. d.*), who was claimed to be Zhaozhou's immediate disciple.

The *Jōshū zenji goroku* 趙州禪師語錄, edited by Suzuki Daisetz and Akizuki Ryūmin, is a text based upon the abovementioned Ming *Zhaozhou heshang yulu* (*Jōshū oshō goroku*), revised and edited on the basis of the earlier extant texts, with critical notes and Japanese reading of the text.

Zhengfayanzang 正法眼藏 (*Shōbōgenzō*) Treasury of the True Dharma Eye, by Jingshan Dahui Zonggao Chanshi 徑山大慧宗杲禪師 (Kinzan Daie Sōkō Zenji), in 6 *juan* [*ZZ* 2: 23.1].

This is a collection of old koans and mondos compiled between 1141 and 1150 by Dahui Zonggao 大慧宗杲 (Daie Sōkō, 1089–1163), a master of the Yangqi (Yōgi) line of Linji (Rinzai) Zen, while he was in retirement at Hengyang 衡陽 (Kōyō), in modern Hunan. To some of the koans and mondos the Master appended his own explanations. Dahui's work should not be confused with the *Shōbōgenzō* by Dōgen Kigen 道元希玄 (1200–1253), founder of the Japanese Sōtō 曹洞 Sect.

Zhenzhou Linji Huizhao chanshi yulu 鎮州臨濟慧照禪師語錄 (*Chinjū Rinzai Eshō zenji goroku*) The Record of the Zen Master Linji Huizhao of Zhenzhou; also known as the *Linji lu* 臨濟錄 (*Rinzai roku*) The Record of Linji [or Rinzai]. Compiled by Sansheng Huiran 三聖慧然 (Sanshō Enen, *n. d.*), in 1 *juan* [*T* 47: 495a–506c].

This is the record of the sayings of Linji Yixuan 臨濟義玄 (Rinzai Gigen, *d.* 866), founder of the Linji 臨濟 (Rinzai) School of Chinese Zen, compiled by his disciple Sansheng Huiran. Linji's posthumous title was Huizhao Chanshi 慧照禪師 (Eshō Zenji). The work comprises three sections: *yulu* 語錄 (*goroku*), recorded sermons and sayings; *kanbian* 勘辨 (*kamben*), short conversations with various monks and laymen in which the Master's purpose is to probe the degree of their understanding; and *xinglu* 行錄 (*anroku*), the record of Linji's enlightenment and subsequent pilgrimage, during which he visited various Zen masters. The *taji* 塔記 (*tōki*)—sometimes called the *lüezhuan* 略傳 (*ryakuden*)—or short biography, now generally found at the conclusion of the *Linji lu*, is the inscription from Linji's memorial stone, written by Yanzhao 延沼 (Enshō, *n. d.*), an otherwise unknown person, and is a later addition to the *Record*.

The traditional view that Huiran was the compiler of the work is open to question. In doubt, also, is the date of the first printing. The *yulu* and *kanbian* sections are at present generally conceded to have been compiled by Huiran but revised by another disciple, Xinghua Cunjiang 興化存獎 (Kōke Zonshō, 830–888), who may also have been responsible for the *xinglu*. A second edition was in preparation by 1120, and for this MA Fang 馬防 (BA Bō), a Court official of the Song about whom nothing more is known, provided a preface.

No translation of the complete work in a western language has as yet been published. The longest excerpts translated into English will be found in the following: *Sources of Chinese Tradition*, edited by Wm. Theodore DE BARY, pp. 400–403; *Essays in Zen Buddhism*, Third Series, by D.T. SUZUKI, pp. 51–55; and *Zen Buddhism and Psychoanalysis*, by D.T. SUZUKI, Erich FROMM, and Richard DEMARTINO, pp. 32–43.

ZONGMEN LIANDENG HUIYAO 宗門聯燈會要 (*Shūmon rentō eyō*) A Collection of Essential Material from the Zen Sect's Successive Records of the Lamp; also known as the *Liandeng huiyao* 聯燈會要 (*Rentō eyō*) Essential Material from the Successive Records of the Lamp, and the *Liandeng* 聯燈 (*Rentō*) Successive Records of the Lamp. Compiled in 1183 by Huiweng Wuming 晦翁悟明 (Maiō Gomyō, *n. d.*), in 30 *juan*, with an additional *juan* devoted to a detailed Table of Contents (*mulu* 目錄 *mokuroku*) [*ZZ* 2乙: 9.3–5].

This compilation is composed entirely of material taken from the *Jingde chuandeng lu* (1004), the *Tiansheng guangdeng lu* (1036), the *Jianzhong Jingguo xudeng lu* (1101), and the records (*yulu* 語錄 *goroku*) of several Zen masters of the Song. Chronologically it covers the entire history of Zen from the Seven Buddhas of the Past (*guoqu qifo* 過去七佛 *kako shichibutsu*) through the twenty-eight generations of Indian patriarchs, the six generations of Chinese patriarchs, and their descendants in the various lines up to and including men of the compiler's own time, that is, the middle of the Southern Song dynasty (1127–1279).

The compiler of this Zen "history," Huiweng Wuming, was a monk in the 8th generation of the Yangqi (Yōgi) line of Linji (Rinzai) Zen through Dahui Zonggao 大慧宗杲 (Daie Sōkō). The publication date is not mentioned in the work, but printing is believed to have followed soon after the compilation was completed.

The work opens with a detailed Table of Contents, which lists the various masters under their names and lines of descent. *Juan* 1–29 of the text proper comprise accounts of the satori experiences and other episodes in the lives of the old masters, together with the koans that developed from them, and the important sermons, lectures, and talks of these men, some with short commentaries by masters of the Song. *Juan* 30 is devoted to fifteen short compositions by Zen writers of earlier periods.

Zudokko 塗毒鼓 The Poison-painted Drum. Edited by Fujita Genro 藤田玄路 (1880–1935); first published in 1917, in 1 volume.

This anthology contains the major Zen koan collections and a few important Chinese and Japanese Zen texts. Among the works included are the *Kōzen Daitō kokushi yuikai*, the *Wumenguan*, the *Xuedou baize songgu*, the *Kattō shū*, the *Tōjō goi henshō kuketsu*, the *Linji lu*, the *Xutang lu: daibie*, and a short selection from the *Kaiankoku go*.

Zudokko (*Zokuhen*) 塗毒鼓（續編）The Poison-painted Drum (Second Series). Edited by Fujita Genro; first published in 1922, in 1 volume.

This companion anthology to the *Zudokko* contains twenty-four short but important writings by Chinese and Japanese Zen masters, among which will be found Hakuin Zenji's *Dokugo shingyō*, the *Shiniutu song*, the *Zuochan yi* 坐禪儀 (*Zazen gi*) Rules for Zazen, the *Baojing sanmei*, and the *Cantongqi*. It concludes with *Kushū* 句集 A Verse Collection, an anthology of phrases and verses patterned upon the *Zenrin kushū*.

The *Zudokko* and the *Zudokko* (*Zokuhen*) are pocket-sized handbooks compiled especially for the use of Zen monks and lay students. In every case only the Chinese character text is given, without authors' names, prefaces, introductions, or explanatory notes, and no indication is given as to the sources or versions of the texts included.

Index To Translations And Modern Works

"The Altar Sutra of the Sixth Patriarch." Eng. trans. of Yuan text of *Liuzu tanjing* 六祖壇經, by Lu K'uan Yü (Charles Luk), in *Ch'an and Zen Teaching*, Third Series, pp. 15–102: 362–63

"Amitāyur-Dhyāna-Sūtra: The Sutra of the Meditations on Amitāyus." Eng. trans. of *Guan wuliangshoufo jing* 觀無量壽佛經, by J. Takakusu, in *Buddhist Mahāyāna Texts*, Part II, pp. 159–201: 344

"Avalokiteśvara-Sūtra." Eng. trans. of Chap. XXIV of *Saddharma-puṇḍarīka-sūtra*, by H. Kern, in *The Saddharma-Puṇḍarīka*, pp. 406–418: 302

"Bendōwa." Eng. trans. of *kan* 1 of *Shōbōgenzō* 正法眼藏 of Dōgen Kigen 道元希玄, by Masunaga Reihō 増永靈鳳, in *The Sōtō Approach to Zen*, pp. 133–161: 354–55

Bi-yän-lu: Meister Yüan-wu's niederschrift von der Smaragdenen Felswand. Verdeutscht und erläutert von Wilhelm Gundert. Ger. trans. of *Biyan lu* 碧巖錄 [München: Carl Hanser, 1960]: 322

The Blue Cliff Records: The Hekigan Roku. Eng. trans. of *Biyan lu*, edited and with commentary by R.D.M. Shaw D.D. [London: Michael Joseph, 1961]: 322

The Bodhisattva Doctrine in Buddhist Sanskrit Literature, by Har Dayal [London: Kegan Paul, 1931]: 303

Bombun nyū Ryōga kyō 梵文入楞伽經. Skr. text of *Laṅkāvatāra-sūtra*, edited by Nanjio Bunyiu 南條文雄 [Kyoto: Otani University Press, 1923]: 334–35

The Book of Chao. Eng. trans. of *Zhaolun* 肇論, with introduction, notes, and appendices, by W. Liebenthal. Monumenta Serica, Monograph XIII [Beijing: The Catholic University of Beijing, 1948]: 381

The Book of the Discipline. Eng. trans. of Pāli *Vinaya-piṭaka*, by Isabel Horner. Sacred Books of the Buddhists, Vols. X, XI, XIII, XIV, XX [London: Humphrey Milford, Oxford University Press, 1938, 1940, 1942, 1951, 1952]: 370

"Das Buch *Genjōkōan* 現成公案 aus dem *Shōbōgenzō* 正法眼藏 des Zen Meisters Dōgen 道元." Ger. trans. of *kan* 3 of *Shōbōgenzō*, with introduction and notes, by Heinrich DUMOULIN, S.J. *Monumenta Nipponica*, Vol. XV, 3–4 (1959–1960), pp. 217–232: 355

A Buddhist Bible, Revised and Enlarged. Edited by Dwight GODDARD [New York: E.P. Dutton & Co., 1938] and [London: George G. Harrap & Co., Ltd., 1956]: 362

Buddhist Mahāyāna Texts. Sacred Books of the East, Vol. XLIX [Oxford University Press; London: Humphrey Milford, 1927]: 342, 343, 344

Buddhist Wisdom Books: The Diamond Sutra and The Heart Sutra. Eng. trans. of Skr. texts, with explanation, by Edward CONZE [London: George Allen & Unwin Ltd., 1958]: 342, 367

Bukka hekigan hakan kyakusetsu 佛果碧巖破關擊節. The Kaga Daijō-ji加賀大乘寺 text of *Biyan lu*, edited and annotated by SUZUKI Daisetsu 鈴木大拙, 2 vols. [Tokyo: Iwanami Shoten, 1924]: 322

Bukkyō no kompon shinri 佛教の根本眞理 The Fundamental Truth of Buddhism. Edited by MIYAMOTO Shōson 宮本正尊 [Tokyo: Sanseido, 1957]: 202

A Catalogue of the Chinese Translation of the Buddhist Tripiṭaka. Compiled by NANJIO Bunyiu [Oxford: The Clarendon Press, 1883]: 302

A Catena of Buddhist Scriptures. Eng. trans. of excerpts from Chinese texts, by Rev. S. BEAL [London: 1871]: 302, 339, 344

Cat's Yawn: The Miscellaneous Writings and Translations of Sokei-an SASAKI [New York: The First Zen Institute of America, Inc., 1947]: 72

Ch'an and Zen Teaching, First Series. Edited, translated, and explained by LU K'uan Yü (Charles LUK) [London: Rider & Co., 1960]: 342, 367

Ch'an and Zen Teaching, Second Series. Edited, translated, and explained by LU K'uan Yü (Charles LUK) [London: Rider & Co., 1961]: 290, 331, 307, 373

Ch'an and Zen Teaching, Third Series. Edited, translated, and explained by LU K'uan Yü (Charles LUK) [London: Rider & Co., 1962]: 362

Ch'anmen nien-sung chi 禪門拈頌集. See *Sŏnmun yŏmsong chip*

Change: Eight Lectures on the *I Ching*. By Hellmut WILHELM. Trans. from the Ger. by Cary F. BAYNES. Bollingen Series LXII [New York: Pantheon Books, 1960]: 379

"A Chapter on the Golden Lion." Eng. trans. of *Jinshizi zhang* 金師子章, in *Sources of Chinese Tradition*, pp. 369–373: 163

Chodang chip 祖堂集 (*Sodō shū*). Mimeographed copy of original Haein-sa text, in 5 vols. [Kyoto: Hanazono Daigaku, 1962]: 309–310

"Complément aux Entretiens du Maître de Dhyâna Chen-houei." By Jacques GERNET. In *Bulletin de l'Ecole Française d'Extrême-Orient*, XLIV (1954), pp. 453–458: 352, 353

"Daitō Kokushi's Admonitions." Eng. trans. from the Japanese of *Kōzen Daitō kokushi yuikai* 興禪大燈國師遺誡, by Daisetz Teitaro SUZUKI, in *Manual of Zen Buddhism*, pp. 147–148: 333

"Dankyō." Dunhuang text of *Liuzu tanjing*, edited by UI Hakuju 宇井伯壽, in *Zenshūshi kenkyū*, Vol. II, pp. 117–172: 361

Daśabhūmika-sūtra et Bodhisattvabhūmi. Skr. text, edited by J. RAHDER [Paris: 1926]: 303

Daśabhūmīśvaro nāma Mahāyānasūtram. Skr. text revised and edited by KONDŌ Ryūkō 近藤隆晃 [Tokyo: 1936]: 303

"The Dates of Kumārajīva 鳩摩羅什 and Sêng-chao 僧肇 Reexamined." By TSUKAMOTO Zenryū 塚本善隆, and trans. from the Japanese by Leon HURVITZ. In *Silver Jubilee Volume of the Zinbun Kagaku Kenkyusyo*, pp. 568–584: 254, 382

DCZ. Abbr. for *The Development of Chinese Zen after the Sixth Patriarch*, for which *see below*

"Deux Documents de Touen-houang sur le Dhyâna chinois." By Paul DEMIÉVILLE, in *Essays on the History of Buddhism Presented to Professor Zenryū Tsukamoto*, pp. 1–27: 352

The Development of Chinese Zen after the Sixth Patriarch. By Heinrich DUMOULIN, S.J., and trans. from the Ger. by Ruth Fuller SASAKI [New York: The First Zen Institute of America, Inc., 1953]: 142. Abbr. DCZ

"The Diamond Cutter of Doubts." Eng. trans. of *Jingang jueyi* 金剛決疑, a comy. on the *Diamond Sutra*, by LU K'uan Yü (Charles LUK), in *Ch'an and Zen Teaching*, First Series, pp. 149–206: 367

"The Diamond Sutra." Eng. trans. of Skr. text of *Vajracchedikā-prajñāpāramitā-sūtra*, with commentary by Edward CONZE, in *Buddhist Wisdom Books*, pp. 21–71: 367

The Diamond Sutra. Eng. trans. from the Chinese, by A.F. PRICE [London: The Buddhist Society, 1955]: 421. Idem *The Jewel of Transcendental Wisdom*, q.v.

Les documents chinois découverts par Aurel Stein dans les sables du Turkestan oriental, by Ed. CHAVANNES [1913]: 352

"Elucidating the Doctrine." Eng. trans. of *Heze dashi xianzong ji* 荷澤大師顯宗記, by Wing-tsit CHAN, in *Sources of Chinese Tradition*, pp. 396–400: 354

The Empire of Min. By Edward H. SCHAFER [Rutland, Vermont: Charles Tuttle Co., for the Harvard-Yenching Institute, 1954]: 264

"English Translation of the Shingyo." Trans. of *Prajñāpāramitā-hṛdaya-sūtra*, by Daisetz Teitaro SUZUKI, in *Manual of Zen Buddhism*, pp. 26–30: 342

L'Enseignement de Vimalakīrti. Traduit et annoté par Étienne LAMOTTE. Bibliothèque du Muséon, Vol 51. French trans. of Tibetan and Chinese (Xuanzang) versions of *Vimalakīrti-nirdeśa* [Louvain: Publications Universitaires, 1962]: 370

Entretiens du Maître de Dhyâna Chen-houei du Hotsö. French trans. from the Chinese of sermons of Heze Shenhui 荷澤神會, by Jacques GERNET. Publications de l'École Française d'Extrême-Orient, Vol. XXXI [Hanoi: 1949]: 351, 352, 354

"Essay on the Golden Lion." Eng. trans. of *Jinshizi zhang*, with explanation, in *A History of Chinese Philosophy*, by FUNG Yu-lan, trans. by Derk BODDE. Vol. II, pp. 341–359: 163

Essays on the History of Buddhism Presented to Professor Zenryū Tsukamoto (*Tsukamoto Hakushi shōju ki'nen bukkyō shigaku ronshū* 塚本博士頌壽記念佛教史學論集) [Kyoto: Tsukamoto Hakushi Shōju Ki'nenkai, 1961]: 352

Essays in Zen Buddhism, First Series. By Daisetz Teitaro SUZUKI [London: Rider & Co., for The Buddhist Society, London, 2nd Imp., 1958]: 357

Essays in Zen Buddhism, Second Series. By Daisetz Teitaro SUZUKI [London: Rider & Co., for The Buddhist Society, London, 2nd Imp., 1958]: 158, 203, 309, 312. 313, 322

Essays in Zen Buddhism, Third Series. By Daisetz Teitaro SUZUKI [London: Rider & Co., for The Buddhist Society, London, 1958]: 341, 347, 382, 410

The Essence of Buddhism. By Daisetz Teitaro SUZUKI [London: The Buddhist Society, 1957]: 163, 209

The Essentials of Buddhist Philosophy. By J. TAKAKUSU [Honolulu: The University of Hawaii, 1947]: 163

"The Five Positions of Prince and Minister." Eng. trans. of *Dongshan wuwei song* 洞山五位頌, by LU K'uan Yü (Charles LUK), in *Ch'an and Zen Teaching*, Second Series, pp. 135–136: 307

The Gaṇḍavyūha-sūtra. Skr. text critically edited by SUZUKI Daisetsu 鈴木大拙 and IDUMI Hōkei 泉芳璟 [Tokyo: The Society for the Publication of Sacred Books of the World, 1949]: 303

"The Gateless Gate." Eng. trans. of *Wumenguan* 無門關, by Nyogen SENZAKI and Paul REPS, in *Zen Flesh, Zen Bones*, pp. 109–161: 309

"Genjōkōan." Eng. trans. of *kan* 3 of Dōgen Kigen's *Shōbōgenzō*, by MASUNAGA Reihō, in *The Sōtō Approach to Zen*, pp. 125–132: 355

"Gensha on the Three Invalids." Eng. trans. of Case 88 in *Biyan lu*, by Daisetz Teitaro SUZUKI, in *Manual of Zen Buddhism*, pp. 120–127: 322

"On the Golden Lion." Eng. trans. of *Jinshizi zhang*, by Daisetz Teitaro SUZUKI, in *The Essence of Buddhism*, pp. 54–60: 163

Haiku, Vol. I. By R.H. Blyth [Kamakura: Kamakura Bunko, 1949]: 72

"Hakuinkei kanna no ichikanken" 白隠系看話の一管見. An Interpretation of the Koan in the Hakuin School. By SHIBAYAMA Zenkei 柴山全慶, in *Zengaku kenkyū*, No. 38 (Dec. 1943), pp. 1–30: 202

"Hakuyūshi no hito to sho" 白幽子の人と書. Hakuyūshi, the Man and His Calligraphy. By ITŌ Kazuo 伊藤和男, in *Zenbunka*, Vol. II, No. 6 (Nov. 1956), pp. 40–48: 194

"The Heart Sutra." Romanized Skr. text of *Prajñāpāramita-hṛdaya-sūtra* with Eng. trans. and comy., by Edward CONZE, in *Buddhist Wisdom Books*, pp. 77–107: 342

The History of Buddhist Thought. By Edward J. THOMAS [London: Kegan Paul, Trench, Trubner & Co., Ltd., 1933]: 303

A History of Chinese Philosophy. By FUNG Yu-lan, and trans. from the Chinese by Derk BODDE, in 2 vols. (Princeton: Princeton University Press, 1952, 1953]: 163

A History of Zen Buddhism. By Heinrich DUMOULIN, S.J., and trans. from the Ger. by Paul PEACHY [New York: Pantheon Books, Random House, 1963]: 202–203, 290

"Hōkyōzammai." Eng. trans. of *Baojing sanmei* 寶鏡三昧, by MASUNAGA Reihō, in *The Sōtō Approach to Zen*, pp. 188–192: 306

"From Hui-neng's Tanjing." Eng. trans. of passages from Dunhuang text of *Liuzu tanjing*, by Daisetz Teitaro SUZUKI, in *Manual of Zen Buddhism*, pp. 82–89: 361

The I Ching, or Book of Changes. The Richard WILHELM German Translation Rendered into English by Cary F. BAYNES. Bollingen Series XIX [New

York: Pantheon Books, 1950]: 379

An Introduction to Zen Buddhism. By Daisetz Teitaro SUZUKI [London: Rider & Co., for The Buddhist Society, London, 1949]: 203

The Invention of Printing in China. By Thomas Francis CARTER. Second ed. rev. by L. Carrington GOODRICH [New York: The Ronald Press Co., 1955]: 368

Inzan roku 隱山錄. Japanese text, edited by TSUJI Tōzan 辻東山 [Gifu: Zuiryō-ji, 1942]: 327

The Jewel of Transcendental Wisdom. Eng. trans. of Ch. text of *Diamond Sutra*, by A.F. PRICE [London: The Buddhist Society, 1947]: 421. Early ed. of *The Diamond Sutra*, by same trans., for which *see above*

Jōron kenkyū 肇論研究: Studies in the *Chao-lun*. Edited by TSUKAMOTO Zenryū [Kyoto: Hōzōkan, 1955]: 382

Jōshū zenji goroku 趙州禪師語錄. Ch. text, revised and edited by SUZUKI Daisetzu and AKIZUKI Ryūmin 秋月龍珉 [Kamakura: Matsugaoka Bunko, 1962]: 383

"Katakushū no seisui" 荷澤宗の盛衰. The Rise and Fall of the Kataku School. By UI Hakuju, in *Zenshūshi kenkyū*, Vol. I, pp. 195–268: 172

"The Koan." By Daisetz Teitaro SUZUKI, in *An Introduction to Zen Buddhism*, pp. 99–117: 203

"The Koan Exercise." By Daisetz Teitaro SUZUKI, in *Essays in Zen Buddhism*, Second Series, pp. 17–189: 203

"Koan no rekishiteki hatten keitai ni okeru shinrisei no mondai" 公案の歷史的發展形態における眞理性の問題. The Problem of Truth in the Historical Development of the Koan. By FURUTA Shōkin 古田紹欽, in *Bukkyō no kompon shinri*, 807–840: 202

Kōkan Shōshitsu issho oyobi kaisetsu 校刊少室逸書及解說. Revised Edition of Lost Writings from Shōshitsu (Dunhuang), with an Interpretation. By SUZUKI Daisetsu and KŌDA Rentarō 公田連太郎, 2 vols. [Osaka: Ataka Bukkyō Bunko, 1936]: 353

"The Kongokyo or Diamond Sutra." Partial Eng. trans. of *Jingang jing* 金剛經, Kumārajīva's Ch. version of *Vajracchedikā-sūtra*, by Daisetz Teitaro SUZUKI, in *Manual of Zen Buddhism*, pp. 38–50: 367

"The Kwannon Sutra." Eng. trans. of *Guanyin jing* 觀音經, Kumārajīva's Ch. version of Chap. XXIV of *Saddharma-puṇḍarīka-sūtra*, by Daisetz Teitaro SUZUKI, in *Manual of Zen Buddhism*, pp. 30–38: 302

Lalitavistara. French trans. from the Skr. text, by P. FOUCAUX. *Annales du Musée Guimet* [Paris: 1889–1892]: 334

The Lankavatara Sutra. Eng. trans. from original Skr. text, by Daisetz Teitaro SUZUKI [London: Routledge & Kegan Paul Ltd., reprint 1956]: 335

"The Larger Sukhāvāti-vyūha." Eng. trans. of Skr. text, by F. Max MÜLLER, in *Buddhist Mahāyāna Texts*, Part II, pp. 1–75: 343

Le Lotus de la bonne loi. French trans. of *Saddharma-puṇḍarīka-sūtra*, by Eugène BURNOUF [1852]: 349

The Lotus of the Wonderful Law, or *The Lotus Gospel*. Abbr. Eng. trans. *Miao-fa lianhua jing* 妙法蓮華經, Kumārajīva's Ch. version of *Saddharma-puṇḍarīka-sūtra*, by W.E. SOOTHILL [Oxford: The Clarendon Press, 1930]: 230, 302, 349

Mahāyānasūtralaṁkāra. French trans. of Skr. text, by Sylvain LÉVI, in 2 vols. [Paris: Champion, 1907, 1911]: 340

Manual of Zen Buddhism. By Daisetz Teitaro SUZUKI [New York: Grove Press, Inc., First Evergreen Edition, 1960]: 289, 302, 322, 333, 342, 361, 367

"Meditation on the Four Acts." Eng. trans. of *Nishu'nyū* 二種入, in *Shōshitsu rokumon* 小室六門, by Daisetz Teitaro SUZUKI, in *Essays in Zen Buddhism*, First Series, pp. 179–183: 357

"The Mu Mon Kwan: The Gateless Barrier to Zen Experience." Eng. trans. of *Wumenguan* 無門關, by Sōhaku OGATA, in *Zen for the West*, pp. 79–134: 309

Muji myō kyō 無字妙經. By SEIGO Hōgaku 棲梧寶嶽. Edited and annotated by RIKUGAWA Taiun 陸川堆雲 [Nagano: Sairaizen-sō, 1936]: 242

Der Ochs und sein Hirte: Eine altchinesische Zen-Geschichte erläutert von Meister Daizohkutsu R. OHTSU mit japanischen Bildern aus dem 15. Jahrhundert übersetzt von Kôichi TSUJIMURA und Hartmut BUCHNER. Ger. trans. of *Shiniutu song* 十牛圖頌, with commentary [Pfullingen: Verlag Günther Neske, 1958]: 289

The Platform Scripture. Eng. trans. of Dunhuang text of *Liuzu tanjing*, with introduction and notes, by Wing-tsit CHAN. Asian Institute Translations, No. 3 [New York: St. John's University Press, 1963]: 361

"Prajñāpāramitā-hṛidaya Sūtra." Eng. trans. of Skr. text by Daisetz Teitaro SUZUKI, in *Essays in Zen Buddhism*, Third Series, pp. 216–219: 342

"The Precious Mirror Samadhi." Eng. trans. of *Baojing sanmei*, by LU K'uan

Yü (Charles Luk), in *Ch'an and Zen Teaching*, Second Series, pp. 149–154: 307

The Saddharma-Puṇḍarīka, or The Lotus of the True Law. Eng. trans. of Skr. text, by H. Kern. Sacred Books of the East, Vol. XXI [Oxford: The Clarendon Press, 1909]: 230, 301, 349

"Sandōkai." Eng. trans. of *Cantongqi* 參同契, by Masunaga Reihō, in *The Sōtō Approach to Zen*, pp. 183–187: 271

"The Sermon of Shênhui." Eng. trans. of a Dunhuang MS, by W. Liebenthal, in *Asia Major*, Vol. III, Part 2 (1953), pp. 132–155: 353

Shenhui heshang yiji 神會和尚遺集. Four Dunhuang MSs compiled, edited, and with textual emendations, by Hu Shi 胡適 [Shanghai: Oriental Book Co., 1930]: 173, 175, 351, 352, 354

"Shōji." Eng. trans. of *kan* 92 of Dōgen Kigen's *Shōbōgenzō*, by Masunaga Reihō, in *The Sōtō Approach to Zen*, pp. 91–99: 355

Shōju rōjin shū 正受老人集. Edited by the Shinano Kyōiku Kai 信濃教育會 [Nagano: Shinano Mainichi Shimbunsha, 1937]: 192–93, 356

Shōshitsu issho 少室逸書. Photographic reproduction of MSs from Dunhuang [Kyoto: Suzuki Teitarō, 1935]: 353

Silver Jubilee Volume of the Zinbun Kagaku Kenkyusyo, Kyoto University. Edited by Tsukamoto Zenryū [Kyoto: 1954]: 254, 382

"The Smaller Sukhāvatī-vyūha." Eng. trans. of Skr. text, by F. Max Müller, in *Buddhist Mahāyāna Texts*, Part II, pp. 87–103: 344

Sodō shū 祖堂集. See *Chodang chip*

Sŏnmun yŏmsong chip 禪門拈頌集 (*Zemmon nenju shū*). Mimeographed copy of original Haein-sa text, in 10 vols. [Kyoto: Hanazono Daigaku, 1960–1962]: 364

The Sōtō Approach to Zen. By Masunaga Reihō [Tokyo: Layman Buddhist Society Press, 1958]: 355

Sources of Chinese Tradition. Compiled by Wm. Theodore de Bary, Wing-tsit Chan, and Burton Watson [New York: Columbia University Press, 1960]: 163, 354, 361, 384

"A Straight Talk on the Heart Sutra." Eng. trans. of *Bore boluomiduo xinjing zhishuo* 般若波羅蜜多心經直説, by Lu K'uan Yü (Charles Luk), in *Ch'an and Zen Teaching*, First Series, pp. 207–223: 342

Studies in the Lankavatara Sutra. By Daisetz Teitaro Suzuki [London: Routledge & Kegan Paul Ltd., reprint, 1957]: 335

Studies Presented to Yuen Ren Chao on His Sixty-fifth Birthday: Academia

Sinica, Bulletin of the Institute of History and Philology, Vol. XXIX, Part II [Taipei: 1958]: 353

"The Sutra Spoken by the Sixth Patriarch." Eng. trans. of Yuan text of *Liuzu tanjing*, by WONG Mu-lam. Edited by Dwight GODDARD, in *A Buddhist Bible*, pp. 497–561: 362

Das Sūtra Vimalakīrti. Übersetz von Jakob FISCHER und YOKOTA Takezō 横田武三. Ger. trans. of a Japanese rendering of a Ch. version of *Vimalakīrti-nirdeśa* [Tokyo: The Hokuseido Press, 1944]: 370

The Sutra of Wei-lang [*or Hui-Neng*]. Eng. trans. of Yuan text of *Liuzu tanjing*, by WONG Mu-lam. Edited by Christmas HUMPHREYS [London: Luzac & Co., for The Buddhist Society, London, 1947]: 362

Suvarṇaprabhāsottama-sūtra: Das Goldglanz-sūtra. Ein Sanskrit-text des Mahāyāna-Buddhismus. I-tsing's Chinesische Version und ihre Tibetische Übersetzung, in 2 bände, von Johannes NOBEL. A Ger. trans. of *Jinguangming zuishengwang jing* 金光明最勝王經 [Leiden: E.J. Brill, 1958]: 365

"10 Bulls." Eng. trans. of *Shiniutu song*, by Nyogen SENZAKI and Paul REPS, in *Zen Flesh, Zen Bones*, pp. 165–187: 289

"The Ten Oxherding Pictures." Eng. trans. of *Shiniutu song*, by Daisetz Teitaro SUZUKI, in Manual of Zen Buddhism, pp. 127-144 : 289

Tonkō shutsudo Kataku Jinne zenji goroku 敦煌出土荷澤神會禪師語錄. Photographic reproduction of Dunhuang MSs [Kyoto: SUZUKI Teitarō, 1932]: 351

Idem. Steel type edition, critically edited by SUZUKI Teitarō and KŌDA Rentarō [Tokyo: Morie Shoten, 1934]: 351

Tonkō shutsudo Rokuso dankyō 燉煌出土六祖壇經. Dunhuang text of *Liuzu tanjing*, critically edited by SUZUKI Teitarō and KŌDA Rentarō [Tokyo: Morie Shoten, 1934]: 361

"Two Newly Edited Texts of the Ch'an Master Shênhui from the Pelliot Collection of Tun-huang Manuscripts at the Bibliotèque Nationale in Paris." By HU Shih, in *Studies Presented to Yuen Ren Chao on His Sixty-fifth Birthday*, pp. 827–882: 353

"Uji." Eng. trans. of *kan* 11 of Dōgen Kigen's *Shōbōgenzō*, by MASUNAGA Reihō, in *The Sōtō Approach to Zen*, pp. 81–90: 355

"Vimalakīrti's Discourse on Emancipation." Eng. trans. of *Weimojie suoshuo jing* 維摩詰所説經, with introduction, by Hōkei Idumi, in *The Eastern Buddhist*, Vol. II (1922–1923), pp. 358–366; Vol. III (1924–1925), pp. 55–69, 138–153, 224–242, 336–349; Vol. IV (1926–1928), pp. 48–55, 177–190, 348–366: 370

"The Wan-ling Record." Eng. trans. of *Huangbo Duanji chanshi Wanling lu* 黄檗斷際禪師宛陵錄. By John Blofeld (Chu Ch'an), in *The Zen Teaching of Huang Po on the Transmission of Mind*, pp. 67–132: 327

Das Wu-mên-kuan 無門關: Der Pass ohne Tor. Übersetz und erklärt von Heinrich Dumoulin, S.J. Monumenta Nipponica Monographs, No. 13 [Tokyo: Sophia University Press, 1935]: 309

"Yasen Kanna 夜船閑話: A Chat on a Boat in the Evening." Eng. trans. from the Japanese of Hakuin Zenji, by R.D.M. Shaw D.D. and Wilhelm Schiffer, S.J. *Monumenta Nipponica*, Vol. XIII, Nos. 1–2 (1956), pp. 101–127: 193

The Yi King. Eng. trans. of *Yi jing* 易經, by James Legge, Unabridged text printed by photo-offset from Sacred Books of the East, Vol. XVI [New York: Dover Publications Inc., 1963]: 379

Zemmon nenju shū 禪門拈頌集. See *Sŏnmun yŏmsong chip*

Zen Buddhism and Psychoanalysis. By D.T. Suzuki, Erich Fromm, and Richard DeMartino [New York: Harper & Bros., 1960]: 290, 384

Zen in English Literature and Oriental Classics. By R. H. Blyth [Tokyo: The Hokuseido Press, 1948]: 72

Zen Flesh, Zen Bones. A Collection of Zen and Pre-Zen Writings. Compiled by Paul Reps, and transcribed by Nyogen Senzaki and Paul Reps [Rutland, Vt., and Tokyo, Japan: Charles E. Tuttle & Co,, 1957]: 289, 309

Zen, der lebendige Buddhismus in Japan. Ausgewählte Stücke des Zen-Textes übersetzt und eingeleitet von Schûej Ōhasama, herausgegeben von August Faust, mit Geleitwort von Rudolf Otto [Gotha/Stuttgart: Friedrich Andreas Perthes A.-G., 1925]: 309

"The Zen Master Dōgen." By Heinrich Dumoulin, S.J., in *A History of Zen Buddhism*, pp. 151–174: 202–203

"The Zen Mysticism of Hakuin.', By Heinrich Dumoulin, S.J. in *A History of Zen Buddhism*, pp. 242–268: 203

The Zen Teaching of Huang-po on the Transmission of Mind. Eng. trans. of

Huangbo Duanji chuanxin fayao 黃蘗斷際傳心法要 and *Wanling lu*, by John BLOFELD (CHU Ch'an) [London: Rider & Co., 1958] and [New York: Grove Press, Inc., 1959]: 327

The Zen Teaching of Hui Hai on Sudden Illumination. Eng. trans. of *Dunwu rudao yaomen lun* 頓悟入道要門論, by John BLOFELD (CHU Ch'an) [London: Rider & Co., 1962]: 319

Zen for the West. By Sōhaku OGATA [London: Rider & Co., for The Buddhist Society, London, 1959]: 309

Zenkai ichiran 禪海一瀾. By IMAKITA Kōsen 今北洪川 (Kōsen Sōon 洪川宗温), in 2 *kan* [Yamaguchi City: Abe Junsuke, 1876]: 201

Zenrin kushū 禪林句集. Edited by SHIBAYAMA Zenkei [Kyoto: Kichūdo, 1952]: 72

Zenshūshi kenkyū 禪宗史研究. By UI Hakuju, in 3 vols [Tokyo: Iwanami Shoten, 1939, 1942, 1943]: 158, 172, 271, 274, 361

Zudokko 塗毒鼓. Edited by FUJITA Genro 藤田玄路 [Kyoto: Kennin Sōdō, 1957]: 333, 358, 377–78, 385

Zudokko (*Zokuhen*) 塗毒鼓 (續編). Edited by FUJITA Genro [Kyoto: Kennin Sōdō, 1957]: 72, 385

Journals

Asia Major: A British Journal of Far Eastern Studies [London: Percy Lund, Humphries & Co., Ltd., Intro, vol. 1920; First Series (10 vols.), 1923–1949; New Series, 1949–]. Semi-annual

Bulletin de l'École Française d'Extrême-Orient [Paris: École Française d'Extrême-Orient, 1901–; Hanoi, –1952; Saigon, 1954; Paris subsequently]. Semi-annual

The Eastern Buddhist: A Bi-monthly Devoted to the Study of Mahayana Buddhism [Kyoto: Eastern Buddhist Society, Otani University, 1921–1937: 1949–1957]. Temporarily suspended

Monumenta Nipponica: Studies on Japanese Culture Past and Present [Tokyo: Sophia University, 1938–]. Semi-annual

Zenbunka 禪文化 Zen Culture [Kyoto: Institute of Zen Studies, Hanazono University, 1955–]. Issued irregularly

Zengaku kenkyū 禪學研究 Studies in Zen Buddhism [Kyoto: Hanazono University, 1925–]. Originally issued irregularly, now annual.

Index To Sanskrit, Chinese, And Japanese Texts

"Bodai bon" 菩提品: idem "Puti pin," q.v.

Bodaidaruma nanshū tei zehi ron 菩提達摩南宗定是非論: idem *Putidamo nanzong ding shifei lun*, q.v.

"Bodaidaruma ryakuben daijō nyūdō shigyō" 菩提達磨略辨大乘入道四行: idem "Putidamo lüebian dacheng rudao sixing," q.v.

Bommō kyō 梵網經: idem *Fanwang jing*, q.v.

Book of Changes: idem *Yi jing*, q.v.

Bore boluomiduo xinjing 般若波羅蜜多心經: (*Hannya haramitta shingyō*); *Bore xinjing* 般若心經 (*Hannya shingyō*); *Xinjing* 心經 (*Shingyō*); *Heart Sutra*: 23, 266, 333, 342. Xuanzang's Ch. trans. *Prajñāpāramitā-hṛdaya-sūtra*

Bore boluomiduo xinjing zhishuo 般若波羅蜜多心經直説 (*Hannya haramitta shingyō jikisetsu*): 342

"Bore wuzhi lun" 般若無知論 (Hannya muchi ron): 253, 381. In *Zhaolun*

Bore xinjing 般若心經: abbr. title *Bore boluomiduo xinjing*, q.v.

Bukka Engo Shinkaku zenji shin'yō 佛果圜悟眞覺禪師心要: idem *Foguo Yuanwu Zhenjue chanshi xinyao*, q.v.

Bukka Engo zenji hekigan roku 佛果圜悟禪師碧巖錄: idem *Foguo Yuanwu chanshi biyan lu*, q.v.

Bukkyo hennen tsūron 佛教編年通論: see *Longxing fojiao biannian tonglun*

Bushū Sōzan Genshō zenji goroku 撫州曹山元證禪師語錄: 316

Bushū Sōzan Honjaku zenji 撫州曹山本寂禪師: idem *Fuzhou Caoshan Benji chanshi*, q.v.

Bussetsu hōdō hatsunaion gyō 佛説方等般泥洹經: idem *Foshuo fangdeng boniyuan jing*, q.v.

Bussetsu Yuimakitsu kyō 佛説維摩詰經: idem *Foshuo Weimojie jing*, q.v.

Busso rekidai tsūsai 佛祖歷代通載: idem *Fozu lidai tongzai*, q.v.

"Butsu fusen ron" 物不遷論: idem "Wubuqian lun," q.v.

Butsuun tsūki 佛運通記: see *Longxing fojiao biannian tonglun*

"Buzhenkong lun" 不眞空論 (Fushinkū ron): 345. In *Zhaolun*

Cantongqi 參同契 (*Sandōkai*): 166, 271, 306, 341, 385

Cao'ange 草庵歌 (*Sōanka*): 271

Chang ahan jing 長阿含經 (*Jō agon kyō*): 253. Ch. trans. *Dīrghāgama*

"Changti pusa pin" 常啼菩薩品 (Jōtai bosatsu bon): 213. In *Dabore boluomiduo jing*

Changuan cejin 禪關策進 (*Zenkan sakushin*): 341–342; quoted, 316

Chanlin sengbao zhuan 禪林僧寶傳 (*Zenrin sōbō den*): quoted, 307–308

Chanzong wumenguan 禪宗無門關 (*Zenshū mumonkan*); *Wumenguan* 無門關 (*Mumonkan*): 17, 24, 138, 145, 180, 181, 183, 184, 225, 245, 294, 295, 308–309, 385; quoted, 39–40, 45–46, 49–50, 53, 225, 239, 241, 244, 246, 256, 294, 308, 309

Chinjū Rinzai Eshō zenji goroku 鎮州臨濟慧照禪師語錄: idem *Zhenzhou Linji Huizhao chanshi yulu*, q.v.

Chinjū Rinzai Gigen zenji 鎮州臨濟義玄禪師: idem *Zhenzhou Linji Yixuan chanshi*, q.v.

Chishū Nansen Fugan zenji goyō 池州南泉普願禪師語要: idem *Chizhou Nanquan Puyuan chanshi yuyao*, q.v.

Chizhou Nanquan Puyuan chanshi yuyao 池州南泉普願禪師語要 (*Chishū Nansen Fugan zenji goyō*): 246

Chodang chip 祖堂集 (*Sodō shū*): 309–310; quoted, 260, 262–63

Chongke guzunsu yulu 重刻古尊宿語錄 (*Jūkoku kosonshuku goroku*); *Guzunsu yulu* 古尊宿語錄 (*Kosonshuku goroku*): 244, 246, 312, 325, 326, 382, 383

Chuanfa zhengzong ji 傳法正宗記 (*Dembō shōjū ki*): 376

Chuandeng lu 傳燈錄: abbr. title *Jingde chuandeng lu*, q.v.

Chūhō kōroku 中峰廣錄: see *Tianmu Zhongfeng heshang guanglu*

Chūhō oshō kōroku 中峰和尚廣錄: see *Tianmu Zhongfeng heshang guanglu*

Chūhō zatsuroku 中峰雜錄: see *Tianmu Mingben chanshi zalu*

Chū Yuimakitsu kyō 注維摩詰經: idem *Zhu Weimojie jing*, q.v.

"Ciliwang xueshi pin" 慈力王血施品 (Jirikiō kesshi bon): 213–14. In *Xianyu jing*

Ciming chanshi wuhui zhuchi yulu 慈明禪師五會住持語錄 (*Jimyō zenji goe jūji goroku*); *Ciming heshang wuhui yulu* 慈明和尚五會語錄 (*Jimyō oshō goe goroku*); *Shishuang Chuyuan chanshi yulu* 石霜楚圓禪師語錄 (*Sekisō Soen zenji goroku*); *Ciming lu* 慈明錄 (*Jimyō roku*): 190, 310–12; quoted, 44, 235

Ciming heshang wuhui yulu 慈明和尚五會語錄: abbr. title *Ciming chanshi wuhui zhuchi yulu*, q.v.

Ciming lu 慈明錄: abbr. title *Ciming chanshi wuhui zhuchi yulu*, q.v.

Ciming sijia lu 慈明四家錄 (*Jimyō shike roku*): 311

Congrong lu 從容錄: abbr. title *Wansong laoren pingchang Tiantong Jue heshang songgu Congrong'an lu*, q.v.

Dabore boluomiduo jing 大般若波羅蜜多經 (*Daihannya haramitta kyō*): 213. Xuanzang's Ch. trans. *Mahāprajñāpāramitā-sūtra*

Daboniepan jing 大般涅槃經 (*Daihatsu nehan gyō*); *Niepan jing* 涅槃經 (*Nehan gyō*); *Nirvana Sutra*: "Northern Text": 151, 205–206, 218, 250, 286, 335, 339; quoted, 51–52, 62, 137; "Southern Text," rev. by Huiyan: 339. Dharmakṣema's Ch. trans. *Mahāparinirvāṇa-sūtra*

Daboniepan jing jijie 大般涅槃經集解 (*Daihatsu nehan gyō shūge*); quoted, 206

Dacheng ru Lengqie jing 大乘入楞伽經 (*Daijō nyū Ryōga kyō*): 336. Śikṣānanda's Ch. trans. *Laṅkāvatāra-sūtra*

Dacheng zhuangyanjing lun 大乘莊嚴經論 (*Daijō shōgongyō ron*); *Zhuangyanjing lun* 莊嚴經論 (*Shōgongyō ron*): 281, 282, 340; quoted, 60, 281–82. Ch. trans. *Mahāyāna-sūtrā-laṁkāra*

Dafantianwang wenfo jueyi jing 大梵天王問佛決疑經 (*Daibontennō mombutsu ketsugi kyō*): 137

Dafangguang fohuayan jing 大方廣佛華嚴經 (*Daihōkō butsukegon kyō*); *Huayan jing* 華嚴經 (*Kegon kyō*); *Wreath Sutra*: "Old Trans." (*jiuyi* 舊譯 *kuyaku*), in 60 *juan*: 161, 162, 163, 164, 165, 234, 290, 304, 305; "New Trans." (*xinyi* 新譯 *shin'yaku*), in 80 *juan*: 162, 165, 228, 290, 304–305, 306; quoted, 228. Ch. trans. *Avataṁsaka-sūtra*

Dafangguang fohuayan jing: *Ru busiyi jietuo jingjie*; *Puxian xingyuan pin* 大方廣佛華嚴經：入不思議解脱境界；普賢行願品 (*Daihōkōbutsukegon kyō*: *Nyū fushigi gedatsu kyōgai*; *Fugen gyōgan bon*): *Huayan jing* 華嚴經 (*Kegon kyō*): 165, 304–305. Ch. trans. *Gaṇḍavyūha-sūtra*

Dahui Jue chanshi pushuo 大慧覺禪師普説 (*Daie Kaku zenji fusetsu*); *Dahui pushuo* 大慧普説 (*Daie fusetsu*); 149, 312, 313

Dahui lu 大慧錄: abbr. title *Dahui Pujue chanshi yulu*, q.v.

Dahui Pujue chanshi zongmen wuku 大慧普覺禪師宗門武庫 (*Daie Fukaku zenji shūmon buko*); *Dahui wuku* 大慧武庫 (*Daie buko*): 149, 313

Dahui Pujue chanshi yulu 大慧普覺禪師語錄 (*Daie Fukaku zenji goroku*); *Dahui yulu* 大慧語錄 (*Daie goroku*); *Dahui lu* 大慧錄 (*Daie roku*): 149, 312–13; quoted, 40, 147, 229

Dahui pushuo 大慧普説: 313. Also abbr. title *Dahui Jue chanshi pushuo*, q.v.

Dahui wuku 大慧武庫: abbr. title *Dahui Pujue chanshi zongmen wuku*, q.v.

Dahui yulu 大慧語錄: abbr. title *Dahui Pujue chanshi yulu*, q.v.

Daibie 代別 (*Daibetsu*): of Xutang Zhiyu, see *Xutang lu*: *daibie*

Daiyu 代語 (*Daigo*): of Fenyang Shanzhao: 320; of Xutang Zhiyu: 378; of Yunmen Wenyan: 380

Daibetsu 代別: idem *Daibie*, q.v.

Daibirushana kyō 大毘盧遮那經: idem *Dapiluzhena jing*, q.v.
Daibontennō mombutsu ketsugi kyō 大梵天王問佛決疑經: idem *Dafantianwang wenfo jueyi jing*, q.v.
Daichido ron 大智度論: idem *Dazhidu lun*, q.v.
Daie buko 大慧武庫: see *Dahui Pujue chanshi zongmen wuku*
Daie Fukaku zenji goroku 大慧普覺禪師語錄: idem *Dahui Pujue chanshi yulu*, q.v.
Daie Fukaku zenji shūmon buko 大慧普覺禪師宗門武庫: idem *Dahui Pujue chanshi zongmen wuku*
Daie fusetsu 大慧普説: see *Dahui Jue chanshi pushuo*
Daie goroku 大慧語錄: see *Dahui Pujue chanshi yulu*
Daie Kaku zenji fusetsu 大慧覺禪師普説: idem *Dahui Jue chanshi pushuo*, q.v.
Daie roku 大慧錄: see *Dahui Pujue chanshi yulu*
Daigo 代語: idem *Daiyu*, q.v.
Daihannya haramitta kyō 大般若波羅蜜多經: idem *Dabore boluomiduo jing*, q.v.
Daihatsu nehan gyō 大般涅槃經: idem *Daboniepan jing*, q.v.
Daihatsu nehan gyō shūge 大般涅槃經集解: idem *Daboniepan jing jijie*, q.v.
Daihōkō butsukegon kyō 大方廣佛華嚴經: idem *Dafangguang fohuayan jing*, q.v.
Daihōkō butsukegon kyō: *Nyū fushigi gedatsu kyōgai*; *Fugen gyōgan bon* 大方廣佛華嚴經：入不思議解脱境界；普賢行願品: idem *Dafangguang fohuayan jing*: *Ru busiyi jietuo jingjie*; *Puxian xingyuan pin*, q.v.
Daijō nyū Ryōga kyō 大乘入楞伽經: idem *Dacheng ru Lengqie jing*, q.v.
Daijō shōgongyō ron 大乘莊嚴經論: idem *Dacheng zhuangyan jing lun*, q.v.
Dainichi kyō 大日經: see *Dapiluzhena jing*
Daiō goroku 大應語錄: abbr. title *Enzū Daiō kokushi goroku*, q.v.
Daishōgon kyō 大莊嚴經: see *Fangguang dazhuangyan jing*
Daitō kokushi goroku 大燈國師語錄: abbr. title *Ryūhō kaisan tokushi Kōzen Daitō Kōshō Shōtō kokushi goroku*, q.v.
"Daitō kokushi gyōjō" 大燈國師行狀: 347; quoted, 208. In *Ryūhō kaisan tokushi Kōzen Daitō Kōshō Shōtō kokushi goroku*
Daitō kokushi hōgo 大燈國師法語: 210, 313–14, 333
"Daitō kokushi sanshō goyō" 大燈國師參詳語要: 347. In *Ryūhō kaisan tokushi Kōzen Daitō Kōshō Shōtō kokushi goroku*
Daitō roku 大燈錄: abbr. title *Ryūhō kaisan tokushi Kōzen Daitō Kōshō Shōtō kokushi goroku*

"Daitoku goroku" 大德語錄: 331, 346. In *Ryūhō kaisan tokushi Kōzen Daitō Shōtō kokushi goroku*
Damamūka-sūtra: for Ch. trans. see *Xianyu jing*
Dankyō 壇經: *Liuzu dashi fabao tanjing*
Dapiluzhena jing 大毘盧遮那經 (*Daibirushana kyō*): *Dari jing* 大日經 (*Dainichi kyō*): 190. Ch. trans. *Mahāvairocana-sūtra*
Dari jing 大日經: alt. title *Dapiluzhena jing*, q.v.
Daśabhūmika-sūtra: *Shidi jing* 十地經 (*Jūji kyō*): 161, 303, 304. See also *Avataṁsaka-sūtra*
Dazhidu lun 大智度論 (*Daichido ron*): 287. Ch. trans. *Mahāprajñāpāramitā-śāstra*
Dazhuangyan jing 大莊嚴經: abbr. title *Fangguang dazhuangyan jing*, q.v.
Dembō shōjū ki 傳法正宗記: idem *Chuanfa zhengzong ji*, q.v.
Denkō roku 傳光錄: 314; quoted, 62, 286
Dentō roku 傳燈錄: see *Jingde chuandeng lu*
Dharmagupta-vinaya: 159. For Ch. trans. see *Sifen lü*
Dhyana Sutra: idem *Guan wuliangshoufo jing*, q.v.
Diamond Sutra: idem *Vajracchedikā-prajñāpāramitā-sūtra* and *Jingang bore boluomi jing*, q.v.
Dirghāgama: for Ch. trans. see *Chang ahan jing*
"Dokugo shingyō" 毒語心經: 333, 385. In *Keisō dokuzui shūi*
The Dongshan Records: 314–17
Dongshan wuwei song 洞山五位頌 (*Tōzan goi no ju*); *Wuwei song* 五位頌 (*Goi no ju*): *Verses on the Five Ranks*: 58, 60, 268, 277, 307, 315–16; quoted, 60, 61–62, 63, 64, 65, 283, 285, 288, 289, 290
Dongshan wuwei xianjue 洞山五位顯訣 (*Tōzan goi kenketsu*); *Wuwei xianjue* 五位顯訣 (*Goi kenketsu*): 316, 317
Dongshan yulu 洞山語錄: abbr. title *Ruizhou Dongshan Liangjie chanshi yulu* (Yufeng Text), q.v.
Doushuai Yue chanshi yu 兜率悅禪師語 (*Tosotsu Etsu zenji go*): 239
Duiji 對機 (*Taiki*): in *Xutang lu*: 328; of Yunmen Wenyan: 380
Dunwu rudao yaomen lun 頓悟入道要門論 (*Tongo nyūdō yōmon ron*); *Dunwu yaomen* 頓悟要門 (*Tongo yōmon*): 282, 317–19; quoted, 282
Dunwu wusheng bore song 頓悟無生般若頌 (*Tongo mushō hannya ju*): 354
Dunwu yaomen 頓悟要門: abbr. title *Dunwu rudao yaomen lun*, q.v.

Egen 會元: see *Wudeng huiyuan*
Eki kyō 易經: idem *Yi jing*, q.v.

Emmyō kokushi gyōjitsu nempu 圓明國師行實年譜: quoted, 180
Engo Bukka zenji goroku 圜悟佛果禪師語錄: idem *Yuanwu Foguo chanshi yulu*, q.v.
Engo goroku 圜悟語錄: see *Yuanwu Foguo chanshi yulu*
Engo roku 圜悟錄: see *Yuanwu Foguo chanshi yulu*
Engo shin'yō 圜悟心要: see *Foguo Yuanwu Zhenjue chanshi xinyao*
Enryō roku 宛陵錄: see *Huangbo Duanji chanshi Wanling lu*
Enshū Kyōzan Ejaku zenji 袁州仰山慧寂禪師: idem *Yuanzhou Yangshan Huiji chanshi*, q.v.
Enzū Daiō kokushi goroku 圓通大應國師語錄; *Daiō goroku* 大應語錄: 319, quoted, 185
"Erzhongru" 二種入 (Nishu'nyū); 356, 357. In *Shōshitsu rokumon*

Fahua jing 法華經: abbr. title *Miaofa lianhua jing*, q.v.
Fanwang jing 梵網經 (*Bommō kyō*): 160
Fangguang dazhuangyan jing 方廣大莊嚴經 (*Hōkō daishōgon kyō*); *Dazhuangyan jing* 大莊嚴經 (*Daishōgon kyō*): 334: Divākara's Ch. trans. *Lalitavistara*
Fayan chanshi yulu 法演禪師語錄 (*Hōen zenji goroku*): 256
Fayu 法語 (*Hōgo*): of Hongzhi Zhengjue: 326; of Dahui Zonggao: 313; of Yuanwu Keqin: 322–23, 380. See also *Hōgo*
Fengxue chanshi yulu 風穴禪師語錄 (*Fuketsu zenji goroku*): 244; quoted, 244
Fenyang lu 汾陽錄: abbr. title *Fenyang Wude chanshi yulu*, q.v.
Fenyang Wude chanshi yulu 汾陽無德禪師語錄 (*Fun'yō Mutoku zenji goroku*); *Fenyang lu* 汾陽錄 (*Fun'yō roku*): 11, 143, 319–20
Foguo Yuanwu chanshi biyan lu 佛果圜悟禪師碧巖錄 (*Bukka Engo zenji hekigan roku*); *Biyan lu* 碧巖錄 (*Hekigan roku*): 11, 12, 24, 45, 145, 146, 147, 225, 232, 233, 238, 240, 245, 253, 320–22, 331, 341, 372, 377; quoted, 44, 45, 49, 53, 54, 63, 233, 246, 248, 249, 254, 264, 265, 277, 284, 286, 289
Foguo Yuanwu Zhenjue chanshi xinyao 佛果圜悟眞覺禪師心要 (*Bukka Engo Shinkaku zenji shin'yō*); Yuanwu xinyao 圜悟心要 (*Engo shin'yō*): 147, 322–23, 380
Fojiao biannian tonglun 佛教編年通論: abbr. title *Longxing fojiao biannian tonglun*, q.v.
Foshuo fangdeng boniyuan jing 佛說方等般泥洹經 (*Bussetsu hōdō hatsunaion gyō*): 339. Dharmarakṣa's Ch. trans. *Mahāparinirvāṇa-sūtra*
Foshuo Weimojie jing 佛說維摩詰經 (*Bussetsu Yuimakitsu kyō*): 252, 369.

Earliest Ch. trans. *Vimalakīrti-nirdeśa*
Four Section Vinaya: idem *Sifen lü*, q.v.
Foyun tongji 佛運通記: alt. title *Longxing fojiao biannian tonglun*, q.v.
Fozu lidai tongzai 佛祖歷代通載 (*Busso rekidai tsūsai*): quoted, 168
"Fu daishi den" 傅大士傳: idem "Fu dashi zhuan," q.v.
Fu daishi goroku 傅大士語錄: see *Shanhui dashi yulu*
Fu dashi yulu 傅大士語錄: alt. title *Shanhui dashi yulu*, q.v.
"Fu dashi zhuan" 傅大士傳 (Fu daishi den): 350. In *Shanhui dashi yulu*
Fugen bosatsu gyō bon 普賢菩薩行品: idem *Puxian pusa xing pin*, q.v.
Fuketsu zenji goroku 風穴禪語錄: idem *Fengxue chanshi yulu*, q.v.
Fun'yō Mutoku zenji goroku 汾陽無德禪師語錄: idem *Fenyang Wude chanshi yulu*, q.v.
Fun'yo roku 汾陽錄: see *Fenyang Wude chanshi yulu*
Fuō kokushi Genjū-an shingi 普應國師幻住庵清規: idem *Puying guoshi Huanzhu'an qinggui*, q.v.
"Fushinkū ron" 不眞空論: idem "Buzhenkong lun," q.v.
Futō roku 普燈錄: see *Jiatai pudeng lu*
Fuyō kyō 普耀經: idem *Puyao jing*, q.v.
Fuzhou Caoshan Benji chanshi 撫州曹山本寂禪師 (*Bushū Sōzan Honjaku zenji*): 376. In *Wujia yulu*

Gaṇḍavyūha-sūtra: 165, 303, 305–306. For Ch. trans. see *Dafangguang fohuayan jing: Ru busiyi jietuo jingjie*; *Puxian xingyuan pin*. See also *Avataṁsaka-sūtra*
Gaofeng heshang chanyao 高峰和尚禪要 (*Kōhō oshō zen'yō*): 221; quoted, 221, 230
Geju 渴頌: of Hakuin Ekaku: 333. See also *Jiesong*
"Genchūmei" 玄中銘: idem "Xuanzhongming," q.v.
Genjū-an shingi 幻住庵清規: see *Puying guoshi Huanzhu'an qinggui*
Gentō 嚴統: see *Wudeng yantong*
Gesan 偈贊: idem *Jiezan*, q.v.
Gobun ritsu 五分律: see *Mishasaibu [hexi] wufen lü*
Goi kenketsu 五位顯訣: see *Dongshan wuwei xianjue*
Goi no ju 五位頌: see *Dongshan wuwei song*
Goke goroku 五家語錄: idem *Wujia yulu*, q.v.
Goke sanshō yōro mon 五家參詳要路門: 197, 323–24
Goke shōjū san 五家正宗贊: idem *Wujia zhengzong zan*, q.v.
"Goshō ron" 悟性論: idem "Wuxing lun," q.v.

Goshū genryūzu 五宗源流画: idem *Wuzong yuanliutu*, q.v.
Goshū roku 五宗錄: see *Wujia yulu*
Gotō egen 五燈會元: idem *Wudeng huiyuan*, q.v.
Gotō gento 五燈嚴統: idem *Wudeng yantong*, q.v.
Gotō gentō gewaku ron 五燈嚴統解惑論: idem *Wudeng yantong jiehuo lun*, q.v.
Gotō roku 五燈錄: idem *Wudeng lu*, q.v.
Guangdeng lu 廣燈錄: abbr. title *Tiansheng guangdeng lu*, q.v.
Guanshiyin pusa pumen pin 觀世音菩薩普門品 (*Kanzeon bosatsu fumon bon*); *Guanyin jing* 觀音經 (*Kannon gyō*); *Guanyin Sutra*: 23, 301–302, 349. Kumārajīva's Ch. trans. *Avalokiteśvara-sūtra*
Guan wuliangshoufo jing 觀無量壽佛經 (*Kan muryōjubutsu kyō*); *Dhyana Sutra*: 156, 156, 344
Guanyin jing 觀音經: abbr. title *Guanshiyin pusa pumen pin*, q.v.
Guanyin Sutra: see *Guanshiyin pusa pumen pin*
The *Guzunsu* Collections: 324–25
Guzunsu yulu 古尊宿語錄: abbr. title *Chongke guzunsu yulu*, q.v.
Guzunsu yuyao 古尊宿語要 (*Kosonshuku goyō*): 324, 383

"Hachidainingaku" 八大人覺: 355. In *Shōbōgenzō*
Hannya haramitta shingyō 般若波羅蜜多心經: idem *Bore boluomiduo xinjing*, q.v.
Hannya haramitta shingyō jikisetsu 般若波羅蜜多心經直說: idem *Bore boluomiduo xinjing zhishuo*, q.v.
"Hannya muchi ron" 般若無知論: idem "Bore wuzhi lun," q.v.
Hannya shingyō 般若心經: see *Bore boluomiduo xinjing*
"Hasō ron" 破相論: idem "Poxiang lun," q.v.
Heart Sutra: see *Prajñāpāramitā-hṛdaya-sūtra*; *Mohebore boluomi damingzhou jing*, and *Bore boluomiduo xinjing*
Hekigan roku 碧巖錄: see *Foguo Yuanwu chanshi biyan lu*
Hennen tsūron 編年通論: see *Longxing fojiao biannian tonglun*
Heze dashi xianzong ji 荷澤大師顯宗記 (*Kataku daishi kenjū ki*): 354
Hōen zenji goroku 法演禪師語錄: idem *Fayan chanshi yulu*, q.v.
Hōgo 法語: of Daitō Kokushi: 314; of Hakuin Ekaku: 333. See also *Fayu*
Hoke kyō 法華經: see *Miaofa lianhua jing*
Hōkō daishōgon kyō 方廣大莊嚴經: idem *Fangguang dazhuangyan jing*, q.v.
Hōkyō zammai 寶鏡三昧: idem *Baojing sanmei*, q.v.
Honzamban 本山版 (ed. of *Shōbōgenzō*): 355

Hōrin den 寶林傳: idem *Baolin zhuan*, q.v.
Hōzō ron 寶藏論: idem *Baozang lun*, q.v.
Hṛdaya-sūtra: see *Prajñāpāramitā-hṛdaya-sūtra*
Huangbo Duanji chanshi Wanling lu 黃蘗斷際禪師宛陵錄 (*Ōbaku Dansai zenji Enryō roku*): *Wanling lu* 宛陵錄 (*Enryō roku*): 139, 326–27; quoted, 139
Idem: *Sijia yulu* text: 326, 360
Huanzhu'an qinggui 幻住庵清規: abbr. title *Puying guoshi Huanzhu'an qinggui*, q.v.
Huayan jing 華嚴經: abbr. title *Dafangguang fohuayan jing* and *Dafangguang fohuayan jing: Ru busiyi jietuo jingjie*; *Puxian xingyuan pin*, q.v. See also *Avataṁsaka-sūtra* and *Gaṇḍavyūha-sūtra*
Huayanjing su 華嚴經疏 (*Kegon-kyō sho*): 166
Huayan wujiao zhiguan 華嚴五教止觀 (*Kegon gokyō shikan*): 234
Huayan yicheng shixuanmen 華嚴一乘十玄門 (*Kegon ichijō jūgemmon*): 234
Huiyuan 會元: abbr. title *Wudeng huiyuan*, q.v.
Hongzhi chanshi guanglu 宏智禪師廣錄 (*Wanshi zenji kōroku*); *Hongzhi guanglu* 宏智廣錄 (*Wanshi kōroku*); *Hongzhi lu* 宏智錄 (*Wanshi roku*): 154, 325–26; quoted, 154
Hongzhi guanglu 宏智廣錄 abbr. title *Hongzhi chanshi guanglu*, q.v.
Hongzhi lu 宏智錄: abbr. title *Hongzhi chanshi guanglu*, q.v.
Hungzhou Baizhangshan Dazhi chanshi yulu 洪州百丈山大智禪自帀語錄 (*Kōshū Hyakujōzan Daichi zenji goroku*): 360. In *Sijia yulu*
Hyaku ron 百論: idem *Bailun*, q.v.
Hyakujō kōroku 百丈廣錄: idem *Baizhang guanglu*, q.v.
Hyakusoku juko 百則頌古: see *Xuedou baize songgu*

Inshū Ōbakuzan Dansai zenji denshin hōyō 筠州黃蘗山斷際禪師傳心法要: idem *Yunzhou Huangboshan Duanji chanshi chuanxin fayao*, q.v.
Inshū Tōzan Gohon zenji goroku 筠州洞山悟本禪師語錄; *Tōzan daishi goroku* 洞山大師語錄; *Tōzan goroku* 洞山語錄 (Shigetsu Text): 268, 306, 316–17; quoted, 61, 266–68, 285
Inzan roku 隱山錄: 199, 327. *See also* Index To Translations And Modern Works

The Jeweled-mirror Samadhi: idem *Baojing sanmei*, q.v.
Jiangxi Mazu Daoyi chanshi yulu 江西馬祖道一禪師語錄 (*Kōzei Baso Dōitsu zenji goroku*): 360. In *Sijia yulu*

Jianzhong Jingguo xudeng lu 建中靖國續燈錄 (*Kenchū Seikoku zokutō roku*); *Xudeng lu* 續燈錄 (*Zokutō roku*): 327–28, 329, 372, 384
Jiatai pudeng lu 嘉泰普燈錄 (*Katai futō roku*); *Pudeng lu* 普燈錄 (*Futō roku*): 328–29, 372: quoted, 255–56
Jiesong 渴頌 (*geju*): in *Xudeng lu*: 328; of Hongzhi Zhengjue: 326; of Shishuang Chuyuan, 311; of Yunmen Wenyan: 380
Jiezan 偈贊 (*gesan*): in *Jiatai pudeng lu*: 329
Jimyō oshō goe goroku 慈明和尚五會語錄: see *Ciming chanshi wuhui zhuchi yulu*
Jimyō roku 慈明錄: see *Ciming chanshi wuhui zhuchi yulu*
Jimyō shike roku 慈明四家錄: idem *Ciming sijia lu*, q.v.
Jimyō zenji goe jūji goroku 慈明禪師五會住持語錄: idem *Ciming chanshi wuhui zhuchi yulu*, q.v.
Jingang bore boluomi jing 金剛般若波羅蜜經 (*Kongō hannya haramitsu kyō*); *Jingang jing* 金剛經 (*Kongō kyō*); *Diamond Sutra*: 151, 172, 253, 336, 360, 366–68; quoted, 136, 367–68. Kumārajīva's Ch. trans. *Vajracchedikā-prajñāpāramitā-sūtra*
Jingang jing 金剛經: abbr. title *Jinggang bore boluomi jing*, q.v.
Jingang jueyi 金剛決疑 (*Kongō ketsugi*): 367
Jingde chuandeng lu 景德傳燈錄 (*Keitoku dentō roku*); *Chuandeng lu* 傳燈錄 (*Dentō roku*): 138, 139, 150, 152, 167, 310, 314, 318, 327, 329–31, 350, 354, 357, 372, 373, 377, 384; quoted, 44, 139, 207, 216–17, 221–22, 230, 231, 232–33, 240, 242, 245–46, 247, 251–52, 253, 257–58, 259, 261–62, 269, 270–71, 272–73, 374–75, 284, 287, 321
Jinguangming jing 金光明經 (*Konkōmyō kyō*): 214, 365. Ch. trans. *Suvarṇa-prabhāsa-sūtra*
Jinguangming zuishengwang jing 金光明最勝王經 (*Konkōmyō saishō-ō kyō*); "Jirikiō kesshi bon" 慈力王血施品: idem "Ciliwang xueshi pin" q.v.
Jinling Qingliangyuan Wenyi chanshi 金陵清凉院文益禪師 (*Kinryō Shōryō-in Bun'eki zenji*): 376. In *Wujia yulu*
Jinshizi zhang 金師子章 (*Konjishi shō*): 163
Jō agon kyō 長阿含經: idem *Chang ahan jing*, q.v.
Jōdō 上堂: of Daiō Kokushi: 319. See also *Shangtang*
Jōron 肇論: idem *Zhaolun*, q.v.
Jōshū oshō goroku 趙州和尚語錄: see *Zhaozhou Zhenji chanshi yulu*
Jōshū roku 趙州錄: see *Zhaozhou Zhenji chanshi yulu*
Jōshū Shinsai zenji goroku 趙州眞際禪師語錄: idem *Zhaozhou Zhenji chanshi yulu*, q.v.

"Jōshū Shinsai zenji gyōjō 趙州眞際禪師行狀: idem Zhaozhou Zhenji chanshi xingzhuang," q.v.
Jōshū soshi goroku 趙州祖師語錄: see *Zhaozhou Zhenji chanshi yulu*
"Jōtai bosatsu bon" 常啼菩薩品: idem "Changti pusa pin," q.v.
Jūgyūzu ju 十牛圖頌: idem *Shiniutu song*, q.v.
Jūji kyō 十地經: see *Daśabhūmika-sūtra*
Jūju ritsu 十誦律: idem *Shisong lü*, q.v.
Juko 頌古: of Daitō Kokushi: 331, 347; of Hakuin Ekaku: 333. See also *Songgu*
Juko hyakusoku 頌古百則: idem *Songgu baize*, q.v.
Jūkoku kosonshuku goroku 重刻古尊宿語錄: idem *Chongke guzunsu yulu*, q.v.
"Jūniji ka" 十二時歌: idem "Shi'ershi ge," q.v.

Kaiankoku go 槐安國語: 331–32, 347, 385
Kaien fusetsu 開筵普説: abbr. title *Sokkō roku kaien fusetsu*, q.v.
Kaisan Shidō Bu'nan anju zenji anroku 開山至道無難庵主禪師行錄: 197, 332
Kamben 勘辨: idem *Kanbian*, q.v.
Kanbian 勘辨 (*Kamben*): of Linji Yixuan: 384; of Shishuang Chuyuan: 311; of Yunmen Wenyan; 381
"Kankin bō" 看經榜: 323. In *Goke sanshō yōro mon*
Kan muryōjubutsu kyō 觀無量壽佛經: idem *Guan wuliangshoufo jing*, q.v.
Kannon gyō 觀音經: see *Guanshiyin pusa pumen pin*
Kanzan shi Sendai kimon 寒山詩闡提記聞: 285; quoted, 285
Kanzeon bosatsu fumon bon 觀世音菩薩普門品: idem *Guanshiyin pusa pumen pin*, q.v.
Katai futō roku 嘉泰普燈錄: idem *Jiatai pudeng lu*, q.v.
Kataku daishi kenjū ki 荷澤大師顯宗記: idem *Heze dashi xianzong ji*, q.v.
Kattō shū 葛藤集: abbr. title *Shūmon kattō shū*, q.v.
Kegon gokyō shikan 華嚴五教止觀: idem *Huayan wujiao zhiguan*, q.v.
Kegon ichijō jūgemmon 華嚴一乘十玄門: idem *Huayan yicheng shixuanmen*, q.v.
Kegon kyō 華嚴經: see *Dafangguang fohuayan jing* and *Dafangguang fohuayan jing: Ru busiyi jietuo jingjie*; *Puxian xingyuan pin*
Kegon-kyō sho 華嚴經疏: idem *Huayanjing su*, q.v.
Keisō dokuzui 荊叢毒蘂: 56, 268, 290, 332–33; quoted, 57–64
Keisō dokuzui shūi 荊叢毒蘂拾遺: 333

Keitoku dentō roku 景德傳燈錄: idem *Jingde chuandeng lu*, q.v.
Kenchū Seikoku zokutō roku 建中靖國續燈錄: idem *Jianzhong Jingguo xudeng lu*, q.v.
Kengu kyō 賢愚經: idem *Xianyu jing*, q.v.
"Ketsumyaku ron" 血脈論 idem "Xuemo lun," q.v.
Kidō oshō goroku 虛堂和尚語錄: idem *Xutang heshang yulu*, q.v.
Kidō roku 虛堂錄: see *Xutang heshang yulu*
Kidō roku: daibetsu 虛堂錄: 代別: idem *Xutang lu: daibie*, q.v.
Kinryō Shōryōyin Bun'eki zenji 金陵清涼院文益禪師: idem *Jinling Qingliangyuan Wenyi chanshi*, q.v.
Kissa yōjō ki 喫茶養生記: 176
Kōhō oshō zen'yō 高峰和尚禪要: idem *Gaofeng heshang chanyao*, q.v.
Kongō hannya haramitsu kyō 金剛般若波羅蜜經: idem *Jingang bore boluomi jing*, q.v.
Kongō ketsugi 金剛決疑: idem *Jingang jueyi*, q.v.
Kongō kyō 金剛經: see *Jingang bore boluomi jing*
Konjishi shō 金師子章; idem *Jinshizi zhang*, q.v.
Konkōmyō kyō 金光明經: idem *Jinguangming jing*, q.v.
Konkōmyō saishō-ō kyō 金光明最勝王經: idem *Jinguangming zuishengwang jing*, q.v.
Kōshū Hyakujōzan Daichi zenji goroku 洪州百丈山大智禪師語錄: idem *Hongzhou Baizhangshan Dazhi chanshi yulu*, q.v.
Kosonshuku goroku 古尊宿語錄: see *Chongke guzunsu yulu*
Kosonshuku goyō 古尊宿語要: idem *Guzunsu yuyao*, q.v.
Kōtō roku 廣燈錄: see *Tiansheng guangdeng lu*
Kōzei Baso Dōitsu zenji goroku 江西馬祖道一禪師語錄: idem *Jiangxi Mazu Daoyi chanshi yulu*, q.v.
Kōzen Daitō kokushi yuikai 興禪大燈國師遺誡: 211, 333, 385; quoted, 34
Kōzen gokoku ron 興禪護國論: 176
Ku zōshi 句雙紙: 71
"Kushū" 句集: 385. In *Zudokko* (*Zokuhen*)

Lalitavistara: 334, 339. For Ch. trans. see *Puyao jing* and *Fangguang dazhuangyan jing*
Laṅkāvatāra-sūtra: 48, 168, 172, 217, 242, 244, 334–37. For Ch. trans. see *Lengqie abaduoluo bao jing*, *Ru Lengqie jing*, and *Dacheng ru lengqie jing*
Laozi 老子 (*Rōshi*): 252
Larger Sukhāvatī: see *Sukhāvatī-vyūha* [Larger]

Ledao ge 樂道歌 (*Rakudō ka*): 230; quoted, 231
Lengqie abaduoluo bao jing 楞伽阿跋多羅寶經 (*Ryōga abattara hō kyō*); *Lengqie jing* 楞伽經 (*Ryōga kyō*): 217, 242, 336. Guṇabhadra's Ch. trans. *Laṅkāvatāra-sūtra*
Lengqie jing 楞咖經: abbr. title *Lengqie abaduoluo bao jing*, q.v.
Lengqie shizi ji 楞伽師資記 (*Ryōga shiji ki*): 357
Liandeng 聯燈: abbr. title *Zongmen liandeng huiyao*, q.v.
Liandeng huiyao 聯燈會要: abbr. title *Zongmen liandeng huiyao*, q.v.
Linji Huizhao chanshi yulu 臨濟慧照禪師語錄 (*Rinzai Eshō zenji goroku*): 360. In *Sijia yulu*
Linji lu 臨濟錄: abbr. title *Zhenzhou Linji Huizhao chanshi yulu*, q.v.
Linji zongzhi 臨濟宗旨 (*Rinzai shūshi*): 375. In *Wujia yulu*
Liuzu dashi fabao tanjing 六祖大師法寶壇經 (*Rokuso daishi hōbō dankyō*); *Liuzu tanjing* 六祖壇經 (*Rokuso dankyō*); *Tanjing* 壇經 (*Dankyō*); *Sixth Patriarch's Platform Sutra*; *Platform Sutra*: 151, 204, 223, 361–62; quoted, 60, 283. (Yuan Text)
Liuzu tanjing 六祖壇經: abbr. title *Liuzu dashi fabao tanjing*, q.v.
Longxing fojiao biannian tonglun 隆興佛教編年通論 (*Ryūkō bukkyō hennen tsūron*); *Fojiao biannian tonglun* 佛教編年通論 (*Bukkyō hennen tsūron*); *Biannian tonglun* 編年通論 (*Hennen tsūron*); *Longxing foyun tonglun* 隆興佛運通論 (*Ryukō butsuun tsūron*); *Foyun tongji* 佛運通記 (*Butsuun tsūki*): 228, 337–38; quoted, 228
Longxing foyun tonglun 隆興佛運通論: abbr. title *Longxing fojiao biannian tonglun*, q.v.
Luojing Heze Shenhui dashi yu 洛京荷澤神會大師語 (*Rakukei Kataku Jinne daishi no go*): 354
Luoyang qielan ji 洛陽伽藍記 (*Rakuyō garan ki*): 212
Lotus Sutra: see *Saddharmapuṇḍarīka-sūtra* and *Miaofo lianhua jing*

Mahāparinibbāna-suttanta: 338
Mahāparinirvāṇa-sūtra; *Nirvana Sutra*: 205–206, 272, 334, 335, 338–39. For Ch. trans. see *Foshuo fangdeng boniyuan jing* and *Daboniepan jing*
Mahāprajñāpāramitā-śāstra: 287. For Ch. trans. see *Dazhidu lun*
Mahāprajñāpāramitā-sūtra: 213. For Ch. trans. see *Mohebore boluomi jing* and *Dabore boluomiduo jing*
Mahāsāṅghika-vinaya: for Ch. trans. see *Mohesengqi lü*
Mahāvaipulya buddhāvataṁsaka-sūtra: restored Skr. title *Avataṁsaka-sūtra*, q.v.

Mahāvairocana-sūtra: for Ch. trans. see *Dapiluzhena jing*
Mahāyāna-sūtrālaṁkāra: 339–40. For Ch. trans. see *Dacheng zhuangyan jing lun*
Mahīśāsaka-vinaya: for Ch. trans. see *Mishasebi* [*hexi*] *wufen lü*
Makahannya haramitsu daimyōju kyō 摩訶般若波羅蜜大明咒經: idem *Mohebore boluomi damingzhou jing*, q.v.
Makahannya haramitsu kyō 摩訶般若波羅蜜經: idem *Mohebore boluomi jing*, q.v.
Makashikan 摩訶止觀: idem *Mohezhiguan*, q.v.
Makasōgi ritsu 摩: idem *Mohesengqi lü*, q.v.
Mazu sijia lu 馬祖四家錄: alt. title *Sijia yulu*, q.v.
Miaofa lianhua jing 妙法蓮華經 (*Myōhō renge kyō*): *Fahua jing* 法華經 (*Hoke kyō*); *Lotus Sutra*: 20, 160, 169, 170, 188, 189, 272, 287, 301–302, 349; quoted, 287. Kumārajīva's Ch. trans. *Saddharma-puṇḍarīka-sūtra*
Miaofalianhua jing xuanyi 妙法蓮華經玄義 (*Myōhōrenge-kyō gengi*): 287
Miaoli yuanchengguan 妙理圓成觀 (*Myōri enjōkan*): 166
Mingjue chanshi yulu 明覺禪師語錄 (*Myōgaku zenji goroku*); *Xuedou Chongxian yulu* 雪竇重顯語錄 (*Setchō Jūken goroku*); *Xuedou lu* 雪竇錄 (*Setchō roku*): 144, 340–41, 347; quoted, 64, 290
Mingben chanshi zalu 明本禪師雜錄: abbr. title *Tianmu Mingben chanshi zalu*, q.v.
Mishasebu [*hexi*] *wufen lü* 彌沙塞部[和醯]五分律 (*Mishasokubu* [*wakei*] *gobunritsu*); *Wufen lü* 五分律 (*Gobunritsu*): 371. Ch. trans. *Mahīśāsaka-vinaya*
Mishasokubu [*wakei*] *gobun ritsu* 彌沙塞部[和醯]五分律: idem *Mishasebu* [*hexi*] *wufen lu*, q.v.
Mohebore boluomi jing 摩訶般若波羅蜜經 (*Makahannya haramitsu kyō*): 213, 252. Kumārajīva's Ch. trans. *Mahāprajñā-pāramitā-sūtra*
Mohebore boluomi damingzhou jing 摩訶般若波羅蜜大明咒經 (*Makahannya haramitsu daimyōju kyō*): 342. Kumārajīva's Ch. trans. *Prajñāpāramitā-sūtra*
Mohesengqi lü 摩訶僧祇律 (*Makasōgi ritsu*): 371. Ch. trans. *Mahāsāṅghika-vinaya*
Mohezhiguan 摩訶止觀 (*Makashikan*): quoted 63, 288
Muji myō kyō 無字妙經: 242; quoted, 48. *See also* Index to Translations and Modern Works
Mujintō ron 無盡燈論: abbr. title *Shūmon mujintō ron*, q.v.
Mukushō kyō 無稱經: see *Shuo Wugoucheng jing*

Mūlasarvāstivādin-vinaya: 159
Mumon oshō goroku 無門和尚語錄: idem *Wumen heshang yulu*, q.v.
Mumonkan 無門關: see *Chanzong wumenguan*
Muryōju kyō 無量壽經: idem *Wuliangshou jing*, q.v.
Myōgaku zenji goroku 明覺禪師語錄: idem *Mingjue chanshi yulu*, q.v.
Myōhō renge kyō 妙法蓮華經: idem *Miaofa lianhua jing*, q.v.
Myōhon zenji zatsuroku 明本禪師雜錄: see *Tianmu Mingben chanshi zalu*
Myōhōrenge-kyō gengi 妙法蓮華經玄義: idem *Miaofalianhua jing xuanyi*, q.v.
Myōri enjōkan 妙理圓成觀: idem *Miaoli yuanchengguan*, q.v.

Nanka no yume 南柯夢: idem *Nanke meng*, q.v.
Nankemeng 南柯夢 (*Nanka no yume*): 332
Nanshū tongyō saijō daijō makahannya haramitsu kyō: Rokuso Enō daishi Shōshū Daibon-ji ni oite sehō suru no dankyō 南宗頓教最上大乘摩訶般若波羅蜜經：六祖慧能大師於韶州大梵寺施法壇經: idem *Nanzong dunjiao zuishang dacheng mohebore boluomi jing: Liuzu Huineng dashi yu Shaozhou Dafansi shifa tanjing*, q.v.
Nanyang heshang dunjiao jietuo chanmen zhiliaoxing tanyu 南陽和上頓教解脱禪門直了性壇語 (*Nan'yō oshō tongyō gedatsu zemmon jikiryōshō dango*): 353–54
Nanyang heshang wenda zazheng yi 南陽和尚問答雜徵義 (*Nan'yō oshō mondō zatchō gi*): 351–52, 354
Nan'yō oshō mondō zatchō gi 南陽和尚問答雜徵義: idem *Nanyang heshang wenda zazheng yi*, q.v.
Nan'yō oshō tongyō gedatsu zemmon jikiryōshō dango 南陽和上頓教解脱禪門直了性壇語: idem *Nanyang heshang dunjiao jietuo chanmen zhiliaoxing tanyu*, q.v.
Nanzong dunjiao zuishang dacheng mohebore boluomi jing: Liuzu Huineng dashi yu Shaozhou Dafansi shifa tanjing 南宗頓教最上大乘摩訶般若波羅蜜經: 六祖慧能大師於韶州大梵寺施法壇經 (*Nanshū tongyō saijō daijō makahannya haramitsu kyō: Rokuso Enō daishi Shōshu Daibon-ji ni oite sehō suru no dankyō*): 204, 361; quoted, 207, Dunhuang text *Liuzu dashi fabao tanjing.*
Nehan gyō 涅槃經: see *Daboniepan jing*
"Nehan mumyō ron" 涅槃無名論: idem "Niepan wuming lun," q.v.
Nempyō sambyakusoku funō go 拈評三百則不能語: 178–79
Nenju shū 拈頌集: see *Sŏnmun yŏmsong chip*
Nenko 拈古: of Daitō Kokushi: 331, 347. See also *Niangu*

Nenko hyakusoku 沾古百則: idem *Niangu baize*, q.v.

Niangu 拈古 (*Nenko*): in *Jiatai pudeng lu*: 329; in *Xudeng lu*: 328; of Xuedou Chongxian: 341; of Hongzhi Zhengjue, see *Niangu baize*; of Yuanwu Keqin: 380. See also *Nenko*

Niangu baize 沾古百則 (*Nenko hyakusoku*): 154, 326. In *Hongzhi chanshi guanglu*

Niepan jing 涅槃經: abbr. title *Daboniepan jing*, q.v.

"Niepan wuming lun" 涅槃無名論 (Nehan mumyō ron): 254, 381–82. In *Zhaolun*

Ninden gammoku 人天眼目: idem *Rentian yanmu*, q.v.

Nirvana Sutra: see *Mahāparinirvāṇa-sūtra* and *Daboniepan jing*

"Nishu'nyū" 二種入: idem "Erzhongru," q.v.

"Nyūhokkai bon" 入法界品: idem "Rufajie pin," q.v.

Nyū Ryōga kyō 入楞伽經: idem *Ru Lengqie jing*, q.v.

Ōbaku Dansai zenji Enryō roku 黃檗斷際禪師宛陵錄: idem *Huangbo Duanji chanshi Wanling lu*, q.v.

"Poxiang lun" 破相論 (Hasō ron): 356. In *Shōshitsu rokumon*

Prajñāpāramitā-hṛdaya-sūtra; *Hṛdaya-sūtra*; *Heart Sutra*: 302, 341–42. For Kumārajīva's Ch. trans. see *Mohebore boluomi damingzhou jing*; for Xuanzang's Ch. trans. see *Bore boluomduo xinjing*

Pudeng lu 普燈錄: abbr. title *Jiatai pudeng lu*, q.v.

"Puti pin" 菩提品 (Bodai bon): quoted, 281–82. In *Dacheng zhuangyanjing lun*

"Putidamo lüebian dacheng rudao sixing" 菩提達磨略辨大乘入道四行 (Bodaidaruma ryakuben daijō nyūdō shigyō): 357. In *Jingde chuandeng lu*

Putidamo nanzong ding shifei lun 菩提達摩南宗定是非論 (*Bodaidaruma nanshū tei zehi ron*): 352–53; quoted, 173

The Pure Land Sutras: 155, 343–44

Puxian pusa xing pin 普賢菩薩行品 (*Fugen bosatsu gyō bon*): 305. See also *Avataṁsaka-sūtra* and *Gaṇḍavyūha-sūtra*

Puyao jing 普耀經 (*Fuyō kyō*): 227, 334; quoted 227. Dharmarakṣa's Ch. trans. *Lalitavistara*

Puying guoshi Huanzhu'an qinggui 普應國師幻住庵清規 (*Fuō kokushi Genjū-an shingi*); *Huanzhu'an qinggui* 幻住庵清規 (*Genjū-an shingi*): 137, 345

Rakudō ka 樂道歌: idem *Ledao ge*, q.v.
Rakuyō garan ki 洛陽伽藍記: idem *Luoyang qielan ji*, q.v.
Rakukei Kataku Jinne daishi no go 洛京荷澤神會大師語: idem *Luojing Heze Shenhui dashi yu*, q.v.
Rentian yanmu 人天眼目 (*Ninden gammoku*): 137, 277, 280, 323, 345
Rentō 聯燈: see *Zongmen liandeng huiyao*
Rentō eyō 聯燈會要: see *Zongmen liandeng huiyao*
Rinzai Eshō zenji goroku: 臨濟慧照禪師語錄: idem *Linji Huizhao chanshi yulu*, q.v.
Rinzai roku 臨濟錄: see *Zhenzhou Linji Huizhao chanshi yulu*
Rinzai shūshi 臨濟宗旨: idem *Linji zongzhi*, q.v.
"Rōhatsu jishū" 臘八示衆: 360. In *Goke sanshō yōro mon*
Rokuso daishi hōbō dankyō 六祖大師法寶壇經: idem *Liuzu dashi fabao tanjing*, q.v.
Rokuso dankyō 六祖壇經: see *Liuzu dashi fabao tanjing*
Rōshi 老子: idem *Laozi*, q.v.
"Rufajie pin" 入法界品 (Nyūhokkai bon): 290, 304, 305–306. In *Avataṁsaka-sūtra*. See also *Gaṇḍavyūha-sūtra*.
Ruizhou Dongshan Liangjie chanshi 瑞州洞山良价禪師 (*Zuishū Tōzan Ryōkai zenji*): 376. In *Wujia yulu*
Ruizhou Dongshan Liangjie chanshi yulu 瑞州洞山良价禪師語錄 (*Zuishū Tōzan Ryōkai zenji goroku*); *Dongshan yulu* 洞山語錄 (*Tōzan goroku*) (Yufeng Text): 416. Idem *Ruizhou Dongshan Liangjie chanshi*, in *Wujia yulu*
Ru Lengqie jing 入楞伽經 (*Nyū Ryōga kyō*): 336. Bodhiruci's Ch. trans. *Laṅkāvatāra-sūtra*
Ryōga abattara hō kyō 楞伽阿跋多羅寶經: idem *Lengqie abaduoluo bao jing*, q.v.
Ryōga kyō 楞伽經: see *Lengqie abaduoluo bao jing*
Ryōga shiji ki 楞伽師資記: idem *Lengqie shizi ji*, q.v.
Ryūhō goroku 龍寶語錄: abbr. title *Ryūhō kaisan tokushi Kōzen Daitō Kōshō Shōtō kokushi goroku*, q.v.
Ryūhō kaisan tokushi Kōzen Daitō Kōshō Shōtō kokushi goroku: 龍寶開山特賜興禪大燈高照正燈國師語錄; *Daitō kokushi goroku* 大燈國師語錄: *Daitō roku* 大燈錄; *Ryūhō goroku* 龍寶語錄: 210, 331, 333, 345–47
Ryūkō bukkyō hennen tsūron 隆興佛教編年通論: idem *Longxing fojiao biannian tonglun*, q.v.
Ryūkō butsuun tsūron 隆興佛運通論: see *Longxing fojiao biannian tonglun*

Ryūtaku kaiso Jinki Dokumyō zenji nempu 龍澤開祖神機獨妙禪師年譜: 197, 347

Saddharma-puṇḍarīka; *Lotus Sutra*: 272, 281, 301, 302, 348–50, 364. For Kumārajīva's Ch. trans. see *Miaofa lianhua jing*
Saishō-ō kyō 最勝王經: see *Jinguangming zuishengwang jing*
"Sambō yawa" 山房夜話: idem "Shanfang yehua," q.v.
Sandōkai 參同契: idem *Cantongqi*, q.v.
Sarvāstivāda-vinaya: 159. For Ch. trans. see *Shisong lü*
Śata-śāstra: for Ch. trans. see *Bailun*
Sekisō Soen zenji goroku 石霜楚圓禪師語錄: see *Ciming chanshi wuhui zhuchi yulu*
Setchō hyakusoku juko 雪竇百則頌古: idem *Xuedou baize songgu*, q.v.
Setchō Jūken goroku 雪竇重顯語錄: see *Mingjue chanshi yulu*
Setchō juko 雪竇頌古: see *Xuedou baize songgu*
Setchō roku 雪竇錄: see *Mingjue chanshi yulu*
Setsu Mukushō kyō 説無垢稱經: idem *Shuo Wugoucheng jing*, q.v.
"Shanfang yehua" 山房夜話 (Sambō yawa): 138; quoted 4–6
Shangtang 上堂 (*Jōdō*): of Fenyang Shanzhao; 319; of Dahui Zonggao: 312; of Yuanwu Keqin: 380. See also *Jōdō*
Shanhui dashi yulu 善慧大士語錄 (*Zenne daishi goroku*); *Fu dashi yulu* 傅大士語錄 (*Fu daishi goroku*): 237, 350; quoted, 44, 237–38
Shaozhou Yunmen Kuangzhen Wenyan chanshi 韶州雲門匡眞文偃禪師 (*Shōshū Ummon Kyōshin Bun'en zenji*): 376. In *Wujia yulu*
"Shashin bon" 捨身品: idem "Sheshen pin," q.v.
"Sheshen pin" 捨身品 (Shashin bon): 214–15
The Shenhui Sermons: 351–54
Shibun ritsu 四分律: idem *Sifen lü*, q.v.
Shidi jing 十地經: Ch. trans. *Daśabhūmika-sūtra*
"Shi'ershi ge" 十二時歌 (Jūniji ka): Zhaozhou's, 382; Yunmen's, 380
Shike goroku 四家語錄: idem *Sijia yulu*, q.v.
Shike roku 四家錄: see *Sijia yulu*
"Shimpōgin" 新豐吟: idem "Xinfengyin," q.v.
Shingyō 心經: see *Bore boluomiduo xinjing*
"Shingyō ju" 心經頌: idem "Xinjing song," q.v.
Shiniutu song 十牛圖頌 (*Jūgyūzu ju*): 385; quoted, 64, 289
Shinsan 眞贊: idem *Zhenzan*, q.v.
Shishuang Chuyuan chanshi yulu 石霜楚圓禪師語錄: alt. title *Ciming chan-*

shi wuhui zhuchi yulu, q.v.
Shisong lü 十誦律 (*Jūju ritsu*): 370. Ch. trans. *Sarvāstivāda-vinaya*
Shōbōgenzō 正法眼藏 (of Dahui Zonggao): idem *Zhengfayanzang*, q.v.
Shōbōgenzō 正法眼藏 (of Dōgen Kigen): 17, 178, 179, 354–55, 383; quoted, 17, 62, 286
Shōbōgenzō goshō 正法眼藏御抄: 355
Shōgongyō ron 荘嚴經論: see *Dacheng zhuangyanjing lun*
"Shohō monjin sammon goroku" 諸方門人參問語錄: idem "Zhufang menren canwen yulu," q.v.
Shōju Dōkyō Etan anju anroku 正受道鏡慧端庵主行錄: 193, 197, 355–56
Shōju rōjin shū 正受老人集: 193, 355, 356; quoted, 192. *See also* Index to Translations and Modern Works
*Shōjū san*正宗贊: *Wujia zhengzong zan*
"Shōjūmon" 正宗門: idem "Zhengzongmen," q.v.
Shōsan 小參: of Daiō Kokushi: 319. See also *Xiaocan*
Shōshitsu rokumon 小室六門; *Shōshitsu rokumon shū* 小室六門集: 207, 356–57
Shōshitsu rokumon shū 小室六門集: alt. title *Shōshitsu rokumon*, q.v.
Shōshū Ummon Kyōshin Bun'en zenji 韶州雲門匡眞文偃禪師: idem *Shaozhou Yunmen Kuangzhen Wenyan chanshi*, q.v.
Shōyō roku 從容錄: see *Wansong laoren pingchang Tiantong Jue heshang songgu Congrong'an lu*
Shūeki 周易: see *Yi jing*
"Shūhongi" 宗本義: idem "Zongbenyi," q.v.
*Shū Kegon ōshi mōjin gengen kan*修華嚴奧旨妄盡還源觀: idem *Xiu Huayan aozhi wangjin huanyuan guan*, q.v.
Shūmon kattō shū 宗門葛藤集; *Kattō shū* 葛藤集: 24, 357–58, 385; quoted, 39, 54, 223, 259–60
Shūmon mujintō ron 宗門無盡燈論; *Mujintō ron* 無盡燈論; *Tōron* 燈論: 196, 241, 358–59; quoted, 46, 241
Shūmon rentō eyō 宗門聯燈會要: idem *Zongmen liandeng huiyao*, q.v.
Shuo Wugoucheng jing 説無垢稱經 (*Setsu Mukushō kyō*); *Wugoucheng jing* 無垢稱經 (*Mukushō kyō*): 370. Xuanzang's Ch. trans. *Vimalakīrti-nirdeśa*
Sifen lü 四分律 (*Shibun ritsu*); Four-Section Vinaya: 159, 160, 371. Ch. trans. *Dharmagupta-vinaya*
Sijia lu 四家錄: abbr. title *Sijia yulu*, q.v.
Sijia yulu 四家語錄 (*Shike goroku*); *Mazu sijia lu* 馬祖四家錄 (*Baso shike*

roku); *Sijia lu* 四家錄 (*Shike roku*): 326, 359–60
The Sixth Patriarch's Platform Sutra: 360–63
Smaller Sukhāvatī: see *Sukhāvatī-vyūha* [*Smaller*]
Sōanka 草庵歌: idem *Cao'ange*, q.v.
Sodō shū 祖堂集: idem *Chodang chip*, q.v.
"Sōfuku goroku" 崇福語錄: 331, 346. In *Ryūhō kaisan tokushi Kōzen Daitō Kōshō Shōtō kokushi goroku*
Sogen tsūyō 祖源通要: idem *Zuyuan tongyao*, q.v.
Sōgo bon 宋吾本 (ed. of *Shōbōgenzō*): 355
Sōji 莊子: idem *Zhuangzi*, q.v.
"Sokkō roku hyōshō jōgo" 息耕錄評唱剩語: 363. In *Sokkō roku kaien fusetsu*
Sokkō roku kaien fusetsu 息耕錄開筵普說; *Kaien fusetsu* 開筵普說: 37, 42, 51–52, 363; quoted, 37–39, 42–43, 51–52
Songgu 頌古 (*Juko*): in *Jiatai puteng lu*: 329; in *Xudeng lu*: 328; of Fenyang Shanzhao: 320; of Xuedou Chongxian, see *Xuedou baize songgu*; of Hongzhi Zhengjue, see *Songgu baize*; of Yuanwu Keqin: 380. See also *Juko*
Songgu baize 頌古百則 (*Juko hyakusoku*): 154, 326, 371. In *Hongzhi chanshi guanglu*
Song of Zazen: idem *Zazen wasan*, q.v.
Sŏnmun yŏmsong chip 禪門拈頌集 (*Zemmon nenju shū*); *Yŏmsong chip* 拈頌集 (*Nenju shū*): 228, 363–64; quoted, 50, 228, 249
Sotei jion 祖庭事苑: idem *Zuting shiyuan*, q.v.
Sōtō nishi roku 曹洞二師錄: 317
Sōzan goroku 曹山語錄 (Gimoku Text): 315
Suichutang shumu 遂初堂書目 (*Suishodō shomoku*): 359
Suishodō shomoku 遂初堂書目: idem *Suichutang shumu*, q.v.
Sukhāvatī-vyūha [*Larger*]; *Larger Sukhāvatī*: 155–56, 343. For Ch. trans. see *Wuliangshou jing*
Idem [*Smaller*]; *Smaller Sukhāvatī*: 156, 343, For Ch. trans. see *Amituo jing*
Suvarṇa-prabhāsa-sūtra: 407–408. For Ch. trans. see *Jinguangming jing* and *Jinguangming zuishengwang jing*

Taiki 對機: idem *Duiji*, q.v.
Taishi zuiō hongi kyō 太子瑞應本起經: idem *Taizi ruiying benqi jing*, q.v.
Taizi ruiying benqi jing 太子瑞應本起經 (*Taishi zuiō hongi kyō*): 214
Tanjing 壇經: abbr. title *Liuzu dashi fabao tanjing*, q.v.
Tanshū Isan Reiyū zenji 潭州潙山靈祐禪師: idem *Tanzhou Guishan Lingyu chanshi*, q.v.

Tanzhou Guishan Lingyu chanshi 潭州潙山靈祐禪師 (*Tanshū Isan Reiyū zenji*): 375. In *Wujia yulu*
Temmoku Chūhō oshō kōroku 天目中峰和尚廣錄: idem *Tianmu Zhongfeng heshang guanglu*, q.v.
Temmoku Myōhon zenji zatsuroku 天目明本禪師雜錄: idem *Tianmu Mingben chanshi zalu*, q.v.
Tenshō kōtō roku 天聖廣燈錄: idem *Tiansheng guangdeng lu*, q.v.
Tianmu Mingben chanshi zalu 天目明本禪師雜錄 (*Temmoku Myōhon zenji zatsuroku*); *Mingben chanshi zalu* 明本禪師雜錄 (*Myōhon zenji zatsuroku*); *Zhongfeng zalu* 中峰雜錄 (*Chūhō zatsuroku*): 137, 365
Tianmu Zhongfeng heshang guanglu 天目中峰和尚廣錄. (*Temmoku Chūhō oshō kōroku*); *Zhongfeng heshang guanglu* 中峰和尚廣錄 (*Chūhō oshō kōroku*); *Zhongfeng guanglu* 中峰廣錄 (*Chūhō kōroku*): 4, 137, 138, 365–66; quoted, 4–6
Tiansheng guangdeng lu 天聖廣燈錄 (*Tenshō kōtō roku*); *Guangdeng lu* 廣燈錄 (*Kōtō roku*): 137, 327, 366, 372,373, 384, quoted, 229
"Tōjō goi henshō kuketsu" 洞上五位徧正口訣: 269, 333, 385; quoted, 57–64. In *Keisō dokuzui*
Tongo mushō hannya ju 頓悟無生般若頌: idem *Dunwu wusheng bore song*, q.v.
Tongo nyūdō yōmon ron 頓悟入道要門論: idem *Dunwu rudao yaomen lun*, q.v.
Tongo yōmon 頓悟要門: see *Dunwu rudao yaomen lun*
Tōron 燈論: abbr. title *Shūmon mujintō ron*, q.v.
Tosotsu Etsu zenji go 兜率悅禪師語: idem *Doushuai Yue chanshi yu*, q.v.
Tōzan daishi goroku 洞山大師語錄: abbr. title *Inshū Tōzan Gohon zenji goroku*, q.v.
Tōzan Gohon zenji goroku 洞山悟本禪師語錄; *Tōzan goroku* 洞山語錄 (Gimoku Text): 315–16
Tōzan goi no ju 洞山五位頌: idem *Dongshan wuwei song*, q.v.
Tōzan goi kenketsu 洞山五位顯訣: idem *Dongshan wuwei xianjue*, q.v.
Tōzan goroku 洞山語錄: abbr. title *Tōzan Gohon zenji goroku* (Gimoku Text), q.v.
Idem: abbr. title *Inshū Tōzan Gohon zenji goroku* (Shigetsu Text), q.v.
Idem: see *Ruizhou Dongshan Liangjie chanshi yulu* (Yufeng Text)
Tōzan goroku no yo 洞山語錄之餘: 316
Tripiṭaka: 231, 343; Korean: 310, 364; Song: 328, 349; Ming: 325, 377

Ummon kōroku 雲門廣錄: see *Yunmen Kuangzhen chanshi guanglu*
Ummon Kyōshin zenji kōroku 雲門匡眞禪師廣錄: idem *Yunmen Kuang-*

zhen chanshi guanglu, q.v.
Ummon oshō kōroku 雲門和尚廣錄: see *Yunmen Kuangzhen chanshi guanglu*
Ummon roku 雲門錄: see *Yunmen Kuangzhen chanshi guanglu*

Vajracchedikā: abbr. title *Vajracchedikā-prajñāpāramitā-sūtra*, q.v.
Vajracchedika-prajñāpdi'amitd-sūtra; *Vajracchedikā*; *Diamond Sutra*: 366–67. For Kumārajīva's Ch. trans. see *Jingang bore boluomi jing*
Verses on the Five Ranks: see *Dongshan wuwei song*
Vimalakīrti-nirdeśa: 368–69. For Ch. trans. see *Foshuo Weimo jie jing*; *Weimojie suoshuo jing*, and *Shuo Wugoucheng jing*
Vinaya-pitaka: 158, 370
The Vinaya Texts: 370–71

Wanling lu 宛陵錄: abbr. title *Huangbo Duanji chanshi Wanling lu*, q.v.
Wanshi kōroku 宏智廣錄: see *Hongzhi chanshi guanglu*
Wanshi roku 宏智錄: see *Hongzhi chanshi guanglu*
Wanshi zenji kōroku 宏智禪師廣錄: idem *Hongzhi chanshi guanglu*, q.v.
Wansong laoren pingchang Tiantong Jue heshang songgu Congrong'an lu 萬松老人評唱天童覺和尚頌古從容庵錄 (*Banshō rōjin hyōshō Tendō Kaku oshō juko Shōyō-an roku*); *Congrong lu* 從容錄 (*Shōyō roku*): 326, 371–72
Weimojie suoshuo jing 維摩詰所説經 (*Yuimakitsu shosetsu kyō*); Weimo jing 維摩經 (*Yuima kyō*): 252, 358, 369–70; quoted, 289, 358. Kumārajīva's Ch. trans. *Vimalakīrti-nirdeśa*
Weimo jing 維摩經: abbr. title *Weimojie suoshuo jing*, q.v.
Wreath Sutra: see *Avataṁsaka-sūtra*
"Wubuqian lun" 物不遷論 (Butsu fusen ron): 351. In *Zhaolun*
Wudeng huiyuan 五燈會元 (*Gotō egen*): *Huiyuan* 會元 (*Egen*): 330, 372–73
Wudeng lu 五燈錄 (*Gotō roku*): 329
Wudeng yantong 五燈嚴統 (*Gotō gentō*); *Yantong* 嚴統 (*Gentō*): 373–74; quoted, 183
Wudeng yantong jiehuo lun 五燈嚴統解惑論 (*Gotō gentō gewaku ron*): 374
Wufen lü 五分律: abbr. title *Mishasebu [hexi] wufen lu*, q.v.
Wugoucheng jing 無垢稱經: abbr. title *Shuo Wugoucheng jing*, q.v.
Wujia yulu 五家語錄 (*Goke goroku*); *Wuzong lu* 五宗錄 (*Goshū roku*): 315, 374–76
Wujia zhengzong zan 五家正宗贊 (*Goke shōjū san*); *Zhengzong zan* 正宗贊 (*Shōjū san*): 138–39, 376–77; quoted 138–39

Wuliangshou jing 無量壽經 (*Muryōju kyō*): 155–56, 343. Ch. trans. [*Larger*] *Sukhāvatī-vyūha*
Wumen heshang yulu 無門和尚語錄 (*Mumon oshō goroku*): 184
Wumenguan 無門關: abbr. title *Chanzong wumenguan*, q.v.
Wuwei xianjue 五位顯訣: abbr. title *Dongshan wuwei xianjue*, q.v.
Wuwei song 五位頌: abbr. title *Dongshan wuwei song*, q.v.
"Wuxing lun" 悟性論 (*Goshō ron*): 357. In *Shōshitsu rokumon*
Wuzong lu 五宗錄: alt. title *Wujia yulu*, q.v.
Wuzong yuanliutu 五宗源流圖 (*Goshū genryūzu*): 375. In *Wujia yulu*

Xianyu jing 賢愚經 (*Kengu kyō*): 214. Ch. trans. *Damamūka-sūtra*
Xiaocan 小參 (*shōsan*): of Fenyang Shanzhao: 319; of Yuanwu Keqin: 380. See also *Shōsan*
"Xinfengyin" 新豐吟 (Shimpōgin): 316. In *Inshū Tōzan Gohon zenji goroku* (Shigetsu Text)
Xinglu 行錄 (*Anroku*): of Linji Yixuan: 384; of Shishuang Chuyuan: 311
Xinjing 心經: abbr. title *Bore boluomiduo xinjing*, q.v.
"Xinjing song" 心經頌 (Shingyō ju): 356. In *Shōshitsu rokumon*
Xiu Huayan aozhi wangjin huanyuan guan 修華嚴奧旨妄盡還源觀 (*Shū Kegon ōshi mōjin gengen kan*): quoted, 164
"Xuanzhongming" 玄中銘 (Genchūmei): 316. In *Inshū Tōzan Gohon zenji goroku* (Shigetsu Text)
Xu chuandeng lu 續傳燈錄 (*Zoku dentō roku*): 377; quoted, 143, 154
Xudeng lu 續燈錄: abbr. title *Jianzhong Jingguo xudeng lu*, q.v.
Xuedou baize songgu 雪竇百則頌古 (*Setchō hyakusoku juko*); *Xuedou songgu* (*Setchō juko*); *Baize songgu* 百則頌古 (*Hyakusoku juko*): 11, 144, 320, 321, 377–78, 341, 377–78
Xuedou Chongxian yulu 雪竇重顯語錄: alt. title *Mingjue chanshi yulu*, q.v.
Xuedou lu 雪竇錄: alt. title *Mingjue chanshi yulu*, q.v.
Xuedou songgu 雪竇頌古: abbr. title *Xuedou baize songgu*, q.v.
"Xuemo lun" 血脈論 (Ketsumyaku ron): 357; quoted, 207. In *Shōshitsu rokumon*
Xu gaozeng zhuan 續高僧傳 (*Zoku kōsō den*): 357; quoted, 336
Xu guzunsu yuyao 續古尊宿語要: abbr. title *Xukai guzunsu yuyao*, q.v.
Xukai guzunsu yuyao 續開古尊宿語要 (*Zokkai kosonshuku goyō*); *Xukan guzunsu yuyao* 續刊古尊宿語要 (*Zokkan kosonshuku goyō*); *Xu guzunsu yuyao* 續古尊宿語要 (*Zoku kosonshuku goyō*): 239, 312, 324–25.
Xukan guzunsu yuyao 續刊古尊宿語要: alt. title *Xukai guzunsu yuyao*, q.v.

Xutang heshang yulu 虛堂和尚語錄 (*Kidō oshō goroku*); *Xutang lu* 虛堂錄 (*Kidō roku*): 186, 363, 378–79; quoted, 186
Xutang lu 虛堂錄: abbr. title *Xutang heshang yulu*, q.v.
Xutang lu: daibie 虛堂錄代別 (*Kidō roku: daibetsu*): 24, 186, 378, 379, 385. In *Xutang heshang yulu*

Yantong 嚴統: abbr. title *Wudeng yantong*, q.v.
Yasen kanna 夜船閑話: 193. *See also* Index to Translations and Modern Works
Yi jing 易經 (*Eki kyō*); Book of Changes; also known as Zhouyi 周易 (*Shūeki*): 34, 193, 307, 379; quoted, 222
Yŏmsong chip 拈頌集: abbr. title *Sŏnmun yŏmsong chip*, q.v.
Yuanzhou Yangshan Huiji chanshi 袁州仰山慧寂禪師 (*Enshū Kyōzan Ejaku zenji*): 375–76. In *Wujia yulu*
Yuanwu Foguo chanshi yulu 圜悟佛果禪師語錄 (*Engo Bukka zenji goroku*); *Yuanwu yulu* 圜悟語錄 (*Engo goroku*); *Yuanwu lu* 圜悟錄 (*Engo roku*): 147, 322, 379–80
Yuanwu lu 圜悟錄: abbr. title *Yuanwu Foguo chanshi yulu*, q.v.
Yuanwu xinyao 圜悟心要: abbr. title *Foguo Yuanwu Zhenjue chanshi xinyao*, q.v.
Yuanwu yulu 圜悟語錄: abbr. title *Yuanwu Foguo chanshi yulu*, q.v.
Yuima kyō 維摩經: see *Weimojie suoshuo jing*
Yuimagyō gisho 維摩經義疏: 370
Yuimakitsu shosetsu kyō 維摩詰所說經: idem *Weimojie suoshuo jing*, q.v.
Yunmen heshang guanglu 雲門和尚廣錄: abbr. title *Yunmen Kuangzhen chanshi guanglu*, q.v.
Yunmen guanglu 雲門廣錄: abbr. title *Yunmen Kuangzhen chanshi guanglu*, q.v.
Yunmen Kuangzhen chanshi guanglu 雲門匡眞禪師廣錄 (*Ummon Kyōshin zenji kōroku*); *Yunmen heshang guanglu* 雲門和尚廣錄 (*Ummon oshō kōroku*); *Yunmen guanglu* 雲門廣錄 (*Ummon kōroku*); *Yunmen lu* 雲門錄 (*Ummon roku*): 145, 147, 377, 378, 380–81; quoted, 47, 241, 285
Yunmen lu 雲門錄: abbr. title *Yunmen Kuangzhen chanshi guanglu*, q.v.
Yunzhou Huangboshan Duanji chanshi chuanxin fayao 筠州黃蘗山斷際禪師傳心法要 (*Inshū Ōbakuzan Dansai zenji denshin hōyō*): 360. In *Sijia yulu*

Zazen gi 坐禪儀: idem *Zuochan yi*, q.v.
Zazen wasan 坐禪和讚; *Song of Zazen*: 40, 226, 241; quoted, 40, 48, 226–27
Zemmon nenju shū 禪門拈頌集: idem *Sŏnmun yŏmsong chip*, q.v.

Zenkai ichiran 禪海一瀾: 201. *See also* INDEX TO TRANSLATIONS AND MODERN WORKS

Zenkan sakushin 禪關策進: idem *Changuan ceqin*, q.v.

Zenne daishi goroku 善慧大士語錄: idem *Shanhui dashi yulu*, q.v.

A Zen Phrase Anthology: idem *Zenrin kushū*, q.v.

Zenrin kushū 禪林句集; *A Zen Phrase Anthology*: xiv, xx, 25, 71–73, 385; quoted, 73–107

Zenrin sōbō den 禪林僧寶傳: idem *Chanlin sengbao zhuan*, q.v.

Zenshū mumonkan 禪宗無門關: idem *Chanzong wumenguan*, q.v.

Zhaolun 肇論 (Jōron) 253, 271, 381–82

Zhaozhou heshang yulu 趙州和尚語錄 (*Jōshū oshō goroku*): 382–83. Also, abbr. title *Zhaozhou Zhenji chanshi yulu*, q.v.

Zhaozhou lu 趙州錄: abbr. title *Zhaozhou Zhenji chanshi yulu*, q.v.

"Zhaozhou Zhenji chanshi xingzhuang" 趙州眞際禪師行狀 (Jōshū Shinsai zenji gyōjō): 382. In *Zhaozhou Zhenji chanshi yulu*

Zhaozhou Zhenji chanshi yulu 趙州眞際禪師語錄 (*Jōshū Shinsai zenji goroku*); *Zhaozhou zushi yulu* 趙州祖師語錄 (*Jōshū soshi goroku*); *Zhaozhou heshang yulu* 趙州和尚語錄 (*Jōshū oshō goroku*); *Zhaozhou lu* 趙州錄 (*Jōshū roku*): 225, 382–83. In *Kuzun-su yulu*

Zhaozhou zushi yulu 趙州祖師語錄: alt. title *Zhaozhou Zhenji chanshi yulu*, q.v.

Zhengfayanzang 正法眼藏 (*Shōbōgenzō*), by Dahui Zonggao 大慧宗杲: 148, 149, 383

"Zhengzongmen" 正宗門 (Shōjūmon): 328. In *Xudeng lu*

Zhengzong zan 正宗贊: abbr. title *Wujia chengzong zan*, q.v.

Zhenzhou Linji Huizhao chanshi yulu 鎮州臨濟慧照禪師語錄 (*Chinjū Rinzai Eshō zenji goroku*); *Linji lu* 臨濟錄 (*Rinzai roku*): 24, 43, 141, 142, 311, 324, 325, 366, 383–84, 385; quoted, 43, 48, 64, 140–41, 142, 231, 242, 283, 289

Zhenzhou Linji Yixuan chanshi 鎮州臨濟義玄禪師 (*Chinjū Rinzai Gigen zenji*): 375. In *Wujia yulu*

Zhongfeng guanglu 中峰廣錄: abbr. title *Tianmu Zhongfeng heshang guanglu*, q.v.

Zhongfeng heshang guanglu 中峰和尚廣錄: abbr. title *Tianmu Zhongfeng heshang guanglu*, q.v.

Zhongfeng zalu 中峰雜錄: alt. title *Tianmu Mingben chanshi zalu*, q.v.

Zhouyi 周易 (*Shūeki*): alt. title *Yi jing*, q.v.

Zhuangzi 莊子 (Sōji): 34, 252

Zhuangyanjing lun 莊嚴經論: abbr. title *Dazheng zhuangyanjing lun*, q.v.
"Zhufang menren canwen yulu" 諸方門人參問語錄 (Shohō monjin sammon goroku); 318. In *Dunwu rudao yaomen lun*
Zhu Weimojie jing 注維摩詰經 (*Chū Yuimakitsu kyō*): 252, 253
Zokkai kosonshuku goyō 續開古尊宿語要: idem *Xukai guzunsu yuyao*, q.v.
Zokkan kosonshuku goyō 續刊古尊宿語要: see *Xukai guzunsu yuyao*
Zoku dentō roku 續傳燈錄: idem *Xu chuandeng lu*, q.v.
Zoku kōsō den 續高僧傳: idem *Xu gaoseng zhuan*, q.v.
Zoku kosonshuku goyō 續古尊宿語要: see *Xukai guzunsu yuyao*
Zokutō roku 續燈錄: see *Jianzhong Jingguo xudeng lu*
"Zongbenyi" 宗本義 (Shūhongi): 381. In *Zhaolun*
Zongmen liandeng huiyao 宗門聯燈會要 (*Shūmon rentō eyō*); *Liandeng huiyao* 聯燈會要 (*Rentō eyō*); *Liandeng* 聯燈 (*Rentō*): 329, 372, 384–85; quoted, 229, 256
Zudokko 塗毒鼓: 333, 357, 358, 379, 385. *See also* Index to Translations and Modern Works
Zudokko (*Zokuhen*) 塗毒鼓 (續篇): 72, 385. *See also* Index to Translations and Modern Works
Zuishengwang jing 最勝王經 (*Saishō-ō kyō*): 408. Ch. trans. *Suvarṇaprabhāsa-sūtra*
*Zuishengwang jing*最勝王經: abbr. title *Jinguangming zuishengwang jing*, q.v.
Zuishū Tōzan Ryōkai zenji 瑞州洞山良价禪師: idem *Ruizhou Dongshan Liangjie chanshi*, q.v.
Zuishū Tōzan Ryōkai zenji goroku 瑞州洞山良价禪師語錄: idem *Ruizhou Dongshan Liangjie chanshi yulu*, q.v.
Zuochan yi 坐禪儀 (*Zazen gi*): 385. In *Zudokko* (*Zokuhen*)
Zuting shiyuan 祖庭事苑 (*Sotei jion*): 206; quoted, 206
Zuyuan tongyao 祖源通要 (*Sogen tsūyō*): 330

Appendices

GANSU
INNER MONGOLIA
Dunhuang
Hohhot
Wutaishan
SHANXI
Taiyuan
Yinchuan
Guzang
Qinghai lake
Xining
NINGXIA
SHAANXI
Xizhou
Fenzhou
QINGHAI
Lanzhou
Luoyang
Wulao
Songshan
Longmen
Ruzhou
Xian
Chang'an
Wannian
Zhongnanshan
HENAN
Nanyang
Dengzhou
Suizhou
HUBEI
Pengzhou
Mianzhou
Chengdu
Suizhou
CHONGQING
Dangyangshan
Jiangling
Dongtinghu
Lizhou
Jiashan
Yueshan
Langzhou
Deshan
Guishan
SICHUAN
INDIA
Changsha
Nanyue (Hengshan)
HUNAN
Hengyang
Guiyang
GUIZHOU
Yunmenshan
Kunming
GUANGXI
YUNNAN
Duanzhou
Nanning
Xinzhou
VIETNAM
MYANMAR
LAOS
Haikou
HAINAN

LIAONING
HEBEI
Beijing
Tianjin
BOHAI
NORTH KOREA
SEA OF JAPAN
SOUTH KOREA
Zhenzhou
Zhaozhou
Jinan
Weifu
SHANDONG
YELLOW SEA
JAPAN
Caozhou
Nanhua
Kaifeng
JIANGSU
ANHUI
Nanjing
Yangzhou
Jingkou
Hefei
Taihu
Suzhou
Shanghai
Niutoushan
Xuancheng
Jingshan
Huzhou
Jiaxing
Chizhou
Tianmushan
Xihu
EAST CHINA SEA
Shuzhou
Yuezhou
Mingzhou
Lin'an (Hangzhou)
Ayuwangshan
Qizhou
Lushan
Simingxiangshan
Tiantaishan
Songshan
Poyanghu
Wuzhou
Nanchang
ZHEJIANG
Hongzhou
Caoshan
Yangshan
Qingyuanshan
Qianzhou
Jizhou
Xuefeng
Gushan
JIANGXI
Fuzhou
FUJIAN
Huangboshan
Qianzhou
Dayuling
Quanzhou
Lechang
Shaozhou
Caoxi
Meiyang
TAIWAN
ZEN SITES IN CHINA
GUANGDONG
Guangzhou
HONG KONG
0
500 miles
SOUTH CHINA SEA
0
500 km
PHILIPPINE SEA
© Quirin Press 2015

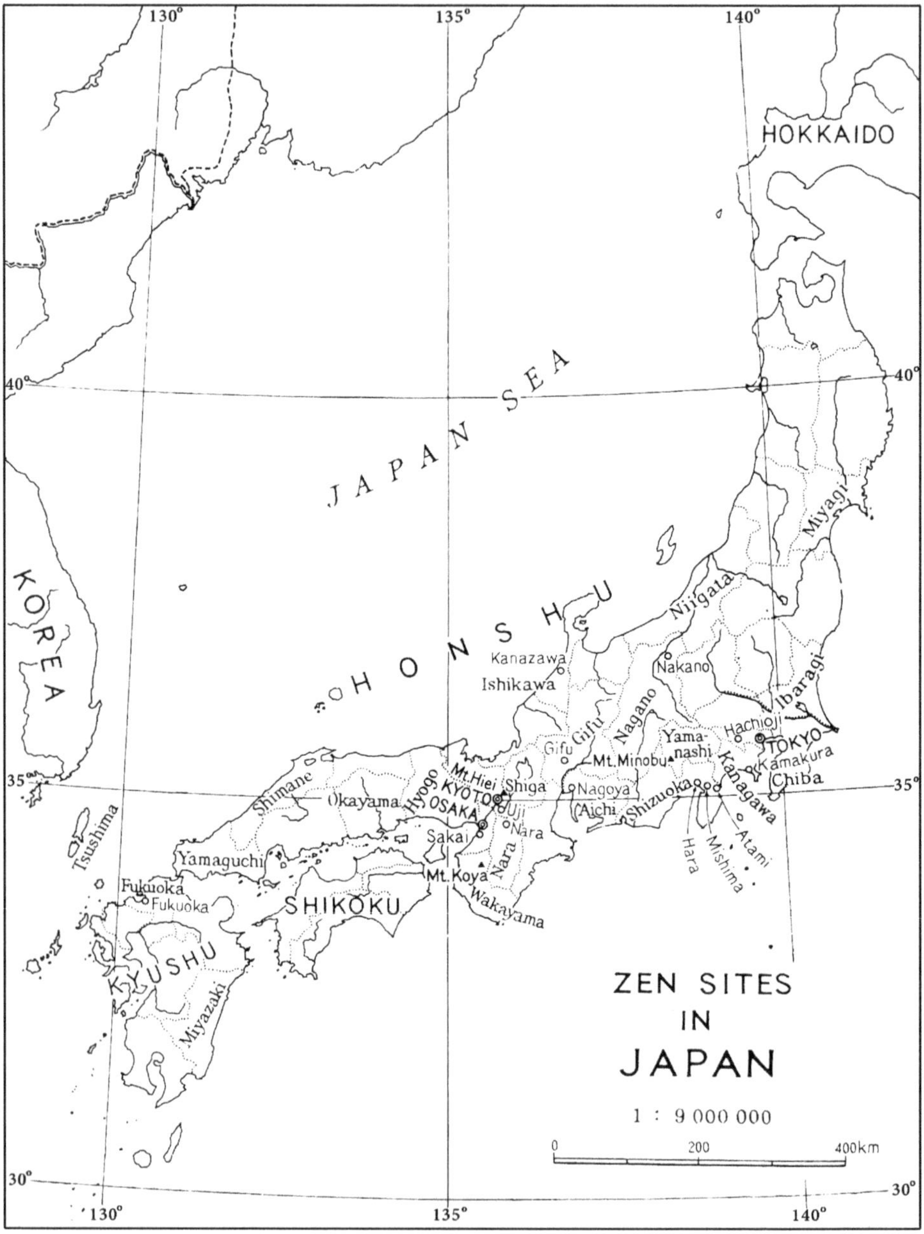

ZEN SITES
IN
JAPAN
1 : 9 000 000
0
200
400km
130°
135°
140°
40°
35°
30°
HOKKAIDO
JAPAN SEA
KOREA
HONSHU
SHIKOKU
KYUSHU
Tsushima
Miyagi
Niigata
Kanazawa
Ishikawa
Nakano
Nagano
Ibaragi
Hachioji
TOKYO
Kamakura
Chiba
Kanagawa
Yama-
nashi
Mt. Minobu
Gifu
Nagoya
Aichi
Shizuoka
Atami
Mishima
Hara
Shimane
Okayama
Hyogo
Mt. Hiei
KYOTO
Shiga
OSAKA
Uji
Nara
Sakai
Mt. Koya
Wakayama
Yamaguchi
Fukuoka
Miyazaki

Table of Chinese Dynasties

Former (Qian) Han 前漢 (Zen Kan)		206 BCE–25 CE
Later (Hou) Han 後漢 (Go Kan)		25–220
Wèi 魏 (Gi)		220–265
Wu 呉 (Go)	222–280	
Western (Xi) Jin 西晉 (Sei Shin)		265–316
Earlier (Qian) Liang 前涼 (Zen Ryō)	313–376	
Eastern (Dong) Jin 東晉 (Tō Shin)		317–420
Later (Hou) Zhao 後趙 (Go Chō)	319–352	
Earlier (Qian) Qin 前秦 (Zen Shin)	351–394	
Later (Hou) Qin 後秦 (Go Shin)	384–417	
Northern (Bei) Liang 北涼 (Hoku Ryō)	397–439	
Northern (Bei) Wèi 北魏 (Hoku Gi)	386–534	
Liu Song 劉宋 (Ryō Sō)		420–479
Qi 齊 (Sei)		479–502
Liang 梁 (Ryō)		502–557
Western (Xi) Wèi 西魏 (Sei Gi)	535–556	
Chen 陳 (Chin)		557–589
Northern (Bei) Zhou 北周 (Hoku Shū)	557–581	
Sui 隋 (Zui)		581–618
Tang 唐 (Tō)		618–907
Five Dynasties (Wudai) 五代 (Godai)		907–960
Northern (Bei) Song 北宋 (Hoku Sō)		960–1127
Southern (Nan) Song 南宋 (Nan Sō)		1127–1279
Yuan 元 (Gen)		1260–1368
Ming 明 (Min)		1368–1644
Qing 清 (Shin)		1644–1912

Table of Japanese Eras

Nara 奈良	710–794
Heian 平安	794–1192
Kamakura 鎌倉	1185–1333
Nambokuchō 南北朝	1332–1392
Muromachi 室町 (Ashikaga 足利)	1338–1573
Momoyama 桃山	1573–1603
Edo 江戸 (Tokugawa 徳川)	1603–1867
Meiji 明治	1868–1912
Taishō 大正	1912–1926
Shōwa 昭和	1926–

Genealogical Charts of Zen Lines

CHART I

Early Chinese Lines: Niutou 牛頭 (Gozu), Beizong 北宗 (Hokushū), Nanzong 南宗 (Nanshū), and Heze 荷澤 (Kataku).

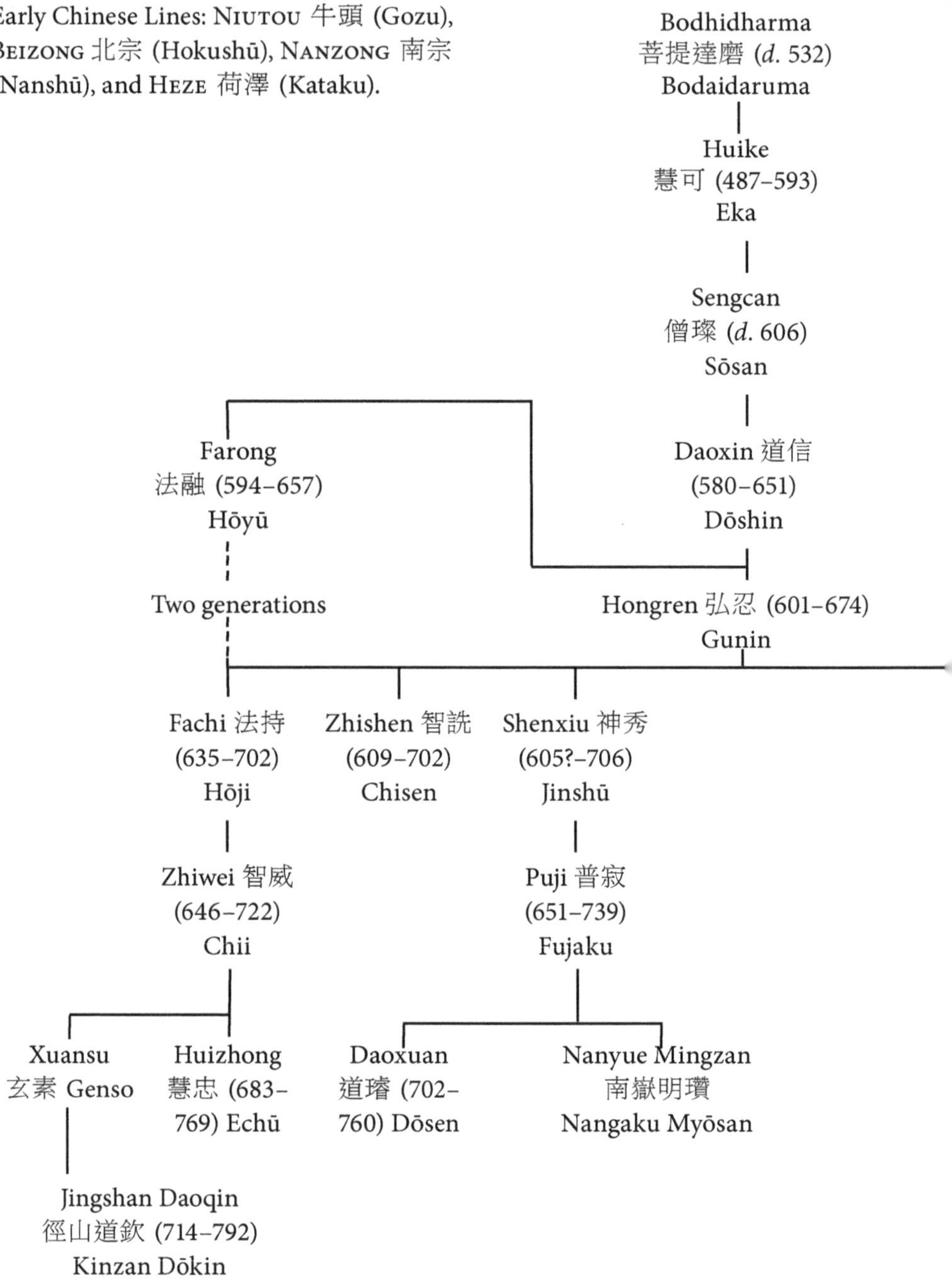

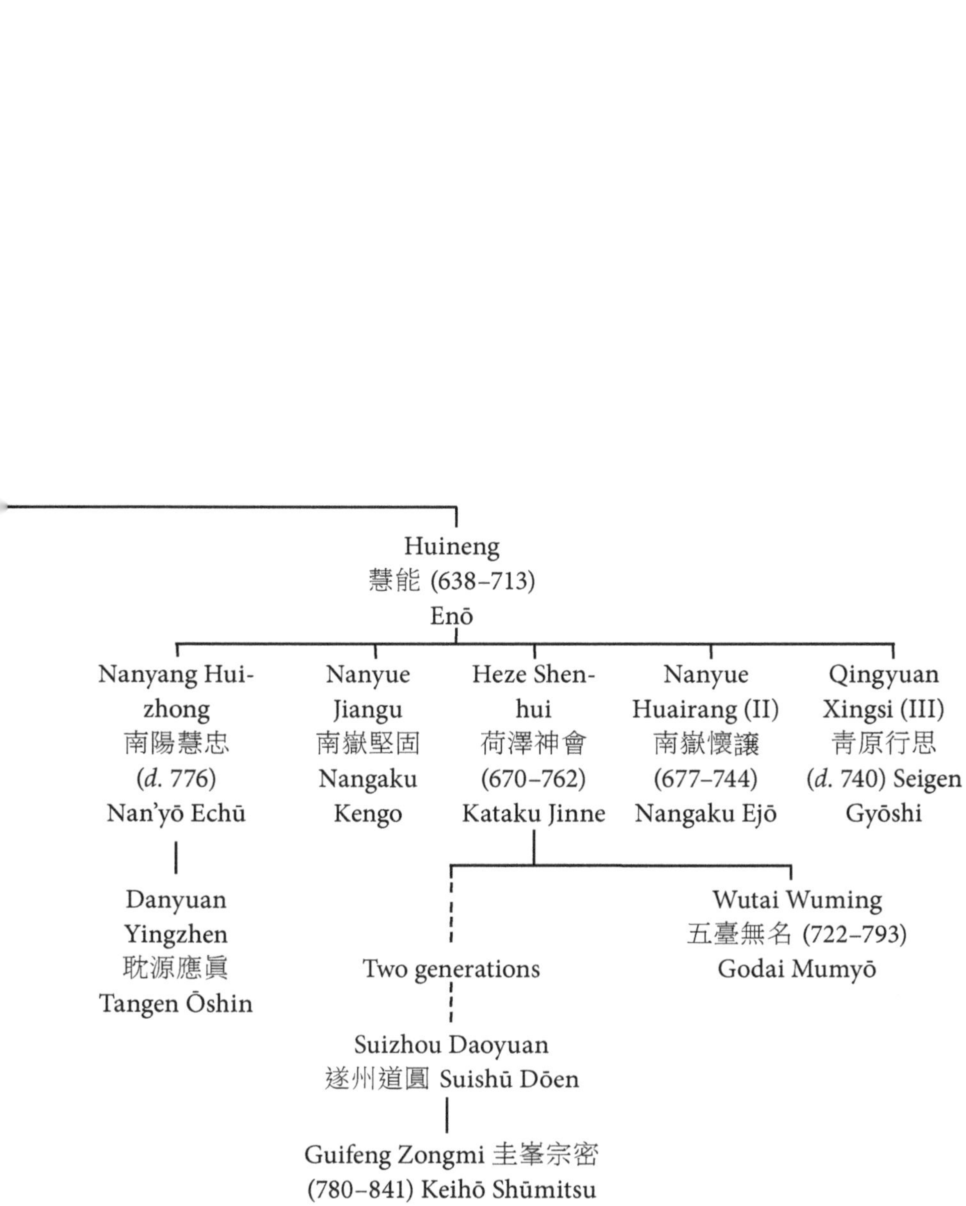
Huineng
慧能 (638–713)
Enō
Nanyang Hui-
zhong
南陽慧忠
(*d.* 776)
Nan'yō Echū
Nanyue
Jiangu
南嶽堅固
Nangaku
Kengo
Heze Shen-
hui
荷澤神會
(670–762)
Kataku Jinne
Nanyue
Huairang (II)
南嶽懷讓
(677–744)
Nangaku Ejō
Qingyuan
Xingsi (III)
青原行思
(*d.* 740) Seigen
Gyōshi
Danyuan
Yingzhen
耽源應眞
Tangen Ōshin
Two generations
Wutai Wuming
五臺無名 (722–793)
Godai Mumyō
Suizhou Daoyuan
遂州道圓 Suishū Dōen
Guifeng Zongmi 圭峯宗密
(780–841) Keihō Shūmitsu

CHART II

NANYUE 南嶽 (Nangaku)
and GUIYANG 潙仰 (Igyō) lines.

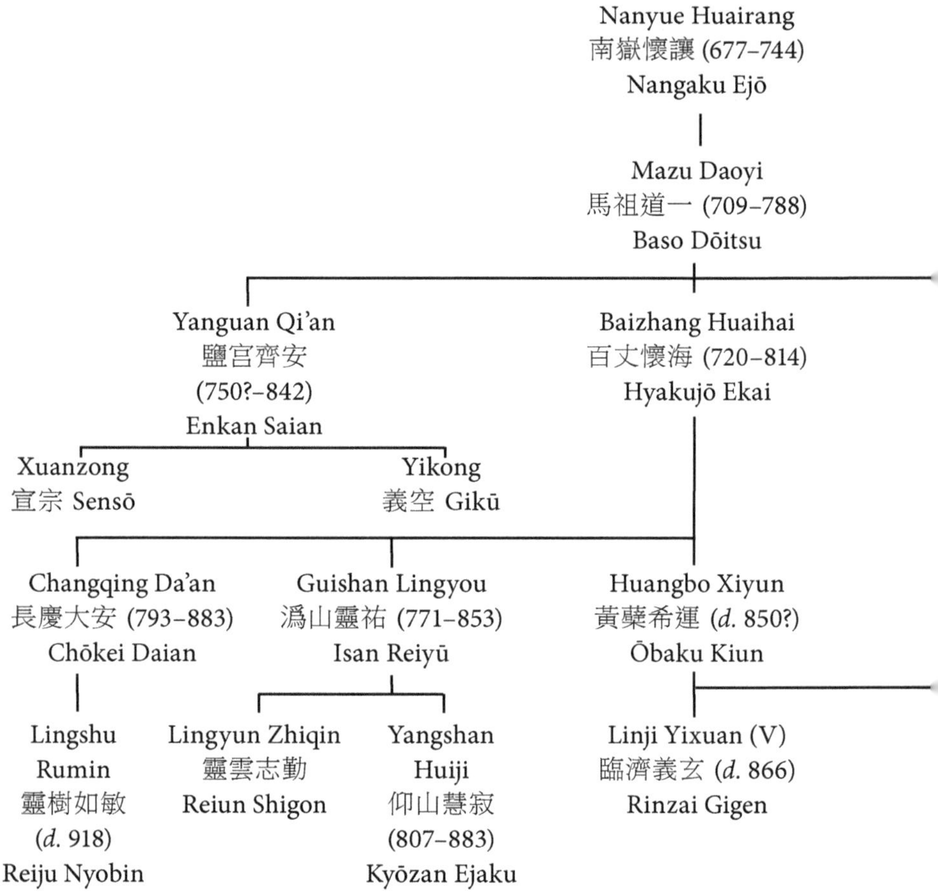

- Guizong Zhichang 歸宗智常 Kisū Chijō
  - Gao'an Dayu 高安大愚 Kōan Daigu
- Wuxie Lingmo 五洩靈默 (747–818) Gosetsu Reimoku
- Nanquan Puyuan 南泉普願 (748–835) Nansen Fugan
  - Changsha Jingcen 長沙景岑 Chōsha Keijin
    - Xuedou Changtong 雪竇常通 Setchō Jōtsū
    - Jinhua Yanling 金華嚴靈 Kinka Genrei
  - Zhaozhou Congshen 趙州從諗 (778–897) Jōshū Jūshin
  - Lu Geng 陸亘 (764–834) Riku Kō

- Chen Zunsu 陳尊宿 (780?–877?) Chin Sonshuku

CHART III

Qingyuan 青原 (Seigen) and Caodong 曹洞 (Sōtō) Lines.

Qingyuan Xingsi 青原行思 (*d.* 740) Seigen Gyōshi

Shitou Xiqian 石頭希遷 (700–790) Sekitō Kisen

Yueshan Weiyan 藥山惟儼 (745–828) Yakusan Igen

Chuanzi Decheng 船子德誠 Sensu Tokujō

Jiashan Shanhui 夾山善會 (805–881) Kassan Zenne

Daowu Yuanzhi 道吾圓智 (769–835) Dōgo Enchi

Shishuang Qingzhu 石霜慶諸 (807–888) Sekisō Keisho

Yunyan Tansheng 雲嚴曇晟 (780?–841) Ungan Donjō

Dongshan Liangjie 洞山良价 (807–869) Tōzan Ryōkai

Caoshan Benji 曹山本寂 (840–901) Sōzan Honjaku

Huixia 慧霞 Eka

Guanghui 廣輝 Kōki

Danxia Zichun 丹霞子淳 (*d.* 1119) Tanka Shijun

Hongzhi Zhengjue 宏智正覺 (1091–1157) Wanshi Shōgaku

Wen'an Sizong 聞庵嗣宗 Mon'an Shishū

Zide Huihui 自得慧暉 Jitoku Eki

Three generations

Dongming Huiri 東明惠日 (1272–1340) Tōmei E'nichi

Yunwai Yunxiu 雲外雲岫 Ungai Unshū

Dongling Yongyu 東陵永璵 (*d.* 1365) Tōryō Eiyo

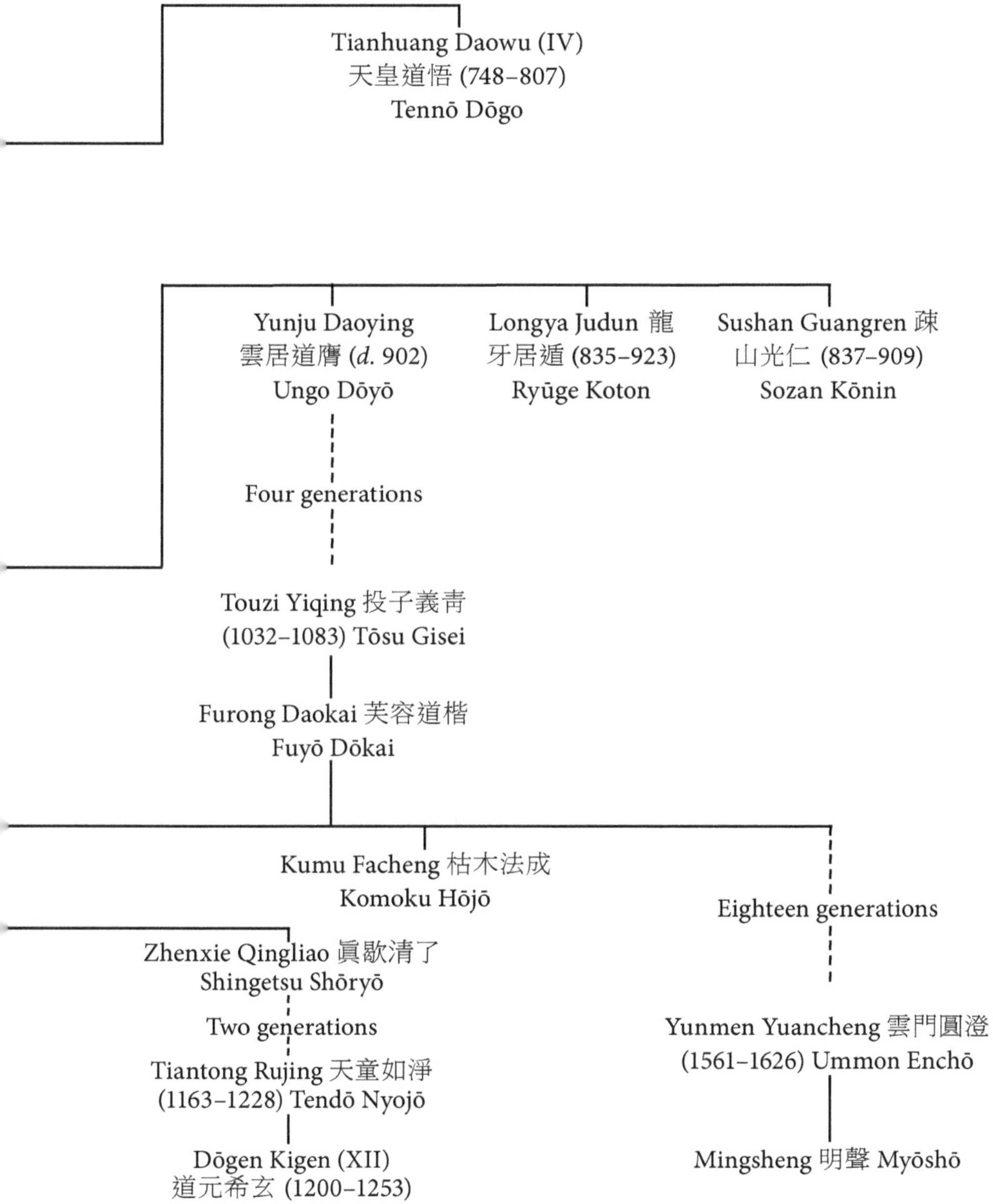
Tianhuang Daowu (IV)
天皇道悟 (748–807)
Tennō Dōgo
Yunju Daoying
雲居道膺 (*d.* 902)
Ungo Dōyō
Longya Judun 龍
牙居遁 (835–923)
Ryūge Koton
Sushan Guangren 疎
山光仁 (837–909)
Sozan Kōnin
Four generations
Touzi Yiqing 投子義青
(1032–1083) Tōsu Gisei
Furong Daokai 芙容道楷
Fuyō Dōkai
Kumu Facheng 枯木法成
Komoku Hōjō
Eighteen generations
Zhenxie Qingliao 眞歇清了
Shingetsu Shōryō
Two generations
Tiantong Rujing 天童如淨
(1163–1228) Tendō Nyojō
Dōgen Kigen (XII)
道元希玄 (1200–1253)
Yunmen Yuancheng 雲門圓澄
(1561–1626) Ummon Enchō
Mingsheng 明聲 Myōshō

CHART IV

Tianhuang 天皇 (Tennō),
Yunmen 雲門 (Ummon), and
Fayan 法眼 (Hōgen) Lines.

Xiantan Ziguo
咸潭資國
Kantan Shikoku

Yantou Quanhuo
巖頭全奯 (828–887)
Gantō Zenkatsu

Baizhao Zhiyuan
白兆志圓
Hakuchō Shien

Luoshan Daoxian
羅山道閑
Rasan Dōkan

Gushan Shenyan
鼓山神晏 (863–939)
Kuzan Jin'an

Cuiyan Lingcan
翠嵌令參
Suigan Reisan

Dalong Zhihong
大龍智洪
Dairyō Chikō

Xuansha Shibei
玄沙師備 (835–908)
Gensha Shibi

Deshan Yuanmi
德山緣密
Tokusan Emmitsu

Luohan Guichen
羅漢桂琛 (867–928)
Rakan Keijin

Two generations

Fayan Wenyi
法眼文益 (885–958)
Hōgen Bun'eki

Qisong
契嵩 (1007–1072)
Kaisū

Baizhang Daoheng
百丈道恆
Hyakujō Dōkō

Tiantai Deshao
天台德韶 (891–972)
Tendai Tokushō

Chengshi
澄諟 Chōshoku

Yongming Yanshou
永明延壽 (904–975)
Yōmyō Enju

- Tianhuang Daowu 天皇道悟 (748–807) Tennō Dōgo
  - Longtan Chongxin 龍潭崇信 Ryōtan Sūshin
    - Deshan Xuanjian 德山宣鑑 (780/2–865) Tokusan Senkan
      - Xuefeng Yicun 雪峰義存 (822–908) Seppō Gison
        - Yunmen Wenyan 雲門文偃 (862/4–949) Ummon Bun'en
          - Xianglin Chengyuan 香林澄遠 Kyōrin Chōon
            - Zhimen Guangzuo 智門光祚 (*d.* 1031) Chimon Kōso
              - Xuedou Chongxian 雪竇重顯 (980–1052) Setchō Jūken
                - Tianyi Yihuai 天衣義懷 Tenne Gikai
                  - Huilin Zongben 慧林宗本 Erin Sōhon
                    - Three generations
                      - Lei'an Zhengshou 雷庵正受 (1146–1208) Raian Shōju
                  - Yuantong Faxiu 圓通法秀 Enzū Hōshū
                    - Foguo Weibai 佛國惟白 Bukkoku Ibyaku
                - Wei Gaizhu 惟蓋竺 I Gaijiku
          - Shoujian 守堅 Shuken
          - Baling Haojian 巴陵顥鑑 Haryō Kōkan
        - Changqing Huileng 長慶慧稜 (854–932) Chōkei Eryō
        - Baofu Congzhan 保福從展 (*d.* 928) Hofuku Jūten
          - Wendeng 文僜 Buntō
            - Jing 靜 Sei *or* Jō
            - Yūn 筠 In

CHART V

LINJI 臨濟 (RINZAI) Line.

Yuyin Yuncong
谷隱蘊聰 (965–1032)
Yokuin Unsō

Li Zunxu
李遵勗 (*d.* 1038)
Ri Junkyoku

Jinshan Tanying
金山曇穎 (985–1060)
Kinzan Don'ei

Xiyu Gongchen 西余拱辰
Seiyo Kōshin

Qingsu
清素 (侍者)
Shōso (Jisha)

Linji Yixuan
臨濟義玄 (d. 866)
Rinzai Gigen

Xinghua Cunjiang
興化存獎 (830–888)
Kōke Zenshō

Sansheng Huiran
三聖慧然
Sanshō Enen

Nanyuan Huiyong
南院慧顒 (*d*. 930)
Nan'in Egyō

Fengxue Yanzhao
風穴延沼 (896–973)
Fuketsu Enshō

Shoushan Shengnian
首山省念 (926–993)
Shuzan Shōnen

Fenyang Shanzhao
汾陽善昭 (947–1024)
Fun'yo Zenshō

Shexian Guisheng
葉縣歸省
Shōken Kisei

Shishuang Chuyuan
石霜楚圓 (986–1039)
Sekisō Soen

Yuanjian Fayuan
圓鑑法遠 (991–1067)
Enkan Hōen

Yangqi Fanghui (VII)
楊岐方會 (992–1049)
Yōgi Hōe

Huanglong Huinan (VI)
黃龍慧南 (1002–1069)
Ōryō E'nan

CHART VI

HUANGLONG 黃龍 (Ōryō)
Line of Linji Sect.

- Huanglong Huinan 黃龍慧南 (1002–1069) Ōryō E'nan
  - Huitang Zuxin 晦堂祖心 Maidō Soshin
    - Five generations
      - Xuan Huaichang 虛庵懷敞 Kian Eshō
        - Myōan Eisai 明菴榮西 (1141–1215)
          - Ryōnen Myōzen 了然明全 (1184–1225)
          - Gyōyū 行勇 (1163–1241)
  - Yunkai Shouzhi 雲蓋守智 (1025–1115) Ungai Shuchi

Baofeng Kewen
賓峯克文 (1025–1102)
Hōbō Kokumon

Juefan Huihong
覺範慧洪
(1071–1128)
Kakuhan Ekō

Doushuai Congyue
兜率從悦
(1044–1091)
Tosotsu Jūetsu

Zhantang Wenjun
湛堂文準
(1061–1115)
Tandō Bunjun

CHART VII

YANGQI 楊岐 (Yōgi) Line of Linji Sect,
including the Japanese Shinchi 心地 Line

Foyan Qingyuan
佛眼清遠 (1067–1120)
Butsugen Seion

Zhu'an Shigui
竹庵士珪 (1083–1146)
Chikuan Shikei

Sengting Shouze
僧挺守賾 Sōtei Shusaku

Dasui Yuanjing
大隋元靜 (*d.* 1135)
Daizui Genjō

Kuo'an Shiyuan
廓庵師遠
Kakuan Shion

Kaifu Daoning
開福道寧
Kaifuku Dōnei

Yue'an Shanguo
月庵善果
Gettan Zenka

Laona Zudeng
老衲祖燈 Rōnō Sotō

Yuelin Shiguan
月林師觀 (1143–1217)
Gatsurin Shikan

Gufeng Dexiu
孤峯德秀
Kohō Tokushu

Huanshan Zhining
皖山止凝
Kanzan Shigyō

Deyi 德異
(*b.* 1231) Tokui

Wumen Huikai
無門慧開 (1183–1260)
Mumon Ekai

Pujing
普敬
Fukei

ZHENG Qingzhi 鄭清之
(*d.* 1251) TEI Seishi. (*or*
Anwan 安晚 Amban)

Yangqi Fanghui
楊岐方會 (992–1049)
Yōgi Hōe

Baiyun Shouduan
白雲守端 (1025–1072)
Hakuun Shutan

Wuzu Fayan
五祖法演 (1024?–1104)
Goso Hōen

Hongfu Ziwen
洪福子文
Kōfuku Shimon

Yuanwu Keqin (VIII)
圜悟克勤 (1063–1135)
Engo Kokugon

Meng Gong
孟珙
(*d.* 1246)
Mō Ko

Zongshao
宗紹
Shūshō

Shinchi Kakushin
心地覺心
(1207–1298)

Kohō Kakumyō
孤峰覺明

Kochiku
虛竹
(*d.* 1298)

Bassui Tokushō
拔隊得勝 (1327–1387)

Shun'ō Reizan
峻翁令山 (1344–1408)

CHART VIII

Yuanwu 圜悟 (Engo) Line.

Huguo Jingyuan
護國景元
Gokoku Keigen

Huo'an Shiti
或菴師體(1108–1179)
Wakuan Shitai

Huqiu Shaolong
虎丘紹隆 (1077–1136)
Kukyū Jōryū

One generation

Mi'an Xianjie (IX)
密菴咸傑 (1118–1186)
Mittan Kanketsu

Puzhao
普照
Fushō

Zuqing
祖慶
Sokei

Jingshan Ruyan
徑山如琰
Kinzan Nyoen

Dachuan Puji
大川普濟 (1179–1253)
Daisen Fusai

Huiyan Zhizhao
晦巖智昭
Maigan Chishō

Juexin
覺心
Kakushin

Yuanwu Keqin
圜悟克勤 (1063–1135)
Engo Kokugon

Dahui Zonggao
大慧宗杲 (1089–1163)
Daie Sōkō

Daoqian
道謙
Dōken

Yunwen
蘊聞
Ummon

Two generations

Huiweng Wuming
晦翁悟明
Maiō Gomyō

Fozhao Deguang
佛照德光 (1121–1203)
Busshō Tokkō

Bojian Jujian
北磵居簡
Hokkan Kokan

Wuchu Daguan
物初大觀
Busso Daikan

Huiji Yuanxi
晦機元熙
Maiki Genki

Xiaoyin Daxin
笑陰大訢
Shōin Daikin

Zongle
宗泐 (1318–1391)
Sōroku

Tingjun
廷俊 (1299–1368)
Teishun

Two generations

Yuansou Xingduan
元叟行端 (1254–1341)
Gensō Gyōtan

CHART IX

Mi'an 密菴 (Mittan) Line,
including Japanese Branches.

Mi'an Xianjie 密菴咸傑
(1118–1186) Mittan Kanketsu

Songyuan Chongyue 松源崇岳
(1139–1209) Shōgen Sūgaku

Wuming Huixing
無明慧性 Mumyō Eshō

Lanxi Daolong 蘭溪道隆
(1213–1278) Rankei Dōryū

Yun'an Puyan 運庵普巖
(1156–1226) Un'an Fugan

Xutang Zhiyu 虛堂智愚
(1185–1269) Kidō Chigu

Nampo Jōmyō (X)
南浦紹明 (1235–1309)

Four generations

Yuanji Juding
圓極居頂 (*d.* 1404)
Enki Kochō

Enni Ben'en
圓爾辨圓
(1201–1280)

Mukan Fumon
無關普門
(1212–1291)

Seven generations

Baiyun Wuliang 白雲無量
Hakuun Muryō

Miyun Yuanwu密雲圓悟
(1566–1642) Mitsuun Engo

Yumi Fazang 於密法藏
(1573–1635) Omitsu Hōzō

Feiyin Tongrong 費隱通容
(1593–1661) Hiin Tsūyō

Yinyuan Longqi 隱元隆琦
(1592–1673) Ingen Ryūki

Po'an Zuxian 破庵祖先
(1136–1211) Hoan Sosen

Wujun Shifan 無準師範
(1177–1249) Bushun Shihan

Xisou Shaotan
希叟紹曇
Kiso Shōdon

Xueyan Zuqin
雪嚴祖欽
Setsugan Sokin

Wuxue Zuyuan
無學祖元 (1226–1286)
Mugaku Sogen

Gaofeng Yuanmiao
高峰原妙 (1238–1295)
Kōhō Gemmyō

Kōhō Kennichi
高峰顯日
(1241–1316)

Zhongfeng Mingben
中峰明本 (1263–1323)
Chūhō Myōhon

Musō Soseki
夢窓疎石
(1275–1351)

Boting Ciji 北庭慈寂
Hokutei Jijaku

Qianyan Yuanchang 千巖元長
(1284–1357) Sengan Genchō

Yuanjing Zuying 遠淨祖應
Onjō Sō

Dazhuo Zuneng 大拙祖能
(1313–1377) Daisetsu Sonō

Eight generations

Huanyou Zhengzhuan 幻有正傳
Gen'yū Shōden

Yufeng Yuanxin 語風圓信
Gofū Enshin

CHART X

NAMPO 南浦 (Daiō Kokushi 大應國師) Line.

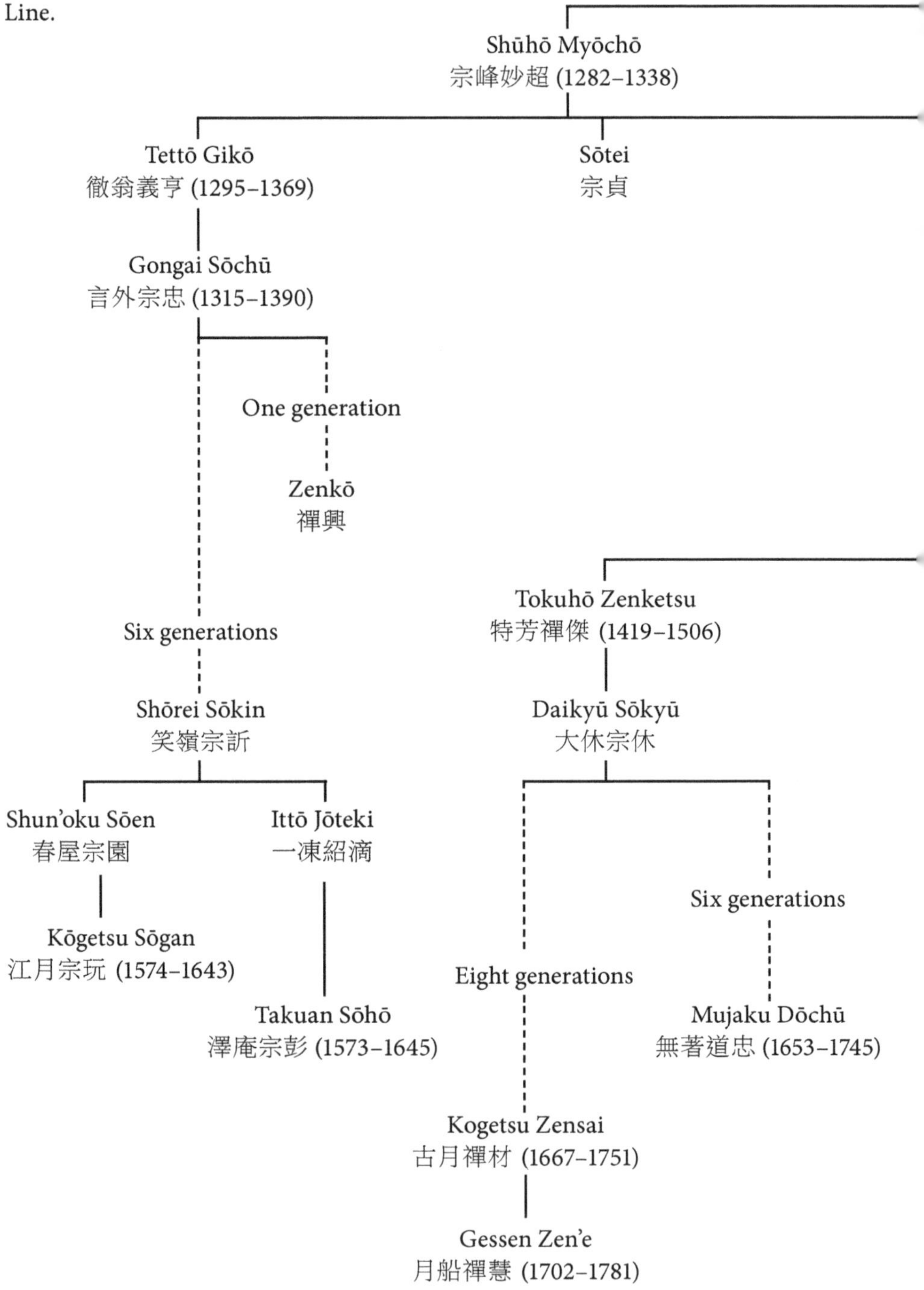

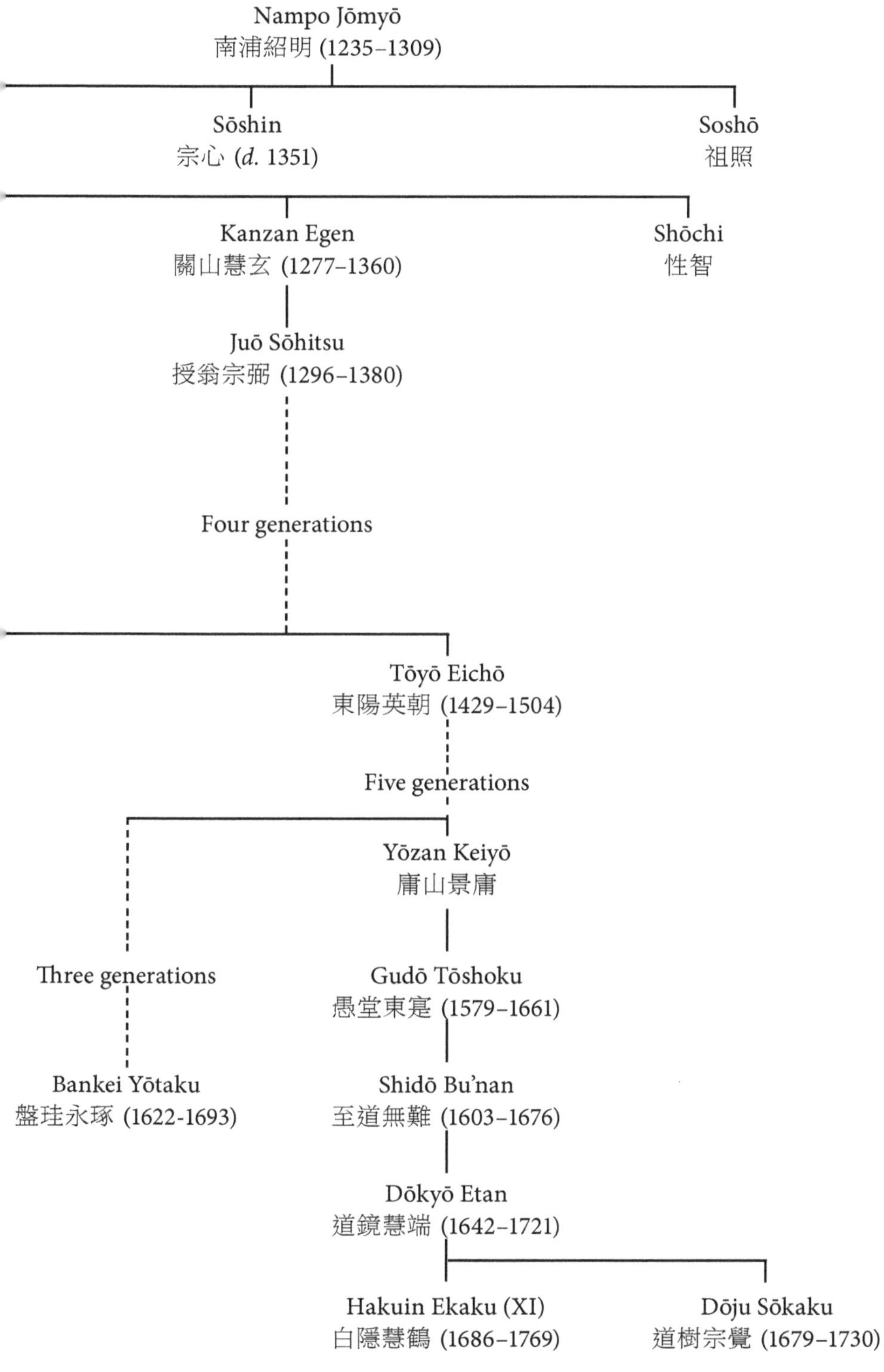
Nampo Jōmyō
南浦紹明 (1235–1309)
Sōshin
宗心 (d. 1351)
Soshō
祖照
Kanzan Egen
關山慧玄 (1277–1360)
Shōchi
性智
Juō Sōhitsu
授翁宗弼 (1296–1380)
Four generations
Tōyō Eichō
東陽英朝 (1429–1504)
Five generations
Yōzan Keiyō
庸山景庸
Three generations
Gudō Tōshoku
愚堂東寔 (1579–1661)
Bankei Yōtaku
盤珪永琢 (1622-1693)
Shidō Bu'nan
至道無難 (1603–1676)
Dōkyō Etan
道鏡慧端 (1642–1721)
Hakuin Ekaku (XI)
白隱慧鶴 (1686–1769)
Dōju Sōkaku
道樹宗覺 (1679–1730)

CHART XI

HAKUIN 白隱 Line.

- Ichidaku 一諾
- Muin 霧隱
- Gen'yaku 原譯
- Genshoku 玄軾
- Zenjo 禪恕
- Zen'ichi 全乙
- Tairei 太靈 (*d.* 1804)
- Inzan Ien 隱山惟琰 (1751–1814)
  - Taigen Shigen 太元孜元
    - Gisan Zenrai 儀山善來 (1802–1878)
      - Kōsen Sōon 洪川宗温 (1816–1892)
        - Kōgaku Sōen 洪嶽宗演 (1859–1919)
          - Hōgaku Jikō 寶嶽慈興 *or* Seigo Hōgaku 棲梧賓嶽
          - Tetsuō Sōkatsu 輟翁宗活 (1870–1954)
            - Zuigan Sōseki 瑞巌宗碩 *or* Gotō Zuigan 後藤瑞巖 (1879–1965)
            - Shigetsu Sōshin 指月宗岑 *or* Sasaki Shigetsu 佐々木指月 (1882–1945)

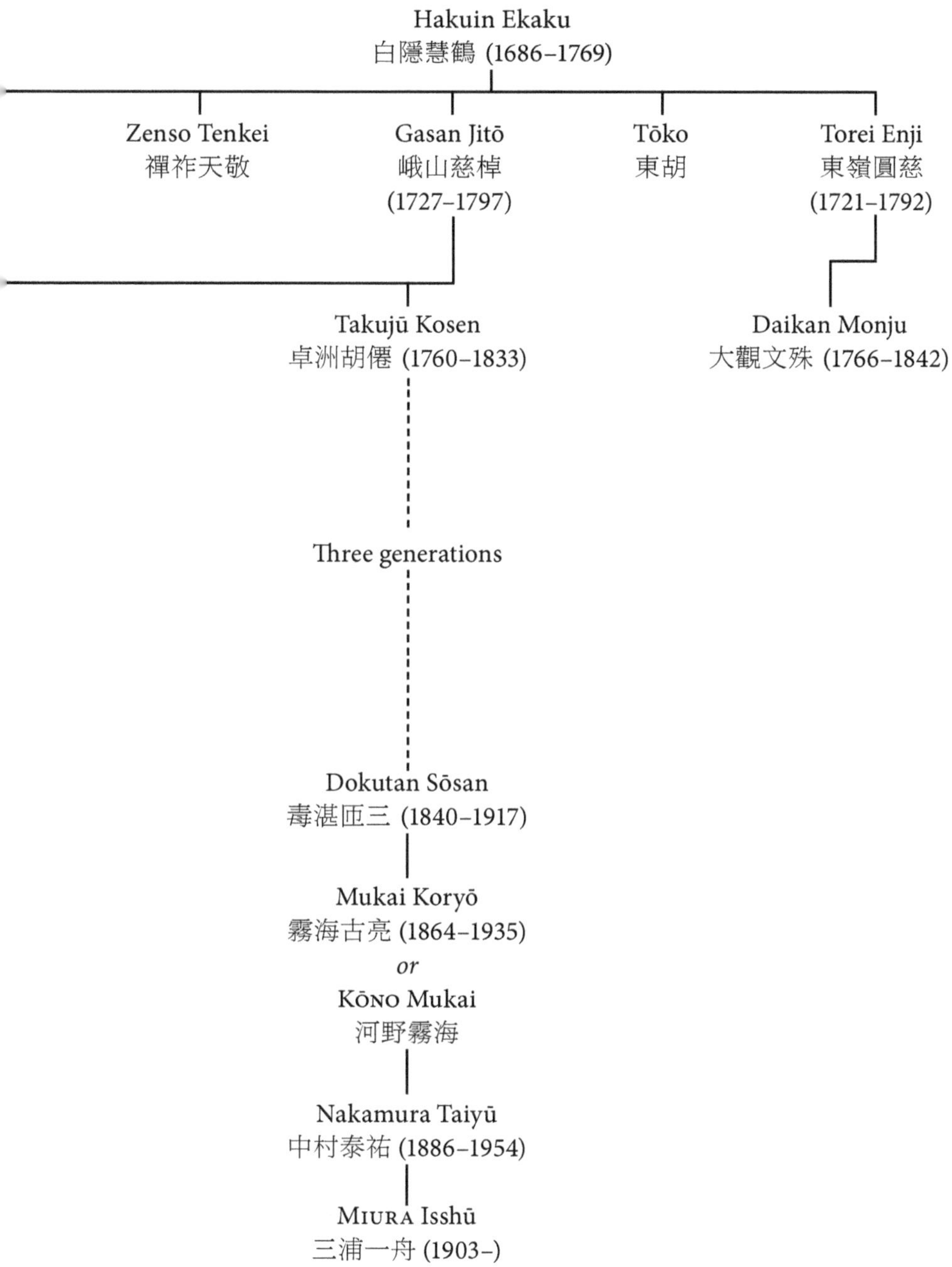
Hakuin Ekaku
白隱慧鶴 (1686–1769)
Zenso Tenkei
禪祚天敬
Gasan Jitō
峨山慈棹
(1727–1797)
Tōko
東胡
Torei Enji
東嶺圓慈
(1721–1792)
Takujū Kosen
卓洲胡僊 (1760–1833)
Daikan Monju
大觀文殊 (1766–1842)
Three generations
Dokutan Sōsan
毒湛匝三 (1840–1917)
Mukai Koryō
霧海古亮 (1864–1935)
or
Kōno Mukai
河野霧海
Nakamura Taiyū
中村泰祐 (1886–1954)
Miura Isshū
三浦一舟 (1903–)

CHART XII

Dōgen 道元 (Japanese Sōtō) Line.

- Dōgen Kigen 道元希玄 (1200–1253)
  - Hōkyō Jakuen 寶慶寂圓
    - Giun 義雲 (1253–1333)
  - Koun Ejō 孤雲懷奘 (1198–1280)
    - Tettsū Gikai 徹通義介
      - Keizan Jōkin 瑩山紹瑾 (1268–1325)
        - Gasan Jōseki 峨山韶碩
          - Twenty three generations
            - Shigetsu Ein 指月慧印 (*d.* 1764)
              - Katsudō Honkō 瞎堂本光
        - Myōhō Sotetsu 明峯素哲
          - Sixteen generations
            - Gesshū Sōko 月舟宗胡
              - Three generations
                - Gentō Sokuchū 玄透卽中 (*d.* 1807)
              - Four generations
                - Gimoku Genkai 宜默玄契

Abbreviations

alt.	alternate
BTT	Buddhist technical term
Bud.	Buddhist
Ch.	Chinese
CBTT	Chinese Buddhist technical term
CTT	Chan technical term
comdt.	commandment
emp.	emperor
fdr.	founder
hdqrs.	headquarters
Ind.	Indian
ISCJT	INDEX TO SANSKRIT, CHINESE, and JAPANESE TITLES
J.	Japanese
JBTT	Japanese Buddhist technical term
med.	meditation
mod.	modern
N.	North or Northern
orig.	originally
pat.	patriarch
posth.	posthumous
RZTT	Rinzai Zen technical term
S.	South or Southern
sch.	school
spec. ref.	specific references
SZTT	Sōtō Zen technical term
ZTT	Zen (Chinese and Japanese) technical term

General Index

This detailed interlocking multilingual INDEX is designed to function not only as a reference to all the names of persons, places, temples, sects, schools, doctrines, terms, etc. appearing in the MAIN TEXT, NOTES, and BIBLIOGRAPHY of *Zen Dust*, but also, within the limits of the material presented, as a dictionary answering the needs of students of Zen. Sanskrit, Japanese, and English entries are, with few exceptions, referred back to the language of their origin where full identification is given.

The more important place names will be found on the accompanying maps of China and Japan. Where the places are ancient or unimportant, the name of the modern province (in China) or prefecture (in Japan) which follows indicates their approximate location.

All persons not otherwise designated may be assumed to be Linji or Rinzai Zen monks. The roman numerals following the names of these latter, or of the lines or schools deriving from them, refer to the accompanying GENEALOGICAL CHARTS on which their lineages are traced. Laymen may be identified by their capitalized family names. Since most modern Japanese roshis are best known under a combination of their family and religious name, this nomenclature has been adopted here. All authors, compilers, and editors mentioned in *Zen Dust* are included in this INDEX, with page reference to the literary material they have produced.

English language titles, terms, or phrases within quotations are the author's translation; those without quotation are the generally accepted English equivalents.

Also available from Quirin Press:

Taoism and Chinese Religion

Revised Edition

by Henri Maspero

Table of Contents

Also available from Quirin Press:

BOOK VIII

BOOK IX
Methods of "Nourishing the Vital Principle" in the Ancient Daoist Religion

Reference Matter:

Original Preface By Max Kaltenmark

When Henri Maspero was deported to Buchenwald, whence he was not to return, he left behind him an immense body of sinological work, only a portion of which had been published during his lifetime. Some of the numerous unpublished materials found among his papers were gathered into three volumes put out by the Bibliothèque de diffusion du Musée Guimet;[1] others, of a more technical kind, were published separately.[2]

There is almost no area of Chinese studies which Maspero did not take up or to which he did not make important contributions,[3] but it is in religious history that his works are most numerous. This is not due to arbitrary choice but is justified by the importance of religious factors which, in China as in all the old traditional civilizations, condition both social structures and individual behavior. But in China these factors happen to be peculiarly numerous, confusing, and varied in origin, so their study presents extraordinary difficulties.

Although the articles reproduced in this volume are already old, they will give the reader quite a complete overview of Chinese religions. More recent work allows us to flesh out Maspero's conclusions, but it never fundamentally invalidates those conclusions. What the first study says about the religion of antiquity remains valid for the classical period, which Maspero knew perfectly. We must now take archaeological and epigraphical data more and more into account. At the time when Maspero was writing, the decipherment of archaic Yin 殷 inscriptions had only begun and the Anyang 安陽 excavations had not yet yielded all the information available to us today. The same is true for excavations of more recent sites. But we must admit that all this new documentation has hardly been used thus far in Western language studies.

The study on modern popular mythology and religion, here republished for the first time, remains one of the best that can be read on that subject. I fear that it does not give a very high opinion of Chinese imagination in this sphere nor, in general, of the religious worth of these popular beliefs. But we must beware of reaching a hasty judgment. We see only the outward appearance of this religion, which is for the most part playful. This is essentially a religion of festivals, and it was at the festivals celebrated during the year that divinities or demons from the immense pantheon took shape, as they were represented by statues either pre-existing or made up for the occasion, or were played by professional or amateur actors. We must likewise bear in mind local differences, necessarily important in so vast a country. Aside from a minority, aware of belonging to a particular religion (Buddhism, Daoism, Islam, Christianity), the religious needs of the Chinese were manifested on the one hand in festivals through which each local community somehow restored its cohesion and heightened its vitality and on the other in two more limited areas: domestic worship (of the ancestors, of the Kitchen God) and professional worship (of the patron divinities of occupational guilds).

During his long stays in Indo-China, Maspero had the chance to study non-Vietnamese peoples, especially the Tai communities, and to gather a great body of documentation about them. Part of this material is used in the article comparing the religion of the ancient Chinese and that of the modern Tai. There we see how the village festivals of the latter allow us to understand those of the Chinese as they can be envisioned through the love-songs of the *Shijing* 詩經, confirming Marcel Granet's interpretation, to which Maspero gives due credit here.

But it is especially through his work on Daoism that Maspero showed himself a pioneer, attacking a practically unexplored realm. Before him, Édouard Chavannes alone had written the first serious study of a Daoist rite.[4] Paul Pelliot, to be sure, had understood the importance of this doctrine very well, and had brought back numerous manuscripts from Dunhuang 燉煌 concerning it. He also has important scholarly notes on this subject in several of his articles, in which, additionally, many questions arose which still await solution. Marcel Granet was likewise interested in this religion but, though he talked about it a great deal in his courses at the École Pratique des Hautes Études, he barely mentioned it in his writings.

In fact, no serious study could be undertaken so long as the Daoist Canon (*Daozang*) remained unknown and almost inaccessible. Chavannes and Pelliot had brought back a number of volumes which they were able to obtain in China and which were deposited in the Bibliothèque Nationale in Paris; but the two collections when brought together remained clearly incomplete. Only when a reproduction of the complete Beijing copy (one of the few, if not the only one, in existence) could researches in Daoism be considered. But it was necessary to begin almost at zero, for only a very few studies on the subject existed. Chinese scholars had scorned this religion and were hardly interested in more than the ancient philosophers, Laozi 老子 and Zhuangzi 莊子. But the *Daozang* represents a considerable mass of texts, since it includes no fewer than 1,120 volumes and 1,476 titled works. The majority of these were then unknown and many did not even bear the author's name or a date. We may imagine the difficulties Maspero encountered when he launched into the examination of this enormous mass of documents. The persistence of his efforts in this area can be traced through his reports in his courses at the Collège de France. As early as 1921–22 one of his courses was entitled "The Origins of the Taoist Religion". From 1926 to 1927 on he regularly gave his students the benefit of his research results. It should be noted that, during 1933–34, he studied the anti-Daoist Buddhist pamphlets, a source that was external, hostile, and prejudiced, but very valuable. It is largely through them that a number of events and writings concerning the history of Daoism can be dated.

It was indeed necessary to seek out chronological benchmarks in order to orient oneself within this immensity of texts. A brief bibliographical introduction is to be found at the beginning of the "Essay on Daoism in the First Centuries CE" (Book VII). Here, as in the notes to several of the articles, corrections would now have to be made, since the history of the Daoist Canon has been the subject of many Chinese, and especially Japanese, works in these recent years. The problem has thus advanced somewhat beyond the time when no guide existed except Father Wieger's *Catalogue* (1911), or when the *Index to the Tao-tsang* appeared in the Harvard-Yenching Sinological Index Series (1935).[5] In this short presentation there can be no question of giving the results of these labors, so I shall limit myself to a few important points.

The *Daozang* which is available to us through the photo-mechanical edition of 1926 was indeed printed under the Ming 明 dynasty, but it is an error to say that there was only a single printing under that dynasty. In reality there was a first wood-block edition in 1445 and several new editions or reprintings with re-engraved plates. The main one of these re-editions was that of 1598 (some of the volumes in the Bibliothèque Nationale bear this date); and there was a supplement which was printed in 1607. Finally, under the Qing 清 dynasty (1644–1911), there were other printings regarding which we do not have precise information.

Another error which it is well to correct concerns the *Taiping jing* 太平經, which he dates from the fifth century in "Methods of 'Nourishing the Vital Principle'" (Book IX, First Part, note 8 of the present edition) and from the sixth century in Book VII (page 379 of this edition). This book is extremely important since it is the first of the revealed texts of religious Daoism and the copy of it which exists in the *Daozang* goes back ultimately to the period of the Later Han 漢. It was the sacred text of the Yellow Turbans and the Celestial Masters and was simply reworked somewhat in the fifth and ninth centuries.

For centuries China has appeared to the West as essentially Confucianist. The importance of Confucian doctrine in the official ideology of the imperial era, the necessity for Sinologists to acquaint themselves with the Classics (*jing* 經) and with the enormous scholarly literature which they inspired, explain this partial view. Among the "three religions," Confucianism was the best known, even though the religious character of this system of thought could be questioned. Buddhism, the writings of which had been accessible for a long time, had been well studied, but the way it had entered China remained obscure. It is one of Maspero's accomplishments to have demonstrated the legendary character of emperor Ming's dream, which according to the old story had occasioned the introduction of the new religion.[6] The problem of the reciprocal influences of the two religions is very thorny and remains much debated. To resolve that, it is clearly necessary to know the history of Daoism better. Maspero's great merit was to have posed the problem and to have opened the way towards a better comprehension of this highly hermetic body of doctrines. The fact that several of his articles, especially those which figure in the "Daoism" of the *Oeuvres posthumes*, have recently been translated into Japanese shows the importance which is attached to these works, even in a country which has the best specialists.

Nowadays Daoism is arousing a growing interest, as much within orientalist circles as among the public at large. The present re-edition, which reassembles studies of a rather technical kind (such as that which sets forth so remarkably "the procedures for nourishing the vital principle," Book IX) with articles easier to read, thus answers a double need, that of a general initiation to the subject and that of an introduction to more advanced researches.[7]

Max Kaltenmark

Lightning Source UK Ltd.
Milton Keynes UK
UKHW010908160322
400148UK00001B/5

9 781922 169129